Health and Healing in the Middle Ages
Volume 2

Ethnicity in Medieval Europe, 950–1250

YORK MEDIEVAL PRESS

York Medieval Press is published by the University of York's Centre for Medieval Studies in association with Boydell & Brewer Limited. Our objective is the promotion of innovative scholarship and fresh criticism on medieval culture. We have a special commitment to interdisciplinary study, in line with the Centre's belief that the future of Medieval Studies lies in those areas in which its major constituent disciplines at once inform and challenge each other.

Editorial Board (2021)

Professor Peter Biller, Emeritus (Dept of History): General Editor
Professor Tim Ayers (Dept of History of Art): Co-Director, Centre for Medieval Studies
Dr Henry Bainton: Private scholar
Dr J. W. Binns: Honorary Fellow, Centre for Medieval Studies
Dr K. P. Clarke (Dept of English and Related Literature)
Dr K. F. Giles (Dept of Archaeology)
Dr Shazia Jagot (Dept of English and Related Literature)
Dr Holly James-Maddocks (Dept of English and Related Literature)
Dr Harry Munt (Dept of History)
† Professor W. Mark Ormrod, Emeritus (Dept of History)
Dr L. J. Sackville (Dept of History)
Professor Elizabeth M. Tyler (Dept of English and Related Literature): Co-Director, Centre for Medieval Studies
Dr Hanna Vorholt (Dept of History of Art)
Dr Sethina Watson (Dept of History)
Professor J. G. Wogan-Browne (English Faculty, Fordham University)
Dr Stephanie Wynne-Jones (Dept of Archaeology)

All enquiries of an editorial kind, including suggestions for monographs and essay collections, should be addressed to: The Academic Editor, York Medieval Press, Department of History, University of York, Heslington, York, YO10 5DD (E-mail: pete.biller@york.ac.uk)

Details of other York Medieval Press volumes are available from Boydell & Brewer Ltd.

Health and Healing in the Middle Ages

Series Editor
Peregrine Horden (All Souls College, Oxford)
Series Adviser
Linda Ehrsam Voigts (University of Missouri-Kansas City)

The subject matter of this series is interpreted broadly, from studies of health or palaeopathology at one end of the spectrum to a medical humanities approach to the history of healing at the other. It welcomes both monographs and focussed edited collections written in English, covering any centuries or geographical areas to which the term 'medieval' can be productively applied.

Enquiries about the series may be sent to Peregrine Horden (peregrine.horden@all-souls. ox.ac.uk) and Linda Voigts (voightsl@umkc.edu). Book proposals should be supported by a one-page prospectus, a brief chapter outline, and a one-page curriculum vitae.

A full list of titles in the series is given at the end of the volume.

This work was supported by the European Research Council (grant no. 724114) and by the H. P. H. Jansen Fund.

© Claire Weeda 2021

All rights reserved. Except as permitted under current legislation no part of this work may be photocopied, stored in a retrieval system, published, performed in public, adapted, broadcast, transmitted, recorded or reproduced in any form or by any means, without the prior permission of the copyright owner

The right of Claire Weeda to be identified as the author of this work has been asserted in accordance with sections 77 and 78 of the Copyright, Designs and Patents Act 1988

First published 2021
Paperback edition 2023

A York Medieval Press publication
in association with The Boydell Press
an imprint of Boydell & Brewer Ltd
PO Box 9, Woodbridge, Suffolk IP12 3DF, UK
and of Boydell & Brewer Inc.
668 Mt Hope Avenue, Rochester, NY 14620–2731, USA
website: www.boydellandbrewer.com
and with the
Centre for Medieval Studies, University of York

ISBN 978 1 91404 901 9 hardback
ISBN 978 1 91404 918 7 paperback

A CIP catalogue record for this book is available from the British Library

The publisher has no responsibility for the continued existence or accuracy of URLs for external or third-party internet websites referred to in this book, and does not guarantee that any content on such websites is, or will remain, accurate or appropriate

Ethnicity in Medieval Europe, 950–1250: Medicine, Power and Religion

Claire Weeda

THE UNIVERSITY *of York*
YORK MEDIEVAL PRESS

Contents

	List of Figures	vii
	Introduction	1

Part I

1	Cataloguing Ethnic Virtues and Vices	41
2	The Naturalization of Ethnicity and Environmental Thought	80
3	Domesticated Spaces, Peoples and Power in Rhetoric	126

Part II

4	Ethnic Slanging Matches	161
5	French Control, German Rage, English Charm: Gender and Military Power	185
6	Imagined Geographies, Colonization and Conquest	230
	Conclusion	253
	Appendix	259
	Bibliography	273
	Acknowledgements	321
	Index	323

Figures

1   T-O map. Isidore of Seville, *Etymologies*, in Auxerre, Bibliothèque Municipale MS 76 fol. 91v., dating to the second quarter of the twelfth century   57

2   Beatus map. Burgo de Osma, Archivo de la Catedral Codex 1, fols. 34v.–35r., dating to 1086   74

3   The impact of air. Bartholomaeus Anglicus, *Livre des propriétés des choses* dating to 1447, in Amiens, Bibliothèques d'Amiens Métropole MS 399 F fol. 131   88

4   Regions, cities and environments. Bartholomaeus Anglicus, *Livre des propriétés des choses* dating to 1447, in Amiens, Bibliothèques d'Amiens Métropole MS 399 F fol. 166   101

5   T-O map. Bartholomaeus Anglicus, *Livre des proprietez des choses* dating to 1482, in London, British Library MS Royal 15 E III fol. 67v.   236

Full credit details are provided in the captions to the images in the text. The author and publisher are grateful to all the institutions and individuals for permission to reproduce the materials in which they hold copyright. Every effort has been made to trace the copyright holders; apologies are offered for any omission, and the publisher will be pleased to add any necessary acknowledgement in subsequent editions.

Introduction

This book's theme is imagining ethnicity. From the comfort of his monastery cell in Wiltshire, William of Malmesbury (*c.* 1090–*c.* 1143) had plenty to say about the supposed character of nations. Three decades after the First Crusade (1095–99), this erudite Benedictine monk crafted a polished account of Pope Urban II's (1035–99) belligerent call in 1095 to embark on a bloody crusade against Muslim rule in Palestine.[1] In his version, inserted into the *Deeds of the English Kings*, a moralistic guide to rulership dedicated to the Scottish King David I (*c.* 1085–1153) and Empress Matilda (1102–67), the librarian of Malmesbury abbey decided to show off his familiarity with Graeco-Arabic environmental theory, which at that time was gaining influence at western European schools and courts.[2] William embellished Pope Urban's call to arms with a parade of various European and western Asian peoples' military skills, wielding ancient Hippocratic climate theory that explained the mental and physical character traits of ethnic groups on physiological grounds.

Allegedly, the pope had deplored the incapacity of Europe's northern regions to produce good knights. In doing so, Pope Urban linked environment to religion and culture: 'There remains Europe, the third zone. How small is the part of it inhabited by us Christians! For none would term Christian those barbarous people who live in distant islands on the frozen ocean, for they live in the manner of brutes.'[3] Far removed from the sun's heat, these men were 'less rational but fight most readily, in proud reliance on a generous and

---

[1] C. Tyerman, *God's War: A New History of the Crusades* (London, 2006), pp. 58–91.
[2] B. Weiler, 'William of Malmesbury, King Henry I and the Gesta Regum Anglorum', *Anglo-Norman Studies* 31 (2009), 157–76; J. E. Phillips, 'William of Malmesbury: Medical Historian of the Crusades', in *Discovering William of Malmesbury*, ed. R. M. Thomson, E. Dolmans and E. A. Winkler (Woodbridge, 2017), pp. 129–38; J. Titterton, 'Bloodless Turks and Sanguine Crusaders: William of Malmesbury's Use of Vegetius in His Account of Urban II's Sermon at Clermont', *The Medieval Chronicle* 13 (2020), 289–308.
[3] William of Malmesbury, *Gesta regum Anglorum* iv.347, ed. and trans. R. A. B. Mynors, R. M. Thomson and M. Winterbottom, 2 vols. (Oxford, 1998–99), i, 600–1: 'Tertium mundi clima restat Europa, cuius quantulam partem inhabitamus Christiani! Nam omnem illam barbariem quae in remotis insulis glatialem frequentat oceanum, quia more belvino victitat, Christianum quis dixerit?' I have made slight alterations to the translation.

exuberant supply of blood'. William looks towards regional environment to explain the French army's prowess as well. The Turkish foe, on the other hand, suffered from a contrasting ineptitude, shooting arrows at a distance out of cowardice, for 'it is in fact well known that every nation born in an eastern clime is dried up by the great heat of the sun; they may have more good sense, but they have less blood in their veins, and that is why they flee from battle at close quarters'. Only the French – Pope Urban was addressing a crowd assembled in the Auvergne in present-day central France – produced excellent armies, endowed with the courtly ideals of both rational thought and courage: 'You are a nation originating in the more temperate regions of the world, men whose readiness to shed your blood leads to contempt for death and wounds, though you are not without forethought; for you observe moderation in camp, and in the heat of battle you find room for reason.'[4]

William of Malmesbury's comments form an adaptation of fourth-century military strategist Vegetius's popular manual *De re militari*.[5] William's use of Graeco-Arabic environmental theory, which grounds groups' traits in their environment, did not just serve to demonstrate his learning, however. Significantly, it lent him a voice of epistemic authority, helping the monk to frame the perceived geopolitical transition of power from south-west Asia to north-west Europe in scientific and religious terms. It also allowed him to portray western Europe's military recruits – rational and courageous men – as the just defenders of Christendom, entitling them to take possession of lands and properties in lands yonder and afar as part of the crusader movement.

William of Malmesbury made this argument while northern Europe was undergoing an agricultural revolution and rapid urbanization, and its market economy was expanding exponentially. Europe's population almost tripled between 800 and 1300, to 70 million.[6] It was under these conditions, as the cul-

---

[4] Ibid., pp. 602–3: 'Contra, populus qui oritur in Arctois pruinis, et remotus est a solis ardoribus, inconsultior quidem sed largo et luxurianti superbus sanguine promptissime pugnat'; 'Constat profecto quod omnis natio quae in Eoa plaga nascitur, nimio solis ardore siccata, amplius quidem sapit, sed minus habet sanguinis; ideoque vicinam pugnam fugiunt, quia parum sanguinis se habere norunt'; 'Vos estis gens quae in temperatioribus mundi provintiis oriunda, qui sitis et prodigi sanguinis ad mortis vulnerumque contemptum et non careatis prudentia; namque et modestiam servatis in castris, et in dimicatione utimini consiliis.'

[5] Vegetius, *Epitoma rei militaris* i.ii, ed. M. D. Reeve (Oxford, 2004); C. T. Allmand, *The De Re Militari of Vegetius: The Reception, Transmission and Legacy of a Roman Text in the Middle Ages* (Cambridge, 2011).

[6] R. C. Hoffmann, *An Environmental History of Medieval Europe* (Cambridge, 2014), pp. 116–17. The transformation is often described as a 'renaissance', an organic term I wish to avoid. The term was coined by C. H. Haskins, *The Renaissance of*

ture of literacy also spread, that monks, schoolmen and courtiers applied ideas about the impact of environment on character and culture in their histories, school texts, poetry and letters, encouraging and justifying holy conquest while conceiving their own territory as a *patria*, a domesticated space. Graeco-Arabic science and Roman rhetoric thereby allowed these men to self-confidently, brazenly position western Europe as the 'natural' repository of disciplined, rational manliness, in distinction to the religious-environmental other.

How did environmental determinism allow for this ethnic rhetoric to emerge and flourish in the heyday of universalizing political and religious ideas and structures? How was it employed, and in what context? This book argues that over the period 950–1250 environmental theory merged with religious and cultural narratives of progress, allowing north-western Europeans to imagine and present themselves as *natural, moral, rational communities* dwelling in temperate domesticated spaces and endowed with good speech, contrasted with irrational, undisciplined others living outside Europe or Christendom. Communities of well-spoken, rational and strong persons, living under good laws, qualified for good rulership, whereas irrational or weak beings in lawless societies invited subjugation. In due course, existing religious-genealogical constructions of ethnicity became grounded in environment, and ethnic character became considered to be geographically determined. This happened while northern Europe was undergoing transformations in the spheres of urbanization and literacy,[7] education and economy and was waging wars of colonization and conquest.

Monks, schoolmen and courtiers disseminated in their prose, poetry, treatises and histories representations of ethnic traits in three specific contexts: in mnemonic textual devices aimed to reflect on collective sins and virtues; in classifications of military qualities considered necessary for the security and protection of the *patria*; and in ethnographies falsely constructing an image of laziness, absence of reason, barbaric speech and lawlessness in regions of settlement and conquest. These images served as cultural arguments for establishing rulership over 'primitive peoples' and seizing their property, drawn

---

the Twelfth Century (Cambridge MA, 1927). It is reproduced in R. L. Benson, G. Constable and C. D. Lanham (ed.), *Renaissance and Renewal in the Twelfth Century* (Cambridge MA, 1982); C. R. Young (ed.), *The Twelfth-Century Renaissance* (New York, 1969); C. Warren Hollister (ed.), *The Twelfth-Century Renaissance* (New York, 1969); and R. N. Swanson, *The Twelfth-Century Renaissance* (Manchester, 1999). See also R. W. Southern, *Medieval Humanism, and Other Studies* (reprint Oxford, 1970).

[7] M. Mostert, 'Studying Medieval Urban Literacy: A Provisional State of Affairs', available at https://medievalliteracy.wp.hum.uu.nl/wp-content/uploads/sites/34/2013/01/Medieval-Urban-Literacy.pdf (accessed 1 September 2020).

from Ciceronian ideas about the relationship between reason, speech and the development of societies. The ideas were expanded in thirteenth-century legal and philosophical treatises discussing the acquisition of property, the role of government, Aristotelian natural law and climate.[8]

To make these arguments, and to learn how to perform ethnicity, fresh manuals of rhetoric actively taught the schoolmen how to stereotype, reproducing and validating the knowledge of groups' constitutions. These manuals were studied at the new, emerging schools where the *artes liberales* programme prepared students to read theology, law or medicine.[9] The schoolmen and court poets, as part of the upper strata, thereby adopted imagery pertaining to the socio-economic and military elite – emphasizing its urbanity, good manners, strength and discipline – to construct reputations of ethnic character, comparing their own urbanity, manliness and rationality to the lawless, beastlike, irrational, rustic status of others. The aspiring schoolmen took and utilized this outlook in their further careers as professional advisors and administrators working in government. A network of educated clerics and court poets, who often found employment in centres of power, reproduced there the classical and religious tropes, defining their ethnicity using images associated with elite traits and values. Underscoring the performative aspect of ethnicity, mirror literature (*specula*) and regimens for the good governance of households, cities and kingdoms thereby spurred the lay and religious aristocracy to reflect upon and regulate their behaviour, virtue and apparel, to further enhance the

---

[8] J. Coleman, 'Medieval Discussions of Property: "Ratio" and "Dominium" According to John of Paris and Marsilius of Padua', *History of Political Thought* 4/2 (1983), 209–28; C. J. Nederman, 'Nature, Sin and the Origins of Society: The Ciceronian Tradition in Medieval Political Thought', *Journal of the History of Ideas* 49/1 (1988), 3–26.

[9] The historiography concerning the rise of the schools and universities in the twelfth century is vast. A selection: J. Verger, *Histoire des universités en France* (Toulouse, 1986); J. Verger, *Les gens de savoir dans l'Europe de la fin du Moyen Âge* (Paris, 1997); W. Rüegg and H. de Ridder-Symoens (ed.), *A History of the University in Europe*, 4 vols. (Cambridge, 1992–2011), I, *Universities in the Middle Ages*; S. C. Ferruolo, *The Origins of the University: The Schools of Paris and their Critics 1100–1215* (Stanford, 1985); G. Leff, *Paris and Oxford Universities in the Thirteenth and Fourteenth Centuries: An Institutional and Intellectual History* (London, 1968); A. B. Cobban, *The Medieval English Universities: Oxford and Cambridge to c. 1500* (Berkeley, 1988). For the study of medicine at the universities, see C. O'Boyle, *The Art of Medicine: Medical Teaching at the University of Paris, 1215–1400* (Leiden, 1998); P. Skinner, *Health and Medicine in Early Medieval Southern Italy* (Leiden, 1997); N. G. Siraisi, *Medieval and Early Renaissance Medicine: An Introduction to Knowledge and Practice* (Chicago, 1990), pp. 48–77. For Galenism as a pedagogical tool, B. Parsons, *Punishment and Medieval Education* (Melton, 2018).

reputations that they carved for themselves. Thus, the ethnic images of both Europeans and others, rather than the natural outcome of protracted cultural and political processes, were shaped and exploited by the authoritative voices of schoolmen and courtiers.

To understand how this particular frame of nationhood developed between 950 and 1250, this book taps into and analyses, from the fresh perspective of the changing discursive impact of religion and science, a rich vein of hitherto untouched as well as more familiar sources, from monastic lists, encyclopaedias and histories, to medical texts, student manuals, sermons, letters, poems and prose texts. It spans the period from the emergence in Benedictine monasteries of catalogues of ethnic traits, in the tenth century, to the period when mendicant friars like Thomas Aquinas (*c.* 1215–74) and John of Paris (*c.* 1255–1306) looked towards Aristotelian ideas about the natural body politic's pursuit of sufficient life, welding together the natural and political processes of *zoē* and *bíos* in their organic concept of man and society, now viewed through a Christian prism, as a form of biopolitics.[10] The approach and main arguments of this book will be further explained below, placing them within existing historiographical traditions and setting out the book's method and the terminology used. This introduction serves as a conceptual and interdisciplinary discussion of how ethnic character was constructed, that is, made concrete and embellished, with examples in the book's six chapters.

New approaches straddling the modern/premodern divide

This book explores how the application of environmental theory and the focus on the *patria* in the courts in their military aspect were entangled with eschatological schemata and classical concepts of civility, allowing monks and schoolmen to imagine European ethnic groups to be moral-natural communities dwelling in domesticated spaces. As it argues, in the process, environmental theory inflected existing genealogical, kinship constructions of what binds peoples together in networks. The authoritative voices of the schoolmen considered the ethnic traits to be geographically determined, as well as embedded in religious and cultural narratives proclaiming an alleged

---

[10] B. Sère, 'Aristote et le bien commun au Moyen Âge: Une histoire, une historiographie', *Revue française d'histoire des idées politiques* 32 (2010), 277–92; M. Meloni, 'Porous Bodies: Environmental Biopower and the Politics of Life in Ancient Rome', *Theory, Culture & Society*, published online 11 June 2020 at Porous Bodies: Environmental Biopower and the Politics of Life in Ancient Rome – Maurizio Meloni, 2020 (sagepub.com); P. Rabinow and N. Rose, 'Thoughts on the Concept of Biopower Today', *BioSocieties* 1 (2006), 195–217.

'civilising process'.[11] The biological categories which these authoritative voices created thereby built upon intersecting religious, social and cultural norms, classifying the physical strengths, weaknesses and mental states of peoples in a gendered language in which male able-bodiedness prevailed. Thus, this book's approach, which is discussed further below, postulates that the marker of 'ethnic character' featured alongside and intersected with other nodes of differentiation, such as physical appearance and cultural practices, which were given meaning and embedded within religiously imbued, social reference frameworks of power, space and time, the past, the present and the future. Configurations of these markers produced imaginary, naturalized 'ethnotypes' – ethnic avatars – symbolizing nationhood in its allegedly most essential form and populating sacralized territories.[12] Instructed by manuals and regimens, the elite endeavoured to perform these ethnotypes.

Before discussing this approach in more detail, it is necessary to first explain where this book stands in relation to the vast corpus of studies on nation, nationhood, ethnicity and race. In my view, exploring the imagination of and identification with ethnic groups from the different perspectives of moral, physical and legal boundary-making allows historians to fracture the modern/premodern divide in which studies of national identity, nation-states, nationalism and racism are currently entrenched.[13] The existing divide is intrinsically bound up with the dominant framing of the nation-state as

[11] S. J. Ball, *Foucault, Power, and Education* (New York, 2013), pp. 13–15. The alleged civilizing process that monks and clerics allude to as a rhetorical argument in the twelfth century, as well as the social-cultural and medical norms and values propagated in household and health regimens, predate any civilizing process that Norbert Elias believed became manifest in the fifteenth century; cf. N. Elias, *Wandlungen der Gesellschaft: Entwurf zu einer Theorie der Zivilisation* (Basel, 1939).

[12] J. Leerssen, *National Thought in Europe: A Cultural History* (rev. edn, Amsterdam, 2006), p. 17.

[13] For discussions about this divide, see L. E. Scales and O. Zimmer, 'Introduction', in *Power and the Nation in European History*, ed. L. E. Scales and O. Zimmer (Cambridge, 2005), pp. 1–29; P. Hoppenbrouwers, 'The Dynamics of National Identity in the Later Middle Ages', in *Networks, Regions and Nations: Shaping Identities in the Low Countries, 1300–1650*, ed. R. Stein and J. Pollmann (Leiden, 2010), pp. 19–42. For a general discussion of approaches to ethnic and national identity in premodernity: L. Johnson, 'Imagining Communities: Medieval and Modern', in *Concepts of National Identity in the Middle Ages*, ed. S. Forde, L. Johnson and A. V. Murray (Leeds, 1995), pp. 1–19; A. D. Smith, 'National Identities: Modern and Medieval?', in Ibid., pp. 21–46; P. Hoppenbrouwers, 'Medieval Peoples Imagined', in *Imagology: The Cultural Construction and Literary Representation of National Characters: A Critical Survey*, ed. M. Beller and J. Leerssen (Amsterdam, 2007), pp. 45–62. For race and ethnicity, see pp. 14–22 below.

being – rather than *self-representing* itself as – the inevitable outcome of community-formation processes managed by a secular, modern elite who, from the eighteenth century, organized and engaged its workforce to facilitate the economy's industrialization and thereby evoked the argument of serving national interests.[14] This process was spearheaded by elites taking rational, bureaucratic decisions, while arousing group emotions through expressions of banal nationalism, via symbols and rituals.[15] Highlighting the cultural construction of national identity, twentieth-century historians were responding to the earlier rise around 1900 of ethnic nationalism, a racist political ideology claiming that modern nations had older, exclusive, 'medieval' genealogical and linguistic roots. An example of the latter is Paul Kirn's *Aus der Frühzeit des Nationalgefühls*, published in Leipzig in the middle of the Second World War, and to date the most extensive publication on nationhood from the eighth to thirteenth centuries in French, British and German territories.[16] Kirn's choice of subject – the historical boundaries of German territories and 'medieval national consciousness' – was relevant to Nazi *Lebensraum*-politics, as was his plea for a strong national community and state, calling on his readers to acknowledge their duties in 'racial and colonisation politics'.[17]

After the Second World War, in reaction to nineteenth- and early twentieth-century romantic ethnic nationalism, (post-)modernists accordingly

[14] Highly influential are E. Gellner, *Nations and Nationalism* (Oxford, 1983); C. Tilly, *Coercion, Capital, and European States, AD 990–1992* (Cambridge, 1992); J. Breuilly, *Nationalism and the State* (New York, 1982); E. J. Hobsbawm, *Nations and Nationalism since 1780: Programme, Myth, Reality* (Cambridge, 1990). See also the series of contributions in E. Hobsbawm and T. Ranger (ed.), *The Invention of Tradition* (Cambridge, 1983), which argue that many national traditions, cultural customs and symbols were in fact nineteenth-century inventions.

[15] For the concept of banal nationalism in the nineteenth century: M. Billig, *Banal Nationalism* (London, 1995).

[16] P. Kirn, *Aus der Frühzeit des Nationalgefühls: Studien zur deutschen und französischen Geschichte sowie zu den Nationalitätenkämpfen auf den Britischen Inseln* (Leipzig, 1943).

[17] C. Kretschmann, 'Einsatz für Deutschland? Die Frankfurter Historiker Walter Platzhoff und Paul Kirn im "Dritten Reich"', in *Frankfurter Wissenschaftler zwischen 1933 und 1945*, ed. J. Kobes and J. O. Hesse (Göttingen, 2008), pp. 5–32 (pp. 26–8). Notably, a copy of Kirn's book was used to send encoded messages (lightly tipping a letter on every other page from back to front) by Dietrich Bonhoeffer, a member of the German resistance group of Abwehr officers who attempted to overthrow the Nazi regime in 1939. Bonhoeffer was imprisoned and later sentenced to death by the Germans in April 1945 after the failed attempt to assassinate Hitler in 1944. R. Bethge and C. Gremmels, *Dietrich Bonhoeffer: Zijn leven in beeld*, ed. H. Sweers (Kampen, 2005), p. 142.

stressed the constructed and recent dimensions of nationhood, being the outcome of politically and economically driven rational processes of modernity and institutionalization.[18] Studies of the religious contribution to the imagination of nations, as *moral communities* defending sacralized spaces, thereby partially slipped into the background. Moreover, the community held together and governed by dynastic networks, which drew their power from God – the counterpoint of the secular, rational, bureaucratic and ultimately democratic nation-state – was described as a thing of the past, as irrational, ultimately 'feudal' and hence 'medieval'. Indeed, the dynastic realm had been supplanted by a state bound by enlightened, universal and national laws, based upon a social contract willed by the people who made up the body politic, and upheld by institutions. Significantly, this perceived shift was said to have occurred in the same period as the global colonization by European powers was in full swing.[19] From this perspective, modern historians and political scientists set store on identifying the period in which sufficient numbers within the population adopted a 'national identity', to be able to speak of nations and nation-states.

Historians of earlier periods, aware of the existence in the archives and libraries of sources mentioning ethnic character, responded by arguing for the existence of a premodern national consciousness, yet in doing so applied modernity's categories. The handful of scholars who took up the challenge of examining these earlier sources often searched for evidence for the beginnings of a Weberian rational, bureaucratic and centralizing state in earlier periods, or else for the existence of older natural communities, or both. Either way, they agreed that national community formation was inherently propelled by political state-formation processes that eventually would lead to the mature materialization of modernity's nation-states. In doing so, however, while reaffirming the constructed rather than primordial or organic nature of nations, historians studying the 'medieval period' continued to infer that nationhood

---

[18] A. D. Smith, *The Nation in History: Historiographical Debates about Ethnicity and Nationalism* (Hanover, 2000), pp. 5–13. For a recent and outspoken perspective on nations as 'rooted in the past': A. Gat, with A. Yakobson, *Nations: The Long History and Deep Roots of Political Ethnicity and Nationalism* (Cambridge, 2012).

[19] The onset of the framing of the 'medieval' and 'feudalism' in conjunction with colonization efforts beginning in the sixteenth century, is brilliantly argued by K. Davis, *Periodization and Sovereignty: How Ideas of Feudalism and Secularization Govern the Politics of Time* (Philadelphia, 2008); and G. Heng, *The Invention of Race in the European Middle Ages* (Cambridge, 2018), pp. 20–4. M. S. Champion, 'A History of Temporalities: An Introduction', *Past & Present* 243/1 (2019), 247–54; A. R. P. Fryxell, 'Time and the Modern: Current Trends in the History of Modern Temporalities', *Past & Present* 243/1 (2019), 285–98.

existed if and when the numbers added up (i.e., when sufficient numbers of the population could imagine the community) and the relevant boxes could be ticked off representing elements of ethnicity (a belief in having shared customs, a sense of having a shared past, language etc.). The question historians posed thus seemed to revolve around pinpointing *when the nation was constructed*, came into existence, rather than *how it was represented, why so and to what end*.

A few examples. Susan Reynolds argued for the longevity and naturalness of political communities, contending that the collective nature of medieval government *ipso facto* meant that the nation was a 'natural, given, objectively existing human community' bound by descent and culture, whereby the existence of kingdoms and shared laws promoted a sense of solidarity.[20] Hugh Seton-Watson argued that rulers from the thirteenth century onwards paved the way for the *political construction* of nation-states through bureaucratization, the centralization of taxation and imposition of a monopoly of violence, nurtured by evolving discourses of sovereignty.[21] Earlier, Joseph Strayer in *On the Medieval Origins of the Modern State*, was quite explicit in his attempt to identify forms of state formation that pre-emptively drew the contours of the modern state.[22] It was only more recently that Caspar Hirschi inversely and innovatively began to re-evaluate the impress of *concepts*, underscoring the lasting influence of the ancient political ideology of *imperium* that was adapted to the world of Germanic peoples and which in his view created a new form of nationalism in which multi-polar nations sought self-definition through claims to honour. In doing so, his approach was one of the first to look at the impact of ideas.[23] In that sense, his book responded to Benedict Anderson's *Imagined Communities*, which earlier had opened up new vistas on the phenomenon of national identity and nationalism by emphasizing the impact of mental concepts on community formation processes. Nonetheless, Anderson again maintained that national identity was inherently modern, and he juxtaposed the horizontal bonds of modernity with premodernity's 'fundamental conceptions about "social groups"', which in his view 'were

---

[20] S. Reynolds, 'The Idea of the Nation as a Political Community', in *Power and the Nation in European History*, ed. L. E. Scales and O. Zimmer (Cambridge, 2005), pp. 54–66 (pp. 56–61); S. Reynolds, *Kingdoms and Communities in Western Europe 900–1300* (Oxford, 1984), pp. 250–31.

[21] H. Seton-Watson, *Nations and States: An Enquiry into the Origins of Nations and the Politics of Nationalism* (London, 1977). However, see A. Hastings, *The Construction of Nationhood: Ethnicity, Religion and Nationalism* (Cambridge, 1997).

[22] J. Strayer, *On the Medieval Origins of the Modern State* (Princeton, 1970).

[23] C. Hirschi, *The Origins of Nationalism: An Alternative History from Ancient Rome to Early Modern Germany* (Cambridge, 2012).

centripetal and hierarchical, rather than boundary-oriented and horizontal'.[24] Part of Anderson's argument relied upon his understanding of 'medieval time' as being non-historical or analogical, a viewpoint that has since been contested as a misconception of religious allegory.[25] Embracing this temporal argument, Anderson himself contributed to the stagist othering of the 'Middle Ages' in a manner analogous to how twelfth-century schoolmen and monks framed earlier spheres of power as locked in a past left behind in the *translatio studii et imperii*, which is further explained below. Moreover, neither Hirschi nor Anderson analysed the underlying religious and scientific discourses, social norms and values informing the manner in which nations are imagined. Thus, as this book argues, the imagined nation, or ethnotype, stands in a long and fluid textual and oral tradition, whereby the relevance and power of those images depends on the context in which they are employed, the discourses on which their validity is based, the authoritative voices that wield them and the arguments made based upon them – arguments that often, be they 'ancient', 'medieval' or 'modern', revolve around the alleged presence or absence of rational thought, discipline, order and strength in comparison to others, to past feats and future destinies.

In the past, confusing discussions accordingly emerged about whether a premodern political ideology of nationalism existed, meaning a doctrine of sovereignty providing 'legitimate state power' emanating from the 'will of the nation'.[26] For example, the rhetoric of the Scottish Declaration of Arbroath of 1320 ('As long as only one hundred of us remain alive, we will never on any condition be brought under English rule') was used as evidence for the existence

---

[24] B. Anderson, *Imagined Communities: Reflections on the Origin and Spread of Nationalism* (London, 1983; 3rd, rev. edn, London, 2006), p. 15.

[25] The concept of eschatological time: R. Koselleck, *Vergangene Zukunft: Zur Semantik geschichtlicher Zeiten* (Frankfurt am Main, 1979). For discussions of messianic time see the references in C. Weeda, 'Meanwhile in Messianic Time: Imagining the Medieval Nation in Time and Space and English Drinking Rituals', in *Imagining Communities: Historical Reflections on the Process of Community Formation*, ed. G. Blok, V. Kuitenbrouwer and C. Weeda (Amsterdam, 2018), pp. 21–40 (pp. 22–30).

[26] For such as discussion about nationalism in earlier times, see J. Leerssen, 'The Baton and the Frame. Or, Tradition and Recollection', *Studies on National Movements* 2 (2014), 13–23; C. Hirschi, 'Duck or Quack. On the Lack of Scholarly Soundness and Decorum in Joep Leerssen's Review', *Studies on National Movements* 2 (2014), 25–37; and J. Leerssen, 'Response to Caspar Hirschi', *Studies on National Movements* 2 (2014), 35–48. For definitions of nationalism as a political ideology, see Leerssen, *National Thought in Europe*, pp. 14–15

of political nationalism by Susan Reynolds and Rees Davies.[27] Scholars did, however, proceed cautiously when evaluating the extent to which references to nationhood directly represented a broad, popular voice. Most historians of earlier periods, although speaking of nationalism, indeed carefully underlined the different scales of political ideology and widespread national sentiment, yet still used modernity's vocabulary of nationalism.[28]

Although, to date, relatively little attention has been paid to the impact of religious ideas and environmental theory on the construction of ethnicity, valuable studies are available for later periods and subtopics covering the impact of legal ideas and political concepts. A well-conceived study, incorporating the concept of the metaphorical body politic, is Albert Rigaudière's *Penser et construire l'État dans la France du Moyen Âge*, which argues that the ancient concept of the body politic shaped discourses of power accelerating state-formation processes in western Europe in the fourteenth–fifteenth century.[29] As Gaines Post and more recently Caspar Hirschi have proposed, from the second half of the thirteenth century, legal court discussions reviewed Ciceronian concepts of the *patria* – although, as this book shows, these were preceded by earlier military exhortations to protect the *patria* inspired by Vegetius's *De re militari*. Arguments circulated that the polity deserved a *defensio patriae* and, on occasion, that rights and obligations were tied to subjects' loyalty based on

---

[27] R. R. Davies 'Presidential Address: The Peoples of Britain and Ireland 1100–1400 III. Laws and Customs', *Transactions of the Royal Historical Society* 6 (1996), 1–23 (p. 11); Reynolds, *Kingdoms and Communities*, pp. 274–6. Leerssen, *National Thought in Europe*, p. 25.

[28] J. Szücs, '"Nationalität" und "Nationalbewußtsein" im Mittelalter: Versuch einer einheitlichen Begriffssprache', *Acta Historica Academiae Scientiarum Hungaricae* 18 (1972), 1–38, 245–66; B. Zientara, 'Nationale Strukturen des Mittelalters: Ein Versuch zur Kritik der Terminologie des Nationalbewußtseins unter besonderer Berücksichtigung osteuropäischer Literatur', *Saeculum* 32 (1981), 301–16; K. F. Werner, 'Les nations et le sentiment national dans l'Europe médiévale', *Revue historique* 244/2 (1970), 285–304; B. Grevin, 'De la rhétorique des nations à la théorie des races', available at http://gas.ehess.fr/docannexe/fichier/107/grevin.pdf (accessed 30 August 2020)gas.ehess.fr/docannexe.php?id=107. See also Strayer, *On the Medieval Origins of the Modern State*, pp. 45–56.

[29] A. Rigaudière, *Penser et construire l'État dans la France du Moyen Âge (XIIIE–XVE siècle)* (Paris, 2003). There are myriad studies on fourteenth- and fifteenth-century state formation, bureaucracy, legal, fiscal and military expansion and the 'rationalization' of government that cannot be included here. I refer, for instance, to R. Stein, *Magnanimous Dukes and Rising States: The Unification of the Burgundian Netherlands, 1380–1480* (Oxford, 2017).

descent.[30] Deciding who is eligible to die for the fatherland, *pro patria mori*, is a stark indication of the inclusivity or exclusivity of community membership, for it indicates whose body communities might consider to represent a rightful sacrifice, a qualification which did not pertain to allegedly weak Jewish, Muslim or women's bodies.[31] Loyalty could also be framed in terms of ethnicity. The Welsh of Snowdon claimed in 1282 that 'even if their prince should give seisin of them to the king, they themselves would refuse to do homage to any foreigner, of whose language, customs and laws they were thoroughly ignorant'.[32]

Since the early 1970s, anthropologists, sociologists and political scientists have developed new methods and approaches that deserve attention if we want to understand the value of cultural constituents to constructions of nationhood.[33] Scholars engaging these approaches have identified the fragile heralds of what are considered the later constitutive building blocks of nations: a collective name, a claim to a historical territory, ties through genealogical descent, collective memories, cultural customs, language and laws. To emphasize differences in scale and cogency, historians writing about these constituents in earlier centuries often preferred to use the term ethnicity rather than national identity, stressing the disjointed nature of a central state's infrastructure and economy as well as the weight of genealogy over legal definitions of nationality in the period 1100–1300. One of the most structured and comprehensive attempts in the 1990s to explore these constituents was the series of four articles in which Rees Davies unwrapped ethnic identity in the British Isles by looking at the significance of ethnic names, boundaries, regnal solidarities, laws

---

[30] Hirschi, *The Origins of Nationalism*, pp. 50–71; G. Post, 'Two Notes on Nationalism in the Middle Ages', *Traditio* 9 (1953), 281–320 (pp. 288–91); E. H. Kantorowicz, *The King's Two Bodies: A Study in Medieval Political Theology* (Princeton, 1957), p. 247; B. Guenée, *States and Rulers in Later Medieval Europe*, trans. J. Vale (Oxford, 1985), p. 55. For the meaning of *patria*: T. Eichenberger, *Patria: Studien zur Bedeutung des Wortes im Mittelalter (6.–12. Jahrhundert)* (Sigmaringen, 1991).

[31] Rabinow and Rose, 'Thoughts on the Concept of Biopower Today', pp. 195–217, discussing Giorgio Agamben's concept of *homo sacer*.

[32] *Registrum Epistolarum Fratris Johannis Peckham Archiepiscopi Cantuariensis*, ed. C. T. Martin, 3 vols. (London, 1882–85), II, 471: '[L]icet princeps vellet dare regi seysinam eorundem, ipsi tamen nollent homagium facere alicui extraneo, cujus linguam, mores, legesque penitus ignorant'; translation in Davies, 'The Peoples of Britain and Ireland 1100–1400 III. Laws and Customs', p. 11.

[33] C. Geertz, *The Interpretation of Cultures: Selected Essays* (London, 1973), pp. 259–60; A. D. Smith, *The Ethnic Origins of Nations* (Oxford, 1987); A. D. Smith, *National Identity* (London, 1991); A. D. Smith, *Myths and Memories of the Nation* (Oxford, 1999); Smith, *The Nation in History*; A. D. Smith, *The Cultural Foundations of Nations: Hierarchy, Covenant, and Republic* (Malden, 2008).

and customs, language and historical myths, concluding that 'the medieval world was a world of peoples' whose boundaries did not necessarily coincide with political structures.[34] Bernard Guenée professed that notions of ethnicity in the fourteenth and fifteenth centuries fed off ideas of shared biological origins, of 'blood', alongside values, customs and language.[35] Likewise, Robert Bartlett considered the ethnic group in this period to be a community that perceived itself to be held together by descent, customs, law and language, underscoring its fluid composition and the relevance of cultural attributes: dress fashions, haircuts, eating and drinking habits, festivities and weaponry, as well as shared social practices and *mores*.[36] Hugh Thomas's detailed study *The English and the Normans* went on to examine how the Anglo-Saxons and Normans assimilated after the Normans' violent conquest of 1066, arguing for the fluidity of their ethnic identities.[37]

Yet these constituents, as this book argues, do not in themselves by necessity set communities on the teleological path of national community formation. For them to do so, abstract organic and/or legal concepts, like the body politic, and authoritative beliefs about the naturalness of communities, such as Hippocratic environmental theory, and Aristotelian ideas about the common good, helped to trigger the imagination and emotions to envisage what supposedly bound and distinguished people in relation to the spaces they inhabited, in past, present and future. These concepts of the bounded, yet porous, community could be laid across existing genealogical–dynastic constructions of networks of power. Moreover, such ideas hooked onto a religious world, in which for instance the celebration of saints' vital dates commanded communal bonding and gave meaning to the calendar and landscapes. King Louis VI of France (*c.* 1081–1137), for instance, adopted St Denis as patron

---

[34] R. R. Davies, 'Presidential Address: The Peoples of Britain and Ireland 1100–1400 I. Identities', *Transactions of the Royal Historical Society* 4 (1994), 1–20 (p. 13); R. R. Davies, 'Presidential Address: The Peoples of Britain and Ireland 1100–1400 II. Names, Boundaries and Regnal Solidarities', *Transactions of the Royal Historical Society* 5 (1995), 1–20; Davies, 'The Peoples of Britain and Ireland 1100–1400 III. Laws and Customs'; and R. R. Davies, 'Presidential Address: The Peoples of Britain and Ireland 1100–1400 IV. Language and Historical Mythology', *Transactions of the Royal Historical Society* 7 (1997), 1–24.

[35] Guenée, *States and Rulers*, pp. 49–65.

[36] R. Bartlett, 'Medieval and Modern Concepts of Race and Ethnicity', *Journal of Medieval and Early Modern Studies* 31/1 (2001), 39–56 (pp. 48–9); R. Bartlett, *Gerald of Wales 1146–1223* (Oxford, 1982; unaltered text reprinted under a new title, *Gerald of Wales: A Voice of the Middle Ages* (Stroud, 2006), p. 155.

[37] H. Thomas, *The English and the Normans: Ethnic Hostility, Assimilation, and Identity, 1066–c. 1220* (Oxford, 2003).

and protector of *Francia* and in 1124 allegedly raised the saint's banner from the altar of the abbey of St Denis, calling upon the French territories to unite against the Germans' threat to take Reims.[38] These ideas and concepts were eagerly adopted at the centres of dynastic power, as convincing arguments in the military sphere, in conquest and colonization and social conflicts.

Defining race and ethnicity

This book explores images' efficacy as mental representations, or ethnotypes, and not necessarily as visual images. Several major studies have already focused on the, sometimes racialized, visualization of difference in manuscript illuminations, frescos and paintings. In 1979, the first volumes of the monumental *The Image of the Black in Western Art* appeared, preceded by Bernhard Blumenkranz's study of the Jew in medieval Christian art and followed by R. Mellinkoff's *Outcasts: Signs of Otherness in Northern European Art of the Late Middle Ages*, and Debra Strickland's study of depictions of Saracens, Jews and monstrous beings.[39] Yet where do conceptualizations in the mind, stereotypical images of groups, stand in regard to racialization and racism? To answer this question, it is necessary to discuss how race and ethnicity are defined, and the relevance of essentialization and the positioning of individuals and groups in hierarchies of power.

Scholars distinguish between ethnicity and race on two levels: the extent to which races and ethnic groups are attributed essentialized, fixed or fluid traits; and the strategic positioning of ethnotypes in hierarchies of power. Ethnicity is generally considered to rest on social and cultural practices: an ethnic

---

[38] G. M. Spiegel, 'The Cult of Saint Denis and Capetian Kingship', *Journal of Medieval History* 1 (1975), 43–70; R. Barroux, 'L'abbé Suger et la vassalité du Vexin en 1124', *Le Moyen Âge* 64 (1958), 1–26.; X. de Planhol and P. Claval, *A Historical Geography of France*, trans. J. Lloyd (Cambridge, 1994), originally published as *Géographie historique de la France* (Paris, 1988), pp. 100–8. In 1222, the Council of Oxford proclaimed St Georges's Day as a 'national feast day'; Guenée, *States and Rulers*, p. 59.

[39] L. Bugner e.a., *L'image du noir dans l'art occidental. II: Des premiers siècles chrétiens aux 'Grandes Découvertes'*, 2 vols. (Fribourg, 1979), trans. as *The Image of the Black in Western Art. II: From the Early Christian Era to the 'Age of Discovery'*, 2 vols. (Cambridge MA, 1979); B. Blumenkranz, *Juden und Judentum in der mittelalterlichen Kunst* (Stuttgart, 1965) and *Le Juif médiéval au miroir de l'art chrétien* (Paris, 1966); R. Mellinkoff, *Outcasts: Signs of Otherness in Northern European Art of the Late Middle Ages*, 2 vols. (Berkeley, 1993); D. H. Strickland, *Saracens, Demons, and Jews: Making Monsters in Medieval Art* (Princeton, 2003); S. Lipton, *Images of Intolerance: The Representation of Jews and Judaism in the Bible moralisée* (Berkeley, 1999).

group shares a language, customs, memories and laws.⁴⁰ Nonetheless, kinship relations and descent also creep in, factoring in the belief that biology plays a part in defining ethnic communities. Races – which can exist as rhetorical, imagined ethnotypes but are not real – are assigned predominantly fixed, innate characteristics, tying physical features to mental qualities.⁴¹ The extent to which ethnotypes in this book qualify as racial depends on the position groups hold in the hierarchy of power and the degree to which they are attributed more or less fixed, innate physical and mental qualities – 'ethnic/racial character traits'. This book observes that those groups in a more disadvantaged position are assigned less fluid traits than those ethnotypes higher up in the hierarchy of power.

Imagined ethnotypes (French, Jewish, Afro-American) surface within a spectrum of intersectional categories (gender, age, education and so forth). Anthropologists and sociologists argue that these categories are attributed to groups by others; individuals, interacting in a social world, are confronted with the perceptions others have, with which they, as members of groups, may (or may not) identify.⁴² However, the illusion of perceived difference is produced through practices embedded in structures of inequality, rather than the outcome of *actual* perceptions of difference.⁴³

Less explored is how positive self-categorizations emerge, which may for instance refer to alleged inherited or acquired qualities of 'civilized behaviour', rationality and virtuousness. Positive, essentialized traits claimed by ethnic groups from an elevated position in a hierarchy can in that sense be termed racial as well, just as the mirrored images of negative stereotypes of others are. Positive self-categorizations are adapted and applied to own group members holding positions of power: the master is qualified as rational and virtuous, which is practised and replicated through his elevated position in a hierarchy of power, governing the more irrational in an alleged 'virtuous pursuit of a common good'. Such self-authorized positive qualities of disciplined and

---

⁴⁰ Smith, *National Identity*, p. 21. In this book nation and ethnic group are used synonymously, in distinction to nation-states.

⁴¹ B. Isaac, *The Invention of Racism in Classical Antiquity* (Princeton, 2004), pp. 23, 33–4; R. Jenkins, *Rethinking Ethnicity: Arguments and Explorations* (2nd edn, London, 2008), pp. 77–85; G. M. Fredrickson, *Racism: A Short History* (Princeton, 2002). Still useful are M. Banton, *Racial Theories* (Cambridge, 1987) and *The Idea of Race* (London, 1977) for discussions of the meaning of 'race' in modernity.

⁴² H. Barker, *That Most Precious Merchandise: The Mediterranean Trade in Black Sea Slaves, 1260–1500* (Philadelphia, 2019), pp. 45–8; D. Shaw, *Necessary Conjunctions: The Social Self in Medieval England* (Basingstoke, 2005), p. 15.

⁴³ K. E. Fields and B. J. Fields, *Racecraft: The Soul of Inequality in American Life* (London, 2012).

rational behaviour are framed as cultural, yet are often embedded within the Hippocratic–Aristotelian framework and essentialized as well, as natural and innate, whereby culture itself is considered the product of environment.

When speaking of racism, we often consider a hierarchy of power in which the category of skin colour dominates differentiation. The Atlantic slave trade in the west is a most heinous manifestation. Skin colour is a visible, and hence dominant, signifier. If we consider racism to imply the essentialization of differences, however, its manifestation becomes broader. Geraldine Heng argues that race is the product of 'specific historical occasions in which strategic essentialisms are posited and assigned through a variety of practices and pressures, so as to construct a hierarchy of peoples for differential treatment'. The differences are essentialized 'to distribute positions and powers differentially to human groups'.[44] Significantly, she expands race's scope by observing that essentialization also stretches to ethnic/religious groups where genealogy and descent are meaningful – in Europe this holds, among others, for Jews, Muslims, Gypsies, serfs – the latter framed as descendants of Cain – and, lest we forget, Christians.

Racial categorization is used to justify differential treatment in hierarchic power relations in various, entangled contexts: in the competitive sphere (for instance through allusion to alleged corruption of power or unreliability) and in the sphere of labour exploitation (referencing physical features such as skin colour and physical strength and an alleged lack of discipline).[45] Racial categorizations reinforce hierarchies and inequalities in rewarding labour and ownership rights, justifying subjugation, exploitation and colonization. In the period studied in this book, such categorizations, commenting on strength and rationality, serve to portray which bodies were well or less equipped to protect territory and property in the military sphere, and which bodies more or less fitted to labour in the service of others. In this regard, self-categorizations of those wielding power tended to emphasize their own manly strength in combination with rationality.

Racism and discrimination are not uniquely European phenomena, nor can they be traced to a specific era. Discriminatory practices exist beyond the sphere of scientific racism. Nonetheless, exploring the impact of environmental determinism on group categorizations in Graeco-Roman antiquity, and its dissemination in the Mediterranean region, in Arabic science and hence in north-western Europe, is helpful in understanding how centres of knowledge

---

[44] Heng, *The Invention of Race*, p. 27. M. Banton, *Racial Theories* (Cambridge, 1987) and *The Idea of Race* (London, 1977) for older discussions of the meaning of 'race' in modernity.

[45] I would like to thank Anne-Ruth Wertheim for her insightful comments.

and power could talk about natural and moral communities, based on the belief that places shaped mental and physical characteristics. This book thereby focuses on the efficacy of these ideas in north-western Europe via patristic commentaries, the work of Vegetius and, from the twelfth century, via more substantial translations and adaptions of Hippocratic texts; but environmental determinism's impact on other regions and periods would merit attention as well. This book stops where environmental thought took on greater significance with the Latin translation of the *Politics* of Aristotle (384–322 BC) in about 1260, a hugely influential text that justified the exploitation of enslaved peoples through climate theory. The relevance of the concept of natural slavery, the influence and interaction of environmental theory, concepts of the common good, religion and capitalism, and the practical role of mendicant friars, physicians, notaries and merchants in organizing (forced) labour deserves a substantial study in its own right.[46]

In *Politics*, Aristotle defined the enslaved person as a piece of property, an instrument of action (labour), whose function was reflected in his strong but non-erect body but inferior rationality. Significantly – and here the attribution of mental qualities comes explicitly to the fore – Aristotle considered the enslaved to have the capacity to perceive reasoning, but not to actively reason which finest action was achievable – and these capacities were determined by climate and environment. The enslaved person's primary function, as Rachana Kamtekar explains insightfully, was bodily (similar to animals), whereas the master of enslaved persons enjoyed superior rational activity and virtue, and hence a claim to rule – so the argument goes. This capacity became actual because of education and experience, and an ability to distinguish, through deliberation, the advantageous from the opposite, the just from the unjust, 'to reason well about the good and the bad in life', which Aristotle terms *logos*. This allowed the natural master to flourish, from which the enslaved could benefit, all in pursuit of a common good. More broadly, Aristotle argued that the good state of the citizens determined how good ruling them was; political actions needed to be in accord with nature.[47] However, as this book

---

[46] Discussions in A. Pagden, 'The Peopling of the New World: Ethnos, Race and Empire in the Early-Modern World', in *The Origins of Racism in the West*, ed. M. Eliav-Feldon, B. Isaac and J. Ziegler (Cambridge, 2009), pp. 292–312; A. Wear, 'Place, Health, and Disease: The *Airs, Waters, Places* Tradition in Early Modern England and North America', *Journal of Medieval and Early Modern Studies* 38/3 (2008), 443–65; M. Harrison, *Climates and Constitutions: Health, Race, Environment and British Imperialism in India, 1600–1850* (New Delhi, 1999).

[47] R. Kamtekar, 'Studying Ancient Political Thought Through Ancient Philosophers: The Case of Aristotle and Natural Slavery', *Polis: The Journal for Ancient Greek*

makes clear, these explicitly formulated ideas were already implicitly present and foreshadowed in the ethnographies of subjected peoples that stood in an unbroken Ciceronian tradition as well. They are reflected in the self-presentations of rational activity and deliberative speech of those engaged in urbane and courtly life, aided by regimens and manuals.

Race and ethnicity in historiography

So, how has historiography treated the relevance of environmental theory in the period 950–1250, before the translation Aristotle's *Politics*? And to what extent, according to historians, were ethnic traits between 950 and 1250 considered natural or fluid features, under the influence of divine grace, upbringing, social contacts and migration?

To date, Clarence Glacken's monumental *Traces on the Rhodian Shore*, published in 1967, is the only extensive study on climate theory that spans the period from antiquity to the eighteenth century.[48] Although dedicating 180 pages to environmental thought in 'The Christian Middle Ages', Glacken was quite dismissive of the period's contribution to it, a study of which 'would not be rewarding since it would only tediously and repetitiously accumulate examples of a few basic ideas'.[49] However, his judgement rests more on an evaluation of the systematic, scientific development of climate theory than on its impact. Nonetheless, Glacken's critique left its mark, as it was copied into Robert Bartlett's formidable biography of the cleric Gerald of Wales (c. 1146–c. 1223), first published in 1982. Although Bartlett identified the use of environmental theory in the chapter dedicated to Gerald of Wales's ethnographic achievement, he argued that its application was unsystematic, fragmented and disjointed.[50] This was in keeping with the fact that Gerald of Wales was educated in Paris in the 1160s or 1170s – when environmental medicine was not yet a standard element of school curricula. Bartlett acknowledged that Gerald of Wales, in his ethnography of Wales and Ireland, like the German chronicler and bishop Otto of Freising (c. 1112–58), in his description of Pannonia, was making specific arguments about civilization, environment,

---

Political Thought 33 (2016), 150–71 (pp. 151–3, 157, 164); N. D. Smith, 'Aristotle's Theory of Natural Slavery', *Phoenix* 37/2 (1983), 109–22 (pp. 110, 119).

[48] C. J. Glacken, *Traces on the Rhodian Shore: Nature and Culture in Western Thought from Ancient Times to the End of the Eighteenth Century* (Berkeley, 1967). An earlier contribution is M. J. Tooley, 'Bodin and the Mediaeval Theory of Climate', *Speculum* 28/1 (1953), 64–83.

[49] Glacken, *Traces on the Rhodian Shore*, pp. 255–6. Bartlett, *Gerald of Wales*, p. 204.

[50] Bartlett, *Gerald of Wales: A Voice of the Middle Ages*, pp. 204–5.

economic development and lawlessness in the sphere of colonization and conquest – as did, among others, William Jones, John Gillingham and James Muldoon.⁵¹ Yet the underlying rhetorical argument, that environments shaped bodies and minds and justified power hierarchies, was not explored further. Indeed, Bartlett stated that the manner in which Gerald of Wales contrasted degrees of self-control in less or more civilized peoples was 'hardly the raison d'être of the work'.⁵² This book, conversely, argues that such representations of the natural ability of human beings to rationally engage in political life formed a core argument to justify a status of servility or freedom, and hence colonization and conquest.

In his major study *The Making of Europe*, published in 1993 – the first comprehensive attempt to understand the impact of ethnic identification on institutional practices and the Church's expansion in Europe's 'fringes' – Bartlett observed that 'it is worth stressing at the outset that, while the language of race – *gens*, *natio*, "blood", "stock", etc. – is biological, its medieval reality was almost entirely cultural'.⁵³ He continued this argument in Thomas Hahn's special issue 'Race and Ethnicity in the Middle Ages' in the *Journal of Medieval and Early Modern Studies*, published in 2001, arguing that peoples (*gentes* or *nationes*) were perceived to be 'ethnic' genealogical descent groups distinguished by fluid cultural features, rather than 'timeless descent groups of fixed nature'. Climate theory did not imply, in Bartlett's view, that people believed groups sharing a common ancestry also shared fixed traits. Instead, according to Bartlett, climate theory 'contradicts the idea of a constant national character'. However, as Bartlett concluded, 'medieval conceptions of race [here meaning ethnicity, fluid, cultural] and nation are so tightly linked that is virtually impossible to draw up a bibliography of medieval nationalism that is not also a bibliography of medieval ethnicity'.⁵⁴ It is a comment with far-reaching implications, for what if environmental theory did infer that group characteristics were natural, inherited and not so easily changeable, and

---

51 W. R. Jones, 'England against the Celtic Fringe: A Study in Cultural Stereotypes', *Journal of World History / Cahiers d'histoire mondiale* 13 (1971), 155–71; J. Gillingham, *The English in the Twelfth Century: Imperialism, National Identity and Political Values* (Woodbridge, 2000); J. Muldoon, *Identity on the Medieval Irish Frontier: Degenerate Englishmen, Wild Irishmen, Middle Nations* (Gainesville, 2003).
52 Bartlett, *Gerald of Wales*, p. 186.
53 R. Bartlett, *The Making of Europe: Conquest, Colonization and Cultural Change 950–1350* (London, 1993), p. 197.
54 Bartlett, 'Medieval and Modern Concepts of Race and Ethnicity', pp. 46–7, 53. Again, in 'Illustrating Ethnicity in the Middle Ages', in *The Origins of Racism in the West*, ed. M. Eliav-Feldon, B. Isaac and J. Ziegler (Cambridge, 2009), pp. 132–56, Bartlett barely touches upon climate theory.

what if these ideas carried more weight in this period than expected? Does it suggest, perhaps, that race is not so much produced by nations but evolves along with them?

This partial neglect of environmental theory's impress after antiquity obfuscated how environmentally deterministic ideas about communities' natural character traits became entangled with religious ideas about sin and salvation, genealogy, language and cultural norms. It also underestimated the contribution of scientific knowledge in this period to ideas about the governance of kingdoms, urban communities, households and selves and the generation of stereotypes of the people being governed and those governing. Robert Moore's *The Formation of a Persecuting Society*, first published in 1987, was the first major study to address the stereotypical classification of various minority groups.[55] Moore observed that the negative representation, hostile attitudes, behaviour towards and legislation concerning Jews, lepers, heretics and prostitutes between 950 and 1250 emerged as the evolving Church sought to define a more exclusive, universal Christian community. The expansion of power of the centralizing Church and state led to the creation of more distinct boundaries, sharply distinguishing between in and out groups. However, Moore's envisioning of incremental stereotyping and hostility towards others was also criticized. David Nirenberg's *Communities of Violence*, published in 1996, underscored the situational aspect and non-linearity of hostile othering.[56] This ground-breaking study, distinguishing between systemic and cataclysmic violence against minorities, showed how hostile acts against minorities reflected measured strategy rather than a blind fury and hatred fuelled emotionally by ethnic stereotyping. An economy of hostility served to buttress economic and legal struggles; attacks on minorities with various different legal and economic statuses were a deflection of claims directed at central authorities.

Jeffrey Jerome Cohen's contribution 'On Saracen Enjoyment: Some Fantasies of Race in Late Medieval France and England' to the above-mentioned 2001 'Race and Ethnicity' issue was the first substantial publication to directly address the question of the relevance of environmental determinism to constructions of race and ethnicity in this period.[57] However, the first monograph about the impact of environmental theory to appear since Glacken's again

---

[55] R. I. Moore, *The Formation of a Persecuting Society: Authority and Deviance in Western Europe, 950–1250* (Oxford, 1987; 2nd rev. edn, Malden, 2007).

[56] D. Nirenberg, *Communities of Violence: Persecution of Minorities in the Middle Ages* (Princeton, 1996).

[57] J. J. Cohen, 'On Saracen Enjoyment: Some Fantasies of Race in Late Medieval France and England', *Journal of Medieval and Early Modern Studies* 31/1 (2001), 113–46.

focused on antiquity. Published in 2004, Benjamin Isaac's *The Invention of Racism in Classical Antiquity* is an important study that argues that Hippocratic and Aristotelian thought led to 'proto-racist thinking', because it considered mental and physical group characteristics to be shaped by climate, intergenerational transmission, as well as ideas about pure lineage.[58] Looking ahead to eighteenth-century scientific racist constructions, Isaac nonetheless skipped the period from early Christendom until the eighteenth century. Again, the argument surfaced that racial constructs in modernity were more structural and systematic, and in earlier times disjointed. Exploring the views of Greeks and Romans about Phoenicians, Carthaginians, Syrians, Egyptians, Mountaineers and Plainsmen, Gauls, Germans and Jews, Isaac also paid little attention to racism based on skin colour. Afterwards, this omission was addressed by David Goldenberg in the volume *The Origins of Racism in the West* (co-edited by Isaac), examining skin colour, hermeneutic blackness and racist descriptions of black people in antiquity in the context of death and sin.[59]

A recurrent claim, in this context, that runs like a thread through the historiography of the 'Middle Ages', is that Christendom's universalistic claims rendered ethnic or racial distinctions less relevant. Yet the perspective that Christianity's universalism inherently takes a non-racial view is problematic. In particular Denise Buell has shown, in my view convincingly, that *gentes* continued to be relevant categories in Christianity, which talks in physiological terms about undergoing a rebirth in Christ.[60] Moreover, as this book discusses in chapter 2, schoolmen pathologized the common descent of humanity in response to original sin, considering some peoples to be of lesser descent than others. Genealogy and environmental thought in early Christianity and scholastic thought were also addressed, in 2009, in the significant volume *The Origins of Racism in the West*, covering the period from antiquity until 1700.[61] In particular the chapter by Peter Biller about the application of medical science to ethnic groups and Joseph Ziegler's discussion of physiognomy for

---

[58] Isaac, *The Invention of Racism in Classical Antiquity*.
[59] D. Goldenberg, 'Racism, Color Symbolism and Color Prejudice', in *The Origins of Racism in the West*, ed. M. Eliav-Feldon, B. Isaac and J. Ziegler (Cambridge, 2009), pp. 88–108. For the term hermeneutic blackness, coined by Geraldine Heng, see p. 106 in chapter 2.
[60] D. K. Buell, *Why This New Race: Ethnic Reasoning in Early Christianity* (New York, 2005). See also D. K. Buell, 'Early Christian Universalism and Modern Forms of Racism', in *The Origins of Racism in the West*, ed. M. Eliav-Feldon, B. Isaac and J. Ziegler (Cambridge, 2009), pp. 109–31.
[61] M. Eliav-Feldon, B. Isaac and J. Ziegler (ed.), *The Origins of Racism in the West* (Cambridge, 2009).

the first time substantially reviewed the relevance of Hippocratic and Galenic thought for race and ethnicity in the twelfth and thirteenth centuries. Charles de Miramon's original work on race in the context of animal breeding and its relevance to social group hierarchy also stands out.[62]

Finally, in recent years, two important books have appeared centring race in this period. In 2018, Geraldine Heng's *The Invention of Race in the European Middle Ages* took on the monumental task of exploring, through a close reading of case studies, how instances of *race-making* worked in practices and language, essentializing and institutionalizing differences.[63] This rich study incorporated a range of sources: narrative, visual and hagiographical, looking at racial representations, both within and beyond Europe, of Jews, Muslims, Mongols, Gypsies and others. It makes several important points. Firstly, that talking about others is talking about selves, and that virtues of prowess and chivalry are benchmarks for making distinctions in a hierarchy of power. Secondly, Heng too acknowledges that a universalizing Christendom engaged an essentializing language talking about race, and that badges and ordinances concerning Jews transformed a language of difference into practice. However, less discussed is the unstable and fragmented apparatus of the 'state' in this period. In addition, in 2019 Lindsay Kaplan's *Figuring Racism in Medieval Christianity* made the important argument that the discourse of racism pertaining to Jews concerned, above all, narratives of servitude in a hierarchy of power.[64]

This book argues that images of others and selves, representing various levels of rationality and strength, virtue and vice, served to buttress forms of subjugation with the voice of religious and scientific authority. For, in conjunction with practices, it is necessary to look closely at the underlying scientific conceptions, ideas and attitudes as well, in particular pertaining to the perceived relationship between bodies and environments, as authoritative knowledge supported images and ideologies that allowed for such hierarchies. This will help in understanding the interactions between ideas and praxis and move *race-making* beyond any 'medieval' frame.

---

[62] P. Biller, 'Proto-Racial Thought in Medieval Science', in *The Origins of Racism in the West*, ed. M. Eliav-Feldon, B. Isaac and J. Ziegler (Cambridge, 2009), pp. 157–80; J. Ziegler, 'Physiognomy, Science, and Proto-racism 1200–1500', in *The Origins of Racism in the West*, ed. M. E. Eliav-Feldon, B. Isaac and J. Ziegler (Cambridge, 2009), pp. 181–99; C. de Miramon, 'Noble Dogs, Noble Blood: The Invention of the Concept of Race in the Late Middle Ages', in *The Origins of Racism in the West*, ed. M. Eliav-Feldon, B. Isaac and J. Ziegler (Cambridge, 2009), pp. 200–16.

[63] Heng, *The Invention of Race*.

[64] M. L. Kaplan, *Figuring Racism in Medieval Christianity* (New York, 2019).

Fresh approaches: discourses and images

After the discussion of the main arguments of this book and the historiography in broad terms, it is now useful to say more about the approach the book takes. In no way does *Ethnicity in Medieval Europe* wish to underplay the undeniable force of political argument – expressed in language but also in buildings or artefacts – and practices of power, effected through institutions, in national community-formation processes or race-making practices. Yet, as this book argues, it is necessary to also look at how authoritative voices of power tapped religious and scientific discourses and ideas, alongside emotive, popular, cultural and social assumptions, to understand how images of ethnicity resonated in relation to territory, space and power. In this context, discourse is considered not to be present in the object itself but enabling it to appear, rendering statements possible.[65] Discourses shape the ways in which reality is perceived and constructed, and discursive fields lay out the normative parameters by which we process the world around us.[66] Hence, ethnotypes, and by extension ethnic identities feeding off discourses, are not stable and inherited but, rather, continuously renegotiated. By asking *how, why and in which reference frameworks ethnic groups, nations or races are imagined*, by looking at how nationhood is talked about, we can historicize the processes and contingencies underlying their conceptualization.

To this end, this book recontextualizes the influence of environmental determinism on conceptions of peoples and spaces. It is here that my book takes a different approach from Geraldine Heng's *The Invention of Race*, looking first at the authoritative knowledge that informed ethnic images, that is to say, what religion and science by process *did with* ethnic stereotypes, rather than considering them to be outcomes. Thus, this book raises the question, firstly, of how and on what grounds people imagined the tangible or metaphorical boundaries of their communities in the period 950–1250; secondly, how and on what grounds community members were classified; and thirdly, how, or how convincingly, courtiers and schoolmen employed these markers or stereotypes in arguments of colonization and conflict. The highly stereotypical, generic ethnotypes flowing from these religious and environmental-medical discourses thereby foregrounded shared mental and physical features and customs, or *habitus*.[67]

---

[65] Ball, *Foucault, Power, and Education*, pp. 19–20.
[66] M. E. Farrar, *Building the Body Politic: Power and Urban Space in Washington, D.C.* (Urbana, 2008), pp. 6–7.
[67] For general approaches to the body and ethnicity: J. W. Burton, *Culture and the Human Body: An Anthropological Perspective* (Prospect Heights, 2001), pp. 51–68.

This book thereby departs from the premise that, instead of exploring constitutive elements or mapping population numbers that demonstrate awareness of nationhood, we should look at the discourses feeding into representations (ethnotypes or memes) of ethnic categories.[68] The ethnotype, it must be added, can serve as a synecdoche for individual members of what were in reality diverse communities. The representations shaped by these discourses drive and reflect changes in the configurations of the labels (such as language, physical appearance, fixed natural traits, cultural traits, descent, laws and territory) that set out the perceived boundaries of groups, producing ethnic categories. The contents of the representations have meanings attached to them that are generated from intergroup and intragroup relations, comparing and mirroring others. What the intergroup and intragroups are depends on context, i.e., on the referential group boundaries. Representations are thus always relational and imbued with meaning, drawn from beliefs, norms and actions. Changes in meaning occur through communicative processes, via rituals and *images*. This method draws upon the work of Ivana Marková and Stephen Reicher.[69]

Ethnotypes are defined here as representations, whereas ethnicity is the ascribed/self-belief of falling under a certain category. My perspective is thereby that people in communities accept (or reject) categories whose imaginary representations are fed by discourses, and that people are born into worlds structured by these categories, which are changeable. Chapters 1–3 look at the religious and scientific discourses informing these categories' representation and their rhetorical use, whereas chapters 4–6 explore the strategic use of these representations in intra- and intergroup relations, social conflicts, war and colonization efforts. Over the period 950–1250, monks and schoolmen reshuffled the labels shaping the representations because they had access to different authoritative texts, but also lived and worked in a changing world marked by encounters and confrontations with others both inside and outside Christendom.

This approach can be used for other periods and communities as well (such as urban ones), which are just as significant in their own context. It does not work with beginnings and outcomes of the development of nationhood, but

---

[68] I refrain from using the term 'meme' throughout this study as it in my view makes obscure the human agency involved in spreading images and symbols before the digital age of algorithms. For the term: R. Dawkins, *The Selfish Gene* (Oxford, 1976).

[69] I. Marková, 'Social Identities and Social Representations: How are They Related?', in *Social Representations and Identity: Content, Process, and Power*, ed. G. Moloney and I. Walker (Basingstoke, 2007), pp. 215–36; S. Reicher, 'The Context of Social Identity: Domination, Resistance, and Change', *Political Psychology* 25/6 (2004), 921–45.

instead looks at processes in which constellations of labels are negotiated, arguing that the focus of historical research should look at the choreography of configurations of markers maintaining boundaries rather than at beginnings and endings of the existence of categories. Hence, this book is not interested in identifying when 'the' ethnic group emerges but, rather, in how boundaries are reconfigured depending on context.

Expanding the enquiry into how boundaries are reconfigured, this book argues that it is necessary to complicate how perceptions of time and space inform a sense of nationhood as well. Historians have mostly looked at how concepts of time in societies contributed to intergroup community formation. Thus, Anderson argued that, with the rise of print capitalism, the experience of 'horizontal time' allowed community members to imagine their co-members' daily regimes, in distinction to the earlier supposedly vertical or messianic experience of time.[70] The impact of narratives of a shared past, shared traumas and victories and future destinies in the shaping of a collective memory has also been researched extensively.[71] However, we need to expand our enquiry into how *intragroup comparisons* created a hierarchy of ethnicities as well, by positioning various coeval groups unevenly on a temporal-geographical axis. Known as stagism, a term coined by Dipesh Chakrabarty who applied it to later periods, authoritative voices thereby represent coeval groups as dwelling in different timeframes, which reflects their supposed position on the ladder of civilizational progress.[72] From circa 1100, historiographers, political theorists and poets writing *chansons de geste* thereby infused the eschatological *translatio* motif about the progress of power and knowledge in time and space, from east to west and past to present with environmental determinism. The combination allowed for intragroup mirroring in which the Latinate man could stand for masculine self-discipline, rationality and urbanity, the prize of progress. Historians in French and English monasteries and courts mirrored these Europeans with images of Muslims, southerners, Jews, Slavs, Irish, Scandinavians, heathens, women, rustics and heretics, marked by a range of negative traits of effeminacy, weakness, irrationality, cunning, lack of discipline and rurality. Intragroup comparison thereby fed intergroup alignment, especially in the context of the wars and colonization. Yet, alongside intragroup mirroring, intergroup competition under the umbrella (or field, in Bourdieu's

---

[70] Anderson, *Imagined Communities*, p. 24.
[71] J. Pollmann, *Memory in Early Modern Europe, 1500–1800* (Oxford, 2017).
[72] D. Chakrabarty, *Provincializing Europe: Postcolonial Thought and Historical Difference* (Princeton, 2009), pp. 4–10.

terminology) of Christendom also occurred, in the urban schools, courts and armies, over levels of devoutness and cultural finesse.

Character, capital and identification

A specific aspect of ethnotypes involves the grafting onto the body of shared *mental affects* or stereotypes of ethnic character.[73] It is here that Hippocratic environmental theory and Galenic humoral theory become particularly relevant. Before turning to these ideas, however, it is necessary to first address a few persistent assumptions about premodern categorization.

To date, premodern notions of ethnic character have been set off against those of modernity, whereby scholars consider the latter period to be dominated by method, taxonomy and systematic comparison, and the earlier by chaos and irrationality. For instance, Michel Foucault claimed that before modernity, writers arranged characteristics unsystematically and based upon similarities rather than comparisons.[74] Nonetheless, ethnic classifications in earlier periods were probably more stable than scholars have assumed. Firstly, they were arranged in accordance with the contemporary temporal-spatial framework of order, from past to present, east to west, based upon *moral* comparative classification. Secondly, although scientific categorizations based on environmental medicine were qualitative (based on colour, dryness or wetness, heat or coldness), by means of which human and non-human species were

---

[73] G. Blaicher (ed.), *Erstarrtes Denken: Studien zu Klischee, Stereotyp und Vorurteil in englischsprachiger Literatur* (Tübingen, 1987) for the prominence of ethnic character as an index marker in stereotyping. Especially useful references to ethnic stereotypes circa 1200 are found in Bartlett's 'Race and Ethnicity', and Ibid., 'Illustrating Ethnicity in the Middle Ages', pp. 132–56 P. Meyvaert, '"Rainaldus est malus sciptor Francigenus" – Voicing National Antipathy in the Middle Ages', *Speculum* 66/4 (1991), 743–63; H. Beumann, 'Zur Nationenbildung im Mittelalter', in *Nationalismus in vorindustrieller Zeit*, ed. O. Dann (Munich, 1986), 21–33; G. Cerwinka, 'Völkercharakteristiken in historiographischen Quellen der Salier- und Stauferzeit', in *Festschrift für Friedrich Hausmann*, ed. H. Ebner (Graz, 1977), 59–80; C. Brühl, *Deutschland, Frankreich: Die Geburt zweier Völker* (Cologne 1990), 243–302; G. Blaicher, 'Zur Entstehung und Verbreitung nationaler Stereotypen in und über England', *Deutsche Vierteljahrschrift für Literaturwissenschaft und Geistesgeschichte* 51 (1977), 549–74.

[74] M. Foucault, *The Order of Things: An Archaeology of the Human Sciences* (New York, 1994), p. xviii. Leerssen, *National Thought*, p. 56, contends that the 'Middle Ages had, to be sure, known many commonplaces, stereotypes and prejudices about certain sets of people, but these were generally speaking neither stable or systematic. Nobody was sure how the category "French" related to the category "Picardian", what was an Irishman and what a good subject of the King of England.'

lumped together (i.e. phlegmatic women, phlegmatic fish), this does not imply that the method was unsystematic either.

Historians also claimed that moral character in the period before modernity denoted a person's external *reputation in society* rather than her or his internal *personality*, and as such was non-essential. Character was said to be 'behavioural, [and] social, referring to the various manners of our times; not a mode of being, but a mode of speaking, dressing, posturing'.[75] Robert Bartlett argued that *mos* (pl. *mores*) in the twelfth–thirteenth centuries frequently designated 'manner', 'way of life' or social practice, although he acknowledged that in the work of the cleric Gerald of Wales the meaning of *mores* slipped from customs into morals.[76] Yet, although this conception of *mos* as a custom certainly is omnipresent, regimens linked behavioural manners to self-discipline, to morals and character traits as well. A person's physiology, moreover, was impacted by such manners, behaviour, religious virtue and climate. Graeco-Arabic medical theory, influenced by Hippocrates and Galen, viewed the mental and physical features of men, women, ethnic and age groups to be intersectional, whereby both the inner workings of the body *and* the mind were subject to external influences known as the non-naturals. Indeed, the metabolic effects of the non-naturals on the balance of the four humours (explained in chapter 2) meant that bodies were considered to be porous, for external factors such as the air, smells, sights and emotions constantly impacted on the inner body, mind and emotional state, manipulating the complexion or temperament. Mortal beings, vice versa, could regulate the body and mind through the release of bodily excretions, bloodletting, spit, mucus, sweat and breath. These medical ideas had not disappeared entirely from sight before the twelfth century. The monthly health *Regimen duodecim mensium*, of which an eighth-century manuscript survives from Lorsch and that was included in the Carolingian calendar, was perhaps produced for the clergy in the chapter-houses.[77] It gave advice on diet, bloodletting and bathing in accordance with the seasons. Certainly in texts engaging environmental

---

[75] J. Leerssen, 'Character (Moral)', in *Imagology: The Cultural Construction and Literary Representation of National Characters: A Critical Survey*, ed. M. Beller and J. Leerssen (Amsterdam, 2007), 284–90 (pp. 284–6).

[76] R. Bartlett and R. Davies observe that manners (*mores*) and customs (*consuetudines*) might refer to exterior badges of identity such as clothing, hair style, modes of warfare and use of weaponry. Bartlett also interprets *cultus* as dress, but it can also mean 'care for', education or culture. Bartlett, *Gerald of Wales*, pp. 147–71; Davies, 'The Peoples of Britain and Ireland 1100–1400 III. Laws and Customs', pp. 13–15.

[77] J. M. van Winter, *Middeleeuwers in drievoud: Hun woonplaats, verwantschap en voeding* (Hilversum, 2017), 205–47, 269–79, 305–10; R. Jansen-Sieben, 'Een Middelnederlands maandregimen uit de 14ᵉ eeuw', in *Verslagen en mededelingen van de*

theory, such as William Fitzstephen's *Description of London* (written between 1170 and 1183), it is hard to distinguish between good manners and inner traits like softness and kindness.[78] Moreover, social customs could evolve into nature through acculturation, while natural dispositions could be modified through external environmental, cultural, religious and social conditions.

Based upon these ideas, ethnic groups were attributed shared features: innate mental dispositions (cowardice) and physical qualities (weak bodies) that in part were environmentally determined, yet which remained fluid and subject to free will, vices and virtues.[79] The ethnic virtue or *vitium* – a vice inherited at the fall of mankind and materializing in a person's complexion – resonated in the manner of life or *habitus* that by means of education, arduous moral introspection and hard practice could potentially be altered, although only through great effort.[80] While religious and medical discourses became entangled, vice thereby continued to be a stain that man was urged to wipe out. It was, for that matter, considered a factor that allegedly determined the outcome of ethnic groups' capacity to embrace Christendom, as well as their fate in history and the history of mankind itself. However, the bodily corruption that arose with the original sin came with a dysfunctional capacity to change that revealed itself in the willingness, or lack thereof, to experience a rebirth in Christ. Jews, like serfs, were said, in a biblical–genealogical narrative, to be essentially cursed by the 'mark of Cain', a prefiguring of the rejection of Jesus, that destined them to a life of unfreedom.[81] Racist thinking is ensconced in such ideas. The medical–religious narratives thereby gave authority and substance to Jews' and serfs' separate legal status and were sometimes tacked onto the inhabitants of regions being colonized as well, as discussed in chapter 6.

Looking at the contexts and beliefs underlying the employment of ethnic character types, we can consequently pinpoint instances where its potentiality was capitalized on in the act of imagining the community. Ethnotypes in the

---

Koninklijke Academie voor Nederlandse taal- en letterkunde (nieuwe reeks). Jaargang 1971 (Gent, 1972), pp. 171–209.

[78] William Fitzstephen, *Descriptio Nobilissimae Civitatis Londoniae*, ed. J. C. Robertson, Materials for the History of Thomas Becket, Archbishop of Canterbury, 7 vols. (London, 1877), iii, 3–5, 8.

[79] C. Weeda, 'The Fixed and the Fluent: Geographical Determinism, Ethnicity, and Religion c. 1100–1300 CE', in *The Routledge Handbook of Identity and the Environment in the Classical and Medieval Worlds*, ed. R. F. Kennedy and M. Jones-Lewis (London, 2016), pp. 93–113.

[80] C. J. Nederman, 'Nature, Ethics, and the Doctrine of "Habitus": Aristotelian Moral Psychology in the Twelfth-Century', *Traditio* 45 (1989–90), 87–110.

[81] J. Cohen, *Living Letters of the Law: Ideas of the Jew in Medieval Christianity* (Berkeley, 1999), pp. 28, 247; R. Mellinkoff, *The Mark of Cain* (Berkeley, 1981), pp. 92–8.

tenth to thirteenth centuries shared several features with early modern characterizations of peoples, as outlined by Franz Stanzel: they were potentially ethnocentric, especially in texts making use of climate theory, and morally schematized within the reference frameworks of religion, *imperium*, colonization and the body politic.[82]

Now schematization flows from the relational aspect of identity, whereby self-perceived boundaries develop by contrasting the self, or autogroup, and its perceived and normative cultural–social values, with the other, or heterogroup.[83] The juxtaposition often has recourse to wielding stereotypes that are homogenizing and resistant, constituting, according to Aronson, Wilson and Akert, 'a generalisation about a group of people in which incidental characteristics are assigned to virtually all members of the group, regardless of actual variation among the members'.[84] Images of the other, be they derogatory or commendatory, thereby reflect, mirror, reaffirm, sharpen and accelerate self-images.[85] Thus, in a situational context, stereotypical markers are affirmative and constitutive, shaping social relations and encouraging behavioural acts.[86] We can see such schematizations at work in the stagist narrative of the *translatio studii et imperii* – a *temporal* and *spatial* comparison – conceiving peoples of the past to be situated in the east, a locus of bygone power, learning and religion, and the disciplined peoples of the present to be dwelling in the west. Thus, places of otherness, and the peoples living in them, are framed in a temporal, forward-looking narrative of progress.[87] In the context of the

---

[82] F. Stanzel, *Europäer: Ein imagologischer Essay* (Heidelberg, 1998), p. 85. M. Beller, 'Stereotypes', in *Imagology: The Cultural Construction and Literary Representation of National Characters: A Critical Survey*, ed. M. Beller and J. Leerssen (Amsterdam, 2007), pp. 429–34.

[83] T. Hylland Eriksen, *Ethnicity and Nationalism: Anthropological Perspectives* (2nd edn, London, 2002), pp. 10, 23–4. Eriksen's approach to ethnicity is socio-anthropological, stressing the relational aspects of ethnicity and the role that *boundary maintenance* plays in forging ethnic identity, which was first set out by Fredrick Barth. Autostereotypes are stereotypes about the own group; heterostereotypes are typologies of the other.

[84] E. Aronson, T. D. Wilson and R. M. Akert, *Social Psychology* (Upper Saddle River, 2005), p. 434.

[85] Brühl, *Deutschland, Frankreich*, p. 275.

[86] L. E. Scales, 'Bread, Cheese and Genocide: Imagining the Destruction of Peoples in Medieval Western Europe', *History* 92 (2007), 284–300 (pp. 284–5).

[87] D. L. Gassman, '*Translatio studii*': *A Study of Intellectual History in the Thirteenth Century*, 2 volumes (Ann Arbor, 1973); U. Krämer, '*Translatio imperii et studii*': *Zum Geschichts- und Kulturverständnis in der französischen Literatur des Mittelalters und der frühen Neuzeit* (Bonn, 1996), pp. 113–68; H. Grundmann, 'Sacerdotium – Regnum – Studium. Zur Wertung der Wissenschaft im 13. Jahrhundert', *Archiv*

twelfth-century drive to expand the settlements to the north-west, north-east and east of Europe, the narrative of cultural and religious ascendancy likewise justified colonization and conquest, which was mirrored in legal and political discussions about *dominium*, property rights and labour. The ethnic self-images in this period in confrontation with the other drew on affects of anxiety or desire by depicting regions of colonization as desirable and bountiful landscapes squandered by allegedly barbaric local populations, as discussed in chapters 5 and 6.[88]

Ethnic reputations also serve as an asset or liability in negotiations within the social or political sphere, depending on and in dialogue with contemporary values. The sources suggest that the ethnic categories in this period invariably were linked to class distinctions – e.g. mentioning Anglo-Saxon rustics in a pejorative sense while praising Anglo-Norman courtliness – and hence that the ethnotypes were shaped in the milieu of the higher social strata. Henri Tajfel's social identity theory postulates that positive social images enhance the attractiveness of a group, strengthening its members' self-confidence and drawing outsiders in.[89] The potency of the discourse of difference in this sense depends upon the openness of a society and the prospect of social mobility.

By extension, in *White Nation*, a study of nationalism in present-day Australia, Ghassan Hage argued that denigrating stereotypes of the other feed off the privileged relationship that a community allegedly has with the territorial space it inhabits – a sense of *patria*.[90] Nationalists fantasize about a homely, domesticated space that is in need of protection while it is supposedly threatened by undesirable others. For multicultural Australia, Hage argues that its population strives to accumulate whiteness – and its alleged concomitant psychological traits and moral positions – because *nationality* might be considered a form of physical–cultural or naturalized capital – 'the sum of valued knowledge, styles, social and physical (bodily) characteristics and practical behavioural dispositions within a given field'.[91] Whiteness and its

---

für Kulturgeschichte 34 (1952), pp. 5–21; É. Jeauneau, Translatio studii: *The Transmission of Learning: A Gilsonian Theme* (Toronto, 1995).

[88] S. L. Gilman, *Difference and Pathology: Stereotypes of Sexuality, Race, and Madness* (Ithaca, 1985), p. 19, for stereotypes as the projection of anxiety.

[89] H. Tajfel, *Human Groups and Social Categories: Studies in Social Psychology* (Cambridge, 1981).

[90] G. Hage, *White Nation: Fantasies of White Supremacy in a Multicultural Society* (New York, 2000); P. Bourdieu, 'The Forms of Capital', in *Handbook of Theory and Research for the Sociology of Education*, ed. J. G. Richardson (New York, 1986), pp. 241–58.

[91] Hage speaks of 'practical nationality': the sum of accumulated nationally sanctified and valued social-physical cultural styles and dispositions as well as valued

mental traits are in this sphere bargaining chips which powerful elite groups supposably possess naturally, often through birth, and which others in an open society can, at least in theory, appropriate. Along with physical qualities such as whiteness, alleged ethnic affects corresponding with social values thus can be valuable assets (cultural capital), which, especially in open rather than more closed, corporative societies, can be wielded to gain social standing or to amass power (symbolic capital).[92] This also means that stereotypes can be either an asset or detrimental when attempting to gain access to and influence in higher stations.

Hage's approach sheds light on how the imagined boundaries of ethnic groups became more pronounced in a spatial and social context between 950 and 1250, utilizing moral and bodily markers. This happened by entangling climate theory with concepts of the sacralized *patria* and eschatology, presenting the outer reaches of western and north-eastern Europe as imaginary, highly desirable, future promised lands.[93] In- and outgroups consequently became more sharply defined, within communities as well as vis-à-vis other territories.[94] Hage's approach also helps us to explore how elites, competing within the field of Christendom, in a bid to appropriate Christian values contributed to the stronger demarcation of territorial identities vis-à-vis the referential framework of the Church. Particularly in the crusader movement emerging in the late eleventh century, the Church's forcibly articulated religious norms of behaviour incited the western European aristocracy to claim for itself the

---

characteristics (such as character) within a given field. This capital is, according to Hage, transformed into the symbolic capital of national belonging. Cf. Hage, *White Nation*, pp. 20, 33–42, 53, 62–4, 73–9.

[92] This is related to what Bourdieu termed '*habitus*', the cultural dispositions of the elite. These dispositions, naturalized by the aristocracy claiming they are innate, give access to the symbolic capital of power; P. Bourdieu, *Distinction: A Social Critique of the Judgement of Taste*, trans. R. Nice (Cambridge MA, 1984), pp. 23–4. Hage, *White Nation*, p. 62.

[93] For the concept of imaginary geographies see E. Said, *Orientalism* (reprint with a new preface, London, 2003), pp. 49–72; D. Gregory, 'Imaginative Geographies', *Progress in Human Geography* 19 (1995), 447–85.

[94] L. Schmugge, 'Über "nationale" Vorurteile im Mittelalter', *Deutsches Archiv für Erforschung des Mittelalters* 38 (1982), 439–59 for the rise of ethnic stereotyping in the twelfth century among crusaders, students and pilgrims. J. Huizinga, 'Patriotisme en nationalisme in de Europeesche geschiedenis tot het einde der negentiende eeuw', in *Verzamelde werken*, ed. J. Huizinga, 9 vols. (Haarlem, 1948–53), IV, 497–554; C. Weeda, 'Ethnic Stereotyping in Twelfth-Century Paris', *Difference and Identity in Francia and Medieval France*, ed. M. Cohen and J. Firnhaber-Baker (Farnham, 2010), 115–35 for the increase of stereotypes at the University of Paris in relation to boundary maintenance theory.

reputation of embodying ideal forms of rational behaviour, which sparked competition between various self-proclaimed chosen peoples.[95] Thus, on the crusades, the French, the Normans and the Teutons fight over their position in 'God's army', operating a gendered language. As discussed in chapter 5, the English, conspicuously avoiding this battle over martial talents, instead took to positioning themselves as paragons of urbane civility, charm and intelligence, compared to the backward rustics dwelling in the Irish regions where they attempted to settle.

Such instances underscore that the employment of ethnotypes bore far more significance than the primitive emotional expressions of hatred and xenophobia that Carlrichard Brühl once assigned to them.[96] Nor was ethnic consciousness incongruent with Christian universalism, as Benedict Anderson argued.[97] The Church, in fact, organized in provinces, made use of a nomenclature that specifically distinguished between polities such as Gallia, Anglia, Germania and Italia.[98] Ethnicity had always remained a significant label marking difference within religious discourse, as is discussed extensively in chapter 1.

There is a caveat, however, for this book explores the imaginations of schoolmen, courtiers and monks, whose views do not reflect the diversity of

---

[95] A. D. Smith, *Chosen Peoples* (Oxford, 2003), pp. 95–130; M. Garrison, 'The Franks as the New Israel? Education for an Identity from Pippin to Charlemagne', in *The Uses of the Past in the Early Middle Ages*, ed. Y. Hen and M. Innes (Cambridge, 2000), pp. 114–61; A. Murray, 'Bede and the Unchosen Race', in *Power and Identity in the Middle Ages: Essays in Memory of Rees Davies*, ed. H. Pryce and J. Watts (Oxford, 2007), pp. 52–67 (p. 56).

[96] Brühl, *Deutschland, Frankreich*, p. 275.

[97] Anderson, *Imagined Communities*, pp. 7, 12–19. See for counter-arguments D. K. Buell and C. J. Hodge, 'The Politics of Interpretation: The Rhetoric of Race and Ethnicity in Paul', *Journal of Biblical Literature* 123/2 (2004), 235–51 (p. 238); Buell, *Why this New Race*. Cf. for the older idea of Christian universalism H. Kohn, *The Idea of Nationalism: A Study in its Origins and Background* (New York, 1944), who observed that national sentiment first arose in Germany in the sixteenth-century Peasant War; Kirn, *Frühzeit des Nationalgefühls*, p. 15; R. Wallach, *Das abendländische Gemeinschaftsbewusstsein im Mittelalter* (Leipzig, 1928), p. 24; M. de Wulf, 'The Society of Nations in the Thirteenth Century', *International Journal of Ethics* 29/2 (1919), 210–29.

[98] G. Kisch, 'Nationalism and Race in Medieval Law', in *Ausgewählte Schriften*, ed. G. Kisch, 3 vols. (Sigmaringen, 1978–80), iii, 179–204 (pp. 182–4, 193), discussing German settlers and law in Slavic territory. H. Münkler, 'Nation als politische Idee im frühneuzeitlichen Europa', in *Nation und Literatur im Europa der Frühen Neuzeit: Akten des I. Internationalen Osnabrücker Kongresses zur Kulturgeschichte der Frühen Neuzeit*, ed. K. Garber (Tübingen, 1989), pp. 56–86 (pp. 59–60).

knowledge and experiences within a society marked by sociocultural hierarchies. Moreover, this book is about the religious, environmental-medical and legal-rhetorical discourses that address a macrolevel rather than the individual contexts, attitudes and practices shaped by local circumstances, socio-economic interactions and personal values. In *Communities of Violence*, David Nirenberg justly warned against taking a structuralist approach that assumes 'medieval people' were locked as passive agents in a continuous discourse of difference.[99] Steven Epstein also argued that, in daily social life, individuals often ignored or considered irrelevant conceptual divisions, instead engaging in social and trade relations, sexual alliances and friendships disregarding social boundaries.[100] People can resist or disregard prejudiced opinions voiced by authorities. Also, the wide range of sources probed for this study – from biblical exegesis and encyclopaedias, to medical and historiographical texts, manuals, letters and poetry – almost exclusively were produced by educated religious men.[101] This choice is owing to an overall scarcity of written or visual sources representing ethnic characteristics engendered by the laity in this period, an exception being the proverbs discussed in chapters 3 and 4.[102] The extent to which these discourses featured in the minds of people going about their day-to-day lives will have depended on levels of urbanization and access to texts and education, as well as socio-economic, cultural, political and legal contexts and individual circumstances, as the works of David Nirenberg and Brian Catlos succinctly demonstrated concerning the attitudes towards Jewish and Muslim populations in Christian Mediterranean communities.[103]

---

[99] Nirenberg, *Communities of Violence*, pp. 5–7.

[100] S. A. Epstein, *Purity Lost: Transgressing Boundaries in the Eastern Mediterranean, 1000–1400* (Baltimore, 2007).

[101] The starting point for source references of ethnic stereotypes is H. Walther, 'Scherz und Ernst in der Völker- und Stämme-Charakteristik mittellateinischer Verse', *Archiv für Kulturgeschichte* 41 (1959), 263–301; W. Wackernagel, 'Die Spottnamen der Völker', *Zeitschrift für deutsches Altertum und deutsche Literatur* 6 (1848), 254–61 and the many literature references in this study.

[102] I refer to p. 14n.39 in the Introduction to visual images of Jews, Muslims and black people not included in this study.

[103] Nirenberg, *Communities of Violence*; B. A. Catlos, *Kingdoms of Faith: A New History of Islamic Spain* (New York, 2018).

Writing about premodern nations is a hazardous exercise, for they are like a spray of soap bubbles that burst open when you try to catch them. Fissiparous *nationes* and *gentes* populate histories, poems, letters and legal documents from this period, yet they are not embedded in a material infrastructure or systematically integrated in governance. Indeed, whereas modern nation-states have accustomed us to border fences and (the memory of) national railway systems, televised news and centralized school programmes, those were absent in the period 950–1250. Yet *nationes* did thrive in the imagination, as William of Malmesbury's comments attest, or those made by students entering into brawls and hurling insults, calling one another 'drunken English', 'arrogant French' or 'raging Teutons', as Jacques de Vitry (1160/1170–1240) observed when looking back on his student days in Paris in the 1180s.[104] So it is important to understand where these group images or stereotypes came from, how and why they were employed and what they meant to those using them, when we talk about ethnicity.

The usage of ethnic markers in this period was not at all random, as historians have argued in the past.[105] It occurred, as this book observes, against the backdrop of several processes that converged and fed into each other. Both the programme of conquest and the imagined naturalization of communities occurred in the sphere of tensions and competition over *dominium*, hierarchic governmental authority and control over labour and property rights in the Christian *imperium* and Roman Church. Environmental theory's focus on the impact of space on cultural, physical and mental traits, and by extension on political systems, thereby allowed court poets to, firstly, distinguish between military recruits in God's army defending a *patria aeterna*, and, secondly, spur them on to secure and protect their territorial *patria*, by using emotive arguments. It gave schoolmen and courtiers a conceptual toolkit to reshape their position vis-à-vis the *imperium christianum* and the institutionalizing Church in the second half of the thirteenth century, allowing political philosophers to fashion the community as a self-referential body politic, a legal persona

---

[104] Jacques de Vitry, *Historia occidentalis*, in *The* Historia Occidentalis *of Jacques de Vitry: A Critical Edition*, ed. J. F. Hinnebusch, Spicilegium Friburgense 17 (Fribourg, 1972), p. 92.

[105] J. Breuilly, 'Changes in the political uses of the nation: continuity or discontinuity', in *Power and the Nation in European History*, ed. L. E. Scales and O. Zimmer (Cambridge, 2005), pp. 67–101 (pp. 76–80) argued that ethnographic distinctions barely played a role in, for example, medieval Anglo-French or Anglo-Scottish relations, his main premise being that ethnicity was an empty concept for broad layers of medieval society.

separate from a universal body of believers.¹⁰⁶ In this context, the geographical and religious other served as a counterpoint and object of desire. Engaging a triangular relationship with both the empire and the other, poets and clerics at the courts described the society and religion of regions beyond Europe as backward, lawless and undisciplined, hence creating a legal argument for seizing those possessions and lands.¹⁰⁷ The ethnotypes, of others and selves, in and outside Christendom, aided a rhetoric to organize labour and property relations in a hierarchical setting, engaging with concepts of slavery, human and animal features. In the centuries thereafter the regions to the east, west, and south of Europe became the object of Europe's 'self-authorizing missions', as Geraldine Heng aptly put it.¹⁰⁸

To understand how monks, schoolmen and courtiers classified ethnic communities, *catalogues* of ethnic groups and their characteristics – drawn up first by Benedictine monks but in the twelfth century increasingly by the secular clergy – take centre stage in this book. In doing so, the writers appropriated religious, environmental-medical and legal discourses and used them rhetorically at the courts and schools. Thus, chapters 1–3 examine the *truth regimes* underlying schematizations of perceived ethnic characteristics, arguing that these partially shift between 950 and 1250. Religious schematizations discussed in chapter 1, produced at monasteries, and medical-environmental theories developed at the schools, discussed in chapter 2, become entangled with the cultural appropriation of Graeco-Arabic climate theory.¹⁰⁹ The imagined ethnotypes gain meaning with the reappraisal of humoral typology – physically cataloguing individuals and groups based, *inter alia*, on environmental determinism. New and revived rhetorical strategies set out in manuals exploring the relationship between image, memory and reality, and in military textbooks advising to evoke loyalty to the *patria*, discussed in chapter 3, encourage students and courtiers to employ stereotypes. Thus, the ethnotypes created potent arguments in the military sphere, firstly classifying the mental and physical capacity to protect both the heavenly and worldly fatherlands, and secondly making an environmentally determined, cultural argument of governance to justify the conquest, colonization and expropriation of property

---

[106] T. Struve, *Die Entwicklung der Organologischen Staatsauffassung im Mittelalter* (Stuttgart, 1978).

[107] Bartlett, *The Making of Europe*.

[108] Heng, *The Invention of Race*, p. 24.

[109] A truth regime, a Foucauldian term, is constructed and upheld by 'an array of authorities considered competent to speak that truth'. For a discussion of truth discourses and biological thought, see Rabinow and Rose, 'Thoughts and Concepts of Biopower Today'.

belonging to so-called lawless, weak, sinful peoples, which was mirrored in coeval legal discussions.

Ethnicity in Medieval Europe is therefore divided into two parts. The first part, encompassing chapters 1–3, examines the changes in thinking about what binds ethnic groups in learned texts from the period 950–1250. These chapters analyse ideas about the characteristics of ethnic groups, firstly, in monastic lists produced from 950 onwards, often written within an eschatological context, in historiographical, encyclopaedic and biblical commentaries pertaining to salvation history; secondly, in scientifically informed texts disseminating environmental theory from circa 1100; and thirdly, in manuals, produced in second half of the twelfth century, teaching a military and poetic rhetoric that evoked the *patria*. In the second part, the book explores the conceptualization and application of these ethnic typologies – the process of imagining the community – in social conflicts, warfare and colonization efforts, by students and courtiers. The manipulation of these ethnotypes served as a form of spatial and temporal othering, engaging a language of progress and *civilitas* using the concept of the *translatio studii et imperii*.[110] As we shall see, from 950 onward, the *moral* classification of peoples, which proliferated in the form of lists – of peoples, towns, professions – becomes entangled with the ethnic classification based upon environmental theory, in which territory is imagined to be a domesticated space, a *patria* under the protection of military recruits. Positive self-representations of ethnicity correspond with the urbane values and norms propagated in manuals and regimens for governing the household, cities and territories. These ideas spawned biological ethnotypes such as the melancholy Jew or charming Englishman, who fitted into or were excluded from the moral community.[111]

---

[110] Bartlett, *The Making of Europe*; J. R. S. Phillips, *The Medieval Expansion of Europe* (Oxford, 1988). For these so-called frontier societies, see furthermore R. Bartlett and A. MacKay (ed.), *Medieval Frontiers Societies* (Oxford, 1989); J. Muldoon and F. Fernández-Armesto (ed.), *The Medieval Frontiers in Latin Christendom: Expansion, Contraction, Continuity* (Aldershot, 2008).

[111] I. M. Resnick, *Marks of Distinctions: Christian Perceptions of Jews in the High Middle Ages* (Washington, 2012), pp. 175–214; P. Biller, 'A "Scientific" View of Jews from Paris Around 1300', *Micrologus: Natura, scienze e società medievali – Nature, Sciences and Medieval Societies* 9 (2001), 137–68; W. Johnson, 'The Myth of Jewish Male Menses', *Journal of Medieval History* 24 (1998), 273–95; B. Bauchau, 'Science et racisme: les juifs, la lèpre et la peste', *Stanford French Review* 13 (1989), 21–35. For the late medieval impact of humoral theory on thinking about ethnicity, see especially the contributions of P. Biller and J. Ziegler in Eliav-Feldon, Isaac and Ziegler, *The Origins of Racism in the West*.

At the close of the period under review here, the metaphor of the body politic – imagining the royal or civic community as an organic, hierarchically organized entity – opened the door to a corporative view of society as being made up of the integrated, hierarchically balanced sum of bodies – be they individuals, households, artisanal corporations or guilds, institutions, officials and governing bodies – which pursued a 'common good' through (self-)governance.[112] It allowed philosophers to imagine the king's body as an avatar representing and embodying the entire community, a divinely appointed proxy and synecdoche. It also presented the nobility and urban elite with a prototype to which they could aspire within a network of power relations. Crucially, it offered a focus point of imposed shared interests – the common good of the *patria* – whose sustainability, it claimed, superseded internal conflicts and inequalities.[113] In this manner, the body politic and the bounded space it populated were increasingly imbued with meaning, as being natural and sacred homelands worthy of effort and protection as sites of *civilitas*.

Before the fourteenth century, as Keechang Kim argues, nationality based on territory and civil law did not serve as a ground for the *divisio personarum*, the legal organization of differences between self and other.[114] Legal status was inherited, obtained through wealth, professional status and marriage, creating myriad legal rights and obligations within the Christian society. *Ius gentium* was Roman customary international law, to which all rational peoples (and not brutish animals!) were subject, and dealt with issues such as warfare, slavery and the prohibition of mixed marriages. A notable exception, however, concerns the legal status of Jews, who early on in Visigothic Iberia, as well as

---

[112] J. Kaye, *A History of Balance, 1250–1375: The Emergence of a New Model of Equilibrium and its Impact on Thought* (Cambridge, 2014); V. Syros, 'Galenic Medicine and Social Stability in Early Modern Florence and the Islamic Empires', *Journal of Early Modern History* 17/2 (2013), 161–213.

[113] E. Lecuppre-Desjardin and A.-L. Van Bruaene (ed.), *De Bono Communi: The Discourse and Practice of the Common Good in the European City (13th–16th c.)/ Discours et pratique du Bien Commun dans les villes d'Europe (XIIIe au XVIe siècle)* (Turnhout, 2010); M. S. Kempshall, *The Common Good in Late Medieval Political Thought* (Oxford, 1999).

[114] K. Kim, *Aliens in Medieval Law: The Origins of Modern Citizenship* (Cambridge, 2000), p. 12; M. Prak, *Citizens Without Nations: Urban Citizenship in Europe and the World, c. 1000–1789* (Cambridge, 2018). According to the concept of personality of law, individuals in judicial proceedings could fall under the law of the place of birth or that of their parents. But the principle of settling disputes by the law of the territory where they were committed gained a foothold. Davies, 'The Peoples of Britain and Ireland 1100–1400 III. Laws and Customs', pp. 6–8; Bartlett, 'Race and Ethnicity', pp. 52–3; Bartlett, *The Making of Europe*, pp. 197–220.

under the Church legislation of the Fourth Lateran Council of 1215 and later, for instance in 1275 under the Statute of the Jewry issued by the English King Edward I (1239–1307), fell directly under the ruler's jurisdiction and were subjected to specific taxation, rules of inheritance and clothing regulations. This exceptionality extended to constructions of the Jewish body and inherited character traits as well. In the colonization movement, authoritative voices attached such qualities to peoples inhabiting the lands of settlement likewise, classifying them as weak, stubborn, lawless and barely Christian. Stereotypes in this period were utilized as a validation of what John Gillingham termed the imperial politics of the Anglo-Norman royal government and aristocracy in its attempts, for instance, to subjugate the Irish and Welsh in the twelfth century.[115] The ethnic stereotypes thus gave weight to legal arguments pertaining to property and *dominium*, while classifying who was well equipped to lead the defence of the *patria* and who was not, using arguments drawn from science. Eventually, these arguments slipped into legal and philosophical constructions of membership of the body politic, of nations.

---

[115] Gillingham, *The English in the Twelfth Century*, pp. 3–18.

PART I

1

Cataloguing Ethnic Virtues and Vices

About the year 900, the Benedictine Abbot Regino of Prüm (*c.* 840–915) drafted a letter to Hatto, the archbishop of Mainz (*c.* 850–913), wherein he gave a definition of what in his view constituted ethnicity: 'Just as various peoples are different in descent, manners, language, and laws, so the holy and universal church throughout the world, although joined in the unity of faith, nevertheless upholds various ecclesiastical customs.'[1] As his remark attests, although a fluid social category, ethnicity featured on the imagined world stage of Christendom from late antiquity onwards. It did so in language, politics and law, on world maps, in military and cultural traditions and in memories.[2] On a rhetorical level, there existed unity in diversity, for the universal Church of western Europe nominally bound together the assemblage of ethnic groups. The umbrella or *tertium comparitionis* under which the manly, warrior *gentes* dwelled was the *imperium christianum*, the Christian imperial successor to the Roman empire, which, monks and clerics after the death of

---

[1] Regino of Prüm, 'Epistola Reginonis ad Hathonem Archiepiscopum missa', in *Reginonis abbatis Prumiensis Chronicon*, ed. F. Kurze, Monumenta Germaniae Historica [hereafter MGH] SS rerum Germanicarum 50 (Hanover, 1890), p. xx: 'Sicut diversae nationes populorum inter se discrepant genere moribus lingua legibus, ita sancta universalis aecclesia toto orbe terrarum diffusa, quamvis in unitate fidei coniungatur, tamen consuetudinibus aecclesiasticis ab invicem differt.' Cf. Reynolds, *Kingdoms and Communities*, p. 257 whose translation I have used. H. Beumann, 'Die Bedeutung des Kaisertums für die Entstehung der deutschen Nation im Spiegel der Bezeichnungen von Reich und Herrscher', in *Aspekte der Nationenbildung im Mittelalter: Ergebnisse der Marburger Rundgespräche 1972–1975*, ed. H. Beumann and W. Schröder (Sigmaringen, 1978), pp. 317–66 (pp. 341–52).

[2] P. J. Geary, 'Ethnic Identity as a Situational Construct in the Early Middle Ages', in *Writing History: Identity, Conflict, and Memory in the Middle Ages*, ed. P. J. Geary, F. Curta and C. Spinei (Bucharest, 2012), pp. 19–32; W. Pohl and G. Heydemann (ed.), *Post-Roman Transitions: Christian and Barbarian Identities in the Early Medieval West* (Turnhout, 2013); W. Pohl and G. Heydemann (ed.), *Strategies of Identification: Ethnicity and Religion in Early Medieval Europe* (Turnhout, 2013); H. Ebling, J. Jarnut and G. Kampers, 'Nomen et gens: Untersuchungen zu den Führungsschichten des Franken-, Langobarden- und Westgotenreiches im 6. und 7. Jahrhundert', *Francia* 8 (1980), 687–745; R. Wenskus, *Stammesbildung und Verfassung: Das Werden der Frühmittelalterlichen Gentes* (Cologne, 1961) emphasizing the growing importance of language.

Charlemagne in 814 more frequently claimed, spanned an expanding world of west and east under the hegemonic power of a world emperor.[3] Within the religious community, however, monks eagerly compared the alleged character and customs of descent groups, their virtues and vices, while juxtaposing them with the supposed features of groups outside Christendom, including Jews, Persians, Egyptians and Greeks. The comparative schema according to which the monks arranged the groups was predicated on their, from a Christian perspective, assigned role in time and space.

It is this temporal and geographical framework with which monks schematized ethnic groups that is the topic of the present chapter. It commences circa 950 when monks in Spanish monasteries, but soon thereafter across western Europe, began to record lists cataloguing ethnic characteristics, virtues and vices. The Benedictine monks compiling these lists dealt closely with the descendants of migratory warrior bands, categorized as Franks, Longobards, Angles and Goths, who in earlier histories had settled and converted to Catholicism. Claiming genealogical, linguistic and cultural ties, monks traced back the lineage of royal dynasties to Trojan, biblical or Scandinavian origins in so-called *origo gentis* myths.[4] In particular, however, the lists drawn up by the Benedictine monks now turned to and interwove biblical patristic traditions commenting on the propensity of groups to succumb to or overcome sinfulness with regard to their role in salvation history. Arranged in time and space from past to present, and from east to west, the groups mentioned in these texts were conceived to be driven by their virtues and vices, shaping past and present events and future destinies. More concretely, in the schema the east was framed as the locus of the religious and imperial past – of Judaism, and the Babylonian, Persian, Greek and Roman empires – while the *imperium christianum* represented the present and main actor in the eschatological future. Compared to later catalogues discussed in the following chapters, these early lists pay little explicit attention to environmental factors or geographical determinism shaping group characteristics, although environmental thought does reverberate through the images taken from patristic commentaries.

This chapter examines religious-genealogical classifications of and ideas about group kinship within and outside the *populus christianorum* in the period 950–1100. Chapter 2 will look at how environmental-medical theory impacted

---

[3] Gabriele, *Empire of Memory*; A. A. Latowsky, *Emperor of the World: Charlemagne and the Construction of Imperial Authority, 800–1229* (Ithaca, 2013).

[4] P. J. Geary, *The Myth of Nations: The Medieval Origins of Europe* (Princeton, 2002), pp. 41–62; S. Reynolds, 'Medieval *Origines Gentium* and the Community of the Realm', *History* 68 (1984), 375–90; Hoppenbrouwers, 'Medieval Peoples Imagined', pp. 45–50.

on ethnic categories from the twelfth century onward. In the early lists, Benedictine monks framed ethnic categories of character within an eschatological context. To understand what ethnicity meant within this religious narrative, it is thus helpful to first explore the meaning inscribed upon geographical spaces, the stage upon which the events in time occurred and the purported essence of the named groups that were thought to inhabit them. This chapter accordingly first addresses ethnic name giving, the meaning of geographical space and its relevance to time in salvation history in early encyclopaedic and historiographical sources, before turning to the lists cataloguing ethnic virtues and vices. For, from a spatial perspective, surviving written attestations of ethnic character from this early period mostly featured within the framework of salvation history and are found primarily in the *Etymologies*, the early seventh-century encyclopaedia of Isidore of Seville, in exegetical texts and in ethnographic-geographical descriptions injected into the prologues of the histories of peoples, such as the *Getica* of Jordanes (d. c. 552), the *History of the Goths, Vandals and Sueves* by Isidore of Seville (560–636), the *Ecclesiastical History of the English People* by Bede (672/3–735), the *History of the Longobards* by Paul the Deacon (c. 720–99) and the *Deeds of the Bishops of the Hamburg Church* by Adam of Bremen (before 1050–85). The tradition extends into the twelfth century, for instance in *History of the English* by Henry of Huntingdon (1080/90–1155) or *History of the Danes* by Saxo Grammaticus (1150–c. 1220).[5]

Stages and actors

The portrayals of ethnic character inserted into the introductory passages of histories are not random. Historical narratives about the origins and deeds of Christianized peoples viewed history and geography as two inseparable disciplines to process the activity of humanity in time and space in accordance with God's plan. In this sense, geography served the purpose of localizing events on the world's stage, signposting them in the history of salvation.[6] Thus, the temporal-spatial relationship was interpreted through the prism of God's design,

---

[5] A. H. Merrills, *History and Geography in Late Antiquity* (Cambridge, 2005); N. Lozovsky, *'The Earth Is Our Book': Geographical Knowledge in the Latin West ca. 400–1000* (Ann Arbor, 2000); S. Tomasch and S. Gilles (ed.), *Text and Territory: Geographical Imagination in the European Middle Ages* (Philadelphia, 1998); M. B. Campbell, *The Witness and the Other World: Exotic European Travel Writing, 400–1600* (Ithaca, 1988). Still useful guides to primary sources are J. K. Wright, *The Geographical Lore of the Time of the Crusades: A Study of the History of Medieval Science and Tradition in Western Europe* (rev. edn, New York, 1965) and C. R. Beazley, *The Dawn of Modern Geography*, 3 vols. (London, 1897–1906).

[6] Merrills, *History and Geography in Late Antiquity*, pp. 1–4, 8.

in which geography provided the spatial context where historical events were set, performed and interpreted by the various ethnic groups. Spaces thereby garnered meaning through the collective memory of events in which individuals and communities had participated. The Christian historian Paulus Orosius (380/385–c. 420), accordingly, claimed in the first book of his *Seven Books of History Against the Pagans* that he would disclose, both in time and space, the conflicts of humanity and the different parts of a world burning with vice, just as Augustine (354–430) had viewed them 'from the watchtower' of his high position in the Church.[7]

If geography set the stage for historical salvation drama, its troupe of actors was made up of communities who cultivated narratives of kinship, claiming descent from a royal agnate. In this regard, the ethnic body was considered to be the historical product of descent, encapsulated in migratory origin myths, recalled and symbolized in collective memories, rituals and artefacts.[8] The words *gens* and *natio*, denoting peoples, derived from the Latin words for birth and generation (*generatio, generare, natus, nasci*); the words used for peoples: *gens, natio* generally were employed interchangeably.[9] *Gens* and *natio* might

---

[7] Orosius, *Historiarum adversum paganos libri VII* i.1, ed. K. F. W. Zangemeister (New York, 1966), p. 8: 'de specula ecclesiasticae claritatis elati sunt'.

[8] For origin myths in early medieval times: Geary, *The Myth of Nations*, p. 61. A. Borst, *Der Turmbau von Babel: Geschichte der Meinungen über Ursprung und Vielfalt der Sprachen und Völker*, 4 vols. (Stuttgart, 1957–63) offers a wealth of sources with references to origin myths. S. Reynolds, 'Medieval *Origines Gentium* and the community of the realm', *History* 68 (1983), 375–90; Hoppenbrouwers, 'Dynamics of National Identity'. For a collective Frankish memory, M. Gabriele, *An Empire of Memory: The Legend of Charlemagne, the Franks, and Jerusalem before the First Crusade* (Oxford, 2011). For the Normans: C. Carozzi, 'Des Daces aux Normands. Le mythe et l'identification d'un peuple chez Dudon de Saint-Quentin', in *Peuples du Moyen Âge: Problèmes d'identification: Seminaire Sociétés, Idéologies et Croyances au Moyen Âge*, ed. C. Carozzi and H. Taviani-Carozzi (Aix-en-Provence, 1996), pp. 7–25; R. H. C. Davis, *The Normans and their Myth* (London, 1976), pp. 49–69; E. Albu, *The Normans in Their Histories: Propoganda, Myth and Subversion* (Woodbridge, 2001).

[9] Davies, 'The Peoples of Britain and Ireland 1100–1400 I. Identities', pp. 6–7; B. Zientara, '*Populus – Gens – Natio*: Einige Probleme aus dem Bereich der ethnischen Terminologie des frühen Mittelalters', in *Nationalismus in vorindustrieller Zeit*, ed. O. Dann (Munich, 1986), pp. 11–20. In some cases, *gentes* together made up a *nation*: Bartlett, 'Race and Ethnicity', p. 48; Huizinga, 'Patriotisme en nationalisme', iv, 506–7; F. W. Müller, 'Zur Geschichte des Wortes und Begriffes "nation" im französischen Schrifttum des Mittelalters bis zur Mitte des 15. Jahrhunderts', *Romanische Forschungen* 58–9 (1947), 247–321. Hastings, *The Construction of Nationhood*, p. 38; N. Berend, *At the Gate of Christendom: Jews, Muslims and 'Pagans' in Medieval Hungary, c. 1000–c. 1300* (Cambridge, 2001), pp. 192–3.

also refer to what we today would call regional communities and/or seignorial entities.[10] Interpreted through a religious prism, however, in particular the Franks, the Anglo-Saxons and the Visigoths considered their *gentes* to have a special alliance with God.[11] The bonds between a territory and its populace, commemorated in the latter's collective memory, inevitably invited contemplation of the community's fate, its relation to divine providence, the fleeting nature of humanity and the effects of group guilt.[12] This narrative paved the way for the interpretation of ethnic character – which was embedded in textual and oral, classical, biblical and migratory traditions – as a factor driving salvation history in the past, present and future.

Following the tradition of ancient geography, religious men addressing the conceptualized ties between language and things from late antiquity thereby invested names with ontological meaning.[13] Etymological deduction was, accordingly, considered a relevant tool for understanding peoples' position in the history of mankind and their willingness to embrace Christianity. Augustine, in the same vein, had maintained that knowledge of scriptural toponymy was essential for understanding the Bible's historical message.[14] It tallied with the theological axiom that the world and all things and beings in it were signs of God's providence, foresight and mystery. Hence the creation was viewed as something which could be read, a book of nature in which God revealed his truth.[15] Knowledge of places gained through etymology offered a tool to understand the Bible's hidden messages.[16] This actually worked both ways, as, hermeneutically, nature and all things created were also 'legible according to Scripture and understood and interpreted through the Bible and the Church

---

[10] P. Moraw (ed.), *Regionale Identität und soziale Gruppen im deutschen Mittelalter* (Berlin, 1992); A. Czacharowski (ed.), *Nationale, ethnische Minderheiten und regionale Identitäten in Mittelalter und Neuzeit* (Toruń, 1994).

[11] See the Introduction, p. 32n.95 for further references.

[12] Lozovsky, *The Earth Is Our Book*, p. 153.

[13] B. Pabst, 'Die Antike im Welt-Buch: Zum Umbang mit antiken Wissenssystemen und -inhalten im Bereich der mittelalterlichen Enzyklopädik', in *Persistenz und Rezeption: Weiterverwendung, Wiederverwendung und Neuinterpretation antiker Werke im Mittelalter*, ed. D. Boschung and S. Wittekind (Wiesbaden, 2008), pp. 33–64.

[14] Merrills, *History and Geography*, pp. 241–2.

[15] J. B. Friedman, *The Monstrous Races in Medieval Art and Thought* (2nd rev. edn, New York, 2000), p. 122. Cf. M. Foucault, *The Order of Things: An Archaeology of the Human Sciences* (New York, 1994), p. 126.

[16] Lozovsky, *The Earth Is Our Book*, p. 48.

Fathers'.¹⁷ Natural artefacts like the Seven Wonders of the World indeed deserved marvel, for, as John Block Friedman put it, in Christian thought 'every creature is a shadow of truth and life, and the natural world holds in its depths the reflections of Christ's sacrifice, the image of the Church militant and the various virtues and vices'.¹⁸ The objective was to interpret the literal or figurative signs of Scripture as conveyed through nature, for fathoming these signs opened up perspectives on understanding God and his word.¹⁹ As a hermeneutical tool, the English monk Bede, like Eusebius of Caesarea (260/264–c. 339) and Jerome (c. 347–419/420) before him, correspondingly drew up an alphabetical guide to his commentary on the New Testament Book of Acts entitled *The Names of Regions*, which topographically portrayed the stage for the expansion of Christianity in south-west Asia.²⁰

Combining biblical and ancient panegyric, Isidore of Seville's depiction of Spain and Bede's representation of Britain did also frame God's creation in terms of salubriousness and sweetness, drawing from a classical tradition of panegyric celebrating various regions' natural features and climate.²¹ In doing so, they alluded to environmental theory that traces back to Hippocrates'

---

[17] M. Tamm, 'A New World into Old Words: The Eastern Baltic Region and the Cultural Geography of Medieval Europe', in *The Clash of Cultures on the Medieval Baltic Frontier*, ed. A. V. Murray e.a. (Farnham, 2009), pp. 11–36 (p. 12); A. Pagden, *European Encounters with the New World: From Renaissance to Romanticism* (New Haven, 1993), p. 12, 52.

[18] Friedman, *The Monstrous Races*, pp. 122–3.

[19] N. Howe, *The Old English Catalogue Poems* (Copenhagen, 1985), pp. 46–7.

[20] Merrills, *History and Geography*, p. 242, 247. Presenting knowledge in alphabetical order is generally considered a thirteenth-century development: M. A. Rouse, 'The Development of Research Tools in the Thirteenth Century', in *Authentic Witnesses: Approaches to Medieval Texts and Manuscripts*, ed. M. A. Rouse and R. H. Rouse (Notre Dame, 1991), pp. 221–55; R. H. Rouse and M. A. Rouse, '"Statim Invenire": Schools, Preachers, and New Attitudes to the Page', in *Renaissance and Renewal in the Twelfth Century*, ed. R. R. Benson, G. Constable and C. D. Lanham (Cambridge MA, 1982), pp. 201–25; A.-D. von den Brincken, 'Tabula Alphabetica: Von den Anfängen alphabetischer Registerarbeiten zu geschichtlichen Werken (Vincenz von Beauvais OP, Johannes von Hautfuney, Paulinus Minorita OFM)', in *Festschrift für Hermann Heimpel zum 70. Geburtstag am 19. Septemper 1971*, ed. T. Schieder e.a., 3 vols. (Göttingen, 1971–73), ii, 902–7.

[21] Bede, *Historia ecclesiastica gentis Anglorum* I.1, in *Bede's Ecclesiastical History of the English people*, ed. and trans. B. Colgrave and R. A. B. Mynors (Oxford 1969), pp. 14–15; Isidore of Seville, *Historia de regibus Gothorum, Wandalorum et Suevorum*, ed. T. Mommsen, MGH Auctores Antiquissimi XI (Berlin, 1894), p. 267.

Airs, Waters, Places.²² Before 1100, the transmission of Hippocratic ideas, holding that the natural environment, climate and altitude affected mental and physical traits, ran mostly via late Roman classical texts like the *Natural History* of Pliny the Elder (23–79 AD).²³ It was deployed in Vegetius's military manual *De re militari*, of which at least sixteen Latin manuscripts have survived predating 1100.²⁴ This handbook contained advice on choosing military recruits based on their physical and mental qualities, taking into account any differences between urban and rural recruits, age groups, professional backgrounds and different climates.²⁵ Commentaries on classical authors, such as the patristic exegesis of Lactantius (*c.* 250–325) or *On the Soul* by Tertullian, who died in about 220, engaged climate theory as well.²⁶ Yet it was not until the twelfth century, when schoolmen and courtiers absorbed climate theory in their crusade histories, court *chansons* and poems praising military virtues and in environmental-medical treatises produced at the universities, that environmental theory began to be explicitly applied. Hippocrates' *Airs, Waters, Places* became available in Latin at the end of the twelfth century, as did sections on environmental theory in translations of Graeco-Arabic medicine, inviting commentaries on the relationship between the natural environment and peoples. This is discussed in further detail in chapter 2.

Etymology and ethnicity: names and character

If nature was to be explored for its hidden meanings, and words signifying things were to be interpreted etymologically, group names themselves served as beacons of identity – be they stamped upon a person at birth, voluntarily embraced or rejected as a derogatory slur. They were, in this regard, explicit markers of group membership. Group names often suggested a common denominator (kinship, shared character or territory) that bound the members of the collectivity, whereby the ontology of the ethnic name allegedly signified

---

[22] Hippocrates, *Ancient Medicine. Airs, Waters, Places. Epidemics 1 and 3. The Oath. Precepts. Nutriment*, trans. by W. H. S. Jones, Loeb Classical Library 147 (Cambridge MA, 1923).

[23] Pliny the Elder, *Historia naturalis* iii.v.40–2, in Pliny, *Natural History, books III–VII*, ed. and trans. H. Rackham, Loeb Classical Library 330, 352–3, 371, 392, 394, 418–19, 10 vols. (Cambridge MA, 2006), ii, 32–3.

[24] Number based on Allmand, *The De Re Militari of Vegetius*, pp. 354–66, including excerpts.

[25] Meloni, 'Porous Bodies', p. 17.

[26] Lactantius, *De origine erroris*, II.x, *Patrologia Latina* [hereafter *PL*] 6, col. 307A–311A; Tertullian, *De anima* XX, *PL* 2, col. 682C–684A

a people's very essence. Ethnic toponyms also translated, sustained or established certain fundamental myths about group characteristics.[27] Genealogy and geography thereby took a central position, for historians, geographers and encyclopaedists signalled that ethnic names sprang from mythical rulers (e.g. the Franks allegedly descended from Francus, the son of Hector of the Trojans, as the appendix to the *Chronicle of Fredegar* claims), or conversely inspired territorial name giving (e.g. the territory Francia was named after the people of the Franci, Britannia after Brutus through his eldest son Locrinus).[28] Physical geography might inspire peoples' names as well; for instance Alemannia was considered to be named after the River Alemannus, or after *alle mannen* – all men.[29] Biblical genealogy was utilized, monks embracing the narrative of the dispersion of peoples after the Flood or asserting that various peoples descended from the progeny of Noah's sons, Shem, Japheth and Ham. For instance, the toponym Africa was said to derive from Afer, the son of Abraham.[30] Chroniclers asserted that the mythological founders of European peoples had undertaken long migratory journeys since earlier biblical times.[31] The Anglo-Saxons, for instance, claimed descent from the Scandi-

[27] Guenée, *States and Rulers*, pp. 50–2.

[28] Fredegar, *Historia Daretis Frigii de origine Francorum*, ed. B. Krusch, MGH Scriptores rerum Merovingicarum 2 (Hanover, 1888), p. 199.

[29] Bartholomaeus Anglicus, *De proprietatibus rerum* xv.13, ed. H. Knochlobtzer (Heidelberg, 1488), 'De Alemannia'. A modern edition of book xv of Bartholomaeus Anglicus's encyclopaedia has not been published to date; separate editions of books i–iv, vi and xvii appeared in the series 'De diversis artibus', edited by C. Meier (Turnhout, 2007–). B. Van den Abeele and H. Meyer, 'Etat de l'edition du *De proprietatibus rerum*', in *Bartholomaeus Anglicus, De proprietatibus rerum: Texte latin et réception vernaculaire / Lateinischer texte und volkssprachige Rezeption: Actes du Colloque international = Akten des Internationalen Kolloquiums, Münster, 9–11 October 2003*, ed. B. Van den Abeele and H. Meyer (Turnhout, 2005), pp. 1–25. I have used Heinrich Knochlobtzer's print edition published in Heidelberg in 1488.

[30] Isidore of Seville, *Etymologiae, Livre ix: Les langues et les groups sociaux* ix.ii.115, ed. M. Reydellet (Paris, 1984), p. 107; Bartholomaeus Anglicus, *De proprietatibus rerum* xv.19, ed. Knochlobtzer, 'De Affrica'. At times, however, even the most ingenious exegetes could not find a way to employ etymology and some regions were said to be named after an otherwise unknown ruler or tribe, such as Crete; Bartholomaeus Anglicus, *De proprietatibus rerum* xv.42, ed. Knochlobtzer, 'De Creta'.

[31] P. Eley, 'The Myth of Trojan Descent and Perceptions of National Identity: the Case of "Eneas" and the "Roman de Troie"', *Nottingham Medieval Studies* 35 (1991), 27–40; J. Garber, 'Trojaner-Römer-Franken-Deutsche: "Nationale" Abstammungstheorien im Vorfeld der Nationalstaatsbildung', in *Nation und Literatur im Europa der Frühen Neuzeit: Akten des I. Internationalen Osnabrücker Kongresses zur Kulturgeschichte der frühen Neuzeit*, ed. K. Garber (Tübingen, 1989), pp. 108–63; F. Graus, 'Troja und trojanische Herkunftssage im Mittelalter', in *Kontinuität und*

navian mythical siblings Hengist and Horsa. In a biblical interpretation, the Bavarians trekked from Armenia – where Noah landed his ark – to southern Germany.[32] In this manner, names encapsulated intricate cultural-religious narratives of migration, symbolizing chosenness and heroism or, where religious others were concerned, alleged perfidy. A poignant case that Geraldine Heng aptly dubbed an 'ingenious lie' was the name assigned by Jerome and Isidore to the Arabs, dubbing them Saracens. The name giving was cunning and misleading, for the Arabs never utilized the name Saracen themselves. Yet the appellative suggested that the Arabs falsely claimed descent from Sarah, Abraham's wife, to conceal their true lineage as descendants of Abraham's enslaved bondswoman Hagar, who bore Ishmael, father of Kedar. In doing so, Christian writers drew attention to the supposedly lesser lineage of the children of Abraham and Hagar, whereas Abraham's wife Sarah had mothered Isaac, God's promised child. Likewise, in order to defile the Jewish lineage, although not using etymology, theologians also alluded to the stain of the 'mark of Cain', the curse that God issued after Cain's fratricide. Like serfs, Jews in the thirteenth century were described by Thomas Aquinas as 'slaves of the Church' whose property could be expropriated.[33]

Not only did these ethnic toponyms draw upon mythical origins of descent and territory. Theologians also considered the close ties between names and groups to be *inherent*. In biblical exegesis, theologians sought knowledge of the significance of regions and the populations dwelling in them to interrogate God's plan, by searching for the original, core meaning of words.[34] For understanding a signifier (e.g. a name) meant fathoming the signification of the thing itself. In this context, names or words were considered to be factual, for they were assumed to be linked to the active lives and deeds of their bearers. In practice, encyclopaedists attempted to understand names and words by means of etymological deduction, which Nicholas Howe defined 'a hermeneutical principle according to which knowledge of a given thing may be realized from

---

Transformation der Antike im Mittelalter: Veröffentlichung der Kongreßakten zum Freiburger Symposion des Mediävistenverbandes, ed. W. Erzgräber (Sigmaringen, 1989), pp. 25–43. B. Braude, 'Cham et Noé. Race, esclavage et exégèse entre islam, judaïsme et christianisme', *Annales: Histoire, Sciences Sociales* 57/1 (2002), 93–125.

[32] Hoppenbrouwers, 'Medieval Peoples Imagined', pp. 45–7.

[33] Thomas Aquinas, *Summa theologiae* 2a-2ae.10.10, ed. T. Gilby, 61 vols. (London, 1964–80), xxxii, 70. Cohen, *Living Letters of the Law*, pp. 164, 367; Heng, *The Invention of Race*, pp. 111–12.

[34] D. Greetham, 'The Fabulous Geography of John Trevisa's Translation of Bartholomaeus Anglicus' *De proprietatibus rerum*' (unpublished dissertation, City University, New York, 1974), pp. 282–301.

an understanding of its name', whereby two similar words must somehow, or so it was believed, be inherently bound to one another.[35] Clerics tied this principle to God's act of creation. Isidore of Seville, whose Latin *Etymologies* was one of the most influential books between 700 and 1200, contended that at the moment of creation Adam had spoken 'true words' when assigning names to things (although assumedly he did not speak in Latin). Thus, compilers of encyclopaedias believed ethnonyms to reflect a transcendental entity; by examining the form of a word, one might understand the essence of the thing.

Because names ostensibly reflected divine truths, the practice of explaining ethnic groups' names etymologically formed an essential element of a fossilized intellectual tradition of thinking about ethnicity and the ties between a region's geography, its population and its rulers. To identify names and peoples correctly, the exegetes turned to biblical and classical texts as well as oral traditions, in the process reaffirming ethnic typologies. Isidore of Seville tapped Jerome's alphabetical gazetteer commenting on the peoples mentioned in Genesis.[36] Encyclopaedists such as Hrabanus Maurus (*c.* 780–856), Gervase of Tilbury (*c.* 1150–*c.*1222), Vincent of Beauvais (before 1200–64) and Bartholomaeus Anglicus (before 1203–72) later copied, elaborated upon and modified Isidore's etymologies.[37] Thus, at the end of the period under review here, Bartholomaeus Anglicus's *On the Properties of Things*, written circa 1240, administered four categories of etymology, based on, firstly, foundation

---

[35] Howe, *Old English Catalogue Poems*, pp. 34, 59–60 (p. 60); M. de Boüard, 'Les encyclopédies médiévales: Sur "La connaissance de la nature et du monde au Moyen Âge"', *Revue des questions historiques* 112 (1930), 258–304 (p. 286); H. Kästner, 'Der großmächtige Riese und Recke Theuton: Etymologische Spurensuche nach dem Urvater der Deutschen am Ende des Mittelalters', *Zeitschrift für deutsche Philologie* 110 (1991), 68–97 (pp. 75–7); Greetham, 'Fabulous Geography', pp. 282–301. W. Haubrichs, 'Veriloquium nominis: Zur Namensexegese im frühen Mittelalter', in *Verbum et signum: Beiträge zur mediävistischen Bedeutungsforschung* ed. H. Fromm, W. Harms, U. Ruberg and E. F. Ohly, 2 vols. (Munich, 1975), i, 231–56.

[36] Genesis 10. Jerome's *Liber de nominibus Hebraicis*, PL 23. P. Gautier Dalché, *Géographie et culture: La representation de l'espace du vie au xiie siècle* (Aldershot, 1997), pp. 278–9; originally published as 'Isidorus Hispalensis, *De gentium vocabulis* (Etym. IX, 2): Quelques sources non repérées', *Revue des études augustiniennes* 31 (1985), 278–86.

[37] Hrabanus Maurus, *De universo*, PL 111; Vincent of Beauvais, *Speculum quadruplex sive Speculum maius* (Baltazar Bellerus, Douai, 1624; reprint Graz, 1964); Gervase of Tilbury, *Otia imperialia: Recreation for an Emperor*, ed. and trans. S. E. Banks and J. W. Binns (Oxford, 2002) For Gervase of Tilbury's work see M. Rothmann, 'Totius orbis descriptio: Die "Otia Imperialia" des Gervasius von Tilbury: Eine höfische Enzyklopädie und die scientia naturalis', in *Die Enzyklopädie im Wandel vom Hochmittelalter bis zur frühen Neuzeit*, ed. C. Meier (Munich, 2002), pp. 189–224.

or *origo gentis* (kinship) myths; secondly, topographical-environmental features; thirdly, the physical appearance of peoples; and fourthly, alleged internal character traits or affects that now were also informed by climate theory, discussed in chapter 2. Bartholomaeus's origin myths, intimating that populations descended from an eponymous founder, thus upheld earlier narratives of descent drawn from Isidore and from histories produced by, for instance, Jordanes, Paul the Deacon or Bede. These origin myths had become increasingly popular in Latin and vernacular epic histories and romances.[38] The tradition assigning meaning to names indeed enjoyed longevity, yet the employment of names could by then, depending on context, serve different functions: to understand God's design, to frame the religious other as perfidious, or to attack others in social and territorial conflicts.

Names, appearances, character

The Isidorean encyclopaedic tradition also pays significant attention to the perceived intricate relationship between ethnic names, physical appearance and character. Isidore, drawing from ancient texts, explained ethnic names by attributing them to cultural practices such as dress or haircuts.[39] For instance, a famous origin myth narrated that a voice from the heavens bestowed upon the Longobards their name, referring to their long beards depicted on their seals and weaponry.[40] The episode occurred when they entered into battle with the Huns and their women tied the hair on their heads onto their cheeks and chins to look like men. The Picts, tattooing their bodies, similarly bore the

---

[38] Reynolds, *Kingdoms and Communities*, pp. 258–9. Reynolds questions the extent to which the laity was familiar with descent myths before the thirteenth century.

[39] In *Commentarii de bello Gallico* i.1, Julius Caesar's three Gauls – Gallia Togata (later Lombardy), Gallia Comata (Burgundia and Francia) and Gallia Braccata (Germania) – were distinguished with reference to the toga, hair (the long-haired Burgundians and Franks) and trousers (the Germans wearing long trousers) of the peoples living there. Copied for instance by Gervase of Tilbury, *Otia imperialia* ii.10, ed. and trans. Banks and Binns, pp. 298–9.

[40] Fredegar, *Chronicarum Fredegarii libri IV cum continuationibus* iii.65, ed. B. Krusch, MGH Scriptores rerum Merovingicarum 2 (Hanover, 1888), p. 110, echoed for example by Honorius of Autun, *Imago mundi* xxvi, ed. V. I. J. Flint, 'Honorius Augustodunensis, *Imago Mundi*', *Archives d'histoire doctrinale et littéraire du Moyen Âge* 57 (1982), 7–153 (pp. 61–2) and Gervase of Tilbury, *Otia imperialia* ii.10, ed. and trans. Banks and Binns, pp. 286–9. W. Pohl, 'Memory, Identity and Power in Lombard Italy', in *The Uses of the Past in the Early Middle Ages*, ed. Y. Hen and M. Innes (Cambridge, 2000), pp. 9–28 (pp. 18–19).

label *picti*, painted.⁴¹ The Albanians took their name, Isidore of Seville said, from the colour of their hair: *albus*, white, because of the incessant snowfall.⁴² Skin colour also determined names: the Mauri (Moors) of Mauretania, burnt by the heat of the sun, took their name from *maron*, Greek for black.⁴³ Inversely, white-skinned people in Galilea, Galicia (who apparently descended from the Greeks and thus were more intelligent) and Gaul took their name from their milky-white-skinned bodies, for '*gala* is Greek for milk'.⁴⁴ This was a tenacious explanation interweaving Virgilian verse claiming that Gallia had 'thus been named since antiquity because of the whiteness of its people. For in Greek γάλα means milk, and therefore the Sybille called them Gauls, that is to say white, saying that their milky necks are circled with gold.'⁴⁵ Parroting Isidore, Bartholomaeus Anglicus in about 1240 accordingly elaborated that 'Ethiopia was originally named after the colour of its people, who live in the vicinity of the sun [...]. Indeed, the colouring of the people demonstrates the force of the sun, for it is always hot.'⁴⁶ These etymologies suggest that

---

⁴¹ Isidore of Seville, *Etymologiae* ix.ii.103, ed. Reydellet, p. 101; Bartholomaeus Anglicus, *De proprietatibus rerum* xv.152, ed. Knochlobtzer, 'De Scottia'.

⁴² Isidore of Seville, *Etymologiae* ix.ii.65, ed. Reydellet, p. 75; cf. Honorius of Autun, *Imago mundi* xviii, ed. Flint, p. 58; Bartholomaeus Anglicus, *De proprietatibus rerum* xv.7, ed. Knochlobtzer, 'De Albania'.

⁴³ Isidore of Seville, *Etymologiae* ix.ii.122, ed. Reydellet, p. 111.

⁴⁴ Ibid., ix.ii.110, ed. Reydellet, p. 105: 'Galleci a candore dicti, unde et Galli.' Also, Isidore of Seville, *Etymologiae* ix.ii.104; xiii.xix.5; xiv.iii.23 and xiv.iv.25; Bartholomaeus Anglicus, *De proprietatibus rerum* xv.66, ed. Knochlobtzer, 'De Gallia'; Gervase of Tilbury, *Otia imperialia* ii.10, ed. and trans. Banks and Binns, pp. 284–5; Honorius of Autun, *Imago mundi* i.26, ed. Flint, p. 61.

⁴⁵ Bartholomaeus Anglicus, *De proprietatibus rerum* xv.66, ed. Knochlobtzer, 'De Gallia': 'Quae etiam a candore populi sic est antiquitus nuncupata. Γάλα enim graece lac dicitur, et ideo Sibylla eos Gallos, id est, canditos vocat, dicens, tunc lactea colla auro innectuntur.' Isidore's association of the Gauls with milky white skin traces back to Jerome's commentary on St Paul's letter to the churches in Galatians 3:1, citing the Latin rhetorician Lactantius, who, in the third volume of his no longer extant work admonishing the Galatians, said that the Gauls were named Galatians because of the whiteness of their bodies. Cf. Jerome, *Commentariorum in epistolam ad Galatos*, PL 26, col. 0353D. The verse 'their milky necks encircled with gold' is ultimately derived from Virgil's *Aeneid* viii, line 660, in *Aeneid VII–XII, Appendix Vergiliana*, ed. G. P. Goold, Loeb Classical Library 64 (Cambridge MA, 2002), p. 104.

⁴⁶ Bartholomaeus Anglicus, *De proprietatibus rerum* xv.52, ed. Knochlobtzer, 'De Aethiopia': 'Aethiopia a colore populi est primitus vocata, quos Solis vicinitas tenet [...] Denique vim sideris prodit hominum color. Est enim iugis aestus.' Cf. Isidore of Seville, *Etymologiae* xiv.v.14 in *Étymologies xiv: De terra*, ed. O. Spevak (Paris, 2011), pp. 92–5. Bartholomaeus also inserted Pliny's explanation that the men of

skin colour was significant in cultural and scientific classification, which is discussed further in chapter 2.[47]

Above all, etymology based on character traits or inner dispositions was brought into play to explain the appellations of the courageous, fear-inspiring Germanic peoples, who spawned (*germinare*) many peoples.[48] The Thuringians acted 'hard', *durus*, in the face of the enemy.[49] In his encyclopaedia compiled between 1210 and 1214 for the German emperor Otto IV (1175–1218), the English canon Gervase of Tilbury conveyed that the toponym of the Saxons, whom he declared to be the strongest of men pursuing their enemies over land and sea, was grounded on 'their endurance and strength, in which they resemble rocks' (*saxa*).[50] A tenacious encyclopaedic tradition held that the Franci were *feroces*, fierce, although the name Francus might designate 'free' as well.[51] Chapters 4 and 5 show that students, clerics and military men actively applied these etymologies in warfare and in political discussions about *imperium*, crying out the names on the battlefield and on pieces of vellum to boast their own innate ferocity or steadfastness and to instil fear in others. For example, the canon jurist Alexander of Roes (died after 1288) of Cologne interpreted

---

Ethiopia were named after a black river. Cf. Pliny the Elder, *Historia Naturalis* v.44–46, ed. Rackham, ii, 250–2.

[47] M. van der Lugt, 'La peau noire dans le science médiévale', *Micrologus: Natura, scienze e società medievali* 13 (2005), 439–75 (pp. 455–6). For colour and names in a different Eastern European tradition, see H. Ludat, 'Farbenbezeichnungen in Völkernamen: Ein Beitrag zu asiatisch-osteuropaïschen Kulturbeziehungen', *Saeculum* 4 (1953), 138–54.

[48] More examples in Wenskus, *Stammesbildung und Verfassung*, pp. 513–14, esp. note 557; Isidore of Seville, *Etymologiae* xiv.iv.4, pp. 53–5; Bartholomaeus Anglicus, *De proprietatibus rerum* xv.13, ed. Knochlobtzer, 'De Alemannia'; Honorius of Autun, *Imago Mundi* xxiii, ed. Flint, pp. 59–60.

[49] Bartholomaeus Anglicus, *De proprietatibus rerum* xv.166, ed. Knochlobtzer, 'De Thuringia'.

[50] Gervase of Tilbury, *Otia imperialia* ii.7, ed. and trans. Banks and Binns, pp. 242–3: 'propter sui fortitudinem et robur quasi saxorum sic appellatur'.

[51] E.g. the ninth-century Aquitanian monk Ermoldus Nigellus's remark in Ermoldus Nigellus, *Carmen in honorem Hludowici* i, line 378 in *Poème sur Louis le Pieux et Épitres au roi Pepin*, ed. and French trans. E. Faral (Paris, 1964), p. 32 that the name of the Franks brings shudders of fear. It is a classical stereotype that could be interpreted in conjunction with the Trojan descent myth; I. Wood, 'Defining the Franks: Frankish Origins in Early Medieval Historiography', in *Concepts of National Identity in the Middle Ages*, ed. S. Forde, L. Johnson and A. V. Murray (Leeds, 1995), pp. 47–57 (p. 50). Wenskus, *Stammesbildung und Verfassung*, pp. 513–14.

the Franks' character politically in his prophetic *Noticia seculi*, claiming that the German Franks were free because of their imperial status.[52]

These etymologies suggest that members of ethnic groups shared an innate disposition. However, over time peoples' names changed and were interpreted differently in accordance with various diverse textual traditions. A range of etymological explanations was hence created, which became a convenient store of images from which to take one's pick. Thus, circa 1240 the Franciscan friar Bartholomaeus Anglicus presented a string of etymologies of the British and English, cross-referencing and entangling Britannia and Anglia.[53] His encyclopaedia claims that the inhabitants of Britannia, or Anglia, descended from the Trojan founder Brutus, but were also Angli living in a remote corner, *angulus*, of the world, serving as a cornerstone of Christendom; that the Angli descended from Queen Engelia, the daughter of a Saxon duke; and that their name was a pun on their beautiful angelic faces, upon which Pope Gregory the Great (*c.* 540–604) had set eyes at a slave market in late sixth-century Rome.[54] That multiple names meant confusion was something a few compilers of encyclopaedias recognized. Early on, Isidore of Seville affirmed: 'There appear to be more names of nations that have been altered than names remaining, and afterwards a rational process has given diverse names to these.'[55] Nonetheless, the compilers made little effort to tidy up the various names; nor were classical names structurally discarded for contemporary denominations reflecting changes as a result of migration, conquest or dynastic reconfigurations. The ensuing chaos perhaps was driven by a deference for *auctoritas*, framing the

---

[52] L. E. Scales, 'France and the Empire: The Viewpoint of Alexander of Roes', *French History* 9/4 (1995), 394–416 (p. 408).

[53] Bartholomaeus also cross-references Gallia and Francia, indicating that both names were considered to be more or less synonymous in the first half of the thirteenth century.

[54] Bartholomaeus Anglicus, *De proprietatibus rerum* xv.14, ed. Knochlobtzer, 'De Anglia'. The remark about Queen Engelia is repeated by Ranulf Hidgen in the fourteenth century but it does not seem to have been picked up on by other writers. Gervase of Tilbury, on the other hand, says that the Saxons come from the island of Engla in Saxony; see *Otia imperialia* ii.10, 17, ed. and trans. Banks and Binns, pp. 306–7, 418–19. The story about the Angles' angelic faces was narrated by Bede, *Historia ecclesiastica* ii.1, ed. and trans. B. Colgrave and R. A. B. Mynors, pp. 133–5. K. Lavezzo, *Angels on the Edge of the World: Geography, Literature, and the English Community, 1000–1534* (Ithaca, 2006), pp. 27–8, 85–6.

[55] Isidore of Seville, *Etymologiae* ix.ii.39, ed. Reydellet, p. 61, trans. *The* Etymologies *of Isidore of Seville*, trans. S. A. Barney and M. Hall (Cambridge, 2006), p. 194: '[P]lura tamen gentium mutata quam manentia vocabula apparent; quibus postea nomina diversa dedit ratio.'

new as a thing of the past, but it is more likely the theological perspective was resonating that the past functioned as a blueprint for deciphering the meaning of present acts and understanding future events, and hence remained cogent, as discussed further below.[56]

Peoples in time and space

Not only did the early histories, encyclopaedias and maps (*mappae mundi*) represent the world and all things and beings in it as part of God's creation, but they also firmly situated ethnic groups in the historical narrative of salvation, in the biblical past, the present and the apocalyptic future. In this context peoples fulfilled their role in the history of mankind by either opening their ears and minds to the apostolic message or, because of their allegedly innate ethnic vices, remaining sinfully deaf and stubborn. Monks and clerics assigned different time slots and spaces to various peoples, framing Jews, Persians, Egyptians and Greeks as 'peoples of the past', left behind, dwelling in the east. This is a form of othering through comparison that is embedded in a Christian historical narrative of salvation, in which time and space coalesce on an east–west axis. From the viewpoint of Christian theologians, the east was the stage of the creation, the biblical past and, adopting a classical schema, the cradle of power and knowledge, which over time had translated to the west, eventually reaching Francia.[57] In this manner, the east was described as a place of the past, and home to religions of the past such as Judaism. Two strains of thought by that means shaped the discourse positioning peoples in the past, present and future: eschatology and the related concept of the

---

[56] H.-W. Goetz, 'The Concept of Time in the Historiography of the Eleventh and Twelfth Centuries', in *Medieval Concepts of the Past: Ritual, Memory, Historiography*, ed. G. Althoff, J. Fried and P. J. Geary (Cambridge, Washington DC, 2002), pp. 139–65; C. Weeda, 'Meanwhile in Messianic Time'; Lozovsky, *The Earth Is Our Book*, pp. 139–47. But see also Gervase of Tilbury's comment that he uses names old and new, doing homage to the past and adhering to oral knowledge; *Otia imperialia* ii.25, ed. and trans. Banks and Binns, pp. 524–7.

[57] Especially in theological, exegetical and encyclopaedic texts and images up till the thirteenth century. Hrabanus Maurus in the ninth century stated that the world can be divided into two parts, East and West; cf. *Commentariorum in Genesim* 2, 6, *PL* 107, col. 513C, echoing Jerome, *Liber interpretationis Hebraicorum nominum*, in *Opera*, Corpus Christianorum. Series Latina 72, ed. P. de Lagarde (Turnhout, 1959), p. 63. S. Akbari, 'From Due East to True North: Orientalism and Orientation', in *The Postcolonial Middle Ages*, ed. J. J. Cohen (Basingstoke, 2000), pp. 19–34 (p. 28, 33); A. Pagden, *The Idea of Europe: From Antiquity to the European Union* (Washington, 2002), pp. 35–6. From a northern perspective, east and south are sometimes blurred.

prophesied translation of power and knowledge from east to west (*translatio studii et imperii*).⁵⁸ For whereas the east was the stage of biblical drama's past, the peoples in the west would be key players in the unfolding apotheosis of the history of humankind.

Depicted at the top of T-O *mappae mundi* (fig. 1) in time and space, the Orient was the alpha and omega of the creation and the three monotheistic religions.⁵⁹ Although some schoolmen maintained that the earthly paradise was a spiritual place rather than a real location, Eden was often situated geographically in the east, as were the successive earlier empires of Babylon, the Medes, the Persians and the Greeks.⁶⁰ From Europe's perspective, the Orient also symbolized the future: not only was the east the place where the world began, but it was the site where it would come to an end. At the centre – the navel – of the Earth stood Jerusalem, in the Christian tradition represented as the future bride of Christ, and, from the late eleventh century onwards, the prize of the crusader movement.⁶¹ The T-O *mappae mundi*

---

⁵⁸ Gassman, '*Translatio studii*'; Krämer, *Translatio imperii et studii*; Grundmann, 'Sacerdotium – Regnum – Studium'.

⁵⁹ A T-O map is a world map based upon Isidore of Seville's description of the world in *De natura rerum* and the *Etymologiae*. It depicts the three continents Asia (at the top), Africa and Europe, which are divided by water. E. Edson, *Mapping Time and Space: How Medieval Mapmakers Viewed their World* (London, 1997); E. Edson, 'World Maps and Easter Tables: Medieval Maps in Context', *Imago Mundi* 48/1 (1996), 25–42; D. Woodward, 'Reality, Symbolism, Time, and Space in Medieval World Maps', *Annals of the Association of American Geographers* 75/4 (1985), 510–21. For the interplay between text and image, see Uwe Ruberg, 'Mappae Mundi des Mittelalters im Zusammenwirken von Text und Bild', in *Text und Bild: Aspekte des Zusammenwirkens zweier Künste in Mittelalter und früher Neuzeit*, ed. C. Meier and U. Ruberg (Wiesbaden, 1980), pp. 550–92; M. Kupfer, 'Medieval World Maps: Embedded Images, Interpretive Frames', *Word & Image* 10/3 (1994), 262–88; K. Biddick, 'The abc of Ptolemy. Mapping the World with the Alphabet', in *Text and Territory: Geographical Imagination in the European Middle Ages*, ed. S. Tomasch and S. Gilles (Philadelphia, 1998), pp. 268–93. Important studies of *mappae mundi* are K. Miller, *Mappae Mundi: Die ältesten Weltkarten*, 6 vols. (Stuttgart, 1895–98); M. Hoogvliet, *Pictura et scriptura: Textes, images et herméneutique des 'mappae mundi' (XIIIe–XVIe siècle)* (Turnhout, 2007); N. R. Kline, *Maps of Medieval Thought: The Hereford Paradigm* (Woodbridge, 2001); P. D. A. Harvey, *The Hereford World Map: Medieval World Maps and Their Context* (London, 2006).

⁶⁰ Minnis, *From Eden to Eternity*, pp. 75–6; For the location of Paradise or the Garden of Eden in the East, see A. Scafi, *Mapping Paradise: A History of Heaven and Earth* (London, 2006).

⁶¹ J. Rubenstein, *Nebuchadnezzar's Dream: The Crusades, Apocalyptic Prophecy, and the End of History* (New York, 2019). Cf. Psalm 73. 12; Ezechiel 5. 5. The location of Jerusalem at the centre of the Earth is a commonplace. See Akbari, 'From Due East

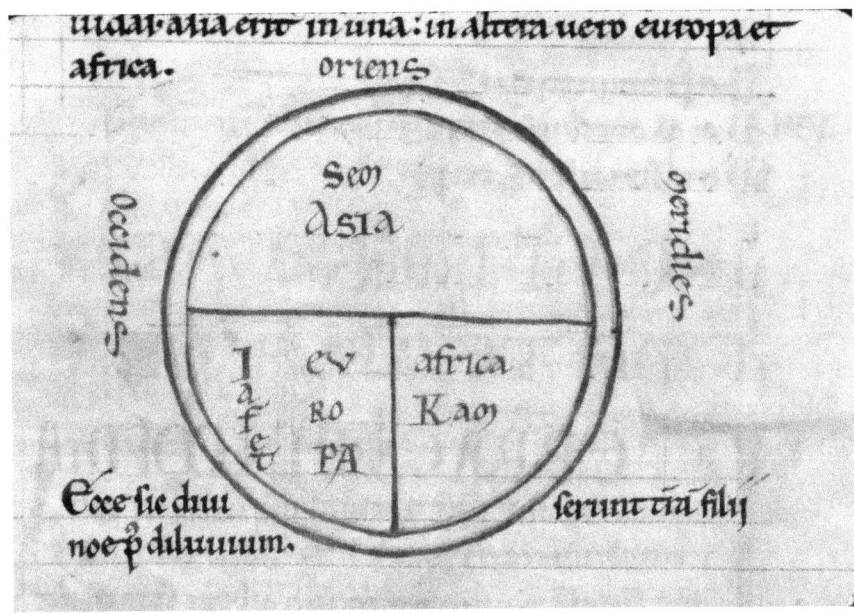

Figure 1. T-O map. Isidore of Seville, *Etymologies*, in Auxerre, Bibliothèque Municipale MS 76 fol. 91v., dating to the second quarter of the twelfth century.

visualized history's path of redemption, coursing linearly from beginning to end yet simultaneously spherically, spanning the entire world and creating a tripartite genealogical-territorial division of the world in Asia, Europe and Africa that formed the basic scheme of an abundance of geographical treatises. Hence, commentaries on passages in Genesis often – although inconsistently – assigned the three continents to the descendants of Noah's children: Shem (allotted by far the largest part: Asia), Japheth (obtaining Europe) and Ham (given hot Africa).[62] On some of the maps, embracing the world and the whole ecumenicity of human diversity with his hands and feet, stood Christ.

---

to True North', p. 21 for further references, commenting that Jerusalem is imagined to be a place of return rather than departure, hence its emotive pull in the three monotheistic religions.

[62] Cf. Ambrosius of Milan, *De noe et arca* i.xxxii, *PL* 14, cols. 414C–415A. Bartholomaeus Anglicus, *De proprietatibus rerum*, ed. Knochlobtzer, xv.1, 'De orbe'. J. Williams, 'Isidore, Orosius and the Beatus Map', *Imago mundi* 49 (1997), 7–32. Benjamin Braude argues that the maps are inconsistently divided up between Shem, Japheth and Ham; B. Braude, 'The Sons of Noah and the Construction of Ethnic and Geographical Identities in the Medieval and Early Modern Periods',

For Hugh of St Victor (c. 1096–1141), who taught at the Augustinian school of St Victor in Paris, the positioning on the axis of the Orient and Occident fitted into an explicitly eschatological context. The expectation was that the world would cease to exist once Christendom had reached the farthest parts of the west, followed by an apocalyptic struggle in the east and the eventual return of Christ.[63] Apocalyptic thought, in this respect, provided the foundation for the appropriation of the 'four corners of the world' through the *imperium christianum*. Foretold in the Old Testament book of Psalms, the apostles had the task of extending God's rule from sea to sea, 'all the nations serving him', from the eastern Mediterranean to the west by means of proselytization.[64] Once the farthest reaches of the world had succumbed to the apostolic message and the *populus christianus* had fully spread, humanity would find salvation. This narrative was inspired by the biblical rendition of Christ's speech upon his ascension to heaven, where he conveyed to his disciples that although only God knew when the end of time would come, his followers 'shall be witnesses to me in Jerusalem, and in all Judea and Samaria, and to the end of the earth'.[65] Rather than a centrifugal evangelization sprouting in the Levant and moving from there across the spherical globe, however, theologians imagined Christendom as slowly progressing linearly from east to west, eventually setting foot on the farthest islands in the Atlantic Ocean.[66] Hugh of St Victor thus observed:

> [T]he order of space and time seems to be in almost complete correspondence. Therefore, divine providence's arrangement seems to have been that what was brought about at the beginning of time would also have been brought about in the East – at the beginning of the world as space – and then as time proceeded toward its end, the centre of events would have

---

The William and Mary Quarterly 54/1 (1997), 103–42; Braude, 'Cham et Noé', 93–125. On allegorical and literal division cf. Akbari, 'From Due East to True North', p. 23.

[63] Hugh of S. Victor, *De arca Noë morali libri iv*, PL 176, col. 667D. The fourth-century Syrian bishop Severian of Gabala's *De mundi creatione* v is an early example that expresses this claim. Cf. Wright, *Geographical Lore*, pp. 233–5.

[64] Psalm 71. 8; L. E. G. Donkin, '"Usque ad ultimum terrae": Mapping the Ends of the Earth in Two Medieval Floor Mosaics', in *Cartography in Antiquity and the Middle Ages: Fresh Perspectives, New Methods*, ed. R. J. A. Talbert and R. W. Unger (Leiden, 2008), 189–218 (pp. 199–201).

[65] Acts 1. 8.

[66] S. McKenzie, 'The Westward Progression of History on Medieval Mappaemundi: An Investigation of the Evidence', in *The Hereford World Map: Medieval World Maps and Their Context*, ed. P. D. A. Harvey (London, 2006), pp. 335–44.

shifted to the West, so that we may recognise out of this that the world nears its end in time as the course of events has already reached the extremity of the world in space.[67]

In this framework, the willingness of peoples to take on the Christian message and to overcome ethnic dispositions allowing them to fall into sin went hand in hand. The westward progression of Christendom was grounded in the spatial-temporal succession of the four empires derived from the prophecies of Daniel.[68] The Church historian Paulus Orosius, who was probably born on the Iberian Peninsula, had described these empires as rising and falling centres of power, successively toppling one another.[69] Jerome awarded the four empires mentioned in the Book of Daniel historical meaning, identifying the Roman empire as the fourth centre of power.[70] Although the western Roman empire collapsed in the fifth century, from the perspective of ninth-century theologians and historians, the *translatio imperii et studii* continued through the revival of the Roman empire as the *imperium christianum*, led by a world emperor associated with the Carolingians.[71] At the end of the first millennium, the translation motif invited

---

[67] Hugh of St Victor, *De arca Noë morali libri IV*, PL 176, col. 677D: 'Ordo autem loci, et ordo temporis fere per omnia secundum rerum gestarum seriem concurrere videntur, et ita per divinam providentiam videtur esse dispositum, ut quae in principio temporum gerebantur in Oriente, quasi in principio mundi gererentur, ac deinde ad finem profluente tempore usque ad Occidentem rerum summa descenderet, ut ex ipso agnoscamus appropinquare finem saeculi, quia rerum cursus jam attigit finem mundi'; translation is cited from Edson, 'The Medieval World View', pp. 507–8.

[68] Cf. Daniel 2.31 and 7.2–28. In Daniel's dream, the four empires appear as animals: a lion with the wings of an eagle; a bear; a four-headed panther with four wings; and a ten-horned beast. Cf. Edson, *Mapping Time and Space*, p. 158.

[69] Orosius, *Historiae adversum Paganos* ii.iii.2–4 and vi.4–6, ed. Zangemeister, pp. 85–6, 95–6. Orosius draws parallels between the histories of Rome and Babylonia, arguing that Babylonia had fallen as a result of its vices, whereas Rome still stood strong because of the Christian religion and God's protection. Cf. Bartholomaeus Anglicus, *De proprietatibus rerum* xv.33, ed. Knochlobtzer, 'De Chaldea'. Lozovsky, *The Earth Is Our Book*, pp. 73–4.

[70] C. Weeda, 'Violence, Control, Prophecy and Power in Twelfth-Century France and Germany', in *Reading the Bible in the Middle Ages*, ed. J. Nelson and D. Kempf (London, 2015), pp. 147–66.

[71] Gabriele, *Empire of Memory*; J. L. Nelson, 'Kingship and Empire in the Carolingian World', in *Carolingian Culture: Emulation and Innovation*, ed. R. McKitterick (Cambridge, 1994), pp. 52–87; Latowsky, *Emperor of the World*; B. McGinn, *Visions of the End: Apocalyptic Traditions in the Middle Ages* (New York, 1998), pp. 44–50;

stories of how a world emperor would lead the battle against the Antichrist, heralding the expiration of the fourth Roman empire.[72] Debates about the identity of this world emperor subsequently laid bare the transient and fragile nature of power, as various Frankish, Saxon and Swabian writers competed for his legacy, particularly during the early crusades. The German chronicler and bishop Otto of Freising, the nephew of the German emperor Frederick Barbarossa (1122–90), articulated the translation in his *Chronicle or History of the Two Cities* written between 1143 and 1145. He recalled that scientific and religious knowledge had travelled from Babylonia to the Greeks, the Romans, the Gauls and the Spaniards, yet that the transfer of power had flowed to the Germans, while others, as discussed in chapter 5, argued that military power had moved to the French.[73]

Sinful dispositions and salvation history

Returning to the tenth century, from an eschatological perspective, peoples' alleged collective moral dispositions etched the boundaries of their communities vis-à-vis humankind, as did their language and customs. Monks and clerics classified and compared ethnic groups as moral communities shaped by their religious beliefs, while implicitly essentializing the traits grounded on Graeco-Roman environmental theory. For, as Christianity purportedly seeped to the four corners of the world, peoples in theory functioned as actors in the drama of salvation unfolding on the world stage. Successful proselytization, whereby Christendom gained a firm foothold, depended upon individual and collective readiness to receive God's word and embrace Christian values and virtues by overcoming individual as well as collective sinful

---

M. Gabriele, 'Asleep at the Wheel? Messianism, Apocalypticism and Charlemagne's Passivity in the Oxford Chanson de Roland', *Nottingham Medieval Studies* 47 (2003), 46–72; M. Gabriele, 'Otto III, Charlemagne, and Pentecost A.D. 1000: A Reconsideration Using Diplomatic Evidence', in *The Year 1000: Religious and Social Response to the Turning of the First Millennium*, ed. M. Frassetto (New York, 2002), pp. 111–32; J. Weiss, 'Emperors and Antichrists: Reflections of Empire in Insular Narrative, 1130–1250', in *The Matter of Identity in Medieval Romance*, ed. P. Hardman (Cambridge, 2002), pp. 87–102.

[72] Merrills, *History and Geography*, pp. 51–3.

[73] Otto of Freising, *Chronica sive Historia de duabus civitatibus*, ed. W. Lammers, German trans. A. Schmidt (Darmstadt, 1961), Prologue. S. Phillips, 'The Outer World of the European Middle Ages', in *Implicit Understandings: Observing, Reporting, and Reflecting on the Encounters between Europeans and other Peoples in the Early Modern Era*, ed. S. B. Schwartz (Cambridge, 1994), pp. 23–63 (pp. 44–5).

dispositions. Disasters, war and famine, conversely, marked God's anger over collective transgressions, particularly those perpetrated by his chosen peoples or New Israelites.[74]

The 'New Israelites', the self-proclaimed successors of the Old Testament Jews who were party to the covenant of the law, advocated an ecumenical contract between God and humanity based upon the *logos* of Christ. In their doing so, the ethnic–religious bond between the Judaic people and God was theoretically replaced with a contract between the deity and the whole of mankind. On paper, the heterogeneity of ethnic communities dissolved into a Christian body politic, a *corpus mysticum*, to which believers were admitted after they were reborn in the body of Christ.[75] In the Epistle to the Colossians (3:5–11), the apostles Paul and Timothy pointedly commanded the people of Colossae to 'put to death, therefore, whatever belongs to your earthly nature: sexual immorality, impurity, lust, evil desires and greed', to discard their old self and put on a new self, having acquired knowledge in God's image. In consequence, the letter claimed, there no longer existed 'Gentile or Jew, circumcised or uncircumcised, barbarian, Scythian, slave or free, but Christ is all, and is in all'. This comment reflects a utopian ideology of universalism that in practice, however, never materialized. Early Christian texts regularly continued to wield terms like *ethnos* to express membership of Christendom, and the religious community institutionally remained organized along ethnic lines. The essentialized dispositions of the barbarian, Scythian or the enslaved proved intractable, continuing to make imagined forays on the desired rectitude of mankind. That ethnicity retained its effectiveness within a religious discourse, was, as Denise Buell has argued extensively, contingent on the rhetoric of Christian universalism which envisaged itself in explicitly corporal terms of rebirth, where descent and the flesh dominated.[76] Thus, the clergy admonished and encouraged members of the religious body of Christ, as well as outsiders, to deploy their free will and act as 'true Christians', mastering their innate sinful ethnic dispositions. The rhetoric of conversion utilized references to the corporal innateness of the moral dispositions of peoples, urging to discard old inclinations. Raoul Ardent of Poitou (died *c.* 1200), master of theology at the university of Paris, preached to the brethren on the Feast of the Holy Trinity, telling each to overcome his ethnic vice. The Jews (assumedly not present in

---

[74] For chosen peoples, see p. 32n.95 in the Introduction.
[75] A. D. Harvey, *Body Politic: Political Metaphor and Political Violence* (Newcastle, 2007), p. 10.
[76] Buell, 'Early Christian Universalism and Modern Racism', pp. 109–31.

the audience) needed to rise above their 'innate disbelief', relating to their 'stiff-necked' nature, their refusal to accept the Christian message; the French should overcome their 'innate arrogance'; the Romans, their 'innate avarice'; and the people of Poitou their 'innate gluttony and garrulity'.[77] In sum, divisions along genealogical–ethnic lines remained authoritative in Christendom, allotting to peoples distinct roles and paths of salvation in light of the history of mankind.

Jewish believers, however, were singled out strategically as incapable of embracing the new because of their *innate disbelief*, leaving them behind in vice, outside the Christian body politic. The attribution of inherited incredulity runs parallel with the assignment to Jews of a separate legal status, reflected in the oppressive legislation issued on the Iberian Peninsula between the sixth and eighth centuries pertaining to the dwindling Jewish population. The rhetoric of obstinacy resonates in Visigoth King Egica's Law promulgated after 687, aiming to convert Jews to Christianity through tax relief and other measures, which likewise complains that Jews 'persevere in the perfidy of their heart and take no heed to convert to the Catholic faith', 'in the obstinacy of their perfidy'.[78] From the twelfth century, the alleged corporality of Jewishness subsequently translated into conspiracies about Jewish thirsting for blood because of their cursed state, physical impairment and bleeding, suggesting that they, as outsiders of the Christian body politic, have no qualms about spilling Christian blood. Like serfs, another distinct legal category whose lineage God 'cursed', Jews occasionally ranked as melancholy types as well, discussed in chapter 2. Powerful abbots like Bernard of Clairvaux (1090–1153) and Peter the Venerable (1092/94–1156) questioned their rationality in not choosing the Christian faith, denouncing the 'bovine intellect' shown by their failure to understand such a simple message.[79] Nonetheless, this did not mean that the Church allowed its believers to attack Jews with impunity, for Jews, Augustine had said, acted as witnesses to the Christian faith.

---

[77] Raoul Ardent, *Homilia* ii.2, 'In die Trinitatis', *PL* 155, col. 1949C-D: 'Judaeis innatam incredulitatem', 'Gallis innatam superbiam'; 'Romanis innatam avaritiam'; 'Pictavinis innatam ingluviem et garrulitatem'.

[78] *The Jews in the Legal Sources of the Early Middle Ages*, ed. A. Lindner (Detroit, 1997), pp. 281–4, no. 542: 'in perfidia cordis sui perseverantes, ad catholicam fidem converti neglexerint'; 'Iudeis in perfidie duritia so permanentibus'. *Perfidia* also in nos. 445, 527, 528, 535, 538–9, 541–2, 544, 556, 570, 579, 722, 811, 841, 850–4, 857–8, 860–1, 867, 979, 1000, 1012, 1020, 1032, 1042, 1049, 1058, 1095, 1112, 1141, 1148, 1191, 1231. M. Toch, *The Economic History of European Jews: Late Antiquity and Early Middle Ages* (Leiden, 2013), p. 106, 108, 110–16. The Jewish population in northern Iberia increased from the tenth century.

[79] Resnick, *Marks of Distinctions*, p. 37.

Grasping boundaries in lists

The final part of this chapter will now explore how Benedictine monks strategically compared and sorted peoples' moral dispositions within such a temporal-geographical framework in a specific type of text listing the virtues and vices of ethnic groups. The oldest surviving Latin lists of this kind emerged in the tenth century in Benedictine monasteries on the Iberian Peninsula.[80] To date, scholars have barely explored these ethnic catalogues listing peoples' virtues and vices. Although he acknowledged their existence, when discussing the emergence of catalogues of nations Franz Karl Stanzel claimed that it was impossible to trace the origins of these catalogues and that he could not detect much order within them.[81] On the surface level, historians summarily (if at all) interpreted lists of this kind to reflect the deficient state of pragmatic geographical knowledge in this period. Such an interpretation assumes that the function of knowledge is to reproduce the pre-existing and rather static boundaries of the – in this case – imagined territories and peoples. On a more abstract level, Umberto Eco argued that listing (accidental)

[80] These lists are not exclusive to the Latin world. An Armenian text of the early eighth century, copied by archbishop Stephen of Siunik, sums up ten peoples and their speech characteristics. Cf. Borst, *Der Turmbau von Babel*, i, 282; P. de Lagarde, 'Agathangelos', *Abhandlungen der Königlichen Gesellschaft der Wissenschaften zu Göttingen, Historisch-Philologische Klasse* 35 (1889), 150–63 (p. 151). In the thirteenth century, this perhaps fifth-century list was incorporated by the Armenian Wardan Areveltsi in his history of the world until 1267. In it, language reflects a group's perceived character: the Greek language is soft natured, the Latin strong, that of the Huns audacious, the Assyrian humble or suppliant, the Persian language rich, the Alan friendly, the Goth pleasant, the Egyptian tongue guttural, the Indian twittering like birds and the Armenian agreeable, attaining all the qualities of the other languages.

[81] F. K. Stanzel, 'Das Nationalitätenschema in der Literatur und seine Entstehung zu Beginn der Neuzeit', in *Erstarrtes Denken: Studien zu Klischee, Stereotyp und Vorurteil in englischsprachiger Literatur*, ed. G. Blaicher (Tübingen, 1987), pp. 84–96 (pp. 86–7). F. K. Stanzel, 'Zur literarischen Imagologie: Eine Einführung', in *Europäischer Völkerspiegel: Imagologisch-ethnographische Studien zu den Völkertafeln des frühen 18. Jahrhunderts*, ed. F. K. Stanzel, I. Weiler and W. Zacharasiewicz (Heidelberg, 1999), pp. 9–39 (p. 20). Cf. Meyvaert, 'Voicing National Antipathy', 747; Brühl, *Deutschland, Frankreich*, 274; H. Fichtenau, 'Gentiler und europäischer Horizont an der Schwelle des ersten Jahrtausends', *Römische Historische Mitteilungen* 23 (1981), 227–43; Bartlett, 'Concepts of Race and Ethnicity', p. 49. S. Kot, 'Old International Insults and Praises: I. The Medieval Period', *Harvard Slavic Studies* 2 (1954), 181–210 discusses the development of catalogues in the fourteenth and fifteenth centuries in Eastern Europe. M. Jeay, *Le commerce des mots: L'usage des listes dans la littérature médiévale médiévale (xiie–xve siècles)* (Geneva, 2006) discusses the emergence of lists in literature, but not specifically of ethnic catalogues.

properties served to aid *those having difficulty in grasping* the boundaries of a thing portrayed. However, properties that serve as classifying markers can also actively *produce* rather than simply *reproduce* the boundaries of imagined peoples populating territories, as well.[82] In other words, such lists can help to actively contemplate imagined ethnic categories, to strategically sort them and not just to serve as reminders. Indeed, there are several indications that these early lists summing up the virtues and vices, rather than serving a pragmatic function, rather should be considered to be rhetorical devices, serving as tools of education and contemplation for actively grasping the boundaries of humanity. The manuscript context, period and location also suggest that these lists sprang from a milieu where monks mused upon the impending end of time on the Spanish peninsula in the ninth–tenth centuries, while a struggle was being waged against Muslim armies. The form of the lists similarly suggests a translatory concept of salvation history, arranging peoples from east to west, and from the past to the present. To explain this, it is helpful to look at these lists in more detail.

Lists of ethnic groups are multifarious and appear in different forms and frameworks, including the biblical genealogies summing up the seventy-two nations descending from Noah's progeny.[83] Many of these catalogues do not necessarily reference ethnic character traits. The earliest lists that do classify and compare ethnic dispositions can be arranged loosely into two groups: those predominantly cataloguing sets of vices, although often commencing with the glory or wisdom of the Greeks or Egyptians; and those contrasting virtues and vices, usually headed by the 'envy of the Jews'.

---

[82] U. Eco, *The Infinity of Lists: An Illustrated Essay* (London, 2009), p. 18, whose division of lists into pragmatic and poetic lists does not adequately accommodate eschatological concepts of time, in which events of the past were considered to simultaneously take place in the present. Howe, *Old English Catalogue Poems*, p. 24 also argued that catalogues present information firstly for knowledge's sake. For discussions of empirical-geographical knowledge, however, Lozovsky, *The Earth Is Our Book*, pp. 139–55; A. C. Gow, 'Fra Mauro's World View: Authority and Empircal Evidence on a Venetian mappamundi', in *The Hereford World Map: Medieval World Maps and their Context*, ed. P. D. A. Harvey (London, 2006), pp. 405–14; Edson, *Mapping Time and Space*, pp. 3, 7–9.

[83] Genesis 10. Borst, *Der Turmbau von Babel*, contains a wealth of source material concerning ethnic genealogy. I have not been able to identify early genealogical tables mentioning ethnic virtues or vices, however. Cf. W. Goffart, 'The Supposedly "Frankish" Table of Nations: An Edition and Study', *Frühmittelalterliche Studien* 17 (1983), 98–130; on ethnic genealogies Reynolds, 'Medieval *Origines Gentium*', pp. 375–90.

Cataloguing Ethnic Virtues and Vices   65

The earliest extant list out of a total of nine clusters of catalogues identified between the ninth and thirteenth centuries and often rubricated *De proprietatibus gentium* (On the Properties of Peoples), is found in the late tenth-century Codex Aemilianensis that was produced in the Benedictine monastery of Suso in San Millán de la Cogolla, in mountainous La Rioja in northern Spain.[84] The manuscript lists twelve peoples and their characteristics, virtues or vices:

The wisdom of the Greeks

The strength of the Goths[85]

The knowledge of the Chaldeans[86]

The arrogance of the Romans[87]

The ferocity of the Franks[88]

The wrath of the Britons

The lust of the Scots[89]

The rigidity of the Saxons[90]

The cupidity of the Persians

The envy of the Jews

---

[84] This earliest surviving list is inserted in the *Albelda Chronicle* (first completed in November 883). The manuscript containing the Codex Aemilianensis is Madrid, Biblioteca Real Academia de la Historia MS 39. For the *Albelda Chronicle*: *Conquerors and Chroniclers of Early Medieval Spain*, trans. and ed. K. B. Wolf (Liverpool, 1999), pp. 1–56; Y. Bonnaz, 'Introduction', in *Chroniques Asturiennes* (fin IXe siècle), ed. Y. Bonnaz (Paris, 1987), pp. xxix–xxx. This section of the manuscript is entitled *Liber Chronica*.

[85] Cf. Isidore of Seville *Etymologiae* ix.ii.89, ed. Reydellet, pp. 91–3.

[86] The knowledge of the Chaldeans refers to astrology; cf. Daniel 1. 4. See also the Arabic-Iberian *Book of the Categories of Nations* by Said al-Andalusi, who praises the Chaldeans' scientific knowledge; S. I. Salem and A. Kumar (ed. and trans.), *Science in the Medieval World: Book of the Categories of Nations*' (Austin, 1991), pp. 18–19. However, the Chaldeans also feature as enemies of Israel and in ninth-century Asturia, Muslims were called Chaldeans who opposed the Goths, the 'New Israelites'.

[87] The arrogance of the Romans possibly alludes to Augustine's criticism that ancient Rome merely desired justice in order to achieve fame and arrogantly created its gods to enhance its power; J. Benzinger, *Invectiva in Romam: Romkritik im Mittelalter vom 9. bis zum 12. Jahrhundert* (Lübeck, 1968), pp. 20–1.

[88] See note 53 in this chapter.

[89] Here and below, the Scots can refer to people living in Ireland.

[90] Cf. Isidore of Seville, *Etymologiae* ix.ii.100, ed. Reydellet, p. 99.

The peace of the Ethiopians[91]

The commerce of the Gauls[92]

The texts enveloping the list 'Wisdom of the Greeks' are similar catalogues inviting the user to memorize and contemplate natural landmarks and resources in a Christian landscape, to marvel at God's creation and bounty, the spread of Christianity and the relationship to language.[93] The list is preceded by several geographical items, such as an 'Enquiry of the Whole World' based on Julius Honorius's fifth-century *Cosmography*, recording the number of seas, islands, mountains and provinces; an 'Enquiry of Spain', based on Isidore's *Etymologies*; a list of Visigoth episcopal provinces; a list of the lengths of Spanish rivers; and the Seven Wonders of the World.[94] The catalogue is succeeded by a list of commodities to be found in the region of Iberia, such as Narbonne chicken, Baeza figs, Galician honey and science and education in Toledo under Visigothic rule before it fell to the Umayyads; a list of the five vowels, semivowels and consonants based on Priscian; and a list of distances between Roman towns.[95] In the eleventh-century section of the Roda Codex, the same catalogue features alongside similar Isidorean texts, including a list of the seventy-two languages of the world, arising from God's anger over mankind's hubris when it built the Tower of Babel.[96]

Both the milieu in which the monks produced these catalogues of peoples – the scattered nations across the face of the Earth – and the manuscript contents have an apocalyptic context.[97] The earliest recorded catalogue, the

---

[91] Cf. Orosius, *Historiae adversum paganos* i.iv.5–6, ed. Zangemeister, pp. 43–4.
[92] See Appendix, I for the Latin text and manuscripts.
[93] Bonnaz, 'Introduction', pp. lxviii–lxx; Howe, *Old English Catalogue Poems*, p. 15.
[94] These Seven Wonders deviate from the traditional list; see: Bonnaz, 'Introduction', p. lxxi, note 4.
[95] *Chroniques Asturiennes*, ed. Y. Bonnaz (Paris, 1987), pp. 8–13. The list of distances between Roman towns in the Codex Aemilianensis stems from the ancient itinerary tradition recording routes to specific destinations. Some of these lists, such as the late third-century Antonine Itinerary charting land and sea routes, were carefully preserved in several manuscript collections. E. Albu, 'Imperial Geography and the Medieval Peutinger Map', *Imago Mundi* 57/2 (2005) 136–48 (pp. 137–8).
[96] Madrid, Biblioteca Real Academia de la Historia MS 78 fol. 196v. In Madrid, Biblioteca Nacional de España MS 8831 (formerly X 161), dating to the eleventh or twelfth century, the same catalogue again precedes the seventy-two languages and the Six Ages of the World. The lists in both manuscripts are preceded by a section containing Orosius's *Historiae adversum paganos*.
[97] The catalogue in the thirteenth-century Paris, Bibliothèque nationale de France, MS Latin 2874 fol. 64v. contrasting virtues and vices, for example, is preceded

'Wisdom of the Greeks', for instance, is found in an Iberian manuscript containing the *Albelda Chronicle*, which is closely related to two other texts, the *Chronicle of Alfonso III* compiled at the behest of Alfonso III of Asturias (*c.* 848–910) bridging pre-conquest Visigoth Spain to Catholic Iberia, and the *Prophetic Chronicle*.[98] The *Alfonso Chronicle* and the *Prophetic Chronicle* both narrate the reconquest of Iberia from the Umayyads in an overtly apocalyptic language. Within eighteen months the Goths, God's chosen people, so the chronicles prophesize, will overcome their foes just as the Israelites had in Babylon, and liberate Iberia, their Judea. Notably, these texts were produced while war was actually being waged against the Umayyads, fostering anti-Islam sentiment in Iberia and leading monks to portray Muhammad as the Antichrist.[99] Perhaps inspired by Mozarab churchmen actively encouraging the Asturian kings to present themselves as successors of the Goths, the *Prophetic Chronicle*, alluding to Ezekiel 38–39, associates both the 'Saracens' and the Goths with the apocalyptic people of Gog. Israel, the promised land of past and future, is accordingly transformed into a territory populated by the Ishmaelites, a Canaanite land of health-giving milk and honey, as it had been in Isidore's panegyric of Spain.[100] Because of the sins of the fornicating clergy, God has sent the Muslims as a scourge to punish the Goths. Reflecting a wider tradition on the Iberian Peninsula, in the *Alfonso Chronicle* the Muslims are in similar, typological vein also called Chaldeans, referring back to the Book of Habbakuk, where God releases his wrath on the people of Israel, devastating its lands. In the *Prophetic Chronicle*, the Ishmaelites, or Chaldeans, will, however, rule only for a mere 170 years, which in Ezekiel 38 numerically symbolizes the length of presence of the 'cloud' of Gog (here the Ishmaelites) over the Israelites.[101] To calculate how long the Ishmaelites had already reigned

---

directly by 'On the End of the World' (*De fine mundi*) and 'On Simon the Sorcerer' (*De Simone mago*).

[98] Both the *Albelda* and the *Alfonso Chronicle* also contain continuations of Isidore's *History of the Goths*.

[99] Wolf, *Conquerors and Chroniclers*, pp. 45–7, 56. For the Goths as a chosen people, see J. N. Hillgarth, 'Historiography in Visigothic Spain', *La storiografia altomedievale: 10–16 aprile 1969*, ed. G. Vinay (Spoleto, 1970), pp. 261–311. The first extant catalogue does not mention Saracens, however.

[100] J. V. Tolan, *Saracens: Islam in the Medieval European Imagination* (New York, 2002), pp. 98–100.

[101] P. S. Marschner, 'The Depiction of the Saracen Foreign Rule in the Prophetic Chronicle through Biblical Knowledge', *Journal of Transcultural Medieval Studies* 5/2 (2018), 215–39 (pp. 225, 228); Wolf, *Conquerors and Chroniclers*, pp. 52–4. G. Barrett, 'Hispania at Home and Abroad', in *Beyond the Reconquista: New Directions in the History of Medieval Iberia (711–1085)*, ed. S. Barton and R. Portass (Leiden,

over Iberia, the *Prophetic Chronicle* in 883 inserts genealogies and lists of the reigns of the Saracen leaders, emphasizing their untrue lineage descending from Sarah instead of their real descent from Hagar. This leads to the convenient prophesy that they will be driven out in the following year, in 884.[102] Similar apocalyptic overtones, fashionable in Iberia, jump off the pages of the illustrated copies of the Asturian monk Beatus of Liébana's commentary on Revelation, produced in the last quarter of the eighth century at the time of the expected end of the Sixth Age of Man.[103] These texts argue that moral weakness within the Christian community invites catastrophe by means of war, famine or natural disaster, on this occasion brought about by religious others of an untrue bloodline. Notably, the *Prophetic Chronicle* also includes a life of Muhammad claiming that the Prophet initially was raised in Christian doctrine, before taking the errant and untrue path of Islam.

In the eleventh century, monks in other parts of Europe began to produce similar catalogues of ethnic virtues and vices, delineating the moral boundaries of the members of the *populus christianorum* and arranging their place in history and geography, encapsulated through their names, genealogies and traits. Anglo-Saxon monks, yet another of God's self-professed chosen peoples, apprehended the imminent end of time in the catalogue 'Victory of the Egyptians'. The list is inserted directly after the so-called Tribal Hidage in a manuscript now held at the British Library. At this time Wulfstan, bishop of

---

2020), pp. 52–119 (pp. 84–5). For other examples of the Saracens portrayed as Chaldeans, Tolan, *Saracens*, pp. 88, 94.

[102] Tolan, *Saracens*, pp. 98–9.

[103] Wolf, *Conquerors and Chroniclers*, p. 61. J. Williams (ed.), *The Illustrated Beatus: A Corpus of the Illustrations of the Commentary on the Apocalypse*, 5 vols. (London, 1994–2003); I. Baumgärtner, 'Die Welt im kartographischen Blick: Zur Veränderbarkeit mittelalterlicher Weltkarten am Beispiel der Beatustradition vom 10. bis 13. Jahrhundert', in *Der weite Blick des Historikers: Einsichten in Kultur-, Landes- und Stadtgeschichte. Peter Johanek zum 65. Geburtstag*, ed. W. Ehbrecht, A. Lampen, F.-J. Post and M. Siekmann (Cologne, 2002), pp. 527–49. K. B. Steinhauser, 'Narrative and Illumination in the Beatus Apocalypse', *The Catholic Historical Review* 81/2 (1995), 185–210; W. D. Wixom and M. Lawson, 'Picturing the Apocalypse: Illustrated Leaves from a Medieval Spanish Manuscript', *The Metropolitan Museum of Art Bulletin* 59/3 (2002), 1–56. It is unclear whether Beatus thought Christ's Second Coming to be imminent. K. R. Poole, 'Beatus of Liébana: Medieval Spain and the Othering of Islam', *End of Days: Essays on the Apocalypse from Antiquity to Modernity*, ed. K. Kinane and M. A. Ryan (Jefferson, 2009), pp. 47–66 (pp. 49–51) and, conversely, J. Williams, 'Purpose and Imagery in the Apocalypse Commentary of Beatus of Liébana', *The Apocalypse in the Middle Ages*, ed. R. K. Emmerson and B. McGinn (Ithaca, 1992), pp. 217–33. Also B. E. Whalen, *Dominion of God: Christendom and Apocalypse in the Middle Ages* (Cambridge MA, 2009).

London and of Worcester and archbishop of York (d. 1023), was issuing dark sermons about the shower of destruction that rained upon the Anglo-Saxon people in retribution for their sins. Scholars suggest that the Tribal Hidage, representing a division of thirty-four Anglo-Saxon kingdoms and groups in hides of land, reflected the division of the Promised Land in Joshua 15–22.[104] Also apocalyptic in tone are the lists of animal comparisons injected, among others, into the catalogue beginning with the 'Envy of the Jews', owned by the Benedictine monastery of Einsiedeln. In it the Saxons are allegorized as horses, the Britons as goats, the Picts as beasts of burden and the Scots/Irish as birds.[105] Eschatological animal imagery also features in city comparisons, or in the *On the Victory of God's Word*, where Rupert of Deutz (1075/80–c. 1129) ties the apocalyptic seven heads of the dragons to the kingdoms of Egypt, Israel, Babylon, the Persians and Medes, the Greeks, Romans and the Antichrist, the lioness symbolizing Babylon, the bear the Persians and Medes, the leopard the Greeks and the beast with the ten horns the Romans.[106] Eschatological animal allegories continue to crop up in later sources such as John of Fordun's *Scotichronicon*, which in the context of subjugation of the Welsh compares the English with crafty foxes, the French with lambs, the Normans with large

---

[104] Appendix, VI. D. Anlezark, 'Understanding Numbers in London, British Library, Harley 3271', *Anglo-Saxon England* 38 (2010), 137–55 (p. 154). Mary P. Richards, 'Wulfstan and the Millennium', *The Year 1000: Religious and Social Response to the Turning of the First Millennium*, ed. M. Frassetto (New York, 2002), pp. 41–8.

[105] Appendix, V.

[106] Rupert of Deutz, *Commentaria in apocalypsim*, PL 169, cols. 1066A–1069D; Whalen, *Dominion of God*, p. 80. See Revelation 6. 1–8. G. Cames, 'A propos de deux monstres dans l'*Hortus deliciarum*', *Cahiers de civilisation médiévale* 11 (1968), 587–603 (pp. 587–9) for animal imagery in the context of apocalyptic thought. Honorius of Autun's *Imago mundi* xxvi, ed. Flint, pp. 61–2 compares several cities with animals; Koht, H., 'The Dawn of Nationalism in Europe', *The American Historical Review* 52/2 (1946/47), 265–80 (p. 276). Other examples at: Stanzel, 'Zur literarischen Imagologie', p. 19; K. F. W. Wander, *Deutsches Sprichwörter-Lexicon: Ein Hausschatz für das Deutsche Volk*, 5 vols. (Leipzig, 1867–80), iv, 648; *The Book of the Mysteries of the Heavens and the Earth and Other Works of Bakhayla Mikâ'êl (Zôsimâs)*, ed. and trans. E. A. W. Budge (London, 1935), pp. v–xx. Much has been written about medieval bestiary literature in general; e.g. W. B. George, *The Naming of the Beasts: Natural History in the Medieval Bestiary* (London, 1991); D. Hassig, *The Mark of the Beast: The Medieval Bestiary in Art, Life, and Literature* (New York, 1999). More research needs to be done on imagery in twelfth- and thirteenth-century *distinctiones* and biblical glosses explaining animal allegory in relation to ethnicity, however. See also Friedman, *The Monstrous Races*, pp. 122–4.

bears, the Britons with boars and the Scots with lions.[107] Just as animals were allegorically compared with peoples, so they too could symbolize capital sins, a popular tradition in, for instance, fables and visual imagery.[108]

Lists representing the passage of time and space

The role of time in the alleged shaping of ethnic group dispositions is multi-layered in the catalogues tallying and comparing ethnic virtues and vices. The spatial-temporal framework not only engages with collective memories of past feats or disasters, or, for that matter, with the territorial or genealogical ties of group members' forebears. It also offers a structure for placing coeval peoples in different stages of progress led by 'advanced European peoples', which Dipesh Chakrabarty has called a stadial approach to history.[109] Thus, whereas the east and, for instance, Judaism are 'of the past' and the stage where future events are prophesized, Christianity is set in the present and future, as indeed is the younger, straying religion of Islam. At the same time, the form of the list – resembling numerical matter through its accumulative nature, similar to the tool of gematria in which words represent numbers and vice versa – represents the embodiment of the divine order. Daniel Anlezark has suggested that the catalogue 'Victory of the Egyptians' in the manuscript containing the Tribal Hidage shows an 'apocalyptic interest in numbers' as the historical ages of man proceed towards 'a new Christian order promised in the symbolic numbers of the Old Testament, and fulfilled in the New'.[110]

The relation to time is borne out by the fact that many of these earlier ethnic catalogues feature in composite manuscripts recording computus material, calculating the Easter calendar and measuring time.[111] In this manner, the lists of peoples, landmarks, words and churches served as tools to fathom the

---

[107] John of Fordun, *Scotichronicon cum supplementis et continuatione Walteri Boweri*, 2 vols. (Edinburgh, 1752), ii, 126; Walther, 'Scherz', no. 153a.

[108] M. W. Bloomfield, *The Seven Deadly Sins: An Introduction to the History of a Religious Concept, With Special Reference to Medieval English Literature* (Ann Arbor, 1967), p. 60.

[109] See Weeda, 'Meanwhile in Messianic Time' for discussions about the role of time and ethnic self-identification as well as references to relevant literature. Chakrabarty, *Provincializing*, pp. 4–10.

[110] Anlezark, 'Understanding Numbers', pp. 140, 155.

[111] For example, in the tenth-century manuscript Einsiedeln, Stiftsbibliothek MS 321 p. 136. E. Edson, 'The Medieval World View: Contemplating the Mappamundi', *History Compass* 8/6 (2010) 503–17 (p. 508); Edson, *Mapping Time and Space*, pp. 61, 73–4. Especially, 'centrifugal computus manuscripts' contain a miscellany of subjects related to time, geography, genealogy, prognostication and medical texts

relationship between the cosmos and humanity in time and space, for numbers were seen to reflect the harmony of the cosmos and the perfection of the creation. Perusing them meant enveloping the passage of time, measured in annals, genealogies, lists of bishops and rulers. Accordingly, as Evelyn Edson argued, *mappae mundi*, more than a realistic representation of geographical fact, reflected the prophesized history of the world from its creation to the day of reckoning, depicting time in relation to space, from the genesis in the east, in slow progression to the west. The Book of the Apocalypse was the cornerstone to this concept of creation, foretelling the end of the world and of time.[112] Studying these images and lists, using them as mnemonic tools, allowed monks to ponder the creation and salvation history.

As a representation of time and space, the ethnic catalogue follows the principle of the *translatio* from east to west, classifying the former as a place of bygone religion and power, foretelling future history, and the latter as the site on which God's eyes are fixed, the stage of the events leading up to the final apocalyptic showdown. Most of the earlier ethnic catalogues indeed commence with the ancient peoples of the east: the Greeks, Jews, Persians, Chaldeans and Egyptians, and then travel towards Rome and finally westwards to the Franks, the Britons, the Saxons and the Picts.[113] Both in space (from east to west) and in time (from past to present and future) the lists reflect and are arranged from the viewpoint of eschatological progress – later transformed into cultural and civilizational progress, that fetish of modernity – concluding with the ethnic groups to whom the scribes belonged, as history came home, so to speak. Here are two such lists side by side:

The wisdom of the Greeks	The victory of the Egyptians
The envy of the Jews	The envy of the Jews
The arrogance of the Romans	The wisdom of the Greeks
The generosity of the Longobards	The cruelty of the Picts
The sobriety of the Goths	The strength of the Romans
The enthronement of the Franks	The generosity of the Longobards

---

and recipes; F. E. Wallis, 'MS Oxford, St John's 17: A Medieval Manuscript in its Context' (unpublished dissertation, University of Toronto, 1985), pp. 610–39.

[112] Edson, *Mapping Time and Space*, pp. 75, 80; Woodward, 'Reality, Symbolism, Time', p. 514; Baumgärtner, 'Die Welt', p. 537. In some cases, geographical information is listed on the maps. Cf. Edson, 'World Maps and Easter Tables', figure 4 on p. 31, for a 'list map' in London, British Library, Cotton MS Vitellius A XII fol. 64r. from the tenth century.

[113] Howe, *Old English Catalogue Poems*, pp. 24–5.

The gluttony of the Gauls
The wrath of the Britons
The stupidity of the Saxons
The lust of the Scots
The cruelty of the Picts

The gluttony of the Gauls
The arrogance or ferocity of the Franks
The wrath of the Britons
The stupidity of the Saxons or Angles
The lust of the Scots[114]

Biblical exegesis and ethnic dispositions

In their entirety, the catalogues of ethnic virtues and vices represented all of mankind, its virtues and fallacies, from the creation to the end days. In this context, the strategic positioning of Jews at or near of the top of most lists serves as the reference point for monks to measure and compare other groups with, in the process of evangelization. The evangelical viewpoint is distinctly present in at least two manuscripts where peoples' vices (*De vitiis gentium*) are contrasted with their virtues (*De virtutibus gentium*).[115]

---

[114] See Appendix, I and IV for the Latin texts and manuscripts. The manuscript containing the first list further has entries on medicine, the moon, stars and winds. The second list is attached to the Tribal Hidage and is dated to circa 1032; Anlezark, 'Understanding Numbers', pp. 154–5. Pierre Hamon, who in the sixteenth century compiled the first 'palaeographic tract', inserted the same list in his manuscript (now Paris, Bibliothèque nationale de France, MS Latin 19116 fol. 40v.) as an example of Saxon writing. H. Omont, 'Le recueil d'anciennes écritures de Pierre Hamon', *Bibliothèque de l'École des Chartes* 62 (1901), 57–73 (p. 70). J. Flach, *Les origines de l'ancienne France: Xe et Xie siècles*, 4 vols. (Paris, 1886–1917), iii, 128, dates the manuscript to 1064, although it is unclear on what grounds (the entry before the list mentions the date 969 in a charter).

[115] Printed in J. M. Burnam, 'Miscellanea Hispanica', *Modern Philology* 12/3 (1914), 165–70 (p. 169) (from Madrid, Codex Matritensis, Biblioteca Nacional MS 7814 fol. 114v. (formerly V 191; catalogued as the Glossary of Isidore) and Namur, Fonds de la Ville, MS 118 fols. 6v–7r.). A thirteenth-century hand has inserted the list at the end of the Codex Matritensis. However, the earliest known manuscript containing a similar contrastive list (Bern, Burgerbibliothek, MS 48 fol. 1r.) dates to the tenth century. The Namur manuscript, containing the letter collection, dates to the twelfth century; P. Faider, *Catalogue des manuscrits conservés à Namur (Musée archéologique, Evêché, Grand séminaire, Museum Artium S.J., etc.)* (Gembloux, 1934), p. 200. See also *Chronica minora saec. iv. v. vi. vii*, ed. T. Mommsen, MGH Auctores Antiquissimi 11 (Berlin, 1894), pp. 389–90. Cf. Kot, 'Old International Insults', p. 186; Meyvaert, 'Voicing National Antipathy', p. 747.

The envy of the Jews
The perfidy of the Persians
The stupidity of the Egyptians
The deceit of the Greeks
The fickleness of the Chaldeans
The inconstancy of the Africans
The gluttony of the Gauls
The vainglory of the Longobards
The cruelty of Huns
The uncleanness of the Suevi
The ferocity of the Franks
The stupidity of the Saxons
The wantonness of the Normans
The lust of the Scots
The wine drinking of the Spaniards

The hardness of the Picts
The lust of the Suevi
The wrath of the Britons
The filth of the Slavs

The prudence of the Hebrews
The steadfastness of the Persians
The ingenuity of the Egyptians
The wisdom of the Greeks
The gravity of the Romans
The sagacity of the Chaldeans
The intelligence of the Africans
The durability of the Gauls
The strength of the Franks
The perseverance of the Saxons
The agility of the Gascons
The faithfulness of the Scots
The wit of the Spanish
The hospitality of the Britons
The Greek is enraged beforehand, the Frank during, the Roman afterwards. The grave Frank, the fickle Roman, the crafty African, Tullius Marcus said.[116]

Here, the catalogue is succeeded by the Byzantine apocryphal list of Christ's disciples, the preachers of the faith and teachers of peoples, who went out to spread the word, each tackling his own region: 'Peter Rome; Andrew Albania; Jacob Spain; John Asia' and so forth – a list which, according to some scholars, was in fact designed to accompany the map in Beatus of Liébana's commentary on John's Apocalypse.[117] The evangelical work of the apostles is

---

[116] See Appendix, II for the Latin text and manuscripts.
[117] Different versions of the list are also quoted by Beatus of Liébana, *Beati in Apocalypsin Libri Duodecim*, ed. H. A. Sanders (Rome, 1930), pp. 116–17, based on Isidore, *Etymologies, Livre VII: Dieu, les anges, les saints* ix, ed. J-Y. Guillaumin (Paris, 2012), pp. 118–29 and *De Ortu et Obitu Patrum*, PL 83, col. 154, which is sometimes attributed to Isidore but also includes Thaddeus and Matthias. Williams, 'Isidore, Orosius and the Beatus Map', pp. 7–8; T. D. Kendrick, *St James in Spain*

Figure 2. Beatus map, Burgo de Osma, Archivo de la Catedral Codex 1, fols. 34v.–35r., dating to 1086. On the right it depicts a Sciapode, one of the Plinian races, dwelling in the Antipodes.

conceptually depicted on three of the fifteen versions of the map belonging to the Spanish Benedictine monk's text, written between 776 and 786. The apostolic mission is visualized by placing portrait heads of the apostles in their missionary fields, in addition to other symbols of cities (fig. 2).[118]

(London, 1960), pp. 188–9; Baumgärtner, 'Die Welt', pp. 530, 542; Englisch, *Ordo Orbis Terrae*, pp. 336–64.

[118] Edson, *Mapping Time and Space*, pp. 149–59 (p. 153). This map is possibly connected to the reconquest of Toledo in 1085 and its claims to bishopric primacy. B. Englisch, *Ordo Orbis Terrae: Die Weltsicht in den 'Mappae mundi' des frühen und hohen Mittelalters* (Berlin, 2002), pp. 347–62. There are four surviving manuscripts with apostle's heads; Baumgärtner, 'Die Welt', p. 542. The apostolic destinations are mentioned on almost all of the fifteen surviving Beatus maps (without actually depicting the heads). A Beatus map can also be found on the chapel wall of the San Pedro de Rocas in southern Galicia, including the heads of the apostles. S. Moralejo Álvarez, 'El mapa de la diáspora apostólica en San Pedro de Rocas:

The affects attached to peoples in these lists further expose the biblical reference framework. Most of the ethnic character traits listed stem from exegetical commentaries on the Pauline letters in the New Testament – evangelical letters heralding the arrival of the heavenly kingdom and emphasizing peoples' willingness or lack thereof to accept the Christian message.[119] The virtues and vices attributed to the various peoples are soaked in classical environmental theory – the Franks' ferocity, the wrath of the Britons and the stupidity of the Saxons are commonplaces drawn from Hippocratic scientific discussions claiming that the cold north produced headstrong, unintelligent and rather fierce peoples, as discussed in chapter 2.[120] However, rather than inspired directly by scientific works on theory, the Benedictine monks drafting these lists drew the essentialized stereotypes mostly from earlier patristic literature preserving and copying the images into exegetical commentaries, in religious traditions concerned with thinking about the nature of humanity.

Various stereotypes in the catalogues are taken from Jerome's exegetical commentary on the foolish character of the Galatians for choosing the Mosaic Law over the Christian *logos*.[121] Another biblical commonplace featuring in the lists is the envy of the Jews as well as their 'stubbornness' for rejecting

---

notas para su interpretación y filiación en la tradición cartográfica de los "Beatos"', *Compostellanum* 31 (1986), 315–40.

[119] The influence of biblical and theological commonplaces has been overlooked. Stanzel, 'Der Nationalitätenschema', p. 85 noted that most stereotypes in early modernity were drawn from an ethnographic-literary treasure store.

[120] D. Fraesdorff, *Der barbarische Norden: Vorstellungen und Fremdheitskategorien bei Rimbert, Thietmar von Merseburg, Adam von Bremen und Helmold von Bosau* (Berlin, 2005), pp. 187–94.

[121] Weeda, 'Characteristics of Bodies and Ethnicity', pp. 100–1. A range of stereotypes in Jerome, *Commentariorum in epistolam ad Titum liber unus*, PL 26, col. 0574C has for instance been copied in Einsiedeln, Stiftsbibliothek MS 321 p. 136: 'Judei duri cervice et gravi corde Greci leves Cretenses mendaces Dalmate feroces Mauri vani Franci tumidi Athenienses ingeniosi Galate indociles, vecordes, tardiores ad sapientiam', and in 1230 was repeated almost verbatim in Robert Grosseteste, *Opera Roberti Grosseteste Lincolniensis: Vol. 1: Expositio in epistolam sancti Pauli ad Galatas* iii.1, ed. J. MacEvoy (Turnhout, 1995): 'ut Cretenses mendaces, malae bestiae, uentres pigri; Mauri uani; Dalmatae feroces; Phrygae timidi; Athenienses ingeniosi; Graeci leues; Iudaei graues corde et dura ceruice'. P. G. Meier, *Catalogus codicum manu scriptorum qui in Bibliotheca Monasterii Einsidlensis O.S.B. servantur*, 3 vols. (Einsiedeln, 1899), i, 292–4. The Einsiedeln catalogue does not include the fearful Phrygians mentioned by Grosseteste. Cf. also Hrabanus Maurus, *Enarrationes in epistolas Beati Pauli*, PL 111, col. 0672A.

Jesus as the Messiah, which heads several of these lists.[122] Jewish stubbornness was a rhetorical explanation for the suggestion that the older religion of Judaism trailed behind in progressive salvation history. It was fraught with significance, for the Epistle to the Romans taught that the Jews' repentance and conversion to Christianity were providentially necessary preambles to Christ's Second Coming, the *Parousia*, whereby the older served the younger.[123] It encapsulates the ambivalent attitude towards Jews, who Augustine argued should be protected from a metaphorical or physical death so that they could act as witnesses to the truth of the Christian faith, yet whose rejection of Christianity was conceived as inimical. This conflicted view of Jews also features in the rhetoric of *adversus Judaeos* sermons and treatises written for a Christian audience. Although this rhetoric, as scholars such as Jeremy Cohen and Paula Fredriksen have underlined, thus serviced theological debates rather than reflecting actual social relations or legislation, it could serve strategically within hierarchical relations of power or to fuel animosity when employed by authoritative voices.[124] For instance, Jews living on the road between Albelda and Viguera, near to where the monks drew up one of the early lists, were attacked by the local population in the eleventh century.[125]

However, the worst sin of all listed in the catalogues, arrogance or pride (*superbia*), rebellion against God and the root of all evil, was attributed to a

---

[122] Appendix, VI. Acts 13. 45 for the envy of the Jews. Exodus 32. 9 and Deuteronomy 9. 13 for Jewish stubbornness. *The Jews in the Legal Sources of the Early Middle Ages*, ed. A. Lindner (Detroit, 1997), pp. 553–55, no. 874, for the envy of the Jews in documents from the Council of Erfurt in 932. S. Lewis, 'Tractatus adversus Judaeos in the Gulbenkian Apocalypse', *The Art Bulletin* 68/4 (1986), 543–66 (p. 552) for apocalyptical images of Jewish obstinacy or 'stiff-necked' Jews, a reference to the Israelites breaking the covenant by constructing a golden calf in the absence of Moses while he received the Ten Commandments on Mount Horeb. See also chapter 5 p. 200n.49 for stiff-necked Germans.

[123] Romans 11. 25–27. For instance, Augustine, *De civitate Dei* xvi.35, trans. E. M. Sanford and W. M. Green, Loeb Classical Library 411–17, 7 vols. (Cambridge, 2015), v, 165; Lewis, 'Tractatus adversus Judaeos', p. 544, note 4 for further references. J. Richards, *Sex, Dissidence and Damnation: Minority Groups in the Middle Ages* (London, 1990), p. 93; B. Blumenkranz, 'Augustin et les juifs; Augustin et le judaïsme', *Recherches augustiniennes* 1 (1958), 225–41; R. Chazan, *Medieval Stereotypes and Modern Antisemitism* (Berkeley, 1997), p. 11. P. Fredriksen, 'Tyconius and Augustine on the Apocalypse', in *The Apocalypse in the Middle Ages*, ed. R. K. Emmerson and B. McGinn (Ithaca, 1992), pp. 20–37.

[124] P. Fredriksen, *Augustine and the Jews: A Christian Defense of Jews and Judaism* (New York, 2008); cf. J. Cohen, 'Revisiting Augustine's Doctrine of Jewish Witness', *The Journal of Religion* 89/4 (2009), pp. 564–78.

[125] Toch, *The Economic History of European Jews*, pp. 116–17.

community within Christendom: the Romans. This trait reflected Rome's early persecution of Christians and the shift in its reputation from being the centre of civilization and *virtus* in antiquity, to a locus of impiety, avarice, malice and other evils, as expounded in Paul's Epistle to the Romans. This ambivalence continued in the centuries after the Roman empire adopted Christianity, when Rome claimed for itself the most important seat in the western Church. Rome's reputation was, accordingly, frequently satirized in eleventh- and twelfth-century Latin poetry produced further to the north-west by French, English and German clerics, as discussed further in chapter 4.[126]

Conclusion

Within the overarching reference framework of Christendom, the Benedictine monks compiling the lists did so probably with a particular view to introspectively meditate on the Last Things.[127] While classifying the other in relation to humanity, the monks pondered about the self; the lists served as an ethical-mnemonic instrument to ruminate on the virtues and vices of human diversity in the light of the world's transitory nature. In this manner, they helped to recall a thing's essence by chewing on it or ruminating, to cite Mary Carruthers's description of the monastic exercise of meditation. Searching through the 'pockets of memory' in their minds, the men in the cloisters hoped to recognize sin by picturing the images of sinful ethnic–religious peoples, for imagination and memory both use *phantasmata*, mental images, so the rules of rhetoric taught.[128] Comparison with others was in that regard a helpful tool, as Salvian of Marseilles held in *On the Governance of God*, which he wrote in about 440. In it, he condemned the environmentally determined vices of the Christians in the late-antique world through comparison with heathen peoples, rhetorically deemed to be more virtuous as the latter had not received the Christian message:

---

[126] Romans 1. 18–32. I. Weiler, 'Ethnographische Typisierungen im antiken und mittelalterlichen Vorfeld der "Völkertafel"', in *Europäischer Völkerspiegel: Imagologisch-ethnographische Studien zu den Völkertaflen des frühen 18. Jahrhunderts*, ed. F. K. Stanzel, I. Weiler and W. Zacharasiewicz (Heidelberg, 1999), pp. 97–118 (p. 107).

[127] M. Carruthers, *The Craft of Thought: Meditation, Rhetoric, and the Making of Images, 400–1200* (Cambridge, 1998), pp. 152–5.

[128] Ibid., pp. 30–1, 146. Stanzel, 'Zur literarischen Imagologie', pp. 35–6 discusses Jack Goody's hypothesis (in *Domestification of the Savage Mind*) that schematization arose from the transition from an oral to a written culture, in which memory and orality remain dominant. As Mary Carruthers argues throughout *The Craft of Thought*, however, it is especially within an oral culture that such schemas were necessary to memorize.

The Saxons are savage; the Franks are treacherous; the Gepidae are ruthless; the Huns are lewd. In short, the life of all barbarian peoples is corruption itself. Do you think their vices have the same guilt as ours? Is the lewdness of the Huns as blameworthy as ours? Is the perfidy of the Franks as reprehensible as ours? Is the drunkenness of the Alemanni as blameworthy as the drunkenness of Christians?[129]

Such rhetoric could be transformed into a meditative tool, a mirror for reflection. In a Carolingian manuscript from *c.* 800, possibly compiled at the monastery of St Gall, these two passages have been explicitly excerpted together as an independent list or *centos* for Christians to ponder.[130]

Nevertheless, interpretation by means of contrast – *in bono* and *in malo* – had an admonitory purpose as well, as it did in the Evagrian or Gregorian ethical system.[131] Listing the ethnic virtues and vices, even if serving to acknowledge the sinful self, remained an exercise in the othering of non-Christian religious

---

[129] Salvian of Marseille, *De gubernatione Dei* iv.14, *PL* 53, cols. 0086C–0087A: 'Gens Saxonum fera est, Francorum infidelis, Gepidarum inhumana, Chunorum impudica; omnium denique gentium barbarorum vita, vitiositas. Sed numquid eumdem reatum habent illorum vitia quem nostra, numquid tam criminosa est Chunorum impudicitia quam nostra, numquid tam accusabilis Francorum perfidia quam nostra, aut tam reprehensibilis ebrietas Alani quam ebrietas Christiani …'. Salvian's condescending excuses for the sins of the pagans are further contrasted with their virtues at *De gubernatione Dei* vii.15, *PL* 53, cols. 0142C–0142D. The only exception concerned the Africans, who in Salvian's opinion were steeped in the stereotypical evils of the southerner, such as inhumanity, deception, artifice, lustfulness and perfidy.

[130] Leiden, Universiteitsbibliotheek MS Vossius Latin Q 69 fols. 37r–38v. R. H. Bremmer Jr., 'Leiden, Vossianus Lat. Q. 69 (Part 2): Schoolbook or Proto-Encyclopaedic Miscellany?', in *Practice in Learning: The Transfer of Encyclopaedic Knowledge in the Early Middle Ages*, ed. R. H. Bremmer Jr. and K. Dekker (Paris, 2010), pp. 19–54; R. McKitterick, 'Le pouvoir des mots: Les glossaires, la mémoire culturelle et la transmission du savoir au Haut Moyen Âge', in *Les Cahiers colombaniens, 2013: Les écoles monastiques au haut Moyen Âge*, ed. P. Riché (Luxeuil-les-Bains, 2013), pp. 16–58. The manuscript contains miscellaneous Sibylline prophecies, epigrams and inscriptions, Roman monuments, Anglo-Saxon glosses, excerpts from Pliny the Elder's *Natural History* and from Vegetius's *De re militari*. Like the Codex Aemilianensis, the catalogue of peoples is preceded by (a more detailed version of) the Wonders of the World.

[131] Bloomfield, *The Seven Deadly Sins*, p. 66; R. Newhauser, *The Treatise on Vices and Virtues in Latin and the Vernacular* (Turnhout, 1993), pp. 114–20. In the sixth century, Gregory the Great listed seven principal sins: vainglory, envy, wrath, sadness, avarice, gluttony and lust – all stemming from the sin of pride. Earlier, in fourth-century Egypt, the ascetic monk Evagrius had drawn up an eight-fold system. In 'Nationalitätenschema', p. 87 Stanzel relates the early catalogues to the seven deadly sins.

groups as well, and featured as a counterpoint, as an exemplum of a group failing to successfully convert in the pitched battle between good and evil. The monks emphasize the traits of alleged stubbornness and envy in the case of the Jews left behind, essentializing their incapacity to embrace truth.

Monks and clerics subsequently jotted down such lists of ethnic vices in the margins or on the front or back covers of manuscripts, integrating contemporary observations. Additions to the catalogue 'Envy of the Jews, Perfidy of the Persians' and 'Envy of the Jews, Wrath of the Britons' in thirteenth-century English manuscripts, for instance, mention the rapacity of the Normans. A version of the 'Wisdom of the Greeks' catalogue in a fourteenth-century Karlsruhe manuscript lists the essentialized traits of Saracen wantonness (*luxuria*), the parsimony of the Tuscans, French courtliness and the incomparable generosity of the English – popular reputations at that time in Latin poetry and vernacular court literature.[132] Ethnocentric sentiments surface, for example in a Bohemian catalogue, where the scribe is at odds about what to do about the vices of the Bohemians – and decides to leave the space blank, perhaps in protest.[133] The location of the production of the catalogues also migrates from the south to the north, and from western to eastern Europe, first to German settlers in the east, and later, in the seventeenth century, followed by Polish writers.[134] And where the ethnic catalogue before 1100 is a mnemonic tool, from the twelfth century onwards it enters the literary domain, encouraged by the early handbooks of rhetoric and poetry at the urban schools, and drawing from popular proverbs as well.

Significantly, from the twelfth century, the cultural transfer at the schools of Greek–Arabic environmental and medical theories about the impact of climate and situation on the body led to more elaborate and active discussions about how organic processes interfered with the dispositions of peoples. New translations appear of Hippocrates' *Airs, Waters, Places*. Environmental theory features in the *Pantegni* of Constantine the African (*c.* 1020–87), in travel manuals and in the dozens of copies of Vegetius's *De re militari*. These texts, read by monks, schoolmen and courtiers, gave scientific authority to the categorizations of ethnic character in the histories and poetry produced at the schools and courts classifying peoples' military qualities and serving as a rhetorical argument in power hierarchies. How environmental theory helped to construct ethnic character based upon *place* as well as morality is discussed further in chapter 2.

---

[132] Appendices III, V, VI, VIII. See further especially chapter 5 for images of French courtliness and English generosity. For Saracen lust or wantonness: Tolan, *Saracens*, p. 152; Cohen, 'On Saracen Enjoyment', p. 125–6.

[133] Appendix, VI.

[134] Kot, 'Old International Insults', pp. 182, 185.

2

The Naturalization of Ethnicity and Environmental Thought

Shortly after the First Crusade to Palestine, Benedictine monks in different monastic houses in England and northern France turned towards physiology to contrast their foes with their own armies. They speak of courageous French fighters and weak-blooded, cowardly, cunning Saracens, both of whom are shaped by their regional environment and climate. Guibert of Nogent (*c.* 1060–*c.* 1125) and William of Malmesbury each directly engaged ancient Hippocratic environmental theory that took a geographic deterministic view of peoples' physical and mental character, strength, intelligence and industry.[1] Echoing these ideas, Orderic Vitalis (1075–*c.* 1142) and Baldric of Bourgueil (*c.* 1050–1130) commented on Turkish military cunning, a trait that environmental theory accounted for on the basis of a lack of blood. Environmental (or climate) theory presented an explanatory structure for the classification of essentialized mental and physical qualities based upon topography, which Aristotle had expanded in his *Politics* to clarify groups' status in a hierarchy of power. Aristotle's work, which was unknown in Arabic and was translated into Latin by William of Moerbeke in *c.* 1260, introduced the concept of natural slavery, building upon environmental theory, arguing that the physiognomy and mental traits of large-bodied workers lacking rational qualities rendered them natural slaves. Various climates favoured different political systems, the weaker southerners and irrational northerners being less well equipped for self-rule because they lacked a sufficient capacity for reason. In line with ancient Greek stoicism, environmental theory accordingly held that only the most temperate

---

[1] Guibert of Nogent, *Dei gesta per Francos et cinq autres textes*, i.2, ed. R. B. C. Huygens (Turnhout, 1996), pp. 89–90; William of Malmesbury, *Gesta regum Anglorum* iv.347, ed. and trans. Mynors, Thomson and Winterbottom, i, 600–3; Orderic Vitalis, *Historia ecclesiastica: The Ecclesiastical History of Orderic Vitalis* ix.12, ed. and trans. M. M. Chibnall, 6 vols. (Oxford, 1969–80), v, 132–3 and Baldric of Bourgueil, *Historia Ierosolimitana* ii, ed. S. J. Biddlecombe (Woodbridge, 2014), p. 33, also speak of Turkish military cunning, a trait that often explained in the context of environmental theory. Also I. Wolsing, 'Horsemen of the Apocalypse? Turkish Alterity in Chronicles from the Latin East, 1098–1187', *Viator* (2021), forthcoming.

region, where heat and coldness, moisture and dryness balanced out, nurtured the ideal, rational and brave man, able to defend his territory.² Even before Aristotle's *Politics* was translated, however, climate theory was known through texts produced in the military and monastic spheres.

This chapter is about how the adoption and adaptation of environmental theory fostered a biological mode of thinking about ethnicity, whereby the significance of the salubriousness and sacredness of domesticated spaces on occasion was identified with the translation of power, learning and military qualities. Following a short explanation of what environmental theory and its sibling humoral theory entail, and their dissemination, this chapter will explore how monks and schoolmen copied, adapted and applied these ideas between 1100 and 1250. Environmental and Galenic theory's effectiveness accelerated in two contexts. Firstly, monks and courtiers consulted Vegetius's army manual *De re militari* in the crusader wars in the Mediterranean region to describe Muslim and Christian soldiers. Environmental theory also was the bedrock for military and travel manuals.³ Secondly, the establishment of urban centres of knowledge encouraged the study of scientific treatises on medicine and the natural sciences using translations from Arabic and Greek into Latin. The heightened focus on these theories gave authority to arguments about the differences between Christian Europeans and others in a military context of colonization, tying physiology to environment and landscape, alongside cultural, social and linguistic factors.⁴ This view was part of a broader development wherein natural philosophy and medicine seeped into all kinds of discussions about the materiality of the body, original sin, the soul and life after death.⁵

---

2   Eliav-Feldon, Isaac and Ziegler (ed.), *Origins of Racism*; Isaac, *The Invention of Racism*; I. Metzler, 'Perceptions of Hot Climate in Medieval Cosmography and Travel Literature', *Reading Medieval Studies* 23 (1997), 69–105.

3   G. Geltner, 'In the Camp and on the March: Military Manuals as Sources for Studying Premodern Public Health', *Medical History* 63/1 (2019), 44–60; P. Horden, 'Regimen and Travel in the Mediterranean', in *Mobility and Travel in the Mediterranean from Antiquity to the Middle Ages*, ed. R. Schlesier and U. Zellmann (Münster, 2004), pp. 117–32.

4   Ziegler, 'Physiognomy, Science, and Proto-racism 1200–1500', p. 199; Epstein, *Purity Lost*, pp. 9–51.

5   Minnis, *From Eden to Eternity*; A. Boureau, 'Hérédité, erreurs et vérité de la nature humaine (XIIe–XIIIe siècles)', *L'hérédité entre Moyen Âge et Époque moderne: Perspectives historiques*, ed. M. van der Lugt and C. de Miramon (Florence, 2008), pp. 67–82; C. W. Bynum, 'Material Continuity, Personal Survival, and the Resurrection of the Body: A Scholastic Discussion in Its Medieval and Modern Contexts', *History of Religions* 30/1 (1990), 51–85. For Adam's complexion in Paradise, J. Ziegler, 'Medicine and Immortality in Terrestrial Paradise', *Religion and Medicine*

The translation of Aristotle's *Politics* thereby eventually impacted on political thought and contributed to the environmental determinism underlying the organization of labour and property rights, leading Thomas Aquinas to argue for the natural inferiority of the enslaved, although they fell under *ius gentium* in Roman canon law, not natural law (applied to animals). Economic, civil or legal subjection, arising after the original sin, consequently meant that the ruler managed 'his subjects for their advantage and benefit'.[6] According to the Dominican scholar Albertus Magnus (*c.* 1200–80), who taught at the *studium generale* in Cologne and in Paris, knowledge of climatic and humoral theory spread rapidly and was discussed *vulgariter*, in the vernacular tongue as well. He makes this comment in a text produced in *c.* 1258.[7]

Racism and environmental theory

The impress of the biological discourse has sparked discussions about the early origins of racism, vigorously unpacked in Geraldine Heng's *The Invention of Race in the European Middle Ages*, focusing on the racialization of Jews, Saracens, Mongols, Romani and Native Americans in the North Atlantic until the sixteenth century.[8] As discussed in the Introduction, the racialized language created and sustained hierarchies by assigning traits to specific collectivities in hierarchical power relations through the practical application of social knowledge – which for most people is far more significant than any theoretical, academic construction of race.[9] Less explored, however, are the scientific texts that fed into these representations of ethnic categories, articulated, copied, commented upon and adapted by the authoritative voices of schoolmen and reworked by court poets, historians and advisors. As far as the scientific discourses are concerned, a central discussion point revolves around

---

in the Middle Ages, ed. P. Biller and J. Ziegler (York, 2001), pp. 201–42. An older discussion in R. Klibansky, E. Panofsky and F. Saxl, *Saturn and Melancholy: Studies in the History of Natural Philosophy, Religion, and Art* (rev. edn, London, 1964), pp. 78–80.

[6] Thomas Aquinas, *Summa theologiae*, 1a.92.1 and 2, ed. Gilby, xiii, 36–9. A. Minnis, *From Eden to Eternity: Creations of Paradise in the Later Middle Ages* (Philadelphia, 2015), p. 98. Barker, *That Most Precious Merchandise*, pp. 15–19. G. Fioravanti, 'Servi, rustici, barbari: Interpretazioni medievali della Politica aristotelica', *Annali della scuola normale superiore di Pisa: Classe di lettere e filosofa* 11 (1981), 399–429.

[7] Biller, 'Proto-Racial Thought', p. 179.

[8] Heng, *The Invention of Race*. See the Introduction, pp. 18–22, for discussion and references.

[9] Hage, *White Nation*, pp. 29–31; M. Barker, *The New Racism: Conservatives and the Ideology of the Tribe* (London, 1981).

whether Hippocratic and Galenic environmental and medical ideas claimed that ethnic character was fixed or fluid. This chapter argues that environmental theory, combined with religious constructs of group traits, allowed schoolmen to strategically claim that some group's traits – notably those of Jews – were more fixed, more essential, than others. Racialization was prevalent when the attribution of such traits served rhetorically to position various groups within a hierarchy of power, placing the virtuous and rational above the allegedly weak, irrational, more beastlike. In addition, comments about the unnaturalness of ethnogenesis, for instance to be found in the twelfth-century pilgrim's guide to Santiago di Compostela, touched on biopolitical issues of reproduction. In the pilgrim guide's opinion, the migration to the region of Navarra of the Scots (or Irish), who violently raped its indigenous female population, had produced a degenerate people.[10]

An exploration of environmental discourse and its application in twelfth- and early thirteenth-century learned texts reveals that although science and culture held miscegenation as unnatural, still its benefits were recognized if and when acculturation led to the appropriation of urbane cultural practices. The acknowledgement of groups' capacity for acculturation probably depended on the degree to which writers self-identified with these groups, as well as their allotted position in the hierarchy of power. Significantly, the religious concept of free will meant that, at least theoretically, change was potential and possible, trumping biological or culturally acquired differences.[11] Hence, adaptations of Galenism and Hippocratic thought clearly did not assume that there were 'permanent and unbridgeable' differences, nor did they suggest that anything goes.[12] Scholars theorized that a person's psychosomatic make-up evolved into transferable traits if the parents of a new-born, endowed with an identical complexion, came from the same region. However, a mortal being's complexional balance remained fluid and susceptible to natural and non-natural particulars such as the climate, air, season, exercise, the planets, food and drink, whose impress oscillated depending on time and place.[13] The body, indeed, was porous. Through social practices set out in the pedagogical books of conduct

---

[10] *The Pilgrim's Guide to Santiago de Compostela: A Critical Edition* vii, ed. and trans. P. Gerson, A. Shaver-Crandell and A. Stones, 2 vols. (London, 1998), ii, 28–31.
[11] Weeda, 'The Fixed and the Fluent', pp. 93–113.
[12] Ziegler, 'Physiognomy, Science', p. 188; Goldenberg, 'Racism, Color Symbolism', p. 92.
[13] Ziegler, 'Physiognomy, Science', p. 193; V. Groebner, '*Complexio*/Complexion: Categorizing Individual Natures, 1250–1600', in *The Moral Authority of Nature*, ed. L. Daston and F. Vidal (Chicago, 2004), pp. 361–83 (pp. 368–9); Van der Lugt, 'La peau noire', p. 459.

as part of the pre-university school curriculum, mortal beings could, moreover, train their *habitus*, their behavioural and character traits, negotiating their humoral condition in order to be good citizens.[14] There is a significant caveat in the case of Jews, however, who sometimes were assigned an essentialized, fixed 'biological make-up', in particular when they converted to Christianity, an act that was often met with distrust.[15]

The active exploration of theories of environment gave arguments weight that were put forward in the context of military strength, colonization and the subjugation of workforces. Moreover, the idea that the environment produced essentialized 'character traits' meant that the domesticated territorial space where peoples dwelled was considered to shape culture. Although peoples' natural traits were not considered to be immutable if humans migrated, the process of change was cumbersome. Thus, administering climate theory allowed monks, schoolmen and courtiers to not only describe Jewish or Muslim traits stereotypically. They likewise applied climate theory to construct stereotypical images of European Christian peoples as well, in a hierarchy that placed the aristocracy above labourer and peasant, knight above infantry, man over woman, catholic over heretic and western Europe over the east and north. Presenting north-western Europe as a temperate region, they reconfigured the French and English character traits, transforming them from the uncultured into tokens of urbanity and rationality – typologies of 'national character' that are just as much essentialized constructions as are antisemitic tropes, rather then the outcome of actual religious, cultural, social, political and economic processes. In this sense, the angry German, intelligent Englishman or civilized Frenchman are stereotypical representations strategically produced within the same framework as the envious Jew or cunning Muslim as a means of sorting positions within a hierarchy of power.

These ethnotypes, which environmental theory helped to create, could function in later political arguments as a synecdoche for the entire community of the body politic in discussions of sovereignty.[16] Responding to the social

---

[14] Nederman, 'Nature, Ethics, and the Doctrine of "Habitus"'; C. Weeda, 'Reviewing Conduct Books: Galenic Medicine and the "Civilizing Process" in Western European Households c. 1100–1300', in *Elite Households in England, 1100–1550: Proceedings of the 2016 Harlaxton Symposium*, ed. C. M. Woolgar (Donington, 2018), pp. 167–84.

[15] See Introduction, pp. 36–8; R. Chazan, *Medieval Stereotypes and Modern Antisemitism* (Berkeley, 1997), pp. ix–xiii.

[16] For instance in Jean Bodin, *Les six livres de la république*, ed. G. Mairet (1993), available at http://classiques.uqac.ca/classiques/bodin_jean/six_livres_republique/bodin_six_livres_republique.pdf (accessed 31 August 2020).

hierarchy stratifying the aristocracy, peasantry, artisans, labourers, men and women, young and old, lay and religious, Graeco-Arabic environmental theory was thus adapted from a relativist concept that each individual had his own unique, mutating complexion, to a more essentializing categorization laying emphasis on the dominant complexion in individuals and groups.[17]

Environmental and humoral theory

How is environmental theory relevant to ethnography? The oldest surviving text working with the theory, *Airs, Waters, Places*, dates to the late fifth century BC. Attributed to Hippocrates (*c.* 460–*c.* 370 BC), this treatise argued that the environment – climate, winds, precipitation and terrain – affected the physiology of mortal beings, producing diverse peoples with different physical and mental qualities. The text compares the cold north, populated by fierce Scythians, to the south, Egypt and Libya, the habitat of weaker peoples. Hippocrates' text is also the first known treatise to contrast east and west, taking into account environment and topography, linking mountainous, rough, well-watered regions to endurance, courage and tall bodies, and low-lying and hot places to stocky, fleshy and dark-haired peoples. Thus, Asia's population was gentle, finely built, yet lacked courage, endurance or willpower. Its people were soft and the region was one of pleasure, which provided a strategic argument for the populace's political subjugation. Mortal beings in the west, conversely, lived under harsher conditions, rendering them more belligerent, courageous and free spirited.[18] Hippocrates' dichotomy, contrasting soft and hard environments on the basis of climate, altitude and seasonality, was influential. On a north–south/east axis of identity, Greek and Roman geographers categorized the populations in northern Europe using gendered markers, claiming them to be manly, headstrong, barbarian peoples who yet lacked civilization, restraint, refinement or political organization. The people in the south, on the other hand, qualified as effeminate, weak, unreliable, fickle yet cunning, intelligent and readily subjected by powerful polities that emerged in the temperate centre, populated by rational, bold men.[19] The astronomer and geographer Claudius Ptolemy (80/100–after150) proceeded to develop

---

[17] Groebner, '*Complexio*/Complexion', pp. 365, 373 for the notion of an individual complexion in relation to the species and the development of complexional types from interior to exterior, focusing on skin colour and marks, after 1250. L. Thorndike, 'De complexionibus', *Isis* 49 (1958), 398–408.

[18] Hippocrates, *Airs, eaux, lieux* xxiii.i–iv, ed. J. Jouanna, Collection Budé (Paris, 1996), pp. 241–4. The third part is unfortunately lost.

[19] Isaac, *The Invention of Racism*, pp. 55–168.

a strand of environmental theory relating human beings' physical and mental constitutions to astrological powers as well. He posited that the revolving spheres of the seven planets and the stars transferred their virtues by discharging rays. In the thirteenth century, scientists contended that such astrological influences shaped Jewish physical constitutions, associating Judaism with Saturn, breeding stereotypes about the Jewish melancholy complexion.[20]

Besides the tripartite division of the known world, geographical space was also arranged by subdividing the spherical earth into latitudinal zones, of which only two were considered habitable. Images of zonal divisions are preserved on the so-called Macrobian maps surviving from the fifth century AD.[21] On them, the extreme cold of the frigid zones near the *septentrionalis* and the *australis*, the northern and southern polar zone respectively, and the blistering heat in the equatorial or torrid region between the tropics of Cancer and Capricorn (the *equinoctialis*) represent places where life was unsustainable. In between lay two mirrored temperate zones: the *solstitialis* (the Tropic of Cancer, the northern temperate zone) and the *brumalis* or *hyemalis* (the Tropic of Capricorn or southern temperate zone). Scholars contended whether or not mortal beings dwelled in the *brumalis* in the Southern Hemisphere. This region was sometimes called 'Antipodum', where men dwelled upside down, entirely cut off from the north by a vast equatorial ocean. Its remoteness concerned theologians, for it implied that the population of the *brumalis* did not have access to the Christian message.[22]

Texts about the impact of climate generally remained focused on the northern, habitable hemisphere, hedged in between a frigid and a torrid zone. To complicate matters, the Greek philosopher and astronomer Posidonius of Apameia (*c.* 135–*c.* 51 BC) divided the Earth's northern *habitable* surface into seven climes as well, strips running from east to west along latitudinal lines, from the Dnieper in the north (50°N) to the Meroë in the south (12°N), in present-day Sudan. Visual representations in Europe of this sevenfold division

---

[20] Biller, '"Scientific" view of Jews', pp. 140–1. For the planetary influence of Saturn on the melancholy complexion, and in general astrology and humoral theory, Resnick, *Marks of Distinctions*, pp. 215–67. Tooley, 'Bodin and the Mediaeval Theory of Climate', pp. 66–9.

[21] Edson, *Mapping Time and Space*, pp. 6–7.

[22] The Antipodeans were sometimes depicted as dwelling in a fourth austral continent lying south of the equator, depicted on the so-called Beatus maps accompanying the commentary on the apocalypse mentioned in chapter 1. Friedman, *The Monstrous Races*, pp. 37–58; Campbell, *The Witness and the Other World*, pp. 47–86; P. Freedman, 'The Medieval Other: The Middle Ages as Other', *Marvels, Monsters and Miracles: Studies in the Medieval and Early Modern Imaginations*, ed. T. S. Jones and D. A. Sprunger (Kalamazoo, 2002), pp. 1–26 (p. 3).

remain scarce before the twelfth century, however, although they feature in Arabic map making.²³ It was rumoured that savage peoples loitered on either side of the boundaries of the habitable world, populating the *ante-climata* and *ultra-climata*. Typically, classical theory held that the fourth and fifth zones, roughly corresponding to the Mediterranean area, were the most temperate.²⁴

The Galenic medical theory of the complexions also looked at the impact of environment on the body. Aristotle had posited that *primae qualitates* qualified the four elements (air, fire, water and earth), satisfying three criteria: first, they must be tangible (ἁπτικός *haptikos*, 'sensitive to touch'); second, they must be capable to enact qualitative change; and third, they must be opposites in pairs. Of the seven opposite pairs that Aristotle recognized, only two met the second condition, namely hot/cold and moist/dry, because a body that is, for example, hot can transfer these qualities to another body, but a body that is hard (also a *prima qualitas*) cannot make another body hard. Thus, the elements of the physical world were characterized by four possible combinations: air – hot and moist (sanguine); fire – hot and dry (choleric); water – cold and moist (phlegmatic); earth – cold and dry (melancholic). Disease was believed to set in when these qualities, such as hot and cold, dry and moist, became imbalanced. The application of the so-called six non-naturals, pertaining to air, food and drink, evacuations, exercise, rest and the regulation of the passions, was meant to repair any imbalance.²⁵ Notably in *On the Temperaments* and *The Faculties of the Soul* (written sometime after 193 ad), Galen of Pergamon (129–200/16) further expounded how the elements and qualities together made up the four humours: the sanguine, choleric, phlegmatic and melancholic. The make-up of the humours created a mortal being's complexion; in a healthy person the humours were balanced in a state of *eucrasia*. Medical theory, although relativistic, at the same time cultivated environmental determinism, especially because a location's terrain, temperature and humidity pertained to elements and qualities (fig. 3).

Galenism was relativistic in the sense that the ideal state of health was not absolute, but instead depended on each individual's specific situation,

---

[23] Edson, *Mapping Time and Space*, p. 7.
[24] Van der Lugt, 'La peau noire', p. 448.
[25] L. J. Rather, 'The "Six Things Non-Natural": A Note on the Origins and Fate of a Doctrine and a Phrase', *Clio Medica* 3/4 (1968), 337–47; L. García-Ballester, 'On the Origins of the Six Non-Natural Things in Galen', in *Galen und das hellenistische Erbe: Verhandlungen des IV. Internationalen Galen-Symposiums veranstaltet vom Institut für Geschichte der Medizin am Bereich Medizin (Charité) der Humboldt-Universität zu Berlin 18.–20. September 1989*, ed. J. Kollesch and D. Nickel (Stuttgart, 1993), pp. 105–15.

Figure 3. The impact of air. Bartholomaeus Anglicus, *Livre des propriétés des choses* dating to 1447, in Amiens, Bibliothèques d'Amiens Métropole MS 399 F fol. 131.

age, gender and location as well as seasonality. The objective was to obtain the desired balance of qualities and elements, depending on a person's given circumstances and natural temperament, by constantly administering to the proportions of heat, cold, moisture and dryness within the body, for instance, through food and drink.[26] A healthy person could excrete pernicious surplus through evacuations, by bathing, vomiting or letting blood, retaining a slight excess of a specific humour that determined a person's temperament. A strong imbalance, however, caused sickness and even death.

The Galenic system acknowledged that the inner workings of the body and mind correlated, for the balance of the bodily humours impacted on the functioning of the brain as well. The humours were believed to traverse from the liver via the veins to the organs, and from the heart, mixed with air from the lungs, to the brain via the arteries, carried along by the 'spirits' or *pneumata*, particles transported in the blood. The spirits along the way were

[26] C. Rawcliffe, 'The Concept of Health in Late Medieval Society', in S. Cavaciocchi (ed.), *Le interazioni fra economia e ambiente biologico nell' Europa preindustriale secc.* (Florence, 2010), pp. 317–34 (pp. 318–22).

metamorphosed from natural *pneumata* in the liver via vital *pneumata* in the heart to 'animal' or 'psychic' *pneumata* in the brain.²⁷ The vital pneumata, upon reaching the brain, after being filtered through a network at the top of the spinal cord called the *rete mirabile*, mixed with air from the nostrils. It now actuated the nervous system as well as serving as an intermediary between sense perception and those parts of the brain responsible for the imagination, reason and memory. The spirits also were the primary constituents of the soul and created human intelligence, for all knowledge came from sense perception, and the more acute the sensory impressions, the more intense the thought process. The theory held that sensory impressions became dulled if they were hampered by thick blood in a cold climate, in regions where unruly people lived. Thin blood, produced in the warm southern climate, led to finer sense impressions and thus, allegedly, to a greater intellect and timidity.²⁸

The transfer of environmental theory

The application of environmental theory gained popularity through two strands of transmission: firstly, military manuals and travel writing, sparked by military pilgrimage, and secondly, in the course of the twelfth century, in the schools, in blossoming centres of learning where schoolmen integrated Graeco-Arabic science.

The main source for the monks commenting on the qualities of peoples in Palestine and Europe shortly after the First Crusade is Vegetius's fifth-century military manual *De re militari*. This text circulated in monasteries prior to, and was copied avidly in, the twelfth century. In addition, and related to army health, Arabic travel regimens addressing the maintenance of health while traversing various climates were translated and adapted in Latin in this period. In the following decades, the translations of Graeco-Arabic scientific texts into Latin, beginning in the late eleventh century with Constantine the African's translation of the *Pantegni*, led to the incorporation of texts about medicine and the natural sciences in the curricula of western European schools.²⁹

---

[27] N. Arikha, *Passions and Tempers: A History of the Humours* (New York, 2007), pp. 23, 38–9.

[28] E. R. Harvey, *The Inward Wits: Psychological Theory in the Middle Ages and the Renaissance* (London, 1975), pp. 4–30; Ziegler, 'Physiognomy, science', p. 189. The higher rational soul was located in the brain's ventricles. The two anterior ventricles were thought to house sense perception and imagination, the middle ventricle reason and the posterior ventricle memory.

[29] Biller, 'Proto-Racial Thought in Medieval Science', p. 159. For the rise of the schools and universities, see p. 4n.9 in the Introduction.

Vegetius's fourth-century *De re militari* was an attractive source for monks, clerics and court poets portraying the Muslim enemy in the context of the crusades, for it gave them a scientific framework to commend the European, and in particular French, military qualities based on environmental factors. Thus, although *De re militari*'s textual transmission remained unbroken from the fifth century, it is not unsurprising that another eighteen manuscripts (including excerpts) survive dating to the twelfth century, followed in the thirteenth century by vernacular translations as well.[30] Guibert of Nogent's *Deeds of God through the Franks*, completed at the Benedictine abbey of Nogent near Laon in 1108 and later revised,[31] and William of Malmesbury's *Deeds of the English Kings* both contain adaptations of and responses to Vegetius's passage on climate and military qualities – William's monastery owned a copy of it in his day.

What exactly does Vegetius have to say about climate and military qualities? The manual, offering strategic advice and paying attention to the mental and physical abilities of soldiers, sets out to examine 'what provinces or nations are to be preferred for supplying the armies with recruits. It is certain that every country produces both brave men and cowards; but it is equally as certain that some nations are naturally more warlike than others, and that courage, as well as strength of body, depends greatly upon the influence of the different climates.' Continuing the theme, in the second chapter of book one, Vegetius explains that

> peoples that are near the sun, being parched by great heat, are more intelligent but have less blood, and therefore lack steadiness and confidence to fight at close quarters, because those who are conscious of having less blood are afraid of wounds. On the other hand the peoples of the north, remote from the sun's heat, are less intelligent, but having a superabundance of blood are readiest for wars. Recruits should therefore be raised from the more temperate climes. The plenteousness of their blood gives them contempt for wounds and death, and intelligence cannot be lacking either which reserves discipline in camp and is of no little assistance with counsel in battle.[32]

---

[30] Allmand, *The De Re Militari of Vegetius*, pp. 354–66.

[31] Guibert of Nogent, *Dei gesta per Francos et cinq autres textes*, ed. R. B. C. Huygens (Turnhout, 1996), pp. 89–90.

[32] Vegetius, *Epitoma rei militaris* i.ii, ed. Reeve, pp. 6–7, trans. Milner, pp. 3–4: 'Omnes nationes quae vicinae sunt soli, nimio calore siccatas, amplius quidem sapere sed minus habere sanguinis dicunt ac propetera constantiam ac fiduciam comminus non habere pugnandi, quia metuunt vulnera qui exiguum sanguinem se habere noverunt. Contra septentrionales populi, remoti a solis ardoribus, inconsultiores

The Roman strategist thereby favoured peasants over city dwellers, who 'are nurtured in the open sky in a life of work, enduring the sun, careless of shade, unacquainted with bathhouses, ignorant of luxury'.[33]

Such advice chimed well with monks and clergymen admonishing the decadence and softness of soldiers. For court poets, Vegetius's focus on the combination of intelligence and courage as military qualities, enhanced by environmental conditions, echoed in their praise of the *preudomme*'s intelligence, strength and disciplined courage, the qualities of the chivalrous man. To monks, spiritual soldiers waging war against that devilish enemy in the self, the manual appealed in its focus on rigour and discipline.[34] For that matter, Benedictine monks certainly were familiar with and applied both medical and environmental theory on a daily basis in monasteries, adhering to the monthly *regimen duodecim*, organizing blood-letting and considering environmental and seasonal conditions in their choice of sites and development of technologies.[35] In particular Cistercian monks like Bernard of Clairvaux assiduously used medicine's metaphors of digestion and purification.[36] Cistercian descriptions of the wildernesses they tamed thus also celebrated the salubrious, paradisiacal surroundings, encapsulated in toponyms such as Clara Valla, Bellefontaine or Fountains. The pleasant, health-giving sites, with clear references to the benefits of the Galenic non-naturals of fresh air and soothing sounds, were satirized in the twelfth century by a Cluniac monk as antithetical to the austere wilderness where the Cistercians claimed to dwell.[37]

---

  quidem sed tamen largo sanguine redundantes, sunt ad bella promptissimi. Tirones igitur de temperatioribus legendi sunt plagis, quibus et copia sanguinis suppetat ad vulnerum mortisque contemptum et non possit deesse prudentia, quae et modestiam servat in castris en nont parum prodest in dimicatione consiliis.'

[33] Ibid., i.iii, ed. Reeve, p. 7, trans. Milner, p. 4: '[Q]uae sub divo et in labore nutritur, solis patiens, umbrae negligens, balnearum nescia, deliciarum ignara'.

[34] Allmand, *The De Re Militari of Vegetius*, pp. 13, 19.

[35] F. E. Glaze, 'The Perforated Wall: The Ownership and Circulation of Medical Books in Medieval Europe, ca. 800–1200' (unpublished dissertation, Duke University, 1999); P. Horden, 'What's Wrong with Early Medieval Medicine', *Social History of Medicine* 24/1 (2009), 5–25; A. Meaney, 'The Practice of Medicine in England About the Year 1000', *Social History of Medicine* 13/2 (2000), 221–37.

[36] F. van Dam, *Het middeleeuwse openbare badhuis: Fenomeen, metafoor, schouwtoneel* (Hilversum, 2020), pp. 156–68, who argues that medical theory held that these processes of digestion were metabolic.

[37] *Descriptio positionis seu situationis monasterii Clarae-Vallensis* in *PL* 185, cols. 569A–574B; the *Reprehensio* in A. Wilmart (ed.), 'Une riposte de l'ancien monachisme au manifeste de saint Bernard', *Revue Bénédictine* 36 (1934), 296–344 (p. 335).

In-house physicians at courts and monasteries, like Faritius at William of Malmesbury's abbey who also practised medicine at the court of English King Henry I (c. 1068–1135) and became abbot of Abingdon in 1100, contributed to the spread of knowledge of environmental theory.[38] The active application of environmental and humoral theory was further propelled by the production of medical, geographical, natural-philosophical and astrological translations from the Arabic and Greek languages into Latin in southern Italy in the eleventh and twelfth centuries and slightly later in Spain, in the second half of the twelfth century.[39] Whereas earlier the accessibility in Latin of Hippocrates' *Air, Waters, Places* was limited – a few manuscripts survive of two translations from Greek, the first a fifth- or sixth-century translation probably made in Ravenna in Italy, and the second made in the second half of the eleventh (and in this case to be associated with the circle of Archbishop Alfanus of Salerno [1015/1020–85]) or in the first half of the twelfth century – at the end of the twelfth century, a new translation, this time from Arabic, appeared.[40] It was consulted, among others, by the physicians Arnald of Villanova (c. 1240–1311), Mondino dei Luzzi (1270–1326) and Cecco d'Ascoli (1269–1327).

The transmission of climate theory took place via adaptations and excerpts as well. The medical compendium known as the *Articella*, a collection of treatises that included the *Isagoge* of Hunayn ibn Ishaq al-Ibadi (808–73), known in Latin as Iohannitius, and the *Viaticum peregrinantis* of Constantine the African – a translation of Ibn al-Jazzar's ninth-century *Provisions for the Traveller and Nourishment for the Sedentary* – allowed students to (re)familiarize themselves with the basic tenets of the influence of environment.[41] The *Isagoge* comments on skin colour, the *Viaticum* about the impact of winds. Al-Majusi's (Haly Abbas) *Kitab*, produced in the tenth century and known in Latin as the *Liber regalis*, was partially reworked in the *Liber pantegni* (Encompassing all Arts) by Constantine the African and translated in full by Stephen of Antioch in 1127, applying climate theory in the paragraph 'De mutatione complexionis propter regionem'.[42] There are at least 29 manuscripts extant, dating to the

---

[38] F. Getz, *Medicine in the English Middle Ages* (Princeton, 1998), pp. 25, 27.
[39] Biller, 'Proto-Racial Thought in Medieval Science', pp. 157–80.
[40] There is an authoritative modern guide to the medieval Latin versions within the history of the tradition of the text provided in Hippocrates, *Airs, eaux, lieux*, ed. J. Jouanna, Collection Budé (Paris, 1996), pp. 109–19, 135–6, 138.
[41] Horden, 'Regimen and Travel in the Mediterranean', p. 119.
[42] Constantinus Africanus, *Liber Pantegni, Theorice*, i.20, v.9 and 10, in *Opera omnia Ysaac*, ed. A. Turinus (Lyons, 1515), 'De mutatione aeris propter regionem' and 'De mutatione aeris propter loca'.

twelfth and thirteenth centuries.⁴³ The abbeys of Bury St Edmunds and of Bath, the abbey of St Amand and Durham priory for instance are all known to have owned copies of it in the twelfth century.⁴⁴ Also, Ibn Sina's (973/980–1037, also known as Avicenna) *Canon of Medicine*, which was written in the eleventh century and translated into Latin before 1187, extensively comments on the impact of climate on the physical and mental qualities of men.⁴⁵

In its course, knowledge of climate and humoral theory was transmitted to and via educational centres: the schools and universities in urban communities and via the work of mendicant friars like Bartholomaeus Anglicus from the 1240s.⁴⁶ In the twelfth century, clerics like Gerald of Wales and Walter of Châtillon commented on the popularity of medical studies in Paris and Bologna. Alexander Neckam (1157–1217) registers the prescribed reading in medicine at Paris, reflecting the situation of the late twelfth century. Knowledge of Salernitan medicine is indeed traceable in the works of, for instance, Adelard of Bath (*c.* 1080–*c.* 1152), John of Salisbury (*c.* 1120–80), Gervase of Tilbury and Rutebeuf (*c.* 1245–85).⁴⁷ Ibn Sina's *Canon* became a standard textbook in Bologna and probably also in Montpellier at the end of the

---

⁴³ C. Burnett and D. Jacquart, 'A Catalogue of Renaissance Editions and Manuscripts of the Pantegni', in *Constantine the African and 'Alī ibn al-'Abbās al-Maǧūsī: The Pantegni and Related Texts*, ed. C. Burnett and D. Jacquart (Leiden, 1994), pp. 316–51.

⁴⁴ M. Green, 'The Re-creation of Pantegni, Practica, book VIII', in *Constantine the African and 'Alī ibn al-'Abbās al-Maǧūsī: The Pantegni and Related Texts*, ed. C. Burnett and D. Jacquart (Leiden, 1994), pp. 121–60; W. Black, '"I will add what the Arab once taught": Constantine the African in Northern European Medical Verse', in *Herbs and Healers from the Ancient Mediterranean through the Medieval West: Essays in Honor of John M. Riddle*, ed. A. Van Arsdall and T. Graham (Farnham, 2012), pp. 153–85; C. Burnett, 'Physics before the *Physics*: Early Translations from Arabic of Texts Concerning Nature in MSS British Library, Additional 22719 and Cotton Galba E IV', *Medioevo: Rivista di Storia della Filosofia Medievale* 27 (2002), 53–109. According to Winston Black there are about a thousand manuscripts of his medical works. Winston Black, 'A Star is Born: Reading Constantine the African in Medieval England', available at https://constantinusafricanus.com/2018/08/22/a-star-is-born-reading-constantine-the-african-in-medieval-england/ (accessed 4 September 2020).

⁴⁵ Ibn Sina, *The Canon of Medicine of Avicenna*, trans. O. C. Grunner (New York, 1970), 34, 305–8, 318–32, 480.

⁴⁶ A. Montford, *Health, Sickness, Medicine and the Friars in the Thirteenth and Fourteenth Centuries* (Aldershot, 2004).

⁴⁷ M. H. Green, 'Salerno on the Thames: The Genesis of Anglo-Norman Medical Literature', in *Language and Culture in Medieval Britain: The French of England c. 1100–c. 1500*, ed. J. Wogan-Browne e.a. (Woodbridge, 2009), pp. 220–34.

thirteenth century. Cornelius O'Boyle suggests that we can assume that a systematic programme in medicine, centring on a canon of medical texts known as the *Ars medicinae*, by then shaped the curriculum of universities like Paris and Montpellier.[48] Earlier, schools of medicine are mentioned in Montpellier from the 1130s and in Bologna. Medicine was perhaps also taught in Italy in the early decades of the thirteenth century at the *studia* of Vicenza, Arezzo and Vercelli, and at the universities of Naples and of Toulouse in France.[49] From these centres, knowledge spread to the courts and wider urban communities via pedagogical writings, encyclopaedias, vernacular regimens and word of mouth. One such encyclopaedia that has already featured in chapter 1 is Bartholomaeus Anglicus's *On the Properties of Things*, which applies humoral and climate theory in its ethnography, consulting among others Constantine the African's *Pantegni*, the elusive Herodatus, Ibn Sina, Solinus (who probably lived in the third century), Pliny and Aristotle. It formed part of the staple education of Franciscan monks in the *studium generale* in the second half of the thirteenth century. It also quickly became popular in urban lay circles and was translated into various vernaculars. Other texts engaging natural science included a translation of Aristotle's *On Animals* from Arabic into Latin before 1220, and his *Politics*, which took an organic view of society and was translated in 1260 by William of Moerbeke.

The health regimens translated and adapted in the twelfth century do not explicitly classify ethnic groups, and in this they differ from the strain of texts operating environmental theory. Nonetheless, these texts likewise taught students to categorize on biological grounds, because they focused on groups such as the sanguine youth and the phlegmatic aged, who were susceptible to the influence of climate and the seasons. For instance, the typology of the sanguine was grafted onto the English, discussed in chapter 5; several sources comment upon the Jews' melancholy. In Latin schools, the humours also worked as a pedagogical apparatus to mould and discipline young men, while taking into account their physical and mental traits. The influential pedagogy manual *Disciplina scolarium*, dating to between 1230 and 1240, presented a programme to discipline the fickle, sanguine youth in the school room.[50] In the fourteenth and fifteenth centuries, slave-trade manuals produced by Mamluk physicians

---

[48] O'Boyle, *The Art of Medicine*, pp. 10–20. D. Jacquart, *Le milieu médical en France du xiie au xve siècle: En annexe 2e supplément au 'Dictionaire' d'Ernest Wickersheimer* (Geneva, 1981); Siraisi, *Medieval and Early Renaissance Medicine*, pp. 48–77.

[49] T. Duranti, 'The Origins of the Studium of Medicine in Bologna: A Status Quaestionis', *CIAN-Revista de Historia de las Universidades* 21/1 (2018), 121–49.

[50] Pseudo-Boethius, *De disciplina scolarium*, ed. O. Weijers (Leiden, 1976); Parsons, *Punishment and Medieval Education*, pp. 63–4.

likewise applied the system to appraise the value of young men and women sold at market, as did animal traders examining and evaluating horses.[51]

How far did knowledge of environmental and humoral theory stretch beyond the walls of the monastery and classroom? Two milieux can be identified where it was picked up. First, *speculum* literature ('mirrors') and regimens owned by larger and smaller households advised how to govern the body (and, by extension, the household, city and polity) according to the rhythms of the days and months. The mirrors drew upon the knowledge of the body and physiognomy, in many cases disseminated via translations and adaptations of the *Sirr al-Asrar*.[52] An example is the final section of the household manual by Daniel of Beccles, known as the *Urbanus magnus*, probably dating to the 1180s.[53] These texts do not, however, contain ethnic stereotypes, nor do later vernacular physiognomic tracts copied into miscellanies belonging to larger households. Joseph Ziegler has argued that the paucity of ethnic stereotypes in physiognomic texts has to do with the fact that the fluidity of a person's complexional make-up generally ruled out group classification.[54] It is worth suggesting that the vernacular physiognomic tracts copied into composite manuscripts perhaps served as tools in households for the appraisal of servants and workers, as well as for establishing the individual traits of citizens, discussed in chapter 3.

The broader dissemination and application of environmental theory can be traced in travel reports, romances, *chansons de geste* and in essentializing images and sculptures of Saracens or Jews, offering us glimpses of the prejudiced representations of the religious 'others' as dark or monstrous beings.[55] Verbal representations of Plinian monstrosity became mixed with discussions of climate theory, as in the *Chronicles* of Benoît of St Maure, who died in 1173. Narrating the history of the Norman dukes, written for an audience of aristocratic warriors, Benoît declares the world's 'fringes' uninhabitable because

---

[51] Barker, *That Most Precious Merchandise*, pp. 4, 45–59.

[52] S. J. Williams, *The Secret of Secrets: The Scholarly Career of a Pseudo-Aristotelian Text in the Latin Middle Ages* (Ann Arbor, 2003); C. Gaullier-Bougassas, M. Bridges and J.-Y. Tilliette (ed.), *Trajectoires européennes du 'Secretum secretorum' du Pseudo-Aristote (XIIIe–XVIe siècle)* (Turnhout, 2015); J. Ferster, *Fictions of Advice: The Literature and Politics of Counsel in Late Medieval England* (Philadelphia, 1996).

[53] F. Whelan, *The Making of Manners and Morals in Twelfth-Century England: The Book of the Civilised Man* (Abingdon, 2017).

[54] Ziegler, 'Physiognomy, Science', pp. 182–7. Ziegler does however present references to examples of Mongols/Tartars, menstruating Jews and sixteenth-century physiognomic tracts about Italian city dwellers.

[55] Heng, *The Invention of Race*, pp. 181–256 and Introduction, p. 14n.39, for further references.

of their extreme frigidity. Europe, on the other hand, sits in the centre of the world. It is a pleasant and temperate region,

> right and handsome and delightful and bounteous and abundant in all that a man needs. The men there are handsomely shaped and of wise manners, discrete, reasonable, and well dressed. They are neither too tall nor too short. There they have courteous manners and arts, laws and justice. There they believe in one God, the creator.

The south woefully lacked all of these features; in that part of the world men knew not the difference between right and wrong, nor had they laws, religion or reason. They were worse than dogs, black, chinless, horned and hairy.[56] However, this is an exceptional vernacular source from this early period; in the first instance it was predominantly through the Latin world of scientific knowledge and historiography that climate and humoral theory spread.

Applying environmental theory

Most of the texts utilizing the theory of climate taught that heat and coldness brought about opposite effects: cold climates produced men with hot temperaments, whereas hot temperatures bred cowardly, vengeful, puny yet cunning ethnotypes, the external heat drawing the moisture and spirits from the body and lowering its temperature and vitality. Constantine the African's late eleventh-century *Liber pantegni*, wielding environmental theory, thus mentions the dark men living in the southern intemperate region as having 'curly and thick hair, dry skin, small, thin bodies, round faces, concave eyes, and large noses'. They tended to be deceitful, 'and indeed they are cold within and thus rendered very timid. Although they appear from this sign to be hot, they are not. For the intense heat extracts from the interior to the exterior their natural heat and thus they are cold within.' In the northern, cold region, under the great or small pole, people mirrored them, having 'blond, soft hair, and are white, with a red and white face, broadly built and quick-footed because of the built-up heat in their breast. Their complexion is hot and hence they are

---

[56] Benoît of St Maure, *Chronique des Ducs de Normandie* i.11 lines 185–203; 131–2; 136–40; 141–3, ed. C. Fahlin, 2 vols. (Uppsala, 1951–54), ed. C. Fahlin, i, 5–7: 'En sunt li grant renne abitable / E riche e bel e delitable / E plantaïf e abondos / De quanque hue nest desiros. / De bele forme I sunt les genz / E de saiges contenemenz, / Discret, raisnable e bien vestu; / Trop grant ne sunt ne trop menu. / Cist sevent les afaitemenz, / Les ars, les leis, les jugemenz, / Cist sevent connoistre e veeir / E entendre e aperceveir / Qu'eu n'est cún Dex, c'un criator'; the translation has been adapted from Friedman, *The Monstrous Races*, p. 54.

audacious and strong, and hot, although they seem cold.'⁵⁷ In a similar vein, the English Benedictine monk William of Malmesbury, consulting Vegetius's *De re militari* in his monastery library, claimed that Saracen fighters locked in battle with crusaders lacked courage, for 'it is very well known that every nation born in the eastern clime is dried up by the great heat of the sun; they may have more good sense, but they have less blood in the veins, and that is why they flee from battle at close quarters: they know that they have no blood to spare.'⁵⁸ Wielding the same theory, the Dominican friar Albertus Magnus, who produced a tract on the nature of places about 1250, taught that men in the hot south suffered a shorter lifespan because of a deficiency of natural *virtus*.⁵⁹ Inversely, mortal beings in the cold northern regions retained the internal heat and moisture because the pores of the skin closed, hindering the heat's evaporation. The hot-blooded man dwelling in a cold climate retained larger quantities of blood, rendering him fearless, or, in Marian Tooley's words, 'confident and assertive, impatient, magnanimous, greedy of honour and power, and a great fighter' – conveniently, as we shall see in chapter 5, the makings of a bold aristocratic knight. However, in the *extremely* cold Scandinavian regions, the body's pores remained blocked and an excess of

---

57 Constantinus Africanus, *Liber Pantegni, Theorice* i.20, ed. Turinus: '[P]ili crispi et asperi, sicca cutis, inferior pars corporis subtilis: facies tumida, oculi concavi, nasi magni atque interiora frigida et ideo inanimositas eos debilitat. [...] [P]ili sunt flavi lenes et albi color albus facies rubicunda pectora lata pedes subtiles propter adunationes caloris in pectore fugientis a perdum extremitate. Eorum complexio est calido et ob hoc fiunt audaces atque fortes et tamen cum non sint: videntur esse frigidi. Ergo in humori non est certitudo a colore et pilis sed ex complexione sui.'

58 William of Malmesbury, *Gesta Regum Anglorum* iv.347, ed. and trans. Mynors, Thomson and Winterbottom, i, 600–3: '[H]omines inertissimi, et qui, comminus pugnandi fidutiam non habentes, fugax bellum diligent. [...] [T]ela mortifero suco ebria, in homine quem percutit non virtus sed virus mortem facit. Quicquid igitur agit, fortunae, non fortitudini attribuerim [...]. Constat profecto quod omnis natio quae in Eoa plaga nascitur, nimio solis ardore siccata, amplius quidem sapit, sed minus habet sanguinis; ideoque vicinam pugnam fugiunt, quia parum sanguinis se habere norunt.' Cf. Gerald of Wales, *Descriptio Kambriae* i.15, in *Giraldi Cambrensis Opera, Vols. I–VII*, ed. J. S. Brewer, J. F. Dimock and G. F. Warner (London, 1861–91), vi, 192–4 and Gerald of Wales, *Topographia Hibernica* i.37, in *Giraldi Cambrensis Opera, Vols. I–VII*, ed. J. S. Brewer, J. F. Dimock and G. F. Warner (London, 1861–91), v, 70–1. Bartlett, *Gerald of Wales*, pp. 164–7. Phillips, 'William of Malmesbury: Medical Historian of the Crusades', pp. 129–38; Titterton, 'Bloodless Turks and Sanguine Crusaders', pp. 289–308.

59 Biller, 'Proto-racial Thought', p. 173.

moisture built up, clogging the brain with the snotty substance of phlegm and reducing the body temperature.[60]

Climate engineering in pursuit of temperance

As elsewhere, Hippocratic and Galenic theory presented twelfth-century northern European monks and clerics with a dilemma.[61] Their discomfort concerned the situation of the ideal temperate centre, which in ancient times was located in the Mediterranean south. Applying the theory to the centres of power and culture, ancient Greek naturalists had categorized the men in the north – the northern Europeans – as rash, and those dwelling in the south as weak. From Hippocrates' perspective, Greece was the most temperate region where the ideal population dwelled. In the same tradition, the biblical narrative situated Paradise in the east as the locus of temperance.[62] Adapting the theory to their own lifeworlds, much-read Roman scholars such as Pliny the Elder proposed Campania in Italy as the most balanced temperate zone, where nature excelled, in a joyous mood, rendering 'all that invigorating healthfulness all the year round, the climate so temperate, the plains so fertile, the hills so sunny, the glades so secure, the groves so shady!'[63] Such were the blessings of the forests, the fertile fields yielding corn, vines and olives, such its healthy livestock and numerous ports facilitating commerce, that its populace were 'men of medium bodily stature, with a marked blending even in the matter of complexion; customs are gentle, senses clear, intellects fertile and able to grasp the whole of nature'.[64] Unsurprisingly, in the twelfth century, north-western Europeans pegged northern France and England as their

---

[60] Tooley, 'Bodin and the Mediaeval Theory of Climate', p. 72. Cf. Pseudo-Aristotelian *Problemata* xiv.16, in *The Works of Aristotle*, trans. E. S. Forster, 12 vols. (Oxford, 1910–52), vii, 910a, which discusses whether heat and coldness is naturally counteracted in the bodies of human beings, making men in hot regions naturally cowardly and vice versa.

[61] Cf. Wear, 'Place, Health, Disease', pp. 448–51 for similar concerns about England's position in Elizabethan times.

[62] Scafi, *Mapping Paradise*.

[63] Pliny the Elder, *Historia naturalis* iii.v.40–2, ed. and trans. Rackham, ii, 32–3: '[T]ota ea vitalis ac perennis salubritas, talis caeli temperies, tam fertiles campi, tam aprici colles, tam innoxii saltus, tam opaca nemora'.

[64] Ibid., ii.lxxx.190, trans. Rackham, pp. 320–3: '[M]edicos corporum habitus magna et in colore temperie, ritus molles, sensus liquidos, ingenia fecunda totiusque naturae capacis.' Pliny also connected geography to political institutions, claiming that the northerners conversely lived in lawless savagery.

most temperate zone, a reflection of the political and cultural relevance the region was claiming for itself.

In response, scholars of geography took to dabbling in textual climatic engineering, tampering with the designated coordinates of the region in order to portray north-west Europe as a natural habitat of civilization, knowledge and power. However, situating western Europe as an ideal temperate zone demanded slightly more ingenuity from intellectuals than their ancient Italian forebears necessarily had mustered, for northern Europe was hardly considered a centre or temperate region in ancient texts. In the mid-thirteenth century, the Dominican friar Albertus Magnus, who was born in Lauingen in Bavaria and spent most of his working life in the German territories, tweaked the south position of the temperate clime and pushed it northwards, from the fourth to the sixth–seventh clime (corresponding to the Hellespont). This allowed him to qualify the sixth and seventh climes as the habitat of handsome, noble and fair men, whereas the men living in the fourth clime were now small and dark.[65] The region of extreme cold (90°) lay further north in uninhabitable parts and that of exceeding heat (24°) below the tropic of Cancer. He also underscored the longevity of people in the north, opposing Aristotle's *Length and Shortness* and the pseudo-Aristotelian *Problems*, which argued that men in hot regions enjoyed longer lives.[66] The English Franciscan friar Roger Bacon (*c.* 1214–*c.* 92) comments that Ptolemy erred in his longitudinal and latitudinal measurements. Bacon writes extensively about the impact of climate on the morals of the Ethiopians, Romans and French, expressing wonderment at the fact that the Picardians, neighbours under the same skies as the French, knew such different customs and language.[67]

Classification of peoples based upon natural environment

With the updating of climate theory came the categorization of peoples in the north and south based upon their natural environments. In the process, intellectuals drew fault lines of regional differences in habitat, character and physique of peoples. Not only did they, in this manner, attempt to depict the

---

[65] Albertus Magnus, *De natura loci* i.11–12 in *De natura loci ad fidem autographi; De causis proprietatum elementorum ad fidem autographi; De generatione et corruptione*, ed. P. Hossfeld (Aschendorff, 1980), pp. 18–21.

[66] P. Biller, *The Measure of Multitude: Population in Medieval Thought* (Oxford, 2000), pp. 282–5.

[67] Roger Bacon, *Geographia* in *The 'Opus Majus' of Roger Bacon*, ed. J. H. Bridges, 3 vols. (Oxford, 1897), i, 305; *Mathematicae in physicis utilitas*, ed. Bridges, i, 138; *Judicia astronomie*, ed. Bridges, i, 250–2.

north-west as a region of temperance, but they also turned their minds to the habitat of specific territories and cities. England's situation, surrounded by a cold sea, elicited from a perturbed Robert the Englishman, lecturing on cosmology in Montpellier in 1271, the remark that the boundaries of the seventh clime were 'hardly across the English Channel, so that almost all of England is outside a clime [i.e. beyond the habitable climes of the world]'.[68] Indeed, according to calculations drawn from the Persian astronomer al-Farghānī (800/5–70), who is known in Europe as Alfraganus, and copied into the Parisian astronomer Johannes de Sacrobosco's (c. 1195–c. 1236) widely read *On the Sphere of the World*, the seventh clime ended where the North Pole was raised above the horizon by 50½ degrees, rendering England and Britain beyond the habitable world. In response, a flurry of poetry and histories produced mostly in northern France and England emphatically and somewhat frantically underscored this region's temperate, pleasant, natural habitat and the affable mental and physical qualities of its inhabitants as well as their sociocultural forwardness. In a similar fashion, as in the later urban panegyrics produced in Italy and France, the clerk William FitzStephen in the twelfth century, working in Thomas Becket's (c. 1120–70) administration, praised London's environment as wholesome, with plenty of fresh air, and flattered its urban population, which was liberal and kind, not fierce or bestial, 'conspicuous above all others for their polished manners, for their dress and for the good tables that they keep'.[69]

The distinctions between regional territories and peoples in Europe reflected existing genealogical-religious identities that now were enveloped in environmental, scientific discourse. Thus, in one of its most detailed applications, in circa 1240 the Franciscan friar Bartholomaeus Anglicus presented in his immensely popular encyclopaedia *On the Properties of Things* a hierarchical sub-categorization of peoples *within Europe*, operating a classification of physical appearance and skin colour, religious devotion, language and public order (fig. 4). In it, on a micro level, Bartholomaeus ethnocentrically favours his own region of birth and residence, for he was born in England and worked and wrote for many decades in Saxony in the German territories. He claims, erroneously citing Constantine the African's *Pantegni*, that the north-easterly

---

[68] For a discussion of al-Farghānī's and Sacrobosco's calculation of the climes: L. Thorndike, *The* Sphere *of Sacrobosco and its Commentators* (Chicago, 1949), pp. 16–18, especially note 88. For Robert the Englishman's commentary, Ibid., Thirteenth Lecture, pp. 186–93, translation at pp. 236–42; citation at p. 236.

[69] C. Weeda, 'Cleanliness, Civility, and the City in Medieval Ideals and Scripts', in *Policing the Urban Environment in Premodern Europe*, ed. C. Rawcliffe and C. Weeda (Amsterdam, 2019), pp. 39–68 (p. 59).

Figure 4. Regions, cities and environments. Bartholomaeus Anglicus, *Livre des propriétés des choses* dating to 1447, in Amiens, Bibliothèques d'Amiens Métropole MS 399 F fol. 166.

wind (Aquilo) has a drying and cooling effect, rendering the air clean and pure, refining and cleansing, wherefore 'in the northern region, the men are tall and elegantly built, for the outer coldness of the air clogs up the pores, retaining the natural inner heat'.[70] To create such a benevolent picture effectively, Bartholomaeus also needed to craftily edit his classical sources, continuously presenting the northern habitat of the Germanic peoples as slightly less inhabitable or harsh than his Mediterranean sources imply.

To give one example, Bartholomaeus dutifully asserts that the Germanic territories bring forth 'noble and immense peoples, about whom Isidore spoke in book IX. The German nations are many and they have immense bodies.'[71] So far, so good. However, as discussed above, *too* cold a climate gave birth not only to strength and endurance but also to dull minds and savage behaviour and, by extension, political subjugation. Thus, Bartholomaeus conveniently omits Isidore of Seville's next remark in his *Etymologies* about the Germans: 'They are savage tribes, hardened by very severe cold. They took their behaviour from that same severity of climate.'[72] He then resumes his copying of Isidore's text, writing that 'they are strong, courageously and fiercely brave, indomitable, living by raiding, and hunting'.[73] But where Isidore states: 'There are many tribes of Germani, varied in their weaponry, differing in the colour of their clothes, of mutually incomprehensible languages. The monstrosity of their barbarism gives a fearsome quality even to their names,' Bartholomaeus assures us that they have 'fair and shapely faces, long, blond hair, they are generous, merry and agreeable' – liberality, merry minds and kind hearts being the attributes of the urbane man in twelfth-century learned circles.[74] Bartholomaeus also quickly

---

[70] Bartholomaeus Anglicus, *De proprietatibus rerum* xiv.1, ed. Knochlobtzer, 'De terra': '[I]n terra aquilonari homines sunt procerae staturae et elegantis formae, frigiditate enim exterioris aeris clauduntur pori, et calor naturalis retinetur intrinsecus.'

[71] Ibid., xv.13, ed. Knochlobtzer, 'De Alemannia': 'Generosos enim et immanes gignit populos, de quibus dicitur in libro ix Isidore. Germaniae nationes sunt multae immania corpora habentes.' Cf. Isidore of Seville, *Etymologiae* ix.ii.97, ed. Reydellet, p. 97.

[72] Isidore of Seville, *Etymologiae* ix.ii.97, ed. Reydellet, p. 97, trans. Barney and Hall, p. 197: '[N]ationes sevissimis duratae frigoribus. Qui mores ex ipso caeli rigore traxerunt.'

[73] Bartholomaeus Anglicus, *De proprietatibus rerum* xv.13, ed. Knochlobtzer, 'De Alemannia': '[V]iribus fortes, audaces animo et feroces, indomiti, raptu, captibus et venationibus occupati.' Cf. Isidore of Seville, *Etymologiae* ix.ii.97, ed. Reydellet, p. 97: '[F]erocis animo et semper indomiti, raptu venatuque viventes'.

[74] Cf. Isidore of Seville, *Etymologiae* ix.ii.97, ed. Reydellet, p. 97: 'Horum plurimae gentes, variae armis, discolores habitu, linguis dissonae [...]. [I]nmanitas barbariae etiam in ipsis vocabulis horrorem quendam significat', trans. Barney and Hall,

highlights that the generous, merry and agreeable character 'applies especially to the Saxons, who surpass the others in the aforementioned things. Isidore says of them that the Saxon people live on the ends and coasts of the ocean and are swift and strong.' Yet again, the Franciscan friar injects a minor emendation, for Isidore mentions that they live in 'impassable marshes'; instead, according to Bartholomaeus, the land is 'fruitful and irrigated by the best rivers', and the mountains are rich in metals.[75] Much of present-day Germany is represented as a garden of delights with rivulets, ponds and lakes enveloped in salubrious air, yielding an abundance of livestock, wine and minerals.[76]

Although the Germanic peoples experienced regional differences in language and culture in the 'Diutsche lant', the utilization of climate theory describing peoples in their natural habitat allowed scholars to look for perceived natural, and hence cultural, similarities.[77] Partly in keeping with classical

---

p. 197; Bartholomaeus Anglicus, *De proprietatibus rerum* xv.13 ed. Knochlobtzer, 'De Alemannia': '[F]acie decori et formosi, comati et coma flavi, liberales animo, hilares et iucundi'. Cf. the hugely popular (more than a hundred manuscripts have survived) twelfth-century poem *Regimen Sanitatis Salernitanum* lines 267, 273–4, ed. and trans. P. W. Cummins, *A Critical Edition of Le régime tresutile et tresproufitable pour conserver et garder la santé du corps humain: With the commentary of Arnoul de Villeneuve, corrected by the "docteurs regens" of Montpellier, 1480, Lyon, 1491* (Chapel Hill, 1976), p. 244: 'Natura pingues isti sunt atque iocantes. [...] Largus, amans, hylaris, ridens, rubeique coloris, / Cantans, camosus, satis audax, atque benignus', part of a verse extract of John of Spain's twelfth-century prose translation of the Arabic *Sirr al-Asrar*, the *Secretum secretorum*. For the manuscripts containing the 'Salernitan Regimen of Health', see P. W. Cummins, 'A Salernitan Regimen of Health', in *Allegorica: A Journal of Medieval and Renaissance Literature* 1 (1976), 78–101 (pp. 78–81); P. W. Cummins, 'Introduction', in Ibid., *A Critical Edition of Le regime tresutile*, pp. ix–xi.

[75] Bartholomaeus Anglicus, *De proprietatibus rerum* xv.13, ed. Knochlobtzer, 'De Alemannia': 'Saxonum gens in oceani finibus et litoribus constituta virtute et agilitate agilis.' Isidore of Seville, *Etymologiae* ix.ii.100, ed. Reydellet, p. 99: 'paludibus inviis'. Cf. Orosius, *Historiae adversum paganos* vii.xxxii.10, ed. Zangemeister, pp. 513–14. Bartholomaeus does, however, copy Isidore's statement that the Saxons take their name from 'saxosus', stony, that they are a hard and powerful people, setting them apart from other 'piratical' peoples.

[76] Ibid., xv.170, ed. Knochlobtzer, 'De Westphalia'.

[77] For regional differences: J. I. H. Mendels, 'Nationalismus in der mittelhochdeutschen und mittelniederländischen Literatur', in Actes du IVe Congrès de l'Association Internationale de littérature Comparée, Fribourg, 1964 = Proceedings of the IVth Congress of the International Comparative Literature Association, ed. F. Jost (The Hague, 1966), pp. 298–308 (pp. 300–5). *Diutsch/tiutsch*, the *tiutsche zunge* and *tiutschen liute* are common references alongside regional dialects. Cf. Kästner, 'Der großmächtige Riese und Recke Teuton', pp. 71–3.

tradition but taking a more positive view, Bartholomaeus Anglicus categorizes the Saxons, the people of Raetia (today's eastern and central Switzerland and parts of southern Bavaria and Swabia), the Swabians, the Thuringians, the people of Zeeland, Holland, Flanders, Brabant and Meissen as populous, elegant, tall, strong and courageous, some of whom also are handsome and blond, whereas he notably considers the more westerly situated Germanic peoples to be more chivalrous and devout than those in the east.[78] Even more merry, agreeable, charming and well spoken are the English. Copying an extract of a Latin verse into his encyclopaedia, he strategically claims that the English are 'full of mirth, free, born to jest, a free people, free of spirit and free of tongue', in contrast with the barbaric peoples in the Irish territories, which the English were in the process of colonizing (see further chapters 5 and 6).[79] The imagery fits rhetorically within the political–legal framework presenting naturally eloquent peoples as capable of governing well. However, this does not imply that the older tradition of etymologizing was discarded, for Bartholomaeus also claims the people of Thuringia, 'like the name of the country [to be] harsh and extremely cruel towards their enemies'.[80]

Classifying European ethnotypes based upon skin colour or complexion

In response to theories of environmental determinism, schoolmen also classified ethnic groups administering degrees or shades of whiteness. They had some secure footing, for, in antiquity, Greek and Roman authors had laid the groundwork by disdainfully commenting upon the large-bodied and white-skinned Scythians in the north.[81] Geographers used the imagery of the Scythians for the peoples in the northern German, Scandinavian and Slavic territories, marking their populations' whiteness of skin and scientifically explaining it through the cold climate and distance from the sun. Bartholomaeus Anglicus declared the Icelandic conditions to be so bone-chilling that

---

[78] Bartholomaeus Anglicus, *De proprietatibus rerum* xv.139, ed. Knochlobtzer, 'De Saxonia'; xv.153, 'De Suevia'; xv.166, 'De Thuringia'; xv.170, 'De Westphalia'; xv.143, 'De Selandia'; xv.110, 'De Hollandia'; xv.58, 'De Flandria'; xv.25, 'De Brabantia'; xv.52, 'De Misnia'.

[79] Ibid., xv.14, ed. Knochlobtzer, 'De Anglia': 'Anglia plena iocis gens libera apta iocari / Libera gens cui libera mens et libera lingua'.

[80] Bartholomaeus Anglicus, *De proprietatibus rerum* xv.166, ed. Knochlobtzer, 'De Thuringia': 'Gens quidem secundum nomen patriae Thuringia, id est, dura contra hostes, maxime et severa.'

[81] Goldenberg, 'Racism, Color Symbolism', p. 92.

the mountains of frozen snow resembled glass. Iceland's large-bodied, strong population, who lived by hunting and fishing, clad in the skins of bears and wild beasts, was 'very white'.[82] The Slavs, also, were sluggish, extremely white and phlegmatic because of the extreme cold that clogged up their senses.

The classification of whiteness within Europe rested firstly upon the non-complexional theory, according to which the proximity to the sun determined skin colour, recasting a black/white binary onto geography.[83] Indeed, natural science traditionally did not hold that black skin was effected by a black complexion, for the Galenic colour schema of the four humours pertained only to white-skinned mortals.[84] Yet, in the first century ad Pliny the Elder had conveyed that the Ethiopians, burnt by the heat of the heavenly body, entered the world scorched and with frizzled hair; in the opposite region of the world the population had frosty-white skins and blond, straight hair.[85] Afterwards, Isidore of Seville compared the Maures, black as night, with the Gauls, white as milk. The *Isagoge* attributed to Hunayn ibn Ishaq also contains an elementary distinction between white and black skins, invoking the Scots and the Ethiopians. In the thirteenth century, northern Europeans in Holland, Frisia, Saxony and Dacia ranked among the white-skinned populations living in the frigid regions.[86]

As the perceived ties between environment, territory and population deepened, however, scholars began to organize differentiation based upon *shades of whiteness* as well – either of skin colour or humoral complexion. This occurs beyond myriad comparisons of shades of whiteness and darkness in literary

---

[82] Bartholomaeus Anglicus, *De proprietatibus rerum* xv.174, ed. Knochlobtzer, 'De Islandia': 'valde alba'.

[83] Van der Lugt, 'La peau noire', pp. 446–50.

[84] Ibid., 452–3. Albertus Magnus claimed that colour was an external sign of physiology; mortal beings in the torrid region, who had an abundance of yellow bile (choleric), were naturally agile and dry because of the evaporation of their vital spirits due to the heat. They died at a young age and were less fertile than people in the north. Albertus Magnus, *De natura loci* ii.3, ed. Hossfeld, pp. 26–7.

[85] Pliny the Elder, *Historia Naturalis* ii.80, trans. Rackham, i, 321. Cf. Albertus Magnus, *De natura loci* ii.3, ed. Hossfeld, pp. 26–7.

[86] Vincent of Beauvais, *Speculum naturale* xxxii.13 about the Gauls, cited verbatim from Isidore of Seville, *Etymologiae* xiv.iv.25, ed. Spevak, pp. 76–9. Also in Hrabanus Maurus, *De rerum naturis* xii.4, *PL* 111, col. 350C. For the *Isagoge*, see Biller, 'Proto-racial Thought', p. 165; Van der Lugt, 'La peau noire', p. 447. For the populations of Holland, Frisia, Saxony and Dacia in the commentary on Sacrobosco's *The Sphere* (*Tractatus de Sphera*) ascribed to the Paris-based astronomer Michael Scot in the 1230s: Thorndike, *The Sphere of Sacrobosco*, pp. 335–6.

sources.[87] In about 1280, Alexander of Roes, a church canon from Cologne, proclaimed that the French were whiter skinned than the Spanish, but less so than the Germans or English.[88] He does so in the *Memoriale*, written while residing at the papal court, in which he asserts the German claim to *imperium* over French pretensions.

To complicate matters, the classification of peoples' skin colour eventually became entangled with comments on complexion, religion and morality. Using the aesthetics of colour to classify moral communities was not a new exercise. In antiquity, blackness and whiteness were intermittently laden with value judgements, earmarking the radiance of virtue or stain of sin.[89] Geraldine Heng defined such markers as hermeneutic blackness, to be distinguished from the physiognomic blackness of skin.[90] For instance, the Hellenized Jewish philosopher Philo of Alexandria (20 BC–50 AD) suggested that the blackness of the Ethiopians appertained to their sin. It could also designate the unbaptized, 'black in spirit'.[91] Yet its meaning was ambivalent. Within Christian allegory, the African symbolized both beauty – alluding to the Song of Songs – as well as deformity and sinfulness, such as in Pope Gregory the Great's *Commentary on Job*.[92] These kinds of associations are found in particular in literary sources. Much later, in the fourteenth century, several *chansons de geste* and manuscript images depict black people, described Ethiops, *maurus*, *niger* or Saracen

---

[87] Heng, *The Invention of Race*, pp. 181–256.

[88] Alexander of Roes, *Memoriale* 15, in *Schriften*, ed. H. Grundmann and H. Heimpel, MGH Staatsschriften 1 (Stuttgart, 1958), pp. 105–8; Van der Lugt, 'La peau noire', pp. 442–4.

[89] Goldenberg, 'Racism, Color Symbolism', 89. According to Snowden, in antiquity the image of the black was without prejudice. However, this view is now contested. See F. M. Snowden, *Before Color Prejudice: The Ancient View of Blacks* (Cambridge MA, 1983). For criticism: Van der Lugt, 'La peau noire', 474 note 106 for references.

[90] Heng, *The Invention of Race*, p. 185.

[91] Goldenberg, 'Racism, Color Symbolism', pp. 94–6. Origen of Alexandria, for example, drew from this allegory in the third century.

[92] T. Hahn, 'The Difference the Middle Ages Makes: Color and Race before the Modern World', *Journal of Medieval and Early Modern Studies* 31/1 (2001), 1–37 (pp. 18–23). The Cistercian abbot Bernard of Clairvaux elaborated on the Song of Songs (1:5) 'I am black but beautiful', interpreting blackness to allow 'the soul to acknowledge and internalize an aspect of self-loathing as means of achieving wholeness'. Abelard made erotic allusions to blackness as an element of desire. Friedman, *The Monstrous Races*, pp. 64–5; Heng, *The Invention of Race*, pp. 238–42.

(*maurus* also designated 'Saracen') as monstrous or devilish.[93] The colour white, conversely, might represent concepts of virtue and purity, epitomized in the rebirth in Christ.[94] These affects spilled over into humoral theory. The bitterness of melancholic black bile, on occasion conceived to dominate the complexions of Jews and serfs stained as the cursed progeny of Cain, was deemed a waste product of sin. Inversely, the sanguine was held in the highest regard, of health, status and morality.[95] Thus, the allegorical text *The Medicine of the Soul*, attributed to the Picardian cleric Hugh of Fouilloy (1096/1111–c. 1172), correlates the sweetness of the sanguine with contemplation, and bitterness and grief with the memory and commission of sin.[96]

The aesthetic value assigned to colour depended on the ethnocentric perspective. The ideal colour in northern western sources was, for that matter, a blushing red-white, reflecting the sanguine – male, youthful, healthy – complexion, whereas in antiquity the sanguine mortal being was light brown – a testimony to how ethnocentricity can determine taste, as David Goldenberg signalled.[97] The *Mirror of Doctrine*, written by the Dominican friar Vincent of Beauvais (before 1200–64), drawing on Johannitius's *Isagoge* and the Latin *De aluminibus et salibus*, a translation of al-Rāzī's work (854–925), in the paragraph 'On Colours' expounds that mortals with a balanced complexion are ruddy white and that the complexional colours reflect mental states such as fear, anger or sadness, whereby blondness represents instability and madness, brilliant redness veracity and blackness a paucity of morals.[98] This extensive encyclopaedia focusing on the mechanical arts was produced, with the support of the French King Louis ix (1214–70), for the edification of Vincent's fellow

---

[93] Van der Lugt, 'La peau noire', pp. 442–4. Strickland, *Saracens, Demons, and Jews*, and Heng, *The Invention of Race*, pp. 181–256 for negative stereotyping in relation to the colour black.

[94] G. Constable, *The Reformation of the Twelfth Century* (Cambridge, 1996), pp. 188–93 argues that white was associated specifically with angels and the victorious Christ of the Apocalypse 1:14, where his head and hair would be snowy white as wool.

[95] See pp. 119–21 for references to melancholy and sin. In the seventh century, Isidore already remarked that 'men dominated by blood are pleasant and charming', and Bede's *De temporum ratione* remarked that they are 'cheerful, merry, full of compassion', and that they 'laugh and talk a lot'. Isidore, *Etymologiae* xi, 'De homine et portentis'; Bede, *De temporum ratione* 35, PL 90, cols. 457C–462A.

[96] Hugh of Fouilloy, *De medicina animae*, PL 176, col. 1185A.

[97] Goldenberg, 'Racism, Color Symbolism', p. 90.

[98] Vincent of Beauvais, *Speculum doctrinale* xiii.50 (Baltazar Bellerus, Douai, 1624; reprint Graz, 1965).

Dominican students, the lay aristocracy and for rulers. Being a combination of heat and moisture, the sanguine temperament was considered praiseworthy because it was the outcome of a perfect digestion, although in youth it might also signal lustfulness and unruliness.[99] In physiognomic treatises, the well-tempered man's complexion was a mixture of red and white with a radiant skin.[100] The Christ-figure represented the sanguine type in the apocryphal description recorded in the *Letter of Lentulus*.[101] Christ and the Virgin Mary, the only beings whose bodies had not been corrupted by original sin, retained a perfect, balanced, most rational complexion. Ethiopians, on the other hand, would not be resurrected as black people, Otto of Freising surmised, a colour from which humankind would be liberated.[102]

The hierarchy of complexions concurrently served to strategically classify gender, age, religious and social groups using markers of skin colour and mental affects, occasionally implying that the phlegmatic and melancholic types – sporadically pasted onto women, Scandinavians, Slavs, Jews and serfs respectively – ranked last.[103] Hence, Bartholomaeus Anglicus indexed the white-skinned blond man living in the extreme north as phlegmatic, 'tough-minded and forgetful', 'listless, heavy and slow, dull of wit and forgetful, soft-fleshed and languid. He is bluish of colour, white-faced, fearful, spitting and snivelling, sluggish and slothful, with a small appetite, little thirst. [...] He has soft, blond and straight hair; his pulse weak, thick and slow, his urine white, thick, crude and discoloured. He is fat, stocky and short, his skin

---

[99] R. J. Long, 'Introduction', in *Bartholomaeus Anglicus: De proprietatibus rerum, libri III–IV*, ed. R. J. Long (Turnhout, 2007), p. 194. Parsons, *Punishment and Medieval Education*, pp. 63–4.

[100] Ziegler, 'Physiognomy, Science', pp. 183–4. In the fifteenth century, Savonarola linked it to Christ's facial complexion and moral perfection, just as Adam had been perfectly balanced. See also J. Ziegler, 'Text and Context: On the Rise of Physiognomic Thought in the Later Middle Ages', in *De Sion exibit lex et verbum domini de Hierusalem: Essays on Medieval Law, Liturgy, and Literature in Honour of Amnon Linder*, ed. Y. Hen (Turnhout, 2001), pp. 159–82 (pp. 171–2) for a physiognomic treatise depicting Christ as perfect, fair and sanguine.

[101] Thomas Aquinas, *Scriptum super libros Sententiarum*, ed. P. Mandonnet and M. F. Moos, 4 vols. (Paris, 1927–47), iii, 495; Albertus Magnus, *De anima* 2.3.23, ed. C. Stroick (Monasterii Westfalorum, 1968), p. 133. Resnick, *Marks of Distinctions*, pp. 31–2 for further source references. C. E. Lutz, 'The Letter of Lentulus Describing Christ', *The Yale University Library Gazette* 50/2 (1975), 91–7.

[102] Minnis, *From Eden to Eternity*, p. 154.

[103] The *De disciplina scolarium* speaks of melancholic intelligence as well, which would later evolve into the melancholic genius. Parsons, *Punishment and Medieval Education*, pp. 63–4.

plain and hairless.'¹⁰⁴ In *On the Nature of Places*, produced shortly after 1248, the Dominican scholar Albertus Magnus, specifying the proximity to the sun, engaging environmental and humoral theory, argued that 'conversely, the Goths and the Dacians from the west, and the Slavs from the east, having been born on the boundary of the seventh clime and beyond, are white on account of their cold complexion. Because their bodies are not porous, and because the place in which they live is cold, and the cold constricts their bodies, much moisture remains in them. And this enlarges their bodies and makes them fleshy and phlegmatic.'¹⁰⁵ The oversized, phlegmatic woman was at risk when she went into labour because the firmness of her body hindered her in childbirth. By a stroke of nature, however, women in the north rarely became pregnant, for the cold constricted their veins and, instead of menstrual flow, they tended to suffer from frequent nose bleeds.¹⁰⁶ Albertus classifies German peoples, although hotter bodied, courageous and strong, as leaning towards the phlegmatic because their bodily fluids evaporate less easily, wherefore they have 'a thick head of straight hair, not curly. Their spirits are not active because of its thickness, because their humour is thick and heavy and does not respond to motion and the reception of forms of the animal spirit. Therefore, they are dull-witted and stupid, if they do not exert themselves in study.'¹⁰⁷ Lastly, the

---

[104] Bartholomaeus Anglicus, *De proprietatibus rerum* iv.2, ed. Knochlobtzer, 'De frigiditate': 'Intellectus durus et obliviosus, appetitus parvus et somnus multus, incessus gravis et tardis.' Ibid., iv.9, 'De flegmatis proprietatibus': 'deses, gravis et tardus et sensu hebes, mente obliviosus, carne mollis et fluidus, colore lividus, albidus in facie, timidus, sputis et excreationibus multis plenus, piger et somniculosus, parvi appetitus, parve sitis. [...] Crine mollis est, flavus et laxus, cuius pulsus est mollis, grossus et tardus, urina alba, spissa, cruda et discolorata, statura pinguis et grossa, in extremitatibus brevis et curta, cuius cutis superficies plana et lenis ac a pilis denudata.' K. Park, 'The Meaning of Natural Diversity: Marco Polo on the "Division" of the World', in *Texts and Contexts in Ancient and Medieval Science: Studies on the Occasion of John E. Murdoch's Seventieth Birthday*, ed. E. Sylla and M. McVaugh (Leiden, 1997), pp. 134–47 (pp. 140–2).

[105] Albertus Magnus, *De natura loci* ii.3, ed. Hossfeld, p. 27: 'E contrario autem Daci et Gothi ex parte occidentis et Sclavi et Parthi ex parte orientis, nati in fine septimi climatis et ultra, sunt albi propter frigus complexionale ipsorum. Et quia corpora eorum porosa non sunt et locus eorum est frigidus constringens corpora eorum, remanet umidum multum in eis. Et hoc auget corpora eorum et facit ea carnosa et fleumatica.' Cf. Albertus Magnus, *De homine* i.1.

[106] Ibid., ii.3, ed. Hossfeld, p. 27.

[107] Ibid., ii.3, ed. Hossfeld, p. 27: 'Et sunt pili eorum multi et laxi, non crispi. Operationes autem eorum animales non vigent propter spissitudinem, quippe umor eorum est piger et spissus nec oboedit motui et receptioni formarum animalium. Sunt igitur tales hebetes et stolidi, nisi hoc sit ex studio exercitio.'

Ethiopians were shaped by the choleric rather than the phlegmatic or melancholic humour.[108] The 'sexual hotness' of black women was also interpreted by Albertus Magnus climatically, indicative of how scientific theory might be construed to validate prejudiced attitudes towards the southerner in the course of the thirteenth century.[109]

Fixed or fluid ethnotypes

The categorization of population groups grounded on geography and environment inevitably raised the issue of whether complexions could change. This question is relevant in discussions about the existence of racial classification and racism in this period. Climate theory did not so much lump people together in subspecies, but categorized them based upon external, natural factors as well as allegedly innate traits, sociocultural and religious factors, *habitus* and free will.[110] Complexional change could occur as a result of, firstly, miscegenation; secondly, migration; and thirdly and importantly, the medicalized application of the non-naturals. Lastly, from the twelfth century, theologians considered temperaments to be subject to religious determinism as well, occasionally stating that the humors were the outcome of the fall of mankind. They classified Jews (and sometimes serfs) as having corrupt, melancholy bodies inherited from their forebears, congenital traits befitting their cursed state and resonating in their semi-free legal status. This tendency to attribute to some groups fixed traits, while assigning to other groups the capacity to change, fits into a racializing hierarchy of power. For it was, as the Franciscan friar Roger Bacon stated, the inherited radical complexions that determined humans' dispositions with regard to morals, learning and languages, crafts and workmanship.[111] Nonetheless, the notion that mortals attained the virtuous

---

[108] Albertus Magnus, *De natura loci* ii.3, ed. Hossfeld, p. 26. Biller, 'Proto-Racial Thought', p. 164 note 25, where Bernard de Gordon (fl. 1270–1330) is quoted saying that the Africans are choleric.

[109] P. Biller, 'Black Women in Medieval Scientific Thought', *Micrologus: Natura, scienze e società medievali – Nature, Sciences and Medieval Societies* 13 (2005), 477–92 (pp. 485–9); Heng, *The Invention of Race*, pp. 181–256. The physician Arnald of Villanova, using environmental theory, commented in circa 1308 that black men, like monkeys, were uncivilized, frightened of shedding blood, quick to use trickery and full of lust; in *Speculum medicine*, 'De regionibus', ed. M. R. McVaugh, Opera medica omnia 13 vols. (Barcelona, 2018), xiii; cited in Biller, 'Proto-racial Thought', pp. 174–5.

[110] Ziegler, 'Physiognomy, Science', p. 195. Isaac, *The Invention of Racism*, pp. 34–5. Weeda, 'The Fixed and the Fluent'.

[111] Roger Bacon, *Mathematicae in physicis utilitas*, in *The 'Opus Majus' of Roger Bacon*, ed. J. H. Bridges, 3 vols. (Oxford, 1897), i, 138; see also *Moralis philosophia* ii, in *The*

or evil qualities of *habitus* through practice and education, guided by manuals and regimens, also exerted its influence.[112]

Questions about the fixed or fluid nature of complexions were concentrated in discussions of generation: the complexion of the male semen and female blood at conception. Alongside radical moisture, gained at the first moment of generation from sperm, members and organs, some commentators claimed that mortals possessed an innate or radical complexion (*complexio innata* or *radicalis*) passed down through parental transmission (semen and blood), together with a natural complexion (*complexio naturalis*) which was changeable in response to environmental factors such as climate, the seasons, planetary conjunctions and other non-naturals such as diet, rest and exercise.[113] As the father's semen mixed with the mother's blood, its complexion bearing the *virtus informativa* stamped its mark on the formation of the embryo and its members, as well as on accidental particularities such as sex, complexion and skin colour.[114] Originating in the heart and drawn from blood, the male semen was the definitive factor in the formation of human beings, just as male blood ties were recognized over female blood in law, articulated in thirteenth-century concepts of nobility.[115] Applying these ideas, in his *Questions on Animals*, Albertus Magnus poses the question in Aristotelian tradition of whether philosophers will beget intelligent children. Affirming that this would be the case, Albertus suggests that 'those of noble birth will beget noble and better children, as is the case with horses', for 'the sperm contains both the bodily and the mental virtue [...] thus children resemble their parents in their

---

'*Opus Majus*' *of Roger Bacon*, ed. Bridges, ii, 258–62 for training morals.

[112] Nederman, 'Nature, Ethics', pp. 87–93.

[113] Ziegler, 'Physiognomy, Science', pp. 191–3; D. Jacquart, *Le médicine médiévale dans le cadre Parisien: xive–xve siècle* (Paris, 1998), pp. 392–3; K. van 't Land, 'The Rise and Fall of Human Life: Theory on Life Course, Nutrition and Sperm in Late Medieval University Medicine' (unpublished dissertation, Radboud University Nijmegen, 2020); L. Thorndike, 'De Complexionibus', 398, note 1. The separate theory of pangenesis held that seeds come from all parts of the body and offered a material basis for the inheritance of acquired characteristics and disease. This theory became popular in relation to the intergenerational transmission of characteristics within groups only from the sixteenth century.

[114] For the dominant embryological narrative: J. Ziegler, 'The Scientific Context of Dante's Embryology', in *Dante and the Human Body: Eight Essays*, ed. J. C. Barnes (Dublin, 2007), pp. 61–88 (pp. 74–82).

[115] M. Keen, *Chivalry* (New Haven, 2005), pp. 143–58; A. A. Robiglio, 'The Thinker as a Noble Man (bene natus) and Preliminary Remarks on the Medieval Concepts of Nobility', *Vivarium* 44 (2006), 205–47 (p. 207). Nobility was potentially universally acquirable. However, with the embodiment of differences the fluid boundaries in theory became more impervious.

bodily disposition, to that extent that they are by the same reasoning similar in mental disposition, such as in wisdom and knowledge'.[116] However, natural and non-natural conditions – the seasons, winds, the imagination, nutrition, stellar influences and climate – influenced the active sperm at the moment of generation. The mother's passive blood could hamper the reception of the paternal form, in which case the child was more likely to resemble its mother or grandparents.[117] Therefore, the parental and the offspring's complexions were not necessarily identical. And although a person's innate complexion was relatively stable, still her natural complexion was subject to non-natural factors throughout life, such as diet or climate. Children placed in the care of a wet nurse who received the wrong food or moved to a different climate might, in theory, undergo a complexional change – this explains why the intake of the mother's natural milk is mentioned in national discourses in later centuries, although in practice physicians seem to have cared little about the value of 'national mother milk'.[118] Migration meant that, for instance, an innate sanguine complexion could slowly become more choleric, although the transformation was more cumbersome if the complexions were incompatible (i.e. a phlegmatic cannot easily become choleric).

These ideas touched upon questions of heredity. The scholastic William of Conches (c. 1085–c. 1154), at the school of Chartres, surmised that nature demanded that the similar came from similar things.[119] Encyclopaedists in the thirteenth century considered leprosy to be transmitted by semen, as well as

[116] Albertus Magnus, *Quaestiones super de animalibus* xviii, Quaestio 4, in *Opera omnia*, ed. E. Filthaut, 40 vols. (Aschendorff, 1951–), xii, 299: 'Quod parentes nobiliores generant filios nobiliores et meliores, ut patet in equis [...] in spermate non solum est virtus corporis, sed animae [...] ergo cum filii assimilentur parentibus in dispositionibus corporalibus ut plurimum, pari ratione assimilabuntur in dispositione animae, ut sapientiae et scientiae etc.'

[117] Van der Lugt, 'La peau noire', pp. 458–60. Ziegler, 'Scientific Context of Dante's Embryology', pp. 73, 79 for the notion that the woman also emitted a generative female semen, in contrast to the Aristotelian concept that the embryo is formed from matter from the female's menses.

[118] John of Newhouse, 'Tractatus de complexionibus Magistri Johannis de Nova domo' i, ed. W. Seyfert, 'Ein Komplexionentext einer Leipziger Inkunabel', *Archiv für Geschichte der Medizin* 20 (1928), 272–99, 372–89, pp. 298–9). For the value of wet nurses in the slave trade, R. L. Winer, *Women, Wealth, and Community in Perpignan, c. 1250–1300: Christians, Jews, and Enslaved Muslims in a Medieval Mediterranean Town* (Aldershot, 2006), pp. 152–4. In the seventeenth century, Anthony Weldon relates Scottish identity to the 'savage mother's milk'; M. Floyd-Wilson, *English Ethnicity and Race in Early Modern Drama* (Cambridge, 2003), pp. 56–8.

[119] Cf. William of Conches, *Dragmaticon Philosophiae* vi.xiii.2–3, ed. I. Ronca, Corpus Christianorum Continuatio Mediaevalis 152 (Turnhout, 1997), pp. 204–5.

being caused by a humoral imbalance.[120] By the fourteenth century – and thus beyond the scope of this book – the scholar John of Newhouse claimed that an identical parental complexion strengthened the likelihood that the offspring would inherit the same physical and mental affects. He applied the concept of parental transmission, thus explicating: 'The Saxons and the Frisians, the Polish and the Thuringians all have the same character, because they are nursed in the same place and under the same constellation.'[121] A scribe commenting on this text clarified the rise in criminality on these grounds.[122] In the fifteenth century, Moors and Jews went on to feature in a Spanish *anti-converso* discourse, that was possibly informed by ideas taken from the sphere of horse breeding, creating a language of 'political disability and reproductive fitness', essentializing Jews who converted by force or voluntarily to Christianity and excluding them from government offices, based upon arguments of 'blood'.[123] The transregional entanglement of human and horse medicine, the development of theories of heredity, animal breeding and the appraisal of bodies of the enslaved, labourers and horses at markets is still little understood.[124]

Returning to the twelfth century, ideas also circulated about the corruption or else emendation of offspring by means of migration, acculturation and the training of a virtuous *habitus* that undercut the allegedly innate, collective character of ethnic groups. The German Bishop Otto of Freising, the nephew of the German Emperor Frederick Barbarossa who commissioned the *Gesta Friderici*, claimed that the Lombards inherited their intelligent and gentle character from their mothers' Roman blood as well as from exposure to the temperate climate, rendering them elegant rather than barbaric in speech and manners.[125] Earlier descent myths also could become entangled with Greek

[120] Resnick, *Marks of Distinctions*, p. 111.
[121] John of Newhouse, *Tractatus de complexionibus*, i, ed. Seyfert, pp. 298–9: 'Et ideo Saxones omnes sunt eiusdem moris et Frisones et Poloni et Thuringi, quia in eodem loco et ab eadem constellatione sunt nutriti.'
[122] Zurich, Zentralbibliothek MS Car. C 111 fol. 207ra: '...et ideo in una terra sunt plures fures quam in alia.' Cited by L. Thorndike, 'De Complexionibus', p. 399 note 5.
[123] Nirenberg, 'Was There Race Before Modernity?', pp. 250–2.
[124] See for horse–human comparisons in Egypt: Y. Rāġib, *Actes de vente d'esclaves et d'animaux d'Égypte médiévale*, 2 vols. (Cairo, 2002–6); Barker, *That Most Precious Merchandise*, p. 113; De Miramon, 'Noble Dogs, Noble Blood', pp. 200–16.
[125] Otto of Freising, *Gesta Friderici* ii.14, in *Die Taten Friedrichs oder richtiger Chronica*, ed. F.-J. Schmale (Berlin, 1965), p. 308–9. Compare also the 'Descriptio Norfolciensium' lines 53–5, ed. T. Wright, *Early Mysteries and Other Latin Poems of the Twelfth and Thirteenth Centuries* (London, 1838), pp. 93–8 (p. 94), claiming that a bad tree does not produce good fruits, nor a bad *patria* good people.

climate theory, arguing that purity of blood through descent was tainted by miscegenation. In *On the Properties of Things*, Bartholomaeus Anglicus pointedly explains the character of the people of Poitou in terms of ethnogenesis, combining a descent myth, climate theory and etymology.[126] In this instance, the changes to the biological make-up of migratory peoples were not considered to be commendable but, rather, the hallmark of impurity. The twelfth-century pilgrim who authored the *Guide to Santiago de Compostela*, who presumably came from Poitou, took a dark view of the so-called contaminated origins of his neighbours in the south. The Navarrese, he said, were not true offspring, as they were partially descended from the Scots who had raped the indigenous female population in Julius Caesar's day, creating an illegitimate, corrupt stock, stripped of its humanity, whom the pilgrim also compares to Muslims. Here, the tradition of etymology is used as an explicatory factor: Navarrus comes from *non verus*, untrue. Swarthy, barbaric, evil, they had disgusting, unhygienic table manners, wore shabby clothes following the Scottish fashion and their language resembled that of dogs barking.[127]

Both skin colour and complexion could change after migration. Although, as Ibn Sina had stated, each individual had his own balanced complexion depending on eight variables, travel generally implied that mortal beings experienced different climates that were not conducive to their individual, natural complexions.[128] The same pertained to skin colour. Black-skinned mortals, born in the fourth or fifth clime, whose blackness was caused by the complexion of their parents born in the first or second clime, slowly turned whiter if they moved to more northerly climes.[129] Albertus Magnus believed that travellers grew weaker unless they returned to their 'natural habitat'.[130] Latin medical treatises on complexions, however, affirmed that complexional change as a result of migration brought about benefits as well. Conveniently for Albertus Magnus, born in Lauingen, Bavaria, but educated in Italy's Padua, German students travelling southwards experienced an expedient mental

---

[126] Bartholomaeus Anglicus, *De proprietatibus rerum* xv.122, ed. Knochlobtzer, 'De Pictavia'.

[127] *The Pilgrim's Guide to Santiago de Compostela: A Critical Edition* vii, ed. and trans. P. Gerson, A. Shaver Crandell and A. Stones, 2 vols. (London, 1998), ii, 28–31. The manuscript containing the guide is known as the *Liber Sancti Jacobi* or the *Codex Calixtinus*. It was compiled sometime between 1139 and 1173, when a monk from Ripoll copied the text.

[128] Ziegler, 'Physiognomy, Science', p. 195.

[129] Albertus Magnus, *De natura loci* ii.3, ed. Hossfeld, p. 26.

[130] Likewise, lions survived only in southern regions. Albertus Magnus, *De natura loci* i.2, ed. Hossfeld, pp. 25–6.

transformation from dull-witted, phlegmatic beings into astute intellectuals. He refers to men nurtured in Milan on law and the arts. Tragically, in his view, the Danes and the Slavs in the far north 'care little' for study, cultural inertia in this case being the outcome of environmental determinism. This idea that transmigration could eventually transform a people's complexion remained popular in later centuries.[131] However, the process was considered to be long drawn out. Gerald of Wales underscored the fixity of the character of the Welsh and the English that was shaped by the climate from which they originally came. Thus, the Welsh, who according to Gerald of Wales's *Description of Wales* originally descended from Aeneas's progeny Brutus, could not erase their Trojan blood. The climatic conditions of the arid Trojan plain accounted for their positive boldness of speech, which they held in common with the Romans and Franks, as well as their swarthy colour, natural warmth of character and hot temperament.[132] The cold and wetness, on the other hand, accounted for the phlegmatic nature of the English. As discussed further in chapter 3, the emphasis on the innate qualities of boldness of speech of the Welsh and their attendant condition of freedom suggests that they, despite attempts by the English king to conquer their territory, should not be subjected to the status of servility. Their lawlessness and lack of good political regimen, however, jeopardized their condition. Gerald's text, containing strategic military information about the strengths and weaknesses of the Welsh, in the tradition of Vegetius's manual, is seemingly arguing for their improved governance, yet resisting their subjugation.

Medical theory cut across social categories. Romance writers occasionally depicted the peasant – like the black children of Ham, a cursed descendant of Cain – as dark skinned and deformed, as a beast or a Moor.[133] The peasant's dark-skinned features came, the argument ran, from his proximity to the element earth when tilling the land. In the *Book of Complexions* attributed to a John of Paris (writing in the twelfth or thirteenth centuries and not, it seems, the famous theologian of that name), complexion also pertained to a skill or profession: iron and copper smiths are subjected to heat and dryness (choleric), bath keepers to heat and humidity (sanguine), fishermen to cold and moisture (phlegmatic) and peasants to cold and dryness (melancholy).[134]

---

[131] Albertus Magnus, *De natura loci* ii.3, ed. Hossfeld, pp. 26–7. Floyd-Wilson, *English Ethnicity and Race*, pp. 48–52.

[132] Gerald of Wales, *Descriptio Kambriae* ii.15, ed. Dimock, vi, 192–4. Bartlett, *Gerald of Wales*, p. 203.

[133] P. H. Freedman, *Images of the Medieval Peasant* (Stanford, 1999), pp. 139–40.

[134] John of Paris, *Liber complexionum*, in Paris, Bibliothèque nationale de France, MS Latin 7121, fols. 73r–80r.; cited in Thorndike, 'De Complexionibus', p. 402.

However, there was little clarity about the time-span required for complexional transformation, which was probably open to ethnocentric and racialized manipulation, depending on the desirability of emphasizing change or stability in power hierarchies.

Religious determinism

Environmental theory had a lasting impact on thinking about groups, notably in the Mediterranean trade in the enslaved, where it was engaged to value people and their alleged traits.[135] It was also appropriated and incorporated by learned religious men, who unsurprisingly intertwined religious and medical discourses, creating a language of inherited physiology integrating religious-cultural traditions and traits, in which disease was triggered by sin. This discourse contained ideas about free will – and hence the possibility of complexional change – as well as religious determinism, and was applied to the non-Christian other.

Speaking of Christianity in terms of embodiment was not new. In late antiquity, the language of conversion had been coined in terms of the mutability that was necessary to achieve full humanness.[136] Conversion was thereby envisioned as a *rebirth*, whereupon new members entered the body politic, the Pauline *corpus mysticum* of Christ's Church. Nonetheless, humoral and environmental theory now lent the embodied religious discourse a scientific framework, and thus authority on a different level.

The embodiment or biological construction of religious categories – which were and are frequently mixed up with ethnic-genealogical categories, the Saracen, for example, being used as an umbrella term for Muslims – notably occurred in medicalized discussions of the 'Jewish nature' and Jews' melancholy complexion grounded in astrology. Peter Biller and Irven Resnick have shown that in the ninth century Abu Ma'shar al-Balkhi (787–886) – who in Europe was known as Albumasar and whose work was translated into Latin in the twelfth century by John of Spain (*fl.* 1133–53) and Hermann of Carinthia (*c.* 1100–*c.* 1160) under the title *Liber de magnis coniunctionibus* – claimed that religious faiths arose under the influence of the conjunctions of the planets.[137]

---

[135] Barker, *That Most Precious Merchandise*, pp. 45–59.

[136] Buell, *Why This New Race*; Buell, 'Early Christian Universalism and Modern Racism', pp. 109–31.

[137] Albumasar, *On Historical Astrology: The Book of Religions and Dynasties (on the Great Conjunctions)* 2.8, ed. C. Burnett and K. Yamamoto, 2 vols. (Leiden, 2000), i, 127. Resnick, *Marks of Distinctions*, pp. 225–7; Biller, '"Scientific" View of Jews', pp. 140–1, 154.

Hermann of Carinthia's *On Essences*, written in 1143, managed to connect Judaism, arising under Saturn, with a melancholy complexion and characterizations of fraud, wickedness, envy, perfidy and stubbornness – familiar older stereotypes listed in the catalogues and in biblical exegesis.[138] These are typical anti-Jewish stereotypes mixing theological commentary with science. Such stereotypes also gave a gendered interpretation of alleged religious–ethnic traits. A clear example is the late twelfth-century treatise written in the crusader states, *Tractatus de locis et statu sancte terre ierosolimitane*, classifying Jews as obstinate people who were more unwarlike than women or serfs and suffered from menstrual flow.[139] The concept that Jews suffered from the inherited *curse* of a 'flux of blood' or haemorrhoids subsequently made its way into texts of Albertus Magnus.[140] Jacques de Vitry's *History of the East* is another example where a combination of biblical exegesis and medicine are used to frame Jewish military qualities, tying them to the myth of deicide as well, claiming that Jews, scattered as slaves across the world, had become unwarlike and weak like women.[141] The *Isagoge* of Al-Qabīsī (who was known in Europe as Alcabitius and who died in 967), which survives in more than a hundred Latin copies and vernacular translations, integrated the older theological contention that the child of Saturn emanated a bad smell *(foetor judaicus)*.[142] Saturn's qualities were cold and dryness, associated with melancholy and bad odour. This trope was particularly heinous because stench or miasma was considered to be the cause of disease, such as gout, leprosy or cancer. Bartholomaeus Anglicus, among others, claimed that Saturn produced men dark, wicked and sad.[143]

---

[138] Hermann of Carinthia, *De essentiis*, ed. and trans. C. Burnett (Leiden, 1982), p. 166–9. Islam was said to have arisen under Venus, Christianity under Mercury.

[139] *Tractatus de locis et statu sancte terre ierosolimitane*, in 'Ein Tractat über das heilige Land und den dritten Kreuzzug', ed. G. M. Thomas (Munich, 1865), p. 26; Biller, 'A "Scientific" View of Jews', p. 158 for a transcription.

[140] Resnick, *Marks of Distinctions*, pp. 188–9; Biller, 'A "Scientific" View of Jews', pp. 140–6; Johnson. 'The Myth of Jewish Male Menses'; Bauchau, 'Science et racisme: les juifs, la lèpre et la peste'; J. Gebke, *(Foreign) Bodies Stigmatizing New Christians in Early Modern Spain*, trans. H. W. Schroeder (Vienna, 2020), pp. 110–11. For the 'immutability' of Jews, Resnick, *Marks of Distinctions*; J. M. Elukin, 'From Jew to Christian? Conversion and Immutability in Medieval Europe', in *Varieties of Religious Conversion in the Middle Ages*, ed. J. Muldoon (Gainesville, 1997), pp. 171–89.

[141] Jacques de Vitry, *Historia orientalis*, ed. and trans. J. Donnadieu (Turnhout, 2008), p. 328.

[142] Al-Qabīsī, *The Introduction to Astrology* 2.2.6, ed. and trans. C. Burnett, K. Yamamoto and M. Yano (London, 2004), p. 63.

[143] Resnick, *Marks of Distinctions*, 199, 232–43 (p. 241 for plague and infection); Bartholomaeus Anglicus, *De proprietatibus rerum* viii.23, ed. H. Knochlobtzer.

Discussions of astrology and hereditary characteristics were, however, at loggerheads with the notion of free will, whose relationship to the body engendered a complicated discussion. Theologians took the monistic position that the soul was partly attached to the body, yet that the intellectual will was divinely appointed.[144] William of Conches, in his commentary on the work of Macrobius (*fl.* 400), for instance, claimed that free will prevailed despite the fact that the planets influenced predispositions.[145] Complexion was accordingly said to be not the cause but the sign of a person's natural character, congenital character being born of divine appointment. Nonetheless, especially where the otherness of Jews, Saracens and heretics was concerned, this idea of free will and mutability seemed to fall short, suggesting that salvation required a specific essence. In Paul's Letter to the Romans, all of mankind had been presented as equal, spiritual descendants of Jacob and Esau.[146] All were God's slaves, regardless of status or descent.[147] Many scholars have accordingly stressed that *christianitas* promoted a transnational myth of oneness and unity, seldom acknowledging internal differences.[148] However, as Denise Buell has argued cogently, in early Christendom, rhetorical strategies continued to wield ethnic markers in order to explain what being a member of the Christian community entailed, often in terms of regeneration. Members of the Christian community described themselves as being reborn in Christ; becoming a Christian meant activating a potential of being, developing an acquirable fixed essence that all human beings allegedly possessed and through which a person achieved full humanness. These ontological essences could, moreover, be administered hierarchically, favouring some groups over others, offering a rhetorical argument to marginalize 'those who had failed (in different ways)

P. Lanfranchi, 'Foetor judaicus: Archéologie d'un préjugé', in *Ékklèsia: Approches croisées d'histoire politique et religieuse: Mélanges offerts à* Marie-Françoise Baslez, ed. C. Bonnet and F. Briquel-Chatonnet (Toulouse, 2017), pp. 119–33 (pp. 119); J. Elukin, *Living Together, Living Apart: Rethinking Jewish-Christian Relations in the Middle Ages* (Princeton, 2007), pp. 107–9; S. K. Cohn Jr., 'Popular Insurrection and the Black Death: A Comparative View', *Past and Present*, 195 Issue Supplement 2 (2007), 188–204.

[144] C. W. Bynum, 'Why All the Fuss About the Body? A Medievalist's Perspective', *Critical Inquiry* 22/1 (1995), 1–33.

[145] Ziegler, 'Scientific Context of Dante's Embryology', pp. 64–6; Resnick, *Marks of Distinctions*, p. 225.

[146] Boureau, 'Hérédité, erreurs', p. 70.

[147] Buell, 'Early Christian Universalism', p. 111.

[148] Jeffrey Cohen, for example, claimed the Christian ecumenicity was 'a universal body unmarked by such differentiations'; Cohen, 'On Saracen Enjoyment', p. 116.

to activate the potential available to all humans'.¹⁴⁹ As we shall see in chapter 3, the hierarchy of humanness was indeed framed rhetorically in legal-cultural narratives of progress and property rights.

Schoolmen likewise commented upon the physical lack of equilibrium and ensuing ill-health in the wake of the fall of mankind. Some attributed the decay of species to a complexional imbalance, sin causing disease, dark complexions and ugliness. Earlier, and exceptionally, the Irish theologian John Scottus Eriugena (*fl. c.* 845–*c.* 870) had explicitly interwoven environmental theory into his discussion of the diversity of mankind and early man.¹⁵⁰ In *The Division of Nature*, he hypothesized that, had Adam not sinned, he would not have been split into two sexes.¹⁵¹ No longer in his primordial condition as the image of God, man thereafter suffered further divisions that were also influenced by environmental factors, such as climate and the non-naturals:

> Insofar as the diversity of man is discerned, and of one species from another, and types of stature are different, this does not have its cause in nature [i.e. the primordial condition before the fall] but arises from sin, and from the diversity of place and circumstances of lands, waters, airs, foods and the like, where people are born and nourished.¹⁵²

As humoral and environmental theory became more influential in western Europe – John Scottus Eriugena was exceptional in using Greek sources in the ninth century – this idea was expanded to incorporate the notion that the fall of man had led to a complexional imbalance. The *Dialogue against the Jews*, written circa 1109 by Petrus Alfonsi, a Spanish physician who converted from Judaism and worked at the English royal court, argued that Adam's illicit desire had created an imbalanced complexion and subsequent mortality, even before he had eaten from the forbidden fruit.¹⁵³ The German Benedictine abbess Hildegard of Bingen (1098–1179) claimed in her medical treatise *Causes and Cures* that before the fall Adam was in perfect health and sanguine; however,

---

¹⁴⁹ Buell, 'Early Christian Universalism', pp. 114, 119, 123–6.
¹⁵⁰ Glacken, *Traces on the Rhodian Shore*, p. 262.
¹⁵¹ For earlier discussions about human procreation and sin: G. Boas, *Essays on Primitivism and Related Ideas in the Middle Ages* (New York, 1978), pp. 70–1.
¹⁵² John Scottus Eriugena, *De divisione naturae* ii.7, *PL* 122, cols. 533A–533B: 'Siquidem diversitas hominum a seipsis, qua uniuscujusque species ab aliis discernitur, et staturae modus variatur, non ex natura provenit, sed ex vitio, et diversitate locorum et temporum terrarum, aquarum, aërum, escarum, ceterarumque similium, in quibus nascuntur et nutriuntur.'
¹⁵³ I. M. Resnick, 'Humoralism and Adam's Body: Twelfth-Century Debates and Petrus Alfonsi's *Dialogus Contra Judaeos*', *Viator* 36 (2005), 181–96 (pp. 191–5).

'when Adam knew what was good and by eating the apple did what was evil, black bile rose up within him in reaction to this change', upon the suggestion of the devil. A melancholy disposition in a corrupt body was accompanied by wavering beliefs, 'for at Adam's fall, the devil scorched the melancholy within him, and in this way [the devil] sometimes makes a person subject to doubt and lack of faith'.[154] About 1200, in his encyclopaedic work *On the Nature of Things* written as a preface to his commentary on Ecclesiastes, Alexander Neckam, probably while living as a canon regular at Cirencester, alleged that whereas before the fall 'every animal would be of temperate complexion in his own genus', although some more temperate than others, because of the sin there occurred a difference of degree, as a lapse from the norm. 'Therefore will it not appear to one versed in physical science that complexions may be changed, although many think this to be impossible?'[155] Original sin thus effectuated the heterogeneity of mankind, although, according to Thomas Aquinas, climate and the planets actually even created disparities in the size, constitution and beauty of bodies in Eden, without meaning that inequality represented a defect of nature.[156] The twelfth-century Anglo-Norman cleric Gerald of Wales saw fit to turn the argument on its head, enlacing religious thought with the environmentally deterministic theory that the devil adjusted heresies to the climate. Thus, in his *Instruction for a Ruler*, written at the English court of King Henry II, Muhammad entices the Arabs to enter into polygamous

---

[154] Hildegard of Bingen, *Causae et curae* ii, ed. L. Moulinier (Berlin, 2003), pp. 183–5: 'Nam cum Adam bonum sciuit et pomum comedendo malum fecit, in vicissitudine mutationis illius melancholia in eo surrexit. [...] Quoniam dyabolus in casu Ade melancoliam in ipso conflauit, qua hominem aliquando dubium et incredulum parat.' Trans. by F. Wallis, in ibid. *Medieval Medicine: A Reader* (Toronto, 2010), pp. 357–8. V. Sweet, *Rooted in the Earth, Rooted in the Sky: Hildegard of Bingen and Premodern Medicine* (New York, 2006); F. E. Glaze, 'Medical Writer: "Behold the Human Creature"', in *Voice of the Living Light: Hildegard of Bingen and Her World*, ed. B. Newman (Berkeley, 1998), pp. 125–48.

[155] Alexander Neckam, *De naturis rerum* 156, in *De naturis rerum libri duo. With the Poem of the Same Author, De laudibus divinae sapientiae*, ed. T. Wright (London, 1863), p. 250: 'Nihilominus tamen esset aliquod animal temperatioris complexionis alio. [...] Nonne igitur in physicis instructo videbitur quod complexiones mutatae sint, quamvis hoc multi censeant esse impossibile?' The translation is cited from Boas, *Essays on Primitivism*, p. 83.

[156] Minnis, *From Eden to Eternity*, p. 115. These ideas foreshadow later classifications. In the eighteenth century, French philosopher Georges-Louis Buffon (1707–88) asked how the descendants of Adam and Eve, expelled from paradise and living in inferior climates, suffered 'degeneration'. Buffon believed both in monogenesis and acquired hereditary characteristics as a result of environmental influences. See Banton, *Racial Theories*, p. 5 and Isaac, *Invention of Racism*, pp. 8–11.

relationships because he knows that the Easterners are full of lust, living in a hot region. The heretical Cathars lured avaricious men in the cold climes to not pay tithes.[157] In the *Deeds of God through the Franks*, the Benedictine monk Guibert of Nogent, using climate theory to explain the presence of heresy in the east, commented:

> However, the faith of the Easterners, which has never been stable, but has always been variable and unsteady, searching for novelty, always exceeding the bounds of true belief, finally deserted the authority of the early fathers. Apparently, these men, because of the purity of the air and the sky in which they are born, as a result of which their bodies are lighter and their intellect consequently more agile, customarily abuse the brilliance of their intelligence with many useless commentaries.

Heresies and plagues arose, the territory producing vipers and nettles.[158] These ideas later echoed in remarkable comments about skin-colour transformation involving religious conversion.[159] As Jeffrey Jerome Cohen put it, blackness provided 'the palimpsest for the racialized representation of Islam'. The Saracen occasionally was imagined as a dark-haired, horned, big-nosed and broad-eared monstrosity with alluring sexual appeal in both geographical and literary sources, such as the *Roman de la Rose*, *Aliscans* or *Fierabras*.[160] Vernacular tales such as the romance *King of Tars* (c. 1330) contain narratives about instantaneous skin-colour transformation, by God's grace, following conversion from Islam to Christianity.[161] Similarly, in one of the legends in the encyclopaedic *Cursor mundi* (Runner of the World), written in circa 1300,

---

[157] Gerald of Wales, *De principis instructione: Instruction for a Ruler* i.17, ed. and trans. R. Bartlett (Oxford, 2018), pp. 222–3; Bartlett, *Gerald of Wales*, pp. 166–7.

[158] Guibert of Nogent, *Dei gesta per Francos* i.2, ed. Huygens, pp. 89–90, trans. R. Levine, *The Deeds of God through the Franks: A Translation of Guibert de Nogent's Gesta Dei per Francos* (Rochester, 1997), p. 26: 'Orientalium autem fides cum semper nutabunda constiterit et rerum molitione novarum mutabilis et vagabunda fuerit, semper a regula verae credulitatis exorbitans, ab antiquorum Patrum auctoritate descivit. Ipsi plane homines pro aeris et celi cui innati sunt puritate cum sint leviores corpulentiae et idcirco alacrioris ingenii, multis et inutibilis commentis solent radio suae perspicacitatis abuti.'

[159] Heng, *The Invention of Race*, pp. 181–256.

[160] Cohen, 'On Saracen Enjoyment', pp. 116–20, and Heng, *The Invention of Race*, pp. 181–256.

[161] *The King of Tars*, line 939, in 'The King of Tars: A New Edition', ed. J. H. Chandler (unpublished dissertation, University of Rochester, 2011), p. 87; cf. Hahn, 'The Difference the Middle Ages Makes', pp. 13–15; Friedman, *The Monstrous Races*, pp. 64–5; S. Kinoshita, '"Pagans are wrong and Christians are right": Alterity, Gender,

King David encounters four monstrous Saracens. When David holds out three rods, blessed by Moses, which they kiss, their skin becomes as white as milk, and they are reborn in a completely new religion.[162]

Conclusion

The impact of environmental and humoral theory on constructions of ethnic character is salient. Firstly, Graeco-Arabic ideas about the impress of environmental factors on groups' and individuals' physical and mental features advanced discussions about how virtuous or insidious behaviour was not only the outcome of free will, but also subject to hereditary and external, natural factors. It gave clerics and monks a scientific apparatus to nurture essentializing stereotypes of Jews and Muslims, and also of European peoples, positioning and sorting them within a hierarchy of power and with the voice of authority. Secondly, environmental determinism considered what bound groups to landscapes and regions, enhancing the process of imagining peoples to be dwelling in domesticated spaces. And thirdly, it allowed for the essentialization of representations of civic and social practices as well as of religious difference, notably enhancing a medicalized construction of Jewishness. Representations of groups' environmentally determined natural weakness, cunningness and irrationality, merging with genealogical constructions of (cursed) descent, resonated in the legal structures of inequality affecting, among others, Jews, serfs and women.

Joel Kaye and Cary Nederman observe that the physiological metaphor of the body politic at this time began to prevail over an anatomic vision of the organic society, viewing society as a self-regulatory body whose integrated members made up the various offices and social groups, jointly labouring towards a singular goal.[163] The metaphor, incorporated by John of Salisbury in

---

and Nation in the *Chanson de Roland*, *Journal of Medieval and Early Modern Studies* 31/1 (2001), 79–111 (p. 82).

[162] *Cursor mundi* lines 8119–22, in *Cursor mundi: A Northumbrian Poem of the xivth century in Four Versions / ed. from British Museum MS. Cotton Vespasian A.III, Bodleian MS. Fairfax 14, Göttingen University Library MS. Theol. 107, Trinity College Cambridge MS., R.3.8*, ed. R. Morris, 7 vols. (London, 1874–93), ii, 62; G. Heng, *Empire of Magic: Medieval Romance and the Politics of Cultural Phantasy* (New York, 2003), p. 417. Maternal thoughts about the skin colour of the foetus could also bring about skin change; Van der Lugt, 'La peau noire', pp. 461–9.

[163] J. Kaye, *A History of Balance, 1270–1375: The Emergence of a New Model of Equilibrium* (Cambridge, 2014); C. J. Nederman, 'The Physiological Significance of the Organic Metaphor in John of Salisbury's "Policraticus"', *History of Political Thought* 8/2 (1987), 211–23; C. J. Nederman, 'Body Politics: The Diversification

his mirror for princes, *Policraticus*, reignited an organic biopolitical conceptualization of society. Analogous with the Church, political commentaries might envisage kingdoms and cities as a mystical corpus, regulating professions and offices through royal, urban and guild ordinances.[164] The metaphor of the body politic fell in step with a biopolitical approach to governing communities, for two reasons. Firstly, the metaphor of the body politic allowed officials to imagine the community as an organism that enjoyed health or could become sick. It could be regulated by political regimens, just as the body could be via *regimina sanitatis*, and the household using conduct books, for the quality of governance depended on the condition of the polity's subjects. Thus, from the late thirteenth century, responding to the Latin translation of Aristotle's *Politics* and earlier reworkings of the mirror for princes, *Sirr al-Asrar*, philosophers in Italy and France such as Giles of Rome (c. 1243–1316) and Thomas Aquinas produced new regimens for rulers and urban magistrates, approaching the political community in physiological terms as an organism whose parts together strove toward a shared, common good.[165] The language of the urban ordinances from the late thirteenth century, spearheaded by Italian cities, was concurrently medicalized, governments claiming to work *pro maiori sanitate hominum*.[166] Secondly, humoral categories gave officials the tool to hierarchically classify and measure the position and contribution of groups and individuals within the organic body politic. Coevally, as discussed in chapter 3, law and rhetoric sketched a sacralized landscape where these bodies politic dwelled.

---

of Organic Metaphors in the Later Middle Ages', *Pensiero Politico Medievale* 2 (2004), pp. 59–87; C. J. Nederman, 'The Living Body Politic: The Diversification of Organic Metaphors in Nicole Oresme and Christine de Pizan', in *Healing the Body Politic: The Politic Thought of Christine de Pizan*, ed. K. Green and C. J. Mews (Turnhout, 2005), pp. 19–33; C. J. Nederman, *Community and Consent: The Secular Political Theory of Marsiglio of Padua's* Defensor Pacis (London, 1995); T. Shogimen, 'Treating the Body Politic: The Medical Metaphor of Political Rule in Late Medieval Europe and Tokugawa Japan', *The Review of Politics* 70/1 (2008), 77–104. For early modernity: J. Gil Harris, *Foreign Bodies and the Body Politic: Discourses of Social Pathology in Early Modern England* (Cambridge, 2006).

[164] B. de Munck, *Guilds, Labour and the Urban Body Politic: Fabricating Community in the Southern Netherlands, 1300–1800* (London, 2018); Struve, *Die Entwicklung der Organologischen Staatsauffassung*, p. 107.

[165] Kaye, *History of Balance*.

[166] G. Geltner, 'Healthscaping a Medieval City: Lucca's Curia viarum and the Future of Public Health History', *Urban History* 40/3 (2013), 395–415; G. Geltner, *Roads to Health: Infrastructure and Urban Wellbeing in Later Medieval Italy* (Philadelphia, 2019).

Christian universalism claimed to girdle the whole of humanity. In discussions of social inequality or the origins of nobility, mankind's common descent was evoked. Yet natural law remained relativistic and was interpreted morally, for monks and ecclesiastics contended that a decay of species had occurred, a corruption of health after the fall. It allowed for social inequality to be viewed as the stain of vice, making room for the argument that social, and legal, control sprang from the necessity to curb the alleged bestial nature of those prone to vice, while elevating the virtuous as just masters.[167] Humoral and environmental theory thereby supplemented earlier moral-genealogical divisions of humanity – the outcome of God's wrath – visible in the Earth's sectioning into three regions populated by the descendants of Noah's three sons: Shem, whose progeny populated Asia, cursed Ham, whose descendants lived in Africa, and Japheth, whose children dwelled in Christian Europe or, as Honorius of Autun wrote, made up the nobility.[168] In humoral and environmental theory, however, physiological processes, natural factors and spaces worked in conjunction with descent.

By consequence, the epithets tacked onto the ethnotypes offered the opportunity to strategically, rhetorically position the self and others within a cultural and social narrative of progress. Depending on the environmentally determined reputations attached to the various ethnotypes, the French, German and English aristocracies accentuated their self-proclaimed chivalrous or urbane features, which are discussed in detail in chapter 5. Socio-economically disadvantaged groups were dealt a less fortunate hand and assigned negative traits, considered harder to erase. Representations of regions' features and peoples' work ethic entrenched in environment offered convenient political-rhetorical arguments for legal and territorial colonization and subjugation, in a Ciceronian-Aristotelian tradition.

On a broader level, the earlier Carolingian ideological schema of the translation of knowledge and power surfaced at power bases.[169] The emphasis on

---

[167] Freedman, *Images of the Medieval Peasant*, pp. 69, 75–7; Friedman, *The Monstrous Races*, pp. 92–3.

[168] D. M. Goldenberg, *The Curse of Ham: Race and Slavery in Early Judaism, Christianity, and Islam* (Princeton, 2003); Braude, 'Cham et Noé', pp. 93–125. For serfs' descent from Ham and Cain: Freedman, *Images of the Medieval Peasant*, pp. 86–104.

[169] S. Lusignan, 'L'université de Paris comme composante de l'identité du royaume de France: Étude sur le thème de la *translatio studii*', in *Identité régionale et conscience nationale en France et en Allemagne du Moyen Âge à l'époque moderne: Actes du colloque organisé par l'Université Paris XII – Val de Marne, l'Institut Universitaire de France et l'Institut Historique Allemand à l'Université Paris XII et à la Fondation Singer-Polignac, les 6, 7 et 8 octobre 1993*, ed. R. Babel and J.-M. Moeglin (Sigmaringen, 1997), pp. 59–72 (pp. 59–61).

the salubriousness of territories was the environmental setting for the translation of power and knowledge, wherein the image of '*douce* France' stands out.[170] In 1306, French political philosopher Pierre Dubois (*c.* 1255–after 1321) advised that the French King Philip the Fair's (1268–1314) progeny should be born and raised in Paris in view of its temperate climate, to ensure that the monarch was fit to lead, at a distance, the French army in the hot eastern climes.[171] The ubiquitous regimens of rulership and mirrors of princes produced by university-trained men, advising on the Hippocratic regulation of the health of rulers in their environment, taught how to align the ruler's body with the natural features of the polity it governed. The rhetorical construction of these natural communities was thus forged within a world of learning, in the schools and courts, where the rhetoric of the natural community meshed with military-political efforts to assert power over and expand territory, under the claim of rational strength.

[170] De Planhol and Claval, *A Historical Geography of France*, p. 101.
[171] Pierre Dubois, Appendix to *De recuperatione Terrae Sanctae*, ed. A. Diotti (Florence, 1977), p. 220.

3

Domesticated Spaces, Peoples and Power in Rhetoric

The twelfth-century schools were a hotbed of ethnic stereotyping. It was ignited by students from a diversity of backgrounds organized loosely in student or teacher guilds called *nationes*.[1] From the early stages of the twelfth century, they convened in Paris, Orléans, Chartres, Bologna and Oxford to study the liberal arts, theology, medicine and law.[2] In the multi-ethnic urban environment of higher education, the young men found ethnic categories to be workable material for practising the arts of satire and panegyric. Afterwards, many went on to find employment in lay and church courts, the evolving bureaucratic institutions and chanceries, as well as to work as mendicant preachers. Overall, literacy and communication between groups of various backgrounds increased in this period in urban centres, through trade networks and in warfare against religious others.[3]

In this environment military strategists, court poets and legal theorists, consulting manuals such as Vegetius's *De re militari*, weighed the qualities of the ideal army recruits using environmental theory and advocated a sacrificial death for the *patria*. This had three implications. Firstly, military success and the security of the domesticated space of the *patria*, as well as colonial expansion, rested in the hands of military recruits considered to be naturally endowed with specific manly and rational, physical and mental qualities nurtured by their *patria*'s environment, which according to Daniel of Beccles's manual *Urbanus magnus* was a divine and health-giving place, perfect for those

---

[1] P. Kibre, *The Nations in the Mediaeval Universities* (Cambridge MA, 1948); G. C. Boyce, *The English–German Nation in the University of Paris During the Middle Ages* (Bruges, 1927). Foreign merchants in later guilds in urban communities also were organized in *nationes*: M. Prak, 'Corporate Politics in the Low Countries: Guilds as Institutions, 14th to 18th Centuries', in *Craft Guilds in the Early Modern Low Countries: Work, Power, and Representation*, ed. M. Prak, C. Lis, J. Lucassen and H. Soly (Aldershot, 2006), pp. 74–106.

[2] See Introduction, p.4n.9, for references.

[3] Schmugge, 'Über "nationale" Vorurteile im Mittelalter', pp. 439–59.

who tilled the land.[4] The classification of qualities of strength and rationality by extension justified legal and social inequalities pertaining to property and labour. Secondly, the rhetorical emphasis on such natural characteristics helped military commanders to galvanize their fighters, holding up to them the prize for which they exclusively, honourably fought for the common cause and good of their semi-sacred community. Thirdly, listing the environmentally determined traits of army recruits in the Christian army in epic verse and historiographies meant that poets distinguished explicitly between ethnicities within the *imperium christianum*.

In order to see how this worked, the second part of this book examines how ethnic images slipped into the sphere of social conflict and warfare, in social and physical discord where stereotypes were consciously used to fire up emotions. This chapter will first explore how intellectuals rhetorically reshaped ideas about territory and *patria* in the legal sphere and military manuals, before moving on to the question of how rhetoric stimulated poets imagining peoples and territories, painting mental pictures with common, proverbial images drawn from the wider cultural sphere. Finally, this chapter discusses the political framework where poets configured ethnic stereotypes with reference to Rome, cataloguing regions' own distinct features and products, resisting the acquisitive centrifugal power of the hegemonic Church.

Legal spheres of territory and ethnicity

The framework defining the status of denizens only slowly began to change around 1200, when a shift occurred from a focus on personality of law, according to which a person falls under the law of his forebears, to territory as a legal category of jurisdiction. Historians have argued that rulers at this time tightened their grip on legal procedures in France and England, and strategically positioned themselves, prevailing over territories rather than peoples. Dynastic rulership claimed that it exercised power more over space, a process that was reflected in the adoption of territorialized denominations in royal charters and deeds.[5] Thus, while in eighth-century Germanic territories 'The-

---

[4] Daniel of Beccles, *The Book of the Civilised Man: An English Translation of the Urbanus magnus of Daniel of Beccles* lines 229–30, trans. F. Whelan, O. Spenser and F. Petrizzo (London, 2020).

[5] B. Schneidmüller, *Nomen patriae: Die Entstehung Frankreichs in der politisch-geographischen Terminologie (10.–13. Jahrhundert)* (Sigmaringen, 1987); R. Schieffer, 'Frankreich im Mittelalter', in *Mittelalterliche nationes – neuzeitliche Nationen: Probleme der Nationenbildung in Europa*, ed. A. Bues and R. Rexheuser (Wiesbaden, 1995), pp. 43–60. For early *regna* and ethnic names, see E. Ewig, 'Volkstum und Volksbewußtsein im Frankenreich des 7. Jahrhunderts: Civitas, pagus, Ducatus and

odiscus' designated the Germanic language, from the mid-eleventh century the classical epithet 'Teutonicus' pertained to the peoples inhabiting German territories, and in the twelfth century 'Teutonia' was introduced to denominate territorial space.[6] Before the crusades, Francia designated either the territory north of the Loire or the historical, Carolingian empire. At the beginning of the thirteenth century, Francia came to denote the kingdom nominally governed by the French ruler. King Philip II (1165–1223) dubbed himself *rex Franciae* after the conquest of Normandy's Rouen in 1204. Anglia at this time, however, referred either to the geographical territory of England or the British Isles, for Anglia and Britannia were often muddled.[7] Yet, despite the changing terminology, a national public sphere did not structurally determine the rights and privileges of free denizens. Circa 1300, liberties and privileges within Christendom were mostly defined not by territory, but by economic status, birth and gender. This extended to Jews and serfs, religious and social groups set apart in legislation and status and in genealogical constructs.

---

natio', in *Spätantikes und fränkisches Gallien: gesammelte Schriften (1952–1973)*, ed. E. Ewig and H. Atsma, 2 vols. (Munich, 1976–79), i, 231–73; Davies, 'The Peoples of Britain and Ireland 1100–1400. II Names, Boundaries and Regnal Solidarities', pp. 2–5.

[6] B. Schneidmüller, 'Reich – Volk – Nation: Die Entstehung des deutschen Reiches und der deutschen Nation im Mittelalter', in *Mittelalterliche nationes – neuzeitliche Nationen: Probleme der Nationenbildung in Europa*, ed. A. Bues and R. Rexheuser (Wiesbaden, 1995), pp. 73–102; P. Monnet, 'La "patria" médiévale vue d'Allemagne, entre construction impériale et identités régionales', *Le Moyen Âge* 107 (2001), 71–99; F. Vigener, *Bezeichnungen für Volk und Land der Deutschen vom 10. bis zum 13. Jahrhundert* (Darmstadt, 1976), pp. 48–102; H. Thomas, 'Sur l'histoire du mot "Deutsch" depuis le milieu du XIIe siècle jusqu'à la fin du XIIIe siècle', in *Identité régionale et conscience nationale en France et en Allemagne du Moyen Âge à l'époque modern: Actes du colloque organisé par l'Université Paris XII – Val de Marne, l'Institut Universitaire de France et l'Institut Historique Allemand à l'Université Paris XII et à la Fondation Singer-Polignac, les 6, 7 et 8 octobre 1993*, ed. R. Babel and J.-M. Moeglin (Sigmaringen, 1997), pp. 27–35; H. Thomas, 'Die Deutschen und die Rezeption ihres Volksnamens', in *Nord und Süd in der deutschen Geschichte des Mittelalters* Akten des Kolloquiums veranstaltet zu Ehren von Karl Jordan, 1907–1984, Kiel, 15.–16. Mai 1987, ed. W. Paravicini (Sigmaringen, 1990), pp. 19–50; H. Thomas, 'Das Identitätsproblem der Deutschen im Mittelalter', *Geschichte in Wissenschaft und Unterricht* 43 (1992), 135–56 (pp. 138–9); J. Ehlers, *Die Entstehung des deutschen Reiches* (Munich, 1994).

[7] Thomas, *The English and the Normans*; S. Reynolds, 'What Do We Mean by "Anglo-Saxon" and "Anglo-Saxons"', *Journal of British Studies* 24 (1985), 395–414 (p. 398). A. MacColl, 'The Meaning of "Britain" in Medieval and Early Modern England', *Journal of British Studies* 45 (2006), 248–69.

Yet ethnicity was not irrelevant in the political, administrative and cultural sphere of European courts. As Robert Bartlett observed, in the early thirteenth century the English king implemented a 'policy of deliberate racial exclusion', ordering the justiciar of Ireland to exclusively promote Englishmen to Irish bishoprics.[8] Local magnates in England called for the expulsion of Poitevins as political advisors to King Henry III (1207–72) of England on the basis of their foreign status.[9] However, the context was one of loyalty rather than legal status, that reverberated in the military sphere. The popularity of manuals such as Vegetius's *De re militari*, consulted in the crusade wars, thereby enkindled the glorification of a sacrificial, heroic, meaningful death for the heavenly and worldly *patria*, accentuating the emotional ties to territory.

Legal theorists, military strategists and poets making the emotive case for the *patria* took its meaning beyond the sense of region of birth (*patria nativitatis*). In the epic verse *Philippide*, William le Breton (*c.* 1165–1226), chaplain to the French King Philip II, evoked the good of the political community whose defence was the focus of warfare, substituting Vegetius's *res publica* with the French kingdom.[10] Such claims transformed the landscape into a domesticated, sacralized space, fantasizing the *regnum* to represent the mystical body of Christ and transposing the heavenly *patria aeterna* onto sweet and temperate worldly plots of land dotted with churches and the relics of saints.[11] The glorifying rhetoric was particularly evocative in the circles of the Frankish aristocracy waging war in Palestine, but also served to embolden the martyrs of the religious *communis patria* spiritually battling Christ's enemy at home, in the monasteries and in the self. At court, both Frankish and Teutonic notaries alluded to a sacred territory at the end of the 1150s. Upon appointing Victor IV (1095–1164) as pope instead of Alexander III (1100/5–81) in 1160, the German Emperor Frederick Barbarossa of the *sacrum imperium* evocatively turned towards the memory of Saint Charlemagne by organizing his canonization in 1165.[12] The Benedictine monk and hagiographer Lawrence

---

[8] Bartlett, *The Making of Europe*, p. 225.

[9] Kim, *Aliens in Medieval Law*, pp. 5, 16, 41, 128. M. T. Clanchy, *England and its Rulers, 1066–1272: Foreign Lordship and National Identity* (Oxford 1983), pp. 241–4.

[10] William le Breton, *Philippide* v lines 408–10, in *Œuvres de Rigord et de Guillaume le Breton*, ed. H.-F. Delaborde, 2 vols. (Paris, 1882–85), ii, 140–1; Allmand, *The De Re Militari of Vegetius*, pp. 92–6; Hirschi, *The Origins of Nationalism*, p. 64.

[11] J. Riley-Smith, 'Crusading as an Act of Love', *History* 65 (1980), 177–92 for the rhetoric of love for Christ and brotherly love used to encourage the laity to take the cross. Eichenberger, *Patria*, p. 58; Kantorowicz, *The King's Two Bodies*, p. 241.

[12] K. Görich comments that the political implications of the canonization and the use of the term *sacrum imperium* should not be overstated. Frederick Barbarossa

of Durham (c. 1110–54), whose monastic house owned a copy of Vegetius's manual, lamenting how the city was ravaged by pillaging soldiers in his Latin 'Dialogues', illustrates the sentiment of loss and sacrifice succinctly, wherein public and private interests and the sacred and secular merge: 'Your tears for England's grief – that public loss / Should generate your private woe – I praise. / For reason tells us all to love our land. / No better love exists than for our land. / Sweet love of country fills the pious heart.'[13] Courtiers and monks fostered the emotive process of imagining a *patria* by employing a symbolic imagery of kingship, enforcing the dynastic fantasy of entitlement to territory symbolized in the motif of brothers-in-arms.[14]

The concept of dying for the *patria* was articulated in legal commentaries as well. In the *Glossa ordinaria*, written in about 1228, the Italian jurist Accursius (1185–1263) included comments that obedience to the fatherland, like to parents, was a principle of the Roman *ius gentium* unbeknown to *brutish* animals, and dying for the *dulcissima patria*, the sweetest fatherland, a glorious

---

generally continued to call his empire a *Romanum imperium*; K. Görich, *Friedrich Barbarossa: Eine Biographie* (Munich, 2011), pp. 633–6.

[13] Lawrence of Durham's twelfth-century *Dialogi* i lines 77–81, in *Dialogi Laurentii Dunelmensis Monachi ac Prioris*, ed. J. Raine, Surtees Society 70 (Durham, 1880), p. 3, trans. A. G. Rigg, 'Lawrence of Durham: Dialogues and Easter Poem: A Verse Translation', *The Journal of Medieval Latin* 7 (1997), 42–126 (p. 47): 'Quod patriae fles damna tuae, quod publica fletum / Mors tibi privatum suggerit, ipse probo. / Dictat enim ratio patriae pietate teneri; / Et quis amor patriae major amore subit? Dulcis amor patriae pia pectora dulcius implet.'

[14] Hirschi, *The Origins of Nationalism*, pp. 51–71. In Germany, *patria* referred to the stem duchies; Eichenberger, *Patria*, pp. 25–81. De Planhol and Claval, *A Historical Geography of France*, p. 105. Koht, 'Dawn of Nationalism', p. 266, discusses Abbot Suger's designation of King Louis VI as 'pater patriae', but I have not been able to trace the reference in his *Vita Ludovici*. Cf. J. duQuesnay Adams, 'The Patriotism of Abbot Suger', *Proceedings of the Annual Meeting of the Western Society for French History* 16 (1988), 19–29. G. Dupont-Ferrier, 'Le sens des mots "patria" et "patrie" en France au Moyen Age et jusqu'au début du XVIIe siècle', *Revue historique* 188 (1940), 89–104; J. Ehlers, 'Elemente mittelalterlicher Nationsbildung in Frankreich (10.–13. Jahrhundert)', *Historische Zeitschrift* 231/3 (1980), 565–87 for growing loyalty to the French monarchy in the course of the twelfth century. Cf. Guenée, *States and Rulers*, p. 54. Southern, *Medieval Humanism and Other Studies*, pp. 135–57, argues that attitudes in England developed in opposition to the crown. Many of the sources quoted by Southern comment upon environment and natural resources. H. Koht, 'A Specific Sense of the Word *patria* in Norse and Norman Latin', *Archivum Latinitas Medii Aevi* 2 (1925), 93–6; Kantorowicz, *The King's Two Bodies*, pp. 232–72.

deed.¹⁵ Caspar Hirschi and Gaines Post showed that the legal commentators Johannes Teutonicus Zemeke, who died in 1245, and Odofredus, a law professor at Bologna who died in 1265, commented that the task to defend the *patria* had priority over the duty to defend a lord.¹⁶ By the mid-1200s, taxes were imposed for the defence of the *patria*. The virtue of *caritas* was interpreted politically: love for the fatherland was rooted in charity and put the programme of the common good above private interests, where fighting for France as the true, *verus Israel* was compared to fighting for the Holy Land.¹⁷ Thus, propagating loyalty towards the *patria*, and from the thirteenth century enhancing the Aristotelian programme of the common good, helped members in networks of power to bond over domesticated spaces as well as through genealogy.

Care should be taken, however, not to equate the utterances of the intellectual elite with 'the populace', nor to consider widespread identification of the population with these ideas as a prerequisite for the relevance of nationhood. They are not evidence of a widespread national sentiment, as historians occasionally argued.¹⁸ Advocating loyalty to the *patria* was in first instance a military exercise of the elite targeting men who took up arms. The classification of their physical and mental qualities – ideally strong, rational warriors – helped to fire up loyalty on the battlefield and inspire fear in the enemy, for instance by shouting out ethnic stereotypes of martial qualities in the battle cry, as Vegetius had advised military commanders to do. Ethnic stereotypes thereby carried persuasive force, which stretched to literary representations as well, employed in poetry tailored to crush the enemy. Thus, new manuals of rhetoric encouraged students to use ethnotypes as tokens of persuasion in the context of literary description, diplomatic letter writing and satire.

Besides military exhortations to protect the *patria* and the common good, historians and philosophers took ideas from the works of Marcus Tullius Cicero (106–43 BC) to reflect on the nature of political and social relations. Taking a progressive view of the development of societies, Cicero's *De officiis* and *De inventione*, both widely available in this period, stated that reason and speech held society together and were the prerequisites for public order and the rule

---

[15] Accursius, *Glossa ordinaria* to *Institutiones* 1.2.1; 1.25 and to *Digesta*, 1.1.2, ed. D. Godefroy (Lyon, 1627); Post, 'Two Notes on Nationalism in the Middle Ages', p. 286.
[16] Hirschi, *The Origins of Nationalism*, p. 71; Post, 'Two Notes on Nationalism in the Middle Ages', pp. 288–91 for source references.
[17] Kantorowicz, *The King's Two Bodies*, p. 247.
[18] See the Introduction, pp. 10–1, for references.

of law.[19] Primordial man, conversely, lived erratically, without rationality, law or religion. Primordial society transformed into social existence through urbanization and the acquirement of professional skills. This transformation came from mankind's natural ability for speech and reason, setting it apart from beasts.[20] Speech should be neither effeminate nor coarse. It allowed mortal beings to claim property under the law, by uttering the words '*hoc est meum*' in an act of speech. Through communication and the use of reason came voluntary associations, and 'without the association of men, cities could not have been built or peopled. In consequence of city life, law and customs were established, and then came the equitable distribution of private rights and a definite social system.'[21] The attendant emphasis on the use of reason by humans set them apart from animals; the latter, subjected to humans, being unable to distinguish right from wrong, to make moral choices, hence in scholastic thought were denied the eternal life in the heavenly kingdom.[22] Accordingly, whereas peoples were subject to and protected in various degrees by the *ius gentium*, animals, lacking reason, fell under natural law. Twelfth-century English court historians, ethnographers and poets, discussed in chapter 5, picked up on this evolutionary view of social organization and utilized it to describe societies under colonization as lacking law, reason and religion, while praising the urbanity, good speech and free status of the Anglo-Normans.

Representations of the development of society, the capacity to reason and make moral choices thereby served rhetorically to organize the governance of labour and property ownership. In the second half of the thirteenth century, political philosophers like John of Paris in *De potestate regia et papali* debated the necessity of government to pursue common tasks and goals that individuals after the original sin naturally failed to pursue. After the fall of mankind, mortal beings acquired private property through their own labour – to be distinguished from the energy and strength spent by beasts without property rights – but now, conflicts over property needed to be adjudicated by rulers in

---

[19] For the influence of Ciceronian learning on court ideals and ethics: C. S. Jaeger, *The Origins of Courtliness: Civilizing Trends and the Formation of Courtly Ideals, 939–1210* (Philadelphia, 1985); C. S. Jaeger, *The Envy of Angels: Cathedral Schools and Social Ideals in Medieval Europe, 950–1200* (Philadelphia, 1994).

[20] Nederman, 'Nature, Sin and the Origins of Society', pp. 5–9.

[21] Cicero, *De Officiis* ii.4, ed. and trans. W. Miller, Loeb Classical Library 30 (Cambridge Mass., 1928), p. 183: 'Urbes vero sine hominum coetu non potuissent nec aedificari nec frequentari; ex quo leges moresque constituti, tum iuris aequa discriptio certaque vivendi disciplina.' V. Cox and J. O. Ward, *The Rhetoric of Cicero in its Medieval and Early Renaissance Commentary Tradition* (Leiden, 2006).

[22] Minnis, *From Eden to Eternity*, pp. 91–3.

an organized society, for instance through petitioning.[23] The secular powers, John of Paris argued, that protected the common good were diverse because of climate and the physical traits of men.[24]

Imagining territories and ethnotypes in rhetoric

Topical catalogues classifying group characteristics and the world's riches surface in twelfth-century school texts, poetry and letters. The catalogues, like the lists compiled in monasteries discussed in chapter 1, still might migrate from east to west, representing the *translatio*, the passage of time and space from the creation to the apocalypse. The *ekphrasis* (a textual representation of a work of art) in the widely copied epic *Alexandreis* of Walter of Châtillon from the last quarter of the twelfth century thus represents a T-O map inscribed on the tomb of Darius III, in the tradition of Daniel's prophesy of the four empires.[25] Yet many of the images contained in it are proverbial: 'France is famed for its knights, Campania for its wines, the Britons for King Arthur, Normandy for its customary arrogance, England for its flattery, Liguria for its usury and the Germans for their fury.'[26] Some of these stereotypes, such as the affect of German fury, are drawn from classical poetry applying environmental theory. Yet many are fresh, such as Italian moneylending or the British belief in the mythical return of King Arthur, called 'Breton Hope' (discussed further in

---

[23] Nederman, 'Nature, Sin and the Origins of Society', pp. 15–19; Coleman, 'Medieval Discussions of Property', pp. 210–17; Minnis, *From Eden to Eternity*, p. 120.

[24] John of Paris, *De potestate regia et papali* 3, ed. F. Bleienstein (Stuttgart, 1969), pp. 81–2.

[25] *The Alexandreis of Walter of Châtillon: A Twelfth-Century Epic*, trans. D. Townsend (Philadelphia, 1996), p. 203. The poem, of which more than 200 manuscripts survived, is dedicated to William of the White Hands, the archbishop of Reims between 1176 and 1202; R. T. Pritchard, 'Introduction', in Walter of Châtillon, *The Alexandreis*, trans. R. T. Pritchard (Toronto, 1986), pp. 4–5, 7; M. K. Lafferty, *Walter of Châtillon's Alexandreis: Epic and the Problem of Historical Understanding* (Turnhout, 1998), pp. 10–11. For pictoral *mappae mundi* in manuscripts containing the *Alexandreis*, M. Destombes, 'The Mappamundi of the Poem "Alexandreidos" by Gautier de Châtillon (ca. A.D. 1180)', *Imago Mundi* 19 (1965), 10–12; M. K. Lafferty, 'Mapping Human Limitations: The Tomb Ecphrases in Walter of Châtillon's Alexandreis', *The Journal of Medieval Latin* 4/4 (1994), 64–81.

[26] Walter of Châtillon, *Alexandreis*, ed. M. L. Colker (Padua, 1978), p. 191: '[F]rancia militibus, celebri Campania Bacho, / Arthuro Britones, solito Normannia fastu / Anglia blanditur, Ligures amor urit habendi, / Teutonicusque suum retinet de more furorem.'

chapter 4).²⁷ The same goes for the self-acclaim, in step with Vegetian military ideals but on occasion counter-attacked as arrogance, that the French now embodied the epitome of learning and chivalry that is prevalent in texts ranging from encyclopaedias to *chansons de geste*. A similar topicality is discernible in adaptations of the monastic lists such as 'Invidia Iudeorum', which now catalogue the *luxuria* of the people of Gascony and the bluntness of the Bavarians, produced at the Cistercian monastery of Sawley.²⁸

New manuals of rhetoric produced at the twelfth-century schools invigorated the topicality of these ethnotypes. Towards the end of the twelfth century, several textbooks on grammar, poetry and rhetoric became standard texts in urban school curricula, including the *Doctrinale puerorum* (Teaching Manual for Children) of Alexander of Villedieu (1160/70–1240/50), produced in 1199, and the *Graecismus* of Évrard (or Eberhard) of Béthune, a grammar textbook produced in circa 1212. For the slightly more advanced students of poetry, the *Art of Versification* (early 1170s) of Matthew of Vendôme and the *Art of Versification* (late twelfth century) of the poet Gervase of Melkley (*fl.* 1200–19) set the standard. These taught how to stereotype, to create images in the mind. The manuals encouraged the use of credible, commonplace, proverbial images – inspiring poets like Walter of Châtillon, educated in Paris, to use *dits* or sayings collected in vernacular repositories in descriptions. Also, the rhetorical works of Quintilian (*c.* 35–*c.* 100), Horace (65 BC–8 AD) and Cicero, in the preceding centuries accessed mainly via *florilegia*, in the twelfth century became objects of comprehensive study.

The manuals became a keystone of the production of poetry, and also of administrative letter writing. With the expansion of government institutions,

---

[27] E. Dümmler, 'Über den furor Teutonicus', *Sitzungsberichte der Preussischen Akademie der Wissenschaften zu Berlin* 9 (1897), 112–26. For the Breton Hope, S. Echard, *Arthurian Narrative in the Latin Tradition* (Cambridge, 1998), pp. 68–106; R. Morris, 'King Arthur and the Growth of French Nationalism', in *France and the British Isles in the Middle Ages and Renaissance: Essays by Members of Girton College, Cambridge, in Memory of Ruth Morgan*, ed. G. Jondorf and D. N. Dumville (Woodbridge, 1991), pp. 115–29; M. L. Day, 'The Letter from King Arthur to Henry II: Political Use of the Arthurian Legend in *Draco Normannicus*', in *The Spirit of the Court: Selected Proceedings of the Fourth Congress of the International Courtly Literature Society (Toronto 1983)*, ed. G. S. Burgess, R. A. Taylor and A. Deyermond (Cambridge, 1985), pp. 153–7.

[28] Cambridge, Corpus Christi College, MS 139 fol. 166v. (see Appendix, II). In the list 'Sapientia Grecorum' dating to the fourteenth century, the French are courteous, the English generous and the Tuscans avaricious (see Appendix, VIII). Walther, 'Scherz', no. 91. For two Irish versions of such lists: P. Wadden, '"The Beauty and Lust of the Gaels": National Characteristics and Medieval Gaelic Learned Culture', *North American Journal of Celtic Studies* 2/2 (2018), 85–104.

notaries wielded the rules of rhetoric in letter writing laid down in manuals of *ars dictandi*.[29] The *Palma* (*c.* 1198) and *Ancient Rhetoric* (1215) produced by Boncompagno da Signa (1170–1240) at Bologna, the centre of legal studies, fed future public officials in secular and papal government with a stockpile of ethnic schematizations to be exploited in diplomacy and the politics of communication, in conjunction with the typologies learned in basic medicine discussed in the previous chapter. Boncompagno himself was well versed in medical theory and produced a sharp description of old age.[30]

Rhetoricians continued to present ethnic characteristics by summing them up in lists, reflecting ethnic heterogeneity within the overarching reference framework of the Christian community of the Roman Church. But the textbooks took new paths, drawing self-referential boundaries by claiming that peoples, their traits and the territory they inhabited were synonymous. Rhetoricians defined the coalescent boundaries of territory and people in the metonymic figure of speech known as the *continens pro contento*, wherein one word is substituted for another on the grounds of a close connection. In several manuals, this form of metonymy is explained by stating that a territory – the container – is replete with an ethnic group – the contained – and that ethnic character and social practices are the alleged essence or stuff that fills a territory's people. In his *Parisiana poetria* (*c.* 1240), the lecturer John of Garland (*c.* 1195–*c.* 1258), who in 1229 went on from Paris to teach at the university of Toulouse, explains that metonymy is at work when 'the instrument is put for the act or the wielder, or the material for the thing made of the material, or the inventor for the invention'.[31] A thirteenth-century versified manual of rhetoric originating from the Cistercian nunnery of Clairmarais, preserved at St Omer, exemplifies the relationship between the student population and France – the territories north of the Loire – now famed as the new seat of learning because of the *translatio studii*, in its example of the container and the contained: 'Flanders flowers with delights, France with teaching; / Flanders stands for the Flemish, France for the French.'[32] The domesticated space, the people dwelling

---

[29] M. Camargo, 'Rhetoric', in *The Seven Liberal Arts in the Middle Ages*, ed. D. L. Wagner (Bloomington, 1983), pp. 96–124 (p. 100); Martin, 'Classicism and Style', p. 538.

[30] Boncompagno da Signa, *Amicitia and De Malo Senectutis Et Senii*, ed. and trans. M. D. Dunne (Leuven, 2012).

[31] *The Parisiana Poetria of John of Garland*, vi lines 281–8, ed. and trans. T. Lawler, Yale Studies in English 182 (New Haven, 1974), pp. 126–7: 'quando instrumentum ponitur pro actu vel pro domino, vel materia pro materiato, vel inventor pro invento'.

[32] Printed in J. B. Hauréau, *Notices et extraits des manuscrits de la Bibliothèque Nationale* 31 (1884), i, 106, no. 40 (Saint-Omer, Bibliothèque municipale MS 115 fol. 53v.): 'Hic ponitur continens pro contento, hoc modo: Flandria deliciis, doctrinis Gallia floret; / Flandria designat Flandrenses, Gallia Gallos.' Walther, 'Scherz' no. 52. For

in it and its essentialized trait are thus glued together. The same rhetorical figure is found in one of the most popular of contemporary treatises on the arts of poetry, the *New Poetry* written circa 1208/13 by grammarian Geoffrey of Vinsauf, who was educated in Paris. His manual, of which several hundred copies survive, was dedicated to Pope Innocent III. Invoking metonymy, he advises: 'Use the container for the contained, aptly employing either a noun or an adjective. Apply the noun thus: / Tippling England; weaving Flanders; boastful Normandy. / Thus use the adjective: / The noisy forum; the silent cloister; the doleful prison; the happy house; the quiet night; the busy day.'[33] In another of Geoffrey of Vinsauf's didactical works, the prose treatise *Instruction on the Manner and Art of Writing Letters and Poetry*, into which he recast his *New Poetry*, the English are refashioned as intelligent rather than drunks, and the French as effeminate, an ethnocentric adaptation possibly to accommodate an English audience practising the bureaucratic art of letter writing.[34] A direct application of this advice is found in an early thirteenth-century manuscript of poetry alongside Geoffrey of Vinsauf's *Instruction*. It includes a poem in praise of the English King Henry II in the context of the rebellion against the king in 1173–74. Recounting the king's adversaries' professional activities and their military qualities, the poet lists the knights of France, the weavers of Flanders (who hence lack warrior strength) and the spears of the ragged Scots, tokens of their perceived barbarity. Thus, the manuals of rhetoric helped to classify military adversaries and their qualities, taking an essentialized perspective in court literature.[35]

---

other references to the wealth of Flanders: Walther, 'Scherz', no. 166B, line 23 and no. 171, line 5. For France as the new seat of learning, Lusignan, 'L'Université de Paris', pp. 59–72 and Chapter 5, pp. 195–6.

[33] Geoffrey of Vinsauf, *Poetria nova* lines 1006–17 in *The Poetria Nova and its Sources in Early Rhetorical Doctrine*, ed. and trans. by Ernest Gallo (The Hague, 1971), pp. 67–9: 'Rem vice contenti quae continet accipe, ponens / Verbum, vel fixum, vel mobile quodlibet, apte. / Insere sic fixum: *Potatrix Angia; Textrix / Flandria; Jactatrix Normannia*. Mobile nomen / Sic appone: *Fora clamosa; Silentia claustra; / Luctisonus carcer; Domus exhilarate; Quieta / Nox; Operosa dies*.' For the dissemination of Geoffrey of Vinsauf's work: M. C. Woods (ed.), *An Early Commentary on the* Poetria Nova *of Geoffrey of Vinsauf* (New York, 1985), p. xv; J. F. Huntsman, 'Grammar', *The Seven Liberal Arts in the Middle Ages*, ed. D. L. Wagner (Bloomington, 1983), pp. 58–95 (p. 75); E. Gallo, 'The *Poetria nova* of Geoffrey of Vinsauf', in *Medieval Eloquence: Studies in the Theory and Practice of Medieval Rhetoric*, ed. J. J. Murphy (Berkeley, 1978), pp. 68–84 (p. 68).

[34] Geoffrey of Vinsauf, *Documentum de modo et arte dictandi et versificandi* ii.iii.38, ed. E. Faral (reprint Paris, 1962), p. 291. Stanzel, 'Das Nationalitätenschema', pp. 85–6.

[35] B. Harbert (ed.), *A Thirteenth-Century Anthology of Rhetorical Poems: Glasgow ms Hunterian V.8.14*, no. 11–13 (Toronto, 1975), pp. 18–20.

Painting mental pictures

As a pedagogical tool, twelfth-century textbooks of rhetoric focused on the lifeworld of the students – Geoffrey of Vinsauf's *Instruction* lists the features of the centres of learning of Salerno, Paris, Bologna and Orléans. The manuals give vivacious examples of images that would have struck a chord in the student's mind. Yet the craft of rhetoric tapped a social culture that was more expansive than the Latinate learning of a distinct elite, for it also drew from vernacular, urban sources and troubadour literature associating towns and regions with their natural resources.[36] The Arras poet Jean Bodel's (*c.* 1165–*c.* 1210) and the trouvère Rutebeuf's lively *dits* spring to mind, since they contain a repertoire of lists of goods sold at town markets, enumerating the world's diversity and plenitude.[37] The urban atmosphere of the centres of learning producing these rhetorical texts partly explains this overlap in cultural and social lifeworlds. In later centuries, *rederijkerskamers* in the Low Countries practising rhetoric similarly produced competitive lists of urban traits.[38] Pupils learning foreign languages learned such lists off by heart, to aid them in their future careers as traders. For instance, lists of wares and resources, rulers and territories are found in the Bruges *Livre des mestiers*, teaching urban merchants how to communicate.[39]

Yet the use of ethnic tropes also sprang forth from a desire to produce *convincing* literary images, whose effectiveness hinged on topicality. This had to do with the tradition from which the discipline of rhetoric sprang. In classical times the art of rhetoric was applied above all in the judicial, the political-deliberative or epideictic (rhetoric to praise or blame, for example in ceremonies) sphere. Descriptions of place such as the *locus amoenus* balanced

---

[36] Especially in England, panegyric overviews of regions, small and large, their commodities, natural resources and praiseworthy characteristics was a popular genre. For example, Henry of Huntingdon, archdeacon of Lincoln, inserted an excerpt of a poem into the first book of his twelfth-century *Historia Anglorum: The History of the English People* i.6, ed. and trans. D. Greenway (Oxford, 1996), pp. 20–1, allegedly drawn from a poem in hexameters in praise of Britain, listing the ships of London, the wine of Winchester, the flocks of Hereford, the fruits of Worcester et cetera.

[37] L. M. Paterson, *The World of the Troubadours: Medieval Occitan Society, c. 1100–c. 1300* (Cambridge, 1993), pp. 5, 17–35.

[38] A.-L. Van Bruaene, 'De stad als scheldwoord: De *Baladen van Doornijcke* (1521/1522) van Matthijs de Castelein en de stedelijke literaire praktijk van de rederijkers', *Spiegel der Letteren* 48 (2006), 135–47.

[39] J. Gessler (ed.), *Het Brugsche* Livre des mestiers *en zijn navolgelingen: Vier aloude conversatieboekjes om Fransch te leeren* (Bruges, 1931).

on classical, judicial *argumenta a loco* and on rules of invention for epideictic oratory.[40] Originally embedded in the lifeworld of politics and the legal courts, the imagery by necessity needed to reflect accepted commonplaces in order to be cogent.

In the twelfth century, the art of rhetoric had been stretched to function in various other social settings as well. Beyond administering the precepts of description to judicial or oratorical writing, description became an independent form of poetry, used to praise in panegyrics or to blame in debating or so-called *Streitgedichte* and satire.[41] Handbooks of rhetoric thereby effectively instructed how to stereotype: to identify and describe persons and things according to type, enhancing them with *maneries*.[42] For to 'invent' poetry, as it was said, meant to 'find' relevant images with which to describe, the ultimate goal being moral edification in search of truth. Stereotypes in this context served as useful tropes for moral interpretation and classification.

Such stereotyping followed normative schematizations and stretched to registers of speech. In the new textbooks of composition, the three classical styles of speech – *humilis, mediocris* and *grandiloquus* – reflected a classification of the social order.[43] In the *Parisiana poetria*, John of Garland sets out that the grandiloquent style is befitting to the *miles dominans* (the dominant fighter), courtiers (*curiales*) and citizens (*civiles*); the mediocre style to the *agricola* (the peasant); and the humble style to the *pastor otiosus* (the idle shepherd). He embellishes these three styles with literary examples from military, agricultural and pastoral life, with their appropriate attributes such as the sword, the plough and the shepherd's staff, and suitable locations such as the fortress, field or pasture. Other classifications included aesthetic dichotomies, teaching

[40] J. K. Hyde, 'Medieval Descriptions of Cities', *Bulletin of the John Rylands Library* 48 (1965/1966), 308–40; C. J. Classen, *Die Stadt im Spiegel der Descriptiones und Laudes urbium in der antiken und mittelalterlichen Literatur bis zum Ende des zwölften Jahrhunderts* (Hildesheim, 1980). D. Thoss, *Studien zum locus amoenus im Mittelalter* (Vienna, 1972).

[41] E. R. Curtius, *European Literature and the Latin Middle Ages*, trans. W. R. Trask (New York, 1963), pp. 193–4.

[42] D. Kelly, *The Arts of Poetry and Prose* (Turnhout, 1991), p. 72. For the relation between typology and allegory: W. Ginsberg, *The Cast of Character: The Representation of Personality in Ancient and Medieval Literature* (Toronto, 1983), pp. 78–9, who argues that exemplary figures are increasingly personified in medieval literature, emphasizing the universal over the particular, 'losing sight of individuals in order to consider the moral and psychological categories to which they belonged'.

[43] L. Arbusow, *Colores rhetorici: Eine Auswahl rhetorischer Figuren und Gemeinplätze als Hilfsmittel für akademische Übungen an mittelalterlichen Texten*, ed. H. Peter (Göttingen, 1963), p. 27. The system was known as the *rota Vergilii*.

how to depict the ugly (using descriptions of the 'morally inferior' Ethiopian) and the beautiful, personified by 'elegant' nobles.[44]

In the process, rhetorical textbooks laid out a rather elaborate framework for success in producing convincing compositions, engaging ideas about the relationship between images, language and memory. To successfully invent and describe, a writer should employ images that somehow reverberated in his listener's mind. The trick was to find the right words or linguistic signifiers to create mental images of some thing's or body's essence, achievable by recalling or remembering the supposed essence of things. To this end, the poet could employ ornaments – 'elaborate punning riffs of memory' – that played a pivotal role in catching the reader's attention and orientating cognitive processes.[45] Figures of speech such as metonymy, especially those using unlikely similarities, could by this means arouse emotions in the mind (the technique of *pathos*), rendering them all the more persuasive. Yet, to be meaningful, rhetorical ornaments had to be in tune with the images in memory (known as *loci*, commonplaces) – the images that formed a prerequisite for memory itself to function, otherwise rendering the rhetorical ornaments empty signifiers. The more playful and surprising the images were, the more likely they would stick in a person's mind.[46] In that respect, word (linguistic signifier) and image were considered on equal footing – the pictorial *mappae mundi* served the same function as verbal maps, as did Walter of Châtillon's verbal *ekphrasis* of the imaginary visual world map on Darius's tomb.

The description that the images produced was meant 'to reveal the essential characteristics, the properties of the subject'.[47] In order for description to be meaningful, the rhetorician had tools for placing a person or group in the appropriate scheme of things, in the form of befitting ornaments or attributes, including ethnic characterizations. It is clearly laid out in Matthew of Vendôme's *Art of Versification*, designed in the early 1170s as a schoolbook and introduction to writing poetry. For Matthew, the main purpose of poetry was description, and that meant uncloaking the essential characteristics of the subject – a person, thing or group – and placing it within its appropriate topical milieu by applying proverbial epithets summing up a person's or thing's

---

[44] John of Garland, *Rota Vergiliana*, in *Les arts poétiques du XIIe et du XIIIe siècle: Recherches et documents sur la technique littéraire du Moyen Âge*, ed. E. Faral (reprint Paris, 1962), p. 87. Arbusow, *Colores rhetorici*, pp. 15–16.

[45] Carruthers, *Craft of Thought*, pp. 122, 159. Cf. Jeay, *Commerce des mots*, p. 33, who states that lists cataloguing wares in grammar texts do not necessarily invite to search for inner depths of meaning. Lists here are also practical learning tools.

[46] Carruthers, *Craft of Thought*, pp. 117–44.

[47] Gallo, 'Matthew of Vendôme: Introductory Treatise', p. 53.

essence. It was through *descriptio*, topical invention of the situation of persons and things using found images, that a type was moulded and cast. The writer should choose the epithets carefully, by 'which is strongest in him and for which he is best known'.⁴⁸ Also, the texts had to appeal to the guiding beliefs and ideas of the audience (*ethos*). In antiquity, for example in criminal trials, a speaker thus could try to persuade a legal court by appealing to the common knowledge of character types. Tapping the prejudiced beliefs about character types with regard to gender or social position, an advocate hoped to cast doubt or persuade his audience of the likeliness that his client had acted in a certain manner, based upon his station in life, profession or natural disposition.

Following the tradition set by the rhetorician Quintilian, in order to invent or find the appropriate personal attributes a person was given eleven *argumenta* which were to be observed from the *topoi* or general commonplaces of condition, age, office, sex and place and alluded, among other things, to name, nature, way of life, fortune, acquired disposition, feelings and deeds.⁴⁹ The second of these attributes, arguments from *nature*, was further divided into physical, mental and external traits: *natio, patria*, as well as age, kindred and gender.⁵⁰ General knowledge of a person's character was based on the *argumenta* drawn from one of these eleven categories.

Accordingly, more and more lists appeared in poetic compositions amplifying an *essential attribute* or natural resource which a person or place was allegedly *overflowing* with. For instance, Reginald of Canterbury, a Benedictine monk at St Augustine's in Canterbury who probably originated from Faye-le-Vineuse in Poitou and was active in literary production in the 1100s, breaks

---

⁴⁸ Matthew of Vendôme, *Ars versificatoria* i.44, in *Mathei Vindocinensis opera*, ed. F. Munari (Rome, 1988), p. 62, trans. R. P. Parr, p. 28: '[Q]uod in ea pre ceteris dominatur et a quo maiorem fame sortitur evidentiam.' Matthew of Vendôme, *Ars versificatoria* i.6, ed. Munari, p. 63. E. Gallo, 'Matthew of Vendôme: Introductory Treatise on the Art of Poetry', *Proceedings of the American Philosophical Society* 118/1 (1974), 51–92. Matthew of Vendôme is drawing directly from Horace, *Ars poetica* lines 114–35, in *Satires, Epistles and Ars Poetica*, ed. H. R. Fairclough, Loeb Classical Library 194 (Cambridge MA, 1999), pp. 458–61 and Cicero, *De inventione* i.46, in *On Invention, etc.*, ed. H. M. Hubbel, Loeb Classical Library 386 (Cambridge MA, 2006), pp. 84–7.

⁴⁹ Matthew of Vendôme, *Ars versificatoria* i.41, ed. Munari, p. 60; Ibid. i 75 and 77, ed. Munari, pp. 95–6. Gallo, 'Matthew of Vendôme: Introductory Treatise', p. 55. Cf. Quintilian, *Institutio Oratoria* v.x.19, 24–7, *Institutio Oratoria*, in *Quintilian, The Orator's Education, books I–VIII*, ed. D. E. Russell (Cambridge MA, 2001) ii, 376–7, identifying similar arguments based on birth and ethnicity.

⁵⁰ *Natio* is defined by Matthew of Vendôme to be determined by language, whereas *patria* is a person's place of origin. He is possibly alluding to Isidore of Seville's *Etymologiae* ix.i.1 and i.14, ed. Reydellet, pp. 31, 41.

into a boundless enumeration of places, phenomena in the physical world, peoples and their typical, environmentally determined, overflowing essence, in a poem accompanying an epic *vita* of the fourth-century desert saint Malchus. The sky is filled with stars, the Eastern Sea with blustery storms, the forest with a canopy of leaves, the sun with rays, Rome with marble, the Greek with books, Etna with sparks, the Thracian mountains with sheep, Cluny with monks, England with herds, Gascony with apples, Flanders with knights, Anjou with heroes, Scotland with thorny bushes, Cordoba with sapphires, Tuscany with pigs and the Brits with butter.[51]

To an extent, exhaustive lists like these were drawn from classic schematizations. Possibly imitating a passage from the 'Foreign Lands Scheme' in Virgil's *Georgics*, the earliest chiefly list natural resources.[52] By visualizing the geographical situation and its essential features, the reader or listener could traverse the corners of the Earth, its heights and depths, mountains, towns, regions and cloisters and consider their essence. The *Architrenius* was written in 1184 by John of Hauville, who died in about 1200 and was a master at the cathedral school of Rouen. It is dedicated to its archbishop, and thus navigates the world, only to find that it, the Church, court and schools are overflowing with vice, while enumerating the regions and the natural resources they are teeming with.[53] Poetry in that sense functioned as blame literature, and the essential characteristics of the places and the peoples inhabiting them were interpreted morally from the perspective of the contemporary political life-world of the clergy and laity, squeezed from proverbs.

---

[51] F. Liebermann, 'Raginald von Canterbury', *Neues Archiv der Gesellschaft für Ältere Deutsche Geschichtskunde zur Beförderung einer Gesamtausgabe der Quellenschriften deutscher Geschichten des Mittelalters* 13 (1888), 517–56, poem no. xv (pp. 542–4). Reginald sent it, among other things, as a gift to the hagiographer Goscelin of Saint-Bertin (died *c.* 1100).

[52] See Virgil's *Georgica* i 56–9 and ii 114–35, *Bucolica, Georgica, Hirtengedichte, Landwirtschaft*, ed. N. Holzberg (Berlin, 2016), pp. 116, 154–6. L. P. Wilkinson, *The Georgics of Virgil: A Critical Survey* (London, 1997), p. 87. Curtius, *European Literature*, pp. 190–5, mentions the 'ideal mixed forest' as a subspecies of the catalogue. In his *Daretis Phrygii Ilias* i 516–19, ed. A. K. Bate, p. 68, composed in 1190, Joseph of Exeter likewise assembles a forest not far away across the fields from Troy, where ten species of trees grow including prophetic laurel and bold ash. A later example is Geoffrey Chaucer's catalogue of species of trees and birds in the *The Parlement of Foulys* lines 176–8 and 344–6, ed. D. S. Brewer (Manchester, 1972), pp. 76, 81; cf. Gallo, 'Matthew of Vendôme: Introductory Treatise', pp. 55–6.

[53] John of Hauville, *Architrenius* vii.6 lines 206–19, ed. W. Wetherbee (Cambridge, 1994), pp. 182–5.

Proverbial knowledge

The manuals encouraged students to describe group character traits by means of proverbs. This meant that they actively tapped into vernacular common knowledge for their literary compositions. For that matter, the proverb, expressing a universal character and memorized collectively, could be smoothly translated and encapsulated in accompanying epithets.[54] Students extracted proverbs from existing collections of glosses or *dictons* containing normative and practical admonitions, which probably aided clerics when they compiled their sermons, poetry, prose and letters, for handbooks of rhetoric expressly prescribed the use of proverbs, in particular in the *exordium* or conclusion of texts.[55] Moreover, teachers used vernacular proverbs in the classroom to teach Latin.[56] The earliest known Old French collection is the *Proverbes au villain*, compiled in Flanders between 1174 and 1190.[57] Latin examples include the proverbs of Master Serlo of Wilton (*c.* 1105–81), a teacher at the university of Paris and a Cistercian abbot.[58]

---

[54] Cf. Matthew of Vendôme, *Ars versificatoria* i.16, ed. Munari, pp. 49–50. The huge collection of medieval Latin proverbs is accessible at *Proverbia sententiaeque Latinitatis medii aevi / Lateinische Sprichwörter und Sentenzen des Mittelalters in alpabetischer Anordnung*, ed. H. Walther and P. G. Schmidt, 9 vols. (Göttingen, 1963–86) and S. Singer, *Thesaurus proverbiorum medii aevi: Lexikon der Sprichwörter des romanisch-germanischen Mittelalters*, 13 vols. (rev. edn, Berlin, 1995–2002). For proverb collections and ethnic stereotypes in this period see Walther, 'Scherz'; A.-M. Bautier, A.-M., 'Peuples, provinces et villes dans la littérature proverbiale latine du Moyen Âge', in *Richesse du proverbe; Vol. 1: Le proverbe au Moyen Âge*, ed. F. Suard and C. Buridant, 2 vols. (Lille, 1984), i, 1–22. W. E. Pfeffer, *Proverbs in Medieval Occitan Literature* (Gainsville, 1997), p. 10 and E. Schulze-Busacker, *Proverbes et expressions proverbiales dans la littérature narrative du Moyen Âge français* (Geneva, 1985), pp. 19–20 for references.

[55] Bautier, 'Peuples, provinces', p. 1. For a discussion of the various definitions of the proverb: J. W. Hassell, *Middle French Proverbs, Sentences, and Proverbial Phrases* (Toronto, 1982), pp. 4–9; Pfeffer, *Proverbs in Medieval Occitan Literature*, pp. 1–11; Schulze-Busacker, *Proverbes et expressions*, p. 19. G. Frank, 'Proverbs in Medieval Literature', *Modern Language Notes* 58/7 (1943), 508–15 (pp. 513–14) argues that the *chansons de geste* and *dit* created ready-made axioms.

[56] C. Geudens and T. van Hal, 'The Role of Vernacular Proverbs in Latin Language Acquisition, c. 1200–1600: An Exploratory Study', *Historiographia Linguistica* 44 (2018), 278–305.

[57] J. Morawski, 'Les recueils d'anciens proverbes français analysés et classes', *Romania* 48 (1922), 481–558.

[58] A. C. Friend, 'The Proverbs of Serlo of Wilton', *Medieval Studies* 16 (1954), 179–218.

The knowledge in these texts, instead of being transmitted strictly through Latin repositories accessible to the literate elite, had been passed down through oral transmission and repetition as well. It had been memorized as cultural knowledge, although in some cases the proverbs were translated from Latin into the vernacular or vice versa.[59] A poignant, early Old French example, preserved in a thirteenth-century manuscript, is the collection of proverbs known as the 'Dit de l'Apostoile', which is replete with *dictons* characterizing peoples, animals, professions and regions of France, including types of wines and cheeses such as *fromage de Brie*. Like the thirteenth-century fabliau *La riote du monde*, the dozens of epithets in this collection, both positive and negative, sum up essentialized traits of ethnic groups, expressing cultural assumptions entrenched in geography and partly in climate theory: the ingenious Saracens; the treacherous men of Hungary; the serfs of the land of the Slavs; angry Germans; tall Danes; English drunks and savage Irishmen. The list continues with an enumeration of regional professions, utilizing proverbial knowledge – the best preachers dwell in Spain, the best jugglers in Gascony, the best dancers in the Lorraine, the greatest turnip eaters in the Auvergne; types of regional dress; minerals and metals; vegetables and fruits; animals; fish; and patisseries.[60] Similar lists of shires or towns and their natural resources appear in Middle English, for example in 'The Baronage of London' and the 'Hervordschir, shild and sper' catalogue, dated tentatively to the mid-thirteenth century.[61]

The students compiling poetry took their material mainly from the storehouse of proverbs and sayings, to be amplified or adapted in accordance with the writer's perspective and the assignment to sort and position groups hierarchically. In this way, assessments of group culture and presumed behavioural, mental and physical traits slipped into school poetry, as in an anthology of

[59] Bautier, 'Peuples, provinces', p. 2; W. J. Ong, *Orality and Literacy: The Technologizing of the Word* (reprint, London 2002), p. 34. For translations from the vernacular and Latin: G. Blaicher, *Merry England: Zur Bedeuting und Funktion eines englischen Autostereotyps* (Tübingen, 2000), p. 17.

[60] 'Proverbes et dictons populaires', ed. J.-H.-R. Prompsault, *Discours sur les publications littéraires du Moyen-Âge* (Paris, 1835), pp. 114–40 (pp. 122–4). J. Ulrich, 'Neue Versionen der Riote du Monde', *Zeitschrift für romanische Philologie* 24 (1900), 112–20 (p. 115), which lists the Normans as drinkers; the French as malicious; the English as unreliable; the Scots as felonious; and the Spanish as luxurious, among others.

[61] T. Wright and J. O. Halliwell-Phillips (ed.), *Reliquiae Antiquae: Scraps from Ancient Manuscripts, Illustrating Chiefly Early English Literature and the English Language*, 2 vols. (London, 1845), I, 269–70; II, 41–2. For the Baronage of London: *English Historical Documents* 1189–1327, ed. D. C. Douglas and G. W. Greenaway, 12 vols. (London, 1953–81), ii, 881–4.

fragments of Latin verse produced in large part by head of the chapter school of Le Mans and archbishop of Tours, Hildebert of Lavardin (1056–1134), and by the schoolmaster of Angers and later bishop Marbod of Rennes (1035–1123). The collection was compiled around 1175–80 at the cathedral of St Gatien in Tours. The verses, for example, comment: 'It is not surprising if a Briton eats butter / That the Normans are satiated with beer.'[62]

The naturalized character of regions and their inhabitants was further demarcated using the markers of diet. Comments about communities living off dairy farming or agriculture, milk and butter or olive oil, beer or wine, reflected an environmentally shaped, cultural fault line running between northern and southern Europe, in which Mediterranean, sedentary agriculture was traditionally considered culturally more advanced than northern or eastern dairy farming. Milk and cheese were associated with the northern regions of the Low Countries, Flanders, Brittany and Ireland.[63] Comments about dairy consumption, although occasionally viewed as a token of wealth, retained classical cultural values that, on aggregate, regarded 'barbaric' milk, cheese and beer consumption as culturally inferior to olive oil and wine – the consumption of dairy products is compared to eating excrement in a proverb about the Frisians.[64] The Normans, famed for their excessive bragging, greed and cruelty, are portrayed as beer drinkers, as are the English, who, according to Reginald

---

[62] H. Hagen, *Carmina Medii Aevi maximam partem inedita* (Bern, 1877), pp. 168–9: 'Sic non est mirum, quod quisque moritur, / Ut non est mirum, si mandit Britto butyrum / Quod Normannigenae potu satiantur avenae.' Walther, 'Scherz', no. 158. For Britons eating butter: A. Wilmart, 'Le florilège de Saint-Gatien: Contribution à l'étude des poèmes d'Hildebert et de Marbode', *Revue Bénédictine* 48 (1936), 3–40, 147–81, 235–58 (p. 35); Walther, 'Scherz', no. 88. For Norman beer drinking, see the epigram in P. Lehmann, 'Eine Sammlung mittellateinischer Gedichte aus dem Ende des 12.Jahrhunderts', *Historische Vierteljahrschrift* 30 (1935), 20–58, 415–16 (p. 45). Cf. Baldric of Bourgueil, 'Vinum Normannis et in hoc et in omnibus annis / ferre solet culmus, non subdita uitibus ulmus', ed. J.-Y. Tilliette, *Carmina Baudri de Bourgueil*, 2 vols. (Paris, 1998–2002), ii, 136. C. Wollin, '"Kein Wein für die Normannen". Marginalien zu Baudri de Bourgeuils "carm." 202', *Sacris Erudiri* 44 (2005), 275–83, for a verse debate between Baldric and William of Lisieux about wine and beer.

[63] Hoffmann, *An Environmental History of Medieval Europe*, pp. 43–84.

[64] Walther, 'Scherz', nos. 96, 187, including an example of barbaric Saxons eating butter, possibly referring to Pliny the Elder, *Historia naturalis* xxviii.35, ed. and trans. W. H. S. Jones, Loeb Classical Library, 10 vols. (Cambridge MA, 2006), VIII, 92–4. Lawrence of Durham's *Dialogi* i.128, ed. Raine, p. 4, relates milk-drinking to the peasantry, where the 'savage Scots' are ridiculed for their boorish palates. Rigg, 'Lawrence of Durham: Dialogues', p. 48.

of Canterbury, had been raised on barley.[65] In the thirteenth century, French poets managed to expand their proverbial knowledge with references to the acclaimed chivalric valour of French knights and learning of the clergy. For instance, variations of the proverb 'The French gain victory without bringing harm', through wisdom, exhale the values of warfare propagated by Vegetius and reproduced in the *Song of Roland*, framed as chivalrous.[66] Variants of moralizing classifications of the deeds of the Greek, Franks, Romans and Jews appear, now pertaining to the French, Flemish and Lombards.[67] The contents of the proverbs are not always fixed, however. Variations of one proverb about the character of the Swabians in central–eastern Europe range from noble magnanimousness to treachery.[68]

---

[65] Liebermann, 'Raginald von Canterbury', p. 531.

[66] E.g. a gloss on Évrard of Béthune's *Graecismus* in the thirteenth-century manuscript Paris, Bibliothèque nationale de France MS Latin 18522 fol. 149r.: 'Armis, militia, rebus, probitate, Sophia / Francia munitur, nec eidem par reperitur'; B. Hauréau, *Notices et extraits de quelques manuscrits latins de la Bibliothèque Nationale*, 6 vols. (Paris, 1890–93) iv, 283; Walther, 'Scherz', no. 17. In a manuscript containing the *Graecismus* (Paris, Bibliothèque nationale de France MS Latin 18522 fol. 9v.): 'Anglia, Flandria flent quia Francia, nescia fraudis, / Continet haec tria: praemia, praedia, praelia laudis'; Hauréau, *Notices et extraits* (1893), vi, 115–25 (p. 117); Walther, 'Scherz', no. 10a for other references to later manuscripts. Bautiers, 'Peuples, provinces', p. 9. G. J. Brault, '*Sapientia* dans la *Chanson de Roland*', *French Forum* 1/2 (1976), 99–118.

[67] *Chronica minora*, ed. Mommsen, p. 390; H. Walther, *Initia carminum ac versuum medii aevi posterioris latinorum / Alphabetisches Verzeichnis der Versanfänge mittellateinischer Dichtungen* (Göttingen, 1959), no. 10306.

[68] The possibly earliest, thirteenth-century version of this cluster of stereotypes in T. Haye, 'Deutschland und die deutschen Lande im spiegel einer lateinischen Spruchsammlung', *Beiträge zur Geschichte der deutschen Sprache und Literatur* 131/2 (2009), 308–17 (Rome, Biblioteca Apostolica Vaticana MS Borg. Lat. 200). Other versions in the Sterzinger Miscellaneen-Handschrift; a Berlin manuscript; a manuscript from the monastery of Lubiąz in Poland and a Munich manuscript. I. V. Zingerle, 'Bericht über die Sterzinger Miscellaneen-Handschrift', *Sitzungsberichte der Akademie der Wissenschaften in Wien, Philosophisch-Historische Klasse* 54 (1867), 293–340 (pp. 317–18); W. Wattenbach, 'Aus einer Humanistenhandschrift', *Anzeiger für Künde der deutschen Vorzeit* 21 (1874), 212–16; W. Wattenbach, *Monumenta Lubensia* (Breslau, 1861), 33–4; F. Mone, 'Städte und Völkerspiegel', *Anzeiger für Künde der Teutschen Vorzeit* 7 (1838), 507–8. J. Werner, *Beiträge zur Kunde der lateinischen Literatur des Mittelalters aus Handschriften* (Aarau, 1905), p. 195, refers to a similar text in a manuscript from Sankt Gallen. Cf. Walther, 'Scherz', 165. See also R. Peiper, 'Europäischer Völkerspiegel', *Anzeiger für Kunde der deutschen Vorzeit* 21 (1874), 102–6 and Prague, Metropolitan University Library MS 1641 fol. 171v (fifteenth century).

The contexts in which the poets composed these snatches of verse concern warfare between principalities, social altercations in the schools and satirical attacks on Rome's hypocrisy, which are further discussed in chapter 4. Yet the classification of ethnic stereotypes frequently relates to the membership of the overarching Christian *communitas*, where the virtues or vices attributed to groups make up the parts of the sum total of morality within Christendom. It resonates in the priamel, a poetic genre that was especially popular in the fifteenth century.[69] The priamel is an epigrammatic form which consists of two parts: the 'foil' and the 'climax'. The foil lists seemingly unconnected individual examples one after another; the climax brings these together under a common, often moral, umbrella. Numerous examples produced in Germany and Poland in the fifteenth century list the virtues or vices of nations, in this example summing up how they are all worthless in the face of vice:

> Piety in Italy,
> Truth in Hungary,
> Humility in Austria,
> Poverty in Venice,
> Beautiful women in Ethiopia,
> Devoutness in Bohemia,
> Felicity in Poland –
> All these things are worthless.[70]

As a tool to praise and blame, catalogues of ethnic groups likewise formed ethical exercises in revealing wisdom and recognizing sin, distinguishing right from wrong, expressing wonderment at the diversity of God's creation. Poetry retained its didactic and mnemonic function, which earlier had allowed even Isidore of Seville's prosaic geography to be versified, indicative of a preliterate world where poetry served to reflect the expanse of the universe, its plenitude

---

[69] A priamel which draws directly from the 'Dit de l'Apostoile' collection, ending with 'the pride of the Templars, / the vanity of the Knights Hospitaller – all these things are worthless' is printed in A. J. V. Le Roux de Lincy, *Le livre des proverbes français: Précédée de recherches historiques sur les proverbes français et leur emploi dans la littérature du moyen âge et de la renaissance*, 2 vols. (Paris, 1859), ii, Appendix ii, 471. Cf. the list of social groups and vices printed in Prompsault, *Discours*, p. 118.

[70] Munich, Bayerische Staatsbibliothek, MS Clm 18910 fol. 102, a fifteenth-century manuscript originally from the Benedictine monastery of Tegernsee; Walther, 'Scherz' no. 43: 'Devocio in Italia / Veritas in Ungaria / Humilitas in Austria / Paupertas in Venecia / Formose mulieres in Ethiopia / Religiositas in Bohemia / Foelicitas in Polonia ... Nichil valent per omnia.' Kot, 'Old International Insults', 181–209 (p. 203) gives more examples.

and heterogeneity.⁷¹ Thus, Diego García, the chancellor of Castile who died in 1218, included an extensive catalogue of ethnic tropes in the prologue to his devotional treatise *Planeta*. He describes how the expanse of God's creation is reflected in the persona of the powerful Archbishop Rodrigo Jiménez de Rada of Toledo (*c.* 1170–1247), to whom his treatise is dedicated. The abundance of virtues in Rodrigo parallels the earthly display of the virtues and vices of mankind, 'strewn out in diverse manner over the five zones of the world. Some are to approve of, some to favour, some to reject, some to reproach, some to add to, some to destroy, some to instruct, some to shatter, some not only to retain but to conceal.' Rodrigo 'corrects and commends the Galicians in speech, those from Léon in eloquence, those from Campesinia at the table, the Castilians in battle, the Saracens in rigor, the Aragonese in constancy, the Catalans in joy', whereafter the text praises the bishop's musical skills in comparison to the Bretons and people from the Provence, as well as Norman friendship, French strenuousness, English aptness and German faith.⁷² The same moral purpose of rhetoric, sorting and comparing groups based upon essentialized traits, was retained in later catalogues serving to inculcate devotion to Christianity in various European peoples, along with the damnation of social groups such as monks, clerics, kings and noblemen.⁷³

Politics and rhetoric

The focus on the alleged essence of ethnic groups explicated the *distinct* identity of sacralized territories and the peoples dwelling in them. Bodies politic recalled the essentialized features geopolitically in the triangular, intersecting contexts of regional warfare of dynasties, efforts of territorial colonization and

---

71 'Versus de Asia et de universi mundi rota', ed. F. Glorie, *Corpus Christianorum. Series Latina* 175 (Turnhout, 1965), pp. 441–54, for a seventh-century example of versification of geography probably originating from Spain. D. Norberg, *La poésie latine rythmique du haut moyen age* (Stockholm, 1954); Howe, *Old English Catalogue Poems*, pp. 16–17.

72 Diego Garcia, *Planeta*, ed. P. M. Alonso (Madrid, 1943), pp. 177–8: '[N]ovit enim omnia que per quinque mundi zonas diversimode sunt repersa. Quedam novit ut probet quedam ut approbet, quedam ut recuset, quedam ut accuset, quedam novit ut astruat, quedam ut destruat, quedam ut instruat, quedam novit ut discutiat, quedam ut docet, quedam ut non solum teneat set occultet. Emendat vel commendat Gallecos in loquela, Legionenes in eloquencia, Campesinos in mensa, Castellanos in pugna, Sarranos in duricia, Aragonenses in constancia, Cathalanos in leticia.' He goes on to mention the thieving Hungarians, seafaring Venetians and the power of the Romans, among many others.

73 An example in Nürnberg, Stadtbibliothek, MS Cent. I, 97, Vorderspiegel; Walther, *Carmina* no. 13999.

argumentation against attempts by the universal, institutionalizing Church of Rome to tax its provinces. Caspar Hirschi argued in *The Origins of Nationalism*, for the period after 1250, that the self-positioning of nations responded to the weakening of the efficacy of Roman imperial ideology, even while the Church was attempting forcibly to entrench its religious hegemony.[74] However, vehement attacks launched against Rome's greed occurred earlier, clustering regional peoples set to resist Rome's grip. For example, in his handbook of poetry, Matthew of Vendôme elucidates the commonplace of a *natio* by transferring the Virgilian fear of gift-bearing Greeks onto Byzantine treachery at the time of the crusades.[75] Yet he also draws material from topical eleventh- and twelfth-century anti-Roman satire, in this case turning *against* the overarching reference point of Rome, in defence of the interests of regional territories that increasingly were being squeezed by the administration of Rome to contribute financially to its coffers.[76] For the institutionalizing Church, in the wake of its own Gregorian reform movement combating simony and greed, was drawing resources from the regions to finance not only the crusades but also its own expanding bureaucracy. These endeavours extracted an outcry from the regional clergy, who wished to resist the burden of over-taxation but were also eager to assail a Church that was clamping down on simoniac practices.[77] Thus, the natural resources with which the regions were overflowing, defining their essential feature, should no longer serve to feed the belly of the Christian body politic; the wealth belonged to distinct communities, argued one cleric. For Rome:

> Worships the gold of Arabia,
> The ornate robes of Greece,
> The ivory and jewels of India,
> The delights of France,

---

[74] Hirschi, *The Origins of Nationalism*.

[75] Matthew of Vendôme, *Ars versificatoria* i.82, ed. Munari, p. 97, quoting Virgil's *Aeneid* ii.49, *Eclogues. Georgics. Aeneid: Books 1–6*, ed. H. R. Fairclough and G. P. Goold, Loeb Classical Library 63–4, 2 vols. (rev. edn, Cambridge, 2015), ii, 318. Bautier, 'Peuples, provinces', p. 5. Odo of Deuil used this old prejudice to describe Byzantium during the Second Crusade in *De profectione Ludovici VII in orientem* iv, ed. and trans. V. Gingerick Berry (New York, 1948), pp. 66–7.

[76] Matthew of Vendôme, *Ars versificatoria* i.82, ed. Munari, pp. 97–9. For the popular genre of anti-Roman invective in this period: Benzinger, *Invectiva in Romam*, pp. 74–6; P. Lehmann, *Die Parodie im Mittelalter* (Stuttgart, 1963), pp. 51–2.

[77] Benzinger, *Invectiva in Romam*, pp. 111–13; J. A. Yunck, *The Lineage of Lady Mead: The Development of Medieval Venality Satire* (Notre Dame, 1963), pp. 80–1; Lehmann, *Die Parodie im Mittelalter*, pp. 25–68.

The silver and gold of England,
The milk and butter of Flanders,
The horse and mare mules of Burgundy –
Rome devours them all completely,
With no worthiness left at all.[78]

The genre of *dictamina* or *formulae*, collections of model letters attached to handbooks of letter writing, was a playground for such tropes. It developed in the Italian educational sphere to aid judges and lawyers. The Bolognese doctor of rhetoric Boncompagno da Signa used such formulae to address the political and social issues at hand. Boncompagno's categorizations – his lively readings in rhetoric were extremely popular, attracting large crowds and poor students allowed to attend for free – served to enliven the classroom, presenting a playful arena for mockery.[79] But the objective of the presentation of ethnotypes was also to praise the political liberty of the Italian city-states, harking back to the time when these were embroiled in a struggle with imperial forces.[80]

The rhetorical precept to attack character in a verbal assault, *genus demonstrativum*, was practised in extenso in the passages explaining the use of distinctions in clauses in Boncompagno's letter writing manual the *Palma* (c. 1198). In it, Boncompagno comments on the personal attire of the Armenians and Greeks, the religion of the Indians and the riches of Babylonia. Ridiculed are the ritual ablutions of the Saracens, which are sexualized: 'The minds of the Saracens are so blindly enshrouded in dark gloom, that they daily lave their genitals, in the belief that they are thus appeasing the Lord.' The Ismaili 'Old Man of the Mountain' Rashid ad-Din Sinan, his band of assassins and the Suriani are accused of sexually defiling themselves through the crime of adultery and all kinds of forms of harlotry, by continuously fornicating with

---

[78] 'Gens Romanorum subdola antiqua colit hydola', lines 6–14, in *Libelli de lite imperatorum et pontificum saeculis xi et xii conscripti*, ed. H. Boehmer (Hanover, 1897), III, 705–6: 'Aurum colens Arabiae, / Ornatas vestes Greciae, / Ebur cum gemmis Indiae, / Delitiosa Franciae / Argentum, aurum Angliae, / Lac et butirum Flandriae, / Mulos, mulas Burgundiae, / Roma deglutit penitus, / Digna perire funditus.' F. Mone, 'Nachweising lateinischer Gedichte', *Anzeiger für Künde der teutschen Vorzeit* 8 (1839), p. 597; Lehmann, *Die Parodie im Mittelalter*, p. 52.

[79] N. Applauso, 'Curses and Laughter: The Ethics of Political Invective in the Comic Poetry of High and Late Medieval Italy' (unpublished dissertation, University of Oregon, 2010), p. 111.

[80] Q. Skinner, *The Foundations of Modern Political Thought: Volume 1, The Renaissance* (16th edn, Cambridge, 2008), pp. 28–32.

prostitutes.[81] Boncompagno then, wielding climate theory, turns his eye to northern Africans and Italians: the defenceless Calabrians, the timid Apulians and the Sardinians in the south are the handmaids of jealousy and servility.[82] Africans walk around naked, Ethiopians are savage and the people of the Provence liars.[83] Corsicans would be highly commended for their courtliness, were they not thieves and traitors, and did they not afterwards steal back what they had previously given away. The Romans, always arousing conflict and strife, show no fear of civil war and, unmindful of their former glory, extort money through fraud and violence. The Tuscans use their own resources commendably and sparkle with many virtues, but a cloud of fraud and envy easily casts them into darkness.[84] However, the pinnacle of virtue dwells in Lombardy – for the Lombards are the patrons of liberty, outstanding defenders of the law and the just senators of Italy. Boncompagno is alluding to the struggle against the German emperor's claims to authority over the communes of northern Italy. Bologna had been a member of the Lombard League who pitched against the German Holy Roman Empire since 1164.[85] The diatribe that the Romagni are 'traitors and double-tongued' may in fact be interpreted as a response to the Romagni's disloyalty to the Lombard League in late 1174. The people living in the March, however, 'are judged by all to be

---

[81] Boncompagno da Signa, *Palma* 45, in *Aus Leben und Schriften des Magisters Boncompagno*, ed. C. Sutter (Freiburg i. B., 1894), p. 121: 'Tenebrose caliginis cecitas ita Saracenorum occupavit animos, quod pudenda cotidie lavant, Dominum propter hoc placere credentes.' Suriani were local Christians in the Levant who spoke Arabic or Syriac. C. H. MacEvitt, *The Crusades and the Christian World of the East: Rough Tolerance* (Philadephia, 2008), pp. 102–3.

[82] Apulia had been held successively by the Goths, Lombards and Byzantines. In 1059 the Norman Robert Guiscard created the duchy of Apulia, which, like Calabria, was part of the *regnum Siciliae* until 1282.

[83] The image of Ethiopians (and Africans in general) as savage and monstrous: Friedman, *The Monstrous Races*, pp. 48, 102. Cf. Isidore of Seville, *Etymologiae* ix.ii,125, ed. Reydellet, p. 113. For the inhabitants of the Provence: Gervase of Tilbury, *Otia imperialia* ii.12, ed. and trans. Banks and Binns, pp. 338–41, who accounts for the mendacious and inconstant nature of the people living near the Rhône and the shrewd, untrustworthy, mischievous character of the Provençals by applying climate theory.

[84] Boncompagno's negative representation of the inhabitants of Tuscany is remarkable, given that he came from Signa in Tuscany.

[85] P. J. Jones, *The Italian City-State: From Commune to Signoria* (Oxford, 1997), pp. 336–40. However, D D. Zancani, 'The Notion of "Lombard" and "Lombardy" in the Middle Ages', in *Medieval Europeans: Studies in Ethnic and National Perspectives*, ed. A. P. Smyth (New York, 2002), pp. 217–32 (pp. 223, 227), classifies Lombardy as 'a mere geographic expression, with no civic or broader "political" identity'.

fools', Boncompagno goes on, whereas the devouring of raw flesh by the Bohemians and Poles implies a beastlike inhumanity – you become what you eat. Boncampagno is dehumanizing the peoples in the east, as Raw Meat-Eaters belonged to the Plinian monstrous races.[86] Likewise, the Hungarians, roaming the woodlands, famished, are 'a very ferocious people, more cruel than any monster', just as Remigius of Auxerre had said at the turn of the tenth century, for these *Hungri* had left the regions of Scythia to still their *hunger*. They were also raw flesh-eaters, descendants of Gog and Magog and hunter-gatherers, lacking the civilization of a sedentary agricultural society.[87] 'The fury of the Germans, the rapacity of the [Burgundian] Allobroges, the arrogance of the French, the Spanish for their mules, the English for their tails and the mendacity of the Scots are often cause for derision,' Boncompagno concludes.[88]

Roaming across the plains, and ridiculing almost every ethnic group along the way, Boncompagno played a game of expectation with his heterogeneous student audience.[89] Boncompagno's lectures in the *ars dictaminis* surely brought on jeering and pointing of fingers, sharpening distinctions, yet also unified the clerics in laughter, foregrounding their sameness in diversity, for the clergy belonged to a distinct intellectual and legal category that set them apart from the lay Bolognese community. Thus, through derisory inclusion, sparing only the patrons of liberty, laughter at the expense of others was a shared experience. Yet Boncampagno is also making a specific political claim, based upon ethnic character, arguing that the Lombard territory was inherently free from imperial subjugation, just as Gerald of Wales had argued that the innate hot-blooded character and boldness of speech of the Welsh resonated in their free status. In chapter 5, we will come across an analogous claim to freedom and merry character in English poetry.

Boncompagno's discussion in the *Palma* of suspended, quasi-final and final clauses explicitly refers to the emotional expectancy that the image of

[86] Cf. the later poem 'Gentium quicum mores', where the people of the March, together with those of Lusatia and the Slavs, are described as 'thieves', lazy and vile. Peiper, 'Europäischer Völkerspiegel', pp. 103–6. Walther, 'Scherz', no. 72 lines 18. Friedman, *The Monstrous Races*, pp. 18, 28.

[87] A. Sager, 'Hungarians as "vremde" in Medieval Germany', in *Meeting the Foreign in the Middle Ages*, ed. A. Classen (New York, 2002), pp. 27–44 (pp. 27–30). Remigius of Auxerre's etymology is in *Epistola ad D. episcopum virdunensem*, PL 131, col. 968A.

[88] Boncompagno da Signa, *Palma* 45, ed. Sutter, p. 123: 'Teutonici per furorem, Alobroges per latrocinium, Francigene per arrogantiam, Yspani per mulas, Anglici per caudam et Scoti per mendacitatem a plurimis deridentur.' For English tails, see pp. 178–83 in chapter 4.

[89] Kibre, *The Nations*, pp. 3–6.

'Italy' triggers, appealing to a sense of a unified *Italian political freedom* within an imperial hegemonic context, using classical Roman geography. A display of unity among the communes countered local divisions that rendered Italy vulnerable to submission.[90] The listener, kept in suspense: 'Since Italy alone among all the provinces of the world enjoys the privilege of liberty …', is informed about the meaning of the utterance, namely that 'one should especially defer to the Italians …'. Finally, the lecturer reveals the meaning of the clause, that 'the provinces of the world are deservedly required to be subject to [the Italians]'.[91] It is easy to imagine how Boncompagno delivered this lecture in front of his audience, pausing after the first phrase, thus allowing his students to directly experience what he was teaching: to use suspension to appeal to emotion. More poignantly, his message – freedom means the right to hold *dominium* – hit a political nerve.

Bodies politic

Manuals of poetry, rhetoric, letter writing and military strategy played a key role in the conceptualization and spread of stereotypes. They gave students the tools to categorize peoples based upon their 'natural affects' and physical qualities. The manuals inspired clerics at court, and monks writing histories, to comment on the mental and physical qualities of army recruits, while legal scholars exposed to Roman and canon law began to rethink the idea of loyalty to a sacralized *patria* scattered with holy relics. Rulers at court received advice in mirrors of princes on governance of the body politic and on their own physical and mental health.

The production and use of these textbooks allowed for the integration of popular assumptions about group culture and biological categorizations based

[90] Skinner, *The Foundations of Modern Political Thought*, pp. 28–32. Cf. A. T. Hankey, 'Civic Pride Versus Feelings for Italy in the Age of Dante', in *Medieval Europeans: Studies in Ethnic Identity and National Perspectives*, ed. A. P. Smyth (New York, 2002), pp. 196–216 (p. 196); H. Baron, *The Crisis of the Early Italian Renaissance: Civic Humanism and Republican Liberty in an Age of Classicism and Tyranny*, 2 vols. (Princeton, 1955), ii, 446–8; N. Rubinstein, 'Florence and the Despots: Some Aspects of Florentine Diplomacy in the Fourteenth Century', *Transactions of the Royal Historical Society* 2 (1952), 21–45; Jones, *The Italian City-State*, p. 339, esp. note 16.

[91] Boncompagno da Signa, *Palma*, ed. Sutter, p. 118: 'Cum sola Italia inter cunctas mundi provincias speciali gaudeat privilegio libertatis […] specialius est Italicis deferendum […] et illis universe provincie orbis merito subesse tenentur.' Cf. Boncompagno da Signa, *Liber de obsidione Ancone*, ed. G. C. Zimolo (Bologna, 1937), p. 15.

on ancient environmental theory. It led to a steady trickle of satirical and biting verse about ethnic others, drawing the moral–physiological boundaries of the community in the context of warfare, colonization and internal social relations. At the courts and urban centres, the clergy informed and encouraged the aristocracy to wield 'rational' arguments of civilization and religion in the justification of their efforts of expansion and conquest.

Before turning to several case studies at the schools and courts, in the second part of this book, it is useful to end this chapter with a small example of how religious, legal and scientific narratives combined and allowed clerics to imagine a *body politic* in the early thirteenth century. The context is the struggle between the Church and the English royal authority. It concerns the episode when the archbishop of Canterbury, Stephen Langton (*c.* 1150–1258), returned to England in 1213, after being exiled on the Continent in the wake of a conflict with the English royal house. The fissure was a result of a political dispute over the election of Langton as archbishop, an appointment which King John of England (1167–1216) had refused to accept, partly on the grounds that Langton's loyalty supposedly lay with the French Capetian monarchy.[92] Subsequently, in 1207, a general interdict was pronounced by Pope Innocent III, denying the English denizens access to the sacraments of mass, baptism, marriage and confession – dramatically hitting at the heart of the English community's religious life. Although it was a temporary penalty, the interdict struck the entire English nation as a punishment for its *collective guilt*, sparing only the dying and being intermitted during the periods of Christmas and Easter. Thus the interdict was a collective punishment of the body politic for the transgression of one individual, the king, who stood morally as a *pars pro toto* for the entire English community.[93] The latter was held responsible for not speaking out or admonishing the king, a failure considered almost as reprehensible as the sin itself, as Pope Innocent III argued in an open letter to the English aristocracy in 1207.[94]

When the conflict was finally resolved in July 1213, and England temporarily became a vassal state of the pope, Langton hastily crossed the Channel, and upon arriving in London, addressed a large crowd at St Paul's cathedral on 25 August.[95] In his sermon, perhaps delivered in English rather than Latin, he

[92] R. V. Turner, *King John* (New York, 1994), pp. 157–74.
[93] P. D. Clarke, *The Interdict in the Thirteenth Century: A Question of Collective Guilt* (Oxford, 2007), pp. 31, 41.
[94] *Selected Letters of Pope Innocent III concerning England (1198–1216)* no. 32, ed. C. R. Cheney and W. H. Semple (London, 1953), pp. 97–9, using medical metaphors.
[95] G. Lacombe, 'An Unpublished Document on the Great Interdict (1207–1213)', *Catholic Historical Review* 15 (1929/1930), 408–20 (p. 409); J. W. Baldwin, *Masters,*

bewailed the English trait of excessive drinking as the catalyser of such great misfortune. English drinking, or wassailing, had been a common stereotype since the 500s and features in dozens of chronicles, sermons and poems:[96]

> The English are burdened with the weight of numerous sins, but they are especially weighed down by two which sink them into the basest of things: gluttony and drunkenness. These two vices reign strongest in England, and it is the nature of the English to drink to wassail.[97]

Langton further indicated that English drinking was passed down from father to son and was hereditary, as John of Salisbury had earlier surmised, the Benedictine abbot Peter of Celle (c. 1115–83) stating it to be a sign as visible as Hebrew circumcision.[98] In fact, English drinking was a ubiquitous trope. Walter Daniel (fl. 1150–67), a Cistercian monk at the abbey of Rievaulx who referred to himself as a *medicus*, in the *Centum Sententiae* portrayed the English drinker sitting, holding in one hand a siphon to his mouth to drink, and in his other hand his own pipe – his penis – to eject urine.[99] Accordingly, said Stephen Langton, Adam was banished from Paradise because of gluttony, yet his children, the English, continued to wallow in vice. To convey his message, the archbishop employs a medical metaphor: 'These two, gluttony and drunkenness, rule in us English; but in order that these are abandoned, we set forth an example how to flee from them. You have heard that certain diseases are passed by heredity to the progeny and derivate from father to son, as in the case of gout.'[100] Because the English, however, continued to indulge in these inherited vices, they 'subject themselves to their Lord's judgment and

---

Princes and Merchants: The Social Views of Peter the Chanter and His Circle, 2 vols. (Princeton, 1970), i, 27. P. B. Roberts, *Stephanus de Lingua-Tonante: Studies in the Sermons of Stephen Langton* (Toronto, 1968), pp. 47, 52.

[96] Weeda, 'Meanwhile in Messianic Time', for source references.

[97] Sermon II, *Selected Sermons of Stephen Langton*, ed. P. B. Roberts (Toronto, 1980), p. 7: 'Sarcinas innumeras peccatorum gerunt Anglicani, sed duabus proprie specialiter deprimuntur quibus descendunt ad infima: hee sunt ingluvies et ebrietas. Hec duo vicia maxime regnant in Anglia, et est Anglorum proprietas bibere ad verseil.'

[98] *The Letters of John of Salisbury. vol. 2: The Later Letters (1163–1180)*, ed. and trans. W. J. Millor and C. N. L. Brooke (Oxford, 1979), no. 270; *The Letters of Peter of Celle* no. 172–3, ed. and trans. J. Haseldine (Oxford, 2001), pp. 664–9.

[99] C. H. Talbot, 'The Centum Sententiae of Walter Daniel', *Sacris Erudiri* 11 (1960), 266–383 (p. 326).

[100] Sermon II, *Selected Sermons of Stephen Langton*, ed. Roberts, p. 7: 'Hec duo, gula et ebrietas, in nobis Anglicis principantur; set ut illa recedant de cetero exemplum proponemus ipsa fugiendi. Audistis quod quedam infirmitates iure hereditario transfunduntur in posteros et a patribus in filios deriuantur, ut est pedum egritudo.'

judge themselves worthy of the punishment of traitors. Drunkenness is the rope by which we are bound; gluttony is the vice for which we are reputed to be traitors.'[101]

Although the controversy between the monarchy and the papacy centred on the issue of who was empowered to elect the archbishop of Canterbury, Stephen Langton mentioned in his address a widespread custom exemplifying the moral state of affairs of the body politic, while explaining its transmission with a medical argument. The underlying notion in this sermon was that the English were a chosen people that was being punished for its collective sins. The collective, hereditary custom of the laity, wassailing – daily performed in taverns and at dining tables, and, ironically, communally at important moments of the Church calendar – thus 'decided' the fate of the English people, the kingdom and the English Church. It suggests the existence of a unified moral community, yet equally so is used by the universal Church to explain the internal corruption of an imagined body politic. Corruption of the moral community conflicted with the alleged *raison d'être* of political communities: the pursuit of the common good, of sufficient life, a shared, higher ideal that superseded individual and group interests and was obtainable through the virtuous quality of the community's members.

The rhetorical operation of ethnotypes drawn from natural science and social practices in order to represent the moral condition of the political collective, as well as to classify the qualities of the men destined to protect its domesticated space, inadvertently had consequences for how religious and social others were regarded and positioned in the hierarchy of power, internally and externally. In later centuries, bodies politic, extending to city-states and seignorial powers, might envision political conflict as the outcome of the clash of putrefying humours. The French legal philosopher Jean de Terre Rouge or Terrevermeille (1370–1430) argued in *Contra rebelles suorum regum* that the supporters of the duke of Burgundy were corrupting the French body politic and hence should be amputated.[102] The imagination of political communities as organic bodies politic, invigorated by Graeco-Arabic thought, allowed political commentators to envisage the legal apparatus as the sinews holding the moral community together. The development of institutions dedicated to regulating and policing the community, from this perspective was perhaps not so much the driving force behind the evolution of the body politic but instead

---

[101] Ibid.: 'Et ita domini sui se subicientes iuditio, dignos se iudicant supplicio traditorum. Ebrietas est vinculum quo ligamur, ingluvies est vicium pro quo pro proditoribus reputamur.'

[102] J. Dunbabin, 'Government', in *The Cambridge History of Medieval Political Thought, c. 350–c. 1450*, ed. J. H. Burns (Cambridge, 1988), pp. 477–519 (p. 480).

a correlative development. The administrators, the bureaucrats – rather than actually working out a rational and efficient form of government in a bid to eliminate violence, organize taxation and secure a peaceful society – represented, or performed, the body politic. In reality, feuding and other forms of violence continued deep into the 'modern era'.[103]

Intellectuals went on to dress the bones of the territorialization of political entities with more flesh by arguing that natural communities populated them, from which loyalty to the *provincia* and the *regnum* flowed. The Dominican friar Thomas Aquinas averred that polities sprang from natural groups rather than from the sinful state of humanity, as Augustine once held.[104] Most importantly here, however, the body politic was envisioned as an organic, moral community that aligned with a community of historical descent dwelling in a specific climate, wherein biblical thought, Hippocraticism and Aristotelianism merged. Influential philosophers such as Marsilius of Padua (c. 1275–c. 1342) in the *Defender of Peace* described the features of societal politics, seeking to fulfil humans' desire for 'sufficient life'. The Dominican friar John of Paris claimed that man, following God's insight, chose instinctively to organize itself in diverse societies that sprang from diverse climates, reflected by the great diversity of the physical qualities of their members.[105] French philosophers argued that the *imperium* was a temporary power and that, based on the Roman *ius gentium*, the sovereign power of bodies politic reflected a return to the natural law held in common by mankind.[106] Men living under natural law thereby distinguished themselves from men living before the law, as beasts.

However, living under natural law was bound to Christendom, as Janet Coleman explains in an insightful article about property rights. Thus, Giles of Rome claimed that only those men who enjoyed continual membership in the Church through baptismal rebirth could justly inherit and own property. On the other hand, uncivilized peoples lacked property rights because of the absence of the context of law (different to Jews or Muslims living in

---

[103] A. Zorzi, 'Legitimation and Legal Sanction of Vendetta in Italian Cities from the Twelfth to the Fourteenth Centuries', in *The Culture of Violence in Renaissance Italy: Proceedings of the International Conference; Georgetown University at Villa Le Balze, 3–4 May 2010*, ed. S. K. Cohn Jr. and F. Ricciardelli (Florence, 2012), pp. 27–54.

[104] Ehlers, 'Elemente mittelalterlicher Nationsbildung', p. 566; Zientara, 'Nationale Strukturen', p. 313.

[105] John of Paris, *De potestate regia et papali* 3, ed. Bleienstein, pp. 81–2; Marsilius of Padua, *Defensor pacis* ii.8, ed. and trans. A. Brett (Cambridge, 2005), pp. 213–20.

[106] Dunbabin, 'Government', pp. 481, 488.

Christian society).¹⁰⁷ In the course of the thirteenth century, the increasing focus on property rights thereby replaced older 'feudal' connections. *Dominium* allowed for property rights to be defensible by law, yet the ultimate *dominium* remained in the hands of the *regnum*. Such ideas expose the relevance of discussions about European *regna* as domesticated spaces, *patriae*, where law, and hence property rights, prevailed, protected by 'naturally qualified' armed recruits – so different, so it was said, from the regions of colonization where lawlessness prevailed.

In due course, the rhetorical body politic could be imagined as a legal fiction as well, besides being a rhetorical one. Thus, the political body became a *persona ficta*, one endowed with agency or sovereignty. This was an idea that did not feature in the Justinian Roman law code of the *Corpus Iuris Civilis*.¹⁰⁸ It was new. It marked the beginnings of a new conceptualization of communities as political bodies in a Christian era.

---

¹⁰⁷ Coleman, 'Medieval Discussions of Property', pp. 214–15.
¹⁰⁸ J. P. Canning, 'Law, Sovereignty and Corporation Theory, 1300–1450', in *The Cambridge History of Medieval Political Thought, c. 350–c. 1450*, ed. J. H. Burns (Cambridge, 1988), pp. 454–76 (p. 473).

PART II

4

Ethnic Slanging Matches

The men attending the schools in the twelfth century took pleasure in ridiculing one another's background. Besides the more sober pursuits of medicine, rhetoric and law, the students following the *artes*-programme, practising verse composition, wrote derisory epigrams about English drunkenness, Breton stupidity and Norman boasting. Often they jotted down ethnic jokes, mocking or praising the military talents of the French, in glosses and snatches of verse in the margins of manuals of grammar and rhetoric, for instance in Évrard of Béthune's grammar textbook the *Graecismus*.[1] At the emerging university of Paris, students from all over Europe entered into ethnic slanging matches, or so Bishop Jacques de Vitry alleges, assailing their compeers and rudely hurling a multitude of insults and sneers at each another. Jacques de Vitry studied in Paris and later became bishop of Acre. In his *History of the West* he claims that mutual envy and conflict led to verbal clashes and even physical violence. Students shouted 'drunk' and 'tail-bearer' at the English, called the French arrogant, weak and effeminate, the Normans vain and boastful, the Romans violent and greedy, the Brabanters mercenaries and rapists, the Lombards usurers and the Flemish rich, gluttonous and soft as butter.[2]

---

[1] 'Francis scire, sitis Anglis, nescire Britannis, / Fastus Normannis crescit crescentibus annis.' Printed in Hauréau, *Notices et extraits*, vi, 124 from a thirteenth-century manuscript (Paris, Bibliothèque nationale de France, MS Latin 18522 fol. 149r.) containing Évrard of Béthune's grammar textbook the *Graecismus*. Here, for the French read: the inhabitants of the region of Île de France. The same manuscript contains a Francophone gloss stating France enjoys privileges, land and the rewards of fame, while England and Flanders puff; Hauréau, *Notices et Extraits*, vi, 117. It also states, at fol. 149r., that the Germans have raging minds (*consuetudine furibunda*). Related glosses in Walther, 'Scherz', nos. 10a, 59; Walther, *Initia carminum*, no. 6840–9. See also the gloss to Évrard of Béthune's *Graecismus* in Hauréau, *Notices et Extraits*, iv, 281; Walther, 'Scherz', no. 17; Bautiers, 'Peuples, provinces', p. 9.

[2] Jacques de Vitry, *Historia Occidentalis* vii, ed. Hinnebusch, p. 92. For the circle of De Vitry, see Baldwin, *Masters, Princes and Merchants*. For the accusation of usury of the Lombards, see also Walter of Châtillon's *Alexandreis* vii.413, ed. Colker, p. 191 (see also chapter 3) and Rutebeuf's late thirteenth-century 'La Bataille des VII Ars', ed. A. Jubinal, *Oeuvres complètes de Rutebeuf, trouvère du XIIIe siècle*, 3 vols. (Paris, 1874–75), iii, 330–1, note 3. M. Greilsammer, *L'Usurier chrétien, un Juif métaphorique? Histoire de l'exclusion des prêteurs lombards (XIIIe–XVIIe siècle)* (Rennes,

Underscoring the relational-emotive aspect of identity, the convergence of students from different backgrounds – in an environment where they were encouraged to stereotype – sparked an acceleration of acrimonious attacks on the other, further honing a sense of ethnicity. Mockery homed in on character traits and the etymology of ethnic names, on religious affiliation and peoples' humanity, calling into doubt the full humanness of the English. The velocity of the incorporation of such images in satire and invective – the focus of this chapter – suggests that the authors drew their ammunition from pre-existing images circulating in urban centres, as well as from literary examples and were fed by the rhetorical prescripts discussed in chapter 3. In practice, within the social context of the schools and courts, students used these negative epithets in warfare and conflicts as a battle cry, in keeping with Vegetius's advice in *De re militari* to tap indignation and anger in encounters with the enemy. It was advice which the French chronicler William le Breton heeded directly in his *Philippide*.[3] Taking into account the atmosphere in which the earliest ethnic invective evolved – anti-Roman satire – suggests moreover that the rallying cry of ethnicity emerged in the context of contestations of the growing papal institutionalization.

Jacques de Vitry decried ethnic stereotyping as seditious student behaviour, along with gambling and prostitution. However, his denunciation of ethnic slander and violence is quite exceptional, for, as we have seen in the previous chapter, ethnic stereotyping was in fact actively encouraged in the curricular textbooks of poetry and letter composition. Ethnic stereotyping helped lecturers to enliven their material, bringing a touch of laughter to the classroom. On 26 March 1215, the Bolognese rhetorician Boncompagno da Signa, who was introduced in the previous chapter, read aloud his *Rhetorica antiqua* in front of the college of professors of civil and canon law.[4] In his lecture, he ridiculed the delicate matter of the 'mourning customs' of various peoples, causing what must have been great hilarity, explaining how the deceitful people of Romagna and Lombardy 'display but little wailing and tears, and while thus murmuring, hasten themselves in throngs above the body of the dead. And in

---

2012); W. Reichert, 'Lombarden als "merchant-bankers" im England des 13. und beginnenden 14. Jahrhunderts', in D. Ebeling, V. Henn, R. Holbach, W. Reichert and W. Schmid (ed.), *Landesgeschichte als multidisziplinäre Wissenschaft: Festgabe für Franz Irsigler zum 60. Geburtstag* (Trier, 2001), 77–134. For their comparison to snails, see the poem printed by F. W. Lenz , *Das Pseudo-Ovidische Gedicht 'De Lombardo et Lumaca'* (S. I., 1957).

[3] Allmand, *The De Re Militari of Vegetius*, p. 94. William le Breton, *Philippide* v lines 408–10, ed. Delaborde, ii, 140–1.

[4] Also known as the *Bonconpagnus*, 1215, revised in 1226.

order to simulate lamentation there are many who wet their eyes with saliva or prick their eyelids, so that it seems as if they are lamenting.' He mocked the northern peoples and their typical drinking habits, claiming that 'the English, Bohemians, Poles, Ruthenians and Slavs mix their tears with drink until they reach a state of drunkenness, and thus consoled, they retain their usual merriment', and suggesting that the Germans lamented in soft voices, which is a playful inversion of their stereotypically harsh voices, likened to barking dogs or rattling carts.[5] Indeed, schoolmen seemed to experience a vicious pleasure in attacking the social (the peasant), religious and ethnic other in satire and invective. Such diatribes induced little moral introspection – these were not the tools of meditation but, rather, outward attacks predominantly targeting peoples' vices, *mala*, rather than their virtues, *bona*.

In the past, scholars such as Ludwig Schmugge had remarked that the international universities were 'multipliers of national prejudice'.[6] The students producing ethnic invective actively forged and at the same time underwent processes of identity formation. This had to do with the fact that the young students came from all kinds of diverse regional backgrounds, cultures and languages. The new universities from the early twelfth century were multi-ethnic hubs where young men lived together, sometimes in houses founded for specific regional groups. Student administration was organized in guilds known as *nations*, entry to which was arranged loosely according to region of origin.[7] Using ethnic invective in this milieu was not merely a literary exercise devoid of social context; in some instances dehumanizing verbal insults stemmed from feelings of pride or entitlement.

Thus, it is tempting to view the ethnic insults produced under these circumstances as straightforward agonistic attacks. Yet, as Lawrence Levine has shown in his analysis of ritualized insults (known as the Dozens) in Black American culture, we must be careful not to interpret ethnic invective as the simple expression of a dualistic animosity. Ritualized insults – verbal assaults within a structured setting – can also deflect aggression, releasing feelings

---

[5] Boncompagno da Signa, *Rhetorica antiqua* vi.3 in *Briefsteller und Formelbücher des elften bis vierzehnten Jahrhunderts*, ed. L. Rockinger (reprint New York, 1961), pp. 141–3: 'Lombardi et Romanioli clamosas voces et lacrimas paucas emittunt, et cum ipsis rumoribus catervatim ruunt super corpora defunctorum, et multos ad simulatum planctum inducunt, qui oculos madefaciunt cum salvia vel palpebris apponunt acrumen, ut plangere videantur. […] Anglici, Boemi, Poloni, Ruteni atque Sclavi potum suum cum fletu permiscent donec ebrietate sunt affecti, et ita remanent solito iocundius consolati.' For references to harsh German voices see p. 190–1.

[6] Schmugge, 'Über "nationale" Vorurteile', p. 454.

[7] See p. 126n.1 for references.

of tension and creating order, a community of laughter, through disciplined play. Indeed, verbal, contentious acts, within a disciplined structure, can create intimacy as well. In this manner, in the twelfth century, the international community of young clerics could express distress and perform taboos without being penalized.[8] However, whether or not invective contributed to inter-ethnic group cohesion will have depended on the degree of homogeneity within the students' community based on their legal or social status. The young clerics at the schools – a distinct group that fell under canon law – presumably shared privileges that outweighed the disadvantages their ethnicity would have imposed upon them.

In this chapter, ethnic ridicule is discussed within the context of the genres of satire and invective and its purpose and employment as a rallying cry in a literary, social and military context. Ethnic invective is classified as a literary and social exercise, guided by the curricular reading of classical satirists, to condemn moral weakness, reveal hypocrisy and incite reform. In addition, on several occasions, students of the arts actively deployed such invective in political settings, notably when English, Norman and French dynastic houses waged war – showing that ethnic identities do not necessarily flow from conflict, yet can be sharpened and mobilized if and when circumstances dictate. Significantly, the political use of ethnic invective was not limited to royal centres of power. Local courts and ecclesiastical chapters weighed in too, organizing their own literary production as well.[9] This chapter will therefore first explore the social and cognitive functions of invective and ridicule, after which it looks at how ethnic jibes and satire might have been affected by, as well as shaping, social and political relations in practice.

---

[8] L. W. Levine, *Black Culture and Black Consciousness: Afro-American Folk Thought from Slavery to Freedom* (New York, 1977), pp. 320–1, 344–58. I would like to thank George Blaustein for drawing my attention to this book. Cf. Applauso, 'Curses and Laughter', pp. 3, 12–13. Martha Bayless argued the same, stating that religious humour, instead of being subversive and disruptive, could serve a cathartic function. In repetitive social systems, ritual rebellion acting out conflicts emphasizes the social cohesion in which these conflicts endure, whereby role reversal serves to ease the tension between social groups while visualizing the source of shame and conflict, yet simultaneously controlling and perpetuating the hierarchical order. M. Bayless, *Parody in the Middle Ages: The Latin Tradition* (Ann Arbor, 1996), pp. 189–91.

[9] Mostert, 'Studying Medieval Urban Literacy', pp. 1–28; M. Mostert, 'Some Thoughts on Urban Schools, Urban Literacy, and the Development of Western Civilisation', in *Writing and the Administration of Medieval Towns: Medieval Urban Literacy i*, ed. M. Mostert and A. Adamska (Turnhout, 2014), pp. 337–48.

Categories of ridicule and invective

To understand the effects that ethnic invective (humourless attacks or verbal violence) and satire (ridicule with a moral purpose) had on identity, it is useful to first discuss briefly the socio-psychological workings of invective and ridicule. They are aggressive ethical tools that should be taken seriously in historical research as means of social exclusion, as Nicolino Applauso argued in his study of the use of invective by poets in Italian city-states.[10] Scholars usually distinguish three psychological factors underlying humour and its social functions. Firstly, humour plays with perceptions of reality, taking an incongruent perspective. Secondly, it can be wielded as an internal coping mechanism, explained by Freud using the 'principle of economy': jokes are a disguised form of low-energy release of aggression.[11] Humour can dampen pain. Thirdly, and relevant here, disparaging humour feeds on perceptions of human behaviour that are interpreted morally. Disparaging humour denounces the other as morally inferior in an act of aggression, at the same time claiming one's own ascendancy and strengthening the moral boundaries of the own group. Depending on the legal and social infrastructure in which they are set, such disparaging jokes about ethnotypes can be termed racist. Ridicule and humour may also serve to pinpoint faults in the other and self, to correct social behaviour and to create order, sometimes playfully, through disciplined, antagonistic, verbal acts.[12] Moreover, humour and ridicule can evoke relief or empathy when a shameful behavioural act or situation of another or the self is witnessed. Finally, humour, and the physical response of laughter, create a shared experience, as Henri Bergson once observed.[13]

Accordingly, in the past, scholars emphasized that laughter, a somatic reaction to humour, helps to create communities, excluding and including, evoking feelings of animosity, sympathy or understanding. As Jacques le Goff argued,

---

[10] Applauso, 'Curses and Laughter', pp. 1–11.

[11] Levine, *Black Culture*, pp. 320–1, referring to Sigmund Freud's *Der Witz und seine Beziehung zum Unbewussten* published in 1905.

[12] Jean-Claude Schmitt discusses the normative aspects of invective, which might either be condemned by authorities (i.e. bans on slanderous comments) or else employed to exert authority through, for instance, excommunication. The power of invective and its limitations are thus situational. J.-C. Schmitt, 'Les images de l'invective', in *L'invective au Moyen Âge: France, Espagne, Italie: Actes du Colloque L'invective au Moyen Âge, Paris, 4–6 février 1993*, ed. É. Beaumatin and M. Garcia (Paris, 1995), pp. 11–20 (pp. 11–14). Cf. J. Huizinga, *Homo Ludens: A Study of the Play-Element in Culture* (Boston, 1955), pp. 10, 65; Levine, *Black Culture*, p. 348.

[13] H. Bergson, *Laughter: An Essay on the Meaning of the Comic* (London, 1935), pp. 3–8.

laughter is a social phenomenon and an instrument of power, needing at least two people.[14] Disparaging humour, as an aggressive ethical act, strengthens feelings of moral and cultural ascendancy, advancing social control, forging group awareness and loyalty and offering comfort to the own group. The ring of laughter – the shared somatic experience of laughing together, out loud – creates distinctions, dividing group members into us and them, even if only fleetingly.

Poetry and invective

In the twelfth century, poetry, rather than a genre of texts to be read in silence and solitude, was composed firstly to be performed orally, or at least read aloud in the absence of a live audience. The power of poetry and rhetoric went far beyond the aesthetic and served political, social and ethical functions as well. Invective and panegyric, alongside hymns, are in that regard considered the earliest forms of poetry that, performed orally, could be used to control social relations. In practice, invective, for example, was wielded in public spaces to crush someone's reputation in order to remove a person from a community.[15]

The social power of poetry is evident if we look at its relationship to the judiciary. Poetry, like court rhetoric, was concerned with the art of persuasion and sought to wield powerful images touching the strings of the listener's imagination. Both the poet and the lawyer could turn to humour, wit and mockery in order to amuse, but also to discredit court opponents. This relationship between forensics, literature and invective stands out in the numerous corresponding rules explicated in the manuals of oratory and poetry concerning the employment of invective, where the *oratio invectiva* instructs students of law and diplomats in their letters to use ridicule in the *disputatio*. For example, the ancient Roman *Rhetoricum ad Herennium* teaches the targeting of external markers such as place of birth and physical and mental affects. In the latter part of the twelfth century, the manuals for the *ars dictaminis* and *ars praedicandi* encourage the use of invective in an analogous manner. In the arts of poetry discussed in the previous chapter, both Matthew of Vendôme

---

[14] J. le Goff, 'Laughter in the Middle Ages', in *A Cultural History of Humour: From Antiquity to the Present Day*, ed. J. N. Bremmer and H. W. Roodenburg (Cambridge, 1997), pp. 40–53 (p. 40). A. Classen, 'Laughter as an Expression of Human Nature in the Middle Ages and the Early Modern Period: Literary, Historical, Theological, Philosophical, and Psychological Reflections. Also an Introduction', in *Laughter in the Middle Ages and Early Modern Times: Epistemology of a Fundamental Human Behavior, its Meaning, and Consequences*, ed. A. Classen (Berlin, 2010), pp. 1–140 (p. 3).

[15] Applauso, *Curses and Laughter*, pp. 95–6.

and Geoffrey of Vinsauf distinguish between praise and vituperation as ethical tools of invention, advising to balance ridicule and blame so as to lend serious matters a lighter touch.

The drawing of the moral boundaries of the community was expressed politically in the form of *sirventes*, political debate poems that arose from two classical traditions: the forensic and the eclogue.[16] Battle verse in the forensic tradition, which includes ethnic debate verse, was usually arranged in two blocks, each party making its case whereupon 'judges' adjudicated. Debate verse in the eclogue tradition, on the other hand, contains alternate short verses, modelled on the singing contests of Virgil's shepherds. In the Carolingian era, and especially in the twelfth century, monks and clergymen produced a plethora of dualistic debate verses between, for example, the non-human entities of wine and beer, water and wine, summer and winter, the soul and the body, but also between ethnic groups.[17] The sources under review in this chapter include satirical epigrams, parodies and debate verse composed from the end of the eleventh century.

Presumably, as was the case with Boncompagno da Signa's catalogues of invective discussed earlier, ethnic debate poems and epigrams were written to be performed before a live audience. We can glean how ethnic verse was chanted out loud from an educational treatise on rhetoric compiled by Marbod of Rennes, *De ornamentis verborum* (On the Adornments of Words). Marbod taught at the cathedral school of Angers in present-day France. In his discussion of the *complexio* which Évrard of Béthune later copied into his school grammar book, the *Graecismus*, Marbod extols the preponderance of the Angevins in military affairs thrice in succession. The *complexio*, a repetition of both initial and final words in successive clauses, is deliberately tailored to enhance feelings of pride, control and belonging among the pupils. It is easy to imagine how the teacher posed each clause in the form of a question, whereupon the students chanted the answer in a military drill:

> Who fights with courage? The Angevins.
> Who vanquishes his enemies? The Angevins.
> Who spares the vanquished? The Angevins.
> Malice thus does not touch the excellent Angevins.[18]

---

[16] Ibid., 18–40, 116.

[17] P. Stotz, 'Beobachtungen zu lateinischen Streitgedichten des Mittelalters: Themen – Strukturen – Funktionen' (Zurich, 2001), 1–22 (pp. 2–7), accessed 5 March 2021 at Beobachtungen zu lateinischen Streitgedichten im Mittelalter (uzh.ch).

[18] Marbod of Rennes, 'De ornamentis verborum', in *Opera Omnia*, ed. J. J. Bourassé (Paris, 1854), p. 1688: 'Qui sunt qui pugnant audaciter? Andegavenses. / Qui sunt

Marbod's little verse is a literary exercise complementing the advice given by Vegetius to make use of indignation and anger to foster hostility towards the enemy.[19] It enhanced group emotions of pride and loyalty. However, the core business of invective was to blame others and was steeped in questions of morality. This applies in particular to satire, whose ultimate purpose was to reprehend vice and encourage virtue as a form of constructive criticism. Invective, ridicule and acts of aggression were in this sense not incongruent with religious ethics; they were moral tools administered by men of the Church, and not necessarily specific manifestations of an antagonistic popular culture. Indeed, satirical texts were written by ecclesiastics of high standing: the *cena* (dinner) parodies, for example, were performed for popes and emperors.[20] Twelfth-century criticism was levelled at the corruption of the clergy and hypocrisy in the cloister, at avarice and simony in the Church; in fact all stations, from kings to peasants, could find themselves at the butt end of its ridicule.[21] Satirical literature included parodies like the *Tractatus Garsiae*, drinkers' masses, gamblers' masses, jibes, gabs and witticisms. Depending on the situation, this means that ridiculing the ethnic other could also serve as a mirror to warn the listeners about the pitfalls of moral and physical weakness within the self. And it could be applied to ethnic groups in warfare as well. Fourteenth-century liturgical 'passions' of ethnic groups lamented the fate of the Scots, the French after the battle of Courtrai and the Jews of Prague.[22]

---

qui superant inimicos? Andegavenses. / Qui sunt qui parcunt superatis? Andegavenses. / Egregios igitur livor neget Andegavenses.' See also Évrard of Béthune, *Graecismus* iii lines 10–12, ed. J. Wrobel, p. 12, who repeats the same lines. Bautier, 'Peuples, provinces', p. 13.

[19] Allmand, *The De Re Militari of Vegetius*, p. 94.
[20] Bayless, *Parody in the Middle Ages*, pp. 178–9, 183–4.
[21] V. Gillespie, 'From the Twelfth Century to c. 1450', in *The Cambridge History of Literary Criticism. Vol. 2: The Middle Ages*, ed. A. Minnis and I. Johnson (Cambridge, 2005), pp. 145–236 (pp. 222–5). R. E. Pepin, *Literature of Satire in the Twelfth Century: A Neglected Mediaeval Genre* (Lewiston, 1988), pp. 1–29; R. M. Thomson, 'The Origins of Latin Satire in Twelfth Century Europe', *Mittellateinisches Jahrbuch* 13 (1978), 73–83; A. G. Rigg, 'Satire', in *Medieval Latin: An Introduction and Bibliographical Guide*, ed. F. A. C. Mantello and A. G. Rigg (Washington DC, 1996), pp. 532–68.
[22] The texts are printed in P. Lehmann, *Parodistische Texte: Beispiele zur lateinischen Parodie im Mittelalter* (Munich, 1923). Bayless, *Parody in the Middle Ages*.

Anti-Roman satire and invective

The genre of satire gained momentum at the end of the eleventh century in an anti-Roman sphere, in the context of the Gregorian Reform movement and the institutionalizing Church. A significant number of satirical texts produced at this time contain ethnic digs directed at Roman hegemonic claims and papal institutions. This kind of satire developed at the schools, as is evident from various examples of elaborate punning on grammatical cases in the verses.[23] These little poems are often viewed as the product of exercises in composition influenced by the study of ancient Roman poets including Horace, Juvenal, Persius and Martial.[24] However, the diatribes are also embedded in socio-economic reality and concern a direct reaction to the introduction, at the time of the Investiture Controversy, of the *servitium*, a payment levied by Rome on newly elected ecclesiastics.[25] The attacks reflect a primary concern about a stronger and more worldly papal curia that was expanding its bureaucratic control. The poets worked with an older, well-established tradition of producing diatribes against Roman arrogance and avarice, first articulated in the New Testament in the context of Rome's suppression and domination.[26] Indeed, Rome's double-edged reputation as the imperial powerbase and

---

[23] An example is 'Aurum, Roma, sitis dantes amat absque dativo; / Accusativo Roma favere negat'; Walther, *Lateinische Sprichwörter*, no. 276; *Carmina Burana*, ed. A. Hilka, O. Schumann and W. Meyer (Heidelberg, 1971), p. 23. For more references: A. P. Orbán, 'De omgang met "het verleden" van Rome in de oudchristelijke en middeleeuwse Latijnse literatuur', in *Omgang met het verleden*, ed. R. E. V. Stuip and C. Vellekoop (Hilversum, 2001), pp. 63–90 (pp. 84–5), especially note 59; and H. Walther, 'Lateinische Verseinträge in einem Vocabular des 15. Jhds.', *Historische Vierteljahrschrift: Zeitschrift für Geschichtswissenschaft und für lateinische Philologie des Mittelalters* 26 (1931), 295–311 (pp. 296–7); Zingerle, 'Bericht über die Sterzinger Miscellaneen-Handschrift', p. 312; Walther, *Initia carminum*, no. 26929.

[24] Thomson, 'On the Origins of Medieval Satire', pp. 76–9.

[25] Yunck, *Lineage of Lady Meed*, pp. 71–81. However, many anti-Roman satirical texts were written after the conflict; Thomson, 'On the Origins of Medieval Satire', p. 81. Benzinger, *Invectiva in Romam*, pp. 94–9. W. Goetz, *Die Entstehung der italienischen Kommunen im frühen Mittelalter* (Munich, 1944), p. 63, argues that, especially during the reign of Frederick Barbarossa, anti-Roman sentiment created a stronger sense of unity in the north-western territories of England, France and Germany. The Germans sometimes were attacked by Rome for their stupidity; see, for example, the fictious letter addressed to Frederick Barbarossa, quoted in Benzinger, *Invectiva in Romam*, p. 99.

[26] Orbán, 'Omgang met "het verleden" van Rome', pp. 74–85. R. M. Thomson, 'Satire, Irony, and Humour in William of Malmesbury', in *Rhetoric and Renewal in the Latin West 1100–1540: Essays in Honour of John O. Ward*, ed. C. J. Mews, C. J. Nederman and R. M. Thomson (Turnhout, 2003), pp. 115–27 (pp. 115–16).

example of civic virtue fed a long tradition of both inciting praise and emulation, and extracting accusations of sexual lewdness, unreliability, greed, arrogance and contentious behaviour. Liutprand of Cremona's (c. 922–70/72) scathing attack on Rome in the *Relatio de legatione Constantinopolitana* in the context of his diplomatic mission to Byzantium in 968 at the behest of German Emperor Otto I (912–73) is probably the most well-known example.[27]

In response to the Gregorian Reform movement, accusations now rang out that Rome's greed was damaging the entire Church, in particular the fees owed to Rome by clerics when they took office. It brought forth an outburst of satire on venality, and manifold complaints about how communities' wealth leaked from all corners of the world to Rome. Diatribes against the sale of false relics lamented: 'The empire has fallen, but pride survives in Rome. The cult of greed reigns tightly. [...] You murdered living saints with cruel wounds, and now you are selling their dead limbs. But so long as the earth devours the bones, you will continue to sell false relics.'[28] Satirists ridiculed the sums of money that the English – reputed for their excessive wealth – transferred to the Roman papacy, claiming that they sent large amounts of silver to bribe the avaricious curia.[29] The English Benedictine monk Gervase of Canterbury (c. 1145–c. 1210) asserted in his *Chronicle* that the archbishop of Canterbury sent heaps of relics of the martyrs Albinus (white, silver metal) and Rufinus (red, gold metal) to Rome, evoking the popular image of simony and greed at the Roman Curia.[30]

---

[27] Rome's arrogance (*superbia*) – also documented in the early monastic ethnic lists discussed in chapter 1 – and desire to dominate foreign peoples (*libido dominandi*) is condemned extensively in Augustine's *On the City of God*. Negative representations of Rome appear from the ninth century onwards, primarily though not exclusively in the German territories; Lombardy and Romania are mentioned as places of ruse and poison, where there is little hospitality and things generally come at a price. Orbán, 'Omgang met "het verleden" van Rome', pp. 80–1.

[28] 'Versus Romae', ed. L. Traube, MGH Poetae Latini aevi Carolini 3 (Berlin, 1896), p. 556: 'Transiit imperium mansitque superbia tecum, / Cultus avaritiae te nimium superat / [...] Truncasti vivos crudeli vulnere sanctos: / Vendere nunc horum mortua membra soles. / Sed dum terra vorax animantum roserit ossa, / Tu poteris falsas vendere reliquias.'

[29] Lehmann, *Die Parodie im Mittelalter*, pp. 25–30; Yunck, *Lineage of Lady Meed*, pp. 71–6; P. Dronke, 'Profane Elements in Literature', in *Renaissance and Renewal in the Twelfth Century*, ed. R. L. Benson, G. Constable and C. D. Lanham (Oxford, 1982), 569–92 (p. 584). For England's wealth, see also chapter 5.

[30] Gervase of Canterbury, *Chronica Gervasii*, in *The Historical Works of Gervase of Canterbury*, ed. W. Stubbs, Rerum britannicarum medii aevi scriptores 73, 2 vols. (London, 1965), i, 560. Thomas, *The English and the Normans*, p. 335, who argues that criticism of the papacy was generally divorced from a specific English identity until after the interdict of King John in 1208. Albinus and Rufinus first appear in late

The etymological punning on the name R.O.M.A. by the Welsh–English archdeacon and court satirist Walter Map (d. 1209/10), alleging that it stood for *Radix Omnium Malorum Avaritia* (Avarice is the root of all evil), is indicative.[31] Satirists imagined and situated the local churches in a religious landscape of martyrdom that was now mined, monetized and taxed. In the highly satirical parody *The Treatise of Garcia of Toledo* (1099), Rome whimpers:

> Let us be consoled, let us be consoled, my people; behold Albinus comes, behold the Church of Toledo brings us Rufinus. Behold the three Gauls make offerings; behold England, in which the buried entrails of Albinus are housed, sends them back to you. Behold the rich seat of the Flemish, where the bones of the martyrs lie artfully hidden ...[32]

Ethnic flytings

Where the attacks on Roman avarice resisted the centralizing Church's attempts to extract money and to make moral claims about the behaviour of the clergy, many of the early catalogues of invective signify outbursts of ethnic sentiment in social and political conflicts being played out at the schools. Instead of expressing an intent to reform, they were meant to harm or ridicule, to buttress self-identities and to incite emotions enhancing the willingness to fight against foes, attacking the other by belittling physical appearance, character, eating and drinking habits and, notably, religiosity. Clerics also took to playing games with groups' names.

In the twelfth century, Norman England and the northern regions of France had a special taste for invective and prose satire. Whereas, according to Trevor

---

eleventh-century verse. Other references to them in R. M. Thomson, 'Introduction', in *Tractatus Garsiae or The Translation of the Relics of SS. Gold and Silver lines 277–82*, ed. and trans. R. M. Thomson (Leiden, 1973), p. 8; 'Tractatus Garsiae Toletani Canonici de Albino et Rufino', ed. E. Sackur, MGH *Libelli de lite imperatorum et pontificum*, 3 vols. (Hanover, 1892), ii, 424; Salimbene, *Chronica*, ed. G. Scalia, Corpus Christianorum: Continuatio mediaeualis (Turnhout, 1995–), p. 227, anno 1248. Walther, *Lateinische Sprichwörter*, ii, 83, no. 14460; Lehmann, *Die Parodie im Mittelalter*, pp. 25–9.

[31] Walter Map, *De nugiis curialium* ii.17, ed. and trans. M. R. James, revised by C. N. L. Brooke and R. A. B. Mynors (Oxford, 1983), pp. 168–9.

[32] *Tractatus Garsiae Toletani* lines 277–82, ed. and trans. Thomson, pp. 39–41: 'Consolamini, consolamini, popule meus, ecce Albinus venit, ecce Rufinum praesentat nobis Toletana ecclesia. Ecce tres Galliae offerunt nobis, ecce tellus Anglica, in qua renes Albini sepulti astruuntur, ad nos respicit. Ecce Flandriarum praedives sinus, ubi sanctorum martirum ossa arte condita requiescunt.' The translation is cited from Yunck, *Lineage of Lady Meed*, p. 74.

Dean, the insults directed at individuals in slanging matches in fourteenth- and fifteenth-century Italy focused on three archetypes – sex, defecation and rottenness – the ethnic digs here pertained to categories of vice (arrogance, avarice), cowardice in the military sphere and intemperate eating and drinking customs.[33] Even the French, so often praised as chivalrous, learned pillars of faith, are depicted as arrogant, fickle and effeminate, lacking any real bravery.[34] The Normans, too, are classified as chivalrous yet proud and cruel, possibly a reputation inherited from the past.[35] The Britons are stupid; the Flemish wealthy yet garrulous; the English, besides being intelligent, merry and having a good sense of humour (discussed further in chapter 5), are also drunkards, cowards, treacherous snakes, who speak terrible French.

One of the earliest extant examples of ethnic invective is found in a late twelfth-century miscellany of Latin verse and proverbs, written mostly by Anglo-Norman or northern French clerics, including Serlo of Wilton and Archbishop Hildebert of Lavardin.[36] Twice the scribe has copied into the margins derisory lines about ethnic groups. He perhaps was an English cleric in Paris, reviewing the ethnicity of the students in his midst:

> The French, I see, are fickle, boasting about their
> Wealth of talent, if they pursue their studies.
> The Britons, I see, are girded for altercation,
> Although their Arthur never makes a show.
> The Normans trim their hair, speak with
> elegance – their native soil permitting.
> The English nobility sends me blond pupils,
> Who shine brightly thanks to Albinus.

---

[33] T. Dean, *Crime and Justice in Late Medieval Italy* (Cambridge, 2007), p. 114; T. Dean, 'Gender and Insult in an Italian City: Bologna in the Later Middle Ages', *Social History* 29/2 (2004), 217–31.

[34] Bautier, 'Peuples, provinces', p. 10. The students at Orléans are also called sodomites.

[35] C. W. Potts, '*Atque unum ex diversis gentibus populum effecit*: Historical Tradition and the Norman Identity', in *Anglo-Norman Studies 18: Proceedings of the Battle Conference 1995*, ed. C. Harper-Bill (Woodbridge, 1996), pp. 139–52 (pp. 144–5), argues we might interpret this double-edged reputation as an attempt to protect the Viking identity of the Normans as warriors from accusations of becoming too soft and effeminate as they embraced Frankish ways.

[36] W. D. Macray, *Catalogi codicum manuscriptorum Bibliothecae Bodleianae pars nona codices a viro clarissimo Kenelm Digby, Eq. Aur., anno 1634 donatos, complectens: adiecto indice nominum et rerum* (Oxford, 1883). Reprinted with corrigenda by R. W. Hunt and A. G. Watson (Oxford, 1999), pp. 26–7.

The Teutons are hardly Catholic, nobody's friend:
When they greet you, beware, for they are your foe!³⁷

It is worth pausing for a moment to unpack this one example of an ethnic flyting, to understand how the anonymous author is repeating common jokes and snarls embedded in the political lifeworld of the schools, Church and courts. First, the remark that the Teutons are barely Catholic also appears in proverbs featuring the people of Alsace and Westphalia.³⁸ The warning to be on guard surfaces in verse about English tail-bearers as well as in a misogynist context, suggestive of how stereotypes intersectionally slide from one group into another.³⁹ Allusions to Breton stupidity are found both in Latin and in late twelfth-century vernacular sources, in oxymoronic sayings such as 'Neither a fat chicken nor a wise Breton'.⁴⁰ The image of wrathful Britons (*ira Britonnum* in the earlier monastic lists) echoes in remarks that they readily pick a fight and wave their fists.⁴¹ However, the tendency of the Bretons to resort to violence is here presented as an act of desperation. The reference to King Arthur is also known as 'Breton Hope'. It is a belittling comment on the so-called Breton belief that King Arthur would one day return and release the Bretons from the yoke of Anglo-Norman subordination. It is court waggery, in the darker context of Anglo-Norman claims over Brittany. Derision of the Bretons' belief especially came to a head during the English King Henry II's campaign to assert his claim to Brittany in 1167. The *Draco Normannicus*, a chronicle written between 1167 and 1169 by Etienne de Rouen, a monk at the abbey of Bec in Normandy, for instance, contains spurious satirical letters

---

37 Oxford, Bodleian Library, MS Digby 53 fol. 17r.: 'Instabiles Galli mihi sunt, predivite vena / Freti, si studium perpetuare queant. / Sunt mihi succinti Britones ad iurgia, quorum / Arturus numquam perveniendo venit. / Sunt castigati Normanni crine, faceti / Verbis, natalis si patiatur humus. / Anglica nobilitas flavos mihi legat alumnos, / Quos facit Albinus prerediare comes. / Theutonici vix catholici, nullius amici: / Quando dicit Ave, sicut ab hoste cave!' Walther, 'Scherz', nos. 13, 97, 172, 174, 178.

38 E.g. in the catalogue printed in Wattenbach, 'Aus einer Humanistenhandschrift', p. 823 (from Berlin, Staatsbibliothek, Lat. fol. 49, a manuscript dating to the fifteenth century), where the people of the Alsace are barely Catholic; Walther, 'Scherz' no. 7 and 166B. In the *Carminum proverbalium* (Basel, 1576), p. 69, the Westphalians are 'hardly Catholic'; Walther, 'Scherz', no. 193.

39 Walther, 'Scherz', no. 15.

40 'Ne gras porci ne sage Breton', ed. J. Morawski, *Proverbes français antérieurs au XVe siècle* (Paris, 1925), p. 1340. Wilmart, 'Florilège de Saint-Gatien', p. 32: 'Nec pinguis pullus, Brito nec sapiens erit ullus.'

41 Bautier, 'Peuples, provinces', p. 12.

written by Count Roland to Arthur, who replies from the Antipodes.[42] Finally, although the verse repeats the triumphant boast that France is the home of learning, here the French are also fickle and proud.

In fact, only the Normans seem commendable, well spoken, with neatly trimmed haircuts. This last remark comes with the curious aside that this is only the case if their native soil 'permits it'. Could this be a derisory allusion to the quality of the Anglo-Norman language and culture under the influence of English customs? In the latter part of the eleventh century, the chaplain William of Poitiers (*c.* 1020–90), the author of the *Carmen de Hastingae Proelio* (The Song of the Battle of Hastings), and Baldric, abbot of Bourgueil and bishop of Dol-de-Bretagne, associated long hair with effeminacy and unwarlike qualities. According to Hugh Thomas, long hair became very fashionable first among the Anglo-Norman nobility and afterwards in circles of English burghers and peasants in the early years of the twelfth century.[43]

This was much to the disdain of the Church, which from the 1090s repeatedly issued the command that 'no one should grow his hair long but have it cut as befits a Christian', under the threat of being denied a Christian burial and being excluded from the Church.[44] Moreover, at the end of the twelfth century, the well-spoken French of the Normans was contrasted in Latin and vernacular jokes with the blustering Anglo-Norman tongue.[45] In the *Roman*

---

[42] William of Malmesbury, *Gesta regum Anglorum* i 8, ed. and trans. Mynors, Thomson and Winterbottom, i, 27. Echard, *Arthurian Narrative in the Latin Tradition*, pp. 69, 85–93. Day, 'The Letter from King Arthur to Henry II', pp. 153–7.

[43] William of Poitiers comments upon the astonishingly long hair of some of the English hostages brought back to Normandy by William the Conqueror in *Gesta Guilhelmi* ii.44, ed. R. H. C. Davis and M. Chibnall (Oxford, 1998), pp. 178–80. Thomas, *The English and the Normans*, pp. 50–1, 55, 247; R. Bartlett, 'Symbolic Meanings of Hair in the Middle Ages', *Transactions of the Royal Historical Society* 4 (1994), 43–60; Platelle, H., 'Le problème du scandale: Les nouvelles modes masculines aux XIe et XIIe siècles', *Revue Belge de Philologie et d'Histoire* 53/4 (1975), 1071–96.

[44] Such as at the Council of Rouen in 1096; Orderic Vitalis, *Historia ecclesiastica* ix.3, ed. Chibnall, pp. 22–3; at p. 24 the northern, rough Norman warriors are compared to their softer neighbours. On the other hand, William of Malmesbury denounces the English at Hastings as drunkards who had 'hair short, chin shaven, arms loaded with gold bracelets, skin tattooed with coloured patterns, eating till they were sick and drinking till they spewed'; in *Gesta regum Anglorum* iii.245, ed. and trans. Mynors, Thomson and Winterbottom, i, 458–9.

[45] P. Rickard, *Britain in Medieval French Literature, 1100–1500* (Cambridge, 1956), pp. 163–87; R. Morris, 'King Arthur and the Growth of French Nationalism', in *France and the British Isles in the Middle Ages and Renaissance: Essays by Members of Girton College, Cambridge, in Memory of Ruth Morgan*, ed. G. Jondorf and D.

de Renart, for instance, the fox Renart disguises himself as a *jongleur* in order to deceive the wolf Ysengrimus, but he cannot even conjugate the simple verb *être*.[46] Anglo-Normans were derided as speaking 'Marlborough French', confusing the gender of nouns, forgetting syllables and generally muddling up their vocabulary.

A different collection of proverbial ethnic jabs – 'Italians sell all things both sacred and profane' – in the same manuscript yet again takes as its benchmark the avarice of Rome, although it is now substituted with Italy.[47] Opening with an attack on Italy's insatiable thirst for money, it comments on the eating and drinking customs of the Flemish and English, who drink beer, on Breton writing and on the singing of the people in the Auvergne. This time the compiler is decidedly positive about the French, who are said to be victorious in battle but do not occasion war unless they are provoked. However, the collection of proverbs also appears in an extended version in a thirteenth-century manuscript held at the British Library, where the Germans are denounced as barely Catholic and the Normans are considered to have the most treacherous of characters.[48] These verses contain a mishmash of proverbial, satirical allusions to financial greed, religiosity, eating and drinking habits and behaviour in warfare, collected by and assumedly tailored to the ethnocentric sentiments of the scribe. The tradition is continued in the thirteenth century, when an extensive catalogue focusing predominantly on the German territories, was drawn up, of which many variants appear continuing into the fifteenth century,

---

Dumville (Woodbridge, 1991), pp. 115–29 (pp. 119–20); E. Schulze-Busacker, 'French Conceptions of Foreigners and Foreign Languages in the Twelfth and Thirteenth Centuries', *Romance Philology* 41 (1987–88), 24–47 (pp. 39–40); E. Schulze-Busacker, 'Renart, le jongleur étranger: Analyse thématique et linguistique à partir de la branche Ib du Roman de Renart (vv. 2403–2580 et 2857–3034)', *Third International Beast Epic, Fable, and Fabliau Colloquium*, ed. J. Goossens and T. Sodmann (Cologne, 1981), pp. 380–91; J. E. Matzke, 'Some Examples of French as Spoken by Englishmen in Old French Literature', *Modern Philology* 3 (1905), 1–14; C. H. Livingston, 'The Fabliau "Des deux Anglais et de l'anel"', *Publications of the Modern Language Association of America* 40/2 (1925), 217–24 for other examples of ridicule of the French dialect spoken in England.

[46] Rickard, *Britain in Medieval Literature*, p. 171; R. Bartlett, *England under Norman and Angevin Kings, 1075–1225* (Oxford 2000), p. 489.

[47] 'Romani que non sacra sunt atque que sacra vendunt', in Oxford, Bodleian Library, Digby MS 53 fol. 16r.; Walther, 'Scherz', no. 136. P. Meyer, 'Troisième rapport sur une mission littéraire en Angleterre et en Écosse', *Archives des missions scientifiques et littéraires*, 2ème série 5 (1868), 139–272 (p. 183).

[48] Printed in Wright and Halliwell-Phillips, *Reliquiae Antiquae*, i, 5 (London, British Library, Cotton MS Vespasian B xiii fol. 123r.). Walther, 'Scherz' no. 101; Walther, *Initia carminum*, no. 9661.

culminating in a Goliardic poem which playfully bemoans the flight of a wandering clerk, fleeing from Flemish butter, the drinking of the Bohemians and the fallacious Hungarians.[49]

Name games

In general, the early invective used in this period to attack group character falls back on the tradition of etymology, whether drawn from social practices or environment. This was a particularly effective means of attack, for, as discussed in chapter 1, Isidore of Seville had taught that the etymology of a name reflected a person or thing's essence. Making a play on individual or group names was hence a powerful tool to ridicule and humiliate, as it represented a profound attack on an essential component of identity. Jokes about names were jokes about a core element of group identity.

The etymology of ethnic names sometimes related to eponymous founders of Trojan descent. In his *History of the British Kings*, Geoffrey of Monmouth (*c.* 1090–1154/55) had awarded the Britons a Trojan ancestry descending from Brutus, the grandson of Ascanius. It was not a huge step to make a play on Brutus and claim that the British were brutes. Toying with the idea of British stupidity, a critical William of Newburgh (*c.* 1136–*c.* 1198), who was an Augustinian canon, hinted that the Britons were *bruti*. This might also explain their gullibility in believing Geoffrey of Monmouth's fabulations in his *History of the British Kings*.[50]

The glosses to Évrard of Béthune's popular school text the *Graecismus* are replete with these kinds of ethnic name games, in particular in reaction to Marbod of Rennes's verse, quoted above, about the superiority of the Angevins, which was itself incorporated within the *Graecismus*.[51] In general, the glosses to the *Graecismus* are sympathetic to the French, evoking France's ascendancy in arms and wisdom.[52] Évrard of Béthune, however, elaborates on the passage about the Angevins by also including the 'claim of a common servant' that

---

[49] Haye, 'Deutschland und die deutschen Lande', p. 309. The poem 'Quo miser exul venio turbine perfusus?', ed. P. Lehmann, *Mitteilungen aus Handschriften*, 9 vols. (Munich, 1929–50), i, 28; Walther, 'Scherz', no. 143.

[50] William of Newburgh, *Historia rerum Anglicarum*, i, Prooemium, in *Chronicles of the Reigns of Stephen, Henry II, and Richard I: Volume 1. The First Four Books of Historia rerum Anglicarum of William of Newburgh*, ed. R. Howlett, Rerum Britannicarum Medii Aevi Scriptores, 4 vols. (New York, 1964), i, 14; Koht, 'Dawn of Nationalism', pp. 270–2. Nennius was the first to award the British with Trojan descent in the ninth century.

[51] Évrard of Béthune, *Graecismus* iii lines 10–12, ed. Wrobel, pp. viii, 12.

[52] Cf. Hauréau, *Notices et extraits*, iv, 280–9.

'*astin* means towns and *anda* shit', which hence accounts for the Angevins' name.⁵³ There are earlier instances of the same Latin pun being employed in a political context, in this case the papal election of 1130, in which Poitiers and Angers represented the two rival camps of Pope Anacletus II (d. 1138) and Pope Innocent II (d. 1143).⁵⁴ In the verse, rendered here in Latin to convey the pun, the motif *nomen est omen* is fully present:

> Sicut Pictavis nomen trahit ex ave picta,
> Sic est Andegavis volucris de stercore dicta.
> Stercus avis sonat Andegavis: de stercore nomen
> Urbs tua contraxit, quia sic tibi contulit omen.⁵⁵

The same image is repeated in another gloss on Évrard of Béthune's *Graecismus*, explicitly stating that the city of Anjou was built on a foundation of bird excrement.⁵⁶ In response, another gloss on the text directly targets the etymology of Poitou and Angers:

> Just as Poitevin comes from a 'painted bird',
> Thus Anjou is said to come from bird shit.
> Just as a painted bird does not represent the truth,
> Thus the people here always want to fill words with falsities.⁵⁷

---

53   Évrard of Béthune, *Graecismus* viii, lines 28–9, ed. Wrobel, p. 28: 'Ut mediastinus probat, astin denotat urbem, / Andaque stercus, ab hinc dicitur Andegavis.'
54   The author of the verse was a supporter of Antipope Anacletus II (d. 1138) and Count William X of Aquitaine (1099–1137), who had expelled Bishop William of Poitiers, a supporter of Innocent II (d. 1143), from the town. Bishop Ulger of Angers (d. 1149) also supported Innocent II.
55   'Just as Poitevin derives from a painted bird, / Thus Angers is said to derive from bird shit. / Birdshit sounds like Angevin, your town's name is based on shit, as the omen says of you.' The verse, 'Est ratio quare bafio dici merearis', ed. W. Wattenbach, 'Mittheilungen aus Handschriften', *Neues Archiv der Gesellschaft für Ältere Deutsche Geschichtskunde zur Beförderung einer Gesamtausgabe der Quellenschriften deutscher Geschichten des Mittelalters* 8 (1883), 191–3, from a thirteenth-century manuscript. A little further down, the folio explicitly mentions that in Greek *anda* means excrement: 'Stercus et anda idem dixerunt significare / Qui Grecas voces studuerunt notificare.'
56   Évrard of Béthune, *Graecismus* viii 29, ed. Wrobel, p. 28: 'Anda graece est stercus latine et inde Andegavis et est nomen civitatis et derivatur a stercoribus avium, qui ubi invenerunt stercora avium ibi fundaverunt civitatem.' Cf. Bautier, 'Peuples, provinces', pp. 13–14, notes 71–2.
57   Hauréau, *Notices et extraits*, iv, 280–9 (p. 284) (from Paris, Bibliothèque nationale de France MS Latin 15133 fol. 33r.): 'Sicut Pictavis nomen trahit ex ave picta, / Sic est Andegavis avium de stercore dicta. / Sicut avis picta verum non denotat esse, / Sic gens hinc dicta falsis vult semper inesse.' Cf. *Histoire littéraire de la France*.

In sharp ridicule, the students also targeted the religiosity of peoples. Another gloss etymologized that 'the Allebroges come from *allos*, i.e. foreign, and *broge*, faith, as if foreign to faith', explaining that the men of Burgundy were traitors.[58] Such attacks were directed especially at groups in northern and eastern Europe, the German territories and at the English, all regions of settlement and subjugation. There is a range of proverbs warning to be on one's guard when greeted by a German or Englishman, as they are barely Catholic, or, where the English are concerned, are treacherous.[59] These insults directly questioned the veracity of religious belief and, in the case of the English, their alleged chosenness and humanness.

The joke about the Englishman with a tail, and attacks on the name *Anglus*, were angular assaults on their identity. This needs some explanation, for in learned geography the name Anglus is etymologized in a positive sense. For instance, Bartholomaeus Anglicus, in his encyclopaedic *On the Properties of Things*, elaborately explains how the name Anglus came from *angelus*, angel, or *angulo*, corner. The angelic etymology related back to the story of Gregory the Great's encounter with young, angel-faced slaves at a market in Italy, narrated by Bede.[60] Gregory himself, engaging in some dexterous punning, realizes the potential of their conversion – foreshadowed by their beautiful angelic faces – and sends the Benedictine monk Augustine of Canterbury (d. 604) on a mission to proselytize in this corner, *angulo*, of the world. This episode forms part of the myth of the conversion and chosenness of the Anglo-Saxons.

However, the reputation of the English was double-edged. On the one hand, Anglo-Norman clerics praised the English as intelligent, generous and merry at a time when the English themselves were colonizing 'backward Ireland'. In the aggregate these characteristics corresponded to the sanguine traits of civic urbanity, held in high esteem – the features of a society of good governance. But negative stereotypes of Anglo-Saxon perfidy, cowardice and drunkenness also circulated. A recurring motif was that of the tailed Englishman (*Anglus*

XIII siècle, 46 vols. (Paris, 1733–2018), XXX, 296: 'Andaque, stercus ab hinc, dicitur Andegavis'; Walther, 'Scherz', no. 160. The Florilegium of St Gatien contains the first two lines, in a slightly different version; Wilmart, 'Le florilège de Saint-Gatien', p. 28. The same manuscript (on p. 32) contains a more positive verse about Poitou: 'Pictavis aurea, Gloria terrea, terra quietis, / utilis aere, clarior ethere, plena poetis'; Walther, 'Scherz', no. 128; Bautier, 'Peuples, provinces', p. 13.

[58] Hauréau, *Notices et extraits*, iv, 284: 'Alloboga dicitur ab allos, quod est alienum, et broge, fides, quasi alienus a fide.'

[59] Walther, 'Scherz', no. 7, 15, 178.

[60] Bede, *Historia Ecclesiastica* ii.1, ed. and trans. Colgrave and Mynors, pp. 133–5.

caudatus).⁶¹ The oldest known source, produced by the Flemish Benedictine monk Goscelin of St Bertin (*c.* 1035–*c.* 1107), relates how Augustine of Canterbury, on his mission to convert the Brits, encountered resistance from the inhabitants of Dorset, who were said to have attached fishtails to his behind, thus forever condemning their progeny to bearing beastly tails. Wace (*c.* 1100–71/83), whose French poem *Roman de Brut* was dedicated to Queen Eleanor of Aquitaine (*c.* 1122–1204), asserted that Augustine prayed to God in Dorchester to dishonour and disgrace those who remained deaf to his message, wreaking upon them his anger and judgement, perpetually shaming the inhabitants.⁶² However, the image of the tailed Englishman soon became a popular trope used to ridicule the English, not only in satirical literature such as the *Ysengrimus* but, for example, by the students in Paris, as Bishop Jacques de Vitry tells us.⁶³ In the poet's Layamon's thirteenth-century Old English version of the *Brut*, the myth was extended to include all of the English, shaming red-faced English freemen abroad, where they were called 'muglings'.⁶⁴ The tale also became muddled up with an incident occurring on the night before the murder of Archbishop Thomas Becket, when his adversaries cut

61   G. Neilson, '*Caudatus Anglicus:* A Medieval Slander', *Transactions of the Glasgow Archaeological Society*, new series 2 (1896), 441–77; D. Th. Enklaar, *De gestaarte Engelsman* (Amsterdam, 1955); L. M. C. Randall, 'A Medieval Slander', *The Art Bulletin* 42/1 (1960), 25–38; P. Rickard, '"Anglois coué" and "L'Anglois qui couve"', *French Studies: A Quarterly Review* 7 (1953), 48–55; P. S. Brown, 'Scoundrels and *Scurrilitas* at St-Pierre de Sévignac', in *Difference and Identity in Francia and Medieval France*, ed. M. Cohen and J. Firnhaber-Baker (Farnham, 2010), 197–226 (p. 217).

62   Goscelin of St Bertin, *Vita Sancti Augustini*, I.41, *PL* 80, cols. 82B–82D. According to Goscelin, the inhabitants of Rochester attacked the saint by attaching fish tails to him; this is repeated by William of Malmesbury writing about Dorsetshire, and later by Wace, *Roman de Brut*, lines 13711–44, *A History of the British: Text and Translation*, ed. and trans. J. Weiss (Exeter, 1999), p. 345, where the descendants of the town dwellers are damned. Cf. Neilson, *Medieval Slander*, pp. 4–5; Enklaar, *Gestaarte Engelsman*, pp. 14–15; Randall, 'Medieval Slander', pp. 34–5 for further references.

63   Enklaar, *Gestaarte Engelsman*, p. 3. *Ysengrimus* iii, line 659, *Ysengrimus: Text with Translation, Commentary and Introduction*, ed. and trans. J. Mann, Mittellateinische Studien und Texte, 12 (Leiden, 1987), p. 334. The *Ysengrimus* was attributed to Master Nivardus and written in Ghent in 1148/9. For Jacques de Vitry's comments, see pp. 161–2 in this chapter. Cf. the twelfth-century Provençal poet Peire D'Auvergne's comments, who calls the English *coütz*; *Die Lieder Peire's von Auvergne*, ed. R. Zenker (Erlangen, 1900), p. 110. Neilson, *Medieval Slander*, pp. 7–8.

64   Layamon, *Brut or Hystoria Brutonum*, lines 14756–72, ed. W. R. J. Barron and S. C. Weinberg (Harlow, 1995), pp. 758–9.

off the tail of one of his horses.⁶⁵ This spurious version was encapsulated in sayings such as 'You, laughing Englishman, cut off the mule's tail: or are you an English serpent? I'm not sure, the tail is hidden.'⁶⁶

Images of perfidy and drunkenness, weakness and treachery, and the etymology of the English name, as well as their beastlike tails, slid into one another, tying servility to inhumanity. In a gloss on Alexander Neckam's didactical text *On Instruments*, the etymological attack on the Angevins is transposed onto the English: '*Anglia*, that is to say *Anglicus*, comes from *anda*, that is shit, or from *angue*, because it stings with its tail like a snake, or from *angulo*, or from *angelus*.'⁶⁷ The etymology of the English name is here related to defecation, the evil prelapsarian snake, the tail, the traditional reference to a corner and, lastly and perhaps reluctantly, an angel. In the fourteenth century, in *Ly Myreur des Histors*, Jean d'Outremeuse (1338–99) elaborates by linking the English tail-bearing descendants of 'King Englans' to the progeny of Cain, the forebear of servile peasantry; whether his clarification is original, or older, is difficult to ascertain.⁶⁸ Other remarks relate tail-bearing to the female gender,

---

⁶⁵ Neilson, *Medieval Slander*, pp. 6–7. The event apparently occurred on Christmas Eve, 1170. In the twelfth century, it is also related to the figure of Bevis of Hampton, where tails are attributed to descendants of the giant in Bevis's service. Rickard, '"Anglois coué" and "L'Anglois qui couve"', p. 49.

⁶⁶ *Anecdota Bedae, Lanfranci et aliorum: Inedited Tracts, Letters, Poems etc. of Venerable Bede, Lanfranc, Tatwin*, ed. J. A. Giles (New York, 1851), p. 96: 'Te ridens Anglus mulo caudam amputate: anne / Est Anglus serpens? Nescio, cauda latet'. Cf. Walther, 'Scherz', no. 176.

⁶⁷ Hauréau, *Notices et extraits*, iii, 203–4: 'Anglia, inde Anglicus, ab ande, quod est stercus, vel ab angue, quia pungit cum cauda sicut anguis, vel ab angulo, vel ab angelus.' Hauréau dates the gloss to the first part of the thirteenth century. The glossator was possibly French and he also glosses that Gallus means a bird, a people, a poet and a river and is known for its priests. Cf. the Franciscan friar William Brito's *Summa Britonis: sive, Guillelmi Britonis Expositiones vocabulorum Biblie* (dating to 1250/1270), ed. L. W. Daly and B. A. Daly, 2 vols. (Padua, 1975), i, 295, asserting that the sibyls called the Gallic priest weak and effeminate, and the comments of Alexander of Roes, *Memoriale* 15, ed. Grundmann and Heimpel, pp. 105–8. C.-V. Langlois, 'Les Anglais du Moyen Âge d'après les sources françaises', *Revue historique* 52/2 (1893), 298–315 (p. 309).

⁶⁸ Only the inhabitants of Canterbury and Dorchester still have tails. The first Angles had tails and those of pure lineage kept their tails, the others have been murdered. They are descendants of King Englans, originating from Engle, a region near the Tower of Babel; Enklaar, *Gestaarte Engelsman*, p. 4. In *Oeuvres complètes de Eustache Deschamps: publiées d'après le manuscrit de la Bibliothèque Nationale*, ed. Marquis de Queux de Saint-Hilaire, Société des Anciens Textes Français 8, 11 vols. (Paris, 1878–1903) v, 48–9, Eustache Duchamps, joking about tails and drinking, questions what the Englishman should do with his tail on a visit to Calais; I. Black,

inviting the Dominican friar Etienne de Bourbon (1180/95–1261) to pose the question why females do not have tails akin to the English.[69] At the end of the thirteenth century, a monk from Silly in northern Hainaut produces a scathing political diatribe against English King Edward I, who was embroiled in endless wars against the French, relating scorpions' tales to English treachery.[70] By the late thirteenth century, in good Vegetian tradition, in the wars between England and Scotland men shouted before battle that the English were *canes caudatos*, tailed dogs or apes. In the early fourteenth century, they also are compared to rats or eels.[71] Moreover, in the thirteenth century, the image crops up that the English hatch eggs, as the Old French *cové* meant both to hatch and 'tailed', implying stupidity, brooding and scheming.[72] Finally, in the fourteenth century, in a commentary by Benvenuto da Imola (1320/30–c. 1387), the Gascons are said to have a wolf's tail and the English snakes' tails.[73]

Moving from the schools to the courts, where many students found employment upon or before graduation, etymological attacks entered the political sphere, lending arguments to political commentaries or claims to political power. Between 1157 and 1161, Pierre Riga (1140–1209), a canon of Reims cathedral, attacked King Henry II of England on the occasion of Henry's broken promise to French King Louis VII (1120–80) regarding the marriage alliance of their young progeny.[74] Appertaining to the etymology of *Anglus* derived from the angelic or angular, Pierre Riga retorts: 'Name and deed do

---

'An Accidental Tourist in the Hundred Years' War: Images of the Foreign World in Eustache Deschamps', in *Concepts of National Identity in the Middle Ages*, ed. S. Forde, L. Johnson and A. V. Murray (Leeds, 1995), pp. 171–87 (pp. 177–8).

[69] Randall, 'Medieval Slander', p. 34.

[70] See also the comment made at the end of the thirteenth century in John of Oxenedes's text about the Barons' War, discussed in Neilson, 'Medieval Slander', p. 10.

[71] Enklaar, *Gestaarte Engelsman*, pp. 11–14.

[72] The joke is mentioned in the early second part of the thirteenth century in the *Vie de St Remi*. In fourteenth-century manuscripts there is also mention of Bretons hatching eggs; Cf. Randall, 'Medieval Slander', p. 36 for source references.

[73] Langlois, 'Les Anglais du Moyen Âge', pp. 309–10; Cf. *Notes and Queries: A Medium of Intercommunication for Literary Men, General Readers, etc.* (London, 1849–), 28 January 1893, pp. 83–4; 4 February 1893, p. 108; 18 February 1893, p. 155. Matthew Paris, *Chronica Majora*, ed. R. Luard, 7 vols. (London, 1872–83), v, 134, 151 (anno 1250) and the *The Chronicle of Lanercost, 1272–1346*, ed. H. Maxwell (Glasgow, 1913), p. 167 concerning the defeat of 1217 at Lincoln. Tailed Englishmen are also compared to dogs by the French aristocracy. Cf. Neilson, *Medieval Slander*, pp. 8–9; Enklaar, *Gestaarte Engelsman*, p. 4.

[74] See also chapter 5.

not correspond well. / To scrutinise the purport of the name: Either English sounds / Like an angel or Angelic like English. / Take note: he is English, no angel, not worthy / Of heaven, but a corner of crime, indeed crime itself!'[75]

The itinerant poet Henry of Avranches (d. 1262/63), who possibly came from Cologne, combined the popular stereotype of English drunkenness with their tailed behinds, the butt end of jokes directed at the Anglo-Norman knights in Richard I's (1157–99) army during the Third Crusade (1189–92).[76] Several courts sponsored Henry of Avranches's literary work, including the papal court, the German Emperor Otto IV, Louis IX of France and Henry III of England, and Henry exploits ethnotypes freely and strategically in his verse. Henry clearly was familiar with Graeco-Arabic science, as he produced a debate verse of Aristotle's *On Generation and Corruption*.[77] In his ethnic debate poem (the initial attack by the Englishman is missing), he lets a German called Conrad fiercely attack Anglo-British ethnogenesis: 'When the tailed English, who were born for drinking cups, / Are filled up, it is with the seed of Brutus. / Then they throw themselves into the fray, boasting they are a glorious people, / Bringing death to all, belching with bursting bellies, / For they are unwarlike weavers and fullers.'[78] On this occasion, gender slips into the imagery and

---

[75] Printed in B. Hauréau, 'Un poème inédit de Pierre Riga', *Bibliothèque de l'École des Chartres* 44 (1883), 5–11 (p. 8): 'Nec bene respondent nomen opusque sibi. / Nominis augurium scrutare: vel angelus Anglus / Ille, vel Angelicus Anglicus ille sonat. / Facta notes: Anglus, non angelus est, neque coelo / Dignus, sed sceleris angulus, imo scelus.' Another comment on the treacherous 'angelic' nature of the English, 'Anglicus angelus est cui numquam credere fas est', in Peiper, 'Europäischer Völkerspiegel', p. 104; Walther, 'Lateinische Verseinträge', 308; Walther, 'Scherz', no. 16. The angelic nature of the English is also ridiculed by Peter the Breton, in Lawrence of Durham's twelfth-century *Dialogi* iii, lines 207–22, ed. Raine, p. 37.

[76] J. C. Russell, 'Master Henry of Avranches as an International Poet', *Speculum* 3/1 (1928), 34–63. Heng, *Empire of Magic*, pp. 92–6. Richard of Devises claims that Richard I and his crusader knights at Messina (after 1190) were called *caudati* by the Greeks and Sicilians. Richard of Devises, *The Chronicle of Richard of Devizes of the Time of King Richard the First / Cronicon Richardi Divisensis de tempore Regis Richardi Primi*, ed. J. T. Appleby (London, 1963), pp. 18–19. In *Richard Coer de Lyon*, the Emperor of Cyprus uses the tailed image as a retort when he is captured by the 'King of Allemayne'. Cf. *Der mittelenglische Versroman über Richard Löwenherz*, ed. K. Brunner (Vienna, 1913), pp. 117, 180, 194, 196. Neilson, *Medieval Slander*, pp. 7–8.

[77] P. Binkley, 'Thirteenth Century Latin Poetry Contests Associated with Henry of Avranches with an Appendix of Newly Edited Texts' (unpublished dissertation, University of Toronto, 1991), p. 29.

[78] Henry of Avranches, 'Non valet audire mala plus Conradulus ire', ed. Binkley, pp. 228–30 (p. 228): 'Angli caudati, qui sunt ad pocula nati, / Cum sunt imbuti, tunc

Henry of Avranches specifically ridicules the gluttony, effeminacy and weak military skills of the English from the perspective of profession, as Vegetius advised. The Germans, on the other hand, were not a royal but an imperial people, subject only to Rome, strong, triumphant, impetuous, with golden hair and tall bodies. (Afterwards, the Englishman defends himself by signalling his own generosity, compared to the German who is reviled throughout the world like a dog.) The miserable British – Henry of Avranches uses the words English/British synonymously following their assimilation or miscegenation – might take a leaf out of the Germans' book: 'But you, o miserable British, slow to the battlefield, / Whose belly is your God and abyss of food.[79] / Full of the dregs of beer and without wisdom, / You honour Bacchus when darkness falls; / Then Venus appears, applying her lewd potion ...'[80]

Following Vegetian tradition, Henry of Avranches's attack alluding to the 'essence' of the English and the Germans is set in a military sphere, suggesting that the feebleness of the English army stemmed from the fact that the recruits were scouted among its artisan weavers. Relating the defence of the *patria* to the mental and physical qualities of recruits and their professions in this case inevitably tied the military defence to the territory's economy, the work ethic of its inhabitants as well as their (lack of) discipline. Moreover, the imagery tapped gendered ideas about strength and power that informed the language underlying the struggles between imperium and principalities, which is analysed in chapter 5.

Conclusion

It is often hard to gauge to what extent ethnic jokes actually caused insult – to what extent nationhood superseded class or legal status, or, for that matter, linguistic divisions, for these jokes came from a Latinate world and for the most part target Christian groups. Assumedly, in the cosmopolitan setting of the centres of learning of Paris, Bologna or Oxford, ethnic slanging matches evoked laughter, serving as an escape valve for the schoolmen convening there. In the *scholiae* in a thirteenth-century codex of German provenance, the Teuton is playfully glossed as positioned under the planet of Mars, naturally bellicose

---

    sunt de semine Bruti; / Prelia tunc tractant, quod sunt gens inclita iactant, / Dant omnes leto, ructantes ventre repleto, / Cum sint imbelles textores vel paripelles.'
[79] Phillipians 3. 17–19.
[80] Henry of Avranches, 'Non valet audire mala plus Conradulus ire', ed. Binkley, p. 229: 'Sed vos, O miseri Britones, ad prelia seri, / Est venter quorum deus atque vorago ciborum, / Vos fece cervisie pleni vacuique sophie / Precolitis Bacum suberit cum tempus opacum; / Tunc Venus obscena subit apponendo venen<a>.'

and customarily cruel, for which reason 'the Romans have inserted in their liturgy: "Save us, o Lord, from the German fury"'.[81] This is clerical banter.

On occasion, however, political conflict and colonization gave rise to the use of harsher ethnic invective, disparaging the cultural and moral features of the other while subjecting them to violence or legal subordination. Attacks took on a more truculent and acerbic flavour in the Church and secular courts, where the use of violence was sanctioned and organized. Ethnic flytings expressed the growing resistance to the outreach of the Roman Church and its policies of taxation. At the courts, moreover, poets and historians held up ethnic stereotypes as markers of civility or barbarity, lending group members status-enhancing claims to reputations of chivalry and urbanity, as the outcome of some form of 'civilising process' and religious *translatio*. Conversely, they associated status-diminishing barbarian cruelty, lawlessness, absence of religious devotion and even beastliness with the territories being settled in Palestine, Ireland and the Baltic, whose bountiful lands were ripe for the taking. It is at the courts, also, that these often gendered ethnic attacks were informed by and infused with environmental theory. It is particularly within this urban–courtly world of learning and power where we begin to see how ideas of Arabic-Graeco medicine – framing the body in relation to geography, descent *and* environment – informed and undergirded ideas about the moral community and its culture, social norms and values. Thus, within the Ciceronian tradition, fitness to wield power and hold property was rhetorically measured by referencing reputations of manliness, rationality, discipline, religious and social organization over which various groups within the *imperium* competed.

The final two chapters of this book, 5 and 6, explore how ethnic images pertaining to culture and religion became entangled with Hippocratic environmental theory in court milieus where agendas of colonization and conquest were set. Images of ethnicity were thus employed and lent cogency to arguments of power, to threats and the actual use of violence, in a gendered language that spoke of military prowess and progress that would leave a lasting mark on the language of colonization in the centuries to come.

---

[81] Walter of Châtillon, *Alexandreis*, ed. Colker, pp. 455–6, 482 (from Vienna, Österreichische Nationalbibliothek, Codex Vindobonensis MS 568): 'Teutonici enim constituti sunt sub Marte illo planeta, et ideo naturaliter sunt bellicosi de more quia secundum consuetudinem crudeles sunt. Inde etiam Romani habent in letania sua "A furore Theutonicorum libera nos, Domine".'

5

French Control, German Rage, English Charm: Gender and Military Power

Between 1159 and 1162 a monk from Tegernsee in Bavaria completed *The Play of the Antichrist*. The play, perhaps performed in the open air, relates how the German emperor, to whom several embassies had submitted *dominium*, becomes embroiled in a battle with the Antichrist. The latter is seconded by Hypocrites. The Antichrist summons the other kings – the kings of the Franks, the Greeks and the Babylonians, and the heathen Gentilitas, King of Jerusalem – 'to help him stem this mad Teutonic flood', and they fight. The army of the Antichrist is defeated. Afterwards, the King of the Teutons returns to his throne and sings: 'Bloodshed must preserve our fatherland's honour / And the fatherland's valour drive out all her enemies. / Law is squandered when blood is for sale / And blood will keep the Empire's dignity.'[1]

This dark, belligerent utterance about the wielding of sheer, bloody, imperial power forms the benchmark and counterpoint for ethnic reputations in court literature, contrasting the Teutons with the French and English. Indeed, in the twelfth century, writers at the centres of power engaged popular ethnotypes rhetorically in competing narratives of courtliness, urbanity, manliness, rationality and power set against this violent backdrop. In their histories, poetry and epic narratives produced for the warrior aristocracy, the French, the Teutons and the English, the subjects of this chapter, jostled at the courts over claims to cultural and military dominance in which north-western Europe was presented as the seat of power and civilization. The cultural appropriation of climate theory invited poets and historians to comment upon the manners of the French, Teutons and English within a geographical framework, the French positioning themselves as the rational, disciplined and courageous receptors

[1] *Der Ludus de Antichristo*, ed. F. Wilhem (Munich, 1912), p. 21: 'Teotonicum condempnet furorem'; 'Sanguine patriae honor est retinendus, / virtute patriae est hostis expellendus. / Jus dolo perditum est sanguine venale. / Sic retinebimus decus imperiale'; adaption of trans. by J. Wright, *The Play of the Antichrist* (Toronto, 1967) pp. 88–9. H. Rosenfeld, Die Bühne des Tegernseer Antichristspiels als Orbis terrarum', in *Literatur und Sprache im europäischen Mittelalter: Festschrift für Karl Langosch zum 70. Geburtstag*, ed. A. Önnerfors, J. Rathofer and F. Wagner (Darmstadt, 1973), pp. 63–74 (p. 64).

of the *translatio studii* and chivalry in the domesticated space of sacred, *douce* northern France. The Normans and English attempted to stake similar claims, but the latter focused on the status of urbanity and intelligence rather than military qualities, presumably in response to England's recent conquest by the Normans. The Germans' reputation, considered agents of barbaric, crude violence in a harsher climate, yet holders and defenders of Christian, imperial *dominium*, was double-edged.

This chapter focuses on how, using environmental–Hippocratic arguments, writers appropriated and competed over reputations for wielding degrees of violence as a means to position the body politic vis-à-vis the *imperium* and others. The challenge by French rulership to the inheritance of the Carolingian *imperium* thus was framed as a claim to wielding rational, measured violence in a sweet environment, in contrast with senseless Teutonic rage. The latter might be called upon to crush the religious other, as a form of extreme violence, yet did not suffice to exert control over Europe's principalities, nor its new settlements in Palestine or Ireland. This chapter argues that the competition over reputations, and the negotiation of group boundaries by juxtaposing them with spatial, religious and cultural 'others' – whom the French and English framed as heretic, heathen or semi-Christians, cruel and lazy squanderers of the land they populated – engaged key markers or signposts of identity within the field of cultural norms. Clerics deliberated the level of cultural finesse, defined by the level of control over emotions and rationality, using environmental deterministic arguments that temperate lands produced rational yet strong peoples. This negotiation stretched to the military qualifications of army recruits and their gendered physical and mental traits. Army members' willingness and capacity to act as true and virtuous defenders of the Christian landscape was measured in the Vegetian tradition. It meant walking a tightrope between the wavering categories of disciplined, rationally informed warriorship, using knowledge to draw up strategies, and fearless use of extreme violence in confrontations with the religious other, and a male excess of aggression. Its counter-image was irrational, effeminate, cruel, cunning, weak, sluggish barbarity.

Positioning ethnic reputations occurred in the context of the territorialization of power at the seignorial and royal courts and urban governments. The peripatetic clerics schooled in Paris, Bologna, Oxford and Chartres, among many other places, found employment at hubs of power where, from the twelfth century, after a steep decline of royal power in the tenth century, dynastic rulers attempted to take control over territories, taxation and legal procedures. The French Capetian dynasty, especially King Philip ii, attempted to acquire more than a nominal, titular power, extending its legal and fiscal grip over the territory's domains.² The taking of Normandy in 1204, and the integration of the county of Toulouse after the Albigensian Crusade between 1209 and 1229, brought large tracts of land within the royal sphere. The Capetian chancellery adopted the spatialized term *regnum Franciae*; and in 1254 under Louis IX *rex Franciae* was substituted for *rex Francorum*.³ In England, the same process, albeit in more complicated form, unfolded in the wake of the Norman conquest in 1066. From the tenth century, on charters and coins, kings intermittently designated themselves *rex Anglorum*. In the first half of the twelfth century the concept of Englishness continued to carry weight. Some historians, notably William of Malmesbury, Henry of Huntingdon and Geffrei Gaimar (*fl.* 1136), interpreted the island's past as English history, advancing titles such as *Deeds of the English Kings* or the *History of the English*.⁴ Nonetheless, 'Englishness' was problematic and Norman poets associated it with servility, treachery and cowardice; relations between the Norman settlers and the suppressed English were both strained and assimilative.⁵ The German empire, although entertaining a hegemonic claim to holding *imperium* over the *populus christianorum*, as well as political dominance in northern Italy, was a complex configuration of territorial identities with various, partly overlapping, jurisdictions. In this period, heated competition between the French and German dynasties centred on the claim to holding *dominium* and protecting Christendom, grounded in the geopolitical ancestry of the Carolingian empire and in memories of a shared past. As discussed below, the competition over power was now also framed using environmental theory, for instance by Alexander of Roes in his *Memoriale*.⁶ Relevant in this regard is that in the twelfth

---

2 P. Contamine, 'The Growth of the Nation State', in *Britain and France: Ten Centuries*, ed. D. W. J. Johnson, F. Crouzet and F. Bédarida (Folkestone, 1980), pp. 21–31; Schieffer, 'Frankreich im Mittelalter', pp. 43–59; J. Dunbabin, *France in the Making, 843–1180* (Oxford, 1985), pp. 376–7.

3 Although Francia continued to mean the core area of royal power north of the Loire, it was now at times employed as a synonym for Gallia or designated as *Francia tota*.

4 Davies, 'The Peoples of Britain and Ireland 1100–1400 I. Identities', pp. 7–22.

5 Thomas, *The English and the Normans*.

6 There are a vast number of publications on the imperial and Carolingian legacy and twelfth-century French and German politics. See W. Kienast, *Deutschland und Frankreich in der Kaiserzeit (900–1270): Weltkaiser und Einzelkönige* (Stuttgart, 1974–75); K. F. Werner, 'Das hochmittelalterliche Imperium im politischen Bewusstsein Frankreichs (10.–12. Jahrhundert)', *Historische Zeitschrift* 200 (1965), 1–60; E. A. R. Brown, 'La notion de la légitimité et la prophétie à la cour de Philippe Auguste', in *La France de Philippe Auguste: Le temps des mutations: Actes du colloque*

century the legal meaning of *dominium* had shifted to define both property rights and authority, whereas earlier in Roman law it signalled possession.[7]

Juxtaposing moral norms voiced at centres of power by the clergy, ethnic reputations could be an asset or liability in negotiations in a social or political sphere, depending on contemporary dominant values and the weight of personal relations in kinship and social networks. The twelfth-century resurgence of rhetorical narratives of civility and barbarity, enhanced by discussions of the nature of society, reason and speech influenced by Cicero, bolstered French, English and German competition, for inherited ethnic reputations functioned as spendable sociocultural capital, to use Pierre Bourdieu's terminology. The competition over claims to strength, rationality and discipline found substance in gendered cultural values that hinged upon environment and geography as well as learning and religion, and in which northern France claimed a leading role. In this narrative the use of the epithet 'barbarian', rather than simply a label of abuse, betrays a complicated interplay of allusions to social organization and physical traits that the northern French aristocracy used to affirm their position as Christian paragons of chivalry, with cultural, political and legal implications. Indeed, political tracts considered barbaric lawlessness, laziness, irrationality and the absence of Christian beliefs to weaken claims to land ownership, opening the door to rhetorical justifications for the colonization of foreign territories and subjugation of genealogically 'cursed' groups within society (serfs, Jews).

For individual members of an ethnic group, stereotypes added or detracted from a person's sociocultural capital. For such capital to acquire value meant

---

international organisé par le C.N.R.S. (Paris, 29 septembre–4 octobre 1980), ed. R.-H. Bautier (Paris, 1982), pp. 77–110; M. Gabriele, 'The Provenance of the "Descriptio qualiter Karolus Magnus": Remembering the Carolingians in the Entourage of King Philip I (1060–1108) before the First Crusade', *Viator* 39/2 (2008), 93–117; T. Reuter, 'Past, Present and No Future in the Twelfth-Century Regnum Teutonicum', in *The Perception of the Past in Twelfth-Century Europe*, ed. P. Magdalino (London, 1992), pp. 15–36; S. Burkhardt, 'Barbarossa, Frankreich und die Weltherrschaft', in *Stauﬁsches Kaisertum im 12. Jahrhundert: Konzepte-Netzwerke-politische Praxis*, ed. S. Burkhardt e.a. (Regensburg, 2010), pp. 133–58. This new interest in the Carolingian memory went hand in hand with an increase in texts concerning the prophecy of the Last Emperor, the coming of a Second Charlemagne, and Charlemagne's purported journey to the East; see J. Ehlers, 'Karolingische Tradition und frühes Nationalbewußtsein in Frankreich', *Francia* 4 (1976), 213–35; J. L. Nelson, 'Kingship and Empire in the Carolingian World', in *Carolingian Culture: Emulation and Innovation*, ed. R. McKitterick (Cambridge, 1994), pp. 52–87 (p. 76); G. M. Spiegel, 'The Reditus Regni ad Stirpem Karoli Magni: A New Look', *French Historical Studies* 7/2 (1971), 145–74.

[7] Coleman, 'Medieval Discussions of Property', p. 212.

that it had to be measurable; to quantify and qualify sociocultural and physical capital, ethnic communities hence needed the other as a benchmark to compete or compare with, by which to draw the moral boundaries of one's own group. Consequently, in the sources, the emphasis lies on the distinct characteristics of the French, Teutons and English in relation to each other and religious and geographical 'others', rather than their shared virtues or vices under the all-encompassing umbrella of Christendom.

The benchmark of civility and chivalry

In the twelfth century, the originally Greco-Latin barbarity–civility binary was pasted onto domesticated spaces within the reference framework of the *populus christianorum*. Conduct books and regimens – advising how to govern the self, households and polities in the pursuit of good governance – and panegyrics now extolled the *civilitas* or *urbanitas* of disciplined, Christian communities in temperate spaces. In earlier centuries, the dichotomy barbarian/civilized had been transformed from a sociocultural and political category into a religious one. In antiquity, barbaric chaos was contrasted with the Greek politico-cultural ideal of the polis and associated linguistically with non-Greek-speaking peoples such as the Scyths, dwelling in harsh climates.[8] The frame was adopted under imperial Roman rule, where *Romanitas* allegedly embodied civilization, manners, subjectivity to law and moral probity, whereas barbarity represented lawlessness, savagery and cruelty. These images were grafted onto the invading and migrating bands of Germanic peoples, generally viewed – wielding climate theory – as tough and courageous yet impulsive, or, in the words of Seneca, a wild and free people,

> free by reason of their very wildness, even as they cannot submit to servitude, neither can they exercise dominion; for the ability they possess is not that of a human being but of something wild and ungovernable; and no man is able to rule unless he can also submit to be ruled. Consequently, the peoples who have held empire are commonly those who live in a rather mild climate. Those who lie toward the frozen north have savage tempers – tempers which, as the poet says, are 'Most like their native skies'.[9]

---

[8] The classic study of the Greek view of barbarity is J. Jüthner, *Hellenen und Barbaren: Aus der Geschichte des Nationalbewusstseins* (Leipzig, 1923); T. Harrison, *Greeks and Barbarians* (Edinburgh, 2002); F. Hartog, *The Mirror of Herodotus: The Representation of the Other in the Writing of History* (Berkeley, 1988); E. Hall, *Inventing the Barbarian: Greek Self-Definition Through Tragedy* (Oxford, 1989).

[9] Seneca, *De ira* ii.15, in *Moral Essays: De Providentia. De Constantia, De ira, De clementia*, 3 vols. ed. J. W. Basore (Cambridge MA, 1958), i, 200–1: '[L]eonum

With the spread of the Christian religion in western Europe, monks and clerics interpreted barbarity in religious terms, while Christianity coalesced with the ideals of *Romanitas*. The transformation was said to have run smoothly, for the acculturated Gauls turned from fierce warriors into a 'softer' population thanks to their closeness to Roman civilization and exposure to consumer goods imported by merchants.[10] The distinction between *Romanitas* and Germanic barbarism faded, following the sustained success of Germanic migrants establishing power bases in western Europe. Indeed, these peoples – Burgundians, Ostrogoths, Franks – were less inclined to describe themselves as barbaric. Instead, in search of a new mirror to reflect upon the group's own moral status, a new barbaric other was found in the heathen or heretic, the Silesians, Pomeranians and Prussians dwelling in the north-east, 'the most ferocious of barbarous heathens'.[11] As an expanding Christendom quashed heathen practices or accommodated them, the reputation for barbarity was dispelled more and more to the imaginary fringes of Europe.

The classical connotation of barbarity survived in linguistic terms, where *Latinitas* was contrasted with the vernacular languages or with insufficient mastery of Latin grammar.[12] Concurrently, difference predating but continuing into the twelfth century between the western Franks and, for instance, the Bavarians, Swabians, Franconians and Saxons was clothed in a linguistic dichotomy between Romance and Germanic languages, the latter spoken of as uttering barbaric sounds.[13] Linguistic rivalry flourished along the Walloon–

---

    luporumque ritu ut seruire non possunt, ita nec imperare; non enim humani uim ingenii, sed feri et intractabilis habent. nemo autem regere potest nisi qui et regi. Fere itaque imperia penes eos fuere populos, qui mitiore caelo utuntur. In frigora septemtrionemque vergentibus immansueta ingenia sunt, ut ait poeta: "Suoque simillima caelo".'

[10] Isaac, *Invention of Racism*, pp. 414–15, 430–9. Cf. A. Alföldi, 'The Moral Barrier on Rhine and Danube', in *Congress of Roman Frontier Studies*, ed. E. Birley (Durham, 1952), 1–16.

[11] *Chronicon Polonorum usque ad a. 1113*, ed. I. Szlachtowski and R. Köpke, MGH Scriptores rerum Germanicarum 9 (Hanover, 1851), p. 425: 'Barbarorum gentilium ferocissimas nationes'. W. R. Jones, 'The Image of the Barbarian in Medieval Europe', *Comparative Studies in Society and History* 13/4 (1971), 376–407 (pp. 381–8).

[12] Jones, 'Image of the Barbarian', p. 389.

[13] For instance, Richer of Reims, *Historiae* i.20, ed. H. Hoffmann, MGH Scriptores 38 (Hanover, 2000), p. 57. Meyvaert, 'Voicing National Antipathy', pp. 753–8; Kirn, *Frühzeit des Nationalgefühls*, pp. 37–43; Mendels, 'Nationalismus in der mittelhochdeutschen und mittelniederländischen Literatur', pp. 299–300; Cerwinka, 'Völkercharakteristiken', p. 60; F. Graus, *Die Nationenbildung der Westslawen im Mittelalter* (Sigmaringen, 1980), p. 40; F. Graus, 'Die Entstehung der mittelalterlichen Staaten in Mitteleuropa', *Historica* 10 (1965), 5–65 (p. 60). Cf. E. Maschke,

Germanic border: in the *Ysengrimus*, written in Ghent in the early 1150s, the protagonist ass is described as 'a wretched German, and as crude as a willow-wood pipe, squeezing out guttural words from his Bavarian throat'.[14] Earlier, in the ninth century, John the Deacon in his *vita* of Gregory the Great compared the savage barbarity of German drunken throats in song to the sounds of carts creaking up a hill.[15] The vernacular harshness of the German tongue contrasted brutally with the melodious flow of the Latin language on the Italian peninsula. Clerics claimed that German pilgrims visiting the shrines sounded like wolves singing the sweet Gregorian melodies, and their battle cry was likened to the sound of thunder, which, given the value attached to eloquence in courtly circles, was certainly a dehumanizing qualification. The sounds were interpreted culturally in relation to social status. John of Salisbury explicitly mentions that Theodwin of Porto (*d. c.* 1151), a German bishop and papal legate on the Second Crusade, 'differing from the Franks in customs and language, was considered a barbarian', and as such was not held in high esteem.[16]

Das Erwachen des Nationalbewusstseins im deutsch-slavischen Grenzraum (Leipzig, 1933), p. 4; Mohr, 'Frage des Nationalismus', p. 110. For examples of animosity in Middle High German, see R. F. M. Byrn, 'National Stereotypes Reflected in German Literature', in *Concepts of National Identity in the Middle Ages*, ed. S. Forde, L. Johnson and A. V. Murray (Leeds, 1995), pp. 137–53 (p. 145).

[14] *Ysengrimus* vi lines 381–2, ed. and trans. Mann, pp. 506–7: 'Teutonicus miser et rudis est ut papa salignus, / Stridula Bauarico gutture uerba liquans.' The author was from the Low Countries. Mann interprets this passage as ridiculing 'a certain "snobism"' about using French in Ghent's bilingual society. J. Mann, 'Introduction', in Ysengrimus: *Text with Translation, Commentary and Introduction*, ed. and trans. J. Mann (Leiden, 1987), pp. 165–7. Cf. also ninth-century Wandalbert of Prüm, *Vita et miracula sancti Goaris* vii, ed. H. E. Stiene, Lateinische Sprache und Literatur des Mittelalters 11 (Frankfurt am Main, 1981), p. 51.

[15] *Vita Gregorii Magni* ii.7, *PL* 75, col. 90D–91A; Meyvaert, 'Voicing National Antipathy', p. 754. See also Peter of Eboli, *Raccolta di tutti scrittori dell'istoria del regno di Napoli* xvi (Napels, 1770), 14, lines 122–3.

[16] P. Fedele, 'Accenti d'italianità in Montecassino nel Medio Evo', *Bulletino dell'istituto storico italiano per il medio evo* 47 (1932), 1–16 (p. 15), from an eleventh-century Beneventan manuscript from St Maria di Albaneta on music and chant. Landulf of Milan, *Historiae Mediolanensis* ii 24, ed. L. C. Bethmann and W. Wattenbach, MGH Scriptores 8 (Hanover, 1848), p. 61. Walter Map says the Germans were deeply insulted by the saying 'Tpwrut Aleman': Walter Map, *De nugis curialium* v.5, ed. James, Brooke and Mynors, p. 459. M. Vale, 'Edward I and the French: Rivalry and Chivalry', in *Thirteenth Century England II. Proceedings of the Newcastle Upon Tyne Conference 1987*, ed. P. R. Coss and S. D. Lloyd (Woodbridge, 1988), pp. 165–76 (p. 175). John of Salisbury, *Historia pontificalis*, in *John of Salisbury's Memoirs of the Papal Court (Ioannis Saresberiensis Historia pontificalis)*, ed. and trans.

Besides cultural interpretation, with the popularity of Lucan's epithet *furor Teutonicus* and its implication that the Germans were aggressive, undisciplined madmen with raging minds, the linguistic dichotomy was in the twelfth century augmented with arguments of character and affect grounded on Hippocratic environmental theory as well.[17] Once more, the *barbaricus* represented the savage, cruel, treacherous man who was not subject to law, lacked reason or work ethic, and was driven by lust. Now, however, he was found dwelling beneath the outer rim of the umbrella of Christianity in a broad sweep of land stretching from present-day Ireland, Scotland and Scandinavia eastwards across the German territories towards the Slavic region. The Irish and Welsh, it was said, lived in a pastoral, milk-drinking, meat-eating society, lazily sustained by cattle herds rather than bespoke, industrious agriculture, or trade and commerce in urban settlements, as Gerald of Wales famously claimed.[18] Sexual lewdness, ferocity and a lack of reason, acted out in a politically fragmented, lawless society squandering the benefits of the lands, were tokens of such barbarity, as was their semi-pagan, corrupt religious status.[19]

M. M. Chibnall (London, 1956), p. 54. See also John of Salisbury's letter to Gerard Pucelle, circa May 1168, in *The Letters of John of Salisbury*, ed. and trans. Millor and Brooke, ii, no. 277. In contrast, the French are praised by Otto of Freising for their 'subtlety and eloquence'; Otto of Freising, *Chronica sive Historia de duabus civitatibus* iv.8, ed. Lammers, p. 318. J. Bumke, *Courtly Culture: Literature and Society in the High Middle Ages*, trans. Thomas Dunlap (Berkeley, 1991), p. 72. Also, *Chronicon Ebersheimense*, ed. L. Weiland, MGH Scriptores rerum germanicarum 23 (Hannover, 1874), p. 433 for derision of the German language by the French.

[17] Dümmler, 'Über den furor Teutonicus', pp. 112–26; Jones, 'The Image of the Barbarian in Medieval Europe', p. 398. For the fourteenth–fifteenth century, see L. E. Scales, 'Germen Militiae: War and German Identity in the Later Middle Ages', *Past and Present* 180 (2003), 41–82 (pp. 66–74).

[18] W. R. Jones, 'England against the Celtic fringe: A study in cultural stereotypes', *Journal of World History / Cahiers d'Histoire Mondiale* 13 (1971), 155–71; Lydon, 'Nation and Race', pp. 103–23; R. C. Hoffmann, 'Outsiders by Birth and Blood: Racist Ideologies and Realities around the Periphery of Europe', in *The Medieval Frontiers of Latin Christendom: Expansion, Contraction, Continuity*, ed. J. Muldoon and F. Fernández-Armesto (Aldershot, 2008), pp. 149–80; J. Muldoon, *Identity on the Medieval Irish Frontier: Degenerate Englishmen, Wild Irishmen, Middle Nations* (Gainesville, 2003); J. F. Lydon, 'Nation and Race in Medieval Ireland', in *Concepts of National Identity in the Middle Ages*, ed. S. Forde, L. Johnson and A. V. Murray (Leeds, 1995), pp. 103–24 (p. 104); R. R. Davies, *Domination and Conquest: The Experience of Ireland, Scotland and Wales, 1100–1300* (Cambridge, 1990), pp. 20–3; Bartlett, *Gerald of Wales*, pp. 131–71; and further references in chapter 6, pp. 238–52, for the image of the Scandinavians and Baltic peoples.

[19] Both John Gillingham and David Crouch mention the Anglo-Norman 'shock' when confronted with the 'cruelty' of the Welsh, Scots and Danes. D. Crouch,

This image of barbarity was with wavering success countered particularly by German writers stressing German strength and audacity in the face of the non-religious other, where the use of extreme, irrational violence was required in the struggle with apocalyptic forces.[20]

At the same time the resurgence of classical notions of civility allowed courtiers to present themselves as undergoing a 'civilizing trend', in which classical sociocultural ideals, flavoured with Christian religious norms, were held up to the aristocracy in the form of chivalry and urbanity.[21] As we saw in chapter 2, the military strategist Vegetius, whose work was popular in the twelfth century, had eulogized the qualities of valour and intelligence in a fighter, born out of environment and professional training. With the rise of 'chivalry', we see these ideas articulated in court programmes of conduct that drew upon already circulating Ciceronian learning concerning ideals of harmony, beauty and discipline. David Crouch argued that more than a century before a code of chivalry was established, in about 1170, a standard of noble conduct already existed in the person of the *preudomme*. He was a man of 'mature sense and wisdom', trustworthy, loyal, generous and modest.[22] Above all, the *preudomme* was intelligent and showed restraint in warfare, reflecting both military, physical qualities and mental traits. Bravery, valour and toughness complemented virtuous, rational behaviour; noble men offered wise (*sage*) counsel and practised discretion. Indeed, the epithet *prudens*, which could mean basic worldly wisdom, now applied to the noble layman. Cruelty, greed, pillaging and rapine were its antithesis, as were disloyal, mindless rage and a lack of self-control. By the second half of the twelfth century the ideal of the *preudomme* would be exemplified in many *chansons de geste* serving as a mirror for the aristocratic elite.[23] Using ethnic stereotypes to describe army recruits' qualities, relating peoples to geographical spaces, was an easy means of boasting about a group's

---

The Birth of Nobility: Constructing Aristocracy in England and France: 900–1300 (Harlow, 2005), p. 64 and Gillingham, *The English in the Twelfth Century*, pp. 14–15.

[20] Weeda, 'Violence, Control, Prophecy and Power'.

[21] For an overview of scholarship on the concept of chivalry, see D. Crouch's introduction in *The Birth of Nobility*. In general: Keen, *Chivalry*; R. Barber, *The Knight and Chivalry* (Woodbridge, 2000); C. Brittain Bouchard, *'Strong of Body, Brave and Noble': Chivalry and Society in Medieval France* (Ithaca NY, 1998).

[22] Crouch, *The Birth of Nobility*, pp. 29–86. On the other hand, Jaeger, *The Origins of Courtliness*, pp. 113–26, links the rise of these ideals to courtly clerical norms influenced by Ciceronian learning in the tenth century.

[23] A. Murray, *Reason and Society in the Middle Ages* (Oxford, 1978), pp. 126–7, 132–6; Crouch, *The Birth of Nobility*, pp. 46–67.

own chivalric values and ability to protect the domesticated space, as well as a powerful argument for conquest and colonization of lands farther away.

Besides warrior values, norms ensconced in the sphere of civic, urbane behaviour set the bar for the behaviour of the clergy themselves, the bureaucrats in administrative functions. Civilization, in the Ciceronian tradition, was presented in the form of rationality, good speech, learning and intelligence, and explained through environmental determinism. As we shall see, where the French and the Germans battled over norms of chivalry, the English preferred to appropriate a reputation for urbanity, presumably in response to the more troubling memory of their losses in battle.

Ideas about civilization cater to the western fetish of progress and innovation, a framework present in the concept of the *translatio imperii*, which was now positively reframed as cultural progress expressed by urbanization. Christianity itself, the period of the Church 'under grace', was represented as an improvement from the old law of Judaism; there was an optimism concerning the ages of man, where the new might entail a restoration of the perfection of the past.[24] As discussed in chapter 6, it was a small step to link this idea of progress to the 'necessary', 'beneficial' expansion of western European culture to other regions using a classical, evolutionary narrative of progress from nomadism, to agriculturalism to urbanity, combined with the religious motif of the trek to promised lands of milk and honey. However, this chapter will first further explore the application of ethnotypes within the military sphere of competition within Christendom, between the French, English and Germans.

French control and German fury

In the early decades of the twelfth century, the French, playing a leading role in the crusader movement, prevailed in the competitive struggle for cultural and military ascendancy, and northern French cultural and social customs became the benchmark for noble demeanour in northern Europe as a whole. French fashion dictated taste, French war games or tournaments (the *conflicti Gallicani*) were staged on Flemish, English and German soil and the French image of a heavily armed knight on horseback became the standard for seals.[25] At the end of the twelfth century, German court *Minnesingers* were adopting and adapting Arthurian romances and troubadour verses and translating the ideals of chivalry into *Manheit*, *Milte*, *Zuht* and *Trowve* (manliness, kindness, virtue

[24] Constable, *The Reformation of the Twelfth Century*, pp. 162–7.
[25] For the Germans: Bumke, *Courtly Culture*, pp. 79–82. For admiration for the French in England: Thomas, *The English and the Normans*, pp. 316–17; Southern, *Medieval Humanism and Other Studies*, pp. 158–9.

and loyalty).[26] In the 1210s, the Bavarian court poet Wolfram von Eschenbach (*c.* 1160/80—*c.* 1220) concurred, noting that the French were *gerîten rîterliche,* true knights.[27] The most powerful literary repartee came from Walther von der Vogelweide in a poem probably composed upon his arrival at the Viennese ducal court in 1203, in which he states *tiuschiu zuht gat vor in allen* (German virtue surpasses all else).[28] Passing through many lands, German manners surpass all, from the Elbe to the Rhine to Hungary, where the most beautiful women live and the men are well bred.[29]

Yet the welding of culture and military prowess was on all counts the prerogative of the northern French, whose fame at the close of the twelfth century was compared by troubadours with the Occitan joy of love.[30] This appropriation expanded the earlier Carolingian theme of the translation of knowledge, court writers now expounding the Vegetian idea of the privileged, mutually dependent relationship of knowledge *and* chivalry in temperate Francia.[31] In the 1170s, in the romance *Cligès,* Chrétien de Troyes's (*fl.* 1160–90) self-congratulatory take on the *translatio studii*-motif proclaimed that chivalry, together with learning, moved from Athens via Rome to Paris.[32]

[26] Bumke, *Courtly Culture,* p. 75; Keen, *Chivalry,* p. 37; Kern, 'Der mittelalterliche Deutsche', p. 242; H. Thomas, 'Nationale Elemente in der ritterlichen Welt des Mittelalters', in *Ansätze und Diskontinuität deutscher Nationsbildung im Mittelalter,* ed. J. Ehlers (Sigmaringen, 1988), pp. 345–76 (p. 357).

[27] Wolfram von Eschenbach, *Willehalm nach der Handschrift 857 der Stiftsbibliothek St Galle* 44, lines 3–4, ed. J. Heinzle (Frankfurt am Main, 1991), p. 40.

[28] Müller, 'Deutschland, Deutschland', pp. 118–21.

[29] *Walther von der Vogelweide. Leich, Lieder, Sangsprüche,* ed. K. Lachmann (Berlin, 1996).

[30] *La Chanson de Roland,* line 3047, ed. C. Segre, 2 vols. (Geneva, 1989), i, 246; Jean Bodel, *La chanson des Saisnes: Edition critique,* lines 641–2, 661, 717 (Redaction A(R)), ed. A. Brasseur, 2 vols. (Geneva, 1989), i, 54, 60. J. Malsch, *Die Characteristik der Völker im altfranzösischen, nationalen Epos* (Heidelberg, 1912), p. 51; Paterson, *The World of the Troubadours,* p. 5.

[31] Cf. the *Grandes Chroniques de France,* prologue, ed. J. Viard, 10 vols. (Paris, 1920–53), i, 5–6: 'Si com aucun veulent dire, clergie et chevalerie sont touz jors si d'un acort, que l'une nu puet sanz l'autre.' Gassman, '*Translatio studii*', i, 125–35.

[32] Chrétien de Troyes, *Cligès,* lines 30–5, ed. and trans. L. Harf-Lancner (Paris, 2009), pp. 62–5. Lusignan, 'L'université de Paris', pp. 61–2. The narrative of the translation confuses St Denis with Denis the Aeropagite, from Athens, who had purportedly come to France taking with him knowledge. Krämer, *Translatio imperii et studi,* pp. 113–68. As, for example, also in the early thirteenth-century *Image du monde,* attributed to Gauthier of Metz. The early thirteenth-century Middle High German *Moriz von Craûn* also speaks of chivalry's translation to France, where chivalry is now blossoming.

It is possible that at that time Chrétien was the court poet of Marie of France, countess of Champagne (1145–98). At the end of the period under review here, William of Nangis, a monk at the royal abbey of St Denis in Paris who died in 1300, embellished the fleur-de-lis with the symbolism that Christ had adorned the French kingdom with three graces: faith, learning and military strength, each standing for one petal.[33] The fact that chivalry accompanied learning is indicative of the appreciation for bookish learning at the courts and the use of reason, not only in scholasticism but also in military performance, as Vegetius had propagated. The virtue of learning was succinctly gendered by the canon law jurist of Cologne Alexander of Roes, who in support of the German emperor claimed that learning in France was dominated by a proud, luxury-loving, soft clergy.[34] Both learning and military power were endowed with a religious benediction, fostering the aristocracy's self-ascribed role as men divinely ordained to wield violence for the sake and protection of Christendom. Students in Paris, a university supported by the Capetian monarchy, were quick to capitalize on this motif, using the *topos* to elicit favour from the monarchy in support of its clergy.[35]

Balanced moderation, propagated in health regimens, political mirrors and household conduct manuals, such as Daniel of Beccles's *Urbanus magnus*, was a prerequisite for good fighting skills. Restraint and finesse – core norms the courtly aristocracy was expected to perform – were complementary tokens. Writers outside of French culture admired these supposed qualities in the French. 'Both in martial exercises and in polish of manners the men of France are easily first among the nations of the West', the Anglo-Norman Benedictine monk William of Malmesbury claimed in the 1120s.[36] William extended

---

[33] Lusignan, 'L'université de Paris', p. 63.

[34] Alexander of Roes, *Notitia seculi* 13–14, in *Schriften*, ed. H. Grundmann and H. Heimpel, MGH Staatsschriften 1 (Stuttgart, 1958), pp. 160–1. Chivalry and learning also merge in Alexander of Paris's (or of Bernay) *Li Romanz d'Athis et Prophilias*, lines 160–204, ed. A. Hilka, Gesellschaft für romanische Literatur, 2 vols. (Halle, 1912–16), i, 6–8, where Athens is said to be the seat of the clergy and Rome of chivalry. Afterwards Athens is conquered by Rome and the clergy unites with chivalry in Rome; Krämer, *Translatio imperii et studii*, p. 119.

[35] Lusignan, 'L'université de Paris', pp. 64–5; Krämer, *Translatio imperii et studii*, pp. 126–7.

[36] William of Malmesbury, *Gesta regum Anglorum* ii.106, ed. and trans. Mynors, Thomson and Winterbottom, i, 152–3: 'Est enim gens illa et exercitatione virium et comitate morum cunctarum occidentalium facile princeps.' The high opinion of the French is expressed by William of Malmesbury in the 1120s in a passage referring to Francia shortly before 800, where King Ecgberht lived in exile for several years.

his praise to the Normans, his father's ancestry, for being 'well-dressed to a fault, and particular about their food, but this side of any excess. The whole nation is familiar with war, and hardly knows how to live without fighting.'[37] The Saxon historian Helmold of Bosau (c. 1120–after 1177) even considered the French more intelligent when he recalled how the French King Louis VII managed to outsmart an attempt by the German Emperor Frederick Barbarossa to overcome him.[38] To the detriment of the French – but this was something all knights were guilty of – they were arrogant and overconfident.[39] Most of the time their courtly cheer shone through: jolly and light hearted, the romance *La Chevalerie d'Ogier de Danemarche* sung, 'the French live merrily and joyously, they return from the host with great joy'.[40] And they were brave. Numerous verses assert that the French were the epitome of

---

Ecgberht, according to William, used this period 'as a whetstone with which to sharpen the edge of his mind by clearing away the rust of indolence, and to acquire a civility of manners very different from the barbarity of his native land'.

[37] Ibid., iii 246, ed. and trans. Mynors, Thomson and Winterbottom, i, 460–1: '[V] estibus ad invidiam culti, cibis citra ullum nimietatem delicati. Gens militiae assueta et sine bello pene vivere nescia'. Gillingham, *The English in the Twelfth Century*, pp. 5–6, 28–9; Thomas, *The English and the Normans*, pp. 254, 316, 356.

[38] Helmold of Bosau, *Slawenchronik/Chronica Slavorum* xci, ed. B. Schmeidler, trans. H. H. Stoob, Ausgewählte Quellen zur deutschen Geschichte des Mittelalters 19 (Darmstadt, 1963), p. 318. Cerwinka, 'Völkercharakteristiken', p. 62.

[39] R. Künzel, *The Plow, the Pen and the Sword: Images and Self-Images of Medieval People in the Low Countries*, trans. C. Weeda (Abingdon, 2017), p. 45, argued that *superbia*, pride, was a typical trait tacked onto the aristocracy, who were full of conceit because of their higher station. M. Schmidt-Chazan, 'Le point de vue des chroniqueurs de la France du Nord sur les Allemands dans la première moitié du XIIème siècle', *Centre de recherches internationales de l'Université de Metz: Travaux et Recherches* 5 (1973/2), 13–36 (p. 17); Coulton, 'Nationalism in the Middle Ages', *The Cambridge Historical Journal* 5/1 (1935), 15–40 (pp. 33–4), quoting the Franciscan Salimbene, who in 1287 denounces the arrogance of the French in thinking they rule the world. Compare also the accusation of the English author of the *Itinerarium Peregrinorum et Gesta Regis Ricardi*, ed. W. Stubbs (London, 1864), i, 295, that the French are arrogant, fickle and lazy, in contrast to their Carolingian ancestors; and the remarks made by crusaders quoted in Weeda, 'Violence, Control, Prophecy and Power', pp. 154–8. Also A. V. Murray, 'National Identity, Language and Conflict in the Crusades to the Holy Land, 1096–1192', in *The Crusades and the Near East*, ed. C. Kostick (London, 2011), pp. 107–30 (p. 122).

[40] Raimbert de Paris, *La Chevalerie d'Ogier de Danemarche*, lines 2034–5, ed. M. Eusebi (Milan, 1963), p. 138: 'François repairent baut e lié e joiant; / A l'ost revienent grant joie demenant.'

chivalry in battle: 'Saxons are arrogant, the French noble and brave.'[41] This also manifested itself in their physique: the French were handsome, tall, bearded and heavily armoured.

Yet to stake these claims court writers needed to mirror themselves with the other. And in the process of appropriating and identifying with these norms, the French turned to an exemplary antithesis: the German bellicose warrior.[42] That French writers were able to do so stems from an inherited reputation from antiquity according to which the Germans, although strong knights, used excessive violence and generally lacked measure or balance. Here, the ancient tradition of environmental climate theory again reverberates, explaining the Germans' irrationality based on their geographical situation, dwelling in a cold and wet territory, compensated by an excess of blood. The appropriation of a civilizing reputation by the northern French and their self-confidence in the wake of the Investiture Controversy and the First Crusade in the eleventh century thus chimed with othering German fury. Crucially, it reaffirmed the gendered self-image of masculine self-control and finesse that rhetorically justified power, relying on the shared memory and ancestry of the Carolingians, yet re-evaluating violence as rational instead of extreme and eschatological. It also allowed the French to shake off their own, more troubling, ancient reputation of Frankish ferocity. The same applies to the Normans, who, although now considered elegant and civilized, originally descended from pirates, whose mythological founder Antenor was ill-reputed for his treachery. The Benedictine monk Orderic Vitalis, for example, still called the Normans 'furious' in the early parts of the twelfth century, although he also viewed them as paragons of polish and finesse.[43] Orderic, born in England, was sent to Normandy to the abbey of Saint-Evroul at the age of eleven, where he would spend the rest of his life.

From the late eleventh century, especially although not exclusively in French and Italian court literature, the Germans increasingly feature as extremely

---

[41] Jean Bodel, *La chanson des Saisnes*, line 5257: 'Saisne sont orguillex, Francois gentil et ber.' Malsch, *Die Characteristik der Völker*, pp. 26–30 for many references.

[42] Len Scales has argued convincingly that in the fourteenth and fifteenth centuries the negative stereotype of the German nobility evoked a reappraisal of its self-image. Scales, 'German Militiae', pp. 41–82.

[43] Potts, 'Atque unum', pp. 144–5, argues that the reputation of the Normans' violent behaviour possibly was a reaction to accusations of effeminacy and softness when they acculturated with Frankish culture. N. Webber, *The Evolution of Norman Identity, 911–1154* (Rochester, 2005), pp. 30–1 argues that by the eleventh century the Normans in Normandy had adopted Christianity and more or less 'established' themselves, although outsiders continued to refer to their treachery in the twelfth century; pp. 175–80 for their identity based on territory rather than descent.

violent, treacherous, irrational men who breach the esteemed qualities of the aristocracy in a world shaped by warfare and personal alliances. 'The fierce fury of the Germans', 'German rage' or *rabies* are much-used epithets, such as in the early thirteenth-century *Philippide* written by William le Breton, court poet of King Philip II of France.[44] Or as the author of the *Life of Louis VII*, the French king, puts it: 'The Germans are the most impatient of men, who are thoughtless in matters of war, but instead furious in their own raging minds.'[45] Their irrationality outed itself in a lack of control and a wallowing in the vices of gluttony and drunkenness, a typical accusation that was also directed at the British, Anglo-Saxons and Normans, Bohemians and Slavs.[46] Landulf of Milan, a late eleventh-century historian educated in France, comments that 'their minds were given to gluttony and drunkenness [...] the most cruel Teutons do not know left from right'.[47] Drunkenness here means loss of

[44] William le Breton, *Philippide* ix, line 62, xi, line 292, 401, ed. Delaborde, ii, 250, 330, 335. Dümmler, 'Über den furor Theutonicus' for more references.

[45] *Vita Ludovici VII* xx, in *Historiae Francorum Scriptores*, ed. A. Duchesne, 5 vols. (Paris, 1636–49) iv, 406: 'Teutonici utpote homines impatientissimi et qui non sunt in armorum negotiis circumspecti, sed propria capitis dementia furibundi.' Cf. *Chronicon Sancti Martini Turonense*, ed. O. Holder-Egger, MGH Scriptores rerum Germanicarum 26 (Hanover, 1882), p. 468; Rolandinus Patavinus, *Chronica* iii 9, ed. Ph. Jaffé, MGH Scriptores 19 (Hanover, 1866), p. 60; Suger, *The Deeds of Louis the Fat* x, ed. and trans. R. Cusimano and J. Moorhead (Washington DC, 1992), pp. 52–3. Dümmler, 'Über den furor Teutonicus', p. 122.; F. Curta, 'Furor Teutonicus: A Note on Ethnic Stereotypes in Suger's *Deeds of Louis the Fat*', *The Haskins Society Journal: Studies in Medieval History* 16 (2005), 62–76.

[46] From the thirteenth century more emphasis is laid on heavy drinking, generally associated with the English and Normans. K. L. Zimmermann, 'Die Beurteilung der Deutschen in der französischen Literatur des Mittelalters mit besonderer Berücksichtigung der chansons de geste', *Romanische Forschungen* 29 (1911), 222–316 (pp. 270–311) for German drinking, greed and unhygienic behaviour.

[47] Landulf of Milan, *Historiae Mediolanensis* ii 22, ed. Bethmann and Wattenbach, p. 59: 'Gulositatem et animos vino deditos [...] saevissimi Theutonici qui nesciunt quid sit inter dexteram et sinistram'. The moral lists of epithets compiled in monastic circles in this period also categorize the Teutons as gluttonous, the Saxons as powerful yet stupid and headstrong and the Bavarians as blunt (for instance Einsiedeln, Stiftsbibliothek MS 321 p. 136 from the tenth century and the twelfth-century manuscript Cambridge, Corpus Christi College, MS 139 fol. 166v.). Walther, 'Scherz', no. 99, 74. Cf. also the *Carminum proverbialium*, an anthology of rhyming proverbs from 1576, where the Bavarian 'defiles' and the Saxon drinks. Excessive drinking was already commented on by Salvian of Marseille, *De gubernatione Dei* iv 67–8, *PL* 53, cols. 0086C–0087A. Jacques de Vitry famously recorded that students in Paris said the Germans were furious and had disgusting manners. Jacques de Vitry, *Historia occidentalis* vii, ed. Hinnebusch, p. 92. H. Glück,

control, opening the gates to aggressive emotions.[48] In the same breath, the Germans' religious devotion to Christianity was questioned, classifying them as stiff necked, an epithet applied to Jews for breaking God's covenant and interpreted in Christian exegesis as an unwillingness to embrace Christianity.[49] Overall, rather than *preudommes*, the Germans were thus a *pute gent*, a dirty people.[50] They treacherously broke the bonds of fealty and, lacking cultural refinement or humour, they failed to meet the par of courtly finesse. The pugnacious Germans, tasting defeat at the hands of the French, ignominiously fled the battleground; the so-called dapper Germans repeatedly turn tail in the chanson de geste *Aymeri of Narbonne*, ascribed to the thirteenth-century poet Bertrand de Bar-sur-Aube, who, like Chrétien of Troyes, was employed at the court of Marie of France in the Champagne.[51] In the vernacular French translation of Caesar's *De bello Gallico*, known as the *Faits des Romains* (1213–14), the Germans are barbarous and savage, treacherous, robbers, 'tall people, coarse, disloyal, senseless'.[52] At the end of the twelfth century, the Provençal poet Peire Vidal commenting on the expedition against Pisa of the German Emperor Henry VI (1165–97), observes: 'I find the Germans without grace and like an uneducated common folk. If one of them tries to be courtly and gracious, it is a deadly nuisance and annoying. Their language sounds like

---

Deutsch als Fremdsprache in Europa vom Mittelalter bis zur Barockzeit (Berlin, 2002), p. 254.

[48] Cf. Donizone, *Vita Mathildis* ii 5, line 530, ed. L. C. Bethmann, MGH Scriptores rerum germanicarum 12 (Hanover, 1856), p. 390.

[49] For Germans as stiff-necked envoys, grinding their teeth with German temerity, in Suger, *The Deeds of Louis the Fat*, trans. Cusimano and Moorhead, x, 56, 60. See also pp. 61–2 in chapter 1.

[50] Zimmermann, 'Die Beurteilung der Deutschen', pp. 257, 306; Le Roman de Rou de Wace 3 215, ed. A. J. Holden, Société des Anciens Textes Français 92, 3 vols. (Paris, 1970–73) i, 120; Jean Renart, *Galeran de Bretagne*, lines 5088–9, Jean Renart, *Galeran de Bretagne: roman du XIIIe siècle*, lines 5088–9, ed. L. Foulet, Les classiques français du Moyen Âge, 37 (Paris, 1925), 155; Jean Bodel, *La Chanson des Saisnes*, line 3993 (Redaction L), ed. Brasseur, i, 353 about the Saxons.

[51] *Aymeri de Narbonne*, Bertrand de Bar-sur-Aube (attrib.), *Aymeri de Narbonne: chanson de geste*, lines 2464–5, ed. L. Demaison, Société des Anciens Textes Français 24, 2 vols. (Paris, 1887), ii, 105. Jean Renart, *Galeran de Bretagne*, line 5613, ed. Foulet, p. 171. Zimmermann, 'Die Beurteilung der Deutschen', p. 271.

[52] M. Schmidt-Chazan, 'Les traductions de la "Guerre des Gaules" et le sentiment national au Moyen Âge', in L'historiographie en Occident du Ve au XVe siècle: actes du congrès de la societé des historiens médiévistes de l'enseignement supérieur; Tours, 10–12 juin 1977/1980 (Tours, 1980), pp. 387–407 (pp. 392–3): '[G]ranz genz, corsues, desvees, sans sens'.

the barking of dogs.'⁵³ Adding insult to injury, they also lacked the culture to understand the intricacies of irony or self-deprecation, unable to bear jokes at their own expense.⁵⁴ Nothing was more ridiculous than an 'Aleman who is courteous and wants to love'.⁵⁵ In sum, as the character Jouglet says in Jean Renart's *Roman de la Rose*, when asked who his companions were: 'A whole lot of Germans – I nearly died of boredom!'⁵⁶

Military talents

As the Latin and vernacular literature juxtaposing French chivalry and courtliness with German bellicosity exemplified the merging of the *preudomme*'s virtues with those of the ideal knight, the *preu chevalier* eventually became equated with the nobility.⁵⁷ However, the appropriation by the French of the reputation for valour necessarily implied addressing the relationship between physical strength, military talents and claims to holding *imperium*. The Germans' strength and physical build, grounded in climate theory, was traditionally acclaimed and occasionally interlaced with myth, for instance in the Flemish Dominican friar Thomas of Cantimpré's (1201–72) *Book on the*

---

⁵³ Peire Vidal, *La Poesie de Peire Vidal* 27, ed. J. Anglade (Paris 1966), p. 27: 'Alamans trob deschauzitz e vilans / E quand negus si feing esser cortes, / Ira mortals cozens et enois es; / E lors parlars sembla lairars de cans.' U. Müller, '"Deutschland, Deutschland, Über Alles"? Walther von der Vogelweide, Hoffmann von Fallersleben and the "Song of the Germans": Medievalism, Nationalism and/or Facism', *Medievalism in the Modern World: Essays in Honour of Leslie Workman*, ed. R. Utz and T. A. Shippey (Turnhout, 1998), 117–29 (p. 117), from which the translation is drawn; Byrn, 'National Stereotypes Reflected in German Literature', pp. 143–5.

⁵⁴ Partonopeu de Blois, *A French Romance of the Twelfth Century*, lines 8783–8, ed. J. Gildea, 2 vols. (Villanova, 1967–70), i, 357. The German poet Freidank, in a crusade song about the fall of Acre in 1291, sighed: 'Swer schuldic sî, daz rihte got, daz wir dâ sîn der Wahle spot: und môhten tiusche liute daz lant gewinnen hiute, die wahle sint in sô gehaz, si gunnens den heiden michels baz'; Mendels, 'Nationalismus', p. 300.

⁵⁵ Gautier d'Arras, *Ille et Galeron*, line 3929, Les classiques français du Moyen Age, 109 (Paris, 1988), p. 145: 'Cil est plus gabés c'Alemans / Qui cortois est et velt amer.' F. Kern, 'Der mittelalterliche Deutsche in französischer Ansicht', *Historische Zeitschrift* 108 (1912), 237–54 (p. 241); M. Remppis, *Die Vorstellungen von Deutschland im altfranzösischen Heldenepos und Roman und ihre Quellen* (Tübingen, 1911), p. 115.

⁵⁶ Jean Renart, *Le roman de la rose ou de Guillaume de Dole*, line 2215, ed. F. Lecoy, trans. J. Dufournet, Champion Classiques: Série Moyen Âge, 24 (Paris, 2008), p. 68; *Jean Renart: The Romance of the Rose or Guillaume de Dole*, trans. P. Terry and N. V. Durling (Philadelphia, 1993), p. 48.

⁵⁷ Crouch, *The Birth of Nobility*, p. 30.

Nature of Things, which claimed the Teutons in ancient times descended from giants.⁵⁸ In the many glosses on Lucan's *Pharsalia*, the Germanic god Teutates was identified with the war-god Mars or Mercurius, and in the eleventh century the deity Teutates had been appointed as the name-giver of the Germans; in the middle of the thirteenth century, the discovery of a repository of bones near Vienna was identified as the grave of Teutonic giants.⁵⁹ Their proverbial warrior strength offered German writers some leeway when emphasizing Germans' military qualities as the defenders of Christendom in the most extreme conditions of violent apocalyptic warfare, underscoring their claim to wield *imperium* as the receptacles of the Carolingian legacy.⁶⁰ At its most vehement, competition between the French monarchy and German empire thus projected images of French rational military valour, arrogance or levity vis-à-vis extremely violent German rage (*furor Teutonicus*), for instance in *The Play of the Antichrist*.

Matthew Gabriele, in *Empire of Memory*, attested that the concept of *imperium* essentially entailed fighting pagans as well as maintaining world authority over a Christian population. Holding *imperium* was not necessarily attached to a specific territory, its focus shifting from Rome to Francia and then to the German territories under the Ottonian dynasty (919–1024).⁶¹ However, the emperor and his armies, responsible for *imperium*'s designated task of defending the Church, effectively demanded various degrees of military strength depending on the enemy at hand, which was usually associated with the Church's foes. The negotiation over who held *imperium* could thus revolve around what kind of violence – extreme bloodshed or measured, disciplined aggression – was deemed appropriate and necessary for the holder of *imperium*. The question was raised against whom the holder of *imperium* was allowed to wave his sword. In this context, we must distinguish between comments about German fury evaluated *within* Christian society, for instance signifying Germanic warrior behaviour on the Italian peninsula, on the one hand, and the wielding of Germanic fury against the religious foe *outside* Christendom,

---

[58] Thomas of Cantimpré, *Liber de natura rerum: Editio princeps secundum codices manuscriptos* iii.v.40 ('De monstruosis hominibus orientes'), ed. H. Boese (Berlin, 1973), p. 100.

[59] Jean Renart, *Galeran de Bretagne*, lines 6048–9, ed. Foulet, p. 184; *Anseïs von Karthago*, line 10080, ed. J. Alton, Bibliothek des litterarischen Vereins in Stuttgart, 194 (Tübingen, 1892), p. 363. Kästner, 'Der großmächtige Riese und Recke Teuton', pp. 81–2. Cf. Lucan, *Pharsalia* I.445, ed. J. D. Duff (Cambridge, 1928), p. 34, mentioning the Celtic god Teutates.

[60] Weeda, 'Violence, Control, Prophecy, Power', pp. 146–66.

[61] Gabriele, *Empire of Memory*, pp. 99–101.

most notably the Antichrist, on the other. In the first case, German fury is rejected; in the second case, it could be valued as a form of necessary violence.

Suger (1081–1151), the politically vocal abbot of the royal abbey of St Denis, responded by underscoring French *strenuitas*. Suger differentiated between the *animositas* and *potentia* of France in contrast to the audacious, brazen behaviour of its enemies. Germans displayed arrogance against France, 'the mistress of lands', to whom the German territories had in the past been subject. The Germans brought violence to Rome instead of protection, anger instead of devotion to the papacy. Contrasting such misconduct, Suger strategically underlines the French policy of protecting the realm and the Church.[62] Conversely, the powerful abbot depicts the Romans using stereotypes typical of the effeminate south and east: corrupt, vain, gullible and suffering from levity. In response, on a few occasions, German chroniclers downplay courtliness; three out of four German chronicles nuance the chivalric character of the tournament organized by Frederick Barbarossa in 1184, and Wolfram of Eschenbach interprets the truly chivalric character of France as arrogance.[63]

Frankish authors managed to rhetorically underscore their chivalrous qualities in the First Crusade by appropriating the role of being the vanguard of Christendom, traditionally the claim of an imperial army.[64] Thus, they joined the efforts to align warrior values with the Church's interests that had been undertaken in the decades leading up to the First Crusade, when the Church revived the earlier Peace and Truce of God movements in central and southern France, presenting the warrior aristocracy as protectors of peace and the Church. The Church specifically called upon the aristocracy to fight in God's service against the religious other, earning it penance and remission of sins. The First Crusade was in this sense pivotal in shaping the knighthood's self-image as God's designated defenders of Christendom, for the knights, instead of being embroiled in internecine fighting in western Europe, now operated as God's soldiers, *milites Dei* or *milites sancti Petri*, embarking on a divine mission. It chimed well with the concept of Frankish chosenness and its mission, said

[62] Curta, 'Ethnic Stereotypes', pp. 73–4.
[63] Thomas, 'Nationale Elemente', pp. 351–4. For Suger and French claims to power, Spiegel, 'The Cult of Saint Denis and Capetian Kingship', 43–69; Barroux, 'L'abbé Suger et la vassalité du Vexin en 1124', 1–26. J. duQuesnay Adams, 'The Regnum Francie of Suger of Saint-Denis: An Expansive Ile-de-France', *Historical Reflections/Réflexions Historiques* 19/2 (1993), 167–88.
[64] For Frankish ethnic identity and the Crusades, L. Boehm, 'Gedanken zum Frankreich-Bewußtsein im frühen 12.Jahrhundert', *Historisches Jahrbuch* 74 (1955), 681–7. For the concept of holy war, see Tyerman, *God's War*, pp. 27–57.

to be divinely appointed and foretold in the Scripture, to liberate Jerusalem, mythically foreshadowed by Charlemagne's pilgrimage to Jerusalem.

The myth of French chosenness is highlighted by several monks. The Benedictine abbot Guibert of Nogent's introduction to his account of the First Crusade discusses how 'God ordained holy wars in our time, so that the knightly order and erring mob, who, like their pagan ancient models, were engaged in mutual slaughter, might find a new way of earning salvation'.[65] In order to find deliverance, the crusade armies established a new Christian settlement while awaiting the apocalyptic last battle and new kingdom of Jerusalem. In step with the Frankish self-acclamation of being New Israelites, Robert the Monk (d. 1122), a cleric who claims he was present at Pope Urban II's speech in 1095, draws comparisons between crusaders and biblical personae on their way to the Promised Land.[66] Crucially, Pope Urban II, in his call for a crusade in 1095 in the wake of the Investiture Controversy, had made his appeal not to the German emperor but to the Frankish aristocracy and Church provinces, though not to the French king.[67] There was reluctance on the side of the Germans to join the First Crusade, which Guibert de Nogent explained in terms of their barbaric character, their obstinacy – a trait that, like stiff-necked, was also assigned to Jews as a way of stadial othering. On the other hand, the French were the chosen allies of the papacy: 'More respectful and humble than other nations toward blessed Peter and pontifical decrees, the French, unlike other peoples, have been unwilling to behave insolently against God. For many years we have seen the Germans, particularly the entire kingdom of Lotharingia, struggling with barbaric obstinacy against the commands of Saint Peter and of his pontiffs.'[68] Guibert further relates how the archbishop of Mainz derided the French, calling them 'Francones'. Guibert

---

[65] Guibert of Nogent, *Dei gesta per Francos* i.1, ed. Huygens, p. 87, trans. Levine, p. 25: '[S]ancta deus, ut ordo equestris et vulgus oberrans, qui vetustae paganitatis exemplo in mutuas versabantur cedes, novum repperirent salutis promerendae genus.' Cf. Heng, *The Invention of Race in the European Middle Ages*, p. 125.

[66] C. Sweetenham, 'Introduction', in *Robert the Monk's History of the First Crusade: Historia Iherosolimitana*, trans. C. Sweetenham (Aldershot, 2005), p. 52, comments that in Robert the Monk's *History*, Adhemar of Le Puy is compared to Moses, and the hymn of praise at Dorylaeum is taken from excerpts from the Book of Exodus. J. Riley-Smith, *The First Crusade and the Idea of Crusading* (London, 1986), p. 142. Murray, 'National Identity, Language', p. 124.

[67] Schneidmüller, *Nomen patriae*, p. 114.

[68] Guibert of Nogent, *Gesta Dei per Francos* ii.1, ed. Huygens, p. 108, trans. Levine, p. 40: 'Ceteris enim gentibus erga beatum Petrum ergaque pontificalia decreta timoratius humiliusque se habuit gens eadem nec temeritate, qua alii assolent, velamen malitiae arripere contra deum voluit libertatem. Videmus iam annis emensis pluribus

retorts: 'You think them so weak and languid that you can denigrate a name known and admired as far away as the Indian Ocean, then tell me upon whom did Pope Urban call for aid against the Turks? Wasn't it the French? Had they not been present, attacking the barbarians everywhere, pouring their sturdy energy and fearless strength into the battle, there would have been no help for your Germans, whose reputation there amounted to nothing.'[69]

Although they were acting under the communal umbrella of Christendom, court writers strongly contrasted ethnic groups' character traits and the talents of the armies in the crusades. Some explicated the differences based on climate theory, which will be discussed at the end of this chapter, lending an already existing narrative the voice of scientific authority. But linguistic and cultural differences also take the foreground. The Norman chaplain Ralph of Caen (c. 1080–c. 1120), narrating the events following the siege of Antioch in 1097/98, says that the Latins taunted the Germans after they had been attacked by Turks, shouting in the streets that 'the Germans are shit'.[70] German madness is explicitly mentioned when talking about the company of Peter the Hermit (d. c. 1115) in the First Crusade. Mindless, full of rage, these men are presented as the adversaries to the cause and crusading ideal. The peasant recruits were swollen with native fierceness, displaying heedless courage but without good counsel, and plundering indiscriminately.[71] True to Vegetius's military

---

Teutonicos, immo totius Lotharingiae regnum, beati Petri eiusque pontificum preceptis barbarica quadam obstinatione reniti.'

[69] Guibert of Nogent, *Gesta Dei per Francos* ii.1, ed. Huygens, 108, trans. Levine, 41: "'Si ita eos inertes arbitraris et marcidos ut celeberrimum usque in Oceanum Indicum nomen fede garriendo detorqueas, dic michi ad quos papa Urbanus contra Turcos presidia contracturus divertit: nonne ad Francos? Hi nisi preissent et barbariem undecumque confluentium gentium vivaci industria et impavidis viribus constrinxissent, Teutonicorum vestrorum, quorum ne nomen quidem ibi sonuit, auxilia nulla fuissent.'"

[70] Ralph of Caen, *Gesta Tancredi* lxxviii, *PL* 155, col. 0544A, *The Gesta Tancredi of Ralph of Caen: A History of the Normans on the First Crusade*, trans. B. S. Bachrach and D. S. Bachrach, Crusade Texts in Translation 12 (Aldershot, 2005), p. 100: 'Caco-Alemanni'; cf. Schmugge, 'Über "nationale" Vorurteile', p. 447. For the language difference during the crusades, see further: Cerwinka, 'Völkercharakteristiken', p. 61.

[71] In the *Historia Vie Hierosolimitane*, dating to the first two decades of the twelfth century, the anonymous Charleville Poet (sometimes known as Fulco), who, like Albert of Aachen, writes about the 'heroic' deeds of Godfrey of Bouillon, very explicitly concentrates on the unruly peasant German contingents accompanying Peter the Hermit. See for instance book ii, lines 117–20, 215–20, 225–36, 250–62 of *The* Historia Vie Hierosolimitane *of Gilo of Paris and a Second, Anonymous Author*, ed. C. W. Grocock and J. E. Siberry (Oxford, 1997), pp. 30–1, 36–9.

advice, the German Bishop Otto of Freising recounts that the French and Germans 'enjoyed taunting each other with bitter and hateful jokes',[72] and the clerk Freidank, who died in circa 1233 and was presumably of Swabian origin, chaffed that the *Wahl* (Romance-speaking) crusaders would rather the Holy Land remained in Muslim hands than be conquered by valiant Germans.[73] The Germans accused the French of arrogance.[74] Enmity continued during the Second Crusade (1147–49). Bishop John of Salisbury – himself Francophone – narrates how the Germans refused to cooperate with the French when shipping their baggage across the Hellespont, or to wait for the French King Louis VII; they were punished for their pride when many died of thirst in the desert.[75] German contingents were accordingly stripped of their validity as God's crusaders, while the French nobility was portrayed as the epitome of chivalry. Abbot Guibert of Nogent wrote in his description of the troops at Nicomedia during the First Crusade: 'One could see gathered the flower of the armed force, or the wisdom, the nobility, of the fame of all of France, dressed in the breastplates and helmets of knights.'[76]

The appeal of ethnic stereotypes to the aristocracy on crusading missions continued in the thirteenth century, where the Germans retained a reputation for 'barbaric' strength and cruel violence.[77] In the poem calling for recruits to sign up for King Louis IX of France's crusade of 1270, 'An Exhortation for Christians against Muhammad's People', written by the Franciscan friar and later archbishop of Canterbury John Pecham (*c.* 1230–92) the whole *gens Christiana*, a spectrum of European peoples, is summoned to arms, including 'swift and fearless' Spaniards, the 'exalted regal nation' of the Italians, the

---

[72] Otto of Freising, *Chronica sive historia de duabus civitatibus* vii.5, 508, ed. Lammers, 508: '[H]ic etiam inter Francos Romanos et Teutonicos, qui quibusdam amaris et invidiosis iocis frequenter rixari solent.' Cited in Bumke, *Courtly Culture*, p. 83.

[73] U. Müller, *Kreuzzugsdichtung* (Tübingen, 1969), p. 108; Byrn, 'National Stereotypes Reflected in German Literature', p. 143.

[74] Malsch, *Die Charakteristik der Völker*, pp. 22–3, 31; Murray, *Reason and Society*, p. 252. The 'superbia Gallica' is invoked in the late thirteenth century by, among others, Alexander of Roes, *Noticia seculi* 13–14, ed. Grundmann and Heimpel, pp. 160–1.

[75] John of Salisbury, *Historia pontificalis* xxiv, ed. Chibnall, p. 54.

[76] Guibert of Nogent, *Dei gesta per Francos* iii.7, ed. Huygens, p. 147, trans. Levine, p. 124: 'Erat ergo ibi considerare collectum totius Francorum militia, nobilitatis, prudentiae armorumque claritudinis florem, quos in equestri loricatorum galeatorumque decore hi.' Guibert also calls the *Franci* arrogant on several occasions.

[77] William of Nangis, *Ex primatis chronicis et Guillelmi gestis Ludovici IX*, xii, ed. H. Brosien, MGH Scriptores 26 (Hanover, 1882), 652. At pp. 656, 660, William of Nangis speaks of the German fury, which the French overcome.

Transylvanians and the Slavs, drawing their bows. In keeping with earlier tradition, the vanguard is typically formed by the French, 'gifted in arms', whereas along with the English, the Germans, third in line, are exhorted to rise up with swords of well-wrought steel, disembowelling, lacerating, scourging and mangling innards.[78]

English fighters

Whereas the French and the Teutons struggled over the Carolingian ancestry of imperial *dominium* and military strength, the English contended with an even more insecure legacy. Historiographical sources framed the Anglo-Saxons, dealing with a broken history following a string of conquests, as weak fighters who afterwards had been infused with a strong Norman warrior culture.[79] Both before and after the Norman Conquest, when Duke William of Normandy (*c.* 1027–87) removed the Anglo-Saxon elite from power and ravaged the country, the Anglo-Saxons suffered from ill repute on several counts.[80] Firstly, in post-Conquest writings 'Anglo-Saxon' might relate specifically to a state of servility, according to some clerics and monks God's punishment for the people's collective sins and weaknesses.[81] An unbroken thread in historical writing justified the wave of conquests in the tenth and eleventh centuries as divine wrath incurred by the islanders' ebriety and gluttony.[82] Monks and clerics, in self-deprecating terms, recalled the lust and corruption of the secular clergy and complained that the English fighters had wallowed in drunkenness, showing weakness and effeminacy. Secondly, a general decline in religion and learning, as well as the oppression of the poor, was said to mark the morally debased state of the community. Cunning, conniving, the Anglo-Saxons were accused of perfidy and treachery, both in older pre-Conquest Norman sources

---

[78] W. C. Jordan, 'John Pecham on the Crusade', *Crusades* 9 (2010) 159–71 (pp. 168–9): 'Tu consurge, gens Germana / Robusta, belligera / In spata colomana / Ad certamen propera / Viscera, lacera, / Verbera, vulnera, / Discerpendo viscera. Audi tu, gens Anglicana, / Freta carutis et plana, / Ad Bethel accelera.' I would like to thank William Chester Jordan for drawing my attention to this poem.

[79] See, for example, Thomas, *The English and the Normans*. Cf. William of Malmesbury, *Gesta regum Anglorum*, ed. and trans. Mynors, Thomson and Winterbottom, I, 450–1.

[80] M. Chibnall, *Anglo-Norman England, 1066–1166* (Oxford, 1986), pp. 11–43; Clanchy, *England and its Rulers*, pp. 44–7.

[81] Thomas, *The English and the Normans*, p. 251.

[82] See Weeda, 'Meanwhile in Messianic Time' for further sources.

and later within the context of the English–French wars.[83] Thirdly, a recurring image was the ineptitude of English knights in warfare, who achieved little military prowess or, as John Gillingham put it, fought like country bumpkins. Post-Conquest sources represented English fighters as long-haired effeminates, for instance in Abbot Baldric of Bourgueil's verse composition for countess Adela of Blois.[84] Effeminacy was presented as a corruption of the aristocratic culture and was associated with decadence. In some instances, court writers depicted the English as revelling in extreme luxuriousness and hence given to weakness, the collateral damage of England's proverbial wealth of natural resources, abundance and generosity. All in all, these images were in stark contrast to the brave Normans and chivalrous French, and distinctly set the Anglo-Saxons apart from their Germanic neighbours. The reputations were strong enough for English historians like Henry of Huntingdon and Ailred of Rievaulx (1110–67) to internalize them, depicting the English as bad knights.[85]

However, the other side of the equation, was to contrast English urbane culture with the inferior barbarism of the Welsh and Irish, which is discussed in chapter 6. Moreover, by stressing English intelligence in opposition to German stupidity, the English could distance themselves further from the 'barbaric northerners' with whom the English were shamefully associated in earlier times. As in the case of the competing German and Frankish aristocracy, climate theory offered a learned framework to lend weight to this narrative.

English urbanity

Along with effeminacy came the slur of the inferior barbarity of a *gens rustica*, which clung to the insular Anglo-Saxons before and shortly after the Conquest in 1066.[86] In a sense, it was the flip side of the Germans' reputation for extreme violence and manly barbarity. Thus, writes the English monk Orderic Vitalis dwelling in Normandy, the Norman aristocracy found the English rustic and almost illiterate after the arrival of the Danes and the destruction wrought upon England as a result of their sins, an abundance of food and drink,

---

[83] Cf. Thomas, *The English and the Normans*, pp. 244–6 for pre-Conquest Norman sources. According to Thomas, there was a counter-response from Anglo-Normans such as Orderic Vitalis, emphasizing how the English were faithful to their rulers.

[84] J. Gillingham, 'Henry of Huntingdon and the Twelfth-Century Revival of the English Nation', in *Concepts of National Identity in the Middle Ages*, ed. S. Forde, L. Johnson and A. V. Murray (Leeds, 1995), 75–101 (p. 82).

[85] Thomas, *The English and the Normans*, pp. 247–8, 251 for source references.

[86] Ibid., p. 242.

'shallowness and flabbiness of the people', their neglect of the monasteries and general lack of canonical discipline.[87] The complaint that the English lacked learning features in both Anglo-Saxon and Norman sources, as does that of a morally and intellectually backward Church, perhaps fuelled by its frequent and, in western Europe, exceptional early use of the vernacular instead of Latin. However, the insular, geographically marginal position of the British Isles on the edge of the world presumably helped to frame the English as barbarians, rather than reflecting an actual cultural chasm between the Continent and the island. It is typical that the Norman aristocracy at the centres of power, keen to suggest their own urbanity, talked about English rusticity.

In response, English authors took a different approach to the French and the Teutons. Rather than emphasizing their military strengths, the focus lay upon their comparative urbanity or civility – Ciceronian values that at this time were being propagated in the schools and courts as the marks of the ideal, educated, well-spoken citizens of the body politic. The clerics reproducing these images, themselves often educated at the cathedral schools of Orléans, Tours, Chartres, Laon and, first and foremost, Paris, likewise looked in awe to France as the cultural heartland, regardless of the fact that northern France and England at this time formed a region marked by a network of relations.[88] Praise of France, its schools and French chivalry is thus run-of-the-mill in English sources as well. The panegyric of Paris by the Augustinian canon Alexander Neckam depicts the men as devout, learned, powerful, prudent and good at arms, and is preceded by a summary of the rich natural resources and pleasant landscape of the surrounding area.[89] Herbert of Bosham, a scholar active in the household of Thomas Becket in the third quarter of the twelfth century, glorifies the sweetness of France, in praise of the French kings, through reference to its fertile lands, its sweet, most clement air, yet above all because of the ingenuous, delightful, sweet manners and company of its

---

[87] Orderic Vitalis, *Historia ecclesiastica* iv.2, 208, ed. and trans. Chibnall, ii, 246–7: 'levitas et mollicies gentis'.

[88] M. Aurell, *The Plantagenet Empire 1154–1224*, trans. D. Crouch (Harlow, 2007), p. 54. R. M. Thomson, 'England and the Twelfth-Century Renaissance', *Past & Present* 101 (1983), 3–21 (p. 4). Southern, *Medieval Humanism and Other Studies*, pp. 158–80.

[89] Alexander Neckam, *De laudibus divinae sapientiae*, lines 789–801 in *De naturis rerum libri duo. With the Poem of the Same Author, De laudibus divinae sapientiae*, ed. T. Wright (London, 1863), pp. 413–14; cited by Thomas, *The English and the Normans*, pp. 316–17. William of Newburgh writes that Richard Lionheart introduced tournaments in England because the French were better at fighting.

population.⁹⁰ French Gothic architecture was copied and revered; the French language served as the *lingua Franca* in the blossoming literary romances and English clerics expressed admiration for the French monarchy. Yet scornful anti-French sentiment, copied from the Normans, was growing as the English participated in and supported continental warfare. Consequently, about 150 years after the Norman Conquest, men such as Alexander Neckam and Geoffrey of Vinsauf were juxtaposing the pejorative stereotypes of the English as perfidious, cowardly, drunken traitors with positive stereotypes of fine speech, generosity, intelligence and charm, traits which Cicero considered to be prerequisites of a well-functioning society where the rule of law reigned. Nigel de Longchamps, a monk at Christ Church, Canterbury who died in about 1200, sketched the English in his satirical *Mirror of Fools* in exemplary manner, noting their subtle minds, excellent customs, handsome faces and eloquence, shrewd wit, counsel and generosity. Their only vices were 'Drink health!' and 'Lady friend!'⁹¹

English urbanity partly was fashioned as an achievement through which the English, contrary to their Irish and Welsh neighbours, had wrested themselves from a pastoral or agricultural society.⁹² It is not uncoincidental that after the Conquest English hostility towards the Celts increased, especially from the 1120s, for as a form of othering it allowed the English and Normans to bond in the face of a fictitious common foe.⁹³ Taking an evolutionary view of progress, championed early on by William of Malmesbury and later famously applied by Gerald of Wales in his ethnography of the Irish, ethnographers alleged that society made headway in four stages of history, in which socio-economic groups evolved from hunters into shepherds, to agriculturalists and finally to

---

⁹⁰ Herbert of Bosham, *Epistola Herberti de Boseham ad Baldewinum Cantuariensem Archiepiscopum et ad eius catholicos successores* XXII in *Materials for the History of Thomas Becket, Archbishop of Canterbury (Canonized by Pope Alexander III, AD 1173)*, ed. J. C. Robertson, Rerum britannicarum medii aevi scriptores, or Chronicles and memorials of Great Britain and Ireland during the Middle Ages, 7 vols. (n.p., 1877), iii, 407–8.

⁹¹ Nigel Whireker, *Speculum Stultorum*, lines 1515–24, ed. J. H. Mozley and R. R. Raymo (Berkeley, 1960), 64–5. Clanchy, *England and its Rulers, 1066–1272*, p. 142.

⁹² Davies, 'Boundaries and Regnal Solidarities'; J. Gillingham, 'Civilizing the English? The English Histories of William of Malmesbury and David Hume', *Historical Research* 74 (2001), 17–43 (pp. 5–6, 28–9).

⁹³ Thomas, *The English and the Normans*, pp. 310–14; Gillingham, *The English in the Twelfth Century*, pp. 27–9. For further references to the 'Celtic Fringe', see p. 192n.18 in this chapter..

civilized city dwellers.⁹⁴ The framework they used echoed Cicero's *De officiis* (On obligations) on statesmanship, originally embedded in the Roman urban ideal of civic political sacrifice, which in the twelfth century now was heralded by a peripatetic, in part urban, court setting. The Anglo-Normans probably copied this evolutionary narrative from Norman writers disparaging the Bretons, using similar commonplaces, claiming that Breton life represented a lower level of society, 'living off milk and little bread', that was related to sexual morality (practising polygamy 'like the Moors'), 'ignorance of divine laws' and a propensity for plunder and feuds.⁹⁵ Ireland, worse still, depended on imports of goods from England, as its soil was barren and its cultivators, a ragged mob, unskilled and poor, lived outside of the towns, whereas 'the English and French, with their more civilized way of life, live in the towns, and carry on trade and commerce'.⁹⁶ By trampling on the Irish, who were so rustic that they could barely transform – a racializing classification – Anglo-Normans consciously set themselves apart as men willing to adapt to Norman culture, putting their barbaric, lawless past behind them. King David of Scotland, promising three years of tax exemption to any of his subjects who might live and dress more elegantly and eat with more refinement, had learned courtly manners because of his upbringing among the English, polishing away his innate barbaric ways. David was also credited with facilitating Scotland's first major wave of urbanization.⁹⁷

---

94 William of Malmesbury, *Gesta regum Anglorum* v.409, ed. and trans. Mynors, Thomson and Winterbottom, i, 738–41; Gerald of Wales, *Topographia Hibernica* III.10, ed. Dimock, v, 151, trans. O'Meara, pp. 85–6; Thomas, *The English and the Normans*, pp. 310–16; Gillingham, 'Civilizing the English?', pp. 18–26.

95 William of Poitiers, *The Gesta Guillelmi of William of Poitiers* i.44, ed. and trans. R. H. C. Davis and M. Chibnall (Oxford, 1998), pp. 74–5. Radulfus Glaber, *Rodulfi Glabri Historiarum libri quinque* ii.4, ed. and trans. J. France (Oxford, 1989), pp. 56–9, speaks disparagingly of the vast quantities of milk produced in Brittany, their sole source of wealth. Hoffmann, *An Environmental History*, pp. 43–84.

96 William of Malmesbury, *Gesta regum Anglorum* v.409, ed. and trans. Mynors, Thomson and Winterbottom, i, 738–41: 'Angli vero et Franci cultiori genere uitae urbes nundinarum commertio inhabitant.'

97 Jaeger, *Origins of Courtliness*, p. 181; Gillingham, 'Civilizing the English?', pp. 38, 41–2. See also Ailred of Rievaulx's remarks written in the 1150s, cited by Gillingham, about King David's civilizing of the Scots, refining them with Christian piety, bringing the whole people, who were once rough and rustic, refined and gentle manners, and imposing laws. These were later echoed by Gervase of Tilbury and Bartholomaeus Anglicus, as discussed on pp. 238–46 in chapter 6. Gervase of Tilbury claimed that once Ireland had been allotted by King Henry II to the English in knights' fees, the land became cultivated and religion flourished.

The government run by educated social climbers – 'moderns' as they dubbed themselves, who shook off the shackles of the past – opened the gates for the carving out of new reputations.[98] In twelfth-century England, educational opportunities presented themselves to talented young men from modest social backgrounds who went to Paris or Chartres; at the same time the expansion of the bureaucracy increased the demand for literate clerks. Social mobility existed not only among men of Anglo-Norman descent but also among 'native' Anglo-Saxons.[99] A typical example of an Englishman benefiting from some degree of meritocracy was Alexander Neckam, the son of King John's wet nurse, who in a verse attributed to him painted a markedly benevolent image of the English – even of English knights – wherein urbane ideals are expressly considered to be 'English manners': strong in warfare, energetic, handsome, generous, '[I]t is very praiseworthy to them [to be] refined with a rich table / Cheerful faces always enter no matter what.'[100]

It is noticeably within this urban–courtly world that we begin to see how Hippocratic environmental theory and the more new-fangled Graeco-Arabic regimens – framing the body within the context of location, environment, gender, age and descent – informed and undergirded ideas of culture, social norms, values and behaviour. For the court clergy produced, taught and were themselves educated by conduct books in pre-university schools, books that taught the aristocracy and urban dwellers 'civilized' or urbane behaviour which in part drew upon Graeco-Arabic medicine.[101] The concept of courtliness and civility evinced in Alexander Neckam's poetry – or *urbanitas*, the word they

[98] B. Stock, 'Antiqui or moderni?', *New Literary History* 10/2 (1979), 391–400; M. T. Clanchy, 'Moderni in Education and Government in England', *Speculum* 50/4 (1975), 671–88.

[99] Aurell, *Plantagenet Empire*, pp. 47–59.

[100] 'Quo versu Anglorum possim describere gentem' (attrib.), in W. Camden, *Remains Concerning Britain*, ed. R. D. Dunn (Toronto, 1984), p. 18: 'Lautior est illis cum mensa divite cultus, / Accedunt hilares semper super omnia vultus.' The translation is cited in Thomas, *The English and the Normans*, p. 297. A shorter version in M. Esposito, 'On Some Unpublished Poems Attributed to Alexander Neckam', *English Historical Review* 30 (1915), 450–71 (pp. 456–7).

[101] Aurell, *Plantagenet Empire*, pp. 73–82, dates discussions of civility in intellectual thought to the end of the twelfth century, but Stephen Jaeger has argued extensively that such notions already existed at eleventh-century German courts; Jaeger, *Origins of Courtliness*, pp. 113–26. However, norms and ideals of civility are far more pronounced in the twelfth century and *urbanitas* and civility did not apply strictly to urban communities either; J. Gillingham, 'From "Civilitas" to Civility: Codes of Manners in Medieval and Early Modern England', *Transactions of the Royal Historical Society*, sixth series, 12 (2002), 267–89. But cf. T. Zotz, 'Urbanitas in der Kultur des westlichen Mittelalters: Eine höfische Wertvorstellung im Umfeld von

frequently used – thereby entailed both behavioural-ethical – *elegantia morum* – social *and* physical reform, abiding by the rules of discipline, hygiene and balance. An elegant way of life, controlling impulsive behaviour (*elegans et urbana disciplina*), entailed showing grace, charm, pleasantness and agreeable manners – which in verse was equated with Englishness. Household regimens and books of manners gave courtiers and affluent urban dwellers scripts for how to behave accordingly and to internalize such ideals.[102]

Urbanity in these sources implied having mastered another powerful quality often related to 'Englishness' – having wit. In glosses the words *elegans/ eleganter*, *urbanitas*, *facetus* (fine, polite, humorous behaviour) and *venustas* (charm) are closely tied to the noun *facetias* (jest, witticism) and adverb *iucunditer* (in a delightful manner). In Papias's (*fl*. 1040–1160) *Lexicon*, *facetus*, witty, is thus glossed as *urbana*, *venusta*, *iocosa*, urbane, charming, jesting; *venustas*, charm, is glossed as *pulchritudo*, *urbanitas*, *eloquentia*, handsome, urbane and eloquent; and *iocus*, jesting, as *lepos*, *urbanitas*, charming, urbane. Beautiful manners and harmonious self-control, showing respect for and performatively upholding the social order, suave speech and refined gestures thereby cultivated 'a beautiful and pure temperament' as 'external indicators of inner harmony', an embodiment of cultural traits that clearly engages humoral theory.[103] More ideals mentioned are affability, amiableness, unbroken cheerfulness, humility, modesty, mildness and patience. Although the clergy were at times critical of court life, especially of devious courtly plotting, in general they claimed that these social values were shared by both the churchmen and the aristocracy alike.[104]

However, although emphasis was put on the 'indigenous nature' of English urbanity – as we shall witness in the poetry of Hugh of Montacute – clerics such as Gerald of Wales and Walter Map often thought little of royal officials of low birth, sergeants and foresters, men said to climb the ranks by fawning flattery – to say nothing of the generally base image they had of

---

elegantia morum und elegantia corporis', *Frühmittelalterliche Studien* 45/1 (2011), 295–308.

[102] Weeda, 'Cleanliness, Civility, and the City in Medieval Ideals and Scripts', 39–68. These ideals can also be translated into the Old French *courtoisie* and German *hövesche zühte*, which, according to Stephen Jaeger, was an imperial ideal that existed independently from the French; Jaeger, *Origins of Courtliness*, p. 127.

[103] *Facetia*, jesting, was a secular occupation of the court clergy that was sometimes frowned upon in monastic circles, as were *hilaritas* (merriment) and *iocunditas*. Jaeger, *Origins of Courtliness*, pp. 115–45, 162–3, 171.

[104] Aurell, *Plantagenet Empire*, pp. 57–68, 76. Jaeger, *Envy of Angels*, pp. 297–308, refers to Herbert of Bosham's comments about Thomas Becket's attempts to 'civilize' the young aristocrats at the English court dinner table.

rustics, who in their view were swarthy, grotesque, boorish creatures ignorant of religion.[105] Many clerics criticized ambitious courtiers in search of promotion and rewards. Begging for ecclesiastical benefices in pursuit of bishoprics and prebends through flattery and cunning was bitterly condemned by satirists such as Walter Map, John of Salisbury or Peter of Blois (1125/30–1212). Criticism of parvenus, 'lesser men', was commonly clothed in denouncements of the 'democratisation of knowledge', as Martin Aurell puts it.[106] To quote Walter Map, himself hardly of high noble birth but feeling the urge to trample on those balancing on a lower rung: 'The villeins on the other hand (or rustics, as we call them) vie with each other in bringing up their ignoble and degenerate offspring to those arts which are forbidden to them.'[107] Apparently, the attainment of knowledge and culture was not accessible to the entire English people either. In that regard, the positive image of English urbanity reflected only upon the court and clergy, dividing the population along class lines as well.

Gendered criticism of cultured urbanity

Along with the upsurge of the ideal of courtliness from the eleventh century on, came criticism, especially from Church reformers using a gendered language of manliness versus effeminacy.[108] In step with classical environmental determinist thought, court criticism crept steadily upwards from the south and south-east to the north, each society viewing its southerly neighbours as over-cultured and decadently luxurious, adopting indecent dress styles and haircuts as well as signs of moral degeneration. Outside Europe, the accusation was hurled at the Saracens and easterners dwelling in hot climes.[109] Within Europe, the Benedictine monk Radulfus Glaber (985–1047), who

---

[105] Freedman, *Images of the Medieval Peasant*, pp. 103–73; Aurell, *Plantagenet Empire*, 60–1.

[106] Aurell, *Plantagenet Empire*, pp. 58–61.

[107] Walter Map, *De nugis curialium* i.10, ed. and trans. James, Brooke and Mynors, p. 13: 'Servi vero, quos vocamus rusticos, suos ignominiosus et degeneres in artibus eis debitis enutrire contendunt.'

[108] Jaeger, *Origins of Courtliness*, p. 155; P. Stafford, 'The Meanings of Hair in the Anglo-Norman World: Masculinity, Reform, and National Identity', in *Saints, Scholars, and Politicians: Gender as a Tool in Medieval Studies: Festschrift in Honour of Anneke Mulder-Bakker on the Occasion of her Sixty-Fifth Birthday*, ed. M. van Dijk and R. Nip (Turnhout, 2005), pp. 153–71 (pp. 156–7) for the moral connotations of long hair and the reform movement; Bartlett, 'Symbolic Meanings of Hair in the Middle Ages', 43–60.

[109] Cohen, 'On Saracen Enjoyment'.

lived in Saint-Germain en Auxerre and died at Cluny, had complained that about the year 1000, after the marriage alliance between the southerner Constance of Arles (986–1034) and the king of the Franks, Robert II the Pious (*c*. 970–1031), a band of men from the Auvergne and Aquitaine had flocked to the north indecently dressed and, worse still, beardless like actors.[110] Abbot Siegfried of Gorze, in turn, lamented that Frankish novelties such as scanty clothing were corrupting the German territories after the marriage alliance between German Emperor Henry III (1017–56) and Agnes of Poitou (*c*. 1025–77).[111] In stark contrast to the common stereotype of German coarseness, the Danish cleric Saxo Grammaticus claimed that the northern Saxons had contaminated Danish manliness with their *mores Theutoniae* of weak effeminacy.[112] Critics sketched the court as a platform or 'ring of turpitude and degeneracy', of idle pleasure, undermining the spirit of manly bravery.[113] Sapping the warriors of their machismo, the aristocracy instead strutted about in tight-fitting clothes and pointed shoes. In the early years of the twelfth century, Anglo-Norman monks such as William of Malmesbury and Orderic Vitalis complained that during the reign of the English King William Rufus (*c*. 1060–1100), men 'sweep the dusty ground with the unnecessary trains of their robes and mantles; their long, wide sleeves cover their hands whatever they do; impeded by these frivolities they are almost incapable of walking quickly or doing any kind of useful work'.[114]

Gendered courtliness, in an ethnic context, was represented not only through dress but also in haircuts. At the end of the eleventh century, having long tresses became fashionable, especially among young courtiers in England.[115] In response, hair-cutting rituals, as an act of moral reform, reached their peak at the turn of the century, executed by Norman bishops attempting to reinstate order. Penalties for long hair, including exclusion from the

[110] Radulfus Glaber, *Historiae* iii.40, ed. and trans. France, pp. 164–9.
[111] Siegfried of Gorze, 'Letter to Poppo of Stavelot', in *Geschichte der Deutschen Kaiserzeit. 2. Blüthe des Kaiserthums*, ed. W. von Giesebrecht (Leipzig, 1885), ii, 714–18; Mohr, 'Frage des Nationalismus', pp. 111–12; Jaeger, *Origins of Courtliness*, pp. 178–9 for more references and discussion.
[112] Saxo Grammaticus, *Saxonis gesta Danorum* vi.8, 7 ed. J. Olrik and H. Ræder (Copenhagen, 1931), p. 167.
[113] Jaeger, *Origins of Courtliness*, p. 177.
[114] Orderic Vitalis, *Historia ecclesiastica* viii.3, 325, ed. and trans. Chibnall, iv, 188–9: '[H]umum quoque pulverulentam interularum et palliorum superfluo sirmate verrunt longis et latisque manicis ad omnia facienda manus operiunt, et his superfluitatibus onusti celeriter ambulare vel aliquid utiliter operari vix possunt.'
[115] William of Malmesbury, *Historia Novella* i.4, ed. E. King, trans. K. R. Potter (Oxford, 1998), pp. 10–13, explicitly associates long hair with courtiers.

Church and the denial of a Christian burial, indicate that cultural apparel was considered a matter of political significance.[116] At Easter 1105, on the eve of the English King Henry I's attack on his brother Duke Robert of Normandy (c. 1050–1134), Henry's hair was ritually trimmed by the bishop of Séez at Carentan in Normandy; according to Orderic Vitalis, the bishop on the occasion castigated the idleness and wealth of Normandy, a region that had succumbed to 'trifles and vanities'. To make his point, Orderic uses the mirror of the religious other dwelling in hotter climes, for King Henry and his men are likened to Saracens, who 'grow the tresses of women on their heads, and deck their toes with the scales of scorpions, revealing themselves to be effeminates by their softness and serpent-like by their scorpion stings'.[117] Such was the fear that the ecclesiastics had instilled, such the 'moral panic about hair and fashion' as Pauline Stafford put it, that the nobles of Amiens, denied access to mass, purportedly cut off their hair using swords and knives.[118] According to Orderic Vitalis, God had even allowed wars, disease and tyranny because men pranced about in public with their long tresses.[119]

The comments about dress and haircut are strongly gendered, displaying concerns that a culture was sapped of its masculinity, although they did not extend to concerns over biological reproduction, as they would in later times. Baldric of Bourgueil chided the pre-Conquest Anglo-Saxons for their long hair and overall weakness in battle. In this way the Anglo-Saxons were effeminized, the men lacking strength and control. Before the Conquest of 1066, Bishop Wulfstan II of Worcester (c. 1008–95) – himself allegedly one of the few to abstain from eating and drinking on the eve of the battle at Hastings – had already prophesied that the Englishmen, resembling women with their long hair (*capillorum fluxu feminas*), would cause the kingdom's downfall. The Anglo-Saxons' moustaches and beards indeed were ethnic markers in the pre-Conquest era, whereas the Normans mostly were clean shaven and short

---

[116] Stafford, 'Meanings of Hair', pp. 157–8.

[117] Orderic Vitalis, *Historia ecclesiastica* xi.4, 208, ed. and trans. Chibnall, v, 66–7: '[C]apita sua comis mulierum comunt, et in summitate pedum suorum caudas scorpionum gerunt, quibus se per molliciem femineos et per aculeos nepae serpentinos ostendunt.'

[118] Stafford, 'Meanings of Hair', pp. 153–6; C. Warren Hollister, *Henry I* (New Haven, 2001), pp. 186–7; F. Barlow, *William Rufus* (London, 1983), pp. 101–10; Bartlett, 'Symbolic Meanings of Hair', pp. 50–2; Platelle, 'Le problèm de scandale', pp. 1071–96.

[119] Orderic Vitalis, *Historia ecclesiastica* viii.3, 324–5, ed. and trans. Chibnall, iv, 188–90.

haired.[120] In its worse manifestations effeminacy resulted in girly, luxurious wantonness, men personifying a 'softness of body' in an unnatural attempt to change the existing order. In the elite male world of warriors, appeals to reform subsequently engaged ideals of masculinity, acknowledging physical traits. It is in this context that humoral and Hippocratic climate theory offered a scientific framework to lend validity to these claims, which will be discussed in the final paragraphs of this chapter.

Ethnic traits and environmental theory

The embodiment of ethnicity, by interpreting cultural traits within the context of climate and humoral theory, features mostly in court narratives. In general, the Christian knighthood is praised in conjunction with the temperate environment in which the fighters dwelled, producing a brave yet intelligent, rational, disciplined and cultured nobility. The flower of the aristocracy, the sources attest, came from northern France, receptor of the *translatio studii et chevalrie*. Both twelfth-century Latin and vernacular sources such as the *Chanson de Roland* commend the French lands as a sweet, *douce* territory, 'the most splendid in the world', and their inhabitants as a *beata gens*, a blessed people beloved by God.[121] Guibert of Nogent's *Deeds of God through the Franks* comments that the 'special', wise, war-like, generous French formed the vanguard called upon by the apostolic see before the First Crusade.[122] A plethora of court romances, epics, verses and sayings praise the French wisdom and courage in warfare. The starkest utterance in the context of the crusader movement was issued by William of Malmesbury, cited in the introduction to this book, in his

[120] William of Malmesbury, *Vita Wulfstani* i.16, ed. R. R. Darlington (London, 1928), p. 23; Guy of Amiens, *Carmen de Hastingae Proelio of Guy Bishop of Amiens*, lines 325–6, ed. and trans. F. Barlow (London, 1972), pp. 20–1. Stafford, 'Meanings of Hair', pp. 155–6, 159–64; P. Wormald, 'Engla Lond: The Making of an Allegiance', *Journal of Historical Sociology* 7/1 (1994), 1–24 (p. 18), for Danish hair and dress and attacks on England in the eleventh century. On the other hand, a thirteenth-century Latin verse complains how children sent by English barons to French universities were corrupted, men becoming effeminate, like stallions that resemble mares; T. Wright (ed.), *Anecdota Literaria: A Collection of Short Poems in English, Latin, and French, Illustrative of the Litarature and History of England in the 13th. Century; and more Especially of the Condition and Manners of the Different Classes of Society* (London, 1844), pp. 38–9.

[121] De Planhol, *Historical Geography of France*, pp. 100–8.

[122] Guibert de Nogent, *Dei gesta per Francos* i.1, ed. Huygens, 88–9. Cf. Robert the Monk's remark put into Bohemund of Taranto's mouth, invoking the 'French' descent of his followers, in *Historia Iherosolimitana* iv, ed. D. Kempf and M. G. Bull (Woodbridge, 2013), p. 42.

rendition of Pope Urban II's speech at Clermont-Ferrand in 1095. Adapting the distinction of military qualities laid out in Vegetius's military manual, the northern French, the epitome of chivalry, are environmentally determined to carry the responsibility of leading God's soldiers on the crusading mission.[123] This was aligned with the tradition of chosenness, acting as God's instrument to lead the *populus christianorum*, crush the enemy and restore the Holy Land in Christian hands.[124] Already under the Frankish Pepin the Short (714–68), the revised prologue to the *Lex Salica* expressed the special Christian bond with the courageous and strong Franks and the liturgy positioned the Franci as New Israelites dwelling on sacred land.[125] The eleventh-century *The Discovery of the Body of Judocus* asserted that the Frankish kingdom preceded all others, old and contemporary, as did its tall people, its celebrated name, virtue, wealth and rich supply of relics. As a 'most Christian' people, truly faithful, the French had a distinct mission on earth.[126]

Tying English characteristics to geography and environmental determinism took a slightly different turn. Specific features of English refinement could be matched with the wealth of the territory's natural resources. The rich isle, 'in want of nothing of the world', was famed for its minerals, tin in Cornwall, iron ore in the Forest of Dean and lead in Cumbria, as well as its fertility, its fine pastures producing meat, cheese, milk and huge wool exports. The clergy's interpretation of England's wealth may have had to do with the fact that many of the king's court advisors and officials exacted large amounts of money in court service by relying on royal favouritism.[127] The royal revenue and wealth of England are well attested in many anecdotes.[128] Yet clerics and monks explained England's wealth also by modifying the traditional rhetoric of the

---

[123] Schneidmüller, *Nomen patriae*, p. 105.

[124] Guibert of Nogent, *Dei gesta per Francos* ii.1, ed. Huygens, p. 109.

[125] Garrison, 'The Franks as the New Israel?', pp. 125–36, 152. See, for instance, Theodorik of Amorbach, *Ex illatione Sancti Benedicti*, ed. M. Bouquet, *Recueil des historiens des Gaules et de la France* 9 (1757), 143, speaking of the sacred land of Gallia as God's treasury. Schneidmüller, *Nomen patriae*, p. 49.

[126] *De inventione corporis s. Judoci*, ed. L. Deslisle, *Recueil des historiens des Gaules et de la France* 10 (1874), 366.

[127] Aurell, *Plantagenet Empire*, pp. 56–8.

[128] Cf. Geoffrey of Monmouth, *The History of the Kings of Britain: An edition and translation of* De gestis Britonum ix (*Historia regum Britanniae*), ed. M. D. Reeve, trans. N. Wright, Arthurian Studies 69 (Woodbridge, 2007), pp. 212–13 and Walter Map, *De nugis curialium* v.5, ed. James, Brooke and Mynors, p. 451. It has been estimated that in 1086 nine million silver pennies were circulating in England; R. M. Huscroft, *Ruling England, 1042–1217* (Harlow, 2005), p. 91; P. Sawyer, 'The Wealth of England in the Eleventh Century', *Transactions of the Royal Historical*

geographical situation of the island. Following a conflation of the ancient classical and patristic traditions, England was pictured simultaneously as lying almost under the North Pole and as a delightful horn of plenty on the edge of the boundless ocean.[129] In part, this image again drew on earlier traditions, for the monks Gildas (*fl.* fifth–sixth century), Bede and Nennius (*fl. c.* 770–810), leaning on Solinus and Orosius, had painted a benevolent vision of Britain blessed with plains and agreeable, arable hills, where flowers of different hues decorated the scenery and the salutary flow of waters refreshed the senses, 'whose constant flow drives before it pebbles white as snow, and brilliant rivers that glide with gentle murmur, guaranteeing sweet sleep for those who lie on their banks, and lakes flowing over with a cold rush of living water'.[130] There were salt and warm springs, and hot baths, and the land was rich in metal, copper, iron, lead and silver, all beneficial to its peoples' well-being.

In the twelfth century, such descriptions of Britannia/Anglia as a divinely blessed plot of land and territory rich with natural resources were interlaced with descriptions of the English character. Their reputation for being jolly, intelligent, well spoken and generous flows from the temperate climate of the territory.[131] Comparing England's environment with the more northern territories eased the way for representing it as a more suitable locus for civilization, lawfulness and religious devotion.

This was a necessary endeavour, for England's geographical position was traditionally considered to be liminal. Indeed, although the little-read Tacitus (*c.* 56–117 AD) and earlier Caesar (100–44 BC) had painted England as a pleasant land, Jordanes, an eastern Roman historian, created a different picture, of British bad weather and people living in wattle huts in a country fertile yet barely sustaining human society.[132] From the viewpoint of both Jerusalem and Rome, Britain was positioned on the outskirts of the world. It was a place of exile, 'wholly sundered from the world', situated in an ocean 'roaring with

---

Society, Series 5, 15 (1965), 145–64; Clanchy, *England and its Rulers*, pp. 25, 73, 76, 230, 248.

[129] Bede, *Historia ecclesiastica* i.1, ed. and trans. Colgrave and Mynors, pp. 16–17.

[130] Gildas, *De excidio Britanniae* 3, in *The Ruin of Britain and Other Works*, ed. and trans. M. Winterbottom (London, 2002), p. 17, 90: '[C]rebris undis niveas veluti glareas pellentibus, pernitidisque rivis leni murmure serpentibus ipsorumque in ripis accubantibus suavis soporis pignus praetendentibus, et lacubus frigidum aquae torrentem vivae exundantibus irrigua.'

[131] Blaicher, *Merry England*, pp. 14–15, who does not offer an explanation. Blaicher gives an overview up till the twentieth century. Hugh Thomas, too, remarked that images of England as an abundant country were related to images of ethnicity, *in casu* their generosity and hospitality; Thomas, *The English and the Normans*, p. 300.

[132] Merrills, *History and Geography*, p. 139.

monsters'.[133] On the east–west axis, moreover, England was a far outpost of the Christian community. On the Jerusalem-centred *mappae mundi* portraying the holy city as the world's navel, Britain was an island in the hem of the world's outer sea. In the sixth-century *The Ruin of Britain*, Gildas, who was born near the river Clyde and later moved to Brittany, situated the island of Britain 'virtually at the end of the world'. He described it as 'numb with chill ice and far removed, as in a remote nook of the world, from the visible sun', warmed only by the dazzling rays of Christ.[134] Circa 1240, Britain's marginality still shone through in the Franciscan friar Bartholomaeus Anglicus's learned etymologies of Anglia: 'Isidore says that the name Anglia comes from "a corner" (*angulus*), as if the land were located at the end or corner of the world.'[135] As discussed

[133] Virgil, *Eclogues* i, line 66, in *Eclogues. Georgics. Aeneid: Books 1–6*, ed. H. R. Fairclough and G. P. Goold, Loeb Classical Library 63–4, 2 vols. (rev. edn, Cambridge, 2015), i, 28: 'et penitus toto divisos orbe Britannos'; Horace, *Odes* iv.14, 47–8, ed. N. Rudd, Loeb Classical Library 33 (Cambridge MA, 2004), p. 258: 'beluosus [...] Oceanus Britannis'. N. Howe, 'An Angle on this Earth: Sense of Place in Anglo-Saxon England', *Bulletin of the John Rylands University Library of Manchester* 82/1 (2000), 3–27 (p. 9).

[134] Gildas, *De excidio Britanniae* 3, 8, ed. and trans. Winterbottom, pp. 16, 18, 89, 91: 'in extremo ferme orbis limite'; 'glaciali frigori rigenti [...] et velut longiore terrarium secessu soli visibili'. Clanchy, *England and its Rulers*, p. 22. Earlier, Anglo-Saxon abbot Aelfric of Eynsham (*fl. c.* 1010) described Britain as 'the outer edge of the earth's extent', and the sea flowing between the continent and the British Isles was reason for Isidore of Seville to suggest that Britain was even 'outside our world'. Isidore of Seville, *Etymologiae* ix.ii.102, ed. Reydellet, p. 101; Eadmer, *Historia novorum in Anglia: Et, Opuscula Duo de Vita Sancti Anselmi et Quibusdam Miraculis Ejus* ii, ed. M. Rule (Cambridge, 2012), p. 108.

[135] Bartholomaeus Anglicus, *De proprietatibus rerum* xv.14, ed. H. Knochlobtzer, 'De Anglia': 'Isidore tamen dicit, Angliam ab angulo dictam, quasi terram in fine vel quasi mundi angulo constitutam.' However, this explanation is not in Isidore's *Etymologies*. Nicholas Howe translates *angulus* as 'angle', suggesting that the depiction of England in the oldest *mappa mundi* surviving from England, dating to the early decades of the eleventh century, is angular; Howe, 'An Angle on This Earth', pp. 3–6, 11–12. However, *angulus* also translates into 'corner'. In the early stages of the eleventh century, for example, Thietmar, bishop of Merseburg in Saxony, remarked that 'the English are situated in a corner of the earth'; Thietmar von Merseburg, *Chronik*, ed. W. Trillmich (Berlin, 1957), p. 392. Bede, on the other hand, says that the English 'come from a land called Angulus', a territory between Jutland and Saxony; Bede, *Historia ecclesiastica* i.15, ed. Colgrave and Mynors, pp. 50–1. Also, in the ninth century, the bishop of Utrecht, Radboud, in *Vita altera Bonifatii* vi, ed. W. Levison, MGH Scriptores rerum Germanicarum in usum scholarum separatim editi 57 (Hanover, 1905), p. 66, discussing how the English resisted the invading Danes, suggests that Angli means 'strength drawn from Christ', possibly interpreting *angulus* as coming from 'firmament', drawn from Isidore's etymology of *angulus*

in chapter 2, England's positioning within the scientific division of latitudinal climes also brought home its extreme marginality on the north–south axis in climatic terms.

Just as scientists began to tamper with England's latitudinal position, so also historians and poets counterbalanced the island's liminal position with images of England's salubriousness, benefiting minds and bodies.[136] Archdeacon Henry of Huntingdon related the 'agreeable temperateness which makes Britain extremely healthy for its inhabitants' to its geographical situation, 'for since it is situated in the north-west, the coldness which comes from the north is tempered by the heat which it receives from the western sun'.[137] This remark follows a paean of 'that isle, blessed by its far-famed splendour' that surpasses in fertile fields, milk and honey 'all others which that God rules, from whose foaming mouth the ocean flows'.[138] Again, Gervase of Canterbury, a monk at Christ Church, Canterbury, in the opening sentence of his textual *mappa mundi* lauds 'the isle of England's temperateness, fertility and opulence'.[139] And the Franciscan friar Bartholomaeus Anglicus, who applied humoral theory elaborately in his encyclopaedia, inserts a conflation of two poems attributed to Hugh of Montacute, the prior of the Cluniac house of Montacute and later abbot of the nearby Benedictine abbey of Muchelney in Somerset in the second half of the twelfth century, relating England's abundance of fruits, metals and plenteous game to the character of the English people. England was now a 'fruitful, fertile land, corner of the earth, / A rich

---

meaning a corner that joins two walls into one. Cf. Isidore of Seville, *Etymologiae* xv.viii.4, in *Étymologies xv: Les constructions et les terres*, ed. J.-Y. Guillaumin and P. Monat (Paris, 2016), pp. 64–7.

[136] England's temperate environment was invoked in an anonymous late antique panegyric to Constantine, speaking of its average temperature, abundance of corn, milk cattle and sheep, and absence of serpents. Cf. *In Praise of Later Roman Emperors: The Panegyrici latini. Introduction, Translation and Historical Commentary with the Latin Text of R. A. B. Mynors*, ed. and trans. R. A. B. Mynors, C. E. V. Nixon and B. S. Rodgers (Berkeley, 1994), pp. 231–2; Camden, *Remains Concerning Britain*, ed. Dunn, pp. 6–7.

[137] Henry of Huntingdon, *Historia Anglorum* i.6, ed. and trans. Greenway, 20–1: 'Nec tacendum arbitror quod temperie gratissima, et ideo inhabitantibus saluberrima sit Britannia. Cum enim inter septentrionem et occidentem sita sit, frigus quod recipit a septentrione, temperat calor quem recipit a sole occidente.'

[138] Ibid. (full quotation): 'Illa quidem, longe celebri splendore beata / Glebis lacte favis supereminet insula cunctis, / Quas regit ille deus, spumanti cuius ab ore / Profluit oceanus.'

[139] Gervase of Canterbury, *Mappa mundi* i, in *The Historical Works of Gervase of Canterbury*, ed. Stubbs, ii, 414: 'temperies, fecunditas et opulentia'. Allmand, *The De Re Militari of Vegetius*, p. 66.

isle, in want of nothing in the world' and its people 'full of mirth, free, born to jest', a 'free people, free of spirit and free of tongue'.[140] Hildebert of Lavardin, the bishop of Le Mans, had had no qualms about writing a similar eulogy of England in his verse 'Anglia terra ferax, tibi pax diuturna quietem', flattering King Henry I of England, who had forced Hildebert to follow him to England after his capture at Le Mans.[141] The same laudation is also articulated in verses produced on English soil, where the joyous and generous, urbane character of the English is tied to the island's fecundity as a land of milk and honey.[142] Contextualizing England's sweet environment, these men thus presented the island as a locus where civility flourished and the so-called civilizing process succeeded. Because of England's pleasant climate and environment, its inhabitants were agreeable, displaying many characteristics akin to the sanguine man and attuned to urbane, Ciceronian ideals of eloquence, good cheer and free-spiritedness. This is a clear example of how Hippocratic and Ciceronian thought merged, bringing together environmental determinism and civic norms.

[140] Bartholomaeus Anglicus, *De proprietatibus rerum* xv.14, ed. H. Knochlobtzer, 'De Anglia': 'Unde quidam describens insulam Anglicanam metrice sic dixit. Anglia terra ferax et fertilis, angulus orbis. / Insula predives, qua toto vix eget orbe. / Et cuius totus indiget orbis ope. / Anglia plena iocis gens libera apta iocari. / Libera gens cui libera mens et libera lingua. / Sed lingua melior, liberiorque manus.' For the attribution to Hugh of Montacute: A. G. Rigg, *A History of Anglo-Latin Literature, 1066–1422* (Cambridge, 1992), pp. 135–6. The poems have, in the past, been linked to Richard of Cluny, but this attribution seems to be erroneous; A. B. Scott, 'Some Poems Attributed to Richard of Cluny', in *Medieval Learning and Literature: Essays Presented to Richard William Hunt*, ed. J. J. G. Alexander and M. T. Gibson (Oxford, 1976), pp. 181–99 (pp. 192–3). Printed earlier in W. Wattenbach (ed.), 'Verse aus England', *Neues Archiv der Gesellschaft für Ältere Deutsche Geschichtskunde zur Beförderung einer Gesamtausgabe der Quellenschriften deutscher Geschichten des Mittelalters* 1 (1876), 600–4, who suggests Henry of Blois and Matthew of Vendôme as possible authors. Lines from both poems were circulating separately; cf. Thomas of Otterbourne, *The Work of Thomas of Otterbourne and John Whethamstede*, as *Duo rerum Anglicarum Scriptores veteres*, ed. T. Hearne (Oxford, 1732), pp. 6–7. Scott, 'Some Poems Attributed to Richard of Cluny', p. 189 for further references. Cf. also Baldric of Bourgueil, 'Itinerarium sive episola ad Fiscannenses', *PL* 166, cols. 1173C–1174A.
[141] Hildebert of Lavardin, *Carmina Minora* 37, 'De Anglia', ed. A. B. Scott (Leipzig, 1969), pp. 24–5.
[142] 'Anglia, terrarum decus', in G. Waitz (ed.), 'II. Reise nach England und Frankreich im Herbst 1877', *Neues Archiv der Gesellschaft für Ältere Deutsche Geschichtskunde zur Beförderung einer Gesamtausgabe der Quellenschriften deutscher Geschichten des Mittelalters* 4 (1879), 9–42 (p. 25). The last two lines are from a poem recorded by Henry of Huntingdon and written before 1129.

Again, the self-image of the English was shaped through comparison with others. The subtle minds and elegant speech of the English were incongruent with the allegedly stupid and coarse German, or, as John of Salisbury put it in a letter to Ralph of Sarre dating to 1160, brutal and headstrong madman.[143] The fact that many of the English schoolmen had, during their studies in Paris, been lumped together with Teutonici in the English *natio* (the organization of masters in the arts), perhaps gave an extra incentive to distance themselves from their allegedly barbaric neighbours, although the context also was political. John of Salisbury's negative view of the Germans may follow from his active interest in the papal schism of 1159–78, in which Frederick Barbarossa supported Pope Victor IV, whereas most territories, including England, supported Pope Alexander III. The capacity for rational thought, grounded in environment, resonates in Geoffrey of Vinsauf's treatise *Instruction on the Manner and Art of Writing Letters and Poetry* contrasting the keen Englishman with the blunt Teuton.[144] In a dialogue written at Bridlington manor, a young student is admonished by his master for being slow witted. If 'you were as English in the quickness of your mind as you are by descent', the teacher laments, the student would not display such Teutonic (lack of) intelligence, getting 'stuck on the level and looking for a knot in a bulrush, as that fellow says', for something 'sounds like Greek to Teutons, if it be not explained'.[145] The English canon lawyer Gervase of Tilbury's *Recreation for an Emperor* turns towards Hippocratic theory to account for the inequalities of intelligence. In his world description, written for the German Emperor Otto IV, he boldly explains that the English are more intelligent and the Teutons

[143] John of Salisbury, *The Letters of John of Salisbury, vol. 1: The Early Letters (1153–1161)* no. 124, ed. W. J. Millor and H. E. Butler, rev. C. N. L. Brooke (Oxford, 1986), pp. 204–14; see also his letter to Thomas Becket, dated 1164, in the same volume, no. 55 (p. 229). H. Fuhrmann, 'Quis Teutonicos constituit iudices nationum? The Trouble with Henry', *Speculum* 69/2 (1994), 344–58. T. Reuter, 'John of Salisbury and the Germans', in *The World of John of Salisbury*, ed. M. Wilks (Oxford, 1984), pp. 415–25. For more anti-Germanic sentiment see, for example, Ralph de Diceto's and Ralph of Coggeshall's remarks that the Austrians are huge bodied, stiff-necked, dirty and stupid, cited in Hoppenbrouwers, *Standaardfactor*, p. 20.

[144] Geoffrey of Vinsauf, *Documentum de modo et arte dictandi et versificandi* ii.3, 38, ed. Faral, p. 291.

[145] Robert of Bridlington, *The Bridlington Dialogue: An Exposition of the Rule of St Augustine for the Life of the Clergy, etc.* vi, ed. and trans. by A religious of C. S. M. V. (London, 1960), 66–66a: 'Si sic esses anglus uiuacitate sensus quemadmodum es natione [...]. Sed quia sensu theutonicus es et propterea etiam heres in plano et, ut ille ait, queris nodum in scirpo'; and 133–133a: 'Teutonicus hoc quasi Grecum sonat, si non exponatur.' Looking for a knot in a bulrush was an expression meaning needlessly looking for difficulty; see ed. 66a note 4 for further references.

stronger, because of the nature of their climates.[146] This was a step up from Benedictine abbot Peter of Celle's judgement that the English had humid brains and hence were given to dreaming and phantasies![147]

Using environmental theory to account for the character of the Angli/Britanni could, conversely, invite reflection upon a descent myth wherein German–English shared origins were highlighted. Gerald of Wales's *Description of Wales*, written in the 1190s, elected to glorify the Trojan origins of the Britons. Mirroring their hot temperaments, he acknowledged the phlegmatic temperament of the English, who upon migration from the Saxon territories retained their outward fairness of complexion and their inner coldness. The British, allegedly migrating from Troy, as had the Romans under Aeneas and the Franks under Antenor, retained their courage, magnanimity, blood, quick-wittedness and ability to speak up for themselves.[148] Significantly, the *Description of Wales* and its sibling the *Topography and Conquest of Ireland* contain a wealth of information about the environment, terrain and population that was of high military value, as well as advice on how to govern these territories, while drawing attention to their current state of political decentralization. These texts can be interpreted as military surveys in the Vegetian tradition, strategically informing how to conquer them, while simultaneously presenting ideological, political arguments about the natural – in the case of the British free – status of the population, referring to their customs, economy and environment.

Territorialization of identities and the Christian ecumene

With adoption of the civilizing myth, and the contrasting of Englishness to otherness, the boundaries between the English and Normans faded into the background. On the other hand, anti-French sentiment grew in the wake of the continental wars and the politicization of Englishness. Geoffrey of Vinsauf speaks disdainfully of boastful Gallia and effeminate Gauls; there was a marked antagonism between French and English knights during the Third Crusade.[149] However, the Irish and Welsh, especially, were framed as 'others' in allusions to geography and environment, culture and religion, in order to justify the violent expropriation of their lands. As discussed further in chapter 6, the othering of the Irish and Welsh was expanded to the Baltic territories

---

[146] Gervase of Tilbury, *Otia imperialia* ii.10, ed. and trans. Banks and Binns, pp. 286–7.
[147] *The Letters of Peter of Celle*, no. 158, ed. and trans. J. Haseldine, pp. 578–81.
[148] Gerald of Wales, *Descriptio Kambriae* ii.15, ed. Dimock, vi, 193–4. Bartlett, *Gerald of Wales*, pp. 195–6, 199.
[149] Hoppenbrouwers, *Standaardfactor*, pp. 15–17.

in a language evoking promised lands where lazy semi-pagans dwelled, squandering the potentially bountiful and rich natural resources.

Within Christian Europe, cultural differences and environmentally determined stereotypes allowed courtiers to classify their armies' physical and mental qualities. Thus, linguistic, cultural, dynastic and natural distinctions fragmented the notion of a universal *christianitas*.[150] Yet the lay aristocracy, competing over status in the Christian ecumene in the politics of the crusade warfare, more likely put up a united front and used the denominator 'Frankish' when facing Byzantines and Muslims.[151] Under the *tertium comparitionis* of religion, in the face of the religious other, regional and ethnic differences abated.

The attacks on Muslims in Palestine and Spain heightened awareness of Christian group identity, and *chansons de geste* list the ethnic traits of a variety of army recruits who together made up the Christian army.[152] By listing the diversity of traits, the crusading chronicles in a sense underscored the universal Christian character of the mission to the Holy Land. Indeed, just as the popular lists recording peoples or commodities presented the sum of all things under the heavenly expanse, the heterogeneity of peoples represented the whole of the Christian ecumene as fighting the Saracens. Yet these depictions of the Christian armies unwittingly underlined the differences in them as well. In the crusading sources, there was a cultural–ethnic divide, especially between *Francigenae* (men from northern France), the Normans and the southern Provençals on the one hand, groups from the patchwork of territories held nominally by the French king though largely independent territories in the region known as Occitania, and the Germans and non-romance-speaking recruits on the other.[153]

---

[150] W. M. Daly, 'Christian Fraternity, the Crusaders, and the Security of Constantinople, 1097–1204: The Precarious Survival of an Ideal', *Medieval Studies* 22 (1960), 43–91 (p. 44, note 4), argues that in fact very few writers thought in terms of a universal empire.

[151] Murray, 'National Identity, Language', pp. 107–30.

[152] Boehm, 'Gedanken zum Frankreich', p. 684; V. Epp, 'Die Entstehung eines "Nationalbewußtseins" in den Kreuzfahrerstaaten', *Deutsches Archiv für Erforschung des Mittelalters* 45 (1989), 596–604; Schmugge, 'Über "nationale" Vorurteile', 444–8.

[153] A. Roach, 'Occitania Past and Present: Southern Consciousness in Medieval and Modern French Politics', *History Workshop Journal* 43 (1997), 1–37 (p. 4), argued that the internal collective identification in Occitania was weak in this period. Paterson, *The World of the Troubadours*, p. 5, observes that the Occitan troubadours' identity was contrasted with Saracens and Jews, and not with the Christian world. However, see also Schulze-Busacker, 'French Conceptions of Foreigners', p. 30. For regional identities and the north–south divide, P. Goubert, *La Mosaïque France:*

In keeping with the relational aspect of ethnicity, the question of which groups fitted under the French umbrella depends entirely on the situation. That circumstances determine identities is clear if we take a closer look at the Norman army recruits on the crusades. To begin with, there is a lack of clarity about whom the name Norman signified – men dwelling in northern France or southern Italy?[154] It is unlikely that the knights on the battlefield viewed the Normans who had settled in southern Italy, crusading under Bohemond of Taranto (*c.* 1058–1111), and those from the duchy of Normandy in France, as separate contingents.[155] This resonates in the stereotypes applied to them. Geoffrey Malaterra (*fl. c.* 1098), who was based in Sicily and was possibly of Norman descent, describes the Normans as cunning, quick to avenge injury, eager for profit and flatterers, who enjoyed a warrior life.[156] Stereotypical Norman qualities also include vigour and courage.[157] Again, the name *Franci* might denote the entire crusading army – as adherents to the Christian faith in the face of the enemy (*al-Ifranj* in Arabic) – or specifically men from northern France, and the same applies to the *Francigenae*.[158] Guibert of Nogent's concept of France in the *Deeds of God through the Franks* stretches from Flanders

---

Histoire des étrangers et de l'immigration (Paris 1988), pp. 131–54; Malsch, *Die Charakteristik der Völker*, pp. 40–6 for sources.

[154] Webb, *The Evolution of Norman Identity*, p. 176.

[155] J. France, 'The Normans and Crusading', in *The Normans and their Adversaries at War: Essays in Memory of C. Warren Hollister*, ed. R. P. Abels and B. S. Bachrach (Woodbridge, 2001), pp. 87–101 (pp. 88–9).

[156] N. R. Hodgson, 'Reinventing Normans as Crusaders? Ralph of Caen's *Gesta Tancredi*', in *Anglo-Norman Studies 30: Proceedings of the Battle Conference 2007*, ed. C. P. Lewis (Woodbridge, 2008), pp. 117–32 (pp. 120–1).

[157] Amatus of Montecassino, *L'Ystoire de li Normant* ii 23, in *Amatus of Montecassino: The History of the Normans*, ed. G. A. Loud, trans. P. N. Dunbar (Woodbridge, 2004), p. 23. Bartlett, *Making of Europe*, pp. 86–7.

[158] Raymond of Aguilers calls both the northern and southern French 'Francigenae', *Historia Francorum* 6, in *Le "Liber" de Raymond d'Aguilers*, ed. J. Hugh and L. L. Hill, introduction and notes P. Wolff, Documents relatifs à l'histoire des croisades 9 (Paris, 1969), p. 52. Schneidmüller, *Nomen patriae*, pp. 106–8; Boehm, 'Gedanken zum Frankreich-Bewußtsein', pp. 638–84. For Frankish identity in the crusader states, see A. V. Murray, 'Ethnic Identity in the Crusader States: The Frankish Race and the Settlement of Outremer', in *Concepts of National Identity in the Middle Ages*, ed. S. Forde, L. Johnson and A. V. Murray (Leeds, 1995), 59–73; Murray, 'National Identity, Language and Conflict', 107–30. For an earlier example of the muddled terminology, I refer to H. Taviani-Carozzi, 'Une bataille franco-allemande en Italie: Civitate (1053)', in *Peuples du Moyen Âge: Problèmes d'identification: Seminaire Sociétés, Idéologies et Croyances au Moyen Âge*, ed. C. Carozzi and H. Taviani-Carozzi (Aix-en-Provence 1996), 181–211 (pp. 204–5).

and Normandy in the north, southwards to the region of Clermont-Ferrand in the Auvergne, where the First Crusade was preached by Pope Urban II.[159]

It was not until the thirteenth century, however, that the confident image was advanced through symbols of power such as the fleur-de-lis that the French held *dominium* across all of France.[160] The royal dynasty, cleverly manipulating the image of exerting power over a sacred, sweet territory, became the subject of prayers of affection, and in the thirteenth century was attributed miraculous healing powers identified with the patron saint of St Denis.[161] Alluded to as a sweet, temperate land, France was the 'rampart of Christianity'. In a bull issued by Pope Gregory IX (before 1170–1241) in 1239, the French are called a new tribe of Judah, crowned by the hand of God himself.[162] Poets also alluded to the Franks' Carolingian ancestry, pointing to the Carolingian lineage of French King Philip II and his son Louis VIII (1187–1226) via Isabella of Hainault (1170–90).[163]

In the second half of the thirteenth century, and thus beyond the scope of this book, the use of symbols and ethnotypes was further politicized. In a reversal of the imagery of French arrogance, the French legal thinker Pierre Dubois at the French royal court argued that there should be one ruler in a united Christendom, the French king and descendant of Charlemagne, who through necessity should be raised in the temperate northern France to ensure that environment and the ruler's character dovetailed.[164] *On the Recovery of the Holy Land*, in which he makes such bold claims, contains remarkable biopolitical advice advocating that the young men and women destined to rule in Palestine should receive training in languages and natural sciences,

---

[159] Guibert of Nogent, *Dei gesta per Francos* i.5, ed. Huygens, p. 105; Boehm, 'Gedanken zum Frankreich-Bewußtsein', p. 686.

[160] Ehlers, 'Elemente mittelalterlicher Nationsbildung', pp. 565–87.

[161] Jacques le Goff, 'Reims, City of Coronation', in *Realms of Memory: The Construction of the French Past*, ed. P. Nora, English trans. A. Goldhammer and ed. L. D. Kritzman (New York, 1996), pp. 193–251; J. R. Strayer, 'France: The Holy Land, the Chosen People, and the Most Christian King', in *Action and Conviction in Early Modern Europe: Essays in Memory of E.H. Harbison*, ed. T. K. Rabb and J. E. Seigel (Princeton, 1969), pp. 3–16 (p. 6).

[162] De Planhol, *Historical Geography of France*, pp. 96–100. In the fourteenth century, the image of the French as an elect nation and its king as *rex Christianissimus* (which became popular from the reign of Philip IV the Fair) fed into the notion of royal miraculous blood.

[163] B. Guenée, 'Les généalogies entre l'histoire et la politique: La fierté d'être Capétien, en France, au Moyen Âge', *Annales: Économies, Sociétés, Civilisations* 33/3 (1978), 450–77 (p. 464).

[164] Pierre Dubois, *De recuperatione terre sancte*, ed. Diotti, pp. 119.

and that there should be physicians of soul and body in sufficient numbers for the society's benefit. Pre-existing etymological explanations once again come in handy, as he contended that the name *Franci* meant free men, i.e. 'not subject to the German empire'. Likewise, the Dominican friar Guillaume de Sauqueville, actively preaching in Paris in the early fourteenth century, claimed that whereas empire derived from '*en pire*', evil, to be free (the *Franci*) of evil was to be free of sin.[165] Reminiscent pretensions were rebutted by Alexander of Roes, canon at Cologne, in his *Memoriale* (1281) and *Notitia seculi* (1288). Defending a universal empire as a divine office with a distinct role in salvation history, Alexander set out to prove that the Germans (*Franci Germani*), descending from the Trojan Franks, were the original Franks and true Christian noblemen endowed with outstanding martial virtues.[166] The Italians had inherited the *sacerdotium*, the Germans the *imperium* and the French the *studium*. The French, in contrast, were not pure Franks but of mixed Frankish–Gallic descent.[167] Alexander's *Memoriale*, probably written for the papal curia, although praising the French for their ideal clerical, courtly manners (boldness, jocosity, generosity, amiability), berates them as well in a digression on the qualities of the French cock (*gallus*), using gendered language to denounce their inconstancy and arrogance, as well as their softness and frivolity.[168] In a losing battle, he thus states that the German temperament is ideally equipped for holy warfare.[169]

Conclusion

In this period, the competition over reputations, and the negotiation of group boundaries by juxtaposing moral communities, using key markers of identity – physical strength, mental qualities and devoutness – was embedded in a narrative of cultural progress and environmental theory. The negotiation looked towards military traits of manliness, strength, courage and rationality.

---

[165] Strayer, 'France: The Holy Land', p. 14.
[166] L. E. Scales, 'France and the Empire: The Viewpoint of Alexander of Roes', *French History* 9/4 (1995), 394–416 (pp. 402–7); Mohr, 'Frage des Nationalismus', p. 113.
[167] Hoppenbrouwers, 'Medieval Peoples Imagined', p. 11.
[168] Alexander of Roes, *Memoriale* 15, 18, ed. Grundmann and Heimpel, pp. 105–8, 113–15; *Notitia seculi* 13–14, ed. Grundmann and Heimpel, 160–1. Scales, 'France and the Empire', 408. Notably, Alexander relates French *superbia* and *luxuria* to the clerical order in France. See Weeda, 'Violence, Control, Prophecy and Power' for further source references.
[169] Alexander of Roes, *Memoriale* 33, ed. Grundmann and Heimpel, p. 142; Scales, 'France and the Empire', p. 400.

Attaining these qualities meant having the capacity to act as true defenders of the Christian landscape, as paragons of virtue. It was a gendered classification, according to which an overexertion of manliness and use of sheer, indiscrete violence *within* the Christian community was rejected in favour of measured, rational strength. This did not necessarily pertain to violence against the religious other, however. The evil foe in the guise of the Antichrist accounted for the use of just, extreme force, but not against Christian 'others'.

The court poets, singing of the deeds of the bands of warriors, weighed and categorized the mental and physical qualities of army recruits using ethnic markers. What does this imply? Firstly, it suggested that the military success or failure depended on qualities considered inherent to groups of men in a specific environment and sharing descent and culture. Secondly, by emphasizing that warfare was in the service of the *patria*, court poets and historians told the warriors that they risked their bodily integrity for the domesticated space and environment they dwelled in. Indeed, arguments of ethnicity engaged for the use of violence, fostered by sentiments of loyalty to the *patria*, do not necessarily have to involve large swaths of the population.

From the late thirteenth century, as the physiological concept of the body politic surfaced in political tracts in the Aristotelian tradition, including Giles of Rome's *De regimine principum* and Thomas Aquinas's *De regimine principum*, climate theory folded into a rhetoric of the national sphere. John of Paris's *De potestate regia et papali* thus states that although human species are similar in the possession of a soul, they differ greatly physically as a result of geography and climate, and hence there is much greater diversity in secular powers than in the Church.[170] This process, in which polities attempted to claim sovereignty from an imperial framework, was aided by the construction of a triangular relationship of Christian *imperium*, sacralized body politics and the non-Christian and allegedly uncivilized other. Religious, cultural and scientific discourses merged to create a new language of power restructuring the balance between *imperium* and bodies politic, as well as vis-à-vis the others in the east, north-west and north-east of Europe. This new language justified the violent expropriation of territories that were colonized, and this is discussed in chapter 6.

---

[170] John of Paris, *De potestate regia et papali* 3, ed. Bleienstein, p. 82.

6

Imagined Geographies, Colonization and Conquest

If all humanity was considered potentially a vessel ready to be filled with the Christian message, by the thirteenth century many parts in Europe had – through the use of violence or voluntarily – accepted its teachings, becoming part of the *christiana respublica*. Within its boundaries, various aristocratic dynasties competed to position themselves as protectors of the *imperium christianum*, crusading in Palestine and Spain, while issuing arguments to wrest themselves from the hegemony of empire and Church. The clergy learned and applied scientific knowledge that environment and geography shaped the physique and character of individuals and groups, plying popular symbols of culture and framing them with boasts of civility and urbanity, the values of well-governed society. The entanglement of classical ethnography, environmental determinism and biblical rhetoric, reproduced in a region positioning itself as a heartland of civilization, good governance and military power (the *translatio studii et imperii*), thereby created a very specific rhetoric of colonization, offering a justification of expropriation of 'squandered lands'. There, the establishment of settlements, embellished with the rhetoric of progress, transmuted imperialism into religious colonialism. Texts and images allowed Christian settlers to claim the landscape by attributing meaning to it and its inhabitants. In the narratives, the geographical position, environment, natural resources and social organization intersected with statements about degrees of religiosity.[1] These claims about others in the colonized territories simultaneously reinforced ideas about the self. In this sense, the other was

---

[1] M. S. Cohen, 'The Ethnographic Dimensions of Conversion: A Study of Conversion Narratives in Northern Europe in the Middle Ages' (unpublished dissertation, University of Toronto, 1995), 153–8; M.-D. Chenu, *Nature, Man and Society in the Twelfth Century: Essays on New Theological Perspectives in the Latin West*, ed. and trans. J. Taylor and L. K. Little (Toronto,1997), 4–18; A. Gransden, 'Realistic Observation in Twelfth-Century England', *Speculum* 47/1 (1972), 29–51; J. Babicz and H. M. Nobis, 'Die Entdeckung der Natur in der geographischen Literatur und Kartographie an der Wende vom Mittelalter zur Renaissance', in *Mensch und Natur im Mittelalter*, ed. A. Zimmermann and A. Speer, 2 vols. (Berlin, 1991–92), II, 939–51.

a much-needed mirror to stake claims to the physical, mental and spiritual ascendancy of the aristocracy of western Europe.

In this final chapter we will take stock of this representation of colonized territories. This chapter builds upon Robert Bartlett's earlier *The Making of Europe*, yet takes the perspective of the influence of theories of environmental determinism in colonizing rhetoric, which is less explored in Bartlett's work. In representations of the regions that were settled, court writers welded scientific and religious discourses, assigning to the Celtic, Germanic and Slavic peoples an instability of faith aligned with cultural and geographical marginality. Yet farther to the north-east, in the Baltic regions, the same authors spoke of pagan lands of milk and honey that awaited the crusaders of civilization. The rhetoric clearly ties environmentally determined semi-paganism to the absence of a social and legal structure and hence argues for the use of legitimate violence and expropriation following the Ciceronian tradition. Whereas in the military, the focus lay on strength and rationality, the classification of the physical and mental qualities in colonial rhetoric concentrated on peoples' ethic in working the land, and socio-economic and legal organization and religiosity, rendering arguments for seizing land and claiming ownership rights.

To unpack this discourse, it is helpful to peruse the detailed, though occasionally confused, landscape of territories and peoples sketched in the alphabetically organized ethnographic geography, the first of its kind: *On the Properties of Things* compiled by the Franciscan friar Bartholomaeus Anglicus at the end of the period under review in this book, in the 1240s.[2] A book of the world, Bartholomaeus's encyclopaedia was a tool to gain knowledge of the

---

[2] For the text's editions, see p. 48n.29 in chapter 1. For its reception, see H. Meyer, *Die Enzyklopädie des Bartholomäus Anglicus: Untersuchungen zur Überlieferungs- und Rezeptionsgeschichte von 'De Proprietatibus Rerum'* (Munich, 2000). A French translation was published by B. A. Pitts (ed.), *Barthélemy l'Anglais: Le livre des regions* (London, 2006). A modern edition of Trevisa's Middle English translation was edited by M. C. Seymour, *On the Properties of Things: John Trevisa's Translation [from the Latin] of Bartholomaeus Anglicus 'De proprietatibus rerum': A Critical Text*, 3 vols. (Oxford, 1975–88). Excerpts were also printed by A. E. Schönbach, 'Des Bartholomaeus Anglicus Beschreibung Deutschlands gegen 1240', *Mitteilungen des Instituts für Österreichische Geschichtsforschung* 27 (1906), 54–90. H. C. Darby, 'Geography in a Medieval Text-Book', *The Scottish Geographical Magazine* 49 (1933), 323–31; G. E. Se Boyar, 'Bartholomaeus Anglicus and His Encyclopaedia', *The Journal of English and Germanic Philology* 19 (1920), 168–89. M. C. Seymour e.a., *Bartholomaeus Anglicus and his Encyclopedia* (Aldershot, 1992), 12, 29–31, 34, dates the encyclopaedia's composition to between 1242 and 1247, while Bartholomaeus was at Magdeburg.

hidden messages contained in nature as manifestations of God's creation.[3] Yet it was also a practical school textbook, based on classical, late antique and contemporary sources belonging to the fields of medicine, geography, biblical exegesis, historiography and poetry. We know that between 1284 and 1304, stationers in Paris were supplying it as a textbook to students. More than 180 manuscript copies have survived.[4] Most manuscripts are held in France (especially Paris, nearly forty manuscripts in total), Germany, England and Italy. This points to its key areas of influence.[5] It contains a fresh outlook tailored to the mendicant friars' needs while preparing their sermons in the urban centres across western Europe.[6] The compilation answered the call, made during the Fourth Lateran Council in 1215, for the Dominican and Franciscan orders to teach a lay audience that was insufficiently educated by local parish priests, and it functioned as a reference book usable in the same vein as the many collections of *distinctions*, containing keywords found in the Bible and giving their literal and allegorical meanings.[7]

[3] Seymour, *Bartholomaeus Anglicus*, 13–14. Greetham, 'Fabulous Geography', 193–4; D. C. Greetham, 'The Concept of Nature in Bartholomaeus Anglicus († 1230)', *Journal of the History of Ideas* 41/4 (1980), 663–77. For twelfth-century encyclopaedias and the 'renaissance', see B. Ribémont, *La 'Renaissance' du xiie siècle et l'encyclopédisme* (Paris, 2002) and B. Beyer de Ryke, 'Les encyclopédies médiévales, un état de la question', *Pecia: Ressources en médiévistique* 1 (2002), 9–42. P. Binkley, 'Preachers' Responses to Thirteenth-Century Encyclopaedism', in *Pre-Modern Encyclopaedic Texts: Proceedings of the second COMERS Congress, Groningen, 1–4 July 1996*, ed. P. Binkley (Leiden, 1997), pp. 75–88.

[4] Meyer, *Bartholomäus Anglicus*, p. 238.

[5] M. C. Seymour, 'Some Medieval French Readers of *De proprietatibus rerum*', *Scriptorium* 28 (1974), 100–3. More than fourteen printed editions also appeared in the fifteenth century and it was translated into French in the fourteenth century under King Charles V (1338–80), and also into Dutch, English and Spanish. Book xv containing the geographical entries also circulated separately, which is a further indication of its popularity; Greetham, 'Fabulous Geography', 188–90. For ethnic sentiments in French–English translations of the text, see M. Salvat, 'Quelques échos des rivalités franco-anglaises dans les traductions de *De proprietatibus rerum* (XIIIe–XVe siècles)', *Bien dire et bien aprandre* 5 (1987), 101–12 (pp. 101–9).

[6] Lynn Thorndike classified the *Properties of Things*, 'an illustration of the rough general knowledge which every person with any pretense to culture was then supposed to possess', in *A History of Magic and Experimental Science*, 8 vols. (New York, 1923–58), ii, 406. Versified geographies in this period sometimes also appeared in the vernacular, for instance of England based on Henry of Huntingdon's *Historia Anglorum*; A. Bell (ed.), 'The Anglo-Norman Description of England: An Edition', in *Anglo-Norman Anniversary Essays*, ed. I. Short (London, 1993), pp. 31–47.

[7] J. B. Voorbij, 'Purpose and Audience: Perspectives on the Thirteenth-Century Encyclopedias of Alexander Neckam, Bartholomaeus Anglicus, Thomas of Cantimpré

As a tutor in theology and provincial minister in the Franciscan Order, Bartholomaeus was well travelled, moving from England to Paris, and from there to Magdeburg in Saxony, where he became a lector in 1231. He was a provincial minister in Austria in 1247 and probably travelled on to Bohemia and Poland. This makes him a valuable source, for although his perspective on the so-called centre and fringes of Christianity is forged by contemporary cultural assumptions and science, his working field invited him to catalogue regions and peoples to the further north and east of Europe as well, in a period marked by colonization and conquest. The 175 alphabetical entries are arranged in one of the nineteen books comprising his encyclopaedia, which rest on the foundations of the four elements (making up Galen's humours). For his book he consulted Galen, Ibn Sina, Constantine the African and many others to describe the Franciscan provinces, constituting a vibrant landscape of territories and peoples.[8] He often engages Galenic humoral and Hippocratic environmental theory. On aggregate, moreover, his views are in step with other testimonies from this period, wherein the city of Paris is positioned as the heartland of Europe, a new centre of learning delighting in natural resources, healthy air and refreshing meadows for those weary of study. In Bartholomaeus's vision, the peoples of northern France and England are civilized, courteous, devout defenders of Christendom, while the ports of Flanders are teeming with handsome men engaged in the wool trade. However, beyond these territories the cultural and environmental benefits of the lands had yet to be fully reaped. The Scots are barbarous warmongers, although their manners have improved, thanks to their dealings with the Anglo-Normans. The Irish, fickle, uncivilized pastoralists, are too lazy to benefit from their lands, living in a lawless society. The indurate, strong-bodied Thuringians are cruel towards their enemies, whereas the men in Holland are rated among the more peaceable and devout Germanic peoples.[9] Finally, even more to the north and east dwell the most cruel and superstitious peoples. The Germanic

and Vincent of Beavais', in *The Medieval Hebrew Encyclopedias of Science and Philosophy: Proceedings of the Bar-Ilan University Conference*, ed. S. Harvey (Dordrecht, 2000), pp. 31–45.

[8] H.-J. Schmidt, 'Establishing an Alternative Territorial Pattern: The Provinces of the Mendicant Orders', in *Franciscan Organisation in the Mendicant Context: Formal and Informal Structures of the Friars' Lives and Ministry in the Middle Ages*, ed. M. Robson and J. Röhrkasten (Berlin, 2010), pp. 1–18.

[9] Bartholomaeus Anglicus, *De proprietatibus rerum* xv.58, 57, 151 and 165, ed. Knochlobtzer, respectively. Bartholomaeus Anglicus did not describe Greenland and Norse America or the land of the khans, although contemporaries such as William of Rubrick had travelled to these regions; B. Ribémont, 'L'inconnu géographique des encyclopédies médiévales: Fermeture et étrangeté', in *Espace vécu,*

and Irish territories in this regard fulfil a position of liminality characterized by an instability of faith.

This is not to say that the geographical coordinates of the territories described by Bartholomaeus were precise or in all cases well informed. Nor do they necessarily correspond with political entities. For instance, Belgica Gallica, an ancient geographical concept, stretches across almost the entire territory of present-day France and is populated by a generally fierce people, yet it is also a peaceful and quiet land, where many groups live and speak different languages. Some boundaries are carefully stated, such as Gascony; others, however, are confused, such as Flanders, Lorraine and Brabant. In deference to authority, Bartholomaeus also tends to accumulate sources instead of sifting and choosing the most up-to-date information, thus including cross-referenced entries on both Britannia and Anglia, Francia and Gallia, and Saxony, Alemannia and Germania, although he seems to have forgotten to insert his separate entry on Germania into his encyclopaedia.

Reflecting the author's intellectual background as a mendicant friar educated at the Parisian *studium generale*, Bartholomaeus's encyclopaedia integrates religious thought with the natural sciences.[10] Fed by the theory of environmental determinism, many entries discuss the regions' climate and fertility, the crops and the fruits they bear, in direct relationship to the moral and religious disposition of the regions' inhabitants, the etymology of their names and their origin myths.

Like Gerald of Wales's sketch of Asia as a poisonous space, Bartholomaeus's encyclopaedia sketches the east–west binary ambivalently, explaining it in climatic terms. The east is the location of earthly Paradise, 'a place with everlasting fair weather and temperate', the cradle of humanity and direction of prayer, although it is also a region of sedition where the Saracens dwell.[11] In

---

mesuré, imaginé: Numéro en l'honneur de Christiane Deluz, ed. C. Bousquet-Labouérie (Paris, 1997), pp. 101–11.

[10] J. C. Murphy, 'The Early Franciscan Studium at the University of Paris', in *Studium generale: Studies offered to Astrik L. Gabriel by his former students at the Mediaeval Institute, University of Notre Dame, on the occasion of his election as an Honorary Doctor of the Ambrosiana in Milan*, ed. L. S. Domonkos and R. J. Schneider (Notre Dame, 1967), pp. 161–203.

[11] Gerald of Wales, *Topographia Hibernica* i.34–40, ed. Dimock, v, 68–73, trans. O'Meara, pp. 35–8. For Paradise in the east: Merrills, *History and Geography*, p. 237; Scafi, *Mapping Paradise*, p. 47. J. B. Friedman, 'Cultural Conflicts in Medieval World Maps', in *Implicit Understandings: Observing, Reporting, and Reflecting on the Encounters between Europeans and Other Peoples in the Early Modern Era*, ed. S. B. Schwartz (Cambridge, 1994), pp. 64–95. In his entry on Kedar, where the Ishmaelites live – 'men surpassing the madness of beasts' – Bartholomaeus quotes

keeping with tradition, Ethiopia, *pars pro toto* for Africa, is full of mortal beings with horrible, monstrous faces, of wild beasts and serpents. It is named after the skin colour of its inhabitants, said to be roasted and toasted in Trevisa's Middle English translation because of the scorching heat (fig. 5).[12] The Africans, Bartholomaeus claims, are cowardly, black-skinned men with crispy hair. Beyond the extremes of Ethiopia, where the sun sets, lies a region unknown and inaccessible, the Antipodes, where Christendom has not set foot. In Asia, on the other hand, live 'several or different nations of peoples marvellous in life and manners and wondrous in figure and bodily shape, as well as mental disposition, amazingly different'.[13] However, Europe's superiority to Asia and Africa is unequivocal and is explained using environmental theory in physical and psychological terms: 'This part of the world, although smaller than Asia, is its equal in number of noble men, for as Pliny said, it produces larger bodied peoples, stronger in might, braver, more handsome and shapely than the regions of Asia or Africa.'[14] The Europeans' skin is whiter and they are accordingly bolder than the men in Asia, where the climate is *mediocriter* (in Trevisa's fourteenth-century translation: *meneliche*).[15]

Environment also accounts for prosperity in Bartholomaeus's encyclopaedia. He depicts the regions of western Europe as copious, economically dynamic, urbanized territories. England is fertile, abounding with precious stones and deer. Thankfully, there are few or no wolves, which is advantageous for animal husbandry and the wool trade, and England's population is urbane,

---

the seventh-century Syriac *Apocalypse of Pseudo Methodius*' revelations that the Saracens were sent as God's scourge for the sexual sins (visiting prostitutes, sodomy) of Christians and as a test for true Christians to overcome before the end of time, known as the period of 'anguish and woe'. Cf. Tolan, *Saracens*, pp. 46–50.

[12] Bartholomaeus Anglicus, *De proprietatibus rerum* xv.52, ed. Knochlobtzer. Cf. Isidore of Seville, *Etymologiae* ix.ii.105 and xiv.v.14–17, ed. Reydellet, p. 103, Spevak, pp. 92–7. In keeping with tradition, Bartholomaeus locates the monstrous races in Ethiopia and India; Friedman, *The Monstrous Races*, p. 8.

[13] Bartholomaeus Anglicus, *De proprietatibus rerum* xv.2, ed. Knochlobtzer, 'De Asia': '[D]iversas gentium nationes, in vita et in moribus mirabiles, figuris corporum, sicut et affectibus mentium, mirabiliter differentes'. The 'hapless savage', categorized by Paul Freedman as 'naked, ignorant, subsisting on raw food', was the epitome of otherness. For the Antipodes, see p. 235..

[14] Bartholomaeus Anglicus, *De proprietatibus rerum* xv.50, ed. Knochlobtzer, 'De Europa': 'Haec mundi particula, etsi sic minor quam Asia, ei tamen par est in populorum numerosa generositate, populos enim, ut dicit Plinius, alit corpore maiores, viribus fortiores, animo audaciores, forma et specie pulcriores quam faciunt Asiae vel Affricae regiones.'

[15] Bartholomaeus Anglicus, *De proprietatibus rerum* xv.50, ed. Knochlobtzer, 'De Europa'. Akbari, 'From Due East', p. 27.

Figure 5. T-O map. Bartholomaeus Anglicus, *Livre des proprietez des choses* dating to 1482, in London, British Library, MS Royal 15 E III f. 67v. There is no difference in the level of urbanization of Africa, Asia and Europe on this map. © The British Library Board.

merry and generous. Saxony is full of fruit, moist with water and many rivers, and benefits from a repository of mineral sources.[16] Above all, Paris is a sweet centre of delights, where the air is soothing. It is equipped for a large urban population. Bartholomaeus claims that Paris is now the mother of wisdom for all parts of Europe, knowledge having translated from east to west: 'For as the city of Athens was once the mother of liberal arts and letters, the nourisher of philosophy, and the fount of all knowledge decorated Greece, so in our days Paris is elevated in knowledge and manners, not only above France, but even

[16] Bartholomaeus Anglicus, *De proprietatibus rerum* xv.139, ed. Knochlobtzer, 'De Saxonia'.

above the rest of Europe.'[17] This lofty position in the liberal arts, theology and philosophy, as well as manners, not only rubs off on mortal beings born in the vicinity of Paris, however, for philosophers who suck in Paris's soft air can sharpen their brains. But, in step with the eschatological tradition discussed in chapter 1, the east is also a locus of the past, and the west the site of knowledge and power. The Greek, although once the master of many kingdoms and armies and the mother of philosophy, enjoyed the gift of knowledge and science in times gone by, *antiquitus*.[18]

Sketching a landscape of cultural ascendancy, the residents of Latin Christendom have attained various degrees of courtliness. The Normans, great warriors originating from Norway, now have acquired an elegant *habitus* (*urbana in habitu*), are sober, devout in speech and peaceful in company.[19] The men of Picardy are 'of elegant stature, handsome with pretty faces, audacious of spirit, with nimble and docile minds, of bright intellect, devout affection, with a greater vocabulary than other French nations' – the attention paid to speech aligns with Cicero's norm that elocution is a requisite of a well-governed society.[20]

Migrating northwards and eastwards, cultural and religious reputations are more troubling. The morality of the Germanic peoples, given to thievery and plunder, is rhetorically classified by invoking degrees of Christianization from the west to the north-east. Religious and cultural status accordingly dovetail

---

[17] Bartholomaeus Anglicus, *De proprietatibus rerum* xv.57, ed. Knochlobtzer, 'De Francia': 'Nam sicut quondam Athenarum civitas mater liberalium atrium et literarum, philosophorum nutrix, et fons omnium scientiarum Graecium decoravit, sic Parisiae nostris temporibus non solum Franciam, imo totius Europae partem residuam in scientia et in moribus sublimarunt.' Cf. Alexander Neckam, *De laudibus divinae sapientiae* v, line 563, ed. Wright, ii, 2, 453 and, written circa 1245, Gauthier of Metz, *L'image du monde de Maitre Goussouin* vi, ed. O. H. Prior (Lausanne, 1913), p. 77.

[18] Bartholomaeus Anglicus, *De proprietatibus rerum* xv.68, ed. Knochlobtzer.

[19] Ibid., xv.106, ed. Knochlobtzer, 'De Nortmannia'.

[20] Ibid., xv.122, ed. Knochlobtzer, 'De Picardia': '[E]legantis staturae, faciei decentis ac venustae, audacis animi, levis et docilis ingenii, intellectus clari, affectus pii, idiomatis grossi magis aliarum Galliae nationum'. Cf. Ibid., xv.167, ed. Knochlobtzer, 'De Thuronia'; xv.122, 'De Pictavia'; xv.108, 'De Narbonensi provincia'. Gervase of Tilbury expands on the image of the people of Narbonne by mentioning that they wear such tight clothes in the Spanish and Gascon style that it would seem their bodies have been sewn into their clothes. Gervase of Tilbury, *Otia imperialia* ii.10, ed. and trans. Banks and Binns, pp. 298–9. This remark is typical of late eleventh- and twelfth-century clerical concerns about long-flowing hair and tight-fitting garments worn by the youth, viewed as immoral, decadent fashions from the south pervading northern Europe. See pp. 214–17 in chapter 5.

with geographical position. The population of Alemannia is noble, tall and strong, but also 'fierce, indomitable, occupying themselves with raiding, looting and hunting'.²¹ The Saxons, in whose midst Bartholomaeus probably wrote his book, although elegantly built and 'accomplished in strength and agility', are 'always extremely bellicose'.²² Bartholomaeus takes pains to emphasize that the Westphalians, Swabians and the people of Meissen share physical elegance and beauty, yet that the mortal beings in the West have attained a higher level of devotion and morality.²³ Like the people of Zeeland, Brabant and Flanders, the men in Holland, whose main city is Utrecht – the seat of the episcopacy – form part of Germany 'as regards situation, manners, and lordship, and also language', beauty, elegance, courage and strength, yet they have 'an honest character, are devoted to God, trustworthy and peaceable toward men, and less intent upon spoils and robbery than other German nations'.²⁴ Hence, the level of social organization is a question of scale.

The so-called fringes of Europe

The ethnography depicting the so-called fringes of Europe used a specific language merging environmental determinism with the religious trope of promised lands. Some looked to the climatic conditions of the north, as did William of Malmesbury in his version of Pope Urban's speech at Clermont in

---

[21] Bartholomaeus Anglicus, *De proprietatibus rerum* xv.13, ed. Knochlobtzer, 'De Alemannia': 'Generosos enim et immanes gignit populos, de quibus dicitur in libro IX Isidore. Germaniae nationes sunt multae immania corpora habentes, viribus fortes, audaces animo et feroces, indomiti, raptu, captibus et venationibus occupati.'

[22] Bartholomaeus Anglicus, *De proprietatibus rerum* xv.13, ed. Knochlobtzer, 'De Alemannia': 'constituta virtute et agilitate abilis [...] gens enim semper fuit bellicosissima'.

[23] Bartholomaeus Anglicus, *De proprietatibus rerum* xv.13, ed. Knochlobtzer, 'De Alemannia'; xv.170, 'De Westphalia'; xv.158, 'De Suevia'; xv.102, 'De Misnia'.

[24] Ibid., xv.110, ed. Knochlobtzer, 'De Hollandia': 'Nam ad Germaniam pertinet, quoad situm, quoad mores, et quoad dominium, et etiam quoad linguam, cuius gens elegans est corpore, robusta viribus, audax animo, venusta facie, honesta in moribus, devota Deo, fida hominibus et pacifica, minus praedis intendens et raptibus, quam aliae Germanicae nationes.' Ibid., xv.143, 'De Selandia'; xv.5, 'De Brabantia'; xv.58, 'De Flandria'. But H. Grundmann, 'Rotten und Brabanzonen: Soldner-Heere im 12. Jahrhundert', *Deutsches Archiv* 5 (1942), 419–92 for the Brabantine army recruits' reputation for plunder and rape. See also Ranulf Hidgen, *Polychronicon* i.28, in *Polychronicon Ranulphi Higden Monachi Cestrensis*, ed. C. Babington, Rolls Series 41, 9 vols. (London, 1865–86), i, 288. Hidgen copies a large number of Bartholomaeus's entries.

1095, preaching the First Crusade.²⁵ Yet the regions where such barbaric heathens and semi-pagans dwelled were, for the most part, portrayed in terms of fertility and bounty, amalgamating classical ethnography, environmental determinism and the biblical rhetoric of Promised Lands. By utilizing a discourse of environmental determinism endowed with the weight of salvation history, encyclopaedists like Bartholomaeus thus managed to attribute meaning to, and hence stake claims to, spaces beyond the boundaries of Latin Christendom, in alignment with the aristocracy's efforts to conquer and settle there. The rhetoric of an instability of faith, low work ethic and a bountiful environment produced an argument to wield violence and expropriate property in liminal, future territories of Christendom. Barbarous semi-pagans dwelled in Canaan, the land of *milk and honey*, beyond which lay a wasteland in Adam of Bremen's description of the territory of the Norwegians, who herded empty tracts of land in the manner of the Arabs.²⁶ Such rhetoric served 'greedy eyes', as Robert Bartlett put it.²⁷ The call for crusading missions conveniently met this need.²⁸ The tropes often tempted writers originating from territories that just so were framed as backwaters of civilization. The Franciscan friar Bartholomaeus Anglicus, for example, was born in England; in 1225 he was appointed as the papal legate to Bohemia, Poland, Moravia and Austria.²⁹

The negatively framed depiction of the so-called fringes of Europe encouraged active proselytization. Criminal behaviour was related to paganism; conversion and, ironically, the seizure of territory, to pacification. The missionary priest Henry of Livonia (*c.* 1188–*c.* 1259) claimed that the Livs, one of the first Baltic peoples forcibly converted by the military order of the

---

[25] William of Malmesbury, *Gesta regum Anglorum* iv.347, ed. and trans. Mynors, Thomson and Winterbottom, i, 600–1; Bartholomaeus Anglicus, *De proprietatibus rerum* xv.105, ed. Knochlobtzer, 'De Norvegia'.

[26] Adam of Bremen, *Gesta Hammaburgensis Ecclesiae Pontificum* iv.31–2, ed. B. Schmeidler, MGH Scriptores rerum Germanicarum 2 (Hanover, 1917), pp. 263–7. Tamm, 'A New World into Old Words', pp. 15–17 and notes 24–6 for further literature. Other important sources are Arnold of Lübeck's *Chronica Slavorum* (circa 1210); Henry of Livonia's *Chronicon Livoniae* (circa 1224–27) and the late thirteenth-century anonymous *Descriptiones terrarum*, which describes regions in Eastern and Northern Europe and was possibly produced by a mendicant friar. It was published by M. L. Colker, 'America Rediscovered in the Thirteenth Century?', *Speculum* 54/4 (1979), 712–26. Fraesdorff, *Der barbarische Norden*; V. Scior, *Das Eigene und das Fremde: Identität und Fremdheit in den Chroniken Adams von Bremen, Helmolds von Bosau und Arnold von Lübeck* (Berlin, 2002).

[27] Bartlett, *Gerald of Wales*, pp. 131–2.

[28] Tamm, 'A New World into Old Words', p. 21.

[29] Seymour, *Bartholomaeus Anglicus*, pp. 1–10.

armed monks of the Sword-Brothers in the early 1200s, were 'formerly most perfidious, and everyone stole what his neighbour had, but now theft, violence, rapine and similar things were forbidden as a result of their baptism'.[30] According to Bartholomaeus Anglicus, the same applied to the Danes, who were once fierce and great warriors, but were now elegantly built, fair haired, handsome men, fierce towards their enemies, but naturally devout and kind to all innocent beings.[31]

Despite their long-standing acceptance of Catholicism, remarks about semi-paganism continued to circulate about the Germans and English. A proverb claimed the Teutons to be barely catholic and nobody's friend, and the Germans are likened to 'stiff-necked' Jews during the First Crusade.[32] As discussed in chapter 4, the images of the English as tailed and drunken evoke similar negative associations with the Anglo-Saxon myth of partially failed conversion in times past. However, the most derogatory remarks are uttered by Radulfus Glaber, Otto of Freising, Gerald of Wales, Helmold of Bosau and Bartholomaeus Anglicus about the backwardness of regions further northwards, east- and westwards: Brittany, Ireland, the Scandinavian north, the Slavic east and the Baltic region, where the alleged absence of towns and castles, trade and manufacture, good husbandry, law and order reflected a region populated by lazy, dirty and uncivilized peoples not acquainted with Christianity. The writers accordingly took, often erroneously and deliberately, to stressing the recent conversion of these regions. Gervase of Tilbury's *Recreations for an Emperor* claimed that the Irish – after colonization by the English – now grew in faith:

---

[30] Henry of Livonia, *Chronicon Livoniae* x.15, ed. A. Bauer (Darmstadt, 1959), p. 66, trans. In *The Chronicle of Henry of Livonia*, J. A. Brundage (New York, 2003), p. 67: '[Q]uondam erat perfidissima et unusquisque proximo suo quod habebat auferebat, et ideo in baptismo huiusmodi prohibita sunt violencia, rapina, furta et his similia'. E. Christiansen, *The Northern Crusades: The Baltic and the Catholic Frontier, 1100–1525* (2nd edn, London, 1997), pp. 93–6. Cf. Bartholomaeus Anglicus, *De proprietatibus rerum* xv.171, ed. Knochlobtzer, 'De Vironia'.

[31] Bartholomaeus Anglicus, *De proprietatibus rerum* xv.47, ed. Knochlobtzer, 'De Dacia'. Helmold of Bosau says the complete opposite of the Danes, however: they know only internal strife and are fearful of becoming too effeminate. Cf. Helmold of Bosau, *Chronica Slavorum* l, ed. Schmeidler, trans. Stoob, p. 192.

[32] Walther, 'Scherz', no. 101, 278: 'Theutonici vix catholici, nullius amici' (in London, British Library, Cotton MS Vespasian B. xiii, dating to the thirteenth century). Cf. Walther, 'Scherz', no. 67 (Prague, Metropolitan University Library MS 1641, fol. 171v., dating to the fifteenth century). For the image of stiff-necked Jews see pp. 61–2, 75–6 in chapter 1.

This island too used to be inhabited by Scottish tribes, until the time of the renowned King Henry of England, your grandfather [of German Emperor Otto IV], most worshipful Prince. He was the first to drive out the pestilential tribes of Irishmen and turn the land into an English possession, dividing it into fiefs for his vassals; it was paid for, however, by the shedding of much English and British blood. And so it has come about that a land which from the earliest times was contemptuous of religion, living on cows' milk and ignoring the Lenten fast, eating raw flesh and given over to filthy practices, is growing strong in the new faith brought by its settlers; while it was the last country to adopt the true religion, and then only under compulsion, it is now surpassing all other nations in its sacred worship and religious fervour. It rejoices in its own episcopal ties, and in monasteries of dedicated observance, richly endowed with substantial estates and providing generous hospitality.[33]

Even in light of the earlier tensions and division between Rome/Canterbury and the Irish Church, such a claim that Ireland had converted in recent times is ludicrous. It was needed to rhetorically justify the expropriation of land based on Ciceronian arguments of speech, culture and religion, while at the same time affirming the claimant's own cultural ascendancy. A range of religious men, including the Cistercian abbot Bernard of Clairvaux and Pope Alexander III, the latter sanctioning the invasion of Ireland in 1172 in the bull 'Laudabiliter', indeed stated that the Irish were godless, neglectful of the Christian faith, bad mannered, as well as, according to Bernard, 'not men but beasts'.[34] In his *History and Topography of Ireland*, Gerald of Wales's tale of the two men of Connaught tellingly narrates his encounter with naked beings, wearing animal skins, who had never heard of Christ or Lent and were amazed

[33] Gervase of Tilbury, *Otia imperialia* ii.10, ed. and trans. Banks and Binns, pp. 308–9: 'A Scotorum gentibus pereque colebatus, usque ad tempora illusttissimi regis Anglorum Henrici, avi tui, princeps sacratissime, qui primus, expulsis obscenis Hiberniensium gentibus, terram Anglis possidendam feodis militaribus distinxit, plurimo tamen Anglorum ac Britonum emptam sanguine. Unde factum est ut terra que, ab antiquissimis temporibus lacte pecudum vivens et quadragesimam ieiuniorum spernens, carnibus crudis utens et obscenitati data, religionis contemptrix erat, nova incolatus sui religione polleat et, sicut ultima veram religionem coacta suscepit, sic inter alias nationes ritu sancto ac religionis ardore plus omnibus ferveat. Episcopalibus sedibus gaudet, monasteriis religiosissimis ac affluenter fundatis in copia prediorum et hospitalitate plenissima.'
[34] Bernard of Clairvaux, *Vita sancti Malachiae* viii, 16–17, in *Sancti Bernardi Opera*, ed. J. Leclercq and H. M. Rochais, 9 vols. (Rome, 1957–), iii, 325; 'Laudabiliter', in *Giraldi Cambrensis Opera, Vols. I–VII*, ed. J. S. Brewer, J. F. Dimock and G. F. Warner (London, 1861–91), v, 317–19. Bartlett, *Making of Europe*, pp. 22–3.

at the sight of bread (necessary for mass) or cheese.³⁵ In a letter to Pope Adrian IV (*c.* 1100–59), John of Salisbury states that the Welsh 'live like beasts and despise the Word of Life and though they nominally profess Christ, they deny him in their life and ways'.³⁶ Beasts, of course, had no territorial claim to the land they dwelled upon.

A backward civilization, besides signalling the absence of public order, came with dehumanizing paganism, just as the word barbaric had in an earlier Christian context related to pagan beliefs. Although justly remarking that some of the Slav, Baltic and Scandinavian peoples had not yet converted, assertions about their cruelty and innate wildness unmistakably served as a political and legal justification for aggression, subjugation and land grabbing.³⁷ Indeed, being outside the Church meant not sharing the same social patterns – the Irish allegedly did not pay tithes and their society lacked hierarchy – and hence less entitlement to land. The Bohemians and Saxons, moreover, persecuted the Church despite their incorporation within the Church hierarchy.³⁸ Adam of Bremen claimed that the people of Courland in present-day Latvia were 'exceedingly bloodthirsty because of their stubborn devotion to idolatry', although the land was replete with gold and horses.³⁹ It is a dehumanizing

---

³⁵ Gerald of Wales, *Topographia Hibernica* iii.26, ed. Dimock, v, 170–1, trans. O'Meara, 94–5; cf. Bartlett, *Gerald of Wales*, p. 134. J.-M. Boivin, *L'Irlande au Moyen Âge: Giraud de Barri et la* Topographia Hibernica *(1188)* (Paris, 1993). Gerald's discussion of the Irish bareback riding skills, or the Welsh' musicality and their dental customs (polishing their teeth with green hazel), could be realistic. I refer also to, for example, Ralph de Diceto's discussion of the people of Aquitaine and their food customs; cf. Gransden, 'Realistic Observation', p. 48.

³⁶ John of Salisbury, *Letters of John of Salisbury, vol. 1,* ed. and trans. Millor and Brooke, no. 87, p. 135: '[B]estiali more vivens aspernatur verbum vitae, et Christum nomine tenus profitentes vita et moribus diffitentur.' Ehlers, 'Nationes in mittelalterlichen Europa', pp. 19, 24.

³⁷ Helmold of Bosau, *Chronica Slavorum* XXXVI and CVIII, ed. Schmeidler, trans. Stoob, pp. 149–50, 370–1, on the Rugiani or Rani. Cf. Bartlett, *Gerald of Wales*, pp. 139–40.

³⁸ Cerwinka, 'Völkercharakteristiken', pp. 69–75. See Helmold of Bosau, *Chronica Slavorum* i, ed. Schmeidler, trans. Stoob, pp. 35–8. The Hungarians are cruel and pagan in Otto of Freising, *Gesta Friderici* i.32, ed. Schmale, p. 192. Cf. P. Görlich, *Zür Frage des Nationalbewußtseins in ostdeutschen Quellen des 12. bis 14. Jahrhunderts* (Marburg, 1964) for (many) further sources.

³⁹ Adam of Bremen, *Gesta Hammaburgensis Ecclesiae Pontificum* iv.16, ed. Schmeidler, 244: 'crudelissima propter nimium ydolatriae cultum fugitur [ab omnibus]' and Ibid., iv.17, ed. Schmeidler, p. 244. The translation is in F. J. Tschan and T. Reuter (Introduction), *History of the Archbishops of Hamburg-Bremen: Adam of Bremen* (New York, 2002), p. 197.

rhetoric: the Sembi or Sambians of present-day Prussia purportedly drank blood and milk and ate meat, living in swamps and not enduring a master, although still human beings. Once more, farther east in Ircania, in present-day northern Iran, the men were cruel and bestial, living on man's flesh and drinking blood. The Scyths, descendants of Gog and Magog, or Tartars, were also accused of such atrocities.[40]

A package of images pertaining to social, legal and economic organization was likewise applied to mortal beings living in the north-west, Ireland, Wales, and sometimes Brittany, and stretching north-eastwards to the Baltic lands. John Gillingham, exploring the imagery of the 'medieval barbarian', arranged it into three categories: at work, on the battlefield and in bed.[41] These three categories correspond to laziness – an unwillingness to harvest the benefits of the land's fertility; rash, cruel, bellicose behaviour on the battlefield; and sexual promiscuity, polygamy and incest. However, this repertoire of images was impregnated with political and legal meaning as well in the context of Ciceronian and later Aristotelian discussions. Property, in this context, was considered rightful if obtained through industrious labour, which should be protected under law by rulers. Chaos, lack of eloquence, irrationality and bestial traits, on the other hand, meant the absence of property rights.

In this way, the regions featured in imaginary geographies as ripe for the taking, where the marvellous dwelled.[42] Mirroring the images of the east and

---

[40] Adam of Bremen, *Gesta Hammaburgensis Ecclesiae Pontificum*, iv.18, ed. Schmeidler, pp. 244–6. Tamm classifies it as 'mythological' description; Tamm, 'A New World into Old Words', p. 14. The people of 'Semi Gaul', a region in Latvia, were also barbarous, 'inculta', 'aspera' and 'severa', despite the fact that they half descended from Gauls or Galatians. For Gog and Magog, see A. R. Anderson, *Alexander's Gate, Gog and Magog, and the Inclosed Nations* (Cambridge MA, 1932); for Gog and Magog on medieval maps, S. D. Westrem, 'Against Gog and Magog', in *Text and Territory: Geographical Imagination in the European Middle Ages*, ed. S. Tomasch and S. Gilles (Philadelphia, 1998), pp. 54–75; Friedman, *The Monstrous Races*; for Gog and Magog in Middle English literature: V. I. Scherb, 'Assimilating Giants: The Appropriation of Gog and Magog in Medieval and Early Modern England', *Journal of Medieval and Early Modern Studies* 32/1 (2002), 59–84.

[41] J. Gillingham, 'The Beginnings of English Imperialism', *Journal of Historical Sociology* 5/4 (1992), 392–409 and the references in chapter 5, note p. 192n.18.

[42] Said, *Orientalism*, pp. 49–72; M. Münkler, 'Experiencing Strangeness: Monstrous Peoples on the Edge of the Earth as Depicted on Medieval Mappae Mundi', *The Medieval History Journal* 5 (2002), 195–222; Friedman, *The Monstruous Races*; J. le Goff, 'The Medieval West and the Indian Ocean. An Oneiric Horizon', in Ibid., *Time, Work and Culture in the Middle Ages*, trans. A. Goldhammer (Chicago, 1980), pp. 189–200; L. L. Knoppers and J. B. Landes (ed.), *Monstrous Bodies/Political Monstrosities in Early Modern Europe* (Ithaca, 2004) for early modernity. Strange

south in Gerald of Wales's *Topography of Ireland*, nature produced strange beasts and half-humans: fish with three gold teeth, wolves who talked to priests, a man who was half ox. Likewise, accusations of sexual promiscuity were directed at both the Irish and the Saracens, although the imagery is not identical. Muslims, in the hot south, wallowing in decadence, were seen to live in a place of luxury; the northerners, however, were accused of polygamy, wife swapping and incest.[43] On a more urbane level, the Swedes, Rani, Welsh and Prussians were famed for their hospitality and the absence of a desire for gold, possibly as a mirror for western society.

William Jones, Robert Bartlett, Rees Davies and James Muldoon have already shown how the 'Celtic fringe' was depicted as a barbaric space.[44] This book argues that this frame was entrenched in environmental determinism, tied to ideas of religious and cultural progress. The marvellous, barbarous, primitive societies of the Welsh and Scots were situated in lands rich in deer and fish, milk and herds, woods and pastureland. Although Bartholomaeus Anglicus is slightly milder in judging the Irish than his direct source Gerald of Wales, he too wields common stereotypes of barbarity, combining the wondrous with an uncivilized society living off milk and meat:

> There are many other wonders in that land. On Ireland, Solinus says: Ireland is an island that approximates Britain in size, and is uncivilised and barbarous through the customs of its people. There are no snakes and birds are scarce. Its people are inhospitable and bellicose; in victory they smear their faces with blood shed by those they have killed, good and evil are the same [...]. The Irish people dress strangely, are uncultured, food is sparse, they have savage spirits, wild and threatening faces, barbarous voices. In their own company, however, they are freehearted, affable and friendly, especially the mortal beings living in the wooded areas and swamps and in mountainous areas; these men are content to eat meat, apples and fruits

---

regions far away were seen as places where everything is permissible, something which Ribémont calls 'a writing of desire'. B. Ribémont, *Littérature et encyclopédies du Moyen Âge* (Orléans, 2002), p. 144.

[43] Such as the Swedes by Adam of Bremen, the Welsh by Gerald of Wales, the Bretons by William of Poitiers, and Irish according to many sources. See Bartlett, *Gerald of Wales*, p. 140 for references. Cohen, 'On Saracen Enjoyment', 113–46; Tolan, *Saracens*, pp. 61–2, discusses the image of Muhammad's large sexual powers, in contrast to Christ's abstinence. For a rhetorical interpretation of Gerald's perversion of nature, see D. Rollo, 'Gerald of Wales' *Topographia Hibernica*: Sex and the Irish Nation', *The Romantic Review* 86/2 (1995), 169–90.

[44] See chapter 5, p. 192n.18, for references.

and to drink milk. This people occupy themselves more with games and hunting than with work.⁴⁵

Descriptions of men living off milk, meat and hunting carried the connotation of a rudimentary societal organization; the people are restless, cattle herders roaming the countryside, eating perhaps a little bread.⁴⁶ Similar representations of pastoralism, hunting and plunder are found in Adam of Bremen's accounts of Norway, Sweden and Iceland, and, earlier, in Radulfus Glaber's presentation of Brittany.⁴⁷ The same is also intimated of the lands of the Slavs and Magyars. Although the latter was a grain-exporting region, Bartholomaeus Anglicus thus unjustly claims that the Hungarians came to Pannonia as hunters. The thirteenth-century Italian rhetorician Boncompagno da Signa asserted, through etymology, that the Hungarians were hungry men roaming the woods.⁴⁸

The pastoral way of life fitted socio-economic organization; the barbaric peoples allegedly lacked manufactured goods or a stable agricultural society, let alone the intricacies of urbanization. They did not dwell in proper houses, instead occupying empty tracts of land, which resonated with Cicero's description of primitive lawless society in *De Officiis*. Gerald of Wales, among others, emphasizes the pastoralism of the Irish, living off oats, meat and dairy

---

⁴⁵ Bartholomaeus Anglicus, De proprietatibus rerum xv.80, ed. Knochlobtzer, 'De Hybernia': 'Multa alia sunt mirabilia in terra illa. De Hybernia dicit Solinus. Hybernia est insula, quae proximat Britanniae in magnitudine, inhumana, incolarum ritu aspera, ibi anguis nullus, ibi avis rara. Gens inhospita et bellicosa, sanguine interemptorum hausto prius victores vultus suos obliniunt, fas atque nefas ab eodem loco ducunt. [...] Gens Hybernica est habitu singularis et inculta, victu parca, animo saeva, vultu ferox et torva, affatu aspera, erga suos tamen liberalis et affabilis ac benigna, et maxime illa gens quae nemorosa et paludes inhabitant ac montana, haec carnibus, pomis et fructibus pro esu, et lacte pro potu est contenta, gens dedita ludis et venationi potius quam labori.' Cf. Solinus, *De mirabilibus mundi* XXII, in Collectanea Iulii Solini Collectanea rerum memorabilium, ed. Th. Mommsen (Berlin, 1895), pp. 100–1.

⁴⁶ Possibly also an allusion to 1 Corinthians 3. 1–3. For the fickle character of the Irish, see also Lydon, 'Nation and Race', p. 104.

⁴⁷ Bartlett, *Gerald of Wales*, pp. 132–3; Adam of Bremen, *Gesta Hammaburgensis Ecclesiae Pontificum* iv.31–32, 36, ed. Schmeidler, pp. 263–5, 271–4; Raldulfus Glaber, *Historiae* ii.4, ed. and trans. France, pp. 56–9; Gunther of Pairis, *Ligurinus* vi.37–43, ed. E. Assmann and W. Setz, MGH Scriptores rerum Germanicarum 63 (Hannover, 1987), p. 331.

⁴⁸ See p. 151 in chapter 3. In the *Annales Altahenses maiores* anno 1042, MGH SS rerum Germanicarum 4 (Hanover, 1891), p. 29, the Slavs fight by hiding in the woods, *lupina fraude* and like robbers. Cerwinka, 'Völkercharakteristiken', pp. 69–70.

products instead of bread, which would require preparation: 'While men usually progress from the woods to the fields, and from the fields to towns and communities of citizens, this people despises agriculture, has little use for the money-making of towns, condemns the rights and privileges of citizenship, and desires neither to abandon, nor lose respect for, the life which it has been accustomed to lead in the woods and countryside.'[49] Concurrently, the Irish, Welsh and Danes were said to suffer from political fragmentation and internal strife; blood vengeance, lawlessness and lack of reason reigned.[50] The fact that they did not till the fields suggested that they lacked a historical right to land ownership. This was the opposite of a well-organized political community managing the natural resources in pursuit of a common good. Other accusations included about their unconventional fighting techniques, such as the Frisians' use of the javelin, riding bareback, not wearing breeches and excessive drinking.[51]

The cultural narrative of expropriation was resisted by the Irish. According to Rees Davies, the Irish took pride in their indifference to refined English eating habits.[52] This did not deter the colonizers from alleging, on a few occasions, that contact with Anglo-Normans led to progress. Bartholomaeus Anglicus conceitedly claims that the Scots, who originally came from Ireland, resembled the Irish in language, manners and nature, 'light-hearted, fierce of spirit, cruel towards enemies, envious, superstitious, deeming nobody

---

[49] Gerald of Wales, *Topographia Hibernica* iii.10, ed. Dimock, v, 151, trans. O'Meara, pp. 85–6: 'Cum emin a silvis ad agros, ab agris ad villas, civiumque convictus, humani generis ordo processerit, gens haec, agriculturae labores aspernans, et civiles gazas parum affectans, civiumque jura multum detrectans, in silvis et pascuis vitam quam hactenus assueverat non desuescere novit nec descire.' The same is said of the Welsh in the mid-twelfth century *Gesta Stephani* viii, ed. and trans. K. R. Potter, with new introduction by R. H. C. Davis (Oxford, 1976), p. 15, which claims that the English had been civilized by the Normans after England was conquered, imposing laws and statutes upon them, and making the land productive. Wales, abounding in deer, fish, milk and herds, breeds men of an 'animal type', swift-footed, bellicose and unreliable. Of the Scots the author says (in xxvi, ed. and trans. Potter, pp. 36–7) that they are barbarous and filthy, swift-footed, cruel and fearless of death. He also mentions the excess of cold and hunger. See for early Norman remarks about Breton pastoralism p. 211 in chapter 5.

[50] Bartlett, *Gerald of Wales*, pp. 134–5. In Bartlett's view, there is an element of truth to these claims. France and Germany were more centralized than Ireland or Poland; societies of kinship were subdivided, with tyrannical leadership.

[51] Cerwinka, 'Völkercharakteristiken', p. 77. In this instance, the Danes are accused of drinking, but it was, and is, a commonplace applied to most northern peoples.

[52] R. R. Davies, *The First English Empire: Power and Identities in the British Isles 1093–1343* (Oxford, 2000), pp. 128–9; Lydon, 'Nation and Race', pp. 104–5.

of virtue, probity or audacity but themselves'.[53] Scotland was also a society allegedly without bread; instead the inhabitants ate meat and fish, and drank milk. Although the Scots were quite handsome and well built, their clothes were shabby. However, as a consequence of their mixings and dealings with the Anglo-Normans, so Bartholomaeus claims, some had actually become quite decent and honest, despite the fact that they clung to the customs of their ancestors.[54] Through acculturation, it was therefore possible, and desirable from Bartholomaeus's perspective, to adapt. Depending on context and structures of hierarchy, however, writers could chose to make racialized claims about the immutability of these peoples and absence of true Christianity, as a useful precondition for the expropriation of territory.

Lands of milk and honey

If the liminal regions of Latin Christendom allegedly harboured semi-pagans on the brink of civilization, the farther areas of Europe were placed in two slightly different traditions. Firstly, whereas the heartland was copious and fertile, the outer edges of Christendom were presented as lands of milk and honey, mirrored in the east by the mountains of Israel and the regions of Phoenicia and Judea, the land of destiny for the Israelites living in exile in Egypt.[55] Secondly, in earlier accounts about the expansion of the Church, faraway regions could be portrayed as a microcosm of the created world, as they had been earlier in Bede's *Ecclesiastical History*. Bede was concerned over Britain's role in the stages of divine history and the expansion of the Church in the Sixth Age.[56] The opening passage in his book paints a mouth-watering encomium of Britain, which had good pasturage for cattle and beasts of burden, vines, land- and waterfowl, fish, particularly salmon, eels and shell-fish, and copious springs, metals and pearls.[57] Bede's panegyric of Britain (and Ireland) is not necessarily depicting a prelapsarian state, but rather has a hexameral undercurrent, the sequence of crops, sea creatures and birds reflecting the order

---

[53] Bartholomaeus Anglicus, *De proprietatibus rerum* xv.152, ed. Knochlobtzer, 'De Scottia': '[L]evis, animo ferox, saeviens in hostes, invida, superstiosa, nullius virtutis vel probitatis aliquem reputans sive audaciae praetor semetipsos.'

[54] Cf. Gervase of Tilbury, *Otia imperialia* ii.10, ed. and trans. Banks and Binns, pp. 310–11.

[55] Exodus 3. 7–10.

[56] Merrills, *History and Geography*, p. 238.

[57] Bede, *Historia ecclesiastica* i.1, ed. and trans. Colgrave and Mynors, pp. 14–15.

in the creation in Genesis.⁵⁸ Thus, the purpose was perhaps not so much to paint a second Eden but, rather, to offer a representation of the created world, a microcosm of the *oikoumene*, a place touched by God.⁵⁹ In addition, Britain, located on the edge of the world, as a recipient of divine favour, was the stage for the end of time. Bede's narrative is indeed a story of the evangelization of Britain; from his perspective, Ireland could be viewed as the next destination in the trek westwards and, as such, could be presented as a new Canaan. In similar vein, in the first part of his *History and Topography of Ireland*, Gerald of Wales, copying Bede, presents the geographical measurements of Ireland, followed by a discussion of its fertility, using the imagery of the Promised Land, noting that the 'island is rich in pastures and meadows, honey and milk, and wine, but not vineyards'.⁶⁰

The image of lands of milk and honey is repeatedly employed in descriptions of regions on the edge or beyond the boundaries of Christendom. To the north-east, in his description of Slavia, Bartholomaeus Anglicus employs the same motif directly. The region, divided into two Slavias, is populated by the people of Bohemia, by Poles, Metani, Vandals, Ruthenians, Dalmatians and Carinthians. These share a common language and customs, but observe different religious rites, for some are still pagan, others adhere to the Greek or Latin Church. The inhabitants of Greater Slavia (Dalmatians, Serbs, Carinthians), some of whom live high up in the mountains or in dense woods, some of whom till the fields, are fierce and uncultured, and less pious in God's service, leading the lives of pirates.⁶¹ Conversely, Lesser Slavia, where the Prussians, Vandals and Bohemians live, is a highly fertile region bearing crops and fruit, full of rivers and ponds, woods and pastures, 'abounding with honey and

---

⁵⁸ Merrills, *History and Geography*, pp. 270–2; D. Speed, 'Bede's Creation of a Nation in his Ecclesiastical History', *Parergon* 10 (1992), 139–54 (pp. 146–51); C. B. Kendall, 'Imitation and the Venerable Bede's Historia Ecclesiastica', in *Saints, Scholars and Heroes: Studies in Medieval Culture in Honour of Charles W. Jones*, ed. M. H. King and W. M. Stevens, 2 vols. (Collegeville MN, 1979), i, 161–90 (p. 180); B. Ward, *The Venerable Bede* (Kalamazoo, 1998), pp. 116–17; C. W. Jones, 'Some Introductory remarks on Bede's Commentary on Genesis', *Sacris Erudiri* 19 (1969/1970), 115–98 (pp. 125–6); N. Howe, *Migration and Mythmaking in Anglo-Saxon England* (New Haven, 1989), p. 59; Smith, *Chosen Peoples*, pp. 144–5. Both Speed and Kendall interpret the 'copia motif' as prelapsarian.

⁵⁹ Merrills, *History and Geography*, p. 273.

⁶⁰ Gerald of Wales, *Topographia Hibernica* i.6, ed. Dimock, v, 28, trans. O'Meara, p. 35: 'pascuis et pratis, melle et lacte, vinis, non vineis'. Gerald continues with a discussion of Bede's claim that vineyards were not entirely absent in Ireland, but that in his day the wines were imported from Poitou in exchange for animal hides.

⁶¹ Trevisa's translation at p. 806 says: 'without devotion'.

milk'. Here the people are strong bodied, dedicated to agriculture and fishing, more devoted to God and more peaceable towards their neighbours than the people of Greater Slavia, as a result of their mixing and daily business with the Germans.[62]

The imagery of lands of health-giving milk and honey implies that the inhabitants of these regions are living in a Canaan or a blessed microcosm of the creation, but refuse to make good use of its natural resources.[63] For instance, Otto of Freising's description of Pannonia, produced for Emperor Frederick Barbarossa shortly after the region's subjugation, describes its rivers, streams and wild animals, delightful because of the natural charm of the landscape. It is so rich in arable fields, 'it seems like the paradise of God, or the fair land of Egypt'. However, its population, Hungarians, are barbarians, crude in customs and speech, 'of disgusting aspect with deep-set eyes and short stature', who have built few proper stone or wooden houses.[64] Otto marvels at the divine patience that so delightful a land should be inhabited by such monstrous beings. In a *vita* of Bishop Otto of Bamberg (*c.* 1060–1131), the monk Herbord of Michelsberg (d. 1168) offers a similar geography of Pomerania, which was converted to Christianity by the said bishop. After sketching the geographical dimensions, Herbord claims:

> [I]ts people, experienced fighters on land and sea, are accustomed to living off plunder and depredation, have always been indomitable due to a natural savageness, and totally alien to Christian culture and faith. But this land offers to its inhabitants a plentiful bounty of fish and animals, and is most fertile with every kind of grain and vegetable or plant. No place is richer in honey, pasture, and herbs. They neither have nor seek wine, but their carefully prepared mead surpasses even the wines of Falernum.[65]

---

[62] Bartholomaeus Anglicus, *De proprietatibus rerum* xv.140, ed. Knochlobtzer, 'De Sclavia': '[M]elle abundans atque lacte. Gens fortis corpore, agriculturae dedita et piscaturae, magis pia ad deum et pacifica quoad proximum, quam illi qui habitant in maiori Sclavia, et hoc est propter mixtionem et societatem, quam quotidie contrahunt cum Germanis.' His source is the elusive 'Erodatus'.

[63] Tamm, 'A New World into Old Words', p. 20. See Bartlett, *England under Norman and Angevin Kings*, p. 286 for similar English sources.

[64] Otto of Freising, *Gesta Friderici* i.32, ed. Schmale, p. 192; C. C. Mierow (trans.), *The Deeds of Frederick Barbarossa (Gesta Friderici I Imperatoris)* (Toronto, 1994), pp. 65–6: 'tamquam paradisus Dei vel Egyptus spectabilis esse videatur'; 'facie tetri, profundis oculis, statura humiles'.

[65] Herbord of Michelsberg (or 'Bamberg'), *Dialogus de vita Ottonis episcopi Babenbergensis* ii.1, ed. R. Köpke MGH Scriptores rerum Germanicarum 33 (Hanover, 1868), p. 725, trans. Cohen, *Ethnographic Dimensions*, p. 162: 'Gens ista terra marique bellare perita, spoliis et raptu vivere consueta, naturali quadam feritate semper

However, the potential of agricultural fertility was not maximized, as Gerald of Wales intimated, and this lack of cultivation of the fields was related to a lack of good morals, as William of Poitiers had already remarked about the Bretons in the eleventh century.[66] Although inhabiting a delectable land, the Hungarians were monsters, not men, Otto of Freising snarled. They were unable – as pagans or wayward Christians – to reap the benefits of the land, to enjoy the fruits of milk and honey, as a righteous and obedient people.[67] In this regard, the regions were trailing in the evolution from hunting and pastoralism to urbanity. Thus, defining the inhabitants as pagan, cruel, barbarian pastoralists gave the depiction of these regions as Promised Lands a sense of urgency. For Canaan was a region to which man must journey, which his 'seed would inherit', just as God, it was said, had sent Abraham from Haran to Canaan to inherit that plot of land.

Was the purpose of the rhetoric to urge men – missionaries, settlers, crusaders – to drive out the idolatrous inhabitants?[68] Marek Tamm suggests that Arnold of Lübeck in his *Chronica Slavorum* used the notion of the Promised Land to incite crusaders to hasten to the land of promised felicity.[69] Len Scales went a step further, arguing that 'within the Judaeo-Christian history of salvation, the obliteration and replacement of peoples was a principal motor of advance and historical change'.[70] The depiction of bountiful territories, indeed, invited settlers to expropriate the fertile lands allegedly bestowed upon humanity by God. Above all, the rhetoric used to depict the irrational inhumanity of the groups living in lawless societies gave the settlers valid cultural arguments aligning with Ciceronian and later Aristotelian concepts of the social nature of man and property rights. Whether or not this entailed the

---

erat indomita et a cultu et fide christiana penitus aliena. Terra vero ipsa piscium et ferarum copiosam incolis praebet habundantiam, omnigenumque frumentorum et leguminum sive seminum fertilissima est; nulla mellis feracior, nulla pascuis et gramine fecundior. Vinum autem nec habent nec querunt, sed melleis poculis et cervisia curatissime confecta vina superant Falernica.' Compare also the *Pilgrim's Guide to Santiago*, which uses similar imagery describing the region of Navarra.

[66] William of Poitiers, *Gesta Guillelmi* i.45, ed. and trans. Davis and Chibnall, pp. 74–5; Thomas, *The English and the Normans*, p. 39. Phillips, 'Outer World', p. 51; A. Simms, 'Core and Periphery in Medieval Europe: The Irish Experience in a Wider Context', in *Common Ground: Essays on the Historical Geography of Ireland Presented to T. Jones Hughes*, ed. W. J. Smyth and K. Whelan (Cork, 1988), pp. 22–40 (p. 24).

[67] Smith, *Chosen Peoples*, p. 146.

[68] Ibid., p. 81.

[69] Arnold of Lübeck, *Chronica Slavorum* v.30, ed. I. M. Lappenberg, MGH Scriptores rerum Germanicarum 14 (Hanover, 1868), p. 214.

[70] Scales, 'Bread, Cheese and Genocide', pp. 294–5.

displacement of the peoples dwelling in these regions depended on various factors such as religion and the demand for cheap labour.

Conclusion

The positioning of the western heartland on the east–west axis offered men of letters in the north-west of Europe an image in which to mirror their own identity: Christian us versus pagan, heretical or religious other (heathen, Muslim, Jewish) them.[71] In conjunction, intersecting mechanisms of classification were applied, of past and present, temperate (northern France, England and Italy) versus hot (the east/south) or extremely cold (the upper north); white versus dark-skinned; civilized and urbanized (northern France, Normandy, England) versus pastoral, rustic, lawless and barbarian (Ireland, Wales, the Scandinavian and Baltic regions); and virtuous versus sinful (everywhere). The use of mirroring images was situational, however, and certainly far more complex in practice.

Within the confines of Christendom in western Europe – where the allegedly civilized Christian or potential Christian lived – shades of otherness continued to be expressed most strongly in terms of degrees of sinfulness, devoutness and social status.[72] Thus, from the outset, it is necessary to bear in mind that these ethnocentric perspectives first and foremost remained scalar and relational: not only was the non-Christian other painted in terms of barbarity, but within Christendom degrees of Christian, social and gendered otherness existed as well. From the viewpoint of the so-called heartland of north-west Europe, the Irish, and to an extent that Germans, might be depicted as uncivilized, barely Catholic people. And within Christendom, where crusading knights could view themselves as epitomes of chivalry facing the Saracen enemy – lewd, cowardly, cunning, luxurious – internally the northern French might accuse their more immediate southern neighbours

---

[71] Akbari, 'From Due East to True North', pp. 19–34; N. Daniel, *Heroes and Saracens: An Interpretation of the* Chansons de Geste (Edinburgh, 1984) and *Islam and the West: The Making of an Image* (rev. edn, Oxford, 1993).

[72] P. H. Freedman, 'The Medieval Other: The Middle Ages as Other', in *Marvels, Monsters and Miracles: Studies in the Medieval and Early Modern Imaginations*, ed. T. S. Jones and D. A. Sprunger (Kalamazoo, 2002), pp. 1–24 (pp. 3–4) writes that 'the medieval Other differs from that of the modern period described by Said in that neither the westward course of history, nor occidental technological superiority, nor a global empire were as yet conceived of, let alone confidently maintained'. This, however, I believe to be inaccurate.

of decadence, effeminacy and over-civilization.[73] Likewise, where the French or Italians might regard themselves to be the measure of civilization and the more northern English or Germans as barbarians dwelling in the backwaters of Europe, the latter transfixed the same imagery on *their* northerly neighbours, the Irish or Scandinavians. The blood-drinking, flesh-eating savage lived in remote spaces dangerously close to home: Ireland in the extremities of the west, the Slavs and Tartars in the east. The English could be stripped of their humanity as tailed men, a physical deformity mythically materializing – crucially – when the Anglo-Saxons rejected Augustine of Canterbury's efforts to convert them in 596.

In the course of the twelfth and early thirteenth centuries, a shift occurred in the conception of the cyclical and linear course of history, laying a stronger emphasis on the social and cultural progress of civilization from rural to urban, from lawless to regulated, from heathen to devout and from wasteful to commercial, said to be bound together within the programme of the pursuit of the common good. Intertwining classical and biblical notions of a future return to a golden age with a concept of social and cultural progress, it allowed the clergy and courtiers to frame the expansion to the north-west, north-east and east of Europe on religious, cultural, economic and physiological terms. Above all, in a legal framework, it gave the court centres arguments for the expansion of territory.

These discourses foreshadow later narratives of the colonization of the Americas and strategies used in the slave trade, in the ethnographies produced by new explorers, many of whom were driven by missionary ideas. It is hazardous to underestimate the combined influence of the rhetoric of environmental determinism, religion and culture in these later pursuits as well, which are so often framed as rational, capitalist endeavours, spawned by curiosity rather than religious zeal, under the aegis of emerging bodies politic rather than the 'medieval', violent, feudal men of the past hungry for power and property. Such a view of history is too neat and tidy, however, concealing a far more complicated and intricate range of factors, processes and contingencies in the formation of national spheres and representations of selves and others.

---

[73] The ethnocentric position is of course not restricted to North-West Europe. Ibn Khaldūn (*Muqaddima* i) wrote a negative report of those in the first and second clime (Abessinians, Sudani) as they were located beyond the temperate zone; Iraq and Syria were the most temperate regions in his viewpoint (in Algeria). Higgs Strickland, *Saracens, Demons and Jews*, p. 178.

Conclusion

This book has explored the entanglement of environmental theory with ideas about cultural progress and eschatology in western Europe in the period 950–1250. The new frame that emerged was marked by two strands in particular: the translation motif, articulating the alleged shift of power and learning from east to west and past to present; and the imagination of communities as moral and natural collectivities, enhanced by the dissemination of Graeco-Arabic environmental theory focusing on the situation where peoples dwelled. These two discourses together gave monks, schoolmen and courtiers a rhetorical toolkit to compare ethnotypes, justifying colonization and conquest efforts using Ciceronian and, later, Aristotelian concepts of governance and an ordered society. The extent to which this narrative continued to shape the colonization discourses of Europeans settling in the Americas has yet to be vigorously researched, following the significant steps taken by, among others, Muldoon, Heng and, earlier, Pagden.[1]

In the process, between circa 950 and 1250, learned monks and clerics in western Europe reconfigured the imagined boundaries of ethnic communities, regrouping the markers of the genealogical–religious framework spatially. The rhetorical focus increasingly lay on the sweetness, fecundity or harsh conditions of territories and the rationality, legal and social infrastructure and work ethic of the peoples populating them. The rhetorical use of ethnotypes occurred foremost in the military sphere, advanced by western European courts working out military strategies while positioning themselves as centres of culture. The ethnic self-images that courtiers forged and appropriated thereby reflected the ideal reputation of the elite, emphasizing urbanity, disciplined good manners and speech.

In the course of the thirteenth and fourteenth centuries, beyond the scope of this book, scholars employing the Greek metaphor of the body politic began to comment upon and expand the idea that bodies politic had agency, based on climate theory, and existed in pursuit of a common good. As Joel Kaye argued in *A History of Balance*, society and the marketplace now became considered as a self-referential organism seeking a balanced hierarchy to

---

[1] Muldoon, *Identity on the Medieval Irish Frontier*; Heng, *The Invention of Race in the European Middle Ages*; Pagden, *European Encounters with the New World*.

maintain its vitality, whose boundaries balanced upon specific, physical classification as well as social station.²

The centres of learning played a key role in the articulation of these ideas. Young students at the university of Paris, as Jacques de Vitry describes, called each other arrogant Frenchman, aggressive German, drunken Englishman or raping Brabander. Such ethnotypes, in part drawn from popular, antagonistic sayings and lists of virtues and vices, were also infused with scientific ideas about the relationship between the body and mind. In this way, religious and scientific ideas from the Bible and ancient Greek texts – in both cases, ideas that originated in the Near East and North Africa – become intertwined with ancient Roman and Germanic traditions in Europe, leaning on a warrior culture.

Before the organization of modern nation-states, without the technology of national railways, border surveillance and printing, the *nationes* are imagined especially by drawing moral boundaries, which rhetorically could align with territorial boundaries. The moral boundaries defined groups predicated on cultural traits, such as the alleged discipline in eating and drinking habits, use of violence and sexual practices, in a dialogue with the Christian schema of virtues and sins. Several significant developments thereby occurred in the period 950–1250. Firstly, religious men reflected upon their own moral-cultural ascendancy under the umbrella framework of the Christian imperial *dominium*. Secondly, courtiers underscored how the environment brought disciplined military power in the context of the expansionary wars in southwest Asia, and in the settlement of Ireland and the Baltic regions, juxtaposing rational, urbanized civilization with the barbaric, lawless, beastlike traits of the marvellous non-Christian other, who nonetheless populated future, bountiful lands. The concomitant concept of history as the progression of civilization, which gained popularity from the twelfth century, encouraged a language of competition and justified the expansionary drive and expropriation of land.

The *translatio studii et imperii* motif, which holds that power and knowledge had moved from the east to the west in the course of history, situates twelfth-century western Europe firmly in the present, while the Near East is left behind in an underdeveloped past. In reality, they of course existed in coeval timeframes, frequently meeting through trade contacts and cultural exchanges, and in warfare. In the process, communities repositioned themselves, from entities dwelling under the hegemonic umbrella of the *imperium christianum*, to bodies politic arranged in a triangulate framework, whereby the own body politic related to a *third other*: in the crusade movement the Muslim

---

² Kaye, *A History of Balance*.

in south-west Asia, for England the Irish in the north-west, and for Teutonic knights the Baltic territories in the north-east. The other was defined culturally and morally, and increasingly racially entrenched in biological-environmental thought, as hovering on a lower rung of the ladder of civilization, barbaric, unreliable or decadent. This process of othering was clearly framed in space and time: western European monks and courtiers situated the centres of power, learning – Greece, Rome – and religion (Judaism) in an eastern past, whereas the heathen territories of Ireland and the Baltic, and the Muslim territories in the east, represented future promised lands. Engaging the *translatio studii et imperii* concept, France successfully appropriated the reputation of being the home of balanced and temperate learning, discipline and rationality, residing in the here and now. Yet, within the Church in western Europe there was competition between the French, the English and the Germans about their place in the hierarchy of overarching Christianity, in which differences were emphasized and claims to chosenness were exerted.

Monks, courtiers and legal thinkers might emphasize a love for a heavenly and earthly *patria*. Significant throughout this book is the role played by monks, clergymen and courtiers in shaping and defining the dimensions of communities of culture and descent, and their translation of older, religiously articulated ideas of sacrifice, loyalty and love onto military communities.

Yet the values attributed to groups had unstable meanings depending on context. Significantly, they were gendered: the overly aggressive masculinity of the German empire, although acceptable in the eschatological context challenging the religious other, was contested by Italian, French and English writers. Within Europe, the French and English presented themselves as more rational and disciplined holders of power, laying an emphasis on learning and urbanity, aiding them in their justification of colonization and conquest. Such self-representations are the mirror image of racialized typologies of others, to the extent that they engaged environmental theory and served to position selves and others in a hierarchy of power.

Nations and history

The aim of this book was to unpack the religious ideas and environmental theories informing the rhetoric of monks, schoolmen and courtiers in the period 950–1250 when talking about nationhood, and its application and validation in monasteries, schools and courts in western Europe. The ideas about nationhood discussed in this book do not stem one-directionally from dynastic centres of power embroiled in warfare or churning out political-philosophical treatises about body politics. They are embedded firstly in religious narratives about the *populus christianorum* and the history of mankind; and afterwards more explicitly in Graeco-Arabic scientific discussions about the impact of environment on peoples, scientific ideas hitherto mostly overlooked in studies about national identities in premodernity. Climate theory, and the metaphor of the body politic, were consequential for the evolving rhetoric of nationhood and concepts of sovereignty. For Graeco-Arabic science offered a framework for imagining the community to be bounded, and invested with agency, akin to the legal *persona ficta*. No longer did the community's ruler by necessity preside over the dynastic community as a *pater familias*, tied by the bonds of descent recorded in genealogy. It was also possible to imagine the community as a body, born into a sweet territory. At the head stood a ruler, as its synecdoche; the aristocracy, officials, tradesmen, artisans and peasants played their allotted roles: contributing to the survival of the organic body politic, in pursuit of the shared interests of the common good. At least, that was how it was presented rhetorically; in reality, the pursuit of land and taxes featured on the agenda. The imagining of the body politic paved the way for later discussions about alternative forms of sovereignty and power, which were no longer said to emanate from some external, divine source, but now might arise from within the community. Hence discussions also arose about the nature of tyranny and the body politic, which are already articulated in John of Salisbury's twelfth-century *Policraticus*. The concept of the body politic aided the imagining of the organization of welfare and the exchange of material goods in a developing market system, further facilitated by growing levels of literacy and methods of accounting that allowed people to anticipate the future.[3] In the period 950–1250, however, in a world where control over social welfare, labour and the economy was less state driven, social and religious identities mostly trumped or else shaped those of nationhood. The existing legal infrastructure subjecting the Jewish minority is a significant exception.

The ethnotypes mentioned throughout this book, such as Norman cruelty, English charm or Poitevin garrulity, often did not align with the political centres of power. This underscores ethnotypes' status not as outcomes of political and cultural processes but, rather, as verbal ammunition to be used in rhetorical arguments. The extent to which royal and ecclesiastical courts as centres of power seeking to expand their grip over territories profited from this range of gendered images was dictated by many circumstances and factors. What does stand out, nonetheless, is that the proliferation of ethnic stereotypes and strengthening ideas of nationhood reflected and fed tensions between the *imperium* and bodies politic, in which images of others buttressed rulers' claims to cultural, social and governmental ascendancy in their own polities,

[3] Kaye, *A History of Balance*.

famously articulated in the twelfth-century adage '*rex in regno suo imperator*'.[4] As such, this book argues that the power relations in terms of the increase of a sense of nationhood are triangular rather than binary.

Exploring the changes in the ways in which communities were imagined uncovers new perspectives on nations in history that move beyond questions of their roots in the past. It also complicates the notion of the cultural givenness of the building blocks of nations – for culture itself is not so much handed down but constantly in flux, adapting to and driving social, religious and political change and responding to ideas, knowledge and material environments. As this book attests, religious thought, in consequence, rather than being replaced by rational, secular nationhood, helped to shape the perceived moral boundaries of nations and reshape the self-presentation of such national communities as disciplined, rational bodies politic. In my view, the longevity of religious ideas about power, ideas of self and morality, as well as the emotive experience of rituals, sentiments of loyalty and sacrificial desire, remain underexplored in studies of early modern nationhood.

Researching processes of community identity formation by looking at religious, cultural, legal and moral boundaries allows us to take an approach that sets little store by the premodern/modern divide. It offers insight into the intersecting fluctuations in the definition of group membership as well as into how the often gendered images attached to groups took on value and meaning, scientifically, socially, culturally and politically. It shows that imagined nations do not suddenly emerge out of nothingness but, rather, that the boundary markers used to classify groups reshuffle, depending on the ideas circulating in a society, levels of contact and political and economic circumstances. For instance, whereas in the ninth century historians might suggest that the Franks formed a community based on descent, in the twelfth century court poets take more cognizance of environmental factors, claiming that places shape group characteristics. Centres of learning and power – the schools and the courts – played a significant role in shaping these ideas. Court poets, churchmen and monks actively consulted manuals on warfare and rhetoric to foster sentiments about the defence of the *patria* and the qualities of armies. They also forged a false, biopolitical narrative of how regions' environment justified the colonization of lands and entitlement to property.

Then and now, the boundaries of communities are constantly redefined, following contingent processes, invoking a triangular framework. In the twelfth century, this framework concerned the Christian *imperium* and the

---

[4] J. P. Canning, 'Introduction: Politics, Institutions and Ideas', in *The Cambridge History of Medieval Political Thought, c. 350–c. 1450*, ed. J. H. Burns (Cambridge, 1988), pp. 341–66 (p. 363).

emerging body politic and colonized others. In a pincer movement, the significance attributed to the markers classifying the community thereby waxed and waned, depending on the configuration of religion and universal norms, on the one hand, and laws, and representations of culture, language and traits, viewed as cultural, inherited or environmental, on the other. Exploring these constantly vacillating boundary markers in each period and situation, and from varying perspectives, makes clear that communities are imagined and performed through ideas and processes, rather than being handed down from one generation to the next. This was the case in the twelfth century, and it is no different today. Thus, images of ethnicity, allegedly validated through genealogy, environment, social practice or religion, remain potent rhetorical instruments within the hierarchy of power.

Appendix

The appendix presents eight clusters of ethnic catalogues ordered chronologically, based on the dating of the manuscripts, and arranged according to incipits.

I 'Sapientia Grecorum' (The Wisdom of the Greeks)

Manuscripts

- Codex Aemilianensis, Madrid, Biblioteca Real Academia de la Historia, MS 39; circa 950; geographical texts, many drawn from Isidore of Seville and including a description of Spain, list of Spanish rivers, the seven wonders of the world and grammar texts
- Roda Codex, Madrid, Biblioteca Real Academia de la Historia, MS 78 fol. 196v.; eleventh century
- Madrid, Biblioteca Nacional de España, MS 8831 fol. 165; eleventh or twelfth century

Printed in: *Chroniques Asturiennes*, ed. Y. Bonnaz (Paris, 1987) and in *Chronica minora saec. iv. v. vi. vii*, ed. T. Mommsen, MGH Auctores Antiquissimi 11 (Berlin, 1894), pp. 389–90

> Sapientia Graecorum
>
> Fortia Gothorum
>
> Consilia Chaldaeorum
>
> Superbia Romanorum
>
> Ferocitas Francorum
>
> Ira Britanniae
>
> Libido Scottorum
>
> Duritia Saxonum
>
> Cupiditas Persarum
>
> Invidia Iudaeorum
>
> Pax Aethioporum
>
> Commercia Gallorum.[1]

---

[1] Translation at pp. 65–6.

- London, British Library, Cotton MS Caligula A XV fol. 122v.; eleventh century; computus material, Six Ages of the World, entries on medicine, the moon, stars and winds

T. Wright, *Biographia Britannica Literaria: Or, Biography of Literary Characters of Great Britain and Ireland, Arranged in Chronological Order*, 2 vols. (London, 1842–46), i, 43

> Sapientia Grecorum
>
> Invidia Judeorum
>
> Superbia Romanorum
>
> Largitas Longobardum
>
> Sobrietas Gothorum
>
> Elevatio Francorum
>
> Gula Gallorum
>
> Ira Brittonum
>
> Stultitia Saxonum
>
> Libido Scottorum.
>
> Crudelitas Pictorum.

(The wisdom of the Greeks; The envy of the Jews; The arrogance of the Romans; The generosity of the Longobards; The sobriety of the Goths; The enthronement of the Franks; The gluttony of the Gauls; The wrath of the Britons; The stupidity of the Saxons; The wantonness of the Scots; The cruelty of the Picts.)

II 'Invidia Iudeorum, Perfidia Persarum' (The Envy of the Jews, the Perfidy of the Persians)

Manuscripts

- Bern, Burgerbibliotek, MS 48 fol. 1r.; tenth century; Life of Columbanus
- Rouen, Bibliothèque municipale, Ms Y 41 Omont 1406; eleventh century; Saint-Ouen de Rouen
- Madrid, Codex Matritensis, Biblioteca Nacional, MS 7814 fol. 114v.; twelfth century; dictionary of Papias

- Paris, Bibliothèque nationale de France, MS Latin 4892 fol. 243; possibly thirteenth century; inserted after the *Iter Hierosolymitanum, sive historia Hierosolymitana ab anno 1095* by Baldric of Bourgueil; *Liber de locis sanctis*
- Rome, Biblioteca Apostolica Vaticana, MS Reg. Lat. 630 fol. 22r.; thirteenth century; Isidorean geographic contexts
- Rome, Biblioteca Apostolica Vaticana, MS Reg. Lat. 630 fol. 22r.; thirteenth century; Isidorean geographic contexts
- Paris, Bibliothèque nationale de France, MS Latin 2874 fol. 64v.; twelfth–fourteenth centuries; containing Dares Phrygius and miscellany, including poems by Hildebert of Le Mans; preceded by 'On the End of the World' and 'On Simon the Sorcerer'
- Paris, Bibliothèque nationale de France, MS Latin 3343 fol. 49v.; fifteenth century; miscellaneous verse, proverbs, epigrams, many on vices
- Rome, Biblioteca Apostolica Vaticana, MS Reg. Lat. 554 fol. 228v.; fifteenth century; preceded by, among others, *De Iherusalem et locis sanctis*, and followed by geographical texts such as 'Orbis a rotunditate […] solis ardoribus'

J. M. Burnam, 'Miscellanea Hispanica', *Modern Philology* 12/3 (1914), 165–70 (p. 169)

H. Omont, 'Vices et vertus des différents peuples', in *Bibliothèque de l'Ecole des Chartres* 45 (1884), 580–1

Invidia Iudeorum	Hebreorum prudentia
Perfidia Persarum	Persarum stabilitas
Stulticia Aegyptiorum	Aegyptiorum sollertia
Fallatia Grecorum	Grecorum sapientia
Levitas Chaldeorum	Romanorum gravitas
Varietas Afrorum	Chaldeorum sagatitas
Gula Gallorum	Afrorum ingenium
Vana gloria Langobardorum	Gallorum firmitas
Crudelitas Hunorum	Francorum fortitudo
Inmunditia Suavorum	Saxonorum instantia

Ferocitas Francorum	Wascanorum agilitas
Stultitia Saxonum	Scottorum fidelitas
Luxuria Normannorum	Spanorum argutia
Libido Scottorum	Brittanorum hospitalitas
Vinolentia Spanorum	Tullius Marcus dixit
Duritia Pictorum	[Grecus irascitur]
Libido Suevorum	Francus in causam
Ira Brittanorum	Romanus post causam
Spurcitia Sclavorum	Francus gravis
	Romanus levis
	Afros versipellis.[2]

- Namur, Fonds de la Ville, MS 118 fols. 6v–7r.; twelfth century; abbey of Floreffe, letters by Yves of Chartres, Anselm, Seneca and Cicero

Faider, *Catalogue des manuscrits conservés à Namur*, pp. 200–2

Invidia Judeorum	Ebreorum prudentia
Perfidia Persarum	Egyptiorum sollertia
Astutia Egyptiorum	Romanorum gravitas
Fallacia Grecorum	Afrorum ingenium
Sevitia Saracenorum	Francorum fortitudo
Levitas Chaldeorum	Hispanorum argutia
Varietas Afrorum	Normannorum communio
Gula Gallorum	Persarum stabilitas
Vana gloria Langobardoum	Grecorum sapiencia

[2] See p. 73 for the translation.

Crudelitas Hunorum	Chaldeorum sagacitas
Immundicia Suevorum	Gallorum firmitas
Ferocitas Francorum	Scottorum fidelitas
Stulticia Saxonum	Britannorum hospitalitas
Duritia Pictavorum	Saxonum instantia
Luxuria Guasconum	Guasconum agilitas
Libido Scottorum	Grecus ante causam sapientem Francus in
Vinolentia Hispanorum	causa. Romanus et Judeus post causa. Tullius
Ira Britannorum	Marcus dixit
Spurcitia Sclavorum	Callidus Afer eris semper, Romane disertus
Rapacitas Normannorum	Semper Galle piger, semper Ibere celer.

(The envy of the Jews; The perfidy of the Persians; The adroitness of the Egyptians; The deceit of the Greeks; The cruelty of the Saracens; The levity of the Chaldeans; The fickleness of the Africans; The gluttony of the Gauls; The vainglory of the Longobards; The cruelty of the Huns; The filth of the Suevi; The ferocity of the Franks; The stupidity of the Saxons; The rigidity of the people of Poitou; The wantonness of the Gascons; The lust of the Scots; The wine-drinking of the Spanish; The wrath of the Britons; The filth of the Slavs; The rapacity of the Normans.)

(The prudence of the Hebrews; The ingenuity of the Egyptians; The gravity of the Romans; The intelligence of the Africans; The strength of the Franks; The wit of the Spanish; The alliance of the Normans; The steadfastness of the Persians; The wisdom of the Greeks; The sagacity of the Chaldeans; The durability of the Gauls; The loyalty of the Scots; The hospitality of the Britons; The perseverance of the Saxons; The agility of the Gascons. The Greeks show wisdom before the case, the Franks during, the Romans and Jews afterwards. The African is always hot; the Roman well spoken. The Gaul is always sluggish; The Spaniard quick.)

Appendix

- Cambridge, Corpus Christi College, MS 139 fol. 166v.; twelfth century, various hands; Cistercian monastery of Sawley; contains numerous chronicles, mostly by Anglo-Norman authors

Invidia Iudeorum	Communio Normannorum
Perfidia Persarum	Grecus irascitur ante causam
Fallatia Grecorum	Francus in causa
Astutia Egyptiorum	Romanus propter causam
Sevitia Saracenorum	Francus fortis
Levitas Chaldeorum	Romanus grauis
Varietas Afrorum	Affer semper uersipellis
Gula Gallorum	Spurcicia Sclauorum
Vana gloria Longobardorum	Rapacitas Normannorum
Crudelitas Hunorum	Normanni nimis sunt animosi
Inmunditia Sabinorum	Sollercia Egiptiorum.

Ferocitas Francorum

Stultitia Saxonum

Hebetudo Bavariorum

Luxuria Vuascanorum

Vinolentia Hispanorum

Duritia Pictorum

Libido Scottorum

Ira Brittonum

Spurticia Sclavorum

Rapacitas Normanorum: Normanni nimis sunt animosi [munio Normannorum]

Libido Suevorum

Duritia Pictorum/vel superbia Pictavorum.

(The envy of the Jews; The perfidy of the Persians; The deceit of the Greeks; The adroitness of the Egyptians; The cruelty of the Saracens; The levity of the Chaldeans; The fickleness of the Africans; The gluttony of the Gauls; The vainglory of the Longobards; The cruelty of the Huns; The filth of the Sabines; The ferocity of the Franks; The stupidity of the Saxons; The bluntness of the Bavarians; The wantonness of the Gascons; The wine-drinking of the Spanish; The rigidity of the Picts; The lust of the Scots; The wrath of the Britons; The filth of the Slavs; The rapacity of the Normans: The Normans are very bold [the defence of the Normans]; The lust of the Suevi; The rigidity of the Picts or the arrogance of the people of Poitou.)

(The alliance of the Normans; The Greeks are enraged beforehand, the Franks during, the Romans afterwards. The strong Frank; The grave Roman; The African is always cunning. The filth of the Slavs; The rapacity of the Normans; The Normans are very bold. The ingenuity of the Egyptians.)

III 'Invidia Iudeorum, Astutia Grecorum' (The Envy of the Jews, the Adroitness of the Greeks)

Manuscript

- Einsiedeln, Stiftsbibliothek MS 321 p. 136; tenth century; computus material

    Invidia Judeorum

    Astutia Grecorum

    Superbia Romanorum

    Avaritia Francorum

    Commercia Gallorum

    Fortitudo Saxonum

    Ira Britonum

    Jactantia Pictonum

    Libido Scotorum

    Saxones comparantur equis

    Britones comparantur capris

    Pictones comparantur iumentis

    Scoti comparantur avibus

Judei duri cervice et gravi corde

Greci leves

Cretenses mendaces

Dalmate feroces

Mauri vani

Franci tumidi

Athenienses ingeniosi

Galate indociles, vecordes, tardiores ad sapientiam.

(The envy of the Jews; The adroitness of the Greeks; The arrogance of the Romans; The avarice of the Franks; The commerce of the Gauls; The strength of the Saxons; The wrath of the Britons; The boasting of the Picts; The lust of the Scots; The Saxons are like horses; The Britons are like goats; The Picts are like beasts of burden; The Scots are like birds. The Jews are stiff-necked and grave hearted. The Greek are fickle; The Cretans are liars; The Dalmatians are ferocious; The Moors are idle; The Franks are puffed up; The Athenians are ingenious; The Galatians are indocile, insane, slow witted.)

IV 'Victoria Aegiptiorum' (The Victory of the Egyptians)

Manuscript

- London, British Library, Harley MS 3271 fol. 6v.; eleventh century; attached to the Tribal Hidage

R. H. Hodgkin, *A History of the Anglo-Saxons* (Oxford, 1952), II, plate 53, 388

J. P. McGowan, 'Anglo-Latin Prose', in P. Pulsiano and E. Treharne, *A Companion to Anglo-Saxon Literature* (Oxford, 2001) pp. 296–323 (p. 297)

Victoria Aegiptiorum

Invidia Judeorum

Sapientia Graecorum

Crudelitas Pictorum

Fortitudo Romanorum

Largitas Longobardorum

Gulla Gallorum

Superbia vel ferocitas Francorum

Ira Britanorum

Stulticia Saxonum vel Anglorum

Libido Hibernorum.

(The victory of the Egyptians; The envy of the Jews; The wisdom of the Greeks; The cruelty of the Picts; The strength of the Romans; The generosity of the Longobards; The gluttony of the Gauls; The arrogance or ferocity of the Franks; The wrath of the Britons; The stupidity of the Saxons or the Angles; The lust of the Scots.)

V 'Invidia Iudeorum, ira Britonum' (The Envy of the Jews, the wrath of the Britons)

Manuscripts

- Cambridge, Corpus Christi College, MS 139 fol. 179r.; twelfth century; Cistercian monastery of Sawley; a hodgepodge of the above lists, augmented with other epithets
- Cambridge, University Library, MS Ff. 1.27 10v.; thirteenth century; Durham Cathedral Priory?; two parts; Nennius, Gildas, Gerald of Wales's topography of Ireland

Printed in: T. Wright and J. O. Halliwell-Phillips (ed.), *Reliquiae Antiquae: Scraps from Ancient Manuscripts, Illustrating Chiefly Early English Literature and the English Language*, 2 vols. (London, 1845), i, 127

Invidia Judaeorum

Ira Britonum

Perfidia Persarum

Spurcitia Sclavorum

Fallacia Graecorum

Rapacitas Normannorum [Wright and Halliwell-Phillips: Romanorum]

Astutia Aegiptiorum

Prudentia Hebraeorum

Saevitia Saracenorum

Stabilitas Persarum

Solertia Aegyptiorum

Levitas Caldaeorum

Sapientia Graecorum

Varietas Affrorum

Gravitas Romanorum

Gula Gallorum

Largitas Longobardorum

Vana gloria Longobardorum

Sobrietas Gottorum

Crudelitas Hunorum

Sagacitas Caldaeorum

Inmunditia Sabinorum

Ingenium Affricorum

Ferocitas Francorum

Firmitas Gallorum

Stultitia Saxonum

Fortitudo Francorum

Hebetudo Bavariorum

Instantia Saxonum

Luxuria Vascanorum

Agilitas Walcarorum

Vinolentia Hispaniarum

Magnanimitas Pictorum

Duritia Pictorum

Hospitalitas Britonum

Argutia Hispaniarum

Libido Suevorum

Duritia et superbia Pictavorum.

(The envy of the Jews; The wrath of the Britons; The perfidy of the Persians; The filth of the Slavs; The deceit of the Greeks; The rapacity of the Normans; The adroitness of the Egyptians; The prudence of the Hebrews; The cruelty of the Saracens; The steadfastness of the Persians; The ingenuity of the Egyptians; The levity of the Chaldeans; The wisdom of the Greeks; The fickleness of the Africans; The gravity of the Romans; The gluttony of the Gauls; The generosity of the Longobards; The vainglory of the Longobards; The sobriety of the Goths; The cruelty of the Huns; The sagacity of the Chaldeans; The filth of the Sabines; The intelligence of the Africans; The ferocity of the Franks; The strength of the Gauls; The stupidity of the Saxons; The strength of the Franks; The bluntness of the Bavarians; The perseverance of the Saxons; The wantonness of the Gascons; The agility of the Walcacori?; The wine-drinking of the Spanish; The magnanimity of the Picts; The rigidity of the Picts; The hospitality of the Britons; The wit of the Spanish; The lust of the Suevi; The rigidity and arrogance of the people of Poitou.)

VI 'Gloria Grecorum' (The Glory of the Greeks)

Manuscripts

- Rome, Biblioteca Apostolica Vaticana, MS Ottoboniani Latini 333 fol. 90; thirteenth century; papal penitentiary; lists of church provinces, bishoprics, kings, crowned emperors
- Avignon, Bibliothèque municipal Ceccano, MS 336 fol. 97; fourteenth century; handbook for the papal penitentiary; lists of church provinces, bishoprics, kings
- Budapest, Országos Széchényi Könyvtár, MS 405 fol. 78v.; fourteenth century; *Chronicon Hungarorum acephalum*; deeds of Alexander the Great, lists of dukes, kings and crowned emperors
- Augsburg, Universitätsbibliothek, MS Cod. II.1. 2°.90 fol. 1r.; 1470; 'Ioca monachorum', ages of man, florilegium
- Vienna, Österreichische Nationalbibliothek, Codex Vindobonensis MS 4117 fol. 28; sixteenth century; miscellaneous verse, preamble 'nihil valent omnia'

R. G. Salomon, 'Aftermath to Opicinus de Canistris', *Journal of the Warburg and Courtauld Institutes* 25 (1962), 137–46 (p. 144)
Catalogue général des manuscrits des bibliotheques publiques de France Départements, 66 vols. (Avignon) (Paris, 1894), xxvii, 247–9

Gloria Grecorum

Invidia Romanorum

Ingenium Lombardorum

Ferocitas Francorum

Stultitia Saxonum

Ebrietas Slavorum

Luxuria Saracenorum

Duritia Judeorum

Ingluvies Teutonicorum.

(The glory of the Greeks; The envy of the Romans; The intelligence of the Lombards; The ferocity of the Franks; The stupidity of the Saxons; The drunkenness of the Slavs; The wantonness of the Saracens; The rigidity of the Jews; The gluttony of the Germans.)

- Dolný Kubín, Čaploviča Knižnica MS C 3/45 fol. 69v.; fifteenth century
J. Sopko, *Codices Latini Medii Aevi Bibliothecarum Slovaciae* (Martin, 1981)

Gloria Grecorum

Invidia Romanorum

Fortitudo Teutonicorum

Ferocitas Francorum

Pompa Ispanorum

Luxuria Sarracenorum

Duricia Iudeorum

… Bohemorum

Crudelitas Ungariorum

Est destructio singulorum.

(The glory of the Greeks; The envy of the Romans; The strength of the Germans; The ferocity of the Franks; The pomp of the Spanish; The wantonness of the Saracens; The rigidity of the Jews; … of the Bohemians; The cruelty of the Hungarians is the downfall of each.)

- *Chronique de Saint-Brieuc*; late fourteenth century

Proprietates quarumdam generum:

Gloria Graecorum

Invidia Romanorum

Avaritia Longobardorum

Crudelitas seu superbia Francorum

Proditio Saxonum

Audacia seu stultitia Britonum

Ebrietas Sclavorum

Luxuria Saracenorum

Duritia Iudeorum

Inordinatio seu abhominatio Hispanorum.

(The properties of certain kinds: The glory of the Greeks; The envy of the Romans; The avarice of the Longobards; The cruelty or arrogance of the Franks; The treachery of the Saxons; The courage or the stupidity of the Britons; The drunkenness of the Slavs; The wantonness of the Saracens; The rigidity of the Jews; The disorder or abomination of the Spanish.)

VII 'Invidia Romanorum' (The Envy of the Romans)

Manuscripts

- Graz, Universitätsbibliothek, MS 536 St Lambrecht, fols. 131–132; end of fourteenth century; Gregory the Great, *Dialogues*; Honorius of Autun, *Imago mundi*, historiography, lists of church provinces, bishoprics, kings

    Invidia Romanorum

    Ingluvies Theotonicorum

    Ferocitas Francorum

    Pompa Ispanorum

    Luxuria Saracenorum.

(The envy of the Romans; The drunkenness of the Germans; The ferocity of the Franks; The pomp of the Spanish; The wantonness of the Saracens.)

VIII 'Sapientia Grecorum, Luxuria Sarracenorum' (The Wisdom of the Greeks, the Wantonness of the Saracens)

Manuscript

- Karlsruhe, Badische Landesbibliothek, MS Cod.Aug.perg. 56 fol. 147 rb, fourteenth century; Reichenau; contains commentary by Innocent v

    Sapientia Grecorum

    Luxuria Sarracenorum

    Infidelitas Ampulorum [?]

    Avaritia Romanorum

    Astutia Lumbardorum

    Parcitas Tuscorum

    Ornatus Provincialium

    Curialitas Gallicorum

    Largitas incomparabilis Anglicorum.

(The wisdom of the Greeks; The wantonness of the Saracens; The infidelity of the Ampulori?; The avarice of the Romans; The adroitness of the Lombards; The parsimony of the Tuscans; The ornateness of the Provençals; The courtliness of the French; The incomparable generosity of the English.)

Bibliography

Manuscripts

Augsburg, Universitätsbibliothek, MS Cod. II.1. 2° 90
Avignon, Bibliothèque municipal Ceccano, MS 336
Bern, Burgerbibliotek, MS 48
Budapest, MS Országos Széchényi Könyvtár, MS 405
Cambridge, Corpus Christi College, MS 139
Cambridge, University Library, MS Ff. 1.27
Dolný Kubín, Čaploviča Knižnica, MS C 3/45
Einsiedeln, Stiftsbibliothek, MS 321
Karlsruhe, Badische Landesbibliothek, MS Cod.Aug.perg. 56
Leiden, Universiteitsbibliotheek, MS Vossius Latin Q 69
London, British Library, Cotton MS Caligula A XV
London, British Library, Cotton MS Vespasian B XIII
London, British Library, Cotton MS Vitellius A XII
London, British Library, Harley MS 3271
Madrid, Biblioteca Nacional de España MS 8831 (formerly X 161)
Madrid, Biblioteca Real Academia de la Historia, MS 39
Madrid, Biblioteca Real Academia de la Historia, MS 78
Madrid, Codex Matritensis, Biblioteca Nacional, MS 7814
Munich, Bayerische Staatsbibliothek, MS Clm 18910
Namur, Fonds de la Ville, MS 118
Nürnberg, Stadtbibliothek, MS Cent. I, 97
Oxford, Bodleian Library, MS Digby 53
Paris, Bibliothèque nationale de France, MS Latin 2874
Paris, Bibliothèque nationale de France, MS Latin 3343
Paris, Bibliothèque nationale de France, MS Latin 4892
Paris, Bibliothèque nationale de France, MS Latin 7121
Paris, Bibliothèque nationale de France, MS Latin 15133
Paris, Bibliothèque nationale de France, MS Latin 18522
Paris, Bibliothèque nationale de France, MS Latin 19116
Prague, Metropolitan University Library, MS 1641
Rome, Biblioteca Apostolica Vaticana, MS Borg. Lat. 200
Rome, Biblioteca Apostolica Vaticana, MS Ottoboniani Latini 333
Rome, Biblioteca Apostolica Vaticana, MS Reg. Lat. 554
Rome, Biblioteca Apostolica Vaticana, MS Reg. Lat. 630
Rouen, Bibliothèque municipale, Ms Y 41 Omont 1406
Saint-Omer, Bibliothèque municipale, MS 115
Vienna, Österreichische Nationalbibliothek, Codex Vindobonensis MS 568
Vienna, Österreichische Nationalbibliothek, Codex Vindobonensis MS 4117
Zurich, Zentralbibliothek, MS Car. C 111

Printed sources

Accursius, *Glossa ordinaria*, ed. D. Godefroy (Lyon, 1627)
Adam of Bremen, *Gesta Hammaburgensis Ecclesiae Pontificum*, ed. B. Schmeidler, MGH Scriptores rerum Germanicarum 2 (Hanover, 1917)
——, F. J. Tschan (trans.), T. Reuter (Introduction), *History of the Archibishops of Hamburg-Bremen: Adam of Bremen* (New York, 2002)
Albelda Chronicle, in *Conquerors and Chroniclers of Early Medieval Spain*, trans. and ed. K. B. Wolf (Liverpool, 1999)
Albertus Magnus, *De natura loci ad fidem autographi; De causis proprietatum elementorum ad fidem autographi; De generatione et corruptione*, ed. P. Hossfeld (Aschendorff, 1980)
——, *De anima*, ed. C. Stroick (Monasterii Westfalorum, 1968)
——, *An Appraisal of the Geographical Works of Albertus Magnus and his Contributions to Geographical Thought* (a translation of *De natura loci*), trans. J. P. Tilmann (Ann Arbor, 1971)
——, *Quaestiones super de animalibus*, in *Opera omnia*, ed. E. Filthaut, 40 vols. (Aschendorff, 1951–)
Albumasar, *On Historical Astrology: The Book of Religions and Dynasties (on the Great Conjunctions)*, ed. C. Burnett and K. Yamamoto, 2 vols. (Leiden, 2000)
Alexander Neckam, *De naturis rerum libri duo: With the Poem of the Same Author, De labudibus divinae sapientiae*, ed. T. Wright (London, 1863)
——, 'Quo versu Anglorum possim describere gentem' (attrib.), in W. Camden, *Remains Concerning Britain*, ed. R. D. Dunn (Toronto, 1984)
Alexander of Paris (Bernay), *Li Romanz d'Athis et Prophilias*, ed. A. Hilka, Gesellschaft für romanische Literatur, 2 vols. (Halle, 1912–16)
Alexander of Roes, *Memoriale*, in *Schriften*, ed. H. Grundmann and H. Heimpel, MGH Staatsschriften 1 (Stuttgart, 1958)
——, *Noticia seculi*, in *Schriften*, ed. H. Grundmann and H. Heimpel, MGH Staatsschriften 1 (Stuttgart, 1958)
Amatus of Montecassino, *L'Ystoire de li Normant*, in *Amatus of Montecassino: The History of the Normans*, ed. G. A. Loud, trans. P. N. Dunbar (Woodbridge, 2004)
Ambrosius of Milan, *De noe et arca*, PL 14
'Anglia, terrarum decus et flos finitimarum', ed. G. Waitz, 'II. Reise nach England und Frankreich im Herbst 1877', *Neues Archiv der Gesellschaft für Ältere Deutsche Geschichtskunde zur Beförderung einer Gesamtausgabe der Quellenschriften deutscher Geschichten des Mittelalters* 4 (1879), 9–42
Annales Altahenses maiores, ed. E. von Oefele, MGH SS rerum Germanicarum 4 (Hanover, 1891)
Anseïs von Karthago, ed. J. Alton, Bibliothek des litterarischen Vereins in Stuttgart, 194 (Tübingen, 1892)
'Armis, militia, rebus, probitate', ed. B. Hauréau, *Notices et extraits de quelques manuscrits latins de la Bibliothèque Nationale*, 6 vols. (Paris, 1890–93), iv, 283
Arnald of Villanova, *Speculum medicine*, ed. M. R. McVaugh, *Opera medica omnia*, 13 vols. (Barcelona, 2018)

Arnold of Lübeck, *Chronica Slavorum*, ed. I. M. Lappenberg, MGH Scriptores rerum Germanicarum 14 (Hanover, 1868)

Augustine, *De civitate Dei*, trans. E. M. Sanford and W. M. Green, Loeb Classical Library 411–17, 7 vols. (Cambridge, 2015)

Bartholomaeus Anglicus, *De proprietatibus rerum*, ed. H. Knochlobtzer (Heidelberg, 1488)

——, *On the Properties of Things: John Trevisa's Translation [from the Latin] of Bartholomaeus Anglicus 'De proprietatibus rerum': A Critical Text*, ed. M. C. Seymour, 3 vols. (Oxford, 1975–88)

Barthélemy l'Anglais: Le livre des regions, ed. B. A. Pitts (London, 2006)

Baldric of Bourgueil (Dol), *The Historia Ierosolimitana of Baldric of Bourgueil*, ed. S. J. Biddlecombe (Woodbridge, 2014)

——, 'Itinerarium sive epistola ad Fiscannenses', in *PL* 166

Beatus of Liébana, *Beati in Apocalypsin Libri Duodecim*, ed. H. A. Sanders (Rome, 1930)

Bede, *Historia ecclesiastica gentis Anglorum*, in *Bede's Ecclesiastical History of the English people*, ed. and trans. B. Colgrave and R. A. B. Mynors (Oxford 1969)

——, 'Te ridens Anglus mulo caudam', in *Anecdota Bedae, Lanfranci et aliorum: Inedited Tracts, Letters, Poems etc. of Venerable Bede, Lanfranc, Tatwin*, ed. J. A. Giles (New York, 1851)

Benoît of St Maure, *Chronique des Ducs de Normandie*, ed. C. Fahlin, 2 vols. (Uppsala, 1951–54)

Berckenmeyer, P. L., *Curieuser Antiqvarius* (Hamburg, 1731)

Bernard of Clairvaux, *Vita sancti Malachiae*, in *Sancti Bernardi Opera*, ed. J. Leclercq and H. M. Rochais, 9 vols. (Rome, 1957–)

Bertrand de Bar-sur-Aube (attrib.), *Aymeri de Narbonne: chanson de geste*, ed. L. Demaison, Société des Anciens Textes Français 24, 2 vols. (Paris, 1887)

Boncompagno da Signa, *Briefsteller und Formelbücher des elften bis vierzehnten Jahrhunderts*, ed. L. Rockinger, 2 vols. (New York, 1961)

——, *Palma*, in *Aus Leben und Schriften des Magisters Boncompagno*, ed. C. Sutter (Freiburg i. B., 1894)

——, *Liber de obsidione Ancone*, ed. G. C. Zimolo (Bologna, 1937)

——, *Amicitia and De Malo Senectutis Et Senii*, ed. and trans. M. D. Dunne (Leuven, 2012)

Carmina Burana, ed. A. Hilka, O. Schumann and W. Meyer (Heidelberg, 1971)

Carminum proverbalium (Basel, 1576)

Catalogue général des manuscrits des bibliotheques publiques de France Départements, 66 vols. (Avignon) (Paris, 1894)

La chanson de Roland, ed. C. Segre, 2 vols. (Geneva, 1989)

Chaucer, *The Parlement of Foulys*, ed. D. S. Brewer (Manchester, 1972)

Chronica minora saec. iv. v. vi. vii, ed. T. Mommsen, MGH Auctores Antiquissimi 11 (Berlin, 1894)

The Chronicle of Lanercost, 1272–1346, ed. H. Maxwell (Glasgow, 1913)

Chronicon Ebersheimense, ed. L. Weiland, MGH Scriptores rerum germanicarum 23 (Hannover, 1874)

Chronicon Polonorum usque ad a. 1113, ed. I. Szlachtowski and R. Köpke, MGH Scriptores rerum Germanicarum 9 (Hanover, 1851)
Chronicon Sancti Martini Turonense, ed. O. Holder-Egger, MGH Scriptores rerum Germanicarum 26 (Hanover, 1882)
Chroniques Asturiennes (fin IXe siècle), ed. Y. Bonnaz (Paris, 1987)
Chrétien de Troyes, *Cligès*, ed. and French trans. L. Harf-Lancner (Paris, 2006)
Cicero, *De inventione*, in *On Invention, etc.*, ed. H. M. Hubbel, Loeb Classical Library 386 (Cambridge MA, 2006)
——, *De Officiis*, ed. and trans. W. Miller, Loeb Classical Library 30 (Cambridge MA, 1913)
Constantinus Africanus, *Liber Pantegni*, in *Opera omnia Ysaac*, ed. A. Turinus (Lyons, 1515)
Cursor mundi: A Northumbrian Poem of the xivth century in Four Versions / ed. from British Museum MS. Cotton Vespasian A.III, Bodleian MS. Fairfax 14, Göttingen University Library MS. Theol. 107, Trinity College Cambridge MS., R.3.8, ed. R. Morris, 7 vols. (London, 1874–93)
Daniel of Beccles, *The Book of the Civilised Man: An English Translation of the Urbanus magnus of Daniel of Beccles*, trans. F. Whelan, O. Spenser and F. Petrizzo (London, 2020)
De inventione corporis s. Judoci, ed. M. L. Deslisle, Recueil des historiens des Gaules et de la France 10 (1874), 366
'Descriptio Norfolciensium', ed. T. Wright, *Early Mysteries and Other Latin Poems of the Twelfth and Thirteenth Centuries* (London, 1838), pp. 93–8
Descriptio positionis seu situationis monasterii Clarae-Vallensis in PL 185
Diego Garcia, *Planeta*, ed. P. M. Alonso (Madrid, 1943)
Donizone, *Vita Mathildis*, ed. L. C. Bethmann, MGH Scriptores rerum germanicarum 12 (Hanover, 1856)
Eadmer, *Historia novorum in Anglia: Et, Opuscula Duo de Vita Sancti Anselmi et Quibusdam Miraculis Ejus*, ed. M. Rule (Cambridge, 2012)
Ekkehard of Aura, *Frutolfs und Ekkehards Chroniken und die anonyme Kaiserchronik*, ed. and trans. F.-J. Schmale and I. Schmale-Ott, Ausgewählte Quellen zur deutschen Geschichte des Mittelalters 15 (Darmstadt, 1972)
English Historical Documents 1189–1327, ed. D. C. Douglas and G. W. Greenaway, 12 vols. (London, 1953–81), ii
Ermoldus Nigellus, *Carmen in honorem Hludowici*, in *Poème sur Louis le Pieux et Épitres au roi Pepin*, ed. and French trans. E. Faral (Paris, 1964)
'Est ratio quare bafio dici merearis', ed. W. Wattenbach, 'Mittheilungen aus Handschriften', *Neues Archiv der Gesellschaft für Ältere Deutsche Geschichtskunde zur Beförderung einer Gesamtausgabe der Quellenschriften deutscher Geschichten des Mittelalters* 8 (1883), 191–3
Eustache Deschamps, *Oeuvres complètes de Eustache Deschamps: publiées d'après le manuscrit de la Bibliothèque Nationale*, ed. Marquis de Queux de Saint-Hilaire, Société des Anciens Textes Français 8, 11 vols. (Paris, 1878–1903)
Evrárd of Béthune, *Graecismus*, ed. J. Wrobel (Bratislava, 1887)
'Francis scire, sitis Anglis, nescire Britannis', ed. B. Hauréau, *Notices et extraits de quelques manuscrits latins de la Bibliothèque Nationale*, 6 vols. (Paris, 1890–93)

Fredegar, *Historia Daretis Frigii de origine Francorum*, ed. B. Krusch, MGH Scriptores rerum Merovingicarum 2 (Hanover, 1888)
——, *Chronicarum Fredegarii libri IV cum continuationibus*, ed. B. Krusch, MGH Scriptores rerum Merovingicarum 2 (Hanover, 1888)
Gauthier of Metz, *L'image du monde de Maitre Goussouin*, ed. O. H. Prior (Lausanne, 1913)
Gautier d'Arras, *Ille et Galeron*, ed. Y. Lefèvre, Les classiques français du Moyen Age, 109 (Paris, 1988)
'Gens Romanorum subdola antiqua colit hydola', in *Libelli de lite imperatorum et pontificum saeculis xi et xii conscripti*, ed. H. Boehmer (Hanover, 1897)
Geoffrey of Monmouth, *Historia regum Britanniae*, in *The History of the Kings of Britain: An edition and translation of* De gestis Britonum, ed. M. D. Reeve, trans. N. Wright, Arthurian Studies 69 (Woodbridge, 2007)
Geoffrey of Vinsauf, *Poetria nova*, in *The Poetria Nova and its Sources in Early Rhetorical Doctrine*, ed. and trans. by Ernest Gallo (The Hague, 1971)
——, *Documentum de modo et arte dictandi et versificandi*, in *Les arts poétiques du XIIe et du XIIIe siècle: recherches et documents sur la technique littéraire du moyen âge*, ed. E. Faral (reprint Paris, 1962)
Geoffrey of Vinsauf, Documentum de modo et arte dictandi et versificandi, trans. R. P. Parr (Milwaukee, 1968)
Gerald of Wales, *Topographia Hibernica* in *Giraldi Cambrensis Opera, Vols. I–VII*, ed. J. S. Brewer, J. F. Dimock and G. F. Warner (London, 1861–91)
——, *The first version of the topography of Ireland*, trans. J. J. O'Meara (Dundalk, 1951)
——, *Expugnatio Hibernica*, ed. and trans. A. B. Scott and F. X. Martin (Dublin 1978)
——, *Descriptio Kambriae*, in *Giraldi Cambrensis Opera, Vols. I–VII*, ed. J. S. Brewer, J. F. Dimock and G. F. Warner (London, 1861–91)
Gerald of Wales: The Journey through Wales and the Description of Wales, trans. L. Thorpe (Harmondsworth, 1978)
——, *De principis instructione: Instruction for a Ruler*, ed. and trans. R. Bartlett (Oxford, 2018)
Gervase of Canterbury, *Chronica Gervasii*, in *The Historical Works of Gervase of Canterbury*, ed. W. Stubbs, Rerum britannicarum medii aevi scriptores 73, 2 vols. (London, 1965)
Gervase of Tilbury, *Otia imperialia: Recreation for an Emperor*, ed. and trans. S. E. Banks and J. W. Binns (Oxford, 2002)
Gesta Stephani, ed. and trans. K. R. Potter, with new introduction by R. H. C. Davis (Oxford, 1976)
Gildas, *De excidio Britanniae*, in *The Ruin of Britain and Other Works*, ed. and trans. M. Winterbottom (London, 2002)
Girart de Roussillon: chanson de geste, ed. by W. M. Hackett, Société des Anciens Textes Français 86, 3 vols. (Paris, 1953)
Goscelin of St Bertin, *Vita Sancti Augustini*, in *PL* 80
——, *Les Grandes Chroniques de France*, ed. J. Viard, 10 vols. (Paris, 1920–53)
Guibert of Nogent, *Dei gesta per Francos et cinq autres textes*, ed. R. B. C. Huygens (Turnhout, 1996)
——, *The Deeds of God through the Franks: A Translation of Guibert de Nogent's* Gesta Dei per Francos, trans. R. Levine (Rochester, 1997)

Gunther of Pairis, *Ligurinus*, ed. E. Assmann and W. Setz, MGH Scriptores rerum Germanicarum 63 (Hannover, 1987)

Guy of Amiens, *Carmen de Hastingae Proelio of Guy Bishop of Amiens*, ed. and trans. F. Barlow (London, 1972)

Helmold of Bosau, *Slawenchronik/Chronica Slavorum*, ed. B. Schmeidler, trans. H. H. Stoob, Ausgewählte Quellen zur deutschen Geschichte des Mittelalters 19 (Darmstadt, 1963)

Henry of Avranches, 'Non valet audire mala plus Conradulus ire', ed. P. Binkley, 'Thirteenth Century Latin Poetry Contests Associated with Henry of Avranches with an Appendix of Newly Edited Texts' (unpublished dissertation, University of Toronto, 199), pp. 228–30

Henry of Huntingdon, *Historia Anglorum: The History of the English People*, ed. and trans. D. Greenway (Oxford, 1996)

Henry of Livonia, *Chronicon Livoniae*, ed. A. Bauer (Darmstadt, 1959)

——, *The Chronicle of Henry of Livonia*, trans. J. A. Brundage (New York, 2003)

Herbert of Bosham, *Epistola Herberti de Boseham ad Baldewinum Cantuariensem Archiepiscopum et ad eius catholicos successors*, in *Rerum britannicarum medii aevi scriptores, or Chronicles and memorials of Great Britain and Ireland during the Middle Ages* (n.p., 1877)

Herbord of Michelsberg (or Bamberg), *Dialogus de vita Ottonis episcopi Babenbergensis*, ed. R. Köpke, MGH Scriptores rerum Germanicarum 33 (Hanover, 1868)

Hermann of Carinthia, *De essentiis*, ed. and trans. C. Burnett (Leiden, 1982)

'Hic ponitur continens pro contento', ed. B. Hauréau, *Notices et Extraits de quelques manuscrits Latins de la Bibliothèque Nationale*, 6 vols. (Paris, 1890–93), i, 106

Hildebert of Lavardin, *Hildeberti Carmina minora*, ed. A. B. Scott (Leipzig, 1969)

Hildegard of Bingen, *Causae et curae*, ed. L. Moulinier (Berlin, 2003)

Hippocrates, *Airs, eaux, lieux*, ed. J. Jouanna, Collection Budé (Paris, 1996)

The Historia Vie Hierosolimitane *of Gilo of Paris and a Second, Anonymous Author*, ed. C. W. Grocock and J. E. Siberry (Oxford, 1997)

Honorius of Autun, *Imago mundi*, ed. V. I. J. Flint, 'Honorius Augustodunensis, *Imago Mundi*', *Archives d'histoire doctrinale et littéraire du Moyen Âge* 57 (1982), 7–153

Horace, *Carmina*, in *Odes and Epodes*, ed. N. Rudd, Loeb Classical Library 33 (Cambridge MA, 2004)

——, *Satires, Epistles and Ars Poetica*, ed. H. R. Fairclough, Loeb Classical Library 194 (Cambridge MA, 1999)

Hrabanus Maurus, *De universo*, in *PL* 111

——, *Enarrationes in epistolas beati Pauli*, in *PL* 112

——, *Commentariorum in Genesim*, in *PL* 107

——, *De rerum naturis*, in *PL* 111

Hugh of Fouilloy, *The Medicine of the Soul*, in *PL* 176

Hugh of St Victor, *De arca Noë morali Libri iv*, in *PL* 176

Ibn Sina, *The Canon of Medicine of Avicenna*, trans. O. C. Grunner (New York, 1970)

Selected Letters of Pope Innocent III concerning England (1198–1216), ed. C. R. Cheney and W. H. Semple (London, 1953)

Isidore of Seville, *Etymologiae, Livre ix: Les langues et les groups sociaux*, ed. M. Reydellet (Paris, 1984)

——, *Etymologies, Livre vii: Dieu, les anges, les saints*, ed. J.-Y. Guillaumin (Paris, 2012)
——, *Étymologies xiv: De terra*, ed. O. Spevak (Paris, 2011)
——, *Étymologies xv: Les constructions et les terres*, ed. J.-Y. Guillaumin and P. Monat (Paris, 2016)
——, *The Etymologies of Isidore of Seville*, trans. S. A. Barney and M. Hall (Cambridge, 2006)
——, *De Ortu et Obitu Patrum* (attrib.), *PL* 83
——, *Historia de regibus Gothorum, Wandalorum et Suevorum*, ed. T. Mommsen, MGH Auctores Antiquissimi XI (Berlin, 1894)
Itinerarium Peregrinorum et Gesta Regis Ricardi, ed. W. Stubbs (London, 1864)
Jacques de Vitry, *Historia occidentalis*, in *The Historia Occidentalis of Jacques de Vitry: A Critical Edition*, ed. J. F. Hinnebusch, Spicilegium Friburgense 17 (Fribourg, 1972)
——, *Histoire orientale = Historia orientalis*, ed. and trans. J. Donnadieu (Turnhout, 2008)
Jean Bodel, *La chanson des Saisnes: Edition critique*, ed. A. Brasseur, 2 vols. (Geneva, 1989)
Jean Bodin, *Les six livres de la république*, ed. G. Mairet (1993), available at http://classiques.uqac.ca/classiques/bodin_jean/six_livres_republique/bodin_six_livres_republique.pdf (accessed 31 August 2020)
Jean Renart, *Galeran de Bretagne: roman du XIIIe siècle*, ed. L. Foulet, Les classiques français du Moyen Âge, 37 (Paris, 1925)
——, *Le roman de la rose ou de Guillaume de Dole*, ed. F. Lecoy, trans. J. Dufournet, Champion Classiques: Série Moyen Âge, 24 (Paris, 2008)
Jean Renart: The Romance of the Rose or Guillaume de Dole, trans. P. Terry and N. V. Durling (Philadelphia, 1993)
Jerome, *Commentariorum in epistolam ad Galatos*, in *PL* 26
——, *Commentariorum in epistolam ad Titum liber unus*, in *PL* 26
——, *Liber de nominibus Hebraicis*, in *PL* 23
——, *Liber interpretationis Hebraicorum nominum*, in *Opera*, Corpus Christianorum. Series Latina 72, ed. P. de Lagarde (Turnhout, 1959)
John the Deacon, *Vita Gregorii Magni*, in *PL* 75
John of Fordun, *Scotichronicon cum supplementis et continuatione Walteri Boweri*, 2 vols. (Edinburgh, 1752)
John of Garland, *Rota Vergiliana*, in E. Faral (ed.), *Les arts poétiques du XIIe et du XIIIe siècle: Recherches et documents sur la technique littéraire du Moyen Âge* (reprint Paris, 1962)
——, *The Parisiana Poetria of John of Garland*, ed. and trans. T. Lawler, Yale Studies in English 182 (New Haven, 1974)
John of Hauville, *Architrenius*, ed. W. Wetherbee (Cambridge, 1994)
John of Newhouse, 'Tractatus de complexionibus Magistri Johannis de Nova domo', ed. W. Seyfert, 'Ein Komplexionentext einer Leipziger Inkunabel', *Archiv für Geschichte der Medizin* 20 (1928), 272–99, 372–89
John of Paris, *De potestate regia et papali*, ed. F. Bleienstein (Stuttgart, 1969)
John Pecham, 'Exhortatio Christianorum contra gentem Mahometi', in W. Chester Jordan, 'John Pecham on the Crusade', *Crusades* 9 (2010) 159–71
John of Salisbury, *The Letters of John of Salisbury, vol. 1: The Early Letters (1153–1161)*, ed. W. J. Millor and H. E. Butler, rev. C. N. L. Brooke (Oxford, 1986)

———, *The Letters of John of Salisbury. vol. 2: The Later Letters (1163–1180)*, ed. and trans. W. J. Millor and C. N. L. Brooke (Oxford, 1979)

———, *Historia pontificalis*, in *John of Salisbury's Memoirs of the Papal Court (Ioannis Saresberiensis Historia pontificalis)*, ed. and trans. M. M. Chibnall (London, 1956)

John Scottus, *De divisione naturae*, in *PL* 122

Joseph of Exeter, *Joseph of Exeter: The Iliad of Dares Phrygius*, ed. G. Roberts (Cape Town, 1970)

'The King of Tars: A New Edition', ed. J. H. Chandler (unpublished dissertation, University of Rochester, 2011)

Lactantius, *De origine erroris*, in *PL* 6

Landulf of Milan, *Historiae Mediolanensis*, ed. L. C. Bethmann and W. Wattenbach, MGH Scriptores 8 (Hanover, 1848)

Lawrence of Durham, *Dialogi Laurentii Dunelmensis Monachi ac Prioris*, ed. J. Raine, Surtees Society 70 (Durham, 1880)

———, trans. A. G. Rigg, 'Lawrence of Durham: Dialogues and Easter Poem: A Verse Translation', *The Journal of Medieval Latin* 7 (1997), 42–126

Layamon, *Brut or Hystoria Brutonum*, ed. and trans. W. R. J. Barron and S. C. Weinberg (Harlow, 1995)

Lucan, *Pharsalia*, ed. J. D. Duff (Cambridge, 1928)

Der Ludus de Antichristo, ed. F. Wilhem (Munich, 1912)

———, trans. J. Wright, *The Play of the Antichrist* (Toronto, 1967)

Marbod of Rennes, 'De ornamentis verborum', in *Opera Omnia*, ed. J. J. Bourassé (Paris, 1854)

Marsilius of Padua, *The Defender of the Peace*, ed. and trans. A. Brett (Cambridge, 2005)

Matthew Paris, *Chronica Majora*, ed. R. Luard, 7 vols. (London, 1872–83)

Matthew of Vendôme, *Ars versificatoria*, in *Mathei Vindocinensis opera*, ed. F. Munari (Rome, 1988)

———, *Ars versificatoria*, trans. R. P. Parr (Milwaukee, 1981)

———, E. Gallo, 'Matthew of Vendôme: Introductory Treatise on the Art of Poetry', *Proceedings of the American Philosophical Society* 118/1 (1974), 51–92

'Ne gras porci ne sage Breton', ed. J. Morawski, *Proverbes français antérieurs au XVe siècle* (Paris, 1925)

Nigel Longchamp (Nigel Whireker or Whiteacre), *Speculum Stultorum*, ed. J. H. Mozley and R. R. Raymo (Berkeley, 1960)

———, *A Mirror of Fools: The Book of Burnel the Ass*, trans. J. H. Mozley (Notre Dame, Ind., 1963)

Notes and Queries: A Medium of Intercommunication for Literary Men, General Readers, etc. (London, 1849–)

Odo of Deuil, *De profectione Ludovici VII in orientem*, ed. and trans. V. Gingerick Berry (New York, 1948)

Orderic Vitalis, *Historia ecclesiastica: The Ecclesiastical History of Orderic Vitalis*, ed. and trans. M. M. Chibnall, 6 vols. (Oxford, 1969–80)

Otto of Freising, *Gesta Friderici*, in *Die Taten Friedrichs oder richtiger Chronica*, ed. F.-J. Schmale (Berlin, 1965)

———, trans. C. C. Mierow, *The Deeds of Frederick Barbarossa (Gesta Friderici I Imperatoris)* (Toronto, 1994)

——, *Chronica sive Historia de duabus civitatibus*, ed. W. Lammers, German trans. A. Schmidt (Darmstadt, 1961)
Partonopeu de Blois: A French Romance of the Twelfth Century, ed. J. Gildea, 2 vols. (Villanova, 1967–70)
Paulus Orosius, *Historiarum adversum paganos libri VII*, ed. K. F. W. Zangemeister (New York, 1966)
Peire d'Auvergne, *Die Lieder Peire's von Auvergne*, ed. R. Zenker (Erlangen, 1900)
Peire Vidal, *La Poesie de Peire Vidal* 27, ed. J. Anglade (Paris 1966)
Peter of Blois, *The Later Letters of Peter of Blois*, ed. E. Revell (Oxford, 1993)
——, E. Braunholtz, 'Streitgedichte Peters von Blois und Roberts von Beaufeu über den Wert des Weines und Bieres', *Zeitschrift für Romanische Philologie* 47 (Berlin 1927), 30–8
Peter of Celle, *The Letters of Peter of Celle*, ed. and trans. J. Haseldine (Oxford, 2001)
Peter of Eboli, *Raccolta di tutti scrittori dell'istoria del regno di Napoli* xvi (Napels, 1770)
Pierre Dubois, Appendix to *De recuperatione Terrae Sanctae*, ed. A. Diotti (Florence, 1977)
Pierre Riga, 'Nec bene respondent nomen opusque sibi', ed. B. Hauréau, 'Un poème inédit de Pierre Riga', *Bibliothèque de l'École des Chartes* 44 (1883), 5–11
The Pilgrim's Guide to Santiago de Compostela: A Critical Edition, ed. and trans. P. Gerson, A. Shaver-Crandell and A. Stones, 2 vols. (London, 1998)
Pliny, *Natural History, books I–II*, ed. and trans. H. Rackham, Loeb Classical Library 330, 352–3, 371, 392, 394, 418–19, 10 vols. (Cambridge MA, 1949), i
——, *Natural History, books III–VII*, ed. and trans. H. Rackham, Loeb Classical Library, 10 vols. (Cambridge MA, 2006), ii
——, *Natural History, books XXVIII–XXXII*, ed. and trans. W. H. S. Jones, Loeb Classical Library, 10 vols. (Cambridge MA, 2006), viii
——, *Natural History, books XXXVI XXXVII*, ed. and trans. D. E. Eichholz, Loeb Classical Library, 10 vols. (Cambridge MA, 1962), x
In Praise of Later Roman emperors: The Panegyrici latini. Introduction, Translation and Historical Commentary with the Latin Text of R. A. B. Mynors, ed. and trans. R. A. B. Mynors, C. E. V. Nixon and B. S. Rodgers (Berkeley, 1994)
'Proverbes et dictons populaires', ed. J.-H.-R. Prompsault, *Discours sur les publications littéraires du Moyen-Âge* (Paris, 1835)
Proverbia sententiaeque Latinitatis medii aevi/Lateinische Sprichwörter und Sentenzen des Mittelalters in alpabetischer Anordnung, ed. H. Walther and P. G. Schmidt, 9 vols. (Göttingen, 1963–86)
Pseudo-Aristotelian *Problemata*, in *The Works of Aristotle*, 12 vols. (Oxford, 1910–52)
Pseudo-Boethius, *De disciplina scolarium*, ed. O. Weijers (Leiden, 1976)
Al-Qabīsī, *The Introduction to Astrology*, ed. and trans. C. Burnett, K. Yamamoto and M. Yano (London, 2004)
Quintilian, *Institutio Oratoria*, in *Quintilian, The Orator's Education, books I–VIII*, ed. D. E. Russell (Cambridge MA, 2001)
'Quo miser exul venio turbine perfusus?', ed. P. Lehmann, *Mitteilungen aus Handschriften*, 9 vols. (Munich, 1929–50), i, 28
Radboud of Utrecht, *Vita altera Bonifatii*, ed. W. Levison, MGH Scriptores rerum Germanicarum in usum scholarum separatim editi 57 (Hanover, 1905)

Radulfus Glaber, *Rodulfi Glabri Historiarum libri quinque*, ed. and trans. J. France (Oxford, 1989)
Raimbert de Paris, *La Chevalerie d'Ogier de Danemarche*, ed. M. Eusebi (Milan, 1963)
Ralph of Caen, *Gesta Tancredi*, in *PL* 155
——, *The Gesta Tancredi of Ralph of Caen: A History of the Normans on the First Crusade*, trans. B. S. Bachrach and D. S. Bachrach, Crusade Texts in Translation 12 (Aldershot, 2005)
Ranulf Higden, *Polychronicon Ranulphi Higden Monachi Cestrensis*, ed. C. Babington and J. R. Lumby, Rolls Series 41, 9 vols. (London, 1865–86)
Raoul Ardent, *Homilia*, 'In die Trinitatis', in *PL* 155
Raymond of Aguilers, *Le 'Liber' de Raymond d'Aguilers*, ed. J. Hugh and L. L. Hill, introduction and notes P. Wolff, Documents relatifs à l'histoire des croisades 9 (Paris, 1969)
Regimen Sanitatis Salernitanum, ed. and trans. P. W. Cummins, *A Critical Edition of Le régime tresutile et tresproufitable pour conserver et garder la santé du corps humain: With the commentary of Arnoul de Villeneuve, corrected by the 'docteurs regens' of Montpellier, 1480, Lyon, 1491* (Chapel Hill, 1976)
Reginald of Canterbury, 'Gozelino monacho suo suus, amico amicus Raginaldus', in 'Raginald von Canterbury', ed. F. Liebermann, *Neues Archiv der Gesellschaft für Ältere Deutsche Geschichtskunde zur Beförderung einer Gesamtausgabe der Quellenschriften deutscher Geschichten des Mittelalters* 13 (1888), 519–56
Regino of Prüm, 'Epistola Reginonis ad Hathonem Archiepiscopum missa', in *Reginonis abbatis Prumiensis Chronicon*, ed. F. Kurze, MGH SS rerum Germanicarum 50 (Hanover, 1890)
Registrum Epistolarum Fratris Johannis Peckham Archiepiscopi Cantuariensis, ed. C. T. Martin, 3 vols. (London, 1882–85)
Remigius of Auxerre, *Epistolae duae ad D. episcopum virdunensem*, in *PL* 131
Reprehensio in A. Wilmart (ed.), 'Une riposte de l'ancien monachisme au manifeste de saint Bernard', *Revue bénédictine* 36 (1934), 296–344
Richard Coer de Lyon, in *Der mittelenglische Versroman über Richard Löwenherz*, ed. K. Brunner (Vienna, 1913)
Richard of Devises, *The Chronicle of Richard of Devizes of the Time of King Richard the First / Cronicon Richardi Divisensis de tempore Regis Richardi Primi*, ed. J. T. Appleby (London, 1963)
Richer of Reims, *Historiae*, ed. H. Hoffmann, MGH Scriptores 38 (Hanover, 2000)
Robert of Bridlington, *The Bridlington Dialogue: An Exposition of the Rule of St Augustine for the Life of the Clergy, etc.*, ed. and trans. by A religious of C. S. M. V. (London, 1960)
Robert the Englishman, Thirteenth Lecture, ed. L. Thorndike, *The Sphere of Sacrobosco and its Commentators* (Chicago, 1949)
Robert Grosseteste, *Opera Roberti Grosseteste Lincolniensis: Vol. 1: Expositio in epistolam sancti Pauli ad Galatas*, ed. J. MacEvoy, Corpus Christianorum: Continuatio mediaeualis 130 (Turnhout, 1995)
Robert the Monk, *Historia Iherosolimitana*, ed. D. Kempf and M. G. Bull (Woodbridge, 2013)
Trans. C. Sweetenham, *Robert the Monk's History of the First Crusade: Historia Iherosolimitana* (Aldershot, 2005)

Roger Bacon, *The 'Opus Majus' of Roger Bacon*, ed. J. H. Bridges, 3 vols. (Oxford, 1897)
Rolandinus Patavinus, *Chronica*, ed. Ph. Jaffé, MGH Scriptores 19 (Hanover, 1866)
Rutebeuf, 'La Bataille des vii Ars', ed. A. Jubinal, *Oeuvres complètes de Rutebeuf, trouvère du XIIIe siècle*, 3 vols. (Paris, 1874–75)
Salimbene, *Chronica*, ed. G. Scalia, Corpus Christianorum: Continuatio mediaeualis (Turnhout, 1995–).
Salvian of Marseille, *De gubernatione Dei*, in *PL* 53
'Sapientia Graecorum; fortia Gothorum', in *Chroniques Asturiennes*, ed. Y. Bonnaz (Paris, 1987)
Saxo Grammaticus, *Saxonis Gesta Danorum*, ed. J. Olrik and H. Ræder (Copenhagen, 1931)
Seneca, *Moral Essays: De Providentia. De Constantia, De ira, De clementia*, 3 vols, ed. J. W. Basore (Cambridge MA, 1958)
'Sic non est mirum, quod quisque moritur', in *Carmina Medii Aevi maximam partem inedita*, ed. H. Hagen (Bern, 1877)
Siegfried of Gorze, Letter to Poppo of Stavelot, *Geschichte der Deutschen Kaiserzeit. 2. Blüthe des Kaiserthums*, ed. W. von Giesebrecht (Leipzig, 1885)
Solinus, Collectanea Iulii Solini Collectanea rerum memorabilium, ed. Th. Mommsen (Berlin, 1895)
Suger, *Vita Ludovici*, in *The Deeds of Louis the Fat*, ed. and trans. R. Cusimano and J. Moorhead (Washington DC, 1992)
Tertullian, *De anima*, in *PL* 2
The Book of the Mysteries of the Heavens and the Earth and Other Works of Bakhayla Mikâ'êl (Zôsîmâs), ed. and trans. E. A. W. Budge (London, 1935)
Thesaurus proverbiorum medii aevi: Lexikon der Sprichwörter des romanisch-germanischen Mittelalters, ed. S. Singer, 13 vols. (rev. edn, Berlin 1995–2002)
Thietmar von Merseburg, *Chronik*, ed. W. Trillmich (Berlin, 1957)
Theodorik of Amorbach, *Ex illatione Sancti Benedicti*, ed. M. Bouquet, *Recueil des historiens des Gaules et de la France* 9 (1757), p. 143
Thomas Aquinas, *Summa theologiae*, 61 vols. (London, 1964–80)
——, *Scriptum super libros Sententiarum*, ed. P. Mandonnet and M. F. Moos, 4 vols. (Paris, 1927–47)
Thomas of Cantimpré, *Liber de natura rerum: Editio princeps secundum codices manuscriptos*, ed. H. Boese (Berlin, 1973)
Thomas of Otterbourne, *The Work of Thomas of Otterbourne and John Whethamstede, as Duo rerum Anglicarum Scriptores veteres*, ed. T. Hearne (Oxford, 1732)
'Tractatus Garsiae Toletani Canonici de Albino et Rufino', ed. E. Sackur, MGH *Libelli de lite imperatorum et pontificum*, 3 vols. (Hanover, 1892)
Tractatus Garsiae or The Translation of the Relics of SS. Gold and Silver, ed. and trans. R. M. Thomson (Leiden, 1973)
Tractatus de locis et statu sancte terre ierosolimitane, 'Ein Tractat über das heilige Land und den dritten Kreuzzug', ed. G. M. Thomas (Munich, 1865)
Vegetius, *Epitoma rei militaris*, ed. M. D. Reeve (Oxford, 2004)
——, *Vegetius: Epitome of Military Science*, trans. N. P. Milner (Liverpool, 1996)
'Versus de Asia et de universi mundi rota', ed. F. Glorie, in *Corpus Christianorum. Series Latina* 175 (Turnhout, 1965), 433–54

'Versus Romae', ed. L. Traube, MGH Poetae Latini aevi Carolini 3 (Berlin, 1896), 554–6

Vincent of Beauvais, *Speculum doctrinale* (Baltazar Bellerus, Douai, 1624; reprint Graz, 1965)

——, *Speculum naturale: Speculum quadruplex sive Speculum maius* (Baltazar Bellerus, Douai, 1624; reprint Graz, 1964)

'Vinum Normannis et in hoc et in omnibus annis / ferre solet culmus, non subdita uitibus ulmus', ed. J.-Y. Tilliette, *Carmina Baudri de Bourgueil*, 2 vols. (Paris, 1998–2002)

Virgil, *Opera*, ed. R. A. B. Mynors, Scriptorum Classicorum Bibliotheca Oxoniensis (Oxford, 1969)

——, *Bucolica, Georgica, Hirtengedichte, Landwirtschaft*, ed. N. Holzberg (Berlin, 2016)

——, *Aeneid VII–XII, Appendix Vergiliana*, ed. G. P. Goold, Loeb Classical Library 64 (Cambridge MA, 2002)

——, *Eclogues. Georgics. Aeneid: Books 1–6*, ed. H. R. Fairclough and G. P. Goold, Loeb Classical Library 63–4, 2 vols. (rev. edn, Cambridge, 2015)

Vita Edwardi Secundi, ed. N. Denholm Young and W. Childs (Oxford, 2005)

Vita Gregorii Magni, in *PL* 75

Vita Ludovici VII, Historiae Francorum Scriptores, ed. A. Duchesne, 5 vols. (Paris, 1636–49)

Wace's Roman de Brut: *A History of the British: Text and Translation*, ed. and trans. J. Weiss (Exeter, 1999)

——, *Le Roman de Rou de Wace*, ed. A. J. Holden, Société des Anciens Textes Français 92, 3 vols. (Paris, 1970–73)

Walter of Châtillon, *Galteri de Castellione Alexandreis*, ed. M. L. Colker (Padua, 1978)

——, *The Alexandreis of Walter of Châtillon: A Twelfth-Century Epic*, trans. D. Townsend, (Philadelphia, 1996)

Walter Map, *De nugis curialium*, ed. and trans. M. R. James, revised by C. N. L. Brooke and R. A. B. Mynors (Oxford, 1983)

Walther von der Vogelweide, *Leich, Lieder, Sangsprüche*, ed. K. Lachmann (Berlin, 1996)

Wandalbert of Prüm, *Vita et miracula sancti Goaris*, ed. H. E. Stiene, Lateinische Sprache und Literatur des Mittelalters 11 (Frankfurt am Main, 1981)

William the Breton, *Œuvres de Rigord et de Guillaume le Breton*, ed. H.-F. Delaborde, 2 vols. (Paris, 1882–85)

William Brito, *Summa Britonis: sive, Guillelmi Britonis Expositiones vocabulorum Biblie*, ed. L. W. Daly and B. A. Daly, 2 vols. (Padua, 1975)

William Camden, *Remains Concerning Britain*, ed. R. D. Dunn (Toronto, 1984)

William of Conches, *Guillelmi de Conchis Dragmaticon philosophiae*, ed. I. Ronca, Corpus Christianorum Continuatio Mediaevalis 152 (Turnhout, 1997)

William Fitzstephen, *Descriptio Nobilissimae Civitatis Londoniae*, ed. J. C. Robertson, Materials for the history of Thomas Becket, Archbishop of Canterbury, 7 vols. (London, 1877)

William of Malmesbury, *Gesta regum Anglorum*, ed. and trans. R. A. B. Mynors, R. M. Thomson and M. Winterbottom, 2 vols. (Oxford, 1998–99)

——, *Gesta Pontificum Anglorum*, ed. and trans. M. Winterbottom and R. M. Thomson, 2 vols. (Oxford, 2007)

———, *Historia Novella*, ed. E. King, trans. K. R. Potter (Oxford, 1998)
———, *Vita Wulfstani*, ed. R. R. Darlington (London, 1928)
William of Nangis, *Ex primatis chronicis et Guillelmi gestis Ludovici ix*, ed. H. Brosien, MGH Scriptores 26 (Hanover, 1882)
William of Newburgh, *Historia rerum Anglicarum*, i, Prooemium, in *Chronicles of the Reigns of Stephen, Henry II, and Richard I: Volume 1. The First Four Books of Historia rerum Anglicarum of William of Newburgh*, ed. R. Howlett, Rerum Britannicarum Medii Aevi Scriptores, 4 vols. (New York, 1964)
William of Poitiers, *The Gesta Guillelmi of William of Poitiers*, ed. and trans. R. H. C. Davis and M. Chibnall (Oxford, 1998)
Wilmart, A., 'Le florilège de Saint-Gatien. Contribution à l'étude des poèmes d'Hildebert et de Marbode', *Revue Bénédictine* 48 (1936), 3–40
Wolfram von Eschenbach, *Willehalm: nach der Handschrift 857 der Stiftsbibliothek St Gallen*, ed. J. Heinzle (Frankfurt am Main, 1991)
Wright, T., *Biographia Britannica Literaria: Or, Biography of Literary Characters of Great Britain and Ireland, Arranged in Chronological Order*, 2 vols. (London, 1842–46)
Wright, T. and J. O. Halliwell-Phillips (ed.), *Reliquiae Antiquae: Scraps from Ancient Manuscripts, Illustrating Chiefly Early English Literature and the English Language*, 2 vols. (London, 1845)
Wulfstan, *Vita Wulfstani*, in *The Homilies of Wulfstan*, ed. D. Betherum (Oxford, 1957)
Ysengrimus: Text with Translation, Commentary and Introduction, ed. and trans. J. Mann, Mittellateinische Studien und Texte, 12 (Leiden, 1987)

Secondary literature

Abeele, B. van den and H. Meyer, 'Etat de l'edition du *De proprietatibus rerum*', in *Bartholomaeus Anglicus, De proprietatibus rerum: Texte latin et réception vernaculaire / Lateinischer texte und volkssprachige Rezeption: Actes du Colloque international = Akten des Internationalen Kolloquiums, Münster, 9–11 October 2003*, ed. B. van den Abeele and H. Meyer (Turnhout, 2005), pp. 1–25
Akbari, S., 'From Due East to True North: Orientalism and Orientation', in J. J. Cohen (ed.), *The Postcolonial Middle Ages* (Basingstoke, 2000), pp. 19–34
Albu, E., *The Normans in Their Histories: Propaganda, Myth and Subversion* (Woodbridge, 2001)
Albu, E., 'Imperial Geography and the Medieval Peutinger Map', *Imago Mundi* 57/2 (2005), 136–48
Alföldi, A., 'The Moral Barrier on Rhine and Danube', in *Congress of Roman Frontier Studies*, ed. E. Birley (Durham, 1952), pp. 1–16
Allmand, C. T., *The De Re Militari of Vegetius: The Reception, Transmission and Legacy of a Roman Text in the Middle Ages* (Cambridge, 2011)
Anderson, A. R., *Alexander's Gate, Gog and Magog, and the Inclosed Nations* (Cambridge MA, 1932)
Anderson, B., *Imagined Communities: Reflections on the Origin and Spread of Nationalism* (London, 1983; third rev. edn, London, 2006)
Anlezark, D., 'Understanding Numbers in London, British Library, Harley 3271', *Anglo-Saxon England* 38 (2010), 137–55

Applauso, N., 'Curses and Laughter: The Ethics of Political Invective in the Comic Poetry of High and Late Medieval Italy' (unpublished dissertation, University of Oregon, 2010)

Arbusow, L., *Colores rhetorici: Eine Auswahl rhetorischer Figuren und Gemeinplätze als Hilfsmittel für akademische Übungen an mittelalterlichen Texten*, ed. H. Peter (Götttingen, 1963)

Arikha, N., *Passions and Tempers: A History of the Humours* (New York, 2007)

Aronson, E., T. D. Wilson and R. M. Akert, *Social Psychology* (Upper Saddle River, 2005)

Aurell, M., *The Plantagenet Empire 1154–1224*, trans. D. Crouch (Harlow, 2007)

Babicz, J. and H. M. Nobis, 'Die Entdeckung der Natur in der geographischen Literatur und Kartographie an der Wende vom Mittelalter zur Renaissance', in *Mensch und Natur im Mittelalter*, ed. A. Zimmermann and A. Speer, 2 vols. (Berlin, 1991–92)

Baldwin, J. W., *Masters, Princes and Merchants: The Social Views of Peter the Chanter and His Circle*, 2 vols. (Princeton, 1970)

Ball, S. J., *Foucault, Power, and Education* (New York, 2013)

Banton, M., *The Idea of Race* (London, 1977)

Banton, M., *Racial Theories* (Cambridge, 1987)

Barber, R., *The Knight and Chivalry* (Woodbridge, 2000)

Barker, H., *That Most Precious Merchandise: The Mediterranean Trade in Black Sea Slaves, 1260–1500* (Philadelphia, 2019)

Barker, M., *The New Racism: Conservatives and the Ideology of the Tribe* (London, 1981)

Baron, H., *The Crisis of the Early Italian Renaissance: Civic Humanism and Republican Liberty in an Age of Classicism and Tyranny*, 2 vols. (Princeton, 1955)

Barroux, R., 'L'abbé Suger et la vassalité du Vexin en 1124', *Le Moyen Âge* 64 (1958), 1–26

Bartlett, R., *Gerald of Wales 1146–1223* (Oxford, 1982; unaltered text reprinted under a new title, *Gerald of Wales: A Voice of the Middle Ages* (Stroud, 2006)

Bartlett, R., *The Making of Europe: Conquest, Colonization and Cultural Change 950–1350* (London, 1993)

Bartlett, R., 'Symbolic Meanings of Hair in the Middle Ages', *Transactions of the Royal Historical Society* 4 (1994), 43–60

Bartlett, R., *England under Norman and Angevin Kings, 1075–1225* (Oxford 2000)

Bartlett, R., 'Medieval and Modern Concepts of Race and Ethnicity', *Journal of Medieval and Early Modern Studies* 31/1 (2001), 39–56

Bartlett, R., 'Illustrating Ethnicity in the Middle Ages', in *The Origins of Racism in the West*, ed. M. Eliav-Feldon, B. Isaac and J. Ziegler (Cambridge, 2009), pp. 132–56

Bartlett, R. and A. MacKay (ed.), *Medieval Frontiers Societies* (Oxford, 1989)

Bauchau, B., 'Science et racisme: les juifs, la lèpre et la peste', *Stanford French Review* 13 (1989), 21–35

Baumgärtner, I., 'Die Welt im kartographischen Blick: Zur Veränderbarkeit mittelalterlicher Weltkarten am Beispiel der Beatustradition vom 10. bis 13. Jahrhundert', in *Der weite Blick des Historikers: Einsichten in Kultur-, Landes- und Stadtgeschichte. Peter Johanek zum 65. Geburtstag*, ed. W. Ehbrecht, A. Lampen, F.-J. Post and M. Siekmann (Cologne, 2002), pp. 527–49

Bautier, A.-M., 'Peuples, provinces et villes dans la littérature proverbiale latine du Moyen Âge', in *Richesse du proverbe; Vol. 1: Le proverbe au Moyen Âge*, ed. F. Suard and C. Buridant, 2 vols. (Lille, 1984)
Bayless, M., *Parody in the Middle Ages: The Latin Tradition* (Ann Arbor, 1996)
Beazley, C. R., *The Dawn of Modern Geography*, 3 vols. (London, 1897–1906)
Bell, A. (ed.), 'The Anglo-Norman Description of England: An Edition', in *Anglo-Norman Anniversary Essays*, ed. I. Short (London, 1993), pp. 31–47
Beller, M., 'Stereotypes', in *Imagology: The Cultural Construction and Literary Representation of National Characters: A Critical Survey*, ed. M. Beller and J. Leerssen (Amsterdam, 2007), pp. 429–34
Benson, R. L., G. Constable and C. D. Lanham (eds), *Renaissance and Renewal in the Twelfth Century* (Cambridge MA, 1982)
Benzinger, J., *Invectiva in Romam: Romkritik im Mittelalter vom 9. bis zum 12. Jahrhundert* (Lübeck, 1968)
Berend, N., *At the Gate of Christendom: Jews, Muslims and 'Pagans' in Medieval Hungary, c. 1000–c. 1300* (Cambridge, 2001)
Bergson, H., *Laughter: An Essay on the Meaning of the Comic* (London, 1935)
Bethge, R. and C. Gremmels, *Dietrich Bonhoeffer: Zijn leven in beeld*, ed. H. Sweers (Kampen, 2005)
Beumann, H., 'Die Bedeutung des Kaisertums für die Entstehung der deutschen Nation im Spiegel der Bezeichnungen von Reich und Herrscher', in *Aspekte der Nationenbildung im Mittelalter: Ergebnisse der Marburger Rundgespräche 1972–1975*, ed. H. Beumann and W. Schröder (Sigmaringen, 1978), pp. 317–66
Beumann, H., 'Zur Nationenbildung im Mittelalter', in *Nationalismus in vorindustrieller Zeit*, ed. O. Dann (Munich, 1986), pp. 21–33
Beyer de Ryke, B. 'Les encyclopédies médiévales, un état de la question', *Pecia: Ressources en médiévistique* 1 (2002), 9–42
Biddick, K., 'The abc of Ptolemy. Mapping the World with the Alphabet', in *Text and Territory: Geographical Imagination in the European Middle Ages*, ed. S. Tomasch and S. Gilles (Philadelphia, 1998), pp. 268–93
Biller, P., 'A "Scientific" View of Jews from Paris Around 1300', *Micrologus: Natura, scienze e società medievali – Nature, Sciences and Medieval Societies* 9 (2001), 137–68
Biller, P., *The Measure of Multitude: Population in Medieval Thought* (Oxford, 2000)
Biller, P., 'Black Women in Medieval Scientific thought', *Micrologus: Natura, scienze e società medievali – Nature, Sciences and Medieval Societies* 13 (2005), 477–92
Biller, P., 'Proto-Racial Thought in Medieval Science', in *The Origins of Racism in the West*, ed. M. Eliav-Feldon, B. Isaac and J. Ziegler (Cambridge, 2009), pp. 157–80
Billig, M., *Banal Nationalism* (London, 1995)
Binkley, P., 'Thirteenth Century Latin Poetry Contests Associated with Henry of Avranches with an Appendix of Newly Edited Texts' (unpublished dissertation, University of Toronto, 1991)
Binkley, P., 'Preachers' Responses to Thirteenth-Century Encyclopaedism', in *Pre-Modern Encyclopaedic Texts: Proceedings of the second COMERS Congress, Groningen, 1–4 July 1996*, ed. P. Binkley (Leiden, 1997), pp. 75–88

Black, I., 'An Accidental Tourist in the Hundred Years' War: Images of the Foreign World in Eustache Deschamps', in *Concepts of National Identity in the Middle Ages*, ed. S. Forde, L. Johnson and A. V. Murray (Leeds, 1995), pp. 171–87

Black, W., '"I will add what the Arab once taught": Constantine the African in Northern European Medical Verse', in *Herbs and Healers from the Ancient Mediterranean through the Medieval West: Essays in Honor of John M. Riddle*, ed. A. Van Arsdall and T. Graham (Farnham, 2012), pp. 153–85

Black, W., 'A Star is Born: Reading Constantine the African in Medieval England', at https://constantinusafricanus.com/2018/08/22/a-star-is-born-reading-constantine-the-african-in-medieval-england/ (accessed 4 September 2020)

Blaicher, G., 'Zur Entstehung und Verbreitung nationaler Stereotypen in und über England', *Deutsche Vierteljahrsschrift für Literaturwissenschaft und Geistesgeschichte* 51 (1977), 549–74

Blaicher, G. (ed.), *Erstarrtes Denken: Studien zu Klischee, Stereotyp und Vorurteil in englischsprachiger Literatur* (Tübingen, 1987)

Blaicher, G., *Merry England: Zur Bedeutung und Funktion eines englischen Autostereotyps* (Tübingen, 2000)

Bloomfield, M. W., *The Seven Deadly Sins: An Introduction to the History of a Religious Concept, With Special Reference to Medieval English Literature* (Ann Arbor, 1967)

Blumenkranz, B., 'Augustin et les juifs; Augustin et le judaïsme', *Recherches augustiniennes* 1 (1958), 225–41

Blumenkranz, B., *Juden und Judentum in der mittelalterlichen Kunst* (Stuttgart, 1965)

Blumenkranz, B., *Le Juif médiéval au miroir de l'art chrétien* (Paris, 1966)

Boas, G., *Essays on Primitivism and Related Ideas in the Middle Ages* (New York, 1978)

Boehm, L., 'Gedanken zum Frankreich-Bewußtsein im frühen 12. Jahrhundert', *Historisches Jahrbuch* 74 (1955), 681–7

Boivin, J.-M., *L'Irlande au Moyen Âge: Giraud de Barri et la* Topographia Hibernica *(1188)* (Paris, 1993)

Bonnaz, Y., 'Introduction', in *Chroniques Asturiennes* (fin IXe siècle), ed. Y. Bonnaz (Paris, 1987)

Borst, A., *Der Turmbau von Babel: Geschichte der Meinungen über Ursprung und Vielfalt der Sprachen und Völker*, 4 vols. (Stuttgart, 1957–63)

Boüard, M. de, 'Les encyclopédies médiévales: Sur "La connaissance de la nature et du monde au Moyen Âge"', *Revue des questions historiques* 112 (1930), 258–304

Bouchard, C. B., *'Strong of Body, Brave and Noble': Chivalry and Society in Medieval France* (Ithaca NY, 1998)

Bourdieu, P., *Distinction: A Social Critique of the Judgement of Taste*, trans. R. Nice (Cambridge MA, 1984)

Bourdieu, P., 'The Forms of Capital', in *Handbook of Theory and Research for the Sociology of Education*, ed. J. G. Richardson (New York, 1986), pp. 241–58

Boureau, A., 'Hérédité, erreurs et vérité de la nature humaine (XIIe–XIIIe siècles)', in *L'hérédité entre Moyen Âge et Époque moderne: Perspectives historiques*, ed. M. van der Lugt and C. de Miramon (Florence, 2008), pp. 67–82

Boyce, G. C., *The English–German Nation in the University of Paris During the Middle Ages* (Bruges, 1927)

Braude, B., 'The Sons of Noah and the Construction of Ethnic and Geographical Identities in the Medieval and Early Modern Periods', *The William and Mary Quarterly* 54/1 (1997), 103–42
Braude, B., 'Cham et Noé. Race, esclavage et exégèse entre islam, judaïsme et christianisme', *Annales: Histoire, Sciences Sociales* 57/1 (2002), 93–125
Brault, G. J., '*Sapientia* dans la *Chanson de Roland*', *French Forum* 1/2 (1976), 99–118
Bremmer, R. H. Jr., 'Leiden, Vossianus Lat. Q. 69 (Part 2): Schoolbook or Proto-Encyclopaedic Miscellany?', in *Practice in Learning: The Transfer of Encyclopaedic Knowledge in the Early Middle Ages*, ed. R. H. Bremmer Jr. and K. Dekker (Paris, 2010), pp. 19–54
Breuilly, J., *Nationalism and the State* (New York, 1982)
Brincken, A.-D. von den, 'Tabula Alphabetica: Von den Anfängen alphabetischer Registerarbeiten zu geschichtlichen Werken (Vincenz von Beauvais OP, Johannes von Hautfuney, Paulinus Minorita OFM)', in *Festschrift für Hermann Heimpel zum 70. Geburtstag am 19. September 1971*, ed. T. Schieder e.a., 3 vols. (Göttingen, 1971–73)
Brown, E. A. R., 'La notion de la légitimité et la prophétie à la cour de Philippe Auguste', in *La France de Philippe Auguste: Le temps des mutations: Actes du colloque international organisé par le C.N.R.S. (Paris, 29 septembre–4 octobre 1980)*, ed. R.-H. Bautier (Paris, 1982), pp. 77–110
Brown, P. S., 'Scoundrels and *Scurrilitas* at St-Pierre de Sévignac', in *Difference and Identity in Francia and Medieval France*, ed. M. Cohen and J. Firnhaber-Baker (Farnham, 2010), pp. 197–226
Bruaene, A.-L. Van, 'De stad als scheldwoord: De *Baladen van Doornijcke* (1521/1522) van Matthijs de Castelein en de stedelijke literaire praktijk van de rederijkers', *Spiegel der Letteren* 48 (2006), 135–47
Brühl, C., *Deutschland, Frankreich: Die Geburt zweier Völker* (Cologne, 1990)
Buell, D. K., *Why this New Race: Ethnic Reasoning in Early Christianity* (New York, 2005)
Buell, D. K., 'Early Christian Universalism and Modern Forms of Racism', in *The Origins of Racism in the West*, ed. M. Eliav-Feldon, B. Isaac and J. Ziegler (Cambridge, 2009), pp. 109–31
Buell, D. K. and C. J. Hodge, 'The Politics of Interpretation: The Rhetoric of Race and Ethnicity in Paul', *Journal of Biblical Literature* 123/2 (2004), 235–51
Bugner, L. e.a., *L'image du noir dans l'art occidental. II: Des premiers siècles chrétiens aux 'Grandes Découvertes'*, 2 vols. (Fribourg, 1979), trans. as *The Image of the Black in Western Art. II: From the Early Christian Era to the 'Age of Discovery'*, 2 vols. (Cambridge MA, 1979)
Bumke, J., *Courtly Culture: Literature and Society in the High Middle Ages*, trans. T. Dunlap (Berkeley, 1991)
Burkhardt, S., 'Barbarossa, Frankreich und die Weltherrschaft', in *Staufisches Kaisertum im 12. Jahrhundert: Konzepte-Netzwerke-politische Praxis*, ed. S. Burkhardt e.a. (Regensburg, 2010), pp. 133–58
Burnam, J. M., 'Miscellanea Hispanica', *Modern Philology* 12/3 (1914), 165–70
Burnett, C. and D. Jacquart, 'A Catalogue of Renaissance Editions and Manuscripts of the Pantegni', in *Constantine the African and 'Alī ibn al-'Abbās al-Maǧūsī: The*

Pantegni and Related Texts, ed. C. Burnett and D. Jacquart (Leiden, 1994), pp. 316–51

Burnett, C., 'Physics before the *Physics*: Early Translations from Arabic of Texts Concerning Nature in MSS British Library, Additional 22719 and Cotton Galba E IV', *Medioevo: Rivista di Storia della Filosofia Medievale* 27 (2002), 53–109

Burton, J. W., *Culture and the Human Body: An Anthropological Perspective* (Prospect Heights, 2001)

Bynum, C. Walker, 'Material Continuity, Personal Survival, and the Resurrection of the Body: A Scholastic Discussion in Its Medieval and Modern Contexts', *History of Religions* 30/1 (1990), 51–85

Bynum, C. Walker, 'Why All the Fuss About the Body? A Medievalist's Perspective', *Critical Inquiry* 22/1 (1995), 1–33

Byrn, R. F. M., 'National Stereotypes Reflected in German Literature', in *Concepts of National Identity in the Middle Ages*, ed. S. Forde, L. Johnson and A. V. Murray (Leeds, 1995), pp. 137–53

Camargo, M., 'Rhetoric', in *The Seven Liberal Arts in the Middle Ages*, ed. D. L. Wagner (Bloomington, 1983), pp. 96–124

Cames, G., 'A propos de deux monstres dans l'*Hortus deliciarum*', *Cahiers de civilisation médiévale* 11 (1968), 587–603

Campbell, M. B., *The Witness and the Other World: Exotic European Travel Writing, 400–1600* (Ithaca, 1988)

Canning, J. P., 'Introduction: Politics, Institutions and Ideas', in *The Cambridge History of Medieval Political Thought, c. 350–c. 1450*, ed. J. H. Burns (Cambridge, 1988), pp. 341–66

Canning, J. P., 'Law, Sovereignty and Corporation Theory, 1300–1450', in *The Cambridge History of Medieval Political Thought, c. 350–c. 1450*, ed. J. H. Burns (Cambridge, 1988), pp. 454–76

Carozzi, C., 'Des Daces aux Normands: Le mythe et l'identification d'un peuple chez Dudon de Saint-Quentin', in *Peuples du Moyen Âge: Problèmes d'identification: Seminaire Sociétés, Idéologies et Croyances au Moyen Âge*, ed. C. Carozzi and H. Taviani-Carozzi (Aix-en-Provence, 1996), pp. 7–25

Carruthers, M., *The Craft of Thought: Meditation, Rhetoric, and the Making of Images, 400–1200* (Cambridge, 1998)

Catlos, B. A., *Kingdoms of Faith: A New History of Islamic Spain* (New York, 2018)

Cerwinka, G., 'Völkercharakteristiken in historiographischen Quellen der Salier- und Stauferzeit', in *Festschrift für Friedrich Hausmann*, ed. H. Ebner (Graz, 1977), pp. 59–80

Champion, M. S., 'A History of Temporalities: An Introduction', *Past & Present* 243/1 (2019), 247–54

Chazan, R., *Medieval Stereotypes and Modern Antisemitism* (Berkeley, 1997)

Chenu, M.-D., *Nature, Man and Society in the Twelfth Century: Essays on New Theological Perspectives in the Latin West*, ed. and trans. J. Taylor and L. K. Little (Toronto, 1997)

Chibnall, M., *Anglo-Norman England, 1066–1166* (Oxford, 1986)

Christiansen, E., *The Northern Crusades: The Baltic and the Catholic Frontier, 1100–1525* (2nd edn, London, 199780)

Clanchy, M. T., 'Moderni in Education and Government in England', *Speculum* 50/4 (1975), 671–88
Clanchy, M. T., *England and its Rulers, 1066–1272: Foreign Lordship and National Identity* (Oxford 1983)
Clarke, P. D., *The Interdict in the Thirteenth Century: A Question of Collective Guilt* (Oxford, 2007)
Classen, A., 'Laughter as an Expression of Human Nature in the Middle Ages and the Early Modern Period: Literary, Historical, Theological, Philosophical, and Pyschological Reflections. Also an Introduction', in *Laughter in the Middle Ages and Early Modern Times: Epistemology of a Fundamental Human Behavior, its Meaning, and Consequences*, ed. A. Classen (Berlin, 2010), pp. 1–140
Classen, C. J., *Die Stadt im Spiegel der Descriptiones und Laudes urbium in der antiken und mittelalterlichen Literatur bis zum Ende des zwölften Jahrhunderts* (Hildesheim, 1980)
Cobban, A. B., *The Medieval English Universities: Oxford and Cambridge to c. 1500* (Berkeley, 1988)
Cohen, J., *Living Letters of the Law: Ideas of the Jew in Medieval Christianity* (Berkeley, 1999)
Cohen, J., 'Revisiting Augustine's Doctrine of Jewish Witness', *The Journal of Religion* 89/4 (2009), pp. 564–78
Cohen, J. J., 'On Saracen Enjoyment: Some Fantasies of Race in Late Medieval France and England', *Journal of Medieval and Early Modern Studies* 31/1 (2001), 113–46
Cohen, M. S., 'The Ethnographic Dimensions of Conversion: A Study of Conversion Narratives in Northern Europe in the Middle Ages' (unpublished dissertation, University of Toronto, 1995)
Cohn, S. K. Jr., 'Popular Insurrection and the Black Death: A Comparative View', *Past & Present*, 195 Issue Supplement 2 (2007), 188–204
Coleman, J., 'Medieval Discussions of Property: "Ratio" and "Dominium" According to John of Paris and Marsilius of Padua', *History of Political Thought* 4/2 (1983), 209–28
Colker, M. L., 'America Rediscovered in the Thirteenth Century?', *Speculum* 54/4 (1979), 712–26
Constable, G., *The Reformation of the Twelfth Century* (Cambridge, 1996)
Contamine, P., 'The Growth of the Nation State', in *Britain and France: Ten Centuries*, ed. D. W. J. Johnson, F. Crouzet and F. Bédarida (Folkestone, 1980), pp. 21–31
Coulton, G. G., 'Nationalism in the Middle Ages', *The Cambridge Historical Journal* 5/1 (1935), 15–40
Cox, V., and J. O. Ward, *The Rhetoric of Cicero in its Medieval and Early Renaissance Commentary Tradition* (Leiden, 2006)
Crouch, D., *The Birth of Nobility: Constructing Aristocracy in England and France, 900–1300* (Harlow, 2005)
Cummins, P. W., 'A Salernitan Regimen of Health', *Allegorica: A Journal of Medieval and Renaissance Literature* 1 (1976), 78–101
Cummins, P. W., '*A Critical Edition of Le régime tresutile et tresproufitable pour conserver et garder la santé du corps humain*: With the commentary of Arnoul de Villeneuve,

corrected by the "docteurs regens" of Montpellier, 1480, Lyon, 1491, ed. P. W. Cummins (Chapel Hill, 1976)

Curta, F., 'Furor Teutonicus: A Note on Ethnic Stereotypes in Suger's *Deeds of Louis the Fat*', *The Haskins Society Journal: Studies in Medieval History* 16 (2005), 62–76

Curtius, E. R., *European Literature and the Latin Middle Ages*, trans. W. R. Trask (New York, 1963)

Czacharowski, A. (ed.), *Nationale, ethnische Minderheiten und regionale Identitäten in Mittelalter und Neuzeit* (Toruń, 1994)

Daly, W. M., 'Christian Fraternity, the Crusaders, and the Security of Constantinople, 1097–1204: The Precarious Survival of an Ideal', *Medieval Studies* 22 (1960), 43–91

Dam, F. van, *Het middeleeuwse openbare badhuis: Fenomeen, metafoor, schouwtoneel* (Hilversum, 2020)

Daniel, N., *Heroes and Saracens: An Interpretation of the* Chansons de Geste (Edinburgh, 1984)

Daniel, N., *Islam and the West: The Making of an Image* (rev. edn, Oxford, 1993)

Darby, H. C., 'Geography in a Medieval Text-Book', *The Scottish Geographical Magazine* 49 (1933), 323–31

Davies, R. R., *Domination and Conquest: The Experience of Ireland, Scotland and Wales, 1100–1300* (Cambridge, 1990)

Davies, R. R., 'Presidential Address: The Peoples of Britain and Ireland 1100–1400 I. Identities', *Transactions of the Royal Historical Society* 4 (1994), 1–20

Davies, R. R., 'Presidential Address: The Peoples of Britain and Ireland 1100–1400 II. Names, Boundaries and Regnal Solidarities', *Transactions of the Royal Historical Society* 5 (1995), 1–20

Davies, R. R., 'Presidential Address: The Peoples of Britain and Ireland 1100–1400 III. Laws and Customs', *Transactions of the Royal Historical Society* 6 (1996), 1–23

Davies, R. R., 'Presidential Address: The Peoples of Britain and Ireland 1100–1400 IV. Language and Historical Mythology', *Transactions of the Royal Historical Society* 7 (1997), 1–24

Davies, R. R., *The First English Empire: Power and Identities in the British Isles 1093–1343* (Oxford, 2000)

Davis, K., *Periodization and Sovereignty: How Ideas of Feudalism and Secularization Govern the Politics of Time* (Philadelphia, 2008)

Davis, R. H. C., *The Normans and Their Myth* (London, 1976)

Dawkins, R., *The Selfish Gene* (Oxford, 1976)

Day, M. L., 'The Letter from King Arthur to Henry II: Political Use of the Arthurian Legend in *Draco Normannicus*', in *The Spirit of the Court: Selected Proceedings of the Fourth Congress of the International Courtly Literature Society (Toronto 1983)*, ed. G. S. Burgess, R. A. Taylor and A. Deyermond (Cambridge, 1985), pp. 153–7

Dean, T., 'Gender and Insult in an Italian City: Bologna in the Later Middle Ages', *Social History* 29/2 (2004), 217–31

Dean, T., *Crime and Justice in Late Medieval Italy* (Cambridge, 2007)

Destombes, M., 'The Mappamundi of the Poem "Alexandreidos" by Gautier de Châtillon (ca. A.D. 1180)', *Imago Mundi* 19 (1965), 10–12

Donkin, L. E. G., '"Usque ad ultimum terrae": Mapping the Ends of the Earth in Two Medieval Floor Mosaics', in *Cartography in Antiquity and the Middle Ages: Fresh Perspectives, New Methods*, ed. R. J. A. Talbert and R. W. Unger (Leiden, 2008), pp. 189–218

Dronke, P., 'Profane Elements in Literature', in *Renaissance and Renewal in the Twelfth Century*, ed. R. L. Benson, G. Constable and C. D. Lanham (Oxford, 1982), pp. 569–92

Dümmler, E., 'Über den furor Teutonicus', *Sitzungsberichte der Preussischen Akademie der Wissenschaften zu Berlin* 9 (1897), 112–26

Dunbabin, J., *France in the Making, 843–1180* (Oxford, 1985)

Dunbabin, J., 'Government', in *The Cambridge History of Medieval Political Thought, c. 350–c. 1450*, ed. J. H. Burns (Cambridge, 1988), pp. 477–519

Dupont-Ferrier, G., 'Le sens des mots "patria" et "patrie" en France au Moyen Age et jusqu'au début du XVIIe siècle', *Revue historique* 188 (1940), 89–104

DuQuesnay Adams, J., 'The Patriotism of Abbot Suger', *Proceedings of the Annual Meeting of the Western Society for French History* 16 (1988), 19–29

DuQuesnay Adams, J., 'The Regnum Francie of Suger of Saint-Denis: An Expansive Ile-de-France', *Historical Reflections/Réflexions Historiques* 19/2 (1993), 167–88

Duranti, T., 'The Origins of the Studium of Medicine in Bologna: A Status Quaestionis', *CIAN-Revista de Historia de las Universidades* 21/1 (2018), 121–49

Ebling, H., J. Jarnut and G. Kampers, 'Nomen et gens: Untersuchungen zu den Führungsschichten des Franken-, Langobarden- und Westgotenreiches im 6. und 7. Jahrhundert', *Francia* 8 (1980), 687–745

Echard, S., *Arthurian Narrative in the Latin Tradition* (Cambridge, 1998)

Eco, U., *The Infinity of Lists: An Illustrated Essay* (London, 2009)

Edson, E., 'World Maps and Easter Tables: Medieval Maps in Context', *Imago Mundi* 48/1 (1996), 25 42

Edson, E., *Mapping Time and Space: How Medieval Mapmakers Viewed their World* (London, 1997)

Edson, E., 'The Medieval World View: Contemplating the Mappamundi', *History Compass* 8/6 (2010) 503–17

Ehlers, J., 'Karolingische Tradition und frühes Nationalbewußtsein in Frankreich', *Francia* 4 (1976), 213–35

Ehlers, J., 'Elemente mittelalterlicher Nationsbildung in Frankreich (10.–13. Jahrhundert)', *Historische Zeitschrift* 231/3 (1980), 565–87

Ehlers, J. (ed.), *Ansätze und Diskontinuität deutscher Nationsbildung im Mittelalter* (Sigmaringen, 1989)

Ehlers, J., *Die Entstehung des deutschen Reiches* (Munich, 1994)

Eichenberger, T., *Patria: Studien zur Bedeutung des Wortes im Mittelalter (6.–12. Jahrhundert)* (Sigmaringen, 1991)

Eley, P., 'The Myth of Trojan Descent and Perceptions of National Identity: The Case of "Eneas" and the "Roman de Troie"', *Nottingham Medieval Studies* 35 (1991), 27–40

Elias, N., *Wandlungen der Gesellschaft: Entwurf zu einer Theorie der Zivilisation* (Basel, 1939)

Eliav-Feldon, M., B. Isaac and J. Ziegler (ed.), *The Origins of Racism in the West* (Cambridge, 2009)

Elukin, J. M., 'From Jew to Christian? Conversion and Immutability in Medieval Europe', in *Varieties of Religious Conversion in the Middle Ages*, ed. J. Muldoon (Gainesville, 1997), pp. 171–89

Elukin, J., *Living Together, Living Apart: Rethinking Jewish-Christian Relations in the Middle Ages* (Princeton, 2007)

Englisch, B., *Ordo Orbis Terrae: Die Weltsicht in den 'Mappae mundi' des frühen und hohen Mittelalters* (Berlin, 2002)

Enklaar, D. Th., *De gestaarte Engelsman* (Amsterdam, 1955)

Epp, V., 'Die Entstehung eines "Nationalbewußtseins" in den Kreuzfahrerstaaten', *Deutsches Archiv für Erforschung des Mittelalters* 45 (1989), 596–604

Epstein, S. A., *Purity Lost: Transgressing Boundaries in the Eastern Mediterranean, 1000–1400* (Baltimore, 2007)

Eriksen, T. H., *Ethnicity and Nationalism: Anthropological Perspectives* (2nd edn, London, 2002)

Esposito, M., 'On Some Unpublished Poems Attributed to Alexander Neckam', *English Historical Review* 30 (1915), 450–71

Ewig, E., 'Volkstum und Volksbewußtsein im Frankenreich des 7. Jahrhunderts: Civitas, pagus, Ducatus and natio', in Ibid., *Spätantikes und Fränkisches Gallien: Gesammelte Schriften (1952–1973)*, ed. E. Ewig and H. Atsma, 2 vols. (Munich, 1976–79), i, 231–73

Faider, P., *Catalogue des manuscrits conservés à Namur (Musée archéologique, Evêché, Grand séminaire, Museum Artium S.J., etc.)* (Gembloux, 1934)

Farrar, M. E., *Building the Body Politic: Power and Urban Space in Washington, D.C.* (Urbana, 2008)

Fedele, P., 'Accenti d'italianità in Montecassino nel Medio Evo', *Bulletino dell'istituto storico italiano per il medio evo* 47 (1932), 1–16

Ferruolo, S. C., *The Origins of the University: The Schools of Paris and their Critics 1100–1215* (Stanford, 1985)

Ferster, J., *Fictions of Advice: The Literature and Politics of Counsel in Late Medieval England* (Philadelphia, 1996)

Fichtenau, H., 'Gentiler und europäischer Horizont an der Schwelle des ersten Jahrtausends', *Römische Historische Mitteilungen* 23 (1981), 227–43

Fields, K. E. and B. J. Fields, *Racecraft: The Soul of Inequality in American Life* (London, 2012)

Fioravanti, G., 'Servi, rustici, barbari: Interpretazioni medievali della Politica aristotelica', *Annali della scuola normale superiore di Pisa: Classe di lettere e filosofa* 11 (1981), 399–429

Flach, J., *Les origines de l'ancienne France: Xe et Xie siècles*, 4 vols. (Paris, 1886–1917)

Floyd-Wilson, M., *English Ethnicity and Race in Early Modern Drama* (Cambridge, 2003)

Foucault, M., *The Order of Things: An Archaeology of the Human Sciences* (New York, 1994)

Fraesdorff, D., *Der barbarische Norden: Vorstellungen und Fremdheitskategorien bei Rimbert, Thietmar von Merseburg, Adam von Bremen und Helmold von Bosau* (Berlin, 2005)

France, J., 'The Normans and Crusading', in *The Normans and their Adversaries at War: Essays in Memory of C. Warren Hollister*, ed. R. P. Abels and B. S. Bachrach (Woodbridge, 2001), pp. 87–101

Frank, G., 'Proverbs in Medieval Literature', *Modern Language Notes* 58/7 (1943), 508–15

Fredrickson, G. M., *Racism: A Short History* (Princeton, 2002)

Fredriksen, P., 'Tyconius and Augustine on the Apocalypse', in *The Apocalypse in the Middle Ages*, ed. R. K. Emmerson and B. McGinn (Ithaca, 1992), pp. 20–37

Fredriksen, P., *Augustine and the Jews: A Christian Defense of Jews and Judaism* (New York, 2008)

Freedman, P. H., *Images of the Medieval Peasant* (Stanford, 1999)

Freedman, P. H., 'The Medieval Other: The Middle Ages as Other', in *Marvels, Monsters and Miracles: Studies in the Medieval and Early Modern Imaginations*, ed. T. S. Jones and D. A. Sprunger (Kalamazoo, 2002), pp. 1–24

Friedman, J. B., 'Cultural Conflicts in Medieval World Maps', in *Implicit Understandings: Observing, Reporting, and Reflecting on the Encounters between Europeans and Other Peoples in the Early Modern Era*, ed. S. B. Schwartz (Cambridge, 1994), pp. 64–95

Friedman, J. B., *The Monstrous Races in Medieval Art and Thought* (2nd rev. edn, New York, 2000)

Friend, A. C., 'The Proverbs of Serlo of Wilton', *Medieval Studies* 16 (1954), 179–218

Fryxell, A. R. P., 'Time and the Modern: Current Trends in the History of Modern Temporalities', *Past & Present* 243/1 (2019), 285–98

Fuhrmann, H., 'Quis Teutonicos constituit iudices nationum? The Trouble with Henry', *Speculum* 69/2 (1994), 344–58

Gabriele, M., 'Otto III, Charlemagne, and Pentecost A.D. 1000: A Reconsideration Using Diplomatic Evidence', in *The Year 1000: Religious and Social Response to the Turning of the First Millennium*, ed. M. Frassetto (New York, 2002), pp. 111–32

Gabriele, M., 'Asleep at the Wheel? Messianism, Apocalypticism and Charlemagne's Passivity in the Oxford Chanson de Roland', *Nottingham Medieval Studies* 47 (2003), 46–72

Gabriele, M., 'The Provenance of the "Descriptio qualiter Karolus Magnus": Remembering the Carolingians in the Entourage of King Philip I (1060–1108) before the First Crusade', *Viator* 39/2 (2008), 93–117

Gabriele, M., *An Empire of Memory: The Legend of Charlemagne, the Franks, and Jerusalem before the First Crusade* (Oxford, 2011)

Gallo, E., 'The *Poetria nova* of Geoffrey of Vinsauf', in *Medieval Eloquence: Studies in the Theory and Practice of Medieval Rhetoric*, ed. J. J. Murphy (Berkeley, 1978), pp. 68–84

Garber, J., 'Trojaner-Römer-Franken-Deutsche: "Nationale" Abstammungstheorien im Vorfeld der Nationalstaatsbildung', in *Nation und Literatur im Europa der Frühen Neuzeit: Akten des I. Internationalen Osnabrücker Kongresses zur Kulturgeschichte der frühen Neuzeit*, ed. K. Garber (Tübingen, 1989), pp. 108–63

García-Ballester, L., 'On the Origins of the Six Non-Natural Things in Galen', in *Galen und das hellenistische Erbe: Verhandlungen des IV. Internationalen Galen-Symposiums veranstaltet vom Institut für Geschichte der Medizin am Bereich Medizin (Charité) der Humboldt-Universität zu Berlin 18.–20. September 1989*, ed. J. Kollesch and D. Nickel (Stuttgart, 1993), pp. 105–15

Garrison, M., 'The Franks as the New Israel? Education for an Identity from Pippin to Charlemagne', in *The Uses of the Past in the Early Middle Ages*, ed. Y. Hen and M. Innes (Cambridge, 2000), pp. 114–61

Gassman, D. L., '*Translatio studii*': *A Study of Intellectual History in the Thirteenth Century*, 2 vols. (Ann Arbor, 1973)

Gat, A., with A. Yakobson, *Nations: The Long History and Deep Roots of Political Ethnicity and Nationalism* (Cambridge, 2012)

Gaullier-Bougassas, C., M. Bridges and J.-Y. Tilliette (ed.), *Trajectoires européennes du 'Secretum secretorum' du Pseudo-Aristote (XIIIe–XVIe siècle)* (Turnhout, 2015)

Gautier Dalché, P. 'Isidorus Hispalensis, *De gentium vocabulis* (Etym. IX, 2): Quelques sources non repérées', *Revue des études augustiniennes* 31 (1985), 278–86

Gautier Dalché, P. *Géographie et culture: La representation de l'espace du vie au xiie siècle* (Aldershot, 1997)

Geary, P. J., *The Myth of Nations: The Medieval Origins of Europe* (Princeton, 2002)

Geary, P. J., 'Ethnic Identity as a Situational Construct in the Early Middle Ages', *Writing History: Identity, Conflict, and Memory in the Middle Ages*, ed. P. J. Geary, F. Curta and C. Spinei (Bucharest, 2012), 19–32

Gebke, J., *(Foreign) Bodies Stigmatizing New Christians in Early Modern Spain*, trans. H. W. Schroeder (Vienna, 2020)

Geertz, C., *The Interpretation of Cultures: Selected Essays* (London, 1973)

Gellner, E., *Nations and Nationalism* (Oxford, 1983)

Geltner, G., 'Healthscaping a Medieval City: Lucca's Curia viarum and the Future of Public Health History', *Urban History* 40/3 (2013), 395–415

Geltner, G., *Roads to Health: Infrastructure and Urban Wellbeing in Later Medieval Italy* (Philadelphia, 2019)

Geltner, G., 'In the Camp and on the March: Military Manuals as Sources for Studying Premodern Public Health', *Medical History* 63/1 (2019), 44–60

George, W. B., *The Naming of the Beasts: Natural History in the Medieval Bestiary* (London, 1991)

Gessler, J. (ed.), *Het Brugsche* Livre des mestiers *en zijn navolgelingen: Vier aloude conversatieboekjes om Fransch te leeren* (Bruges, 1931)

Geudens, C. and T. van Hal, 'The Role of Vernacular Proverbs in Latin Language Acquisition, c. 1200–1600: An Exploratory Study', *Historiographia Linguistica* 44 (2018), 278–305

Gillespie, V., 'From the Twelfth Century to c. 1450', in *The Cambridge History of Literary Criticism. Vol. 2: The Middle Ages*, ed. A. Minnis and I. Johnson (Cambridge, 2005), pp. 145–236

Gillingham, J., 'The Beginnings of English Imperialism', *Journal of Historical Sociology* 5/4 (1992), 392–409

Gillingham, J., 'Henry of Huntingdon and the Twelfth-Century Revival of the English Nation', in *Concepts of National Identity in the Middle Ages*, ed. S. Forde, L. Johnson and A. V. Murray (Leeds, 1995), 75–101

Gillingham, J., *The English in the Twelfth Century: Imperialism, National Identity and Political Values* (Woodbridge, 2000)

Gillingham, J., 'Civilizing the English? The English Histories of William of Malmesbury and David Hume', *Historical Research* 74 (2001), 17–43

Gillingham, J., 'From "Civilitas" to Civility: Codes of Manners in Medieval and Early Modern England', *Transactions of the Royal Historical Society*, sixth series, 12 (2002), 267–89

Gilman, S. L., *Difference and Pathology: Stereotypes of Sexuality, Race, and Madness* (Ithaca, 1985)

Ginsberg, W., *The Cast of Character: The Representation of Personality in Ancient and Medieval Literature* (Toronto, 1983)

Glacken, C. J., *Traces on the Rhodian Shore: Nature and Culture in Western Thought from Ancient Times to the End of the Eighteenth Century* (Berkeley, 1967)

Glaze, F. E., 'Medical Writer: "Behold the Human Creature"', in *Voice of the Living Light: Hildegard of Bingen and Her World*, ed. B. Newman (Berkeley, 1998), pp. 125–48

Glaze, F. E., 'The Perforated Wall: The Ownership and Circulation of Medical Books in Medieval Europe, ca. 800–1200' (unpublished dissertation, Duke University, 1999)

Glück, H., *Deutsch als Fremdsprache in Europa vom Mittelalter bis zur Barockzeit* (Berlin, 2002)

Goetz, H.-W., 'The Concept of Time in the Historiography of the Eleventh and Twelfth Centuries', in *Medieval Concepts of the Past: Ritual, Memory, Historiography*, ed. G. Althoff, J. Fried and P. J. Geary (Cambridge, Washington DC, 2002), pp. 139–65

Goetz, W., *Die Entstehung der italienischen Kommunen im frühen Mittelalter* (Munich, 1944)

Goff, J. le, 'The Medieval West and the Indian Ocean. An Oneiric Horizon', in *Time, Work and Culture in the Middle Ages*, ed. J. le Goff, trans. A. Goldhammer (Chicago, 1980), pp. 189–200

Goff, J. le, 'Reims, City of Coronation', in *Realms of Memory: The Construction of the French Past*, ed. P. Nora, English trans. A. Goldhammer, ed. L. D. Kritzman (New York, 1996), pp. 193–251

Goff, J. le, 'Laughter in the Middle Ages', in *A Cultural History of Humour: From Antiquity to the Present Day*, ed. J. N. Bremmer and H. W. Roodenburg (Cambridge, 1997), pp. 40–53

Goffart, W., 'The Supposedly "Frankish" Table of Nations: An Edition and Study', *Frühmittelalterliche Studien* 17 (1983), 98–130

Goldenberg, D. M., *The Curse of Ham: Race and Slavery in Early Judaism, Christianity, and Islam* (Princeton, 2003)

Goldenberg, D., 'Racism, Color Symbolism, and Color Prejudice', in *The Origins of Racism in the West*, ed. M. Eliav-Feldon, B. Isaac and J. Ziegler (Cambridge, 2009), pp. 88–108

Görich, K., *Friedrich Barbarossa: Eine Biographie* (Munich, 2011)
Görlich, P., *Zür Frage des Nationalbewußtseins in ostdeutschen Quellen des 12. bis 14. Jahrhunderts* (Marburg, 1964)
Goubert, P. and Y. Lequin, *La mosaïque France: Histoire des étrangers et de l'immigration* (Paris 1988)
Gow, A. C., 'Fra Mauro's World View: Authority and Empircal Evidence on a Venetian mappamundi', in *The Hereford World Map: Medieval World Maps and their Context*, ed. P. D. A. Harvey (London, 2006), pp. 405–14
Gransden, A., 'Realistic Observation in Twelfth-Century England', *Speculum* 47/1 (1972), 29–51
Graus, F., 'Die Entstehung der mittelalterlichen Staaten in Mitteleuropa', *Historica* 10 (1965), 5–65
Graus, F., *Die Nationenbildung der Westslawen im Mittelalter* (Sigmaringen, 1980)
Graus, F., 'Troja und trojanische Herkunftssage im Mittelalter', in *Kontinuität und Transformation der Antike im Mittelalter: Veröffentlichung der Kongreßakten zum Freiburger Symposion des Mediävistenverbandes*, ed. W. Erzgräber (Sigmaringen, 1989), pp. 25–43
Green, M., 'The Re-creation of Pantegni, Practica, book viii', in *Constantine the African and 'Alī ibn al-'Abbās al-Maǧūsī: The Pantegni and Related Texts*, ed. C. Burnett and D. Jacquart (Leiden, 1994), pp. 121–60
Green, M. H., 'Salerno on the Thames: The Genesis of Anglo-Norman Medical Literature', in *Language and Culture in Medieval Britain: The French of England c. 1100–c. 1500*, ed. J. Wogan-Browne e.a.. (Woodbridge, 2009), pp. 220–34
Greetham, D., 'The Fabulous Geography of John Trevisa's Translation of Bartholomaeus Anglicus' De proprietatibus rerum' (unpublished dissertation, City University, New York, 1974)
Greetham, D. C., 'The Concept of Nature in Bartholomaeus Anglicus († 1230)', *Journal of the History of Ideas* 41/4 (1980), 663–77
Gregory, D., 'Imaginative Geographies', *Progress in Human Geography* 19 (1995), 447–85
Greilsammer, M., *L'Usurier chrétien, un Juif métaphorique?: Histoire de l'exclusion des prêteurs lombards (XIIIe–XVIIe siècle)* (Rennes, 2012)
Grevin, B., 'De la rhétorique des nations à la théorie des races', available at http://gas.ehess.fr/docannexe/fichier/107/grevin.pdf (accessed 20 August 2020) gas.ehess.fr/docannexe.php?id=107
Groebner, V., '*Complexio*/Complexion: Categorizing Individual Natures, 1250–1600', in *The Moral Authority of Nature*, ed. L. Daston and F. Vidal (Chicago, 2004), pp. 361–83
Grundmann, H., 'Sacerdotium – Regnum – Studium: Zur Wertung der Wissenschaft im 13. Jahrhundert', *Archiv für Kulturgeschichte* 34 (1952), 5–21
Guenée, B., 'Les généalogies entre l'histoire et la politique: La fierté d'être Capétien, en France, au Moyen Âge', *Annales: Économies, Sociétés, Civilisations* 33/3 (1978), 450–77
Guenée, B., *States and Rulers in Later Medieval Europe*, trans. J. Vale (Oxford, 1985)
Hage, G., *White Nation: Fantasies of White Supremacy in a Multicultural Society* (New York, 2000)
Hahn, T., 'The Difference the Middle Ages Makes: Color and Race before the Modern World', *Journal of Medieval and Early Modern Studies* 31/1 (2001), 1–37

Hall, E., *Inventing the Barbarian: Greek Self-Definition through Tragedy* (Oxford, 1989)
Hankey, A. T., 'Civic Pride versus Feelings for Italy in the Age of Dante', in *Medieval Europeans: Studies in Ethnic Identity and National Perspectives*, ed. A. P. Smyth (New York, 2002), pp. 196–216
Harbert, B. (ed.), *A Thirteenth-Century Anthology of Rhetorical Poems: Glasgow ms Hunterian V.8.14* (Toronto, 1975)
Harris, J. G., *Foreign Bodies and the Body Politic: Discourses of Social Pathology in Early Modern England* (Cambridge, 2006)
Harrison, M., *Climates and Constitutions: Health, Race, Environment and British Imperialism in India, 1600–1850* (New Delhi, 1999)
Harrison, T., *Greeks and Barbarians* (Edinburgh, 2002)
Hartog, F., *The Mirror of Herodotus: The Representation of the Other in the Writing of History* (Berkeley, 1988)
Harvey, A. D., *Body Politic: Political Metaphor and Political Violence* (Newcastle, 2007)
Harvey, E. R., *The Inward Wits: Psychological Theory in the Middle Ages and the Renaissance* (London, 1975)
Harvey, P. D. A., *The Hereford World Map: Medieval World Maps and Their Context* (London, 2006)
Haskins, C. H., *The Renaissance of the Twelfth Century* (Cambridge MA, 1927)
Hassell, J. W., *Middle French Proverbs, Sentences, and Proverbial Phrases* (Toronto, 1982)
Hassig, D., *The Mark of the Beast: The Medieval Bestiary in Art, Life, and Literature* (New York, 1999)
Hastings, A., *The Construction of Nationhood: Ethnicity, Religion and Nationalism* (Cambridge, 1997)
Haubrichs, W., 'Veriloquium nominis: Zur Namensexegese im frühen Mittelalter', in *Verbum et signum: Beiträge zur mediävistischen Bedeutungsforschung*, ed. H. Fromm, W. Harms, U. Ruberg and E. F. Ohly, 2 vols. (Munich, 1975), i, 231–56
Hauréau, B. (ed.), *Notices et extraits de quelques manuscrits latins de la Bibliothèque Nationale*, 6 vols. (Paris, 1890–93)
Haye, T., 'Deutschland und die deutschen Lande im spiegel einer lateinischen Spruchsammlung', *Beiträge zur Geschichte der deutschen Sprache und Literatur* 131/2 (2009), 308–17
Heng, G., *Empire of Magic: Medieval Romance and the Politics of Cultural Fantasy* (New York, 2003)
Heng, G., *The Invention of Race in the European Middle Ages* (Cambridge, 2018)
Hillgarth, J. N., 'Historiography in Visigothic Spain', in *La storiografia altomedievale: 10–16 aprile 1969*, ed. G. Vinay (Spoleto, 1970), pp. 261–311
Hirschi, C., *The Origins of Nationalism: An Alternative History from Ancient Rome to Early Modern Germany* (Cambridge, 2012)
Hirschi, C., 'Duck or Quack. On the Lack of Scholarly Soundness and Decorum in Joep Leerssen's Review', *Studies on National Movements* 2 (2014), 25–37
Histoire littéraire de la France. XIII siècle, 46 vols. (Paris, 1733–2018)
Hobsbawm, E. and T. Ranger (ed.), *The Invention of Tradition* (Cambridge, 1983)
Hobsbawm, E. J., *Nations and Nationalism since 1780: Programma, Myth, Reality* (Cambridge, 1990)

Hodgkin, R. H., *A History of the Anglo-Saxons*, 2 vols. (Oxford, 1952)
Hodgson, N. R., 'Reinventing Normans as Crusaders? Ralph of Caen's *Gesta Tancredi*', in *Anglo-Norman Studies 30: Proceedings of the Battle Conference 2007*, ed. C. P. Lewis (Woodbridge, 2008), 117–32
Hoffmann, R. C., 'Outsiders by Birth and Blood: Racist Ideologies and Realities around the Periphery of Europe', in *The Medieval Frontiers of Latin Christendom: Expansion, Contraction, Continuity*, ed. J. Muldoon and F. Fernández-Armesto (Aldershot, 2008)
Hoffmann, R. C., *An Environmental History of Medieval Europe* (Cambridge, 2014)
Hollister, C. Warren (ed.), *The Twelfth-Century Renaissance* (New York, 1969)
Hollister, C. Warren, *Henry I* (New Haven, 2001)
Hoogvliet, M., *Pictura et scriptura: Textes, images et herméneutique des 'mappae mundi' (XIIIe–XVIe siècle)* (Turnhout, 2007)
Hoppenbrouwers, P., 'Medieval Peoples Imagined', in *Imagology: The Cultural Construction and Literary Representation of National Characters: A Critical Survey*, ed. M. Beller and J. Leerssen (Amsterdam, 2007), pp. 45–62
Hoppenbrouwers, P., 'The Dynamics of National Identity in the Later Middle Ages', in *Networks, Regions and Nations: Shaping Identities in the Low Countries, 1300–1650*, ed. R. Stein and J. Pollmann (Leiden, 2010), pp. 19–42
Horden, P., 'Regimen and Travel in the Mediterranean', in *Mobility and Travel in the Mediterranean from Antiquity to the Middle Ages*, ed. R. Schlesier and U. Zellmann (Münster, 2004), pp. 117–32
Horden, P., 'What's Wrong with Early Medieval Medicine', *Social History of Medicine* 24/1 (2009), 5–25
Howe, N., *The Old English Catalogue Poems* (Copenhagen, 1985)
Howe, N., *Migration and Mythmaking in Anglo-Saxon England* (New Haven, 1989)
Howe, N., 'An Angle on this Earth: Sense of Place in Anglo-Saxon England', *Bulletin of the John Rylands University Library of Manchester* 82/1 (2000), 3–27
Huizinga, J., 'Patriotisme en nationalisme in de Europeesche geschiedenis tot het einde der negentiende eeuw', in *Verzamelde werken*, ed. J. Huizinga, 9 vols. (Haarlem, 1948–53), iv, 497–554
Huizinga, J., *Homo Ludens: A Study of the Play-Element in Culture* (Boston, 1955)
Huntsman, J. F., 'Grammar', in *The Seven Liberal Arts in the Middle Ages*, ed. D. L. Wagner (Bloomington, 1983), pp. 58–95
Huscroft, R., *Ruling England, 1042–1217* (Harlow, 2005)
Hyde, J. K., 'Medieval Descriptions of Cities', *Bulletin of the John Rylands Library* 48 (1965/66), 308–40
Isaac, B., *The Invention of Racism in Classical Antiquity* (Princeton, 2004)
Jacquart, D., *Le milieu médical en France du xiie au xve siècle: En annexe 2e supplément au 'Dictionaire' d'Ernest Wickersheimer* (Geneva, 1981)
Jacquart, D., *Le médicine médiévale dans le cadre Parisien: xive–xve siècle* (Paris, 1998)
Jaeger, C. S., *The Origins of Courtliness: Civilizing Trends and the Formation of Courtly Ideals, 939–1210* (Philadelphia, 1985)
Jaeger, C. S., *The Envy of Angels: Cathedral Schools and Social Ideals in Medieval Europe, 950–1200* (Philadelphia, 1994)

Jansen-Sieben, R., 'Een Middelnederlands maandregimen uit de 14e eeuw', in *Verslagen en mededelingen van de Koninklijke Academie voor Nederlandse taal- en letterkunde (nieuwe reeks). Jaargang 1971* (Gent, 1972), pp. 171–209

Jeauneau, É., Translatio studii: *The Transmission of Learning: A Gilsonian Theme* (Toronto, 1995)

Jeay, M., *Le commerce des mots: L'usage des listes dans la littérature médiévale (xiie–xve siècles)* (Geneva, 2006)

Jenkins, R., *Rethinking Ethnicity: Arguments and Explorations* (2nd edn, London, 2008)

Johnson, L., 'Imagining Communities: Medieval and Modern', in *Concepts of National Identity in the Middle Ages*, ed. S. Forde, L. Johnson and A. V. Murray (Leeds, 1995), pp. 1–19

Johnson, W., 'The Myth of Jewish Male Menses', *Journal of Medieval History* 24 (1998), 273–95

Jones, C. W., 'Some Introductory remarks on Bede's Commentary on Genesis', *Sacris Erudiri* 19 (1969/70), 115–98

Jones, P. J, *The Italian City-State: From Commune to Signoria* (Oxford, 1997)

Jones, W. R., 'England against the Celtic Fringe: A Study in Cultural Stereotypes', *Journal of World History / Cahiers d'histoire mondiale* 13 (1971), 155–71

Jones, W. R., 'The Image of the Barbarian in Medieval Europe', *Comparative Studies in Society and History* 13/4 (1971), 376–407

Jordan, W. C., 'John Pecham on the Crusade', *Crusades* 9 (2010) 159–71

Jüthner, J., *Hellenen und Barbaren: Aus der Geschichte des Nationalbewusstseins* (Leipzig, 1923)

Kamtekar, R., 'Studying Ancient Political Thought through Ancient Philosophers: The Case of Aristotle and Natural Slavery', *Polis: The Journal for Ancient Greek Political Thought* 33 (2016), 150–71

Kantorowicz, E. H., *The King's Two Bodies: A Study in Medieval Political Theology* (Princeton, 1957)

Kaplan, M. L., *Figuring Racism in Medieval Christianity* (New York, 2019)

Kästner, H., 'Der großmächtige Riese und Recke Theuton: Etymologische Spurensuche nach dem Urvater der Deutschen am Ende des Mittelalters', *Zeitschrift für deutsche Philologie* 110 (1991), 68–97

Kaye, J., *A History of Balance, 1250–1375: The Emergence of a New Model of Equilibrium and its Impact on Thought* (Cambridge, 2014)

Keen, M., *Chivalry* (New Haven, 2005)

Kelly, D., *The Arts of Poetry and Prose* (Turnhout, 1991)

Kempshall, M. S., *The Common Good in Late Medieval Political Thought* (Oxford, 1999)

Kendall, C. B., 'Imitation and the Venerable Bede's Historia Ecclesiastica', in *Saints, Scholars and Heroes: Studies in Medieval Culture in Honour of Charles W. Jones*, ed. M. H. King and W. M. Stevens, 2 vols. (Collegeville MN, 1979), i, 161–90

Kendrick, T. D., *St James in Spain* (London, 1960)

Kern, F., 'Der mittelalterliche Deutsche in französischer Ansicht', *Historische Zeitschrift* 108 (1912), 237–54

Kibre, P., *The Nations in the Mediaeval Universities* (Cambridge MA, 1948)

Kienast, W., *Deutschland und Frankreich in der Kaiserzeit (900–1270): Weltkaiser und Einzelkönige* (Stuttgart, 1974–75)
Kim, K., *Aliens in Medieval Law: The Origins of Modern Citizenship* (Cambridge, 2000)
Kinoshita, S., '"Pagans are wrong and Christians are right": Alterity, Gender, and Nation in the *Chanson de Roland*', *Journal of Medieval and Early Modern Studies* 31/1 (2001), 79–111
Kirn, P., *Aus der Frühzeit des Nationalgefühls: Studien zur deutschen und französischen Geschichte sowie zu den Nationalitätenkämpfen auf den Britischen Inseln* (Leipzig, 1943)
Kisch, G., 'Nationalism and Race in Medieval Law', in *Ausgewählte Schriften*, ed. G. Kisch, 3 vols. (Sigmaringen, 1978–80), iii, 179–204
Klibansky, R., E. Panofsky and F. Saxl, *Saturn and Melancholy: Studies in the History of Natural Philosophy, Religion, and Art* (rev. edn, London, 1964)
Kline, N. R., *Maps of Medieval Thought: The Hereford Paradigm* (Woodbridge, 2001)
Knoppers, L. L. and J. B. Landes (ed.), *Monstrous Bodies/Political Monstrosities in Early Modern Europe* (Ithaca, 2004)
Kohn, H., *The Idea of Nationalism: A Study in its Origins and Background* (New York, 1944)
Koht, H., 'A Specific Sense of the Word *patria* in Norse and Norman Latin', *Archivum Latinitas Medii Aevi* 2 (1925), 93–6
Koht, H., 'The Dawn of Nationalism in Europe', *The American Historical Review* 52/2 (1946/1947), 265–80
Koselleck, R., *Vergangene Zukunft: Zur Semantik geschichtlicher Zeiten* (Frankfurt am Main, 1979)
Kot, S., 'Old International Insults and Praises: I. The Medieval Period', *Harvard Slavic Studies* 2 (1954), 181–210
Krämer, U., '*Translatio imperii et studii*': Zum Geschichts- und Kulturverständnis in der französischen Literatur des Mittelalters und der frühen Neuzeit* (Bonn, 1996)
Kretschmann, C., 'Einsatz für Deutschland? Die Frankfurter Historiker Walter Platzhoff und Paul Kirn im "Dritten Reich"', in *Frankfurter Wissenschaftler zwischen 1933 und 1945*, ed. J. Kobes and J. O. Hesse (Göttingen, 2008), pp. 5–32
Kruger, S. F., *The Spectral Jew: Conversion and Embodiment in Medieval Europe* (Minneapolis, 2006)
Künzel, R., *The Plow, the Pen and the Sword: Images and Self-Images of Medieval People in the Low Countries*, trans. C. Weeda (Abingdon, 2017)
Kupfer, M., 'Medieval World Maps: Embedded Images, Interpretive Frames', *Word & Image* 10/3 (1994), 262–88
Lacombe, G., 'An Unpublished Document on the Great Interdict (1207–1213)', *Catholic Historical Review* 15 (1929/1930), 408–20
Lafferty, M. K., 'Mapping Human Limitations: The Tomb Ecphrases in Walter of Châtillon's Alexandreis', *The Journal of Medieval Latin* 4/4 (1994), 64–81
Lafferty, M. K., *Walter of Châtillon's Alexandreis: Epic and the Problem of Historical Understanding* (Turnhout, 1998)
Lagarde, P. de, 'Agathangelos', *Abhandlungen der Königlichen Gesellschaft der Wissenschaften zu Göttingen, Historisch-Philologische Klasse* 35 (1889)

Land, K. van 't, 'The Rise and Fall of Human Life: Theory on Life Course, Nutrition and Sperm in Late Medieval University Medicine' (unpublished dissertation, Radboud University Nijmegen, 2020)

Lanfranchi, P., 'Foetor judaicus: Archéologie d'un préjugé', in *Ékklèsia: Approches croisées d'histoire politique et religieuse: Mélanges offerts à* Marie-Françoise Baslez, ed. C. Bonnet and F. Briquel-Chatonnet (Toulouse, 2017), pp. 119–33

Langlois, C.-V., 'Les Anglais du Moyen Âge d'après les sources françaises', *Revue historique* 52/2 (1893), 298–315

Latowsky, A. A., *Emperor of the World: Charlemagne and the Construction of Imperial Authority, 800–1229* (Ithaca, 2013)

Lavezzo, K., *Angels on the Edge of the World: Geography, Literature, and the English Community, 1000–1534* (Ithaca, 2006)

Lecuppre-Desjardin, E. and A.-L. Van Bruaene (ed.), *De Bono Communi: The Discourse and Practice of the Common Good in the European City (13th-16th c.)/ Discours et pratique du Bien Commun dans les villes d'Europe (XIIIe au XVIe siècle)* (Turnhout, 2010)

Leerssen, J., *National Thought in Europe: A Cultural History* (rev. edn, Amsterdam, 2006)

Leerssen, J., 'Character (Moral)', in *Imagology: The Cultural Construction and Literary Representation of National Characters: A Critical Survey*, ed. M. Beller and J. Leerssen (Amsterdam, 2007), pp. 284–90

Leerssen, J., 'The Baton and the Frame: Or, Tradition and Recollection', *Studies on National Movements* 2 (2014), 13–23

Leerssen, J., 'Response to Caspar Hirschi', *Studies on National Movements* 2 (2014), 35–48

Leff, G., *Paris and Oxford Universities in the Thirteenth and Fourteenth Centuries: An Institutional and Intellectual History* (London, 1968)

Lehmann, P., *Parodistische Texte: Beispiele zur lateinischen Parodie im Mittelalter* (Munich, 1923)

Lehmann, P., *Mitteilungen aus Handschriften*, 9 vols. (Munich, 1929–50)

Lehmann, P., 'Eine Sammlung mittellateinischer Gedichte aus dem Ende des 12.Jahrhunderts', *Historische Vierteljahrschrift* 30 (1935), 20–58, 415–16

Lehmann, P., *Die Parodie im Mittelalter* (Stuttgart, 1963)

Lenz, F. W., *Das Pseudo-Ovidische Gedicht 'De Lombardo et Lumaca'* (S. I., 1957)

Le Roux de Lincy, A. J. V., *Le livre des proverbes français: Précédée de recherches historiques sur les proverbes français et leur emploi dans la littérature du moyen âge et de la renaissance*, 2 vols. (Paris, 1859)

Levine, L. W., *Black Culture and Black Consciousness: Afro-American Folk Thought from Slavery to Freedom* (New York, 1977)

Lewis, S., 'Tractatus adversus Judaeos in the Gulbenkian Apocalypse', *The Art Bulletin* 68/4 (1986), 543–66

Liebermann, F., 'Raginald von Canterbury', *Neues Archiv der Gesellschaft für Ältere Deutsche Geschichtskunde zur Beförderung einer Gesamtausgabe der Quellenschriften deutscher Geschichten des Mittelalters* 13 (1888), 517–56

Lindner, A., *The Jews in the Legal Sources of the Early Middle Ages* (Detroit, 1997)

Lipton, S., *Images of Intolerance: The Representation of Jews and Judaism in the Bible moralisée* (Berkeley, 1999)

Livingston, C. H., 'The Fabliau "Des deux Anglais et de l'anel"', *Publications of the Modern Language Association of America* 40/2 (1925), 217–24

Long, R. J., 'Introduction', in *De proprietatibus rerum, libri III–IV*, ed. R. J. Long (Turnhout, 2007)

Lozovsky, N., *'The Earth Is Our Book': Geographical Knowledge in the Latin West ca. 400–1000* (Ann Arbor, 2000)

Ludat, H., 'Farbenbezeichnungen in Völkernamen: Ein Beitrag zu asiatisch-osteuropäischen Kulturbeziehungen', *Saeculum* 4 (1953), 138–54

Lugt, M. van der, 'La peau noire dans le science médiévale', *Micrologus: Natura, scienze e società medievali* 13 (2005), 439–75

Lusignan, S., 'L'université de Paris comme composante de l'identité du royaume de France: Étude sur le thème de la *translatio studii*', in *Identité régionale et conscience nationale en France et en Allemagne du Moyen Âge à l'époque moderne: Actes du colloque organisé par l'Université Paris XII – Val de Marne, l'Institut Universitaire de France et l'Institut Historique Allemand à l'Université Paris XII et à la Fondation Singer-Polignac, les 6, 7 et 8 octobre 1993*, ed. R. Babel and J.-M. Moeglin (Sigmaringen, 1997), pp. 59–72

Lydon, J. F., 'Nation and Race in Medieval Ireland', in *Concepts of National Identity in the Middle Ages*, ed. S. Forde, L. Johnson and A. V. Murray (Leeds, 1995), pp. 103–24

MacColl, A., 'The Meaning of "Britain" in Medieval and Early Modern England', *Journal of British Studies* 45 (2006), 248–69

MacEvitt, C. H., *The Crusades and the Christian World of the East: Rough Tolerance* (Philadephia, 2008)

Macray, W. D., *Catalogi codicum manuscriptorum Bibliothecae Bodleianae pars nona codices a viro clarissimo Kenelm Digby, Eq. Aur., anno 1634 donatos, complectens: adiecto indice nominum et rerum* (Oxford, 1883). Reprinted with corrigenda by R. W. Hunt and A. G. Watson (Oxford, 1999)

Malsch, J., *Die Characteristik der Völker im altfranzösischen, nationalen Epos* (Heidelberg, 1912)

Mann, J., 'Introduction', in *Ysengrimus: Text with Translation, Commentary and Introduction*, ed. and trans. J. Mann (Leiden, 1987)

Marková, I., 'Social Identities and Social Representations: How Are They Related?', in *Social Representations and Identity: Content, Process, and Power*, ed. G. Moloney and I. Walker (Basingstoke, 2007), pp. 215–36

Marschner, P. S., 'The Depiction of the Saracen Foreign Rule in the Prophetic Chronicle Through Biblical Knowledge', *Journal of Transcultural Medieval Studies* 5/2 (2018), 215–39

Maschke, E., *Das Erwachen des Nationalbewusstseins im deutsch-slavischen Grenzraum* (Leipzig, 1933)

Matzke, J. E., 'Some Examples of French as Spoken by Englishmen in Old French Literature', *Modern Philology* 3 (1905), 1–14

McGinn, B., *Visions of the End: Apocalyptic Traditions in the Middle Ages* (New York, 1998)

McGowan, J. P., 'Anglo-Latin Prose', in *A Companion to Anglo-Saxon Literature*, ed. P. Pulsiano and E. Treharne (Oxford, 2001), pp. 296–323

McKenzie, S., 'The Westward Progression of History on Medieval Mappaemundi: An Investigation of the Evidence', in *The Hereford World Map: Medieval World Maps and Their Context*, ed. P. D. A. Harvey (London, 2006), 335–44

McKitterick, R., 'Le pouvoir des mots: Les glossaires, la mémoire culturelle et la transmission du savoir au Haut Moyen Âge', in *Les Cahiers colombaniens, 2013: Les écoles monastiques au haut Moyen Âge*, ed. P. Riché (Luxeuil-les-Bains, 2013), pp. 16–58

Meaney, A., 'The Practice of Medicine in England About the Year 1000', *Social History of Medicine* 13/2 (2000), 221–37

Meier, P. G., *Catalogus codicum manu scriptorum qui in Bibliotheca Monasterii Einsidlensis O.S.B. servantur*, 3 vols. (Einsiedeln, 1899)

Mellinkoff, R., *The Mark of Cain* (Berkeley, 1981)

Mellinkoff, R., *Outcasts: Signs of Otherness in Northern European Art of the Late Middle Ages*, 2 vols. (Berkeley, 1993)

Meloni, M., 'Porous Bodies: Environmental Biopower and the Politics of Life in Ancient Rome', *Theory, Culture & Society*, published online 11 June 2020 at Porous Bodies: Environmental Biopower and the Politics of Life in Ancient Rome – Maurizio Meloni, 2020 (sagepub.com)

Mendels, J. I. H., 'Nationalismus in der mittelhochdeutschen und mittelniederländischen Literatur', in Actes du IVe Congrès de l'Association Internationale de littérature Comparée, Fribourg, 1964 = Proceedings of the IVth Congress of the International Comparative Literature Association, ed. F. Jost (The Hague, 1966), pp. 298–308

Merrills, A. H., *History and Geography in Late Antiquity* (Cambridge, 2005)

Metzler, I., 'Perceptions of Hot Climate in Medieval Cosmography and Travel Literature', *Reading Medieval Studies* 23 (1997), 69–105

Meyer, H., *Die Enzyklopädie des Bartholomäus Anglicus: Untersuchungen zur Überlieferungs- und Rezeptionsgeschichte von 'De Proprietatibus Rerum'* (Munich, 2000)

Meyer, P., 'Troisième rapport sur une mission littéraire en Angleterre et en Écosse', *Archives des missions scientifiques et littéraires, 2ème série* 5 (1868), 139–272

Meyvaert, P., '"Rainaldus est malus sciptor Francigenus" – Voicing National Antipathy in the Middle Ages', *Speculum* 66/4 (1991), 743–63

Miller, K., *Mappae Mundi: Die ältesten Weltkarten*, 6 vols. (Stuttgart, 1895–98)

Minnis, A., *From Eden to Eternity: Creations of Paradise in the Later Middle Ages* (Philadelphia, 2015)

Miramon, C. de, 'Noble Dogs, Noble Blood: The Invention of the Concept of Race in the Late Middle Ages', in *The Origins of Racism in the West*, ed. M. Eliav-Feldon, B. Isaac and J. Ziegler (Cambridge, 2009), pp. 200–16

Mitchell, J. B., 'The Matthew Paris Maps', *The Geographical Journal* 81/1 (1933), 27–34

Mohr, W., 'Zur Frage des Nationalismus im Mittelalter', *Annales Universitatis Saraviensis: Philosophie – Lettres* 2 (1953), 106–16

Mone, F., 'Nachweising lateinischer Gedichte', *Anzeiger für Künde der teutschen Vorzeit* 8 (1839), 597

Mone, F., 'Städte und Völkerspiegel', *Anzeiger für Künde der teutschen Vorzeit* 7 (1838), 507–8

Monnet, P., 'La "patria" médiévale vue d'Allemagne, entre construction impériale et identités régionales', *Le Moyen Âge* 107 (2001), 71–99

Montford, A., *Health, Sickness, Medicine and the Friars in the Thirteenth and Fourteenth Centuries* (Aldershot, 2004)

Moore, R. I., *The Formation of a Persecuting Society: Authority and Deviance in Western Europe, 950–1250* (2nd edn, Malden, 2007)

Moralejo Álvarez, S., 'El mapa de la diáspora apostólica en San Pedro de Rocas: notas para su interpretación y filiación en la tradición cartográfica de los "Beatos"', *Compostellanum* 31 (1986), 315–40

Moraw, P. (ed.), *Regionale Identität und soziale Gruppen im deutschen Mittelalter* (Berlin, 1992)

Morawski, J., 'Les recueils d'anciens proverbes français analysés et classes', *Romania* 48 (1922), 481–558

Morris, R., 'King Arthur and the Growth of French Nationalism', in *France and the British Isles in the Middle Ages and Renaissance: Essays by Members of Girton College, Cambridge, in Memory of Ruth Morgan*, ed. G. Jondorf and D. Dumville (Woodbridge, 1991), pp. 115–29

Mostert, M., 'Some Thoughts on Urban Schools, Urban Literacy, and the Development of Western Civilisation', in *Writing and the Administration of Medieval Towns: Medieval Urban Literacy i*, ed. M. Mostert and A. Adamska (Turnhout, 2014), pp. 337–48

Mostert, M., 'Studying Medieval Urban Literacy: A Provisional State of Affairs', available at https://medievalliteracy.wp.hum.uu.nl/wp-content/uploads/sites/34/2013/01/Medieval-Urban-Literacy.pdf (accessed 1 September 2020)

Muldoon, J., *Identity on the Medieval Irish Frontier: Degenerate Englishmen, Wild Irishmen, Middle Nations* (Gainesville, 2003)

Muldoon, J. and F. Fernández-Armesto (ed.), *The Medieval Frontiers of Latin Christendom: Expansion, Contraction, Continuity* (Aldershot, 2008)

Müller, F. W., 'Zur Geschichte des Wortes und Begriffes "nation" im französischen Schrifttum des Mittelalters bis zur Mitte des 15. Jahrhunderts', *Romanische Forschungen* 58–9 (1947), 247–321

Müller, U., *Kreuzzugsdichtung* (Tübingen, 1969)

Müller, U., '"Deutschland, Deutschland, Über Alles"? Walther von der Vogelweide, Hoffmann von Fallersleben and the "Song of the Germans": Medievalism, Nationalism and/or Facism', in *Medievalism in the Modern World: Essays in Honour of Leslie Workman*, ed. R. Utz and T. A. Shippey (Turnhout, 1998), pp. 117–29

Munck, B. de, *Guilds, Labour and the Urban Body Politic: Fabricating Community in the Southern Netherlands, 1300–1800* (New York, 2018)

Münkler, H., 'Nation als politische Idee im frühneuzeitlichen Europa', in *Nation und Literatur im Europa der Frühen Neuzeit: Akten des I. Internationalen Osnabrücker Kongresses zur Kulturgeschichte der Frühen Neuzeit*, ed. K. Garber (Tübingen, 1989), pp. 56–86

Münkler, M., 'Experiencing Strangeness: Monstrous Peoples on the Edge of the Earth as Depicted on Medieval Mappae Mundi', *The Medieval History Journal* 5 (2002), 195–222

Murphy, J. C., 'The Early Franciscan Studium at the University of Paris', in *Studium generale: Studies offered to Astrik L. Gabriel by his former students at the Mediaeval Institute, University of Notre Dame, on the occasion of his election as an Honorary Doctor of the Ambrosiana in Milan*, ed. L. S. Domonkos and R. J. Schneider (Notre Dame, 1967), pp. 161–203

Murray, A., *Reason and Society in the Middle Ages* (Oxford, 1978)

Murray, A., 'Bede and the Unchosen Race', in *Power and Identity in the Middle Ages: Essays in Memory of Rees Davies*, ed. H. Pryce and J. Watts (Oxford, 2007), pp. 52–67

Murray, A. V., 'Ethnic Identity in the Crusader States: The Frankish Race and the Settlement of Outremer', in *Concepts of National Identity in the Middle Ages*, ed. S. Forde, L. Johnson and A. V. Murray (Leeds, 1995), pp. 59–73

Murray, A. V., 'National Identity, Language and Conflict in the Crusades to the Holy Land, 1096–1192', in *The Crusades and the Near East*, ed. C. Kostick (London, 2011), pp. 107–30

Nederman, C. J., 'The Physiological Significance of the Organic Metaphor in John of Salisbury's "Policraticus"', *History of Political Thought* 8/2 (1987), 211–23

Nederman, C. J., 'Nature, Sin and the Origins of Society: The Ciceronian Tradition in Medieval Political Thought', *Journal of the History of Ideas* 49/1 (1988), 3–26

Nederman, C. J., 'Nature, Ethics, and the Doctrine of "Habitus": Aristotelian Moral Psychology in the Twelfth-Century', *Traditio* 45 (1989–90), 87–110

Nederman, C. J., *Community and Consent: The Secular Political Theory of Marsiglio of Padua's Defensor Pacis* (London, 1995)

Nederman, C. J., 'Body Politics: The Diversification of Organic Metaphors in the Later Middle Ages', *Pensiero Politico Medievale* 2 (2004), 59–87

Nederman, C. J., 'The Living Body Politic: The Diversification of Organic Metaphors in Nicole Oresme and Christine de Pizan', in *Healing the Body Politic: The Politic Thought of Christine de Pizan*, ed. K. Green and C. J. Mews (Turnhout, 2005), pp. 19–33

Neilson, G., '*Caudatus Anglicus*: A Medieval Slander', *Transactions of the Glasgow Archaeological Society, new series* 2 (1896), 441–77

Nelson, J. L., 'Kingship and Empire in the Carolingian World', in *Carolingian Culture: Emulation and Innovation*, ed. R. McKitterick (Cambridge, 1994) pp. 52–87

Newhauser, R., *The Treatise on Vices and Virtues in Latin and the Vernacular* (Turnhout, 1993)

Nirenberg, D., *Communities of Violence: Persecution of Minorities in the Middle Ages* (Princeton, 1996)

Nirenberg, D., 'Was there Race before Modernity? The Example of "Jewish" Blood in Late Medieval Spain', in *The Origins of Racism in the West*, ed. M. Eliav-Feldon, B. Isaac and J. Ziegler (Cambridge, 2009), pp. 232–64

Norberg, D., *La poésie latine rythmique du haut Moyen Âge* (Stockholm, 1954)

O'Boyle, C., *The Art of Medicine: Medical Teaching at the University of Paris, 1215–1400* (Leiden, 1998)

Omont, H., 'Le recueil d'anciennes écritures de Pierre Hamon', *Bibliothèque de l'École des Chartres* 62 (1901), 57–73

Orbán, A. P., 'De omgang met "het verleden" van Rome in de oudchristelijke en middeleeuwse Latijnse literatuur', in *Omgang met het verleden*, ed. R. E. V. Stuip and C. Vellekoop (Hilversum, 2001), pp. 63–90

Pabst, B., 'Die Antike im Welt-Buch: Zum Umgang mit antiken Wissenssystemen und -inhalten im Bereich der mittelalterlichen Enzyklopädik', in *Persistenz und Rezeption: Weiterverwendung, Wiederverwendung und Neuinterpretation antiker Werke im Mittelalter*, ed. D. Boschung and S. Wittekind (Wiesbaden, 2008), pp. 33–64

Pagden, A., *European Encounters with the New World: From Renaissance to Romanticism* (New Haven, 1993)

Pagden, A., *The Idea of Europe: From Antiquity to the European Union* (Washington, 2002)

Pagden, A., 'The Peopling of the New World: Ethnos, Race and Empire in the Early-Modern World', in *The Origins of Racism in the West*, ed. M. Eliav-Feldon, B. Isaac and J. Ziegler (Cambridge, 2009), pp. 292–312

Park, K., 'The Meanings of Natural Diversity. Marco Polo on the "Division" of the World', in *Texts and Contexts in Ancient and Medieval Science: Studies on the Occasion of John E. Murdoch's Seventieth Birthday*, ed. E. Sylla and M. McVaugh (Leiden, 1997), pp. 134–47

Parsons, B., *Punishment and Medieval Education* (Melton, 2018)

Paterson, L. M., *The World of the Troubadours: Medieval Occitan Society, c. 1100–c. 1300* (Cambridge, 1993)

Peiper, R., 'Europäischer Völkerspiegel', *Anzeiger für Kunde der deutschen Vorzeit* 21 (1874), 102–6

Pepin, R. E., *Literature of Satire in the Twelfth Century: A Neglected Mediaeval Genre* (Lewiston, 1988)

Pfeffer, W. E., *Proverbs in Medieval Occitan Literature* (Gainsville, 1997)

Phillips, J. E., 'William of Malmesbury: Medical Historian of the Crusades', in *Discovering William of Malmesbury*, ed. R. M. Thomson, E. Dolmans and E. A. Winkler (Woodbridge, 2017), pp. 129–38

Phillips, J. R. S., *The Medieval Expansion of Europe* (Oxford, 1988)

Phillips, S., 'The Outer World of the European Middle Ages', in *Implicit Understandings: Observing, Reporting, and Reflecting on the Encounters between Europeans and other Peoples in the Early Modern Era*, ed. S. B. Schwartz (Cambridge, 1994), pp. 23–63

Planhol, X. de and P. Claval, *A Historical Geography of France*, trans. J. Lloyd (Cambridge, 1994)

Platelle, H., 'Le problème du scandale: Les nouvelles modes masculines aux XIe et XIIe siècles', *Revue Belge de Philologie et d'Histoire* 53/4 (1975), 1071–96

Pohl, W., 'Memory, Identity and Power in Lombard Italy', in *The Uses of the Past in the Early Middle Ages*, ed. Y. Hen and M. Innes (Cambridge, 2000), pp. 9–28

Pohl, W. and G. Heydemann (ed.), *Post-Roman Transitions: Christian and Barbarian Identities in the Early Medieval West* (Turnhout, 2013)

Pohl, W. and G. Heydemann (ed.), *Strategies of Identification: Ethnicity and Religion in Early Medieval Europe* (Turnhout, 2013)

Pollmann, J., *Memory in Early Modern Europe, 1500–1800* (Oxford, 2017)

Poole, K. R., 'Beatus of Liébana: Medieval Spain and the Othering of Islam', in *End of Days: Essays on the Apocalypse from Antiquity to Modernity*, ed. K. Kinane and M. A. Ryan (Jefferson, 2009), pp. 47–66

Post, G., 'Two Notes on Nationalism in the Middle Ages', *Traditio* 9 (1953), 281–320

Potts, C. W., '*Atque unum ex diversis gentibus populum effecit*: Historical Tradition and the Norman Identity', in *Anglo-Norman Studies 18: Proceedings of the Battle Conference 1995*, ed. C. Harper-Bill (Woodbridge, 1996), 139–52

Prak, M., 'Corporate Politics in the Low Countires: Guilds as Institutions, 14th to 18th Centuries', in *Craft Guilds in the Early Modern Low Countries: Work, Power, and Representation*, ed. M. Prak, C. Lis, J. Lucassen and H. Soly (Aldershot, 2006), pp. 74–106

Prak, M., *Citizens without Nations: Urban Citizenship in Europe and the World, c. 1000–1789* (Cambridge, 2018)

Pritchard, R. T., 'Introduction', in Walter of Châtillon, *The* Alexandreis, trans. R. T. Pritchard (Toronto, 1986)

Prompsault, J.-H.-R., *Discours sur les publications littéraires du Moyen-Âge* (Paris, 1835)

Rabinow, P. and N. Rose, 'Thoughts on the Concept of Biopower Today', *BioSocieties* 1 (2006), 195–217

Rāġib, Y., *Actes de vente d'esclaves et d'animaux d'Égypte médiévale*, 2 vols. (Cairo, 2002–6)

Randall, L. M. C., 'A Medieval Slander', *The Art Bulletin* 42/1 (1960), 25–38

Rather, L. J., 'The "Six Things Non-Natural": A Note on the Origins and Fate of a Doctrine and a Phrase', *Clio Medica* 3/4 (1968), 337–47

Rawcliffe, C., 'The Concept of Health in Late Medieval Society', in *Le interazioni fra economia e ambiente biologico nell' Europa preindustriale secc. XIII–XVIII*, ed. S. Cavaciocchi (Florence, 2010), pp. 317–34

Reicher, S., 'The Context of Social Identity: Domination, Resistance, and Change', *Political Psychology* 25/6 (2004), 921–45

Reichert, W., 'Lombarden als "merchant-bankers" im England des 13. und beginnenden 14. Jahrhunderts', in *Landesgeschichte als multidisziplinäre Wissenschaft: Festgabe für Franz Irsigler zum 60. Geburtstag*, ed. D. Ebeling, V. Henn, R. Holbach, W. Reichert, W. Schmid (Trier, 2001), pp. 77–134.

Remppis, M., *Die Vorstellungen von Deutschland im altfranzösischen Heldenepos und Roman und ihre Quellen* (Tübingen, 1911)

Resnick, I. M., 'Humoralism and Adam's Body: Twelfth-Century Debates and Petrus Alfonsi's *Dialogus Contra Judaeos*', *Viator* 36 (2005), 181–96

Resnick, I. M., *Marks of Distinctions: Christian Perceptions of Jews in the High Middle Ages* (Washington, 2012)

Reuter, T., 'John of Salisbury and the Germans', in *The World of John of Salisbury*, ed. M. Wilks (Oxford, 1984), pp. 415–25

Reuter, T., 'Past, Present and No Future in the Twelfth-Century Regnum Teutonicum', in *The Perception of the Past in Twelfth-Century Europe*, ed. P. Magdalino (London, 1992), pp. 15–36

Reynolds, S., 'Medieval *Origines Gentium* and the Community of the Realm', *History* 68 (1984), 375–90

Reynolds, S., 'What Do We Mean by "Anglo-Saxon" and "Anglo-Saxons"', *Journal of British Studies* 24 (1985), 395–414

Reynolds, S., *Kingdoms and Communities in Western Europe 900–1300* (Oxford, 1984)

Reynolds, S., 'The Idea of the Nation as a Political Community', in *Power and the Nation in European History*, ed. L. E. Scales and O. Zimmer (Cambridge, 2005), pp. 54–66

Ribémont, B., 'L'inconnu géographique des encyclopédies médiévales: Fermeture et étrangeté', in Espace vécu, mesuré, imaginé: Numéro en l'honneur de Christiane Deluz, ed. C. Bousquet-Labouérie (Paris, 1997), pp. 101–11

Ribémont, B., *La 'Renaissance' du xiie siècle et l'encyclopédisme* (Paris, 2002)

Ribémont, B., *Littérature et encyclopédies du Moyen Âge* (Orléans, 2002)

Richards, J., *Sex, Dissidence and Damnation: Minority Groups in the Middle Ages* (London, 1990)

Richards, M. P., 'Wulfstan and the Millennium', in *The Year 1000: Religious and Social Response to the Turning of the First Millennium*, ed. M. Frassetto (New York, 2002), pp. 41–8

Rickard, P., '"Anglois coué" and "L'Anglois qui couve"', *French Studies: A Quarterly Review* 7 (1953), 48–55

Rickard, P., *Britain in Medieval French Literature, 1100–1500* (Cambridge, 1956)

Rigaudière, A., *Penser et construire l'État dans la France du Moyen Âge (xiiie–xve siècle)* (Paris, 2003)

Rigg, A. G., *A History of Anglo-Latin Literature, 1066–1422* (Cambridge, 1992)

Rigg, A. G., 'Lawrence of Durham: Dialogues and Easter Poem: A Verse Translation', *The Journal of Medieval Latin* 7 (1997), 42–126

Rigg, A. G., 'Satire', in *Medieval Latin: An Introduction and Bibliographical Guide*, ed. F. A. C. Mantello and A. G. Rigg (Washington dc, 1996), pp. 532–68

Riley-Smith, J., 'Crusading as an Act of Love', in *History* 65 (1980), 177–92

Riley-Smith, J., *The First Crusade and the Idea of Crusading* (London, 1986)

Roach, A., 'Occitania Past and Present: Southern Consciousness in Medieval and Modern French Politics', *History Workshop Journal* 43 (1997), 1–37

Roberts, P. B., *Stephanus de Lingua-Tonante: Studies in the Sermons of Stephen Langton* (Toronto, 1968)

Robiglio, A. A., 'The Thinker as a Noble Man (bene natus) and Preliminary Remarks on the Medieval Concepts of Nobility', *Vivarium* 44 (2006), 205–47

Rollo, D., 'Gerald of Wales' *Topographia Hibernica*: Sex and the Irish Nation', *The Romantic Review* 86/2 (1995), 169–90

Rosenfeld, H., 'Die Bühne des Tegernseer Antichristspiels als Orbis terrarum', in *Literatur und Sprache im europäischen Mittelalter: Festschrift für Karl Langosch zum 70. Geburtstag*, ed. A. Önnerfors, J. Rathofer and F. Wagner (Darmstadt, 1973), pp. 63–74

Rothmann, M., 'Totius orbis descriptio: Die "Otia Imperialia" des Gervasius von Tilbury: Eine höfische Enzyklopädie und die scientia naturalis', in *Die Enzyklopädie im Wandel vom Hochmittelalter bis zur frühen Neuzeit*, ed. C. Meier (Munich, 2002), pp. 189–224

Rouse, R. H. and M. A. Rouse, '"Statim Invenire": Schools, Preachers, and New Attitudes to the Page', in *Renaissance and Renewal in the Twelfth Century*, ed. R. L. Benson, G. Constable and C. D. Lanham (Cambridge MA, 1982), pp. 201–25

Rouse, M. A., 'The Development of Research Tools in the Thirteenth Century', in *Authentic Witnesses: Approaches to Medieval Texts and Manuscripts*, ed. M. A. Rouse and R. H. Rouse (Notre Dame, 1991), pp. 221–55

Ruberg, U., 'Mappae Mundi des Mittelalters im Zusammenwirken von Text und Bild', in Text und Bild: Aspekte des Zusammenwirkens zweier Künste in Mittelalter und früher Neuzeit, ed. C. Meier and U. Ruberg (Wiesbaden, 1980), pp. 550–92

Rubenstein, J., *Nebuchadnezzar's Dream: The Crusades, Apocalyptic Prophecy, and the End of History* (New York, 2019)

Rubinstein, N., 'Florence and the Despots: Some Aspects of Florentine Diplomacy in the Fourteenth Century', *Transactions of the Royal Historical Society* 2 (1952), 21–45

Rüegg, W. and H. de Ridder-Symoens (ed.), *A History of the University in Europe*, 4 vols. (Cambridge, 1992–2011)

Russell, J. C., 'Master Henry of Avranches as an International Poet', *Speculum* 3/1 (1928), 34–63

Sager, A., 'Hungarians as "vremde" in Medieval Germany', in *Meeting the Foreign in the Middle Ages*, ed. A. Classen (New York, 2002), pp. 27–44

Said, E., *Orientalism* (reprint with a new preface, London, 2003)

Salem, S. I. and A. Kumar (ed. and trans.), *Science in the Medieval World: 'Book of the Categories of Nations'* (Austin, 1991)

Salomon, R. G., 'Aftermath to Opicinus de Canistris', *Journal of the Warburg and Courtauld Institutes* 25 (1962), 137–46

Salvat, M., 'Quelques échos des rivalités franco-anglaises dans les traductions de *De proprietatibus rerum* (XIIIe–XVe siècles)', *Bien dire et bien aprandre* 5 (1987), 101–12

Sawyer, P. H., 'The Wealth of England in the Eleventh Century', *Transactions of the Royal Historical Society*, Series 5, 15 (1965), 145–64

Scafi, A., *Mapping Paradise: A History of Heaven and Earth* (London, 2006)

Scales, L. E., 'France and the Empire: The Viewpoint of Alexander of Roes', *French History* 9/4 (1995), 394–416

Scales, L. E., 'Germen Militiae: War and German Identity in the Later Middle Ages', *Past and Present* 180 (2003), 41–82

Scales, L. E., 'Bread, Cheese and Genocide: Imagining the Destruction of Peoples in Medieval Western Europe', *History* 92 (2007), 284–300

Scales, L. E. and O. Zimmer (eds), *Power and the Nation in European History* (Cambridge, 2005)

Scales, L. E. and O. Zimmer, 'Introduction', in *Power and the Nation in European History*, ed. L. Scales and O. Zimmer (Cambridge, 2005), 1–29

Scherb, V. I., 'Assimilating Giants: The Appropriation of Gog and Magog in Medieval and Early Modern England', *Journal of Medieval and Early Modern Studies* 32/1 (2002), 59–84

Schieffer, R., 'Frankreich im Mittelalter', in *Mittelalterliche nationes – neuzeitliche Nationen: Probleme der Nationenbildung in Europa*, ed. A. Bues and R. Rexheuser (Wiesbaden, 1995), pp. 43–60

Schmidt, H.-J., 'Establishing an Alternative Territorial Pattern: The Provinces of the Mendicant Orders', in *Franciscan Organisation in the Mendicant Context: Formal and Informal Structures of the Friars' Lives and Ministry in the Middle Ages*, ed. M. Robson and J. Röhrkasten (Berlin, 2010), pp. 1–18

Schmidt-Chazan, M., 'Le point de vue des chroniqueurs de la France du Nord sur les Allemands dans la première moitié du XIIème siècle', *Centre de recherches internationales de l'Université de Metz: Travaux et Recherches* 5 (1973/2), 13–36

Schmidt-Chazan, M., 'Les traductions de la "Guerre des Gaules" et le sentiment national au Moyen Âge', in L'historiographie en Occident du Ve au XVe siècle: actes du congrès de la societé des historiens médiévistes de l'enseignement supérieur; Tours, 10–12 juin 1977/1980 (Tours, 1980), 387–407

Schmitt, J.-C., 'Les images de l'invective', in *L'invective au Moyen Âge: France, Espagne, Italie: Actes du Colloque L'invective au Moyen Âge, Paris, 4–6 février 1993*, ed. É. Beaumatin and M. Garcia (Paris, 1995), pp. 11–20

Schmugge, L., 'Über "nationale" Vorurteile im Mittelalter', *Deutsches Archiv für Erforschung des Mittelalters* 38 (1982), 439–59

Schneidmüller, B., *Nomen patriae: Die Entstehung Frankreichs in der politisch-geographischen Terminologie (10.–13. Jahrhundert)* (Sigmaringen, 1987)

Schneidmüller, B., 'Reich – Volk – Nation: Die Entstehung des deutschen Reiches und der deutschen Nation im Mittelalter', in *Mittelalterliche nationes – neuzeitliche Nationen: Probleme der Nationenbildung in Europa*, ed. A. Bues and R. Rexheuser (Wiesbaden, 1995), 73–102

Schönbach, A. E., 'Des Bartholomaeus Anglicus Beschreibung Deutschlands gegen 1240', *Mitteilungen des Instituts für Österreichische Geschichtsforschung* 27 (1906), 54–90

Schulze-Busacker, E., 'Renart, le jongleur étranger: Analyse thématique et linguistique à partir de la branche Ib du Roman de Renart (vv. 2403–2580 et 2857–3034)', in *Third International Beast Epic, Fable, and Fabliau Colloquium*, ed. J. Goossens and T. Sodmann (Cologne, 1981), pp. 380–91

Schulze-Busacker, E., *Proverbes et expressions proverbiales dans la littérature narrative du Moyen Âge français* (Geneva, 1985)

Schulze-Busacker, E., 'French Conceptions of Foreigners and Foreign Languages in the Twelfth and Thirteenth Centuries', *Romance Philology* 41 (1987–88), 24–47

Scior, V., *Das Eigene und das Fremde: Identität und Fremdheit in den Chroniken Adams von Bremen, Helmolds von Bosau und Arnold von Lübeck* (Berlin, 2002)

Scott, A. B., 'Some Poems Attributed to Richard of Cluny', in *Medieval Learning and Literature: Essays Presented to Richard William Hunt*, ed. J. J. G. Alexander and M. T. Gibson (Oxford, 1976), pp. 181–99

Se Boyar, G. E., 'Bartholomaeus Anglicus and his Encyclopaedia', *The Journal of English and Germanic Philology* 19 (1920), 168–89

Sère, B., 'Aristote et le bien commun au Moyen Âge: Une histoire, une historiographie', *Revue française d'histoire des idées politiques* 32 (2010), 277–92

Seton-Watson, H., *Nations and States: An Enquiry into the Origins of Nations and the Politics of Nationalism* (London, 1977)

Seymour, M. C., 'Some Medieval French Readers of De proprietatibus rerum', *Scriptorium* 28 (1974), 100–3

Seymour, M. C. e.a., *Bartholomaeus Anglicus and His Encyclopedia* (Aldershot, 1992)

Shaw, D., *Necessary Conjunctions: The Social Self in Medieval England* (Basingstoke, 2005)
Shogimen, T., 'Treating the Body Politic: The Medical Metaphor of Political Rule in Late Medieval Europe and Tokugawa Japan', *The Review of Politics* 70/1 (2008), 77–104
Simms, A., 'Core and Periphery in Medieval Europe: The Irish Experience in a Wider Context', in *Common Ground: Essays on the Historical Geography of Ireland Presented to T. Jones Hughes*, ed. W. J. Smyth and K. Whelan (Cork, 1988), pp. 22–40
Singer, S., *Thesaurus proverbiorum medii aevi: Lexikon der Sprichwörter des romanisch-germanischen Mittelalters*, 13 vols. (rev. edn Berlin, 1995–2002)
Siraisi, N. G., *Medieval and Early Renaissance Medicine: An Introduction to Knowledge and Practice* (Chicago, 1990)
Skinner, P., *Health and Medicine in Early Medieval Southern Italy* (Leiden, 1997)
Skinner, Q., *The Foundations of Modern Political Thought: Volume 1, The Renaissance* (16th edn, Cambridge, 20081978)
Smith, A. D., *The Ethnic Origins of Nations* (Oxford, 1987)
Smith, A. D., *National Identity* (London, 1991)
Smith, A. D., 'National Identities: Modern and Medieval?', in *Concepts of National Identity in the Middle Ages*, ed. S. Forde, L. Johnson and A. V. Murray (Leeds, 1995), pp. 21–46
Smith, A. D., *Myths and Memories of the Nation* (Oxford, 1999)
Smith, A. D., *The Nation in History: Historiographical Debates about Ethnicity and Nationalism* (Hanover, 2000)
Smith, A. D., *Chosen Peoples* (Oxford, 2003)
Smith, A. D., *The Cultural Foundations of Nations: Hierarchy, Covenant, and Republic* (Malden, 2008)
Smith, A. D., *Ethno-Symbolism and Nationalism: A Cultural Approach* (London, 2009)
Smith, N. D., 'Aristotle's Theory of Natural Slavery', *Phoenix* 37/2 (1983), 109–22
Snowden, F. M., *Before Color Prejudice: The Ancient View of Blacks* (Cambridge MA, 1983)
Southern, R. W., *Medieval Humanism, and Other Studies* (Oxford, 1970)
Speed, D., 'Bede's Creation of a Nation in his Ecclesiastical History', *Parergon* 10 (1992), 139–54
Spiegel, G. M., 'The Reditus Regni ad Stirpem Karoli Magni: A New Look', *French Historical Studies* 7/2 (1971), 145–74
Spiegel, G. M., 'The Cult of Saint Denis and Capetian Kingship', *Journal of Medieval History* 1 (1975), 43–70
Stafford, P., 'The Meanings of Hair in the Anglo-Norman World: Masculinity, Reform, and National Identity', in *Saints, Scholars, and Politicians: Gender as a Tool in Medieval Studies: Festschrift in Honour of Anneke Mulder-Bakker on the Occasion of her Sixty-Fifth Birthday*, ed. M. van Dijk and R. Nip (Turnhout, 2005), pp. 153–71
Stanzel, F. K., 'Das Nationalitätenschema in der Literatur und seine Entstehung zu Beginn der Neuzeit', in *Erstarrtes Denken: Studien zu Klischee, Stereotyp und Vorurteil in englischsprachiger Literatur*, ed. G. Blaicher (Tübingen, 1987), pp. 84–96
Stanzel, F., *Europäer: Ein imagologischer Essay* (Heidelberg, 1998)
Stanzel, F. K., 'Zur literarischen Imagologie: Eine Einführung', in *Europäischer Völkerspiegel: Imagologisch-ethnographische Studien zu den Völkertafeln des frühen 18.*

Jahrhunderts, ed. F. K. Stanzel, I. Weiler and W. Zacharasiewicz (Heidelberg, 1999), pp. 9–39

Stein, R., *Magnanimous Dukes and Rising States: The Unification of the Burgundian Netherlands, 1380–1480* (Oxford, 2017)

Steinhauser, K. B., 'Narrative and Illumination in the Beatus Apocalypse', *The Catholic Historical Review* 81/2 (1995), 185–210

Stock, B., 'Antiqui or moderni?', *New Literary History* 10/2 (1979), 391–400

Stotz, P., 'Beobachtungen zu lateinischen Streitgedichten des Mittelalters: Themen – Strukturen – Funktionen' (Zurich, 2001), 1–22, accessed 5 March 2021 at Beobachtungen zu lateinischen Streitgedichten im Mittelalter (uzh.ch)

Strayer, J. R., 'France: The Holy Land, the Chosen People, and the Most Christian King', in *Action and Conviction in Early Modern Europe: Essays in Memory of E.H. Harbison*, ed. T. K. Rabb and J. E. Seigel (Princeton, 1969), pp. 3–16

Strayer, J., *On the Medieval Origins of the Modern State* (Princeton, 1970)

Strickland, D. H., *Saracens, Demons, and Jews: Making Monsters in Medieval Art* (Princeton, 2003)

Struve, T., *Die Entwicklung der Organologischen Staatsauffassung im Mittelalter* (Stuttgart, 1978)

Swanson, R. N., *The Twelfth-Century Renaissance* (Manchester, 1999)

Sweet, V., *Rooted in the Earth, Rooted in the Sky: Hildegard of Bingen and Premodern Medicine* (New York, 2006)

Sweetenham, C., 'Introduction', in *Robert the Monk's History of the First Crusade: Historia Iherosolimitana*, trans. C. Sweetenham (Aldershot, 2005)

Syros, V., 'Galenic Medicine and Social Stability in Early Modern Florence and the Islamic Empires', *Journal of Early Modern History* 17/2 (2013), 161–213

Szücs, J., '"Nationalität" und "Nationalbewußtsein" im Mittelalter: Versuch einer einheitlichen Begriffssprache', *Acta Historica Academiae Scientiarum Hungaricae* 18 (1972), 1–38, 245–66

Tajfel, H., *Human Groups and Social Categories: Studies in Social Psychology* (Cambridge, 1981)

Talbot, C. H., 'The Centum Sententiae of Walter Daniel', *Sacris Erudiri* 11 (1960), 266–383

Tamm, M., 'A New World into Old Words: The Eastern Baltic Region and the Cultural Geography of Medieval Europe', in *The Clash of Cultures on the Medieval Baltic Frontier*, ed. A. V. Murray e.a. (Farnham, 2009), pp. 11–36

Taviani-Carozzi, H., 'Une bataille franco-allemande en Italie: Civitate (1053)', in *Peuples du Moyen Âge: Problèmes d'identification: Seminaire Sociétés, Idéologies et Croyances au Moyen Âge*, ed. C. Carozzi and H. Taviani-Carozzi (Aix-en-Provence 1996), pp. 181–211

Thomas, H., 'Die Deutschen und die Rezeption ihres Volksnamens', in *Nord und Süd in der deutschen Geschichte des Mittelalters: Akten des Kolloquiums veranstaltet zu Ehren von Karl Jordan, 1907–1984, Kiel, 15.–16. Mai 1987*, ed. W. Paravicini (Sigmaringen, 1990), pp. 19–50

Thomas, H., 'Nationale Elemente in der ritterlichen Welt des Mittelalters', in *Ansätze und Diskontinuität deutscher Nationsbildung im Mittelalter*, ed. J. Ehlers (Sigmaringen, 1988), pp. 345–76

Thomas, H., 'Das Identitätsproblem der Deutschen im Mittelalter', *Geschichte in Wissenschaft und Unterricht* 43 (1992), 135–56

Thomas, H., 'Sur l'histoire du mot "Deutsch" depuis le milieu du XIIe siècle jusqu'à la fin du XIIIe siècle', in *Identité régionale et conscience nationale en France et en Allemagne du Moyen Âge à l'époque modern: Actes du colloque organisé par l'Université Paris XII – Val de Marne, l'Institut Universitaire de France et l'Institut Historique Allemand à l'Université Paris XII et à la Fondation Singer-Polignac, les 6, 7 et 8 octobre 1993*, ed. R. Babel and J.-M. Moeglin (Sigmaringen, 1997), pp. 27–35

Thomas, H., *The English and the Normans: Ethnic Hostility, Assimilation, and Identity, 1066–c. 1220* (Oxford, 2003)

Thomson, R. M., 'Introduction', in *Tractatus Garsiae or The Translation of the Relics of SS. Gold and Silver*, ed. R. M. Thomson (Leiden, 1973)

Thomson, R. M., 'The Origins of Latin Satire in Twelfth Century Europe', *Mittellateinisches Jahrbuch* 13 (1978), 73–83

Thomson, R. M., 'England and the Twelfth-Century Renaissance', *Past & Present* 101 (1983), 3–21

Thomson, R. M., 'Satire, Irony, and Humour in William of Malmesbury', in *Rhetoric and Renewal in the Latin West 1100–1540: Essays in Honour of John O. Ward*, ed. C. J. Mews, C. J. Nederman and R. M. Thomson (Turnhout, 2003), pp. 115–27

Thorndike, L., *The Sphere of Sacrobosco and its Commentators* (Chicago, 1949)

Thorndike, L., 'De complexionibus', *Isis* 49 (1958), 398–408

Thorndike, L., *A History of Magic and Experimental Science*, 8 vols. (New York, 1923–58)

Thoss, D., *Studien zum locus amoenus im Mittelalter* (Vienna, 1972)

Tilly, C., *Coercion, Capital, and European States, AD 990–1992* (Cambridge, 1992)

Tipton, C. L. (ed.), *Nationalism in the Middle Ages* (New York, 1972)

Titterton, J., 'Bloodless Turks and Sanguine Crusaders: William of Malmesbury's Use of Vegetius in His Account of Urban II's Sermon at Clermont', *The Medieval Chronicle* 13 (2020), 289–308

Toch, M., *The Economic History of European Jews: Late Antiquity and Early Middle Ages* (Leiden, 2013)

Tolan, J. V., *Saracens: Islam in the Medieval European Imagination* (New York, 2002)

Tomasch, S. and S. Gilles (ed.), *Text and Territory: Geographical Imagination in the European Middle Ages* (Philadelphia, 1998)

Tooley, M. J., 'Bodin and the Mediaeval Theory of Climate', *Speculum* 28/1 (1953), 64–83

Turner, R. V., *King John* (New York, 1994)

Tyerman, C., *God's War: A New History of the Crusades* (London, 2006)

Ulrich, J., 'Neue Versionen der Riote du Monde', *Zeitschrift für romanische Philologie* 24 (1900), 112–20

Vale, M., 'Edward I and the French: Rivalry and Chivalry', in *Thirteenth Century England ii. Proceedings of the Newcastle Upon Tyne Conference 1987*, ed. P. R. Coss and S. D. Lloyd (Woodbridge, 1988), pp. 165–76

Verger, J., *Histoire des universités en France* (Toulouse, 1986)

Verger, J., *Les gens de savoir dans l'Europe de la fin du Moyen Âge* (Paris, 1997)

Vigener, F., *Bezeichnungen für Volk und Land der Deutschen vom 10. bis zum 13. Jahrhundert* (Darmstadt, 1976)

Voorbij, J. B., 'Purpose and Audience: Perspectives on the Thirtheenth-Century Encyclopedias of Alexander Neckam, Bartholomaeus Anglicus, Thomas of Cantimpré and Vincent of Beavais', in *The Medieval Hebrew Encyclopedias of Science and Philosophy: Proceedings of the Bar-Ilan University Conference*, ed. S. Harvey (Dordrecht, 2000), pp. 31–45

Wackernagel, W., 'Die Spottnamen der Völker', *Zeitschrift für deutsches Altertum und deutsche Literatur* 6 (1848), 254–61

Wadden, P., '"The Beauty and Lust of the Gaels": National Characteristics and Medieval Gaelic Learned Culture', *North American Journal of Celtic Studies* 2/2 (2018), 85–104.

Wallach, R., *Das abendländische Gemeinschaftsbewusstsein im Mittelalter* (Leipzig, 1928)

Wallis, F. E., 'MS Oxford, St John's 17: A Medieval Manuscript in its Context' (unpublished dissertation, University of Toronto, 1985)

Wallis, F. (ed.), *Medieval Medicine: A Reader* (Toronto, 2010)

Walther, H., 'Lateinische Verseinträge in einem Vocabular des 15. Jhds.', *Historische Vierteljahrschrift: Zeitschrift für Geschichtswissenschaft und für lateinische Philologie des Mittelalters* 26 (1931), 295–311

Walther, H., 'Scherz und Ernst in der Völker- und Stämme-Charakteristik mittellateinischer Verse', *Archiv für Kulturgeschichte* 41 (1959), 263–301

Walther, H., *Initia carminum ac versuum medii aevi posterioris latinorum / Alphabetisches Verzeichnis der Versanfänge mittellateinischer Dichtungen* (Göttingen, 1959)

Walther, H. and P. G. Schmidt, *Proverbia sententiaeque latinitatis medii aevi / Lateinische Sprichwörter und Sentenzen des Mittelalters in alphabetischer Anordunung*, 9 vols. (Göttingen, 1963–86)

Wander, K. F. W., *Deutsches Sprichwörter-Lexicon: Ein Hausschatz für das Deutsche Volk*, 5 vols. (Leipzig, 1867–80)

Ward, B., *The Venerable Bede* (Kalamazoo, 1998)

Wattenbach, W., *Monumenta Lubensia* (Breslau, 1861)

Wattenbach, W., 'Aus einer Humanistenhandschrift', *Anzeiger für Künde der deutschen Vorzeit* 21 (1874), 212–16

Wattenbach, W. (ed.), 'Verse aus England', *Neues Archiv der Gesellschaft für Ältere Deutsche Geschichtskunde zur Beförderung einer Gesamtausgabe der Quellenschriften deutscher Geschichten des Mittelalters* 1 (1876), 600–4

Wear, A., 'Place, Health, and Disease: The *Airs, Waters, Places* Tradition in Early Modern England and North America', *Journal of Medieval and Early Modern Studies* 38/3 (2008), 443–65

Webber, N., *The Evolution of Norman Identity, 911–1154* (Rochester, 2005)

Weeda, C., 'Ethnic Stereotyping in Twelfth-Century Paris', in *Difference and Identity in Francia and Medieval France*, ed. M. Cohen and J. Firnhaber-Baker (Farnham, 2010), pp. 115–35

Weeda, C., 'Violence, Control, Prophecy and Power in Twelfth-Century France and Germany', in *Reading the Bible in the Middle Ages*, ed. J. Nelson and D. Kempf (London, 2015), pp. 147–66

Weeda, C., 'The Fixed and the Fluent: Geographical Determinism, Ethnicity, and Religion c. 1100–1300 CE', in *The Routledge Handbook of Identity and the Environment in the Classical and Medieval Worlds*, ed. R. F. Kennedy and M. Jones-Lewis (London, 2016), pp. 93–113

Weeda, C., 'The Characteristics of Bodies and Ethnicity *c*. 900–1200', *Medieval Worlds* 5 (2017), 95–112

Weeda, C., 'Meanwhile in Messianic Time: Imagining the Medieval Nation in Time and Space and English Drinking Rituals', in *Imagining Communities: Historical Reflections on the Process of Community Formation*, ed. G. Blok, V. Kuitenbrouwer and C. Weeda (Amsterdam, 2018), pp. 21–40

Weeda, C., 'Reviewing Conduct Books: Galenic Medicine and the "Civilizing Process" in Western European Households *c*. 1100–1300', in *Elite Households in England, 1100–1550: Proceedings of the 2016 Harlaxton Symposium*, ed. C. M. Woolgar (Donington, 2018), pp. 167–84

Weeda, C., 'Cleanliness, Civility, and the City in Medieval Ideals and Scripts', in *Policing the Urban Environment in Premodern Europe*, ed. C. Rawcliffe and C. Weeda (Amsterdam, 2019), pp. 39–68

Weiler, B., 'William of Malmesbury, King Henry I and the Gesta Regum Anglorum', *Anglo-Norman Studies* 31 (2009), 157–76

Weiler, I., 'Ethnographische Typisierungen im antiken und mittelalterlichen Vorfeld der "Völkertafel"', in *Europäischer Völkerspiegel: Imagologisch-ethnographische Studien zu den Völkertafeln des frühen 18. Jahrhunderts*, ed. F. K. Stanzel, I. Weiler and W. Zacharasiewicz (Heidelberg, 1999), pp. 97–118

Weiss, J., 'Emperors and Antichrists: Reflections of Empire in Insular Narrative, 1130–1250', in *The Matter of Identity in Medieval Romance*, ed. P. Hardman (Cambridge, 2002), pp. 87–102

Wenskus, R., *Stammesbildung und Verfassung: Das Werden der Frühmittelalterlichen Gentes* (Cologne, 1961)

Werner, J., *Beiträge zur Kunde der lateinischen Literatur des Mittelalters aus Handschriften* (Aarau, 1905)

Werner, K. F., 'Das hochmittelalterliche Imperium im politischen Bewusstsein Frankreichs (10.–12. Jahrhundert)', *Historische Zeitschrift* 200 (1965), 1–60

Werner, K. F., 'Les nations et le sentiment national dans l'Europe médiévale', *Revue historique* 244/2 (1970), 285–304

Westrem, S. D., 'Against Gog and Magog', in *Text and Territory: Geographical Imagination in the European Middle Ages*, ed. S. Tomasch and S. Gilles (Philadelphia, 1998), pp. 54–75

Whalen, B. E., *Dominion of God: Christendom and Apocalypse in the Middle Ages* (Cambridge MA, 2009)

Whelan, F., *The Making of Manners and Morals in Twelfth-Century England: The Book of the Civilised Man* (Abingdon, 2017)

Wilkinson, L. P., *The Georgics of Virgil: A Critical Survey* (London, 1997)

Williams, J., 'Purpose and Imagery in the Apocalypse Commentary of Beatus of Liébana', in *The Apocalypse in the Middle Ages*, ed. R. K. Emmerson and B. McGinn (Ithaca, 1992), pp. 217–33

Williams, J. (ed.), *The Illustrated Beatus: A Corpus of the Illustrations of the Commentary on the Apocalypse*, 5 vols. (London, 1994–2003)

Williams, J., 'Isidore, Orosius and the Beatus Map', *Imago mundi* 49 (1997), 7–32
Williams, S. J., *The Secret of Secrets: The Scholarly Career of a Pseudo-Aristotelian Text in the Latin Middle Ages* (Ann Arbor, 2003)
Wilmart, A., 'Le florilège de Saint-Gatien: Contribution à l'étude des poèmes d'Hildebert et de Marbode', *Revue Bénédictine* 48 (1936), 3–40, 147–81, 235–58
Winer, R. L., *Women, Wealth, and Community in Perpignan, c. 1250–1300: Christians, Jews, and Enslaved Muslims in a Medieval Mediterranean Town* (Aldershot, 2006)
Winter, J. M. van, *Middeleeuwers in drievoud: Hun woonplaats, verwantschap en voeding* (Hilversum, 2017)
Wixom, W. D. and M. Lawson, 'Picturing the Apocalypse: Illustrated Leaves from a Medieval Spanish Manuscript', *The Metropolitan Museum of Art Bulletin* 59/3 (2002), 1–56
Wollin, C., '"Kein Wein für die Normannen". Marginalien zu Baudri de Bourgeuils "carm." 202', *Sacris Erudiri* 44 (2005), 275–83
Wolsing, I., 'Horsemen of the Apocalypse? Turkish Alterity in Chronicles from the Latin East, 1098–1187', *Viator* (2021), forthcoming
Wood, I., 'Defining the Franks: Frankish Origins in Early Medieval Historiography', in *Concepts of National Identity in the Middle Ages*, ed. S. Forde, L. Johnson and A. V. Murray (Leeds, 1995), pp. 47–57
Woods, M. C. (ed.), *An Early Commentary on the* Poetria Nova *of Geoffrey of Vinsauf* (New York, 1985)
Woodward, D., 'Reality, Symbolism, Time, and Space in Medieval World Maps', *Annals of the Association of American Geographers* 75/4 (1985), 510–21
Wormald, P., 'Engla Lond: The Making of an Allegiance', *Journal of Historical Sociology* 7/1 (1994), 1–24
Wright, J. K., *The Geographical Lore of the Time of the Crusades: A Study of the History of Medieval Science and Tradition in Western Europe* (rev. edn, New York, 1965)
Wright, T. (ed.), *Anecdota Literaria: A Collection of Short Poems in English, Latin, and French, Illustrative of the Litarature and History of England in the 13th. Century; and more Especially of the Condition and Manners of the Different Classes of Society* (London, 1844)
Wright, T. and J. O. Halliwell-Phillips (ed.), *Reliquiae Antiquae: Scraps from Ancient Manuscripts, Illustrating Chiefly Early English Literature and the English Language*, 2 vols. (London, 1845)
Wulf, M. de, 'The Society of Nations in the Thirteenth Century', *International Journal of Ethics* 29/2 (1919), 210–29
Young, C. R. (ed.), *The Twelfth-Century Renaissance* (New York, 1969)
Yunck, J. A., *The Lineage of Lady Meed: The Development of Mediaeval Venality Satire* (Notre Dame, 1963)
Zancani, D., 'The Notion of "Lombard" and "Lombardy" in the Middle Ages', in *Medieval Europeans: Studies in Ethnic and National Perspectives*, ed. A. P. Smyth (New York, 2002), pp. 217–32
Ziegler, J., 'Medicine and Immortality in Terrestrial Paradise', in *Religion and Medicine in the Middle Ages*, ed. P. Biller and J. Ziegler (York, 2001), pp. 201–42
Ziegler, J., 'Text and Context: On the Rise of Physiognomic Thought in the Later Middle Ages', in *De Sion exibit lex et verbum domini de Hierusalem: Essays on*

Medieval Law, Liturgy, and Literature in Honour of Amnon Linder, ed. Y. Hen (Turnhout, 2001), pp. 159–82

Ziegler, J., 'The Scientific Context of Dante's Embryology', in *Dante and the Human Body: Eight Essays*, ed. J. C. Barnes (Dublin, 2007), pp. 61–88

Ziegler, J., 'Physiognomy, Science, and Proto-racism 1200–1500', in *The Origins of Racism in the West*, ed. M. Eliav-Feldon, B. Isaac and J. Ziegler (Cambridge, 2009), pp. 181–99

Zientara, B., 'Nationale Strukturen des Mittelalters: Ein Versuch zur Kritik der Terminologie des Nationalbewußtseins unter besonderer Berücksichtigung osteuropäischer Literatur', *Saeculum* 32 (1981), 301–16

Zientara, B., '*Populus – Gens – Natio*: Einige Probleme aus dem Bereich der ethnischen Terminologie des frühen Mittelalters', in *Nationalismus in vorindustrieller Zeit*, ed. O. Dann (Munich, 1986), pp. 11–20

Zimmermann, K. L., 'Die Beurteilung der Deutschen in der französischen Literatur des Mittelalters mit besonderer Berücksichtigung der chansons de geste', *Romanische Forschungen* 29 (1911), 222–316

Zingerle, I. V., 'Bericht über die Sterzinger Miscellaneen-Handschrift', *Sitzungsberichte der Akademie der Wissenschaften in Wien, Philosophisch-Historische Klasse* 54 (1867), 293–340

Zorzi, A., 'Legitimation and Legal Sanction of Vendetta in Italian Cities from the Twelfth to the Fourteenth Centuries', in *The Culture of Violence in Renaissance Italy: Proceedings of the International Conference; Georgetown University at Villa Le Balze, 3–4 May, 2010*, ed. S. K. Cohn Jr. and F. Ricciardelli (Florence, 2012), pp. 27–54

Zotz, T., 'Urbanitas in der Kultur des westlichen Mittelalters: Eine höfische Wertvorstellung im Umfeld von elegantia morum und elegantia corporis', *Frühmittelalterliche Studien* 45/1 (2011), 295–308

Acknowledgements

I was especially fortunate to be able to explore the representation of embodied communities and biopolitics in a research project about premodern healthscaping in European cities. Many ideas that found their way into this book sprang from the discussions with Janna Coomans, Taylor Zaneri, Lola Digard and Léa Hermenault. I am particularly grateful to Peyman Amiri for his support. I would also like to thank my colleagues at Leiden University, Louis Sicking and Robert Stein. Peter Hoppenbrouwers set me on the path of ethnic stereotyping while I was a graduate student. I thank him for his encouragement and support over the years. Carole Rawcliffe's friendship and comments are, as ever, inspiring.

Eric Storm, Judith Pollmann and Rudi Künzel read early versions of the manuscript and made very insightful suggestions. Conversations with Guy Geltner, his support and comments, have been invaluable. I would also like to extend my profound thanks to Peregrine Horden, Peter Biller and Linda Voigts, as well as to the manuscript reviewers. I am very grateful for their substantial comments. I thank Caroline Palmer and Elizabeth McDonald for their excellent guidance in preparing the manuscript for publication.

Some of the source materials have been presented and discussed in earlier articles and chapters. A section of chapter 2 was originally published, in a revised version, in 'The Fixed and the Fluent: Geographical Determinism, Ethnicity, and Religion *c.* 1100–1300 CE', in *The Routledge Handbook of Identity and the Environment in the Classical and Medieval Worlds*, edited by Rebecca Futo Kennedy and Molly Jones-Lewis, (London, 2016), pp. 93–113. Source materials in chapter 1 and 2 also were discussed in 'The Characteristics of Bodies and Ethnicity *c.* 900–1200', *Medieval Worlds* 5 (2017), 95–112, following the conference organised by Ilja Afanasyev at the University of Oxford, 'Identity, Ethnicity, and Nationhood before Modernity: Old Debates and New Perspectives', in 2015.

Finally, I would like to thank Marcel Haenen, who has taught me about penguins and people, and my family.

Index

Abelard, philosopher 106n.92
Abraham, patriarch 48, 250
Abu Ma'shar al-Balkhi (Albumasar) 116
　Liber de magnis coniunctionibus 116
Accursius, jurist 130
　Glossa ordinaria 130–1
Acts, Book of 46, 76n.122
Adam, first man 50, 108n.100, 119–20, 154
Adam of Bremen, chronicler 239, 242–3, 245
　Gesta Hammaburgensis Ecclesiae Pontificum 43, 239, 242–3, 245
Adela, countess of Blois 208
Adelard of Bath, natural philosopher 93
Aeneas, mythological Trojan figure 115, 224
Afer, son of Abraham 48
　see also Africa
Africa 48, 56n.59, 57, 124, 254
　see also Asia, Europe, *mappae mundi*
Africans 235
　beauty 106
　blackness 235
　choleric 110n.108
　cowardice 235
　cunning 73, 78n.129, 265
　hair 235
　hot 263
　intelligence 73, 263, 269
　inconstancy 73, 263, 265, 269
　lustfulness 78n.129
　naked 150
　savagery 150n.83, 235
　see also Ethiopians, Ham, skin colour, southerners
Agnes of Poitou, empress of the Holy Roman Empire 215
Ailred, abbot of Rievaulx 208, 211n.97
Albanians 52
Albelda, Benedictine monastery 76
　Albelda Chronicle 65n.84, 67
Albert of Aachen, chronicler 205n.71

Albertus Magnus, Dominican friar 82, 97, 99, 109–10, 112, 114–5, 117
　De anima 108n.101
　De homine 109n.105
　De natura loci 99, 105n.84 and 85, 109–10, 114–15
　Quaestiones super de animalibus 112
Albigensian Crusade 187
Albinus, relics of 170–2
Albumasar, see Abu Ma'shar al-Balkhi
Alcabitius, see Al-Qabīsī
Alemannia 48, 234
　see also Alemans
Alemannus, river 48
Alemans 238
　body height 238
　drunkenness 78
　plunderers 238
　see also Germans
Alexander III, pope 129, 223, 241
　'Laudabiliter', bull of 1172 sanctioning invasion of Ireland 241
Alexander Neckam, schoolman 93, 120, 180, 209–10, 212
　De laudibus divinae sapientiae 209
　De naturis rerum 120
　De utensilibus 180
　'Quo versu Anglorum' 212
Alexander of Roes, canon law jurist 53–4, 106, 187, 196, 228
　Memoriale 106, 180n.67, 187, 228
　Noticia seculi 54, 196, 206n.74, 228
Alexander of Villedieu, poet 134
　Doctrinale puerorum 134
Alfanus, archbishop of Salerno 92
Al-Farghānī (Alfraganus), astronomer 100
Alfonso III of Asturias, king of León 67
Alfraganus, see Al-Farghānī
Aliscans, chanson de geste 121
Allebroges, see Burgundians

Al-Majusi (Haly Abbas), physician 92
  Kitab (*Liber regalis*) 92
Al-Qabīsī (Alcabitius), astrologer 117
  Isagoge 117
Al-Rāzī, physician 107
  De aluminibus et salibus 107
Alsace, people of 173
  instability of faith 173
Amatus of Montecassino, Benedictine monk 226n.157
  L'Ystoire de li Normant 226n.157
Ambrosius of Milan, theologian 57n.62
  De noe et arca 57n.62
Anacletus, pope 177
Anderson, Benedict, political scientist 9, 25, 32
Angers 144, 167, 176–7
  pun on name 176–7
Angevins 180
  military skills 167, 176
Anglia, *see* England
'Anglia, terrarum decus' 222n.142
Anglo-Normans 30, 38, 132
  language 174–5
  see also Anglo-Saxons, Britons, English
Anglo-Saxons 13, 30, 42, 45, 48, 68–9
  chosenness 178
  cowardice 178, 207
  drunkenness 174n.44, 178, 199, 207
  military skills 207
  perfidy 178, 207
  stupidity 72
  see also Anglo-Normans, Britons, English
animals 4, 17, 35, 37, 82, 83, 115, 120, 130, 132, 143, 151, 156, 179, 180, 184, 234n.11, 235, 241, 242, 244, 249, 254
  animal allegory 59n.68, 69–70
  breeding 22, 113
  horses 95, 111, 113
  see also Britons, English, French, Gascons, Germans, Greeks, Normans, Persians, Romans, Saracens, Saxons, Scots, traits
Anjou 177

heroes of 141
Annales Altahenses maiores 245n.48
Antenor, mythological figure 198, 224
Antichrist 60, 67, 185, 203, 229
Antipodes 86, 174, 235
Apocalypse of John (Book of Revelation) 71, 73, 107n.94
Apostles, list of 73
Apulians, timid 150
Aquitaine 215
Arabia, gold of 148
Arabs 49, 120, 239
  see also Moors, Muslims, Saracens
Aragonese, constancy of 147
Arezzo, *studium generale* 94
aristocracy, *see* nobility
Aristotle, philosopher 4, 5, 13, 16–18, 21, 80–2, 87, 94, 111, 124, 131, 156, 182, 243, 250, 253
  On Animals 94
  On Generation and Corruption 182
  On Length and Shortness of Life 99
  Politics 17, 80–2, 94, 123
Armenia 49
Armenians, dress of 149
Arnald of Villanova, physician 92
  Speculum medicine 110n.109
Arnold of Lübeck, Benedictine abbot and chronicler 250
  Chronica Slavorum 239n.26, 250
Arras 137
Articella 92
Arthur, king, *see* Britons
Asia 1, 2, 46, 56–7, 85, 124, 234–5, 254, 255
  climate 235
  see also Africa, Europe, *mappae mundi*, Shem, southerners
Asturia 63–8
  mules of 151
  preachers 143
  see also Spain, Spanish, Visigoths
Athens, translation of knowledge 195–6, 236–7
  see also Greece
Athenians ingenious 266
Atlantic 16, 58, 82

Augustine, theologian 44, 45, 62, 65n.87, 76, 156
  De civitate Dei 76, 170n.27
Augustine of Canterbury, missionary 178–9, 252
Austrians humility 146
Auvergne 2, 215, 227
  singers of 175
  turnip eaters 143
Avicenna, *see* Ibn Sina

Bertrand de Bar-sur-Aube, poet
  Aymeri of Narbonne 200
Babel, Tower of 66, 180n.68
Babylonia 42, 56, 59n.69, 60, 67, 185
  compared to a lioness 69
  riches of 149
Baeza figs 66
Baldric of Bourgueil, bishop of Dol-de-Bretagne 80, 144n.62, 174, 208, 216
  Historia Ierosolimitana 80, 261
  'Itinerarium sive episola ad Fiscannenses' 222n.140
Baltic territories 184, 224, 231, 239–40, 242–3, 251, 254–5
barbarity 1, 189–194, 242–4
  dairy diet 144–5, 192, 211, 245
  language 190–1
  lawlessness 3, 4, 35, 36, 132, 157, 186, 188, 189, 192
  paganism 189–90, 192, 242
  sexuality 243
  work ethic 240
  see also Baltic territories, Britons, Brittany, civility, Danes, Germans, Irish, labour, narratives of progress, Scandinavians, Scots, Slavs, Welsh
Baronage of London, catalogue 143
Bartholomaeus Anglicus, Franciscan friar and papal legate to Bohemia, Poland, Moravia and Austria 50–2, 54, 93, 94, 100–5, 108–9, 114, 117, 178, 220, 221, 231–40, 245, 247–9
  De proprietatibus rerum 48n.29, 50, 52–4, 57n.62, 59n.69, 94, 100, 102–5,

109, 114, 117, 178, 220, 222n.140, 233–40, 245, 247, 249
Bavaria 49, 104, 185, 195
Bavarians 190
  barbaric language 190–1
  bluntness 134, 199n.47, 265, 269
  origins in Armenia 49
  see also Germans
Beatus of Liébana, monk 68, 73, 86n.22
  Beati in Apocalysin Libri Duodecim 73n.117
Bede, Benedictine monk and scholar 43, 46, 51, 178, 219, 247–8
  De temporum ratione 107n.95
  Historia ecclesiastica 43, 46, 54n.54, 178, 219, 220n.135, 247
  Nomina regionum et locorum de Actibus Apostolorum 46
Belgica Gallica 234
Benoît of St Maure, poet 95–6
  Chroniques des Ducs de Normandie 95–6
Benvenuto da Imola, scholar 181
Bergson, Henri 165
Bernard of Clairvaux, Cistercian abbot 62, 91, 106n.92, 241
  Vita sancti Malachiae 241
Bernard de Gordon, physician 110n.109
Bevis of Hampton, mythological figure 180n.65
blood 2, 13, 80, 185
  see also Germans, Jews
body politic 5, 8, 11, 13, 29, 34, 37, 38, 84, 116, 122–4, 147, 148, 152–7, 186, 209, 229, 252, 253–8
  corpus mysticum 61–2, 116, 123
Bohemians 79, 242, 248
  devoutness 146
  diet of raw flesh 151
  drinking 163, 176, 199
Bohemond of Taranto, crusader 217n.122, 226
Bologna, university of 93–4, 126, 131, 135, 137, 150, 183, 186
Boncompagno da Signa, rhetorician 135, 149–52, 162–3, 167, 245
  Palma 135, 149–52

Boncompagno da Signa, rhetorician (*continued*)
  Rhetorica antiqua 135, 162–3
Bourdieu, Pierre, sociologist 188
Brabant 104, 234
  mercenaries 161, 254
  urbanity 238
Breton hope, *see* Britons
Bretons 147, 173, 211, 244n.43, 250
  see also Brittany, Britain, Britons
Brie, cheese of 143
Britannia 48, 54, 128, 219, 234, 244, 247–8
  see also Anglia, Brittany, Britons
Britons 7, 71, 133
  brutish 176
  compared to boars 70
  compared to goats 69, 266
  conversion narrative 179
  courage 271
  dairy diet 141, 144, 211
  hospitality 73, 263, 269
  hot temperament 224
  legend of King Arthur (Breton Hope) 133–4, 172–4
  musical skills 147
  stupidity 161, 172–3, 271
  Trojan origins 176, 224
  wrath 65, 72–3, 75, 79, 173, 260, 265, 267, 269
  writing skills 175
  see also Anglo-Normans, Anglo-Saxons, Bretons, Brittany, Britannia, English
Brittany 144, 173, 220, 240, 243, 245
  pastoral society 245, 250
  see also Britannia, Britons
Brutus, mythological Trojan ancestor, grandson of Ascanius 48, 54, 115, 176, 182
  see also Britons, Britannia
Buffon, Georges-Louis, naturalist 120
bureaucratization 8, 9, 126, 136, 148, 156, 169, 194, 212
Burgundians 5n.39, 190
  rapacity 151
  traitors 155

Burgundy 5n.39, 155
  mules of 149
Bury St Edmunds, Benedictine abbey 93
Byzantium 150n.82, 170, 225
  treachery 148

Cain, son of Adam and Eve 16, 28, 49, 107, 115, 180
  see also English, Jews, serfs
Calabrians, weakness of 150
Campania 98
  wines of 133
Campesinians, table manners 147
Canaan, promised land 239, 248–50
Canterbury, seat of the archbishopric 180n.67, 241
Carentan 216
Carmen de Hastingae Proelio 174
Carinthians 248
Carolingians 59, 128, 187, 198, 202, 207
  see also Charlemagne
Carthagians 21
Castilians, military skills of 147
Catalans, joy of 147
Cathars 121
Cecco d'Ascoli, physician 92
Chaldeans 67, 71
  astrologers 65
  fickleness 73, 263, 265, 269
  sagacity 73, 263, 269
  see also Saracens
Chanson de Roland 145, 217
Charlemagne 41, 227
  canonization of 129
  Last Emperor prophecy 187n.6
  mythical journey to Jerusalem 187n.6, 204
  see also Carolingians, *imperium*
Chartres, school of 112, 126, 186, 209
Chaucer, Geoffrey, poet 141n.52
  The Parlement of Foulys 141n.52
chosen peoples (New Israelites) 32, 61–62, 67–8, 178, 203, 217–8, 255
  see also Anglo-Saxons, Franks, Goths
Chrétien de Troyes, poet 195–6, 200
  Cligès 195

Christ 21, 28, 56–8, 61, 107, 118, 129, 196, 220, 241, 242
　perfect complexion 108
　sexual abstinence 244n.43
Christianity 21, 22, 45, 46, 60, 62, 66, 70, 76, 77, 84, 113, 116, 121, 147, 190, 192, 194, 200, 227, 233, 240, 247, 249, 255
　arose under Mercury 117n.138
　conversion (rebirth) to 61, 116, 118–22
　universalism 32, 61, 124
Chronicle of Alfonso III 67
Chronicon Ebersheimense 191n.16
Chronicon Polonorum usque ad a. 1113 190n.11
Chronicon Sancti Martini Turonense 199n.45
Cicero, rhetorician 4, 11, 18, 73, 124, 131–4, 184, 188, 193–4, 209–11, 222, 231, 237, 241, 243, 245, 250, 253
　De inventione 131
　De officiis 131–2, 211, 245, 250, 253
Cirencester 120
Cistercians, salubrious sites of the 91, 103
　Bellefontaine, Cistercian monastery 91
　Clara Valla, Cistercian monastery 91
　Fountains, Cistercian monastery 91
　see also environmental (climate) theory
civility (urbanity) 189–94, 212–7, 222
　see also barbarity, English, French
Clairmarais, Cistercian nunnery 135
Clermont-Ferrand 218, 227, 238
Cluny, abbey 141, 215
Clyde, river 220
Codex Aemilianensis 65, 66n.95, 78n.130, 259
collective memory *see* ethnicity
Cologne 82, 106, 182, 196, 228
colonization 3, 8, 14, 16, 19, 23, 24, 25, 29, 30, 35, 36, 38, 81, 84, 124, 132, 147, 153, 157, 184, 188, 199, 230, 233, 238–51
　of the Americas 252, 253
Colossae, people of 61
common good 13, 15, 17, 37, 123, 131, 133, 155, 246, 252–3, 256
Constance of Arles, queen of France 215

Constantine the African 79, 89, 92, 94, 96–7, 100, 233
　Pantegni 79, 89, 92, 94, 96–7, 100
　Viaticum peregrinantis 92
Cordoba, sapphires of 141
Cornwall 218
Corpus Iuris Civilis, Justinian law code 157
Corsicans, treachery of 150
Courland, in present-day Latvia 242–3
　dehumanizing paganism 242–3
Courtrai, battle of 168
Cretans, liars 266
Crete 48n.30
crusades 56, 129, 225, 251–2, 254
　First Crusade 1–2, 31–2, 80, 89, 198, 203–6, 217–8, 227, 238–40
　siege of Antioch 205
　French-German competition 203–7
　Second Crusade 148n.75, 191, 206
　Third Crusade 182, 224
Cumbria 218
Cursor mundi, poem 121–2

Dacians, whiteness of 105
Dalmatians 248
　ferocious 266
Danes 115, 208, 240
　cruelty 192n.19
　drinking 246n.51
　lawlessness 246
　manliness 215, 217n.120
　pacification of 240
　tall 143
　see also Scandinavians
Daniel, Book of 59, 133
Daniel of Beccles, poet and courtier 95, 126–7, 196
　Urbanus magnus 95, 126–7, 196
Darius III, Persian king 133, 139
David, biblical king 122
David I, king of Scotland 1, 211
De fine mundi 66n.97
De inventione corporis s. Judoci 218
'De proprietatibus gentium' 65
De Simone mago 66n.97

Denis the Aeropagite 195n.32
'Descriptio Norfolciensium' 113n.125
'Descriptio positionis seu situationis monasterii Clarae-Vallensis' 91n.37
Descriptiones terrarum 239n.26
Deuteronomy, Book of 76n.122
Diego García, chancellor 147
  Planeta 147
diet of milk and butter 144–5
  beer and wine 144–5
  see also barbarity, Britons, Flemish, Irish, Low Countries, narratives of progress, Welsh
Dit de l'Apostoile 143
Dits, genre 142–4
Dnieper, river 86
Dominium 30, 34, 38, 152, 157, 185–9, 207, 227, 254
  temperate climate 189, 227–8
Donizone of Canossa, monk 200n.48
  Vita Mathildis 200n.48
Dorchester 179, 180n.68
Dorset 179
Durham priory 93

Eadmer, monk 220n.134
  Historia novorum in Anglia 220n.134
Easter calendar 70
Ecclesiastes, Book of 120
Ecgberht, king of Wessex 196n.36
Eco, Umberto, philosopher 63–4
Eden, earthly paradise 56, 98, 120, 154, 234, 248
Edward I, king of England 38, 181
Egica, Visigothic king 62
Egyptians 21, 42, 55, 69, 71, 85
  glory 64
  ingenuity 73, 263, 265, 268–9
  stupidity 73
  victory 68, 70, 71, 267
Einsiedeln, monastery 69
Ekphrasis 133
Elbe, river 195
Eleanor of Aquitaine, queen of England 179

England 32, 54, 98, 100, 127, 128, 133, 171, 180, 219–20, 234, 232, 239, 251
  angulo, corner of the world 54, 178, 180–2, 220
  cold/temperate climate 218–24
  herds of 141
  interdict of 1207 153–5
  minerals 218–9, 235
  Norman conquest of 187, 210
  wealth of resources 137n.36, 149, 170, 172, 208, 218–9, 221–2, 235
  see also Anglo-Normans, Anglo-Saxons, Britannia, Britons, English
English 32, 54, 124, 164, 185–7, 207–24
  compared to dogs, apes, rats, eels 181
  compared to foxes 69
  compared to serpents 180
  cowardice (weak military skills) 172, 180, 183, 187, 207–8, 216–7
  courtliness, gendered 214–7
  descent from angels 54n.54, 178, 180–2
  descent from Cain 180
  descent from Queen Engelia, daughter of a Saxon duke 54
  drinking 34, 136, 143, 145, 154, 161, 163, 172, 174n.44, 175, 180, 182, 183, 199, 210, 240, 254
  effeminacy 183, 208
  eloquence 104, 209–10, 219, 223
  flattery 133
  freedom 104, 222
  generosity 79, 134n.28, 178, 208, 210, 219, 236, 272
  hair 208, 215–7
  handsome 212
  instability of faith 240
  intelligence 84, 136, 147, 172, 178, 186, 208, 210, 219, 223
  lack of learning 209
  merry 104, 172, 178, 212, 219, 236
  phlegmatic 115, 224
  rusticity 208–9, 213–4
  sanguine 94, 178, 222
  tailed (*caudatus*) 151, 161, 173, 178–83, 240, 252

treacherous 143n.60, 172, 178, 180–1, 187, 210
urbanity 36, 104, 178, 186, 208–16, 236, 256
whiteness 106
wit 172, 210, 213
see also Anglo-Normans, Anglo-Saxons, Britons, Britannia, England
Englans, mythological king from Engle near the Tower of Babel 180n.68
see also English
'Enquiry of the Whole World' 66
'Enquiry of Spain' 66
environmental (climate) theory 1–3, 4, 5, 11, 13, 16–22, 23, 25, 26, 27, 28, 29, 31, 33, 34, 35, 36, 42, 46–7, 51, 60, 75, 79, 80–122, 124–6, 133, 150, 153, 156, 184, 185–7, 189, 192, 194, 198, 212, 214, 217–24, 227, 230–51, 252, 253, 255, 257, 258
   air 27, 83, 87–9, 100, 102, 103, 119, 121, 209, 233, 236, 237
   astrological determinism 116–8
   climate engineering 98–9
   cold 1, 75, 81, 85–9, 96–105, 108–9, 115, 121, 251
   complexions 27–8, 81n.5, 83, 87–9, 95, 96, 98, 104–20, 167, 224
     acculturation 113
     and colour 106–10
     complexional change 110–6
     and generation 111–3, 122
     and migration 110, 113–6
     and miscegenation 110–16, 183
     and mother milk 112
     natural complexion 111–3
     and professions 115
     radical complexion 111–3
     virtus informativa 111
   elements 87, 233
   environmental determinism 3, 16, 17, 20, 23, 25, 35, 87, 104, 115, 122, 194, 218, 222, 230, 231, 234, 238, 239, 244, 252
   eucrasia (balance) 87–8, 253–4
   fluidity/fixity 82–4, 110–22

   heat 1, 81, 85–9, 96–104, 121, 251
   humours 27, 35, 81–4, 105, 233
     choleric 87, 115, 150
     melancholy 36, 87, 107–8, 115, 119–21
     see also Jews, original sin, serfs
     phlegmatic 87, 97–8, 105, 108, 115
       sluggish 108–9
       whiteness 108
       see also Scandinavians, Slavs, women
     sanguine 87, 107, 115
       Christ and Virgin Mary 108
       ideal 108
       reddish-white complexion 107
       see also English, Germans
     and political conflict 155
     see also skin colour, stereotypes of southerners
   and longevity 99
   miasma 117
   non-naturals 27, 83, 87–8, 91, 110–2, 119
   pneumata 88–9
   and rulership 227–8
   and southern/eastern luxuriousness 214
   temperateness 2, 80–1, 84, 87, 91, 96, 98–100, 125, 186, 189, 217, 221–4
   and transfer of knowledge 89–96
   winds 102
   see also physiognomy, race and racism, stereotyping, traits
Ermoldus Nigellus, monk 53n.51
   Carmen in honorem Hludowici 53n.51
eschatology 5, 25, 31, 42, 55, 58–60, 64, 66–71
   numbers 70–1
   Sixth Age of Man 68
Esau, brother of Jacob, biblical figure 118
Etienne de Bourbon, Dominican friar 181
Ethiopians 52, 99, 105–6, 108, 110, 139, 150, 235
   beautiful women 146
   choleric 110, 150
   peace of 66

Ethiopians (*continued*)
  savagery 150, 235
  skin/hair 105–6, 108, 235
ethnic nationalism 7, 30
ethnicity 6, 12, 14–22
  and collective guilt 153
  and collective memory 12, 15, 25, 44, 45, 70, 142
  and competition 16, 25, 32, 188–9, 198
  and conversion (rebirth) 61, 116, 118–22
  customs 27
  diet 13, 144–5
  and discourses 23–26
  dress 13, 51
  ethnogenesis 83, 114, 182
  gendered representations 3, 4, 6, 16, 25, 32, 85, 174, 182–5, 186–7, 198, 214–7, 229, 251, 255, 257
  genealogy 3, 5, 9, 12, 13, 15–16, 19, 21, 28, 44, 57, 62, 64, 70, 100, 124, 128, 131, 216–7, 253, 256
  gens, pl. *gentes* 44–5
  hair 13, 51, 52
  intragroup comparison 24–5, 223
  language 15, 63n.80, 190–2
  moral communities 8, 12, 13, 15, 36, 155–6, 184, 254
  natio, pl. *nationes* 44–5
  natural groups 156
  personality 27
  relational aspect of 29–30, 162–3, 226, 251
  schematization 29–32
  self-(re)presentation 7, 18, 34, 36, 255, 257
  and social practices 13, 15
  and territories 12, 13, 16, 37, 127–8, 156
  and time 25
  see also environmental (climate) theory, ethnogenesis, ethnonyms, ethnotypes, law, military skills, othering, race and racism, stereotyping, traits
ethnonyms 12, 47–55, 162, 170–1, 176–83, 228
  see also etymology

ethnotypes 6, 10, 14–15, 23–32, 36
Etienne de Rouen, monk at the abbey of Bec 173
  Draco Normannicus 173
etymology 45–55, 114, 162, 170, 176–80, 220n.135, 234, 245
  see also ethnonyms
Europe 1, 2, 3, 11, 16, 17, 19, 22, 25, 30, 31, 35, 41, 48, 56–7, 68, 70, 79, 84–6, 89, 90, 98–100, 105, 119, 124, 144, 145, 147, 157, 161, 178, 185, 186, 190, 194, 203, 206, 209, 214, 225, 229, 230–3, 236–9, 247, 251–5
  climate 96, 235
  see also Africa, Asia, *mappae mundi*
Europeans 1–2
  chivalrous 95–6, 235
  whiteness 235
  see also Europe, Japheth
Eusebius of Caesarea, theologian 46
Eustache Duchamps, poet 180n.68
Evagrius Ponticus, ascetic 78n.131
Eve, first woman 120n.156
Évrard (Eberhard) of Béthune, grammarian 134, 161, 167, 176–7
  Graecismus 134, 145n.66, 161, 167–8, 176–7
Exodus, Book of 76n.122, 204n.66, 247n.55
Ezekiel, Book of 67

Faits des Romains, Old French prose chronicle 200
Faritius, physician and abbot of Abingdon 92
Faye-le-Vineuse 140
Fierabras, chanson de geste 121
Flanders 234, 238
Flemish 104, 135–6, 141, 142, 144, 145, 149, 171, 194, 226, 233, 234, 238
  dairy diet 144, 149, 161, 176
  drinking 175
  garrulity 172
  gluttony 161
  knights of 141
  urbane 238

wealth of 135, 161, 172
weavers 136, 233
flood, biblical 48
Fourth Lateran Council 38, 232
France (Francia) 48, 51n.39, 55, 98, 100, 123, 127, 128, 131, 143, 171, 187n.3, 196n.36, 202, 203, 209, 232, 234, 251
   delights 148
   douce 125, 186, 195–6, 209, 217, 227
   knights of 133, 136, 145, 194–6, 201–5
   priesthood of 145, 180n.67, 196
   regnum Franciae 187, 227
   seat of learning 135, 145, 172, 174, 195–6
Francigenae 225–6
Francus, mythological Trojan hero 48, 53
   see also France, Franks, French
'Francis scire, sitis Anglis' 161
Franconians, barbaric language of 190
Franks 42, 45, 48, 51n.39, 53–4, 71, 145, 185, 190, 215, 227–8, 257
   anger 73, 265
   arrogance 72, 174, 266, 267
   avarice 266
   chosenness 45, 203–4, 217–8, 227
   enthronement 71, 260
   ferocity 53n.51, 65, 72–3, 75, 198, 263, 265, 267, 269–71
   freedom 54, 228
   perfidy 78, 143n.60
   strength 73, 147, 218, 263, 265, 269
   treachery 78
   Trojan origins 48, 53n.51, 115, 224, 228
   see also France, Francigenae, Francus, French, Gauls
French 2, 7, 14, 32, 60, 99, 124, 164, 168, 226–8
   arrogance 34, 62, 134, 151, 161, 172, 197, 203, 206, 224, 228, 254
   compared to birds 180n.67
   compared to cocks 228
   compared to lambs 69
   courage 80, 172, 185
   courtliness/chivalry 79, 84, 134, 145, 172, 175, 176, 185, 188, 191, 194–209, 217–8, 228, 272
   definition in crusades 226–7
   disciplined 185, 188
   effeminate 161, 172, 224, 228
   fickle 172, 174
   rationality 185, 188, 255, 263
   receptors of the *translatio studii et chevalrie* 186, 188, 195–6, 217, 228
   relation to *imperium* 185–7, 194–207, 228
   weak 161
   whiteness 106
   see also Franks, Gauls
Fredegar, chronicler 48
   Chronicarum Fredegarii libri IV cum continuationibus 51n.40
   Historia Daretis Frigii De Origine Francorum 48
Frederick Barbarossa, German emperor 113, 129, 169n.25, 197, 203, 249
free will 110, 116–22
Freidank, poet 206
Frisians 105, 113, 144
   excrement 144
   use of javelins 246
   whiteness 105

Galatians 75, 243n.40
   foolish 75, 266
   whiteness 52n.45
Galen, physician 22, 26, 27, 81, 83, 87, 88, 91, 98, 105, 233
   On the Temperaments 87
   The Faculties of the Soul 87
Galicia 52
   honey of 66
Galicians, speech of 147
Galilea 52
Gallia 32, 51n.39, 52, 171, 187n.3, 234
   see also France, Franks, French, Gauls
Gascons, agility 73, 263
   apples of 141
   compared to wolves 181
   jugglers 143
   wantonness 134, 263, 265, 269
Gascony 234
Gauls 21, 52, 60, 105, 190, 243n.40
   commerce 66, 190, 266
   durability 73, 263

Gauls (*continued*)
  gluttony 72, 73, 260, 263, 265, 267, 269
  sluggishness 73, 263
  softness 190, 224
  strength 269
  whiteness 52n.45, 105
  see also France, Franks, French, Gallia
Gautier d'Arras, poet 201
  Ille et Galeron 201
Geffrei Gaimar, chronicler 187
Gematria, art of 70
gendered representations, *see* ethnicity
genealogy, *see* ethnicity
Genesis, Book of 50, 57, 64n.82, 248
Gentilitas, mythical king of Jerusalem 185
'Gentium quicum mores' 151n.86
Geoffrey Malaterra, Benedictine monk and historian 226
Geoffrey of Monmouth, chronicler 176
  Historia regum Britanniae 176, 218n.128
Geoffrey of Vinsauf, grammarian 136–7, 167, 210, 223, 224
  Documentum de modo et arte dictandi et versificandi 136, 223
  Poetria nova 136
Gens, pl. *gentes*, *see* ethnicity
'Gens Romanorum subdola antiqua' 148–9
Gepidae 78
Gerald of Wales, archdeacon and ethnographer 18–19, 27, 93, 115, 120–1, 151, 192, 210–1, 213, 224, 234, 240–2, 244–5, 248, 250
  De principis instructione 120–1
  Descriptio Kambriae 97n.58, 115, 224
  Topographia Hibernica 97n.58, 210–11; 224, 234, 241–2, 244–6, 248
Germania/Teutonia 32, 51n.39, 128, 234
  territories of 146, 232
Germans (Teutons) 7, 9, 14, 32, 49, 53–4, 79, 102–4, 114–5, 124, 175, 182–3, 185–92, 194–207, 225, 231, 238–9, 249, 251, 255
  barbaric 189–90, 204
  and climate 189
  compared to dogs 163, 201
  courage 102, 104
  cowardice 200
  descent from giants 201–2
  drinking 199, 271, 270
  effeminacy 215
  faith 147
  freedom 189
  furor (rage) 34, 84, 133, 143, 151, 161n.1, 184–6, 192, 194–203, 205–6, 208, 254
  hair 102, 104, 183
  and *imperium* 185–7, 228
  instability of faith 173, 175, 178, 200, 231, 238, 240
  lack of chivalry 194–207
  language 128, 163, 190–1, 201
  under Mars 183, 202
  under Mercurius 202
  merry 102
  phlegmatic 109, 114–5
  plunder, thievery 237–8
  strength 102, 104, 183, 206, 270
  stiff-necked 200, 204, 240
  stupidity 114–5, 169n.25, 208, 223–4
  tall 104, 183
  treachery 173, 200
  urbane 103, 195
  whiteness 106
  see also Alemans, Bavarians, Jews, Saxons, Thuringians
Gervase of Canterbury, monk at Christ Church 170, 221
  Chronica Gervasii 170
  Mappa mundi 221
Gervase of Melkley, poet 134
  Ars versificaria 134
Gervase of Tilbury, canon lawyer 50, 52, 93, 211n.97, 223–4, 240–1
  Otia imperialia 50, 51n.39 and 40, 52, 53n.50, 54n.54, 150n.83, 224, 237n.20, 241, 247n.54
Gesta Stephani 246n.49
Ghent 191
Gildas, monk 219–20, 267
  De excidio Britanniae 219–20
Giles of Rome, philosopher 123, 156, 229

De regimine principum 229
Glacken, Clarence, historian 18
Gog and Magog 67, 151, 243
Goscelin of St Bertin, monk 179
   Vita Sancti Augustini 179
Goths 42, 109, 150n.82
   chosenness 67
   phlegmatic 109
   sobriety 71, 260, 269
   strength 65
   see also Visigoths
Grandes Chroniques de France 195n.31
Greece 56, 60, 98, 236, 255
Greeks 21, 42, 52, 55, 56, 60, 71, 145, 148–9, 182n.76, 185
   anger 73, 265
   books of 141
   compared to leopards 69
   deceit 73, 148, 263, 65, 269
   dress 148, 149
   fickle 266
   glory 269–71
   intelligence 52, 265–6
   language 223
   wisdom 64–5, 67, 71, 73, 79, 259–60, 263, 267, 269
   see also Byzantium, *translatio studii et imperii*
Gregorian reform movement 148, 169
Gregory the Great, pope 54, 78n.131, 106, 178, 191
   Moralia, sive Expositio in Job 106
Gregory IX, pope 227
Guibert of Nogent, Benedictine monk 80, 90, 121, 204–6, 217–8, 226–7
   Dei gesta per Francos 80, 90, 121, 204–6, 217–8, 226–7
Guy of Amiens, bishop 217n.120
   Carmen de Hastingae Proelio 217n.120
Gypsies 16, 22

Habbakuk, Book of 67
habitus 23, 31n.92, 84, 110–1, 113
Hagar, bondswoman of Abraham 49, 68
Haly Abbas, *see* Al-Majusi
Ham, son of Noah 48, 57

Haran, biblical city 250
Hastings, battle of 174n.44, 216
Hatto, archbishop of Mainz 41
heathens 25, 77, 186, 190, 251, 252, 255
   criminalisation of 239–40
   see also Baltic territories, barbarity, Ireland
Hebrews, prudence 73, 263, 269
   see also Israel, Israelites, Jews
Hector, Trojan hero 48
Hellespont 99, 206
Helmold of Bosau, chronicler 197, 240
   Chronica Slavorum 197, 240, 242n.37 and 38
Hengist, mythological figure 49
Henry I, king of England 92, 216
Henry II, king of England 120, 136, 173, 181, 211n.97, 241
Henry III, king of England 129, 182
Henry III, German emperor 215
Henry VI, German emperor 200
Henry of Avranches, poet 182–3
Henry of Blois, bishop of Winchester 222n.140
Henry of Huntingdon, chronicler 43, 187, 208, 221, 222n.142
   Historia Anglorum 43, 137n.36, 187, 221
Henry of Huntingdon, archdeacon 43, 221
   Historia Anglorum 43, 221
Henry of Livonia, missionary priest 239–40
   Chronicon Livoniae 239–40
Herbert of Bosham, scholar 209–10, 213n.140
   Epistola 209–210
Herbord of Michelsberg, monk 249–50
   Dialogus de vita Ottonis episcopi Babenbergensis 249–50
heretics 20, 25, 84, 118, 186, 190, 251
   and climate 120–1
   see also barbarity, religious determinism
Hermann of Carinthia, astronomer 116–7
   De essentiis 117
'Hervordschir, shild and sper' 143

'Hic ponitur continens pro contento' 135
Hildebert of Lavardin (le Mans),
    archbishop of Tours 144, 172
Hildegard of Bingen, Benedictine abbess
    119–20
  Causae et curae 119–20
Hippocrates, physician 16, 21, 22, 26, 27,
    46–7, 79, 83, 85, 92, 98, 156, 184, 186,
    212, 217, 222–3, 233
  Airs, Waters, Places 47, 79, 85, 92
  Historia Vie Hierosolimitane 205n.71
Holland, people of 104, 233, 238
  compared to Germans 238
  devoutness 233, 238
  whiteness 105
Honorius of Autun, theologian 124
  Imago mundi 51n.40, 52n.42 and 44,
    53n.48, 106n.69, 271
Horace, Roman poet 134, 169
  Ars poetica 140n.48
  Odes 220n.133
Horsa, mythological figure 49
Hrabanus Maurus, Benedictine monk
    and theologian 50
  Commentariorum in Genesim 55n.57
  De rerum naturis 105n.86
  De universo 50
  Enarrationes in epistolas Beati Pauli
    75n.121
Hugh of Fouilloy, cleric 107
  De medicina animae 107
Hugh of Montacute, abbot of
    Muchelney (Somerset) 221–2
Hugh of St Victor, canon regular and
    theologian 58–9
  De arca Noë morali libri iv 58
Hunayn ibn Ishaq al-Ibadi (Iohannitius),
    physician 92, 105, 107
  Isagoge 92, 105, 107
Hungary, 195
  truth in 146
Hungarians
  hunger of 151, 245
  monsters 250
  paganism 242, 270
  pastoralism 245, 249–50

treachery 143, 147n.72, 151, 176
Huns 51
  cruelty 73, 263, 265, 269
  lewdness 78
Hypocrites, helpers of the Antichrist 185

Ibn al-Jazzar, physician 92
  Provisions for the Traveller and
    Nourishment for the Sedentary 92
Ibn Khaldūn 252n.73
Ibn Sina (Avicenna), philosopher 93, 94,
    114, 233
  Canon of Medicine 93
Icelanders 104–5
  pastoralism 245
  whiteness 105
imperium 9, 29, 34, 41, 42, 53, 58–9, 106,
    127, 129, 156, 183, 184, 201–2, 254–8
  competition over 185–9, 228–9
  forms of violence 202
  protection of the Church 203, 228–30
  world emperor 42, 59–60
  see also Carolingians, Charlemagne,
    dominium
India, language of 63n.80
  Plinian races 236n.12
  precious stones 148
  religion in 149
Indian Ocean 205
Innocent II, pope 177
Innocent III, pope 136, 153
  Epistola 153
Iohannitius, see Hunayn ibn Ishaq
    al-Ibadi
Iraq 252n.73
Ircanians, paganism of 243
Ireland 18, 129, 144, 186, 192, 247–8, 255
  colonization of 104, 240–1, 254–5
  lawlessness 184, 192, 233, 242, 246
  land of milk and honey 248
  pastoralism 244–6
Irish 25, 32, 38, 104, 129, 210–1, 224, 241,
    246
  barbaric 192, 211, 233, 240–1, 251–2
  dairy diet 144, 192, 240–1, 244–5
  instability of faith 184, 241–2

Index   335

savagery 143, 192
sexuality 244
work ethic 192, 233, 245
see also Scots
Isaac, son of Abraham 49
Isabella of Hainault, queen of France 227
Ishmael, father of Kedar 49, 234n.11
Ishmaelites 67
  madness of 234n.11
Isidore of Seville, encyclopaedist 43, 49, 50, 51, 52, 54, 67, 102, 105, 146, 220
  arose under Venus 117n.138
Israel 67, 69, 247
  De Ortu et Obitu Patrum (attrib.) 73n.117
  Etymologiae 43, 48n.30, 50, 52, 53n.48, 54, 56n.59, 65n.85 and 90, 66, 102, 103n.75, 105, 107n.95, 140n.50, 150n.83, 220, 221n.135, 235n.12
  Historia de regibus Gothorum, Wandalorum et Suevorum 43, 46, 67
  'Versus de Asia et de universi mundi rota' 147n.71
Islam 68, 70, 121
  see also Israelites, Hebrews, Jews
Israelites 67, 76n.122, 247
  see also Hebrews, Israel, Jews
Italy 32, 92, 94, 98, 100, 114, 123 172, 175, 178, 187, 191, 198, 202, 206, 226, 228, 232, 251, 255
  greed 175
  freedom of 149–52
  inheritors of the priesthood 228
  piety 146
  see also Romans, Rome
Itinerarium Peregrinorum et Gesta Regis Ricardi 197n.39

Jacob, brother of Esau, biblical figure 118
Jacques de Vitry, bishop of Acre 34, 117, 161–2, 179, 254
  Historia occidentalis 34, 161, 199n.47
  Historia orientalis 117

Japheth, son of Noah 48, 57, 124
Jean Bodel, poet 137
  La chanson des Saisnes 195, 198n.41, 200n.50
Jean Bodin, political philosopher 84
Jean d'Outremeuse 180
  Ly Myreur des Histors 180
Jean Renart, poet 201
  Galeran de Bretagne 200n.50 and 51, 202n.59
  Roman de la Rose 201
Jean de Terre Rouge (Terrevermeille), legal philosopher 155
  Contra rebelles suorum regum 155
Jerome, theologian 46, 49, 50, 59, 75
  Commentariorum in epistolam ad Galatos 52n.45
  Commentariorum in epistolam ad Titum liber unus 75n.121
  Liber de nominibus Hebraicis 50
  Liber interpretationis Hebraicorum nominum 55n.57
Jerusalem 56, 57n.61, 58, 204, 219–20
Jews 14, 16, 20, 21, 22, 25, 28, 33, 36, 37, 38, 42, 49, 55, 61–2, 71, 72, 82–5, 95, 110, 113, 116, 118, 122, 128, 145, 156, 168, 188, 225n.153, 251, 256
  adversus Judaeos sermons 76
  anti-*converso* rhetoric 113
  blood libel 62
  effeminacy 117
  envy 64–5, 69, 71, 73, 75, 79, 84, 117, 260, 263, 265, 267, 269
  foetor judaicus 117
  irrationality 62
  legal status 110, 128
  melancholy 36, 38, 62, 85, 94, 108n.103, 110, 116–7, 266
    and astrology 116–7
  menstrual flux 95n.54, 117
  perfidy 62, 117
  under Saturn 85, 86n.20, 117
  stiff-necked (rigidity) 61–2, 75–6, 79, 117, 204, 240, 267, 270–1
  Statute of the Jewry 38
  wisdom 263

Jews (*continued*)
  see also Hebrews, Israel, Israelites, Judaism, othering in time, religious determinism
Johannes de Sacrobosco, astronomer 100
  Tractatus de Sphera 100, 105n.86
Johannes Teutonicus Zemeke, jurist 131
John (Hymonides), deacon of Rome 191
  Vita Gregorii Magni 191
John I, king of England 153, 170n.130, 212
John of Fordun, chronicler 69–70
  Scotichronicon 69–70
John of Garland, rhetorician 135, 138
  Parisiana poetria 135, 138
John of Hauville, poet 141
  Architrenius 141
John of Newhouse, scholar of medicine 113
  Tractatus de complexionibus 113
John of Paris, Dominican friar 5, 132–3, 156, 229
  De potestate regia et papali 132–3, 156, 229
John of Paris, scholar of medicine 115
  Liber complexionum 115
John Pecham, Franciscan friar 206–7
John of Salisbury, bishop and philosopher 93, 122, 154, 191–2, 206, 214, 223, 242, 256
  Epistola 154, 191–2, 223, 242
  Historia pontificalis 206
  Policraticus 123, 191n.16, 256
John Scottus Eriugena, theologian 119
  De divisione naturae 119
John of Spain (Seville), translator 102n.74, 116
John Trevisa, translator 235
Jordanes, chronicler 43, 51, 219
  Getica 43
Joseph of Exeter, poet 141n.52
  Daretis Phrygii Ilias 141n.52
Joshua, Book of 69
Judaism 42, 55, 70, 76, 194, 255
  arose under Saturn 86, 117
  see also Israel, Israelites, Hebrews, Jews, othering in time
Judea 58, 67, 247
Julius Caesar, Roman general 219
  Commentarii de bello Gallico 51n.39, 200
Julius Honorius, geographer 66
  Cosmographia 66
Jutland 220n.235
Juvenal, Roman poet 169

King of Allemayne, mythological figure 182n.76
King of Tars, romance 121
kinship networks 5, 8, 15, 42, 44, 47, 188
  see also ethnicity, *origo gentis* myths
Kirn, Paul, German historian 7

La riote du monde, fabliau 143
labour 16, 30, 34, 35, 82, 127, 131–2
  work ethic 3, 188, 231
  see also Baltic territories, barbarity, Irish, Moors, Slavs
Lactantius, Christian apologist 47, 52n.45
  De origine erroris 47
Landulf of Milan, chronicler 199
  Historiae Mediolanensis 191n.16, 199
Laon 91, 209
Lauingen (Bavaria) 99, 114
Layamon, poet 179
  Brut 179
law 9, 11, 15
  ius gentium 37, 82, 130, 132, 156
  legal status and territory 127–8
  natural law 4, 156
  personality of law 127
  persona ficta 34, 157, 256
lawlessness, see barbarity
Lawrence of Durham, Benedictine monk 129–30
  Dialogi 130, 182n.75
Le Mans, chapter school 144
Lebensraum politics 7
Leprosy 20, 112–3, 117
Letter of Lentulus 108
Lex Salica 218
Libya 85
Ligurians, usury of 133

lists 63–77, 133–4
   resources 137
   and time and space 70–2
Liutprand of Cremona, diplomat 170
   Relatio de legatione Constantinopolitana 170
Livre des mestiers 137
Livs 239–40
Locrinus, mythological king of the Britons 48
Loire, river 128
London 100, 153
   St Paul's cathedral 153
Lombard League 150
Lombards 113, 145, 150n.82
   deceit 162
   intelligence 113, 272
   patrons of liberty 150
   usury 161, 170n.27
Lombardy 51n.39, 150, 162, 170n.27
Longobards 42, 55
   avarice 271
   beards 51
   generosity 71, 260, 267, 269
   vainglory 73, 263, 265, 269
Lorraine 234
   dancers of 143
Lorsch 27
Lotharingia 204
Louis VI, king of France 13, 130n.14
Louis VII, king of France 181, 197, 206
Louis VIII, king of France 227
Louis IX, king of France 107, 182
Low Countries 137
   dairy diet 144
Lucan, Roman poet 202
   Pharsalia 202
Ludus de Antichristo 185, 202
Lusatia, thieves of 151n.86

Macrobius, scholar 118
Malchus, saint 141
Malmesbury abbey 1, 92
mappae mundi 55–6, 71, 139, 220, 221
   Macrobian maps 86–7
   T-O maps 56, 133

Marbod of Rennes, bishop 144, 167–8, 176
   De ornamentis verborum 167–8
March, foolish people of 150–1
Marie of France, countess of Champagne 196, 200
Marsilius of Padua, philosopher 156
   Defensor pacis 156
Martial, Roman poet 169
Matilda, empress of the Holy Roman Empire 1
Matthew Paris, Benedictine monk and chronicler 181
   Chronica Majora 181n.73
Matthew of Vendôme, poet 134, 139–40, 148, 166, 222n.140
   Ars versificatoria 134, 139–40, 142n.54, 148
Mauretania 52
Medes 56
   compared to bears 69
medieval, periodization 7–8, 252
   'eschatological time' 10
   see also othering
Meissen, people of 104
   urbane 238
Mercury, *see* Christianity
Meroë (Sudan) 86
Metani 248
Michael Scot, astronomer 105n.86
Milan 115
military skills 1, 2, 3, 32, 34, 35, 90–1, 97, 131, 193, 194–208
   battle cry 131, 162
   chivalry 91, 189–94, 201–8
   lack of self-control 193–4
   preudomme 91, 193
   see also English, French, gendered representations, Germans, traits
milk and honey, lands of 67, 194, 221–2, 231, 239, 247–50
Minnesingers 194
mirror literature 4, 107, 122, 123, 152, 210
   see also regimens
mnemonic textual devices 3, 77

mnemonic textual devices (*continued*)
  phantasmata (mental images) 77,
    138–40
Mondino dei Luzzi, physician 92
Mongols 22, 82, 95n.54
Montpellier, university of 93, 94, 100
Moors (Mauri) 52, 105, 113, 115, 211
  idle 266
  see also Arabs, Muslims, Saracens
moral communities *see* ethnicity
Moses, prophet 76n.122, 122, 204n.66
Muhammad, prophet 67–8, 120, 206
  sexual powers 244n.43
Muslims 1, 16, 22, 25, 33, 64, 81, 84, 114, 116,
    122, 156, 206, 225, 251, 254
  cunning 84
  see also Arabs, Islam, Moors, Saracens

Naples, university of 94
Narbonne, chicken of 66
  dress 237n.20
Natio, pl. *nationes*, *see* ethnicity
national identity 6, 8, 9, 12
  see also ethnicity
nationalism 6–7, 9 –11
  see also ethnicity
nation-state 6, 8, 9, 34, 254
  see also ethnicity
nationality 12, 30, 37
  see also ethnicity
nationes, university corporations 126,
    163, 223
Native Americans 82
natural law, *see* law
Navarra 83, 114, 250n.65
Nennius, monk 219
Nicomedia 206
Nigel de Longchamps (Whireker),
    satirist 210
  Speculum Stultorum 210
Noah, biblical figure 48–9, 57, 64, 124
nobility 37, 111, 124, 139, 172, 174, 188, 193,
    196, 197n.39, 198n.42, 199, 201, 203,
    204, 206, 208–9, 212–3, 215, 217, 225,
    231, 256
  arrogance 197

blood 111
Nogent, Benedictine abbey of 90
Normandy 133, 198, 207–8, 216, 226–7
  conquest of in 1204 187
Normans 13, 32, 144, 164, 186, 187, 198, 207,
    210, 216, 224–6, 237, 246n.49
  arrogance 133, 172
  boastful 136, 144, 161
  boldness 265
  chivalrous 172, 186, 197
  compared to bears 70
  cruelty 144, 172, 256
  drinking 143n.60, 144, 199
  eloquence 172, 174
  friendship (alliances) 147, 263, 265
  greed 144, 226
  hair 172, 174, 216
  rapacity 263, 265, 269
  treacherous 175, 198, 226
  urbanity 198, 209, 237, 251
  vain 161
North Pole 100, 219
Norway 237
  pastoralism 245
Norwegians 239
  see also Scandinavians

Odo of Deuil, chronicler 148n.75
  De profectione Ludovici VII in orientem
    148n.75
Odofredus, jurist 131
Orderic Vitalis, Benedictine monk at
    monastery of Saint-Evroul 80, 198,
    208, 215–6
  Historia ecclesiastica 80, 174n.44,
    209n.87, 215–6
Origen of Alexandria, theologian
    106n.91
original sin 21, 28, 82, 108, 110, 119, 120,
    124, 132
  corruption of health 116–22, 124
  social inequality 124
  see also environmental (climate) theory,
    Jews, religious determinism, serfs
origo gentis myths 42, 47–51, 234
  climate theory 113–5, 224

Trojan origins 53n.51, 115, 176, 224
  see also Britons, Franks, Romans, Welsh
Orléans, school 126, 137, 209
  sodomites 172n.34
Ostrogoths 190
  see also Goths, Visigoths
othering, in time 8, 10, 23–6, 29, 42–60, 70–2, 204, 237, 251, 254–5
  in space 23–6, 29, 42–60, 70–2, 204, 237, 251, 254–5
  see also ethnicity, Judaism
Otto of Bamberg, bishop 249
Otto I, German emperor 170
Otto IV, German emperor 53, 182, 223
Otto of Freising, bishop and chronicler 18, 60, 108, 206, 240, 249, 250
  Chronica sive Historia de duabus civitatibus 60, 191n.16, 206
  Gesta Friderici 113, 242, 249
Ottonian dynasty 202
Oxford, university of 126, 183, 186

Padua, university of 114
Palestine 1, 80, 89, 184, 186, 206, 225, 227, 230
Pannonia 18, 245, 249
Papias, grammarian 213
  Lexicon 213
Paris 125, 172, 196
  Franciscan *studium generale* 234
  temperate climate 227, 233, 236–7
  translation of knowledge to 195–6, 236–7
  university of 18, 34, 82, 93–4, 126, 134–5, 137, 142, 161, 179, 183, 186, 209, 232, 233–4, 254
  patria 3, 5, 11–12, 30–1, 35, 36, 37, 38, 113n.125, 126–7, 129–31, 140, 151, 183, 229, 255, 257
  communis patria 129
  dying for the 130–1, 229, 257
  emotions 129–30
  kingdoms 129, 157
  loyalty 156, 229
  patria aeterna 34, 129, 255
  sacralization 129–30
Paul, apostle 61, 74, 75, 77, 116
  Epistle to the Romans 76, 77, 118
  Epistle to the Colossians 61
  first Epistle to the Corinthians 245n.46
Paul the Deacon, chronicler 43, 51
  Historia Langobardorum 43
Paulus Orosius, church historian 44, 59, 219
  Historiarum adversum paganos libri vii 44, 59, 66n.91, 103n.75
Peace and Truce of God movements 203
Peire D'Auvergne, poet 179n.63
Peire Vidal, poet 200–1
Pepin the Short, king of the Franks 218
Persians 42, 55, 56, 71
  compared to bears 69
  cupidity 65
  perfidy 73, 79, 263, 265, 269
  steadfastness 73, 263, 269
Persius, Roman poet 169
Peter, apostle 204
Peter of Blois, scholar 214
Peter of Celle, abbot 154, 224
  Epistola 224
Peter of Eboli, chronicler 191n.15
Peter the Hermit 205
Peter the Venerable, abbot 62
Petrus Alfonsi, physician 119
  Dialogi contra Iudaeos 119
Philip II, king of France 128–9, 186, 199, 227
Philip the Fair, king of France 125
Philo of Alexandria, philosopher 106
Phoenicia 247
Phoenicians 21
Phrygians 75n.121
physiognomy 21, 80, 95
  see also environmental (climate) theory, ethnicity, race and racism, stereotyping, traits
Picardians 99
  urbane 237
  eloquent 237
Picardy 107, 237

Picts 51, 71
  beasts of burden 69, 266
  boasting 266
  cruelty 71, 72, 267
  magnanimity 269
  rigidity 265, 269
  tatoos 51
  see also Irish, Scots
Pierre Dubois, political theorist 125, 227
  De recuperatione terre sancte 125, 227
Pierre Riga, poet 181
Pilgrim's Guide to Santiago di Compostela
  83, 114, 250n.65
Pisa 200
Plinian (monstruous) races 151
  see also Indians
Pliny the Elder, Roman naturalist 47, 94,
    95, 98, 105, 151, 235
  Historia naturalis 47, 52n.46, 78n.130,
    98, 105, 144n.64
poetry 5, 79, 133–48
  social power of 166–76
  see also proverbs, satire
Poitevins 62, 114, 129, 140, 177
  garrulity 62
  gluttony 62
  pun on name 177
  rigidity or arrogance 263, 265, 269
Poitiers 177
Poitou 114
Poland 79, 146
  diet of raw flesh 151
  felicity 146
Polish 113, 248
  drinking 163
Pomerania 249
Pomeranians 190
Posidonius of Apameia, astronomer 86
Prague, Jews of 168
priamel, poetic genre 146
Priscian, grammarian 66
progress, narratives of 3, 25, 29, 36, 71, 124,
    194, 230, 244, 252, 254
  'civilizing process' 6, 184, 193–4, 222, 228
  environmental determinism 244–51
    primordial man 132–3

  evolutionary view of social
    organization 132–3, 194, 210–11,
    243–7, 250, 252
  agricultural society 210–11, 243–51
  dairy diet 144–5, 211, 244
Prophetic Chronicle 67–8
property 3, 16, 30, 34, 35, 38, 82, 127, 131–2,
    156, 231, 243, 250, 257
  see also *dominium*, labour
prostitution 20, 150
Provençals 225
  musical skills 147
  ornateness 272
  untrustworthy 150
proverbs 79, 142–7, 171–83
Proverbes au villain 142
Prussians 190, 248
  hospitality 244
Psalms 58
Pseudo-Aristotle, philosopher 98–9
  Problemata 98–9
Pseudo-Boethius, scholar 94
  Disciplina scolarium 94, 108n.103
Pseudo-Herodatus, geographer 94
Ptolemy, astronomer 85, 99

Quintilian, rhetorician 134, 140
  Institutio Oratoria 140
'Quo miser exul venio turbine perfusus?'
  176

race and racism 6, 7, 14–22, 82–5, 110, 116,
    165, 211, 247, 255
  see also environmental (climate)
    theory, ethnicity, physiognomy,
    stereotyping, traits
Radboud of Utrecht, bishop
  Vita altera Bonifatii 220n.135
Radulfus Glaber, monk 214–5, 240, 245
  Historiae 211n.95, 215, 245
Raetia 104
Raimbert de Paris, poet 197
  La Chevalrie d'Ogier de Danemarche
    197
Ralph of Caen, chronicler 205
  Gesta Tancredi 205

Ralph of Sarre, master 223
Ranulf Higden, Benedictine monk 54n.54
 Polychronicon 238n.24
Raoul Ardent, theologian 61–2
 Homilia 62
Rashid ad-Din Sinan, Ismaili leader of the Assassins 149
 sexualization of 149
Raymond of Aguilers 226n.158
 Historia Francorum 226n.158
Ravenna 92
Rederijkerskamers 137
Regimen duodecim mensium 27, 91
Regimen Sanitatis Salernitanum 102n.74
regimens 4, 6, 27, 36, 111, 123, 125, 189, 196, 212–13
 see also mirror literature
Reginald of Canterbury, Benedictine monk 140
Regino of Prüm, abbot 41, 151
Registrum Epistolarum Fratris Johannis Peckham Archiepiscopi Cantuariensis 12n.32
Reims 14
religious determinism 110, 116–22
 see also ethnicity, heretics, Jews, Saracens
Remigius of Auxerre, Benedictine monk 151n.87
 Epistola ad D. episcopum virdunensem 151n.87
rhetoric 4, 79, 127
 argumenta a loco 137–41
 emotions 7, 13, 127, 139, 152, 168, 171
 letter writing (ars dictandi) 134–5, 149, 151, 166
 manuals of 134–41
 mental images 77, 138–40
 metonymy (continens pro contento) 135–6
 proverbs 142–7
 schematization 138–9
 stereotyping 133–41, 152
Rhetoricum ad Herennium 166
Rhine, river 195

Richard I, king of England 182
Richard Coer de Lyon, romance 182
Richard of Cluny (of Poitiers), Benedictine monk 222n.140
Richard of Devises, chronicler
 Chronicon Ricardi Divisiensis 182n.76
Richer of Reims, Benedictine monk and chronicler 190n.13
 Historiae 190n.13
Rievaulx, Cistercian abbey 154
Robert of Bridlington, Augustinian canon 223
 Bridlington Dialogue 223
Robert II (Curthose), duke of Normandy 216
Robert II the Pious, king of the Franks 215
Robert the Englishman, astronomer 100
Robert the Monk, chronicler 204
 Historia Iherosolimitana 217n.122
Roda Codex 66
Rodrigo Jiménez de Rada, archbishop 147
Roger Bacon, Franciscan friar 99, 110
 Opus majus 67, 110
Rolandus Patavinus, chronicler 199n.45
 Chronica 199n.45
Romagni, cunning 162
 traitors 150
Romans 21, 60, 99, 145, 150
 anger 73, 265
 arrogance 65, 71, 76–7, 169–70, 260, 266
 avarice 62, 77, 148, 150, 161, 168–71, 175, 272
 beast with the ten horns 69
 eloquence 263
 envy 270–1
 fickleness 203
 gravity 73, 263, 265, 269
 hypocrisy 146, 148
 lewdness 170
 skilful 73
 strength 71, 147n.72, 267
 Trojan origins 115, 224
 violence 150, 161
 wisdom 263
 see also Italy, Rome, satire

Romanitas 189–90
  see also Roman empire
Rome 54, 59n.69, 71, 127, 148–9, 183, 202, 219, 241
  false relics 170
  marble of 141
  translation motif 59–60, 195–6, 255
  see also Italy, Romans, satire
Rouen 128
  school 141
Rufinus, relics of 170–1
Rupert of Deutz, Benedictine abbot and theologian 69
  Commentaria in apocalypsim 69
Rutebeuf, poet 93, 137
  'La Bataille des VII Ars' 161n.2
Ruthenians 248
  drinking 163

Sabines, filth of 265, 269
Said al-Andalusi, astronomer 65n.86
  Book of the Categories of Nations 65n.86
Saint-Germain en Auxerre 215
Salerno, university of 137
Salvian of Marseilles, Christian writer 77–8
  De gubernatione dei 77–8, 199n.47
Samaria 58
San Pedro de Rocas 74n.118
Santiago di Compostela 83
Saracens 14, 49, 67–8, 80, 82, 95, 97, 107, 116, 118, 122, 214, 216, 225n.153, 234–5, 251
  compared to scorpions 216
  cowardice 80, 97
  cruelty 263, 265, 269
  cunning 80, 143
  effeminacy 216
  ethnonym 49, 68
  monstrous 107, 121–2
  rigor 147
  wantonness 79, 121, 149, 214, 216, 234–5, 244, 270–2
  weak blooded 80
  see also Arabs, Chaldeans, Moors, Muslims, religious determinism
Sarah, wife of Abraham 49, 68

satire 138, 153, 165–6
  and aggression 163–6
  anti-Roman 148, 162, 169–71
  and humour 165–6
  invective 162–84
  see also poetry, proverbs
Sawley, Cistercian monastery 134
Saxo Grammaticus, chronicler 43, 215
  Saxonis gesta Danorum 43, 215
Saxons 53, 60, 71, 100, 103–5, 113, 190, 242
  arrogant 198
  barbaric language 190
  butter eaters 144n.64
  compared to horses 69, 266
  cowardice 200
  drinking 199n.47
  effeminacy 215
  origins on island of Engla 54n.54
  perseverance 73, 263, 269
  rigidity 65, 199n.47
  savagery 78, 238
  strength 103–4, 238, 266
  stupidity 72, 73, 75, 199n.47, 260, 263, 265, 269–70
  treachery 271
  urbane 103–4
  whiteness 105
  see also Germans
Saxony 54n.54, 100, 220n.135, 234, 236
Scandinavians 42, 49, 97, 104, 108, 192, 240, 242, 251–2
  barbaric 192, 240, 242, 251
  paganism 242
  sluggishness 104–5
  whiteness 104–5
  see also Danes, Norwegians, Swedes
Sciapode, Plinian race 74
Scotland 181
  thorny bushes 141
Scottish Declaration of Arbroath 10
Scythia 151
Scythians 61, 85, 104, 189, 243
  drinking blood 243
  harsh climate 189
  whiteness 104
Second World War 7

Séez, bishop of 216
Sembi (Sambians) drinking blood 243
Seneca, philosopher 189
  De ira 189
Serlo of Wilton, abbot 142, 172
Servitium, Church taxation 169, 184
Seven Wonders of the World 46, 66, 78n.130
Severian of Gabala, bishop 58n.63
  De mundi creatione 58n.63
Shem, son of Noah 48, 57, 124
Sicilians 182n.76
Siegfried of Gorze, abbot 215
Silesians 190
Sirr al-Asrar 95, 102n.74, 123
Sirventes, debate poems 167
skin colour 16, 21, 52–3, 92, 100, 104–10, 114–6, 122n.162
  blackness 21, 52, 104–10, 113–15, 120–1
    beauty 106
    compared to monkeys 110n.109
    Ham 114, 115
    sexuality 110
    sin 106–7
    timidity 110n.109
    and conversion 121–2
  whiteness 30–1, 52, 96, 104–9, 114, 122, 235, 251
    see also Dacians, English, environmental (climate) theory, French, Frisians, Galatians, Gauls, Germans, Hollanders, Icelanders, Saxons, Scandinavians, Scots, Scythians, Slavs, Spanish
slavery 16, 35, 37, 49, 118, 252
  enslaved persons 61, 113, 117
  natural slavery 17–18, 80
Slavia, land of milk and honey 248–30
Slavs 25, 104–5, 108, 143, 207, 231, 242, 245, 252
  barbaric 192, 240, 242, 252
  dirty 73, 263, 265, 269
  drinking blood 252
  drunkenness 163, 199, 265, 270–1
  lazy and thieves 151n.86, 245n.48
  paganism 242–3

pastoralism 245
phlegmatic 105
whiteness 104–5
Solinus, grammarian 94, 219, 244
Song of Songs 106
southerners, stereotypes of 68n.129, 80, 85, 89, 96–9, 110, 144, 150, 203, 214, 221, 237n.20, 244, 251
  see also Africans, environmental (climate) theory, Saracens
sovereignty 9, 10, 84, 156–7, 229, 256
Spain 46, 65–7, 92, 225, 229, 259
  mules of 151
  see also Asturia
Spanish 42, 60, 64, 66, 106, 113, 206, 225, 230, 237n.20
  acuteness 73
  disorder 271
  quick 73, 206, 263
  luxurious 143n.60
  pomp 270–1
  preachers of 143
  whiteness 106
  wine drinking 73, 265, 269
  wit 73, 263, 269
  see also Visigoths
St Augustine's in Canterbury, abbey 140
St Amand, abbey 93
St Denis, patron saint 13, 195n.32, 227
St Denis, royal abbey 14, 196, 203
St Gall, abbey 78
St Gatien, cathedral in Tours 144
St Georges's Day, festivity 14n.38
St Omer, monastery 135
Stephen Langton, archbishop 153–5
Stephen of Siunik, archbishop 63n.80
Stephen of Antioch, translator 92
stereotyping 4, 15, 20, 23, 26–32, 38
  manuals of rhetoric 133–41
  see also environmental (climate) theory, ethnotypes, othering, race and racism, traits
Streitgedichte 138
Suevi, lust of 73, 265, 269
  uncleanness 73, 263
  see also Swabians

Suevia 104n.78, 238n.23
Suger, abbot of St Denis 130n.34, 203
  Vita Ludovici Grossi Regis 199n.45
Suriani, sexualization of 149–50
Suso, monastery 65
Swabians 60, 104, 145, 190, 238
  barbaric language 190
  magnanimous 145
  treacherous 145
  urbane 238
  see also Suevi, Suevia
Swedes, hospitality 244
  pastoralism 245
  see also Scandinavians
Sword Brothers, order of 239–40
Sybille, prophetess 52, 78n.130
Syria 252n.73
Syrians 21

Tacitus, Roman consul and historian 219
Tartars, drinking blood 243, 252
Tegernsee, abbey 146n.70, 185
Tertullian, theologian 47
  De anima 47
Teutates, deity 202
The Chronicle of Lanercost 181n.73
Theodorik of Amorbach (Fleury), Benedictine monk 218
  Ex illatione Sancti Benedicti 218
Theodwin of Porto, bishop 191
Thietmar of Merseburg, bishop
  Chronicon 220n.135
Thomas Aquinas, Dominican friar 5, 82, 120, 123, 156
  De regimine principum 229
  Scriptum super libros Sententiarum 108n.101
  Summa theologiae 49n.33, 82
Thomas Becket, archbishop 100, 179–80, 209, 223n.143
Thomas of Cantimpré, Dominican friar 201–2
  Liber de natura rerum 201–2
Thuringians 53, 104, 113
  strong and cruel 233
  see also Germans

time, *see* ethnicity, othering
Timothy, apostle 61
Toledo 66, 74n.118
Toulouse, county 187
  university of 94, 135
Tractatus Garsiae Toletani 168, 171
Tractatus de locis et statu sancte terre ierosolimitane 117
traits 14–22, 51–55
  and acculturation 28, 83, 113, 247
  bravery 1–3, 80, 85, 91
  cowardice 28, 80, 85, 89, 91, 96
  deceitfulness 16, 80, 85, 96–8; 122
  discipline (moderation) 2, 3, 4, 10, 15, 16, 19, 25, 35, 183–4, 186, 213
  effeminacy 25, 85, 216–17
  essentialized 139–40
  fluidity/fixity 61, 82–4, 110–22
  freedom 53–4, 61, 85, 115, 149–52, 189, 228
  and eloquence 3, 4, 18, 131–3, 213, 253
  innate 61
  intelligence 2, 32, 88–9, 91, 111–12, 121
  pangenesis, theory of 111n.113
  positive self-description 15, 36
  rationality 1–3, 4, 10, 15–18, 22, 25, 32, 80, 83–5, 108, 122, 125, 126–7, 131–3, 184, 185–6, 188
  strength 3, 4, 6, 10, 16, 22, 53, 91, 125, 126–7, 186
  stubbornness 38
  and urbanity 4, 5, 32, 36, 37, 83–4, 100, 186–94; 212–7, 253
  weakness 3, 6, 25, 28, 36, 38, 80, 83, 85, 122
  see also animals, barbarity, environmental (climate) theory, ethnicity, gendered representations, race and racism, stereotyping
translatio studii et imperii 10, 25, 29, 36, 55, 59, 71, 125, 133, 135, 184, 186, 194–6, 217, 230, 253–5
  prophesy of the four empires 59, 133
Transylvanians 207
Tribal Hidage 68, 70, 72n.114
Tours 144, 209

Trojan origins, *see origo gentis* myths
Tropic of Cancer 86, 99
Tropic of Capricorn 86
Turks 2, 205
  cunning 80
  lack of blood 80
Tuscans 150
  fraud 150
  parsimony 79, 134n.28, 272
Tuscany, pigs of 141

Ulger, bishop of Angers 177n.54
Umayyads 66–7
Universities, rise of 4
Urban II, pope 1–2, 204–5, 218, 227, 238

Vandals 248
Vegetius, military strategist 2, 11, 17, 47, 79, 81, 89–91, 97, 115, 126, 129, 130, 131, 134, 145, 162, 183, 186, 193, 195, 196, 205, 218, 224
  De re militari 2, 11, 47, 78n.130, 79, 81, 89–91, 97, 126, 129, 162
Venice, poverty in 146
Venus 117n.138, 183
Vercelli, *studium generale* 94
Vicenza, *studium generale* 94
Victor IV, pope 129, 223
Vienna 195, 202
Viguera 76
Vincent of Beauvais, Dominican friar 50, 107
  Speculum doctrinale 107
  Speculum naturale 105n.86
'Vinum Normannis' 144n.62
Virgil, Roman poet 52, 141, 148, 167
  Aeneid 52n.45, 148
  Eclogues 220n.133
  Georgica 141
Virgin Mary, complexion of 108
Visigoths 37, 45, 62, 66–7
  see also Goths, Spanish, Spain
Vita Gregorii Magni 191n.15
Vita Ludovici VII 199

Wace, poet 179

Roman de Brut 179
Wales 18
  climate 115
  see also Welsh
Walter of Châtillon, poet 93, 133–4, 139
  Alexandreis 133, 161n.2, 184n.81
Walter Daniel, monk 154
  Centum Sententiae 154
Walter Map, satirist 171, 191n.16, 213–4
Walther von der Vogelweide, poet 195
Wandalbert of Prüm, Benedictine monk 191n.14
  Vita et miracula sancti Goaris 191n.14
Wardan Areveltsi, chronicler 63n.80
Welsh 38, 69, 115, 210, 224
  barbarity 246, 251
  dairy diet 192, 246n.49
  eloquence 115, 115
  freedom 151
  hot-blooded 151
  hospitality 244
  Trojan origins 115, 224
  see also Bretons, Britons, Wales
Westphalia 238
  instability of faith 173
  urbane 238
wet nurses 112
William Brito, Franciscan friar 180n.67
  Summa Britonis 180n.67
William le Breton, poet 129, 162, 199
  Philippide 129, 162, 199
William Fitzstephen, cleric 100
  Descriptio Nobilissimae Civitatis Londoniae 28
William of Conches, philosopher 112, 118
  Dragmaticon Philosophiae 112
William of Malmesbury, Benedictine monk 1–2, 34, 80, 92, 97, 187, 196–7, 210, 215, 217, 238–9
  Gesta regum Anglorum 1, 80, 174n.42 and 44, 196–7, 207n.79, 211n.94 and 96, 239
  Historia Novella 215n.115
  Vita Wulfstani 217n.120
William of Moerbeke, scholar 80, 94

William of Nangis, chronicler 196
William of Nangis (*continued*)
   Ex primatis chronicis et Guillelmi gestis Ludovici IX 206n.77
William of Newburgh, Augustinian canon 176, 209n.89
   Historia rerum Anglicarum 176
William of Poitiers, chronicler 174, 250
   Gesta Guilhelmi 174, 211n.95, 250
William of Poitiers, bishop 177n.54
William Rufus, king of England 215

Wolfram von Eschenbach, poet 195, 203
women 25, 117, 122, 181
   phlegmatic 27, 108–9
   see also English, Jews
Wulfstan, bishop of Worcester and archbishop of York 68–9, 216

Ysengrimus, poem attrib. to master Nivardus 175, 179, 191
Zeeland 104
   urbane 238

Health and Healing in the Middle Ages

1 SAINTS, CURE-SEEKERS AND MIRACULOUS HEALING IN TWELFTH-CENTURY ENGLAND
 Ruth J. Salter

2 ETHNICITY IN MEDIEVAL EUROPE, 950–1250
 Medicine, Power and Religion
 Claire Weeda

3 THE GUILD BOOK OF THE BARBERS AND SURGEONS OF YORK (BRITISH LIBRARY, EGERTON MS 2572)
 Study and Edition
 Richard D. Wragg

4 DEATH AND DISEASE IN THE MEDIEVAL AND EARLY MODERN WORLD
 Perspectives from across the Mediterranean and Beyond
 Edited by Lori Jones and Nükhet Varlık

www.ingramcontent.com/pod-product-compliance
Lightning Source LLC
Chambersburg PA
CBHW052056300426
44117CB00013B/2153